Making the Best of Basics

Family Preparedness Handbook

James Talmage Stevens

Making the Best of Basics—Family Preparedness Handbook
© 1974, 1975, 1976, 1980, 1996, 1997 by James Talmage Stevens

Library of Congress Cataloging-in-publication Data
Stevens, James Talmage.
Making the best of basics : family preparedness handbook / by James Talmage Stevens.
p. cm.
Originally published: Salt Lake City, UT : Peton Corp., 1975.
Includes index.
ISBN 1-882723-25-2
1. Food—Storage. 2. Food—Preservation. 3. Cookery. 4. Gardening. I. Title.
TX601.S69   1996   96-7076
641.3—dc20   CIP

Disclaimer: The author and publisher disclaim all liability in connection with the use of this *Family Preparedness Handbook.* It is intended only as an informative guide for those desiring to implement an in-home storage plan in an effort to be prepared for unknown future events over which one has little or no control. We have done our best to provide guidelines for implementing and utilizing in-home food storage. Our recommendations are based on experience and data from sources we believe reliable. Accordingly, the reader must take responsibility for decisions and the ultimate actions regarding his/her choice to effect any idea, suggestion, recommendation, instruction, or recipe in this *Handbook.*

The information offered herein is general and is made without guarantees by either the author or the publisher. The information is as accurate as humanly possible. However, given the amount and variety of choices in the marketplace, the differences in individual needs and tastes, and the fact that we have no control over quality, kinds, and types of possible substitutions and alternatives for virtually every item in our suggested items and quantities, we cannot be held responsible for the reader's ultimate choices or results. You should get advice from local consultants and from government advisors in your area. Their local experience will be invaluable to your in your efforts in **Making the Best of Basics.**

Publication History

Date	Printing	Edition
02/74	First	First
03/74	Second	Second
08/74	Third	Second *(Special)*
08/74	Fourth	Third
03/75	Fifth	Third
07/75	Sixth	Fourth
06/76	Seventh	Fifth *(Special)*
08/76	Eighth	Fifth
10/76	Ninth	Fifth
11/76	Tenth	Fifth
02/77	Eleventh	Fifth
04/77	Twelfth	Sixth
03/80	Thirteenth	Sixth
11/80	Fourteenth	Seventh
02/82	Fifteenth	Eighth
02/96	Sixteenth	Ninth
06/97	Seventeenth	Ninth
11/97	Eighteenth	Tenth

Printed in the United States of America.
24   23   22   21   20   19   18

Making the Best of Basics

Family Preparedness Handbook

James Talmage Stevens

GOLD LEAF PRESS

ACKNOWLEDGMENTS

This 10th Edition of **Basics** would not have been realized without friends, family, and the many professionals from the medical, educational, emergency preparedness, and food storage disciplines who've aided in this journey of realization over the past years. Also, thanks to all the manufacturers, wholesalers, distributors, and individual dealers who've sent information about their businesses to be shared with our readers. Many have shared their personal interests, their knowledge, and their ideas for improvement of **Basics**.

Debi and Bob Rebo, computer technicians who continued to serve with software and hardware upgrades, installing new "stuff" to simplify the process of getting the information from the various sources to the computer's memory.

Continuing the journey during the past several months, we've traveled extensively to gather additional information required to modify the last edition. Those who have made our time away from home much easier include John and Patricia Van Hoecke, Ken and Darlene Anderson, Dick and Donna Miller, and Gloria Arre. Last, but not least, gratitude for my business manager, Mark Schultz, who has maintained the income stream at the insurance company to assure the continuation of our research.

There have been many others along the path who have added to this book with their own stories, insights, suggestions, and information. Thanks to you all. I'm truly grateful for the constant help and support from my wife, LeeDee, who not only believed it could be done, but gave me the means, the time, and the energy to undertake what I knew would be a long journey—and it continues!

Making the Best of Basics
Family Preparedness Handbook

10th Edition

TABLE OF CONTENTS

TABLE OF CONTENTS (continued)

TABLE OF CONTENTS (continued)

TABLE OF DIRECTIONS & RECIPES

TABLE OF DIRECTIONS & RECIPES (continued)

TABLE OF CHARTS, GUIDES, ILLUSTRATIONS & LISTS

TABLE OF CHARTS, GUIDES, ILLUSTRATIONS & LISTS (continued)

FOREWORD

Twenty-four years ago, as a result of an assignment, I wrote **Making the Best of Basics**—*The Family Preparedness Handbook.* My personal motivation at that time was to simplify preparedness practices for my own family using the experiences of my youth. In those early years as we printed copies to share with others, we found we constantly needed to print more. After 7 editions and more than 15 printings, we had sold more than 300,000 copies. The success of **Basics** seemed to be its simplicity and directness.

Basics had been out of print for 10 years. People called and wrote, asking how to get copies because none were available in bookstores. Some folks went to the extreme of illegally photocopying old copies—some entrepreneurs even tried printing them for resale.

Eventually, I began to think seriously about an updated edition. Though many encouraged me to reprint the book exactly as it had been left some years ago just to get it back in print, I was unwilling to do so. Much had changed in the preparedness industry, and I felt strongly those changes ought to be brought to the public's attention.

While in the process of updating **Basics**, I married a woman with no background in preparedness. Her inexperience in the field combined with a prolonged period of ill health (hers) created opportunities for me to examine and experiment with preparedness issues from new perspectives. As I began the work of updating and rewriting, I saw the distinctive need for the following:

1. to **fill in the gaps** in the information currently available
2. to maximize state of the art technology and **provide the general public more knowledge** about the massive resources of the preparedness industry
3. to provide a resource **guidebook to help individuals, families, and groups** to

   • **customize a preparedness plan** to meet their needs
   • **prioritize their selection and collection** of preparedness supplies and equipment
   • **utilize preparedness resources** more effectively

The tenth edition of **Making the Best of Basics** reflects the simplicity of earlier editions, while drawing on much advanced technological capabilities. We've developed more charts to put information into a more useable format. Also, we've collaborated with professionals to share their knowledge of specific fields. We have made an effort to provide more information in this **Basics** edition than has even been written in a single volume about food storage and emergency preparedness. Still, there is more to say. *Don't Get Caught with Your Pantry Down,* a compendium of preparedness resources, is scheduled for release in 1998. *Pantry* will be comprised of information resources, including:

   • **a natural disasters resource guide**
   • **a man-caused disasters resource guide**
   • **a public information resource guide**
   • **a published works resource guide**
   • **a where-to-buy-it resource guide**

Our purpose is to help you establish a preparedness plan for your family's future security. We've spent years updating and improving this edition of **Basics**. We take responsibility for our work—only you can take responsibility for your family state of preparedness.

Please give your attention now to your family's security...

because no one knows what's in store for them on the horizon!

James T. Stevens

DEDICATION

This 10th Edition is dedicated to 3 women. All of them had a strong influence on the fulfillment of my dream to accomplish the results achieved in publishing this revised edition.

First: Ruth P. Stevens, my mother and mentor in the kitchen, who took the time to explain how things worked—a practical woman who had more talent than she could contain. She was a great example of being prepared for whatever—sometimes to excess! However, she wrote the book on pantry lifestyle. She was perspicacious and a great teacher.

Second: Jean Newman, my high school English teacher, who cared enough for her students and had a personal interest in each of them. Without her influence, I would not have understood excellence, gone to college, or ever undertaken such a project as this. Wherever she is, I hope she knows she's remembered well by a former student. She was a great teacher.

Third: LeeDee Teague-Stevens, my wife and companion, who recognized and accepted the inevitability of the work it would take to bring about this edition. Without her sacrifice, love, understanding, and forbearance, you wouldn't be reading this. She is a great teacher.

Thanks to each of you for the memories, the honing of skills, the polishing of the language, and the words of encouragement to accomplish this important work.

Chapter 1

What Is Family Preparedness?

Once upon a time there was an old man who loved to listen to the striking of his grandfather clock. He enjoyed it so much, in fact, that he kept it in his bedroom against the far wall. After retiring each night, he would lie in his bed, half-awake, listening to the striking of the clock. Whenever the clock struck, he would sleepily count the chimes. One night something went wrong with the clock's mechanism. It began to strike and he began to count. He counted to ten, eleven, twelve . . . then thirteen! . . . fourteen! . . . fifteen!. . . Suddenly he realized something had gone wrong and he was immediately wide awake. He reached over, shook his wife, and said, "Wake up, Ma! It's later than I've ever knowed it to be!"

It is later than many of us realize. Those who have lived during the last two or three decades of the 20th century have witnessed unparalleled growth, progress, and constant innovation. Sometimes this progress is accompanied by the belief or hope that science, technology, and government can meet all the challenges of our times, tame the forces of nature, and fix everything that goes wrong. However, our unprecedented progress has been accompanied by social change in which we've seen the eroding of our "traditional" values and by the depletion of our earth's natural resources. Daily we are confronted with the evidence of our progress: ozone alert days; water use restrictions; *"Don't Eat*

> *"In this work, when it shall be found that much is omitted, let it not be forgotten that much likewise is performed."*
>
> Dr. Samuel Johnson, 1775, upon completion of his dictionary

The Fish" signs along polluted rivers and lakes; men, women, and children standing on street corners with signs proclaiming "*Will work for food*"; latchkey kids; metal detectors in schools; increased security at airports; government services shutdowns; . . . the list seems endless.

The old man's "wake-up call"—"It's later than I ever knowed it to be"—serves to remind us during these challenging and chaotic times of the need for personal responsibility and individual creative genius. We need to recognize that each of us is important in our own special way to the survival and well-being of this world. But first, we must take responsibility for our own survival and well-being and actively exercise our creativity to that end—we can't expect science, technology, government, or anyone else to do our part.

PREPAREDNESS IS EXPECTING THE UNEXPECTED

Because no one knows what's in store on the horizon, the individual who takes responsibility for his life and that of his family not only expects the unexpected but prepares accordingly. The premise of **Making the Best of Basics** is that we *know* we are at a high risk for some disaster. The purpose of this edition is to help you become prepared for it.

Family preparedness activities facilitate a proactive, self-sustaining lifestyle and a high level of readiness for circumstances beyond our control. Being prepared means being able to face the potential problems of increasing demand and decreasing supply of basic commodities with a degree of confidence and certainty.

The only way we achieve this level of preparation is by deciding to take control of our own destiny. Although we can't control externally caused life-changing events, we *can* organize a plan and implement it for times when such events occur.

There is a powerful, secure feeling in knowing that you chose to take charge of your personal readiness and your family will be able to eat and sustain a relatively stress-free rebound period after a disaster—because together you made the effort to plan ahead.

If you've prepared for your family's self-sufficiency (security) with both emergency and long-term provisions, you can turn what could have been a life-threatening situation into a manageable problem.

Family preparedness is a practice of being aware and alert to the possible and probable reality of a disaster happening to you.

1. *Preparedness* **is knowing how to**
   - **ascertain potential disasters, whether natural, man-caused or personal, to which one's family is vulnerable, and**
   - **eliminate or minimize risks—and therefore the negative effects— of any disasters to the degree possible.**

2. *In-home storage* **is how you can minimize the negative impact of the unexpected by having stored in your own home adequate resources of water, food, fuel, medical supplies & medications, clothing, money, transportation, bedding—anything you need to be self-sufficient during an emergency or an extended period of time.**

Events Which Could Not Be Controlled

When we understand the importance of self-reliance and being prepared, it's as if we hear the "wake up call" and begin taking responsibility for managing our own lives. In so doing, we understand (paradoxically) that there are many facets of our lives which cannot be managed or "controlled."

Natural Disasters

Consider a partial list of major disasters which occurred in the U.S. since 1989. Even the most responsible among us could not control these events:

1989—Charlotte NC, Charleston SC, and other inland areas devastated by Hurricane Hugo.

1989—Bay Area of San Francisco rocked by an earthquake during World Series playoff.

1991—California residential areas suffer severe fire losses.

1992—Southern Florida suffers worst damage ever from Hurricane Andrew as it destroys public and private property.

1992—Hawaiian Islands pounded by vicious wind and water and suffer heavy property damages due to Hurricane Iniki.

1993—California homes ravaged by fires again and losses exceed previous years.

1993—The Great Flood inundates 8 million acres in 9 states along the Mississippi River, causing $12 billion in damage.

1994—January, several major calamities happen concurrently in the U.S.:
- Los Angeles earthquake (6.8 on the Richter Scale), which disrupts the entire city, kills 60 people, and ultimately costs more than $6.5 billion.
- 24 North Central, Midwest, and Northeastern states are paralyzed by extremely cold and bitter winter weather during the "storm of the century."
- natural gas explosion in Kentucky destroys property and disrupts many communities.
- frozen water distribution system in Atlanta, Georgia, leaves part of city without water for days.
- extreme winter conditions disrupt businesses and federal government offices in many Eastern seaboard cities and towns, including Washington, D.C.

1994—November, Hurricane Gordon rips through southern Florida, destroying winter vegetable crops estimated in excess of $200 million, then proceeds up the Eastern shore to the Carolinas, causing additional losses.

There's little need to continue—the sheer volume of tropical storms and hurricanes during the summer of 1995 alone exhausted the entire alphabet!

Man-Caused Disasters

There are many instances of man-caused disasters—business disasters, political upheavals, nuclear detonations, war, and terrorist acts:

1992—Los Angeles barrios engulfed by civil riots and fires, looting, and vandalism.

1993—World Trade Center bombed by terrorists, killing six people.

1995—April, terrorist bombing of the Federal Building in Oklahoma City, Oklahoma.

1995–1996—continuing saga of elected officials straining to pass legislation on a balanced budget ultimately disrupts the lives and fiscal security of hundreds of thousands of federal employees during the Christmas season.

Note the changes in the number of major airlines which have either been consumed or have totally gone out of business. Or witness the major changes in the *Fortune 500* listings, closures of many military bases, and resultant major cutbacks in the military's civilian support industry. Have you noticed how many *Fortune 50* (yes, that's fifty) companies have downsized their employment force by tens of thousands?

Personal Disasters

But the most frequent disasters in our lives are the ones which don't get headline coverage—the private disasters which occur on a daily basis to people of all ages and incomes:

- serious illness or disability in the family
- death of a family member
- divorce
- loss of home
- losses due to crime
- loss of income or job due to rapid technological change, downsizing, or business closing
- having less than two-weeks' income in savings
- bankruptcy
- isolation of the elderly
- lack of income for retirement years
- struggling to make ends meet
- being technologically unskilled in a technological world
- living impoverished in a world of plenty

"At Risk"

As society becomes increasingly more complex and our space more crowded, greater numbers of us live and work in disaster-prone areas, and the potential for involvement in any of these disasters is enhanced. Today's lifestyle adds further pressure to the chances for "personal" disasters. Greater numbers of communities and individuals are "at risk" of involvement in life-changing events. People become displaced and find themselves without adequate supplies for sustaining life, much less sustaining a near-normal lifestyle. So as the potential grows for more people to face "uncontrollable" life-changing events, economic self-sufficiency becomes a significant focus of life management.

WHY DON'T WE PREPARE?

There are no emergencies for those who are truly prepared!

It's certainly easy enough to understand why we don't prepare as past generations did. "Progress" and the resulting technological advancements of recent years seem to have lulled us into a false sense of security—believing we can have anything we want, anytime we want, anywhere we want it. Control of our personal and family self-sufficiency (which in reality is our *real* security) has been replaced by the ease of obtaining credit, buy-now/pay-later plans, and ready availability in the stores of practically everything we want, regardless of our ability to meet the payments. We take for granted the availability of public services such as water, sewer, electricity, natural gas, telephone lines, and cable TV. Then there are the many privately owned resources such as 24-hour supermarkets, convenience stores, automated banking machines, debit cards, telemerchandising and drop-ship businesses which have addicted most of us to a high-technology, hand-to-mouth lifestyle.

Additionally, as we survey our society and the requirements of daily living, we can see more reasons why preparing for self-reliance and security takes a back seat for most of us. Our nation's families are stretched thin financially, emotionally, and in terms of time.

As companies downsize, employees are asked to work more overtime. Communication technology, with all of its advantages, also keeps people "on call" 24 hours a day. We are a mobile society—families move across town and across country seeking better opportunities. More and more women and men have the responsibility of parenting children alone while maintaining a job to provide money to reduce overwhelming financial obligations.

Unfortunately for the modern family, there have never been so many distractions to interfere with the establishment of a family self-sufficiency program.

Fortunately there has never been more information available to guide today's family in the quest for self-reliance and security. In this the Information Age, there are countless books, periodicals, pamphlets, brochures, videotapes, and computer software programs designed to help families in their effort to become prepared. **Making the Best of Basics** draws on some of the best of these to combine the most important information into one volume.

How Prepared Is Your Family?

How prepared is your family? Perhaps the following questions will alert you to the reality of your vulnerability:

- **To what potential natural or man-caused disasters is your family subject? To what types of personal disasters?**
- **What have you done or can you do to eliminate or minimize the impact of these potential disasters on your family?**
- **If normal distribution of food to the grocery stores were curtailed, what sources of food would you have available to you or under your control?**
- **If electricity were unavailable for an extended period of time, what methods would you use for cooking, heating, and lighting in your home?**
- **If you had to evacuate your home right now, where would you go for shelter?**
- **If you were required to move away from potential harm immediately, how much gasoline is in your vehicle at this moment?**
- **If someone in your family were injured and medical help were unavailable, what resources would you have at your disposal?**
- **What would be the results if your normal source of income were interrupted for 2 weeks or longer?**
- **How much money do you have on hand for emergency situations?**

> *It's better to have it and not need it than to need it and not have it!*
>
> Common Sense 1:1

If these questions, or rather, the answers to them, make you uncomfortable, now is the time for you to start to work on your preparedness by using **Making the Best of Basics** as your *Family Preparedness Handbook*.

In-Home Storage—a Basic Strategy for Family Preparedness

In-Home Storage—an Overview

If you are unfamiliar with in-home storage, the following paragraphs provide a general idea of what you might expect if you choose to pursue your own program. Recognize that this is a lifestyle choice. Being prepared through in-home storage requires a commitment to learn new skills and use resources in ways never before considered.

Your Personal In-Home Grocery Store

Think of your home, apartment, or other safe storage place as your personal in-home grocery store. That's right, a virtual personal shopping center, stocked with the things you need and like to eat—set up where you have unique access to it when needed!

Imagine having supplies of food and other necessary items on hand from which you can draw continuously for up to a year. Imagine everything in constant stock rotation—items consumed are replaced and new items added as they are discovered and enjoyed. Think about having quality foodstuffs to utilize in the preparation of wholesome and nourishing meals…

Making the Best of Basics was compiled to help you and your family develop just such an "in-home grocery store." This *Handbook* provides:

- guidelines for establishing your own "in-home store"
- tools to help personalize your "in-home store" and provision it for dairy, bakery, produce, medications, personal care, and meat departments, with additional storage for water and fuel
- general guidelines for quantities and quality specifications, including listings of what foods, supplies, and equipment to stock
- selected listings of suppliers for suggested storage items
- charts for listing, prioritizing, and budgeting the orderly acquisition of supplies
- recipes for using your "in-home store" provisions

Commitment—the Major Requirement of In-Home Storage

In-home storage requires thoughtful planning and review because family resources will need to be re-allocated in new and perhaps unfamiliar ways. Achieving the goal of preparedness demands change. Change requires commitment. Essential resource demands will be:

- sacrificing immediate gratification for long-term objectives
- setting aside time to establish and maintain a home storage program
- investing financial resources in purchasing adequate food and supplies
- designating and using living space for storage of food and supplies
- using stored foods as a regular part of daily food preparation
- rotating foodstuffs and supplies on a fixed schedule

The great reward for all this planning activity is being self-reliant and self-sustaining!

Though establishing an in-home storage program is not easy, it's worth it. We must realize there's no security without labor; there's no progress today without the experiences of yesterday; and, there's no future prosperity without adhering to sound advice.

Wealth and security seem to increase whenever people exert energy in the right direction and in the right causes.

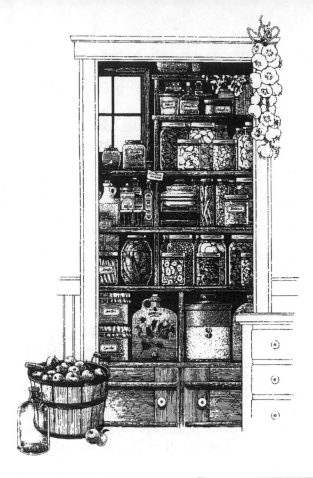

Chapter 2
Basic In-Home Storage

Almost everyone accepts the concept of being prepared for emergencies. However, when it's time to do the actual planning and acquiring the necessary items, most of us are simply overwhelmed by the enormity of it all. Let's face it, most of us have a difficult time getting organized for a Saturday afternoon barbecue, much less planning for and procuring enough foodstuffs to feed ourselves for an entire week, month, or longer.

Your thoughts may be like mine were: "It could take years to acquire all that stuff…" and "Even if money weren't an issue, where and how can I store food and supplies so they can be used and not go to waste?" More basic than that were the details of *what* to store, *how much* of each, and *which* items to buy first. The solution to the problem is found in an age-old saying: "A journey of a thousand miles begins with the first step."

Take the first step by using this ***Family Preparedness Handbook*** as your workbook. The answers to the questions of *what* to acquire first, *how much* to store, and *how long* items should last on the shelf are addressed in this ***Handbook***.

Don't count on the ***Handbook*** for sustenance unless you've applied some of your personal energy and resources to planning and implementing the concepts and principles that will help you meet your storage needs. The ***Handbook*** is not printed on rice paper with vitaminized ink—you won't be able to boil it and eat it if you've otherwise failed to prepare!

> *"A meaningful life is not a matter of speed or efficiency. It's much more a matter of what you do and why you do it, than how fast you get it done."*
>
> Stephen R. Covey

PREPAREDNESS AND IN-HOME STORAGE

The *Family Preparedness Handbook* concept of being prepared is having the resources in your home to live in a near-normal manner for up to a year when natural, man-caused, or personal disasters impact your geographical area, your neighborhood, or your own life. This effort is a choice you make to become self-reliant. Once you make this choice, the negative impact of any disaster is mitigated by your preparedness, and you can provide your family continuing security.

Creating a one-year inventory of foods and nonfoods from which a family can live without need of constant replenishment is no small undertaking. We recognize that the average American family may not be financially capable of having a full-fledged one-year supply of foods and nonfoods, but every family can do a better job of utilizing its resources to attain security—it's simply a matter of choices.

If you are overwhelmed by the magnitude of what it would take to sustain you for a year, then think more in terms of what it would take to keep you alive for a few days, weeks, or months in case you didn't have anything else to eat except what's on hand. Be honest with yourself in both your expectations and the reality of what resources you can commit to creating an in-home store.

There are only three things to remember about building your in-home storage program with the *Family Preparedness Handbook* concept:

1. **Store what you eat!**
2. **Eat what you store!**
3. **Use it or lose it!**

The biggest challenge in procuring an in-home storage supply is financing its acquisition. Creative use of current household items, wise budgeting in accordance with the family's income, and smarter shopping will help minimize costs. But until the in-home storage program is established as a primary financial priority—*after planning the repayment of current debt, of course*—it will not become a reality.

We've found that creating an in-home store is both a journey *and* a destination. Begin planning your journey by determining where you want to be in your preparedness and when you plan to arrive there. Identify where you are on your journey now and commit to move consistently towards your destination and learn along the way. Remind yourself, *"I don't have to do it all at once; I just have to begin, then I can continue from there."*

Most importantly, get everyone in the family involved in the storage program, particularly in decisions about food purchases, because you want to buy only those items your family will consume. As family funds, living and play space, family work assignments, and so many other assets may require redistribution, family discussions about and agreement to changes are important.

A storage program is an opportunity for family members to have a common destination and be on a joint journey—generating shared enthusiasm, building family unity, and instilling a feeling of self-reliance for the entire family. In the remainder of this chapter, we give you practical ways and means, as well as some methods and tools, to set up your own in-home storage plan. In the *Family Preparedness Handbook* you'll discover the following things to do and how to do them. For example, in this chapter, you'll learn:

How to:
- build a basic in-home storage program
- know what items to store for best nutrition, health, and morale maintenance
- select a balance of food and nonfood items and the appropriate quantities

You're also provided the necessary equipment:

Tools to:
- chart inventory quantities needed
- compute a simple numerical value to determine storage quantities
- prioritize storage selections and budget your money for purchases
- use time units to make your storage program more manageable

What's Important to Store

The storage program recommended by the *Family Preparedness Handbook* is comprised of fifteen food and nonfood **In-Home Storage Categories** (see **Chart 2-1** & **Chart 2-2**). Six of the categories, called the *Foundation Categories,* are the *basics* upon which the other categories, the *Building Block Categories,* are added—forming the structure for a viable in-home storage program. By themselves, the food and nonfood items in the six Foundation Categories are capable of sustaining life through a fundamental, no-frills diet. Building Block foods enhance the utility and enjoyment of these basic foods by increasing the variety of recipes and menus possible. Including the Building Block nonfoods in the storage program improves a family's ability to handle emergencies, fosters a healthier existence, and supports a more routine lifestyle when necessary to rely solely on stored items.

Chart 2–1

Basic In-Home Storage Categories

Foundation Categories—the Basics	
1. Water—emergency supplies & treatment	• 2nd in importance only to the air we breathe • we can survive approximately 3 days without it • simplest basic category to store
2. Wheat, other whole grains, flours, & beans	• considered an essential item for any food storage program • assumes family will have other basic foods in storage
3. Powdered milk, dairy products, & eggs	• stored as whole dried milk or skim (nonfat)
4. Sweeteners—honey, sugar, & syrup	• essential sugars for many food preparations
5. Cooking catalysts	• salt, oil, & leaveners essential to food preparation • category essential to body development • least expensive category to store
6. Sprouting seeds & supplies	• fresh, green, live whole foods—any time of the year—for pennies per day

The nine Building Block food and nonfood categories are briefly described in **Chart 2-2**. The listings in the chart are organized arbitrarily. In practice each family must choose how to prioritize its own categories, purchases, and the details of which items to acquire for a workable preparedness plan.

Chart 2–2

In-Home Storage Categories

Building Block Categories	
7. Medical care, medications, & first aid kits	• medications without which a person's life or health is in jeopardy • 30-day supply of all essential medications in an emergency kit • first aid supplies for emergencies or in the event of a disaster
8. Basic supplementation—vitamin, mineral, and herbal supplements	• essential for storage diet to maintain adequate nutrition • processed foods are depleted in vitamins and minerals • additional nutritional losses are incurred from long-term storage of foods • necessary to support the body during stressful times generally accompanying a food-storage-only diet
9. Fuels, energy, & camping gear	• when there are no available public utilities, these commodities will provide the means for cooking your food, as well as heating and lighting your living space • emergency commodities, such as bedding, cooking equipment, and other necessities for away-from-home living, if required
10. Personal, family, infant, & pet care essentials	• clothing, personal items, and body care items • necessities for individual special needs • necessities for babies, infants, or children • food and care items for any pets
11. Canned & dried fruits, vegetables, & soups	• selection of the family's favorite and familiar fruits, vegetables, and soups in quantities adequate to provide regular meals
12. Kitchen staples—condiments & seasonings	• all the meal accessories the family needs to make meals as tasty and normal as possible
13. Meats & seafoods	• selection of meats—fresh, frozen, or canned
14. Domestic maintenance & preparedness	• items needed to maintain the home, yard, garden—all the important things needed for continuing repair and maintenance
15. Pleasure foods—snacks, beverages, sweets, & treats	• morale-lifting, familiar, and convenient foods that would give the family a "lift" when all else seems to be going awry

All fifteen categories together represent a variety of foods and nonfoods that, when stored in your in-home "pantry," would support family life in a near-normal manner. Each category has an associated **Pantry List** (found in the last section of this chapter) which identifies suggested storage foods and nonfoods. You are encouraged to personalize the listings and add any other items your family chooses.

Some items in the **Pantry Lists** have been designated as "essential" and are noted in boldface type. For example, in **Quick-List 2–1**, **potable water**, **aseptic water**, **bleach**, and **treatment tablets** have been selected as essentials. *Essential* items are recommended as first purchases within each category because of their contribution to sustaining life in a reasonably healthy and normal manner, enhancing variety in menu and meal selection, and increasing the utility of your storage.

The other food and nonfood items (not in boldface type) on the **Pantry Lists** are referred to as "supplemental." They are included to offer greater choice and to fulfill personal needs. That means that even though I don't consider *Twinkies®* a personal choice, it doesn't preclude your family from making that choice!

It is each family's challenge and opportunity to decide which foods and nonfoods to store based on individual preference, age, sex, health needs, finances, available storage space, living conditions, job(s), etc. The **In-Home Storage Categories** and **Pantry Lists** are provided as a framework of suggestions from which you make choices to plan your in-home storage program.

The Foundation Categories

The first six categories together are considered the Foundation Categories. Water, wheat (other grains, beans, etc.), powdered milk, honey, salt, and sprouting seeds are the real *basics* of in-home storage. Each of these items is relatively inexpensive to purchase for storage, stores easily for long periods, and provides adequate nutrition to sustain life—though most people won't get fat from them. The true worth lies, however, in their combination because they work synergistically—each adding greater value to the others.

The advantages of using these basics as the foundation of in-home storage are that they maximize

- family dollars available for storage purchases
- available household storage space
- utility of other stored foods
- life-sustaining capability with least number of stored foods and least expense

Chart 2-3 illustrates the significance of the Foundation Categories—individually and in relationship to each other. Note that as each category is added, nutritional value, diet selection, and versatility are increased. Water by itself will sustain life but offers no nutrition. Wheat adds nutrition to the diet. Each additional category multiplies the value of the others. This **Building on Basics** concept is what makes the Foundation Categories so fundamentally important to in-home storage.

Most of the remaining chapters in this *Handbook* focus on the basic foundation foods. The information in these chapters will provide you with greater detail about the foods, instructions for utilizing them, and some basic recipes to enhance these stored foods.

Using the basic foods offers tremendous opportunities to experience a lifestyle that supports personal growth. Integrating basic foods into your present diet is a way to put new skills into operation, develop greater self-reliance and resourcefulness, and improve your ability to adapt to change. Frequently people tell us that their copies of earlier editions of the *Family Preparedness Handbook* are worn out because of the use they received during challenging times when they were raising their families on limited funds.

Now is the time to begin living from in-home resources. Practice new skills and adjust to unfamiliar foods before the necessity of living only on stored supplies arises. These new skills are not acquired overnight, and eating basic foods requires acclimation—the body must adjust gradually to different foods. Incorporating basic foods into your daily lifestyle is a worthy challenge for any family—the rewards will eventually speak for themselves.

Chart 2–3

Building on Basics—Illustration of Incremental Values

					fresh green vegetables provide live whole food year round for excellent nutrition; use alone or with other foods; excellent in salads, soups, sandwiches, add to baked breads, casseroles, etc.
				cooking catalysts enhance recipes; also essential to chemical action in dough; saline preservative for meats and vegetables; pickling & brining; yeast makes finer breads; oils essential to frying, baking & general cooking	
			a catalyst for food preparation; essential to chemical action in certain foods; enhances recipes and all foods; sweet preservative for fruits & vegetables		
	whole-grain cereal (bulgur); soups & stews; side dish; use instead of potatoes; make primitive breads; boil for whole-berry cereals; roast for hot drinks; substitute for rice; sprout as substitute for green vegetables; dry sprouts for sugar; add a grinder and crack grain for cereals, whole-wheat flour for gluten (a substitute for meat); make more advanced non-yeast breads such as sourdough & tortillas	enhances water and wheat use; expands utility of cracked grains and whole-wheat flours; provides milk and dairy products such as yogurt, cottage cheese, & hard cheeses; makes creamy topping when whipped			
a person can live on water alone for many days; add treatment system to assure continuing supply of drinking & cooking water					
water (treatment device)	**wheat / whole grains (grinder or mill)**	**powdered milk**	**sweeteners**	**cooking catalysts (salt, oil, & yeast)**	**sprouts & seeds**
absolute *basic;* has fairly short storage life (3–6 months); heavy, bulky to store, but cheap to acquire; treatment device small & not expensive	addition of wheat to water provides a quantum leap for nutrition and survivability; nutritious & versatile grain; has indefinite (15+ years) storage life; grinder provides ability to increase utility of wheat	stores well (up to 48 months); allows in-home production of yogurt, cottage cheese, and hard cheese when yogurt-maker and cheese press added	stores indefinitely; enhances taste of foods; honey is preferred sweetener due to higher nutritive content, more healthful attributes, & sweeter than sugar	cooking catalysts are essential to cooking; salt stores indefinitely; critical to body cell functioning; very little storage space required for this entire category; oil & yeast essential to baking	easiest method of gardening—requires only small space in kitchen cabinet / on windowsill; equipment: quart jar, piece of gauze, & rubber band; inexpensive seed & very inexpensive equipment; requires very little storage space

GUIDELINES FOR STOCKING YOUR PANTRY

After reviewing potential storage items in the **Pantry Lists** at the end of this chapter, walk through your home taking a "fresh" look at your household goods as supplies for in-home storage. So maybe you don't have a year's supply of food yet, but maybe you have a year's supply of seasonings and lots of canned goods or packaged mixes.

Check out your equipment. What tools do you have for cooking and baking? Do you have camping gear—equipment that might be used for emergencies?

An old lunch box makes a very good container for first aid supplies. What items do you have in the bathroom drawers and in the kitchen cabinets that might go into a first aid kit? Remember the last time you had fast food and threw away the plastic utensils in the plastic sleeve without a care? What about keeping those for your in-home storage in case you don't have water for washing dishes. Picnic supplies may come in handy, too. Emptied plastic soda bottles work well for storing emergency drinking water—which is a good way to reuse these items, too.

Get boxes and begin sorting storage items as you find them. Make the best of the things you already have. Most people are surprised to find how much they have on hand already. You'll soon realize that preparedness is really a matter of awareness of what you have at your disposal for whatever needs you have.

Rebuild, recycle, redo, refinish refurbish, relock, remake, renew, repair, resole, reupholster, rewire re-order your pri-orities...

get back to the basics!

Store What You Eat

The most important part of an in-home storage plan is knowing what you eat now and buying what you'll most likely eat in the future. In-home storage is wasted time, money, and effort if the food stored does not appeal to the family's taste.

This is an excellent time to review carefully your eating habits—becoming even more aware of the "good" foods your family eats as well as the snacks, treats, drinks, and other "junk" foods to which they've become attached. It is also a great teaching moment for parents to urge children (of all ages!) to cut back on all sorts of unhealthy foods, especially since they don't usually store well, as a general rule. It's a good idea to begin to limit your purchases of prepared foods, too.

Your in-home pantry is managed in a similar fashion to the local grocery store—as items are stocked, they are placed behind the goods already on the shelf. As you acquire items for your in-home storage, date them so you'll know which was purchased first. Items with shorter shelf life may be noted and dated *"Use by: _____"* to assure utilization within their useful shelf life period. As items are used, they are restocked. Food items not favored by the family are obviously not restocked. Managing the rotation of all food items will be much easier if you have stored foods that family members are interested in eating.

Inventory management for *Basic* in-home food storage is very simple—and hopefully, by now, very familiar:

1. **Store what you eat.**
2. **Eat what you store.**
3. **Use it or lose it!**

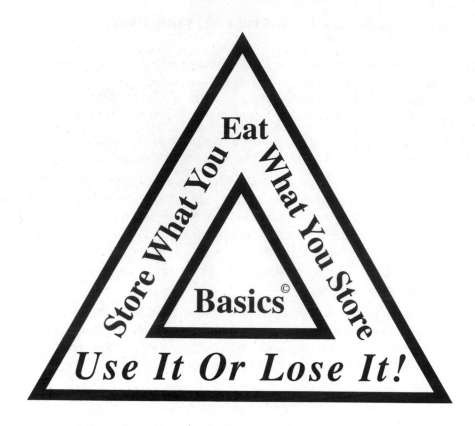

Purchase the "Essentials" First

Realistically, given the need to allocate your financial resources to more areas of your life than just purchasing storage supplies, it becomes critically important to have a way to determine what to buy first. In this edition of **Making the Best of Basics** we provide you with a **Shopping List** that eliminates the guesswork.

The **Essentials Shopping List** at the end of this chapter identifies selected items from each **In-Home Storage Category** that are recommended as *essential* needs or purchases. As noted, essential items have been selected because of their contribution to sustaining life in a reasonably normal and healthy manner, for enhancing variety in meal selection, and to supporting greater utility of the other stored items.

Use the **Shopping List** as a guide to the most useful purchases for your storage supply. If the only items acquired for in-home storage were the essentials, you would have a life- and health-sustaining diet.

The advantages of employing the **Shopping List** are

- provides you with a built-in plan until you gain experience to design your own

- allows you to acquire storage items in an orderly and systematic manner—one at a time—and one that is consistent with your income

- facilitates storing supplies from all categories—insuring greater self-sufficiency

- permits flexibility—can be modified to meet your personal needs

Determine Manageable Time Units

The process of gathering a year's supply can be accomplished more easily if the effort is broken into smaller parts. Do this by setting up *time units* in which to accomplish certain interim objectives or stopping places on your journey. Determine the block(s) of time in which you function most comfortably.

If you're oriented to a week-at-a-time schedule, then plan to store 52 one-week quantities. If you organized on a monthly basis, then plan for 12 one-month quantities—or as we call it in today's parlance, installments. Time units are a good method to relate to your acquisition plan. Once you've decided what to buy, merely divide the family's storage requirements by whatever time unit(s) your family chooses, then buy the item(s) in installments. Make the calendar and time work for you!

Chart Your Progress

There are no deadlines other than those you establish for yourself, and these are established only in relationship to your own circumstances. *Any progress you make is success.* Put a chart on your wall for your family to see the progress being made. This chart can also serve to display the range and balance of items stored, helping avoid imbalances (for example: 6 week's/month's worth of powdered milk, only 1 week/month of wheat, and no water for making milk or bread!).

Chart 2–4 is an example of a chart you could make and place on a wall or the refrigerator door, using colored pens or crayon to show your on-hand position versus your needs. Charting your progress will remind you of your family's achievements in your in-home food storage plan and give encouragement on your journey.

Borrowing money to acquire in-home food storage items is not recommended!

Chart 2–4

Sample Family Progress Chart

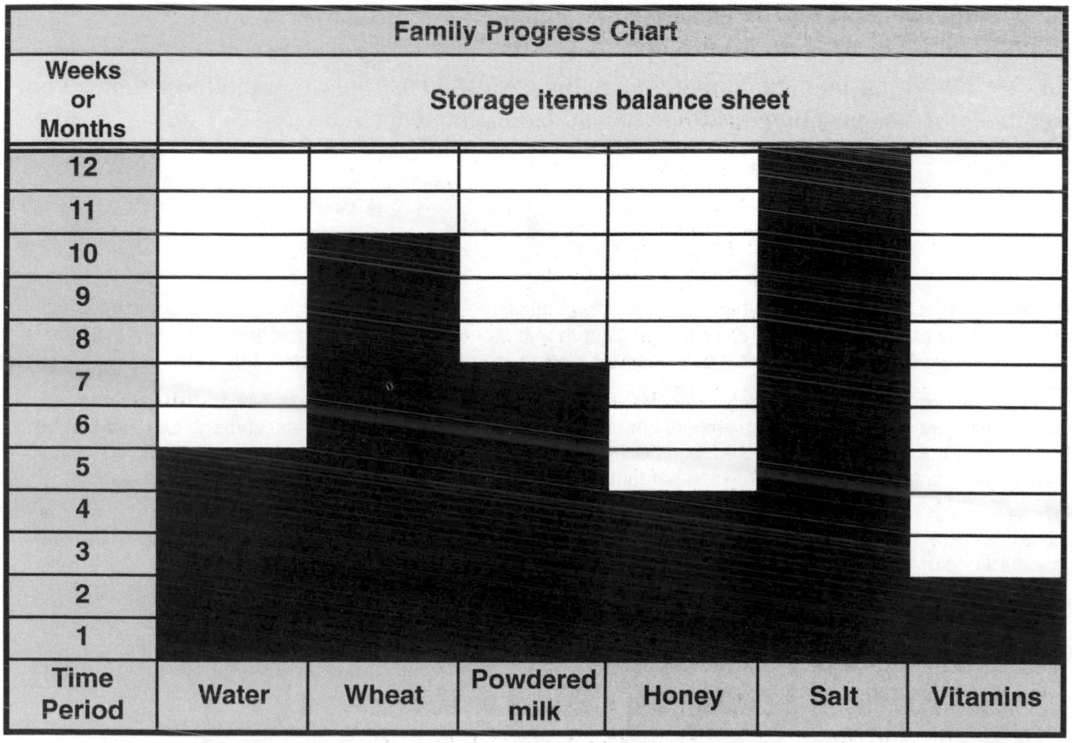

Start In-Home Storage with a "Safety Net" Supply

Having an in-home food storage supply is not an "all or nothing" situation. All food storage is ever-changing and transitional. As you begin your family's in-home food storage project and establish your plan, you may want to experience some immediate progress by starting with *safety net* supply purchasing. This acquisition concept may help you gain momentum immediately by obtaining some items without destroying your overall budget.

Safety net purchases should be food and supplies which would sustain life should an emergency occur before your total preparations are completed—at least you would have some food in your pantry. Buy for your storage program those items consumed in your present diet through a process called *planned copybuying* [1]—a purchasing plan you already utilize, it just wasn't formalized with a name. *Planned copybuying* means buying extra cans, jars, or packages of foodstuffs, medicines, and household products you routinely use.

Safety net purchasing might include either of the following methods of planned copybuying:

- **Dupli-buying:** As you buy food items for immediate use—*buy another for your in-home food storage program*. Do this *every* time you shop. This doesn't include buying extra perishable and low-priority items, of course.

  This method allows you to acquire foods you normally use, while eventually building a reservoir of foodstuffs. Perhaps for the budget-limited, this is the only way to get some foods in the "safety net."

- **Multi-buying:** *Buy a large supply of anything you use when it's on sale*. As seasonal food and product specials are offered by the stores, you'll maximize your purchasing power through bulk buying.

  This is the preferable way to acquire food storage items more quickly, but it requires a greater financial commitment and resources to accomplish.

In essence, either form of copybuying is the easiest and simplest method to balance your acquisitions—you're buying what you eat and eating what you buy.

---

[1] Pat Slaughter is a practicing in-home food storage counselor and has taught many classes on how to save a year's supply and make 72-hour emergency kits. In-home storage is a program she firmly believes in and lives by daily. She can be reached at 373 E. Roosevelt, Salt Lake City UT 84115 ☎(801) 485-6413.

Pat learned about food storage early in life. Her father and grandmother taught her to buy 2 of an item and put 1 away. From her childhood, she remembers her father putting the "extra" in a big metal garbage can and that he was always willing to share his stored foods with others. She remembers all too well when the family was forced to live from stored foods for a year when her father was ill. Once he recovered, he started saving food again.

Three times in her life she has relied on her food storage: the first occasion was when she became very ill and could not work for a year; the second was as a single mother raising three daughters and between jobs; and the third occurred when she gave her food storage to her daughter's family to help them get started in civilian life after leaving the military.

Her children carry on the family food storage tradition. Recently, her daughter in Missouri was able to sustain her own family and also supplied neighbors with food for several weeks after the Midwest floods inundated their area.

Maximize Your Purchasing Power

Here are some hints to help remind you about using all techniques at your disposal to minimize costs and maximize value as you implement your in-home storage plan:

- Learn to use coupons effectively when shopping at retail stores.
- Discover food wholesalers and buying clubs, or establish cooperative grocery clubs with a group of friends, get into a group buying plan, learn to master the feed and grain stores, and even haunt the farmer co-ops or open-air markets—whatever it takes to get lower prices and expand your purchasing dollars.
- Find or establish barter or exchange organizations. If there are no organizations of these types in your area, start one. Consider starting with your extended family, neighbors, church group, or other organizations with which you are familiar.
- Join or start a *shared resources* group. Find others who are willing to share the costs and use of expensive equipment, for example. The equipment then is owned collectively and no one family must bear the entire expense of expensive nonfood items.
- Utilize mail order for those storage items that you cannot obtain locally or are more costly when bought locally.

> *Please write your notes in the margins—that's why they're so wide!*

Capitalize on the Wide Variety of Resources Available

Planning your in-home food storage program is essential. The best knowledge about what your family requires for its subsistence during a time of need—whether it's a short or long period of time—seems always to come *after* your bad experience. That could be far too late for your family when the next emergency situation occurs.

Knowing how to organize, maintain, and fully utilize a sensible, continuing, workable in-home food storage program becomes a matter of self-education and self-implementation for each family in advance of a natural, man-caused, or personal disaster.

Thankfully, there are numerous public and private resources available for those who want to do more homework before launching their journey. Draw on the experience and knowledge of others to establish and maintain proactively your own preparedness and in-home food storage program. At the end of this **Handbook** you will find supplemental materials which provide listings of publications and suppliers of products which you may want to utilize.

PLANNING YOUR ONE-YEAR STORAGE

The kinds of foods and nonfoods and the amounts to be stored for a one-year supply are recommended in this section of the **Family Preparedness Handbook.** This information is compiled from knowledge available as of publication date and intended to provide generic guidelines. These guidelines should be varied according to each family's tastes, situation and circumstances.

A good in-home storage program is based on knowledge of your family's eating habits. You'll also need to take into account the ages, occupation(s), nutritional state, health, climate, and other factors which may alter the kinds of foods desired, supplies needed, and the amount(s) of each to be stored for an entire family.

Quick-Charts

To help you make your one-year, in-home storage a reality, this **Handbook** provides an organized framework for stocking a one-year pantry. This chapter includes detailed charts which will enable you to determine the economic impact on your financial resources through a ready-made inventorying, prioritizing, purchasing, and budgeting system. Amounts are based on living exclusively on your in-home storage for an entire year—without business lunches, dining out, or eating at the parents' or kids'. By assessing your on-hand supplies, you know where you are currently and how far you must go to reach your one-year supply requirements.

Quick-Guide 2–1. Provides an overview of the **In-Home Storage Categories** and recommended one-year storage quantities for the average adult male (*Adult Quantity.*)

Quick-Lists 2–1 through **2–15**. **Pantry Lists** detail for each **In-Home Storage Category** the recommended *essential* and *supplemental Storage Items,* expected *Shelf Life* of these recommended storage items, and the recommended one-year storage quantities for the average adult male (*Adult Quantity.*)

Quick-Shop 2–1 Essential Foods and Nonfoods Shopping List. This listing of *essential* foods and nonfoods from all **In-Home Storage Categories** repeats the *Shelf Life* and *Adult Quantity.* In addition it provides worksheet space for figuring family storage requirements. Use this chart to identify *essential* items needed in your in-home storage.

Quick-Shop 2–2 Supplemental Foods & Nonfoods Shopping List. This blank chart provides worksheet space to write down needed *supplemental* storage items and to determine family storage needs. Refer to the **Pantry Lists** for *Shelf Life* and *Adult Quantity* of needed items.

Quick-Plan 2–1 Planning & Budgeting Worksheet. This blank worksheet provides space to prioritize all of your needed storage items, write down sources and suppliers of storage items, and figure costs of the needed items.

Family Factor

Over the years, our experience in communicating the concept of preparedness through basic in-home food storage has grown. In this edition, we're sharing our easier, simpler method of computing the food and nonfood quantities needed for storage. This method uses a numerical value, based on points assigned to each member of the household. Once derived by simple math, this numerical value is used as a multiplier for each recommended storage item, thus determining the needed family quantity for that item. To help you derive this numerical value, named the *Family Factor,* you use the *Family Factor Formula.*

The Family Factor Formula assigns each family member food consumption points. These food consumption points are percentages ("points"). These are numbers relative to the average adult male consumption level. Using 100 points for the adult male as the base, or index, number, the consumption points for other family members are lesser or greater percentages, depending on age, sex, and appetite, of course. See **Chart 2-5** for other family member "points."

Assume you're part of a family comprised of an average adult male, consumption level @ 100 points (or 100%), an adult female @ 85 points (85% or 0.85 consumption of adult male), 2 male teenagers @ 140 points each (140% per male teenager, or 40% more than adult male), a female teenager @ 95 points (95% or 0.95 of adult male), a female child @ 75 points (75% or 0.75 of an adult male), and an infant @ 50 points (50% or 0.50 of adult male). The Family Factor Formula uses these consumption points or percentages to determine the Family Factor.

Using **Chart 2–5** derive the **Family Factor** by the following steps.

1. Identify the *Number (#) of People* in each *Family Members* category (i.e., 1 male adult, 1 female adult, 2 male teenagers, etc.).

2. Multiply the *Number (#) of People* in each category by the assigned *Consumption Points* to obtain *Total Points*.

3. Add together the *Total Points* to determine the *Family Total Points.*

4. Divide the *Family Points Total* by 100 to determine the Family Factor.

Chart 2–5

Sample Family Factor

Computing Your Family Factor					
Family Members	# People	X	Points	=	Total Points
Male adult	1		100		100
Female adult	1		85		85
Male teenager	2		140		280
Female teenager	1		95		95
Male child			95		
Female child	1		75		75
Infant (1–3 yrs.)	1		50		50
Family Total Points					685
Divide total points by 100					÷ 100
This is the Sample *Family Factor*:					6.85

Below is a chart for deriving your own *Family Factor.*

Chart 2–6

My Family Factor

Computing Your Family Factor					
Family Members	# People	X	Points	=	Total Points
Male adult			100		
Female adult			85		
Male teenager			140		
Female teenager			95		
Male child			95		
Female child			75		
Infant (1–3 yrs.)			50		
Family Total Points					
Divide total points by 100					÷ 100
This is the Sample *Family Factor*:					_____

To derive the maximum benefit from the Family Factor, factor in your experience and knowledge of your family's consumption habits to make adjustments to the *Consumption Point* values, if necessary. Our figures are based on an adult male's average rate.*

For example, say your teenage son can't live without potatoes at every meal. He even rushes home from school to eat a cold boiled potato, or nowadays, heat it in the microwave oven. He then drenches the hot potato with 2 tablespoons of butter and dollops on a quarter-pound of sour cream—just so he can make it to supper time! In such an instance, you'd need to adjust the Family Factor in the potato section of the listings later in this chapter.

Assume for a moment your Family Factor is 6.85, just as the Sample family. Merely "bump up" the Family Factor to 7.0 for this food item. Let's also assume no one in the family likes dehydrated potatoes. Here's what the potato section would be for your family:

Quantities rounded to nearest 5 lb., except where noted ✎			Family Multiplier	Food Storage Requirements			
Storage Item	Shelf Life in months	Adult Quantity	Family Factor	Family Total	On Hand	Needs	Quick-Chart Worksheets (✓)
potatoes & yams (fresh equivalent)—200 lb. minimum assorted from this listing							
potatoes, all dried	36–48	25	0	0	0	0	
potatoes, all, fresh—see Chapter 3	1–6	150	7.0	1050	150	900	✔

* recommended storage quantities are indexed to the yearly requirements for the average adult male

The Family Factor Formula is based on a collection of federal data from the *U.S. Department of Agriculture, U.S. Required Daily Allowance* (USRDA), and other U.S. government publications which establish average yearly consumption levels of most foods for the average adult male. Temper this government information with acquired knowledge and many years of accumulated experience through testing and learning of food storage consultants, food and dietary experts, medical doctors, even holistic medical practitioners—and the result is this simplified formula.

Step-by-Step Planning

1. Review each **Pantry List** for the recommended storage items; checkmark items needed in your personal pantry. Remember, not every item recommended may be suitable for your family.
2. Transfer the checkmarked items to the **Shopping Lists.** (The *essential* items are already listed for you.)
3. On the **Shopping List** calculate the *Family Total* (amount needed for one year) by multiplying the *Adult Quantity* by your *Family Factor.* Remember to adjust your *Family Factor* to meet your needs.
4. Inventory your current supplies. Fill in amounts in the *On-Hand* category of the **Shopping Lists.**
5. On the **Shopping List**, subtract *On Hand* from *Family Total* to determine *Needs.*
6. List needed items on the **Budget Sheets** by priority of need.
7. Identify suppliers and cost of each item on **Budget Sheets.**
8. Total the costs of all items on the **Budget Sheets**.
9. Use this information to plan your shopping.

Quick-Guide 2–1

In-Home Storage Categories

Quantities rounded to nearest 5 lb., except where noted 🐟			In-Home Storage Requirements				
Storage Item ①	Shelf Life (Months) ②	Adult Quantity ③	Family Factor ④	Family Total ⑤	On Hand ⑥	Needs ⑦	Quick-Plan Worksheets (✓) ⑧
In-Home Storage Categories							
water—emergency supplies & treatment (2 weeks)		14 gal.	see Chapter 4 for details ⑨				Quick-List 2–1⑩
wheat, other whole grains, flours, & beans		700 lb.	see Chapter 5 for details				Quick-List 2–2
powdered milk, dairy products, & eggs		200 lb.	see Chapter 12 for details				Quick-List 2–3
sweeteners—honey, sugar, & syrup		100 lb.	see Chapter 13 for details				Quick-List 2–4
cooking catalysts		75 lb.					Quick-List 2–5
sprouting seeds & supplies		10 lb.	see Chapter 15 for details				Quick-List 2–6
medical care, medications, & first aid kits		per need					Quick-List 2–7
basic supplementation		per need	see Chapter 14 for details				Quick-List 2–8
fuels, energy, & camping gear		per need	see Chapter 17 for details				Quick-List 2–9
personal, family, infant, & pet care essentials		per need					Quick-List 2–10
canned & dried fruits, vegetables & soups		2,750 serv.	see Chapter 16 for details				Quick-List 2–11
kitchen staples—condiments & seasonings		per need					Quick-List 2–12
meats & seafoods		700 serv.	see Chapter 3 for details				Quick-List 2–13
domestic maintenance & preparedness		per need					Quick-List 2–14
pleasure foods—snacks, beverages, sweets & treats		2,000 serv.					Quick-List 2–15

Notes for Quick-Guide 2–1

This is an overview sheet for the **In-Home Storage Categories**. **Quick-Lists** (*Pantry Lists*) and **Quick-Shop Charts** (*Shopping Lists*) follow which suggest quantities for many items to help you get started with a *Basics in-home storage* plan. Use the key information noted on the **Quick-Guide** marked with a numbered indicator and explained below to understand the corresponding details on the other **Quick-Charts**.

① **Essential and supplemental storage items** for your in-home storage program are listed in this column.

② **Shelf Life** or maximum period of time an item is edible is detailed in this column.

③ **Adult Quantity** suggested is the recommended storage amount for one year for the average adult male.

④ Insert your **Family Factor** previously computed from the *Family Factor Formula*.

⑤ Multiply the **Adult Quantity** amount by the **Family Factor** to derive the **Family Total** amount needed for each item.

⑥ Determine how much of this item you have **On Hand** and enter in this column.

⑦ Deduct **On Hand** amount from **Family Total** amount to determine **Needs** (needed amount).

⑧ Transfer needed items to the **Quick-Plan Worksheet.**

⑨ Refers to specific chapter of the *Handbook* regarding this category.

⑩ Refer to this **Quick-List** for recommended storage items in this category.

Quick-List 2–1

Water—Emergency Supplies & Treatment Pantry List
see Chapter 4 for additional information

Multiply Adult Quantity by your Family Factor to determine your Family Total

✓	Storage Item	Shelf Life (Months)	Adult Quantity	✓	Storage Item	Shelf Life (Months)	Adult Quantity
water				**containers**			
	water, potable	*6–12*	14 gal.[2]		5-gal. collapsible canvas	*indefinite*	
	water, 4 & 6 oz., aseptic pkg	*indefinite*	2 gal.		6-gal. mylar bag w / box	*indefinite*	
commercial bottled water					15-gal. container	*indefinite*	
	1-gal. bottle	*6–12*			25+ gal. canvas bag	*indefinite*	
	2½-gal. bottle	*6–12*			cups, drinking, 6-oz.	*indefinite*	
	5-gal. bottle	*6–12*			canteen / cup	*indefinite*	
tools				**water treatment equipment & supplies**			
	barrel pump	*indefinite*			portable treatment unit	*indefinite*	1 unit
	barrel spigot	*indefinite*			bleach, 5.25% sodium hypochlorite	*6*	1 gal.
	bung wrench	*indefinite*			tablets, water treatment	*36–60*	1 pkg.
testing kits					iodine tincture, 2%	*indefinite*	2 oz.
	testing kit, water quality	*indefinite*			pot with lid (*for boiling water*)	*indefinite*	

Quick-List 2–2

Wheat, Other Whole Grains, Flours & Beans Pantry List
select 700 lb.minimum from this category
see Chapter 5 for additional information

Multiply Adult Quantity by your Family Factor to determine your Family Total

✓	Storage Item	Shelf Life (Months)	Adult Quantity	✓	Storage Item	Shelf Life (Months)	Adult Quantity
wheat—select 350 lb. assorted from this list				**other whole grains—select 100 lb. minimum**			
	wheat, whole grain (berries)	*indefinite*	350		barley	*60*	
	Dark Hard Winter Wheat	*indefinite*			**corn**	*60*	10
	Dark Turkey Red Wheat	*indefinite*			oats	*60*	
	Golden 86 Hard White Spring	*indefinite*			popcorn, whole kernels	*12–24*	20
	Montana White Wheat	*indefinite*			Quinoa	*60*	
	Spring Wheat	*indefinite*			rye	*60*	
	wheat, mill prepack	*indefinite*			triticale	*60*	
flours, fresh-ground or commercial—select 35 lb. minimum assorted from this list							
	barley	*1–2*			rice	*1–2*	
	beans (from dried beans)	*3–6*			rye	*1–2*	
	buckwheat	*1–2*			wheat / bran	*1*	
	cornmeal / flours	*60*	10		wheat / gluten flour	*6–12*	
rice, whole grain—select 45 lb. minimum assorted from this list							
	rice, white, enriched	*24–48*	10		**rice, wild**	*24–36*	5
	rice, white pre-cooked	*36*	25		brown	*1–3*	
pastas (fresh equivalent)—select 35 lb. minimum assorted from this list							
	lasagna	*18–24*			noodles, egg	*6–9*	
	macaroni	*18–24*			spaghetti	*18–24*	

---

[2] This meets the FEMA emergency guideline for one gallon per person per day for two-week *subsistence-level* storage. *Maintenance-level* storage guidelines are two gallons per person per day. However, you should always store as much water as feasible. See **Chapter 4** for storage details.

Quick-List 2–2 (continued)

✓	Storage Item	Shelf Life (Months)	Adult Quantity	✓	Storage Item	Shelf Life (Months)	Adult Quantity
	**Wheat, Other Whole Grains, Flours & Beans Pantry List**						

Wheat, Other Whole Grains, Flours & Beans Pantry List

Multiply Adult Quantity by your Family Factor to determine your Family Total

✓	Storage Item	Shelf Life (Months)	Adult Quantity	✓	Storage Item	Shelf Life (Months)	Adult Quantity
	**cereals, whole grain—select 50 lb. minimum assorted from this list**						
	barley, pearled	12			kernel, whole grains	1–3	
	buckwheat (kasha)	6–12			oats, groats	1–3	
	granola (see **Ch. 7**)	1–3			oats, rolled (oatmeal)	12	
	hominy & hominy grits	12			Quinoa	1–3	
	**cereals, processed & prepared—select 25 lb. minimum assorted from these lists**						
colspan4	ready-to-eat, dry	colspan4	ready-to-heat, pre-cooked
	corn	12			corn / hominy / posole	12	
	rice	12			oatmeal	12	
	wheat, shredded	12			wheat / rice, creamed		
	**legumes, variety of dried beans & peas—select 75 lb. minimum assorted from this list**						
	bottled & canned, all	24–36			navy	varies	
	dried, all	60+			peas, black-eyed	varies	
	Anasazi	varies			peas, green or split	varies	
	kidney	varies			pinto	varies	
	lentils	varies			soybeans	varies	
	lima, large & small	varies					
	**textured vegetable protein (TVP)—select 10 lb. minimum from this list**						
	TVP, unflavored	24–36	5		flavorings—ham / beef / chicken / vegetable	24–36	1
	**equipment & supplies needed for storage—see Chapter 5 for details**						
	grain mill / grinder	indefinite	1 / family		mixer / breadmaking	indefinite	1 / family
	dry ice	minutes!	depends		containers / tight-fitting lids	indefinite	
	diatomaceous earth	indefinite	depends		liners, plastic, food-grade	indefinite	

Quick-List 2–3

Powdered Milk, Dairy Products & Eggs Pantry List
select 200 lb. minimum assorted from this category
see Chapter 12 for additional information about powdered milk & Chapter 3 for refrigerated item listing details

Multiply Adult Quantity by your Family Factor to determine your Family Total

✓	Storage Item	Shelf Life (Months)	Adult Quantity	✓	Storage Item	Shelf Life (Months)	Adult Quantity
	**dairy products, dried & powdered—150 lb. minimum assorted from this list**						
	milk, non-instant powdered	24–48	100		buttermilk powder	24–36	
	butter, dehydrated	60–96	20		milk, aseptic packaging	pkg. date	
	cheese, dehydrated	60–96	25		non-dairy creamers	24–36	
colspan4	**eggs, powdered—25 dz. minimum (fresh equiv.)**	colspan4	**milk, canned—select 24 cans from this list**
	eggs, dehydr. / freeze-dried	60–96	25 dz.		evaporated milk	24–36	6 cans
colspan4	**cheese-making items**		condensed, sweetened	24–35	12 cans
	cheese press (see **Ch. 12**)	indefinite			**yogurt-making items**
	cooking thermometer	indefinite			yogurt starter / wet type	1–2 wk.	
	cheese cloth, fine mesh	indefinite			cheese bag / cheese cloth	indefinite	
	Rennet / Junket tablets	indefinite			yogurt maker (see **Ch. 12**)	indefinite	

Quick-List 2–4

Sweeteners—Honey, Sugar & Syrup Pantry List
select 100 lb. minimum assorted from this category
see Chapter 13 for additional information

Multiply Adult Quantity by your Family Factor to determine your Family Total

✓	Storage Item	Shelf Life (Months)	Adult Quantity	✓	Storage Item	Shelf Life (Months)	Adult Quantity
	honey—select 70 lb. minimum from this listing				**sugar—select 15 lb. minimum from this listing**		
	honey, unfiltered	*indefinite*	65		sugar, white	*indefinite*	10
	comb, pure & unprocessed	*indefinite*			brown	*indefinite*	
	creamed	*48–60*			confectioners	*indefinite*	
	diluted	*36–48*			maple sugar	*48–60*	
	syrup / equivalents—as needed				substitutes, non-sugar	*indefinite*	
	corn syrup	*indefinite*			**equipment for storage**		
	maple syrup	*indefinite*			containers / tight-fitting lids	*indefinite*	
	molasses	*18–24*			plastic bags, food-grade	*indefinite*	

Quick-List 2–5

Cooking Catalysts—Salt, Oils & Leaveners Pantry List
select 75 lb. minimum assorted from this category

Multiply Adult Quantity by your Family Factor to determine your Family Total

✓	Storage Item	Shelf Life (Months)	Adult Quantity	✓	Storage Item	Shelf Life (Months)	Adult Quantity
	salt—select 5 lb. minimum from this list						
	iodized salt	*indefinite*	5		salt, ice cream	*indefinite*	per need
	salt, pickling	*indefinite*	per need		seasoning, herbs, no-salt	*12–18*	
	leaveners, dry & moist—select 1 lb. minimum from this list				**oils, fats & shortening—15 gal. (60 lb.) minimum assorted from this list**		
	yeast, cake, moist	*pkg. date*	4 oz.		vegetable oil, liquid	*12–24*	10 gal.
	yeast, active dry powdered	*12–24*	12 oz.		lard, commercial rendering	*3–6*	
	sourdough starter	*1–3*			olive, extra virgin	*12–24*	
	powder, baking	*6–9*			sesame	*2–4*	
	soda, baking	*18–24*			shortening, vegetable, all	*12*	

Quick-List 2–6

Sprouting—Seeds & Supplies Pantry List
select 10 lb. minimum assorted from this category
see Chapter 15 for additional information

Multiply Adult Quantity by your Family Factor to determine your Family Total

✓	Storage Item	Shelf Life (Months)	Adult Quantity	✓	Storage Item	Shelf Life (Months)	Adult Quantity
	select 10 lb. minimum assorted beans, grains & seeds						
	for best results, use only untreated or organic beans, grains & seeds						
	alfalfa	*24–36*	1		soybean	*24–36*	
	barley, unhulled	*24–36*			vegetables—your selection	*24–36*	
	mung	*24–36*			wheat	*24–36*	
	peas—your preference	*24–36*					
	equipment for sprouting						
	quart jar w / screw ring	*indefinite*			cheese cloth	*indefinite*	
	sealing ring, canning	*indefinite*			rubber band	*indefinite*	
	colander or strainer	*indefinite*			nylon netting	*indefinite*	

Quick-List 2–7

✓	**Storage Item**	**Shelf Life (Months)**	**Adult Quantity**		✓	**Storage Item**	**Shelf Life (Months)**	**Adult Quantity**
**Medical Care—Medications & First Aid Kits Pantry List**								

✓	Storage Item	Shelf Life (Months)	Adult Quantity	✓	Storage Item	Shelf Life (Months)	Adult Quantity
**personal life-preserving medications[3]**							
	cardiovascular conditions medication				**nervous conditions medications**—for those being treated for emotional, psychological or psychiatric disorders & those whose "normal" functioning is dependent upon medication		
	nitroglycerin—all forms	pkg. date			anti-anxiety medications	pkg. date	
	sub-lingual	pkg. date			anti-depressants	pkg. date	
	patches	pkg. date			tranquilizers	pkg. date	
	digitalis preparations	pkg. date			**respiratory and allergic conditions**		
	blood thinners	pkg. date			allergy medications	pkg. date	
	diuretics	pkg. date			asthma "puffers"	pkg. date	
	heart / blood pressure pre-scriptions	pkg. date			bite & sting medications for severely allergic persons	pkg. date	
	diabetic conditions medication				cortisone	pkg. date	
	insulin—all types used	pkg. date			oral med. / "breathing" relief	pkg. date	
	injectables	pkg. date			**seizure conditions medications**		
	oral dosages	pkg. date			epileptic seizure preventives	pkg. date	
	syringes / needles	pkg. date			seizure medication	pkg. date	
	"stomach" and intestinal medications						
	colitis / irritable bowel medications	pkg. date			ulcer medications	pkg. date	
	gastritis medications	pkg. date					
**other critical conditions medication(s)**							
**prescription medications for preventive care** — ask your physician for a prescription & refills — if you are allergic to Keflex, substitute "Zithromax", a new & often more costly medication							
	twenty (20) tabs or caps 500 mg Cephalexin ("Keflex")	pkg. date			six (6) caps 250 mg Azithromycin ("Zithromax")	pkg. date	
**recommended non-prescription health maintenance medications & supplies** — the following items are useful and helpful in treatment of minor illnesses, aches, pains, and general personal well-being:							
	acetaminophen (reduce fever)	12–24			bicarbonate of soda	12–24	
	antacid medication (for upset stomach)	12–24			syrup of Ipecac (to induce vomiting)	12–24	
	anti-diarrhea medication	12–24			hydrogen peroxide	6–12	
	aspirin (for headaches)	12–24			eye drops	9–12	
	hay fever / cold / sinus tablets	12–24			laxative	indefinite	
	ibuprofen (to reduce pain)	12–24			mineral oil	indefinite	
	alcohol / rubbing	indefinite			moleskin (for foot blisters)	indefinite	

---

[3] This information courtesy of Carlin G. Bartschi, MD, who invested a great deal of his limited spare time to prepare, review and edit the medical material. He also consulted on several other related issues addressed in this new edition, especially the water chapter and charts. Dr. Bartschi has worked more than 18 years in the medical profession beginning with his general practice, then specializing in accident and emergency medical & trauma treatment. He practiced family medicine in Yuma, AZ, for 14 years. From 1991 through 1993, he devoted his medical expertise exclusively to Emergency Medicine in emergency rooms in 4 southeast Texas hospitals. He is practicing currently as an emergency room specialist in a suburban Phoenix hospital though he still commutes to a South Texas hospital to serve as the emergency room doctor. Carlin was born and raised in Montpelier, ID, completed his undergraduate studies at Utah State University, in Logan, UT. He attended medical school at the Universidad Autonoma de Guadalajara (Mexico), then completed post-graduate training in Saskatoon, Saskatchewan (Canada). Carlin and his wife, Joyce, are parents of 10 children and several grandchildren. He and his family strive to manage a lifestyle of preparedness, both philosophically and in real-life.

Quick-List 2–7 (continued)

	Medical Care—Medications & First Aid Kits Pantry List (continued)						
✓	Storage Item	Shelf Life (Months)	Adult Quantity	✓	Storage Item	Shelf Life (Months)	Adult Quantity
	recommended non-prescription health maintenance medications & supplies (continued)						
	anti-itch medication	indefinite			saline solution	indefinite	
	emergency medical care—first aid kits						
	If you choose to develop your own first aid kit, see itemized listing below						
	family first aid kit / prepack	indefinite	1		individual first aid kit / prepk	indefinite	1
	first aid kit itemized listing						
	If you'd prefer to develop your own first aid kit, here are the essentials. Add any other items specific to your needs.						
	absorbent cotton / balls	indefinite			manual, first aid	indefinite	
	applicator sticks, cotton-tip	indefinite			medicine dropper	indefinite	
	bandage, finger-tip	indefinite			oatmeal (mixture stops itching)	indefinite	
	bandage, knuckle	indefinite			ointment, anti-bacterial	12	
	bandage, stretch	indefinite			pad, adhesive, sterile strips	indefinite	
	bandage, triangular	indefinite			pharyngeal airway	indefinite	
	bedpan	indefinite			safety pins / assorted sizes	indefinite	
	blades, single-edge razor	indefinite			shaving supplies	indefinite	
	clippers, fingernail / toenail	indefinite			snake-bite kit	indefinite	
	closure, butterfly	indefinite			soap, surgical / cleansing	indefinite	
	cold pack / ice pack	indefinite			splinting material	indefinite	
	contact lens cleaner	indefinite			sunscreen / sun lotion	indefinite	
	cornstarch	indefinite			surgical scissors	indefinite	
	dental emergency kit	indefinite			suture kit, emergency surgery	indefinite	
	douche equipment	indefinite			syringe / needles / injection	indefinite	
	ear drops	indefinite			syringe, irrigation	indefinite	
	eye pads	indefinite			tape, adhesive, medical, assorted 1" / 2" / 3"	indefinite	
	gauze pads, assorted large sizes 18" / 24" / 72"	indefinite			gauze, rolls, assorted sizes 1" / 2" / 3"	indefinite	
	gauze pads, asstd. 2" / 3" / 4"	indefinite			thermometer	indefinite	
	gloves, rubber / surgical	indefinite			tongue blades / wood	indefinite	
	hand lotion	indefinite			tourniquet	indefinite	
	knife, pocket / multi-blade	indefinite			tweezers	indefinite	
	knife, surgical / blades	indefinite			vinegar	indefinite	
	lubricant, tube, lubricating jelly	indefinite			water, sterile	12	

Quick-List 2–8

Basic Supplementation[4] for Food Storage Pantry List
select items of choice from this category
see Chapter 14 for additional information

Multiply Adult Quantity by your Family Factor to determine your Family Total

✓	Storage Item	Shelf Life (Months)	Adult Quantity	✓	Storage Item	Shelf Life (Months)	Adult Quantity
herbs & whole food supplements				**live whole food concentrates**			
	aloe vera	6–9			*see Chapter 14*		
	apple cider vinegar	36–48		**minerals**			
	bee supplements	12–24			boron	12–24	
	beet root powder	pkg. date			chromium picolinate	18–24	
	bladderwrack	pkg. date			copper	24–36	
	blue-green algae	12–24			selenium	pkg. date	
	fo-ti	pkg. date			zinc	24–36	
	ginger	pkg. date		**vitamins**			
	ginkgo biloba	pkg. date			beta carotene	12–24	
	hawthorne berries	pkg. date			bioflavonoids	12–24	
	kola nut	pkg. date			vitamin C	12–24	
	ma huang	pkg. date			vitamin E	12–24	
	parsley	pkg. date					
	saw palmetto	pkg. date					
	white willow	pkg. date					
	yerba maté	pkg. date					

Quick-List 2–9

Fuels, Energy & Camping Gear Pantry List
see Chapter 17 for additional information

Multiply Adult Quantity by your Family Factor to determine your Family Total

✓	Storage Item	Shelf Life (Months)	Adult Quantity	✓	Storage Item	Shelf Life (Months)	Adult Quantity
light & heat equipment—as needed				**family camping equipment & supplies—per need**			
	flashlight / "D" type, 2- or 3- battery	indefinite			camp cooking set	indefinite	
	"D" batteries	12–24			utensils, camp / kitchen	indefinite	
	lamp, kerosene	indefinite			lantern, two-mantle	indefinite	
	kerosene (gal.)	6–12			lantern fuel (gal.)	12	
	perfumed fuel (qt.)	24–36			mantles, replacement set	indefinite	
	candles, tallow or wax	indefinite			fire starter / magnesium kit	indefinite	
	emergency type	indefinite			matches (waterproof)	indefinite	
	camp stove, 2-burner	indefinite			charcoal cooking unit	indefinite	
	stove fuel (gal.)	12			charcoal / briquettes (lb.)	24–36	
	stove accessories	indefinite			starter (qt.)	indefinite	

---

[4] Thanks to Zoltan P. Rona, MD, M.Sc for this information on vitamins, minerals and herbal supplements in the food storage program. Dr. Rona is a graduate of McGill University Medical School and has a master's degree in biochemistry and clinical nutrition from the University of Bridgeport in Connecticut. He is the author of the Canadian bestseller **The Joy of Health, A Doctor's Guide to Nutrition and Alternative Medicine** and is a past president of the Canadian Holistic Medical Association. He is currently in private medical practice in Toronto and has regular columns in **Alive Magazine**, **Health Naturally** and **The Toronto Star**. Recently he was guest columnist in **The Preparedness Journal**. Dr. Rona is also known for his many public lectures and media appearances. Look for his new book, **Return to the Joy of Health, A Doctor's Guide to Nutrition and Herbal Medicine**, Alive Books, Vancouver, BC, Canada, 1995.

Quick-List 2–9 (continued)

Fuels, Energy & Camping Gear Pantry List
Multiply Adult Quantity by your Family Factor to determine your Family Total

✓	Storage Item	Shelf Life (Months)	Adult Quantity	✓	Storage Item	Shelf Life (Months)	Adult Quantity
light & heat equipment (continued)				**family camping equipment & supplies** (continued)			
	portable heater	indefinite			stick matches (box)	indefinite	
	heater fuel	25			shovel / multi-purpose	indefinite	
	canned fuel (lb.)	12–24					
personal camping equipment—per preferences				**overnight gear—per preferences**			
	air mattress	indefinite			bag, sleeping	indefinite	
	ax	indefinite			blanket(s)	indefinite	1/ person
	camp shovel / multi-purpose	indefinite			cloth, ground, waterproof	indefinite	1/ person
	poncho	indefinite			pad, sleep, cushioning	indefinite	1/ person
	cot	indefinite			pillow	indefinite	1/ person
	rake	indefinite			tent	indefinite	per need
	hatchet	indefinite		**family heat items**			
	ice chest, insulated, 1-gal.	indefinite			coal (ton) / stove	36–60	
	5-gal size	indefinite			firewood (cord)	indefinite	
	portable heater / fuel	12			wood saw, 1-man	indefinite	
					wood saw, 2-man	indefinite	
safety items					hatchet / ax	indefinite	
	carbon monoxide / gas alarm	indefinite			wedge	indefinite	
	fire / smoke detectors	indefinite			sledge hammer	indefinite	
hygiene & sanitation—as needed							
	potty, portable	indefinite			disposable plastic bags 1 / 3 / 5-6 / 20 / 30-gal.	indefinite	
	supplies, sanitary	indefinite			pails or buckets	indefinite	
	disinfectant aerosols	indefinite			chemicals for toilet	indefinite	
communications equipment—as needed							
	AM / FM radio	indefinite			citizens band radio	indefinite	
	batteries	12			batteries	12	

Quick-List 2–10

Personal, Family, Infant & Pet Care Essentials Pantry List

Multiply Adult Quantity by your Family Factor to determine your Family Total

✓	Storage Item	Shelf Life (Months)	Adult Quantity	✓	Storage Item	Shelf Life (Months)	Adult Quantity
	personal essentials				**infant & child care**—*special needs of infants & children*		
	toiletry / travel kit	*indefinite*	personal		formula	*12–18*	**per need**
	toilet paper	*indefinite*	60 rolls		juices, strained	*12–14*	**per need**
	feminine needs / sanitary napkins	*indefinite*	per need		foods, strained	*6–12*	**per need**
	family essentials				**supplies**		
	soap, bath	*indefinite*			diapers, disposable	*indefinite*	**per need**
	soap, hand / face	*indefinite*			clothing	*varies*	**per need**
	sunscreen	*12–18*			medications	*indicated*	**per need**
	toothbrush	*indefinite*			sleepers	*varies*	
	toothpaste	*12–24*			cornstarch	*indefinite*	
	shampoo	*indefinite*			talcum powder	*indefinite*	
	household essentials				toys	*indefinite*	
	soap, laundry	*indefinite*			games	*varies*	
	cleanser, scouring	*indefinite*			bedding, special sizes	*indefinite*	
	soap, cleaning, liquid	*indefinite*			waterproof sheets	*indefinite*	
	towels, bath	*indefinite*			blankets	*indefinite*	
	wash cloths				**infant safety items**		
	kitchen towels				restraints	*indefinite*	
	dish cloth				bicycle	*indefinite*	
	pet care				automotive	*indefinite*	
	food	*6–12*			carrier, back frame	*indefinite*	
	equipment, handling	*indefinite*			**other essentials**		
	immunization / medications	*indicated*					
	maintenance equipment	*per vet*					
	treats	*varies*					

Quick-List 2–11

Canned & Dried Fruits, Vegetables & Soups Pantry List
2,750 assorted servings (fresh equivalent) minimum from this category
see Chapter 16 for additional information about drying fruits & vegetables

Multiply Adult Quantity by your Family Factor to determine your Family Total

✓	Storage Item	Shelf Life (Months)	Adult Quantity	✓	Storage Item	Shelf Life (Months)	Adult Quantity
	fruits—1250 servings minimum assorted				**vegetables—1000 servings minimum assorted**		
	canned, all, except citrus	*12–18*			beans, green—cut / whole	*24–36*	
	citrus products	*6–12*			beans, pinto / kidney	*24–36*	
	bottled, all, except citrus	*18*			beans, red / yellow	*24–36*	
	citrus products	*18*			beets, diced / sliced	*12–24*	
	jam, jelly & preserves	*12–18*			carrots, diced / sliced	*24–36*	
	fruit cocktail	*12–18*			corn, cut / creamed	*24–36*	
	potatoes & yams (fresh equivalent)—200 lb. minimum assorted from this list (see Chapter 3)				greens, all	*24–36*	
	potatoes, all dried	*36–48*	25		peas, all	*24–36*	

Quick-List 2–11 (continued)

Canned & Dried Fruits, Vegetables, & Soups Pantry List
Multiply Adult Quantity by your Family Factor to determine your Family Total

✓	Storage Item	Shelf Life (Months)	Adult Quantity	✓	Storage Item	Shelf Life (Months)	Adult Quantity
	potatoes & yams (continued)				**vegetables** (continued)		
	potatoes, all, fresh	*3–6*	100		tomato, paste / stewed / sauce	*24–36*	
	potatoes, canned, all types	*24–36*			vegetables, all mixed	*24–36*	
	soups—250 servings minimum assorted selected from this list or your preference						
	bean & bacon	*24–36*			mushroom		
	beans & chili	*24–36*			onion	*24–36*	
	cheese	*24–36*			potato	*24–36*	
	chicken—cream / noodle / rice / vegetable	*24–36*			vegetable	*24–36*	
	other selections—100 servings from this list or your preference						
	macaroni & cheese	*24–36*			spaghetti & tomato sauce	*12–24*	

Quick-List 2–12

Kitchen Staples—Condiments & Seasonings Pantry List
select assortment as needed from this category to suit your taste
Multiply Adult Quantity by your Family Factor to determine your Family Total

✓	Storage Item	Shelf Life (Months)	Adult Quantity	✓	Storage Item	Shelf Life (Months)	Adult Quantity
	mixed condiments—as preferred				**nuts & nut butters—select 50 lb. minimum from this list**		
	relish, sweet / dill	*indefinite*			**nut butters**		
	pickles, cut or whole	*indefinite*			peanut butter	*12–24*	15
	olives, canned, all	*12–24*			almond butter	*12–24*	
	mayonnaise	*9–12*			pecan butter	*2–3*	
	salad dressing	*9–12*			**nuts, raw**		
	salsa	*12–24*			shelled	*6–9*	
	salad dressings, bottled, all—as preferred				unshelled	*12–24*	
	bleu cheese	*9–12*			**nuts, roasted**		
	French	*9–12*			shelled, bulk, all	*3–6*	
	Italian	*9–12*			shelled, canned, all	*12–24*	
	ranch	*9–12*			unshelled, bulk, all	*6–12*	
	other	*9–12*			unshelled, canned, all	*12–24*	
	bouillon cubes, granules & liquid—select 1 lb.				**seeds, raw**		
	beef / chicken / ham	*12–24*			pumpkin	*1–3*	
	onion / vegetable	*12–24*			sunflower	*1–3*	
	chocolate—select 5 lb. from this list				sesame butter	*12–15*	
	baking, unsweetened	*12–24*			walnuts	*2–3*	
	chips, baking	*18–24*					
	liquid	*12*			**seeds, roasted**		
	syrup	*12–18*			pumpkin	*1–3*	
					sunflower	*1–3*	
	thickeners, liquid & powder—select 5 lb.				**crackers, table—select 6 lb. from this list**		
	arrowroot	*12–24*			saltines / lite salt	*6–12*	
	cornstarch	*12–24*			seafoods	*6–12*	
	gelatin, dry	*12–18*			stone ground	*8–12*	

Quick-List 2–12 (continued)

Kitchen Staples—Condiments & Seasonings Pantry List
Multiply Adult Quantity by your Family Factor to determine your Family Total

✓	Storage Item	Shelf Life (Months)	Adult Quantity	✓	Storage Item	Shelf Life (Months)	Adult Quantity
	gravy mixes—as preferred				**crackers, specialty**		
	liquid	12–24			graham	12–24	
	powder	24–48			**other items—as preferred**		
	flavored				tapioca	24–36	
	liquid condiments—as preferred						
	catsup	24–36			vinegar, apple cider	indefinite	
	soy sauce	indefinite			Worcestershire sauce	indefinite	
	steak sauce	12-24					
	seasonings & spices, whole & ground—select 2 lb. minimum from this listing						
	herbs & spices				**seasonings, mixed**		
	ground, all	6–9			Italian	12–18	
	whole, all	12–15			Mexican	12–18	
	celery, salt	depends			bouquet garni	6–12	
	dill	depends			herbes fines	6–12	
	garlic, flakes or powder	depends					
	mustard	depends			**flavorings & extracts**		
	onion, flakes or powder	depends			almond	12–24	
	parsley, flakes or powder	depends			banana	12–24	
	pepper, black, ground	**indefinite**	**8 oz.**		lemon	12–24	
	pepper, cayenne	depends			maple	12–24	
	peppers, bell—all	depends			orange	12–24	
	pepper, jalapeño	depends			vanilla	12–24	
	savory	depends					
	sesame seed	depends					

Quick-List 2–13

Meats & Seafoods Pantry List
select 700 minimum servings assorted (fresh equivalent) from this category
see Chapter 3 for additional information about refrigerator & freezer storage
Multiply Adult Quantity by your Family Factor to determine your Family Total

✓	Storage Item	Shelf Life (Months)	Adult Quantity	✓	Storage Item	Shelf Life (Months)	Adult Quantity
	beef—120 servings minimum from list				**luncheon meats—250 servings min. from list**		
	chipped, dried	12–24			spreads, sandwich	12–24	
	corned, canned	12–24			deviled meats	12–24	
	jerky, dried	6–9			sausage, vienna	12–24	
	imitation, flavored	1–3			pepperoni	12–24	
	ground meat	**12–24**	**75**		**seafoods—100 servings minimum from this list**		
	poultry—select 75 servings minimum from list				clams, all	12–24	
	chicken	12–24			crab, chopped / imitation	12–24	
	turkey	12–24			fish—halibut / mackerel / tuna	12–24	
	pork—select 50 servings minimum from list				fish—salmon / sardines	24–36	
	bacon	12–24			shrimp	12–24	
	sausage	12–24					
	other cuts	12–24					

Quick-List 2–14

Domestic Maintenance & Preparedness Pantry List							
Multiply Adult Quantity by your Family Factor to determine your Family Total							
✓	Storage Item	Shelf Life (Months)	Adult Quantity	✓	Storage Item	Shelf Life (Months)	Adult Quantity
garden seeds / plants for growing season				**tools**			
	seeds, garden	*12–24*	**per need**		automotive	*indefinite*	
	supplies, chemicals & mulch	*12–24*	**per need**		general	*indefinite*	
	tools, gardening	*indefinite*			household	*indefinite*	
kitchen equipment					yard	*indefinite*	
	cooking utensils	*indefinite*	per need	**food preparation equipment / supplies**			
	meat grinder, hand-operated	*indefinite*			bottling	*indefinite*	
storage containers—*use only food-grade plastics approved by USDA & FDA*					canning	*indefinite*	
	1-gal. pail / lid	*indefinite*			drying / dehydrating	*indefinite*	
	5-gal., plastic / lid	*indefinite*			freezing	*indefinite*	
	55-gal. drum / metal / lid / locking ring	*indefinite*			pickling	*indefinite*	
	#10 can, sealed	*indefinite*			smoking / curing	*indefinite*	
cleaning equipment & supplies—*expand your current inventory of supplies by copybuying purchases*				**clothing**—*a year's supply of clothing and supplies should be in your storage program*			
	rubber gloves	*indefinite*			clothing, seasonal	*indefinite*	
					shoes, boots	*indefinite*	
sewing—*sewing equipment & items should be stored*							
	sewing supplies	*indefinite*			sewing equipment	*indefinite*	
bedding—*a year's supply of bedding should be maintained*							
	sheets	*indefinite*			comforters	*indefinite*	
	blankets	*indefinite*			pillowcases	*indefinite*	
	quilts	*indefinite*			pillows	*indefinite*	
					inflatable beds	*indefinite*	
additional gardening items							
seeds, slips & plants catalogs				**seed or plant requirements for next growing season**			
	fruit, plant catalog				fruit, plants		
	fruit, tree catalog				fruit, trees		
	fruit, vine catalog				fruit, vines		
	vegetable catalog				vegetable plants, nursery		
soil amendments							
	composted material / mulch				fertilizer, organic / chemical		
gardening tools & equipment							
	hoe				rake		
	mattock				shovel		
	poles, 6' for beans & tomatoes				spade		
72-hour emergency kits				**other emergency provisions**			
	family	12	1 kit		emergency clothing kit	*seasonal*	as needed
	individual	12	1 kit		MREs	*36–48*	selection

Quick-List 2–15

✓	Storage Item	Shelf Life (Months)	Adult Quantity	✓	Storage Item	Shelf Life (Months)	Adult Quantity
	**Pleasure Foods—Beverages, Snacks, Sweets & Treats Pantry List** 2,000 servings minimum assorted from this category Multiply Adult Quantity by your Family Factor to determine your Family Total						
	**beverages—750 servings minimum assorted from this category**						
	juice, fruits				**chocolate & cocoa**		
	aseptic cartons, all	pkg. date			chocolate, regular	18–24	
	canned & bottled, all	12–24			instant mix	12–18	
	apple	12–24			candy, filled	3–6	
	prune	12–24			milk chocolate	6–9	
	grape	12–24			syrup	12–18	
	grapefruit	12			cocoa, regular	18–24	
	orange	12			**coffee**		
	cranberry & mixtures	12–24			canned, ground or instant	12–15	
	pineapple	12			freeze-dried	6–9	
	apricot nectar	12			chicory	12–18	
	non-caffeine hot drinks				**tea**		
	Pero	12–24			regular		
	Postum	12–24			instant	6–12	
	tea, herbal	9–12			leaves, loose & bagged	6–12	
	canned beverages				herbal, black	12–24	
	soft drinks	6–12			**other beverages**		
	bottled sodas	6–12			mixes, powdered	36–48	
	water, carbonated	12–24			liquid concentrates	24–36	
					root beer concentrate / bottle	48–60	
	**snacks: cakes, candy, & chips—750 servings minimum assorted from these listings**						
	cake mixes				**popcorn**		
	chocolate	12–24			popped	2–3	
	lemon	12–24			microwave	pkg. date	
	white	12–24			pre-seasoned	pkg. date	
	candy				**puddings, dry mix**		
	bars	12			vanilla	24–36	
	hard sugar	12			lemon	24–36	
	mixed candies, vacuum-pk.	24–36			banana	24–36	
	gum, chewing				chocolate	24–36	
	chips & filled crackers				gelatin	36–48	
	corn chips	12–18			**puddings, pre-mixed (non-refrigerated)**		
	potato chips	12–18			banana	12–18	
	wheat snacks	12–18			chocolate	12–18	
	crackers, snack	12			topping, whipped / sweet	12–24	

Quick-Shop 2–1

Essential Foods & Nonfoods Shopping List

				In-Home Storage Requirements			
Quantities rounded to nearest 5 lb., except where noted ↘							
Multiply Adult Quantity by your Family Factor to determine your Family Total							
Storage Item	Shelf Life (months)	Adult Quantity	Family Factor	Family Total	On Hand	Needs	Quick-Plan Worksheets (✓)
Quick-List 2–1: Water—Emergency Supplies & Treatment							
water, potable	6–12	14 gal.	per person				
water, 4 or 6 oz. aseptic pack	indefinite	2 gal.	per person				
portable treatment unit	indefinite	1	1 unit				
bleach, 5.25% hypochlorite	6	1 gal.					
tablets, water treatment	36–60	1 pkg.					
Quick-List 2–2: Wheat, Other Whole Grains, Flours & Beans							
wheat, whole grain (berries)	indefinite	350					
grain mill / grinder	indefinite	1 / family					
mixer / breadmaking	indefinite	1 / family					
yeast , cake, moist	pkg. date	4 oz.					
yeast, active dry powdered	12–24	12 oz.					
cornmeal / flours	60	10					
rice, white, fortified / enriched	24–48	10					
rice, white pre-cooked	36	25					
rice, wild	24–36	5					
Quick-List 2–3: Powdered Milk, Dairy Products & Eggs							
milk, non-instant powdered	24–48	100					
butter, dehydrated	60–96	20					
cheese, dehydrated	60–96	25					
eggs, dehydrated / freeze-dried	60–96	25 dz.					
evaporated milk	24–36	12 cans					
Quick-List 2–4: Sweeteners—Honey, Sugar & Syrup							
honey, unfiltered	indefinite	65					
sugar, white	indefinite	10					
Quick-List 2–5: Cooking Catalysts—Salt, Oils & Leaveners							
iodized salt	indefinite	5					
yeast, cake, moist	pkg. date	4 oz.					
yeast, active dry powdered	12–24	12 oz.					
vegetable oil, liquid	12–24	10 gal.					
Quick-List 2–6: Sprouting—Seeds & Supplies							
alfalfa	24–36	1					
Quick-List 2–7: Medical Care—Medications & First Aid Kits							
personal life-preserving medications							
cardiovascular conditions medication							
diabetic conditions medication							
nervous conditions medications							
respiratory and allergic conditions							
seizure conditions medications							

Essential Foods & Nonfoods Shopping List (continued)

Quantities rounded to nearest 5 lb., except where noted ↖				Food Storage Requirements			
Multiply Adult Quantity by your Family Factor to determine your Family Total							
Storage Item	Shelf Life (months)	Adult Quantity	Family Factor	Family Total	On Hand	Needs	Quick-Plan Worksheets (✓)
personal life-preserving medications (continued)							
"stomach" and intestinal medications							
other critical conditions medication(s)							
prescription medications							
emergency medical care—first aid kit							
family first aid kit, commercial prepack	indefinite	1					
individual first aid kit, commercial prepack	indefinite	1					
Quick-List 2–8: Basic Supplementation							
herbs & whole food supplements							
minerals							
vitamins							
live whole food concentrates							
Quick-List 2–9: Fuels, Energy & Camping Gear							
flashlights / "D" type, 2- or 3-battery	indefinite						
"D" batteries	12–24						
lamp, kerosene	indefinite						
kerosene (gal.)	6–12						
candles, tallow or wax	indefinite						
emergency candles	indefinite						
camp stove, 2-burner	indefinite						
stove fuel (gal.)	12						
stove accessories	indefinite						
camp cooking set	indefinite						
utensils, camp / kitchen	indefinite						
lantern, two-mantle	indefinite						
lantern fuel (gal.)	12						
mantles, replacement set	indefinite						
fire starters	indefinite						
magnesium/steel kit	indefinite						
matches (waterproof)	indefinite						
portable heater	indefinite						
heater fuel	25						
Quick-List 2–10: Personal, Family, Infant & Pet Care Essentials							
feminine needs / sanitary napkins	indefinite	per need					
toilet paper	indefinite	60 rolls					
toiletry / travel kit	indefinite	personal					
infant care							
clothing	varies						
diapers, disposable	indefinite						
medications	indicated						
formula / infant	12–18						
juices, strained / infant	12–14						

Essential Foods & Nonfoods Shopping List (continued)

Quantities rounded to nearest 5 lb., except where noted ↖			Food Storage Requirements				
Multiply Adult Quantity by your Family Factor to determine your Family Total							
Storage Item	Shelf Life (months)	Adult Quantity	Family Factor	Family Total	On Hand	Needs	Quick-Chart Worksheets (✓)
pet care							
food	6–12						
equipment, handling	indefinite						
Quick-List 2–11: Canned & Dried Fruits, Vegetables & Soups							
potatoes, all dried	36–48	25					
potatoes, all, fresh	3–6	100					
Quick-List 2–12: Kitchen Staples—Condiments & Seasonings							
peanut butter	12–24	15					
pepper, black	indefinite	8 oz.					
Quick-List 2–13: Meats & Seafood							
ground meat	12–24	75					
Quick-List 2–14: Domestic Maintenance & Preparedness							
seeds, garden	12–24	per need					
storage containers	indefinite	per need					
72-hour emergency kit							
family	12	1 kit					
individual	12	1 kit					
emergency clothing kit	seasonal	as needed					
Quick-List 2–15: Pleasure Foods—Beverages, Snacks, Sweets & Treats							
Add your personal & family needs here							

Quick-Shop 2–2

Supplemental Foods & Nonfoods Shopping List

Personal & Family Supplemental Needs Quantities rounded to nearest 5 lb., except where noted			In-Home Storage Requirements				
Multiply Adult Quantity by your Family Factor to determine your Family Total							
Storage Item	Shelf Life (months)	Adult Quantity	Family Factor	Family Total	On Hand	Needs	Quick-Plan Worksheet (✓)

Quick-Plan Worksheet 2–1

Planning & Budgeting Worksheet

	Foods & Nonfoods Priority List				
R A N K	Item or Description	Source of Supply	Need Am't.	Cost Each Unit	Total Cost
1					
2					
3					
4					
5					
6					
7					
8					
9					
10					
TOTALS: Basic In-Home Storage Items					

Inventory Date: _____ Projected Purchase Date: _____ Budgeted Amount: _____

Chapter 3

In-Home Storage Problems & Solutions

Food has some "enemies" constantly working at different rates with different effects. The net effect of these food enemies, though, is they destroy the eating quality or taste of foods, lessen nutritional values, and create morale problems when you realize your investment of time, energy, and hard-earned money has become garbage!

The major enemies causing the loss of quality and nutrition in foods are
   1. poor food selection
   2. improper packaging and storage techniques
   3. high storage temperatures
   4. moisture and microbial infiltration
   5. insect and rodent infestation
   6. storage period exceeding useful shelf life

Time is the greatest enemy of in-home storage—the other factors increase in probability as time passes. This chapter outlines some of the problems caused by these food enemies and suggests solutions for their effective resolution as summarized in the following charts.

Quick-Guide 3–1

Summary of In-Home Storage Problems & Solutions

1. Poor Food Selection Problems

- **Lost investment of time, money & food if food deteriorates or is not acceptable to family tastes.**

Solutions	Hints

• select high-quality, storage-grade foods for in-home storage
 	
• choose foods with consideration for nutritional value, storage qualities, and in most cases, the taste buds
 	
• store what you normally eat
 	
• eat from stored supplies regularly as part of daily diet to help maintain or develop a taste for the foods available in the storage program
	• never purchase outdated, broken, or dented goods of any kind for food storage
	• damaged, canned, or packaged foods will be contaminated if the airtight seal has been broken
	• especially avoid bulging cans—they're already suspect and dangerous
	• these are the common-sense reasons for storing what you normally eat:
	    –eliminates food spoilage
	    –minimizes food deterioration
	    –stabilizes diet during stressful situations
	    –provides insurance against malnutrition
	    –your year's food supply will not exceed original investment
	    –the one factor of food storage that's entirely under your control is buying what you eat [1]

2. Improper Packaging and Storage Techniques Problems

- **Contamination is made easier when foods are not maintained in proper containers.**
- **Rancidity results when airtight seal of a container is broken.**

Solutions	Hints
• foods must be clean at the time they are purchased • foods must be clean at time of packaging • foods must be placed in clean containers free from insects • foods must be sealed so insects, pests, and moisture cannot gain entrance	**Storage** • rates at which foods deteriorate depend upon the particular food, its purity, the way it's stored, and especially upon its environmental temperature • when a package or can has been opened, the useful life of its contents is greatly shortened **Rancidity** • the warmer the ambient air, the more rapidly rancidity develops • small amounts of natural fats in foods become foul smelling and slightly toxic when the food's protective shell is breached by oxidants • foods which have their natural structure broken up, such as cracked wheat and flour from whole wheat, meal and flour from corn, polished rice, etc., may become rancid when stored unsealed • many dried vegetables, including corn, green beans, and green peas are subject to rancidity when kept in unsealed containers • rancidity may be minimized by storing in properly sealed containers and storage in a cool, dry, and dark location

[1] The belief that a person will eat anything under emergency situations has been proven faulty. Dr. Norman Wright of the British Food Ministry, after experiencing living conditions in England and war-torn Europe following World War II stated, *"A sudden emergency is no time for introducing untried novelties."* He indicated people were more likely to reject unfamiliar or distasteful foods during times of stress than under normal conditions. Isn't this the usual response in times of trouble—reverting to type or habit? When we are frightened, upset, and insecure, don't we tend to return to things with which we are acquainted or familiar? The only way to be certain stored foods will be acceptable to the palate during times of need is to assure our tastes are acquainted with them and tolerate them during normal times.

2. Improper Packaging and Storage Techniques Problems (continued)

Container Suggestions

Glass containers:
- glass bottles and jars are good storage packages; however, they break, don't stack well, let in light, are generally quite expensive, and are always heavy
- when using glass containers, take precautions to place them in a stable position near the floor
- when storing foods in glass containers, store in dark location; some foods deteriorate more rapidly when exposed to light
- as a further precaution for glass containers, hot wax may be poured over the contact point of friction-type lids to ensure protection; with other types of lids, masking tape may be used for sealing cracks where corrosion could begin
- save all glass bottles from salad dressings, pickles, even odd-shaped jars and use them for storage containers
- save gallon jugs and jars for storing rice, beans, powdered milk, etc.
- pack empty bottles with fruit, vegetables, or water
- keep a supply of glass jars and lids on hand for bottling
- some fruits will keep longer in glass containers than in metal cans due to the relatively high acidity of their contents; these include foods and drinks such as pineapple, orange, lemon, lime, apple, and tomato
- fruits, vegetables, and meats properly processed in glass bottles and stored properly will store as well as canned goods

Plastic containers:
- rigid, round plastic containers protect contents better than square ones
- make sure containers are rodent-proof
- bulk-packaged foods, especially flour, granulated sugar, and powdered milk should be immediately repacked in either clean and dry metal, glass, or plastic containers, then sealed with airtight lids
- small, round plastic buckets can be chewed through by rats, but mice will not generally attack plastic buckets

Metal containers:
- food-grade, heavy-duty, sealable plastic liners in new galvanized steel drums provide good storage space capable of excluding both rodents and insects

3. High Storage Temperature Problems

- Chemical reactions and changes occur in foods which may not be apparent & could be dangerous.
- Storage at higher temperatures diminishes shelf life.
- Food quality is lost at increased rates at high temperatures.

Solutions	Hints
• locate food storage in dry, cool place, below 70°F	• generally, changes in color, flavor, or texture are accompanied by loss of nutritional value
• foods should be stored as close to 40°F as possible	• for every 20°F increase in storage temperature, the shelf life of stored food is decreased by almost 50%
• the cooler and drier foodstuffs are kept, the longer they remain tasty and nourishing	• canned fruits and vegetables may soften and become mushy and have an offensive odor

4. Moisture and Microbial Infiltration Problems

- Moisture accumulates inside food containers and increases incidence of microbial infiltration.
- Chemical reactions in food caused by moisture result in food quality loss and nutritional deterioration.
- When both moisture and temperature are high, probability of contamination is greatly increased.

Solutions	Hints
• storage must be properly sealed and located in a dry, cool place • moisture is excluded only by maintaining an airtight seal • place food on shelves when possible • avoid placing any food storage containers directly on concrete or dirt surfaces—use plywood or thick cardboard sheets in layers to prevent cans from direct contact with concrete floors • be observant, and you'll become aware of the indicators of deterioration when you use stored foods	• moisture hardens and spoils all forms of stored foods, whether dried in-home or dehydrated commercially, crystallized (such as sugars, salt, desserts, and drink mixes), powdered products (such as baking powder, flours, cornstarch, baked goods, and boxed mixes), processed foods (such as cereals, chips, and crackers), and canned or bottled vegetables, meats, soups, fish, etc. **Molds:** • mold grows in a very low moisture environment and is the prime cause of spoilage in stored foods • mold spores are abundant in the air and can live on almost any type of food • molds produce the most poisonous toxins known • in seeds, cereals, and nuts, molds are known to produce toxins which can cause permanent damage to internal organs • *moldy foods should always be discarded* **Rust prevention:** • metal containers often rust through and spoil food • prevention is best achieved by keeping storage containers away from moisture inducing surfaces by placing cardboard, plywood, or pieces of lumber beneath metal cans to prevent direct contact with concrete floors • see following instructions for **wax coating treatments**

Wax Coating Treatments

Shelf life of foods in metal containers is extended by coating containers with wax or paraffin to minimize corrosion in high-humidity areas. Following are two treatment methods:

- **Paraffin method**: Paraffin is heated and the container is either dipped into the wax or a brush may be used to spread the wax onto all surfaces, especially at the joints.

- **Wax method**: Make a solution of 2 oz. jelly wax and 1 qt. mineral spirits by warming the minerals spirits in its container in a bucket of hot water—*don't use an open flame!* Stir the jelly wax into the mineral spirits until dissolved. Then, dip the can—including label—into the solution, making certain the entire can is covered. Place on wood blocks to dry, then place in storage. Choose low-humidity days for this task, and be sure to do this project *outside* the house!

5. Insect and Rodent Infestation Problems

- Infestation of insects and rodents causes dangerous food contamination.

Solutions	Hints
• utilize proper packaging to protect contents • use metal cans with heavy-duty, food-grade, waterproof, plastic containers and airtight lids for all powdered products	• four-legged critters and pests generally contaminate more food than they eat • rats, mice, cockroaches, and beetles are "dirty" and carry disease • insects packaged in food products feed and multiply easily inside containers • when evidence of pest or critter presence is seen, the foods they've spoiled must be discarded • weevils found in stored grains and some processed grain products, including flours, are "clean" and edible without harm to the human system

- all glass and crockery containers should have airtight seals
- fumigate with one of basic methods detailed in the section following
- the addition of chemicals ought to be done according to the best information available from local County Extension agents or food storage experts

Commercial Packaging:

- most commercial foods are intact and are generally free from insects
- in paper packaging such as a paper flour sack, even a tiny hole may permit pests to enter and lay eggs; the newly hatched larvae will infest the food quickly
- normally, packaging protects food during shipping and storage on store shelves
- no matter what precautions you take after placing most commercial packaging in storage, paper packaging alone will not preclude pests for very long
- pests may already be in the creases and recesses of packages and with time will enter the paper packaging enclosure

Fumigating Foods for Storage
Basic Dry-Ice Treatment Method

One of the most difficult facets of food storage is repacking or packaging bulk foods into smaller containers while either preventing entry of new or eliminating existing bugs and pests.

Dry ice will eliminate bugs and pests requiring oxygen by replacing the storage atmosphere in the container with carbon dioxide. This is a very simple and easy method of treatment—the most difficult part is finding dry ice and getting it home and into the containers in a timely manner.

Use **Container Requirements Estimator Chart** to determine the number and sizes of containers needed for your bulk storage foods. The **Basic Dry-Ice Treatment Chart** details how much dry Ice you'll need to fumigate containers of different sizes. See charts on page 44.

Basic Dry-Ice Treatment Instructions
- Make sure all equipment, containers, and tools are clean and free of dirt before starting.
- Break dry ice into approximate weight as indicated in the **Basic Dry-Ice Treatment Chart**, using either a hammer or a big knife, chisel, or flat-blade screwdriver.
- Wipe frosty crystals from dry ice with a clean cotton towel to prevent addition of moisture into container.
- Wrap dry ice in newspaper or butcher paper to prevent direct contact with hands and foods. Grain germination or sprouting may be affected by being in contact with dry ice, but will still have the same baking quality.

Notes on Handling Dry Ice

- Use caution when handling dry ice—dry ice burns, or rather, freezes, skin almost instantly!
- Don't use dry ice in glass containers—glass may break if sealed too soon or shatter when dry ice comes in direct contact with glass not designed for subfreezing temperatures.

Caution: keep children away from your work area—dry ice is a temptation for them!

There are two methods for fumigating with dry ice. Each is effective. It's generally a matter of preference, depending on whether you're working with new or existing stored foods.

- For refumigating existing foods, use the *basic on-top method.*

Basic on-top treatment method:
- on top of almost-full container, place required amount of dry ice on folded paper cut from grocery bags or other nonconductive (insulating) material
- press lid down gently, leaving an exit for air to escape
- after 20–30 minutes, check to see if dry ice has completely evaporated
- if not, wait another 5 minutes, then check again
- when dry ice has completely evaporated, remove material and seal container

- When dividing bulk foods into smaller containers, use the *basic on-bottom method.*

Basic on-bottom treatment method:
- on bottom of 5-gallon metal storage bucket, place $1/4$ lb. dry ice wrapped in heavy paper (butcher paper will do nicely, or cut paper grocery bag) or other nonconductive (insulating) material that can be left in bucket
- add storage contents
- press lid down gently, leaving only a small outlet for escaping air (lid will bulge if air/carbon dioxide gas can't escape)
- after 20–30 minutes, check to determine if dry ice has evaporated by sealing container (if lid pops off or container bulges, crack seal and wait another 5 minutes, then check again)
- when dry ice has completely evaporated, seal container

See following information for determining number of containers and quantity of dry ice for treating bulk foods.

Insect and Rodent Infestation Problems (continued)

Container Requirements Estimator for Dry-Ice Treatment Chart

Stored Item / 100 pounds	5-Gallon Containers Required
beans	3
corn, dried	3
flours—all	4
lentils	3
oats, rolled	4
pasta products—large (large macaroni, noodles, ravioli, spaghetti, etc.)	5
pasta products—small (elbow, alphabet, etc.)	4
peas, dried	3
soup mixes	3–4
sugar—all	3
TVP	4
whole grains—wheat, rice, etc.	3

Basic Dry-Ice Treatment Chart

Container Size	Food Quantity (pounds)	Dry Ice Required (ounces)	Expansion Space Required (inches)
Metal Containers			
#10 can	3–5$\frac{1}{2}$	1	$\frac{1}{4}$
5 gallon	15–35	2–3	$\frac{1}{2}$
25–30 gallon	100	8	$\frac{1}{2}$
Plastic Containers			
1 gallon	3$\frac{1}{2}$–7	1	$\frac{1}{4}$
4 gallon	13–30	4	$\frac{1}{2}$
5 gallon	15–35	4	$\frac{1}{2}$

Other Fumigation Methods

There are several other ways to fumigate bulk stored foods. Some of the commercial pesticides, even though food-grade approved, require more skills and equipment than most of us have. The other do-it-yourself methods recommended include the following three described below:

- freezing method
- heating method
- organic method

Fumigation by Freezing

The freezing method will kill all live bugs—but not necessarily the eggs—over an extended period of time.

The advantage of the freezing method is its simplicity. Its major disadvantage is that the pest eggs are not usually killed by freezing—that's what makes it difficult to have foolproof storage conditions.

It's always best to refreeze the previously frozen grains after 30 days to assure eggs hatched are killed.

Basic freezer method: place small quantities in either chest or upright freezer (*not freezer section of refrigerator*) for 72 hours at 0°F or lower.

Fumigation by Heating

The heating method also has the advantage of killing all forms of animal life in foods.

The disadvantage is that it also kills the food if overheated or left in the oven too long!

Basic heating method:
- pour infested foods in shallow baking pan to depth of one-half inch
- place in preheated 150°F oven for *only* 15–20 minutes

Foods will scorch if kept in heat too long. Oven door may be left open to allow moisture and heat to escape.

Insect and Rodent Infestation Problems (continued)

Organic Fumigation Method

Diatomaceous earth is an organic method to eliminate the hungry little critters feeding on your stored grains. It will rid the container of all bug and critter life. It works best with whole grains, beans, dried items, and processed grains such as rolled oats, TVP, and cereals.

This organic treatment is not harmful to humans or animals. It's also relatively inexpensive and simple to use.

Diatomaceous products are available at most lawn & garden shops, building supply centers, and hardware stores.

Basic organic method:

- for each 5-gallon container of food, put 1¼ cup diatomaceous earth into container

- shake vigorously or roll container until all the grains are dusted

6. Storage Period Exceeding Useful Shelf Life Problems

- **Food quality & nutritional values deteriorate continually over time.**
- **Loss of food value is approximately 2–5% each year.**

Solutions	Hints
• store what is already enjoyed by your family and the problem of storage period exceeding the useful life of stored food simply ceases to exist • **Store what you eat.** • **Eat what you store.** • **Use it or lose it!** Rotate→Rotate→Rotate→Rotate→Rotate	• one of the fundamental tenets of a successful storage program is the rotation of supplies to 　—prevent spoilage 　—minimize loss of food value and flavor 　—keep taste buds acquainted with foods one would depend on to sustain life • rotation is a "mechanical" method of keeping your inventory edible and nutritious while preventing spoilage • rotation of storage foods is a continuous process • always place the oldest canned goods in front and mark them so they will be consumed first • chemical reaction with metal containers occurs more rapidly with certain foods • canned foods will remain usable, if not wholesome, as long as the container seals remain intact and cans are not bulged • canned goods should be rotated and replaced with new food as used • solids tend to settle if not rotated • old, out-of-date food is edible but is not as palatable or nutritious • the next section details the typical shelf life of selected canned fruits and vegetables; note shelf life differences in foods: colored fruits, rhubarb, pickles, and sauerkraut have shorter shelf life • **Quick-Guide 3–2** details additional pantry, refrigeration, and freezing information about meats, vegetables, dairy products, baked goods, fish, and other foods

Storage Life of Canned Fruits & Vegetables[2]

Canned Fruits (Western U.S. at 70°F)[3]	Shelf Life (Months)	Canned Vegetables (Western U.S. at 70°F)	Shelf Life (Months)
Apples & applesauce	36	Asparagus	36+
Apricots	36	Beans—blackeye, lima, navy or pinto	96+
Blackberries	12+	Beans—green, snap or stringless	36+
Blueberries	12+	Beets	48+

---

[2] From "Progress in the Tin Plate Industry," *Food Technology*

[3] Note these shelf life projections are based on western U.S. locations, where humidity is not the problem it is in other areas of the country. Depending on where you live, you may need to factor in shorter shelf life periods and higher incidence of inventory turnover.

Storage Life of Canned Fruits & Vegetables (continued)					
Canned Fruits (Western U.S. at 70°F)	Shelf Life (Months)		Canned Vegetables (Western U.S. at 70°F)	Shelf Life (Months)	
Cherries, maraschino	12+		Brussels sprouts	48+	
Cherries, sweet	12+		Cabbage	48+	
Cherries, black	12+		Carrots	96+	
Cranberry sauce	12+		Cauliflower	48+	
Fruit salad	36		Corn	96+	
Grapes	12+		Hominy	96+	
Grapefruit	36+		Peas	96+	
Peaches	36		Pickles	12+	
Pears	36		Potatoes, sweet	48+	
Pineapple	36		Potatoes, whole white	48+	
Plums	12+		Pumpkin	48+	
			Rhubarb	12+	
			Sauerkraut	12+	
			Spinach	36+	
			Squash	48+	
			Tomatoes	48+	

Quick-Guide 3–2

Fresh & Processed Foods Shelf Life Table[4]

NOTES ON REFRIGERATED & FROZEN FOODS

When buying frozen foods:
- Be sure all refrigerated and frozen foods items are bagged separately so they will be stored first when you arrive home. Always place refrigerated items in the coolest area of the car for the trip home from the grocery store, especially during warm months.
- It is important when grocery shopping that refrigerated and frozen food items be selected last. This can help prevent spoilage and safeguard against risk of temperature loss.
- Always check frozen food labels for preparation and serving instructions. Unless otherwise stated on container, do not refreeze.
- Always select items in display cases that are below the "frost line" or "load line" (the line marked on commercial freezer cabinets which indicates the safety level).

Leftover foods:
- Refrigerate leftovers immediately to prevent bacterial growth—do not let them sit unrefrigerated for an extended period.
- Leftovers should be taken from the proper serving temperature (140°F–180°F) to the proper refrigeration temperature (40°F) as quickly as possible.
- Break large food items into smaller portions before refrigerating to promote faster chilling—leaving leftover foods out "to cool down" is not wise as it will promote bacterial growth.
- To prevent contamination in refrigerator, always place cooked food above raw items in the refrigerator. Make sure all food is covered when stacking so particles from the shelf above don't fall onto foods below.

Thawing frozen foods:
- Never thaw frozen food at room temperature! Either thaw in the refrigerator or under cold running water. It's best to let food thaw in a covered container overnight in the refrigerator.

Basic tip: Put your frozen product—fillet of fish, beef steak, or chicken breast—in a sealed plastic bag, eliminating as much air as possible. Thaw under cold running water.

---

[4] Contributors to this section include: USDA; Peggy Gentry-Van Laanen, Assoc. Prof. & Extension Nutrition Specialist, Texas A&M University; Delsa Wilson, food storage consultant; & lecture notes.

Food / Item	Pantry (50°–70°F)	Fridge (40°F)	Freezer (0°F)	Special Handling Notes
				Average Storage Time in Weeks (unless otherwise indicated)
Fresh baked goods				
breads, fresh	3–5 days	1–2	3–6	keep cool & dry; for maximum storage time when opened, store in airtight container; refrigeration generally extends shelf life; homemade breads may have shorter shelf life due to lack of preservatives
refrigerated biscuit / cookie dough		pkg. date	26–52	
rolls, fresh	2–5 days	pkg. date		
tortillas, corn & wheat flour	5–10 days	3–6	26–52	
Fresh dairy products				
butter		4–12	24–36	•butter will keep up to 1 year if melted enough to separate the whey from the pure butterfat •pour off the fat and seal in sterile bottles for pantry storage •the remaining whey can be refrigerated and used in cooking
Cheese				
cream / Neufchatel		12–16		
hard / wax-coated / opened & unopened		12–24		•mold growing on the surface of cheese can be cut off rather than discarding the entire piece of cheese •cheese bricks will not mold if wrapped in vinegar cloth •change vinegar cloth every 6 months •*basic alternative:* rub the entire cheese with a cloth moistened in white vinegar to kill and remove the moldy formation
hard / Parmesan / opened		12–24	24–36	
hard / Parmesan / unopened	52	96	see notes	freezing not recommended
processed cheese products	26	96	see notes	freezing not recommended
soft / ricotta		1–2	see notes	freezing not recommended
Cream, sweet				
half & half / light or heavy		4–12	see notes	freezing not recommended
Cream, sour				
sour cream		1–3	see notes	freezing not recommended
dips, mixed		1–3	see notes	freezing not recommended
Ice cream / ice milk / sherbet				
ice cream			1–2	
ice milk			1–3	
sherbet			1–3	
Milk products, fresh				
milk, fresh / pasteurized		1	3–4	freezing not recommended
buttermilk, fresh / pasteurized		1–2	12–16	
milk-based prepared foods		1		freezing not recommended
milk, nonfat / powdered / dry (opened)		1–2	12	
milk, nonfat / powdered / rehydrated		1		freezing not recommended
yogurt, regular & nonfat		pkg. date	4–6	
yogurt, frozen			36–52	

Fresh and Processed Foods Shelf Life Table (continued)

Food / Item	Pantry (50°–70°F)	Fridge (40°F)	Freezer (0°F)	Special Handling Notes
Average Storage Time in Weeks (unless otherwise indicated)				
Milk products, pantry				
infant formula	52–78	see notes		after opening, maximum refrigeration period is 48 hours
Margarine				
regular & soft		36–52	52	
diet		36–90	see notes	freezing diet varieties not recommended
Canned milk				**all:** turn canned milk upside down every other month to prevent lumps from forming due to fats separating; use evaporated, condensed sweetened, and other canned milks within one year; no need to refrigerate until opened; keeps refrigerated 3 days to 1 week after opening
evaporated / whole	12–24	see notes		
condensed, sweetened	9–12	see notes		
Non-dairy products				
whipped topping, aerosol can		18–52		do not freeze pressurized aerosol products
whipped topping, carton / tub			12	
creamers, powdered	12–24			refrigeration not necessary
creamers, frozen / liquid		1	12–24	
Fresh eggs				
in-shell		1–2		
frozen			36–52	
Fresh fish & shellfish				
fish, fresh / fat types		1 day	12–16	includes bluefish, bonito, eel, grunt, herring, kingfish, mackerel, mullet, porgy, salmon, sardines, sea bass, striped bass, sturgeon, swordfish, lake trout, rainbow trout, tuna, whitefish, whiting & yellowtail
fish, fresh / lean types		1 day	24–30	includes bluegill, carp, catfish, cod, crappie, croaker, dabs, fluke, flounder, grouper, haddock, halibut, monkfish, ocean perch, octopus, pike, pollock, red snapper, rockfish, sand dab, scrod, shark, sole, snapper & squid
fish, cooked		3–4 days	12–16	
fish, smoked / whole		1–2		freezing not recommended
fish, smoked / cut up		3–5 days		freezing not recommended
clams, shucked		1–2 days	12–16	
crabs		1–2 days	12–16	
oysters, shucked		1–2 days	12–16	
scallops		1–2 days	12–16	
shrimp, raw		2–3 days	24–30	do not refreeze previously frozen shrimp
shrimp, fresh		1–3 days	16–26	do not refreeze previously frozen shrimp

NOTES ON STORING FRESH MEATS

Refrigeration
- Prepackaged fresh meats from the meat self-service counter can be stored, unopened, in the refrigerator for 2–7 days.
- Properly wrapped, refrigerated or frozen meats will store well *in the refrigerator* for up to 7 days.
- Unopened vacuum-packed, processed (lunch or table-ready) meats will store in the refrigerator for up to 7 days, depending on cut(s), additives (cheese, pork, etc.), and fat content. Always check the freshness date on these packages when buying. Unopened packages can be kept frozen up to two months without rewrapping or overwrapping.

• For optimal refrigerated storage, temperatures of 28°–32°F are best. However, most refrigerators are equipped to maintain temperatures of 36°–40°F, so this chart is based on 36°–40°F.

Freezing
• Rewrapping, overwrapping, or sealing meat in foil, freezer paper or a heavy plastic wrap (a moisture- and vapor-proof material) will prepare it for freezer storage and extend storage time dramatically.
• Properly wrapped and frozen, fresh meat will store well in the freezer from several months up to a year, depending on cut, as indicated below.
• When freezing meats, label all packages with details about contents, weight, number of servings, or pieces.
• Date should be the date each package was placed in the freezer. Be sure to rotate frozen foods with the same dedication with fresh or canned foods—use oldest packages first.

Cooking fresh & frozen meats
• Meats should be cooked to a minimum internal temperature of 140°F.
• Poultry and stuffed meat items should be cooked to a minimum of 165°F.
• Pork should reach an internal temperature of 150°F.
• Cold meats should be served at a temperature of 40°F or lower.

Food / Item	Pantry (50°–70°F) (Don't!)	Fridge (40°F) Days	Freezer (0°F) Months	Special Handling Notes
Beef / cuts		3–5	6–12	
Beef / ground		1–2	3–4	
Lamb / cuts		3–5	6–9	
Lamb / ground		1–2	3–4	
Leftover cooked meat		4–5	3–4	
Organ meats Brains Heart Kidney Liver Sweetbreads		1–2	3–4	
Lunch meats		3–5	6–12	
Pork / cuts		3–5	6–9	
Pork / ground		1–2	1–2	
Pork / sausage		2–3	1–2	
Tongue		6–7	3–4	
Veal / cuts		3–5	6–9	
Veal / ground		1–2	3–4	

NOTES ON STORING FRESH VEGETABLES

This section briefly describes how fresh vegetables may be stored to preserve their flavor and nutrition. The following information details storing fresh vegetables in the kitchen, pantry, and refrigerated cold storage. Freezing and canning are not a part of this **Quick-Guide.**

Follow these general suggestions to enjoy the results of your selection of fresh vegetables:
• when possible, eat fresh vegetables raw, in salads, in relishes, or sliced as a side dish
• use vegetables as soon as possible after harvesting (or acquiring) to ensure maximum texture, flavor, and food value; cook vegetables in skins when possible, or peel very thinly, since the highest concentration of minerals and vitamins lies near the skin
• when storing a vegetable for only a short time, wash thoroughly, then refrigerate in the refrigerator vegetable drawer or in a heavy-duty, food-grade, freezer-quality, sealable plastic bag
• cook vegetables in a minimum amount of water or use none at all, as many nutrients are water soluble
• start fresh vegetables in boiling water, reduce heat so they boil gently, keeping cooking utensil tightly covered to shorten cooking time and preserve nutrients

Fresh and Processed Foods Shelf Life Table (continued)

- do not stir vegetables more than necessary—air brought in contact with food allows vitamin deterioration and stirring also breaks up the vegetable
- cook only until tender, since overcooking destroys color, texture, and flavor
- cream vegetables in their own cooking liquid to minimize the amount of fat by adding a small amount of milk or yogurt, or thicken with a blend of flour and milk, or cornstarch and water or milk (use *arrowroot* instead, if you're growing your own)
- salt lightly *after* cooking or sprinkle herbal mixes on foods for a healthy taste treat
- use any water from cooking vegetables as soup, sauce base, or put into stock pot
- lemon juice enhances vegetable flavor, making it possible to reduce margarine, butter, or spicy seasonings for a healthy taste treat

Fresh Vegetable Storage without Refrigeration

Food	Pantry (50°–70°F) Weeks	Fridge (0°F)	Freezer (0°F)	Special Handling Notes
Beans, all dried; see separate listings	52			
Garlic	3–8			
Lentils	52			
Onions–white or yellow	1–2			
Onions, pearl or globe	2–3			
Onions, sweet, white or yellow	1–2			
Peas, dried	52			
Peppers, chili	2–3			
Potatoes, new, red	2–3			
Potatoes, white, Russet, Baker	1–2			
Squash—winter (acorn, butternut, spaghetti)	1–2			
Sweet potatoes	5–7			
Tomatillo (Mexican tomato)	1–2			
Tomatoes, green	1–2			
Tomatoes, unripe	1			
Turnips	4–6			
Yams	5–7			substitute in any recipe for sweet potatoes

Fresh Vegetable Storage Requiring Refrigeration

Fresh Vegetables—this listing includes vegetables which may be stored only when refrigerated.
- cold storage in refrigerator at 40°F in heavy-duty, food-grade, sealable plastic bags
- some vegetables should not be refrigerated—check listings of vegetables above
- properly processed and frozen vegetables have shelf life of 10–12 months when stored at 0°F in freezer-quality, food-grade, heavy-duty, airtight plastic bags

Food	Pantry (50°–70°F)	Fridge (40°F)	Freezer (0°F)	Special Handling Notes
Arrowroot		7–14		dishes with arrowroot thickening cannot be reheated
Artichokes		7		
Asparagus		4–6		
Beans—lima, fava		2–3		
Beans—green, snap or string, yellow wax, all long beans		3–5		
Beets		7–10		
Broccoli		3–5		

Item			Notes
Brussels sprouts		3–5	
Cabbage—red		7–14	
Cabbage—green		7–14	
Carrots		7–14	
Cauliflower		4–7	
Celery		7–14	
Chard—Swiss		4–5	
Cilantro (Coriander)		7–10	
Corn—white or yellow		1	
Cucumber		4–5	
Dandelion		3–5	substitutes for spinach in any recipe
Eggplant		3–4	
Endive		3–5	
Ginger root		14–21	
Jicama		10–14	
Kale		2–3	
Kohlrabi		4–5	
Leeks		7–14	
Lettuce—butter		3–4	
Lettuce—iceberg & romaine		7–14	
Mushrooms		4–5	
Okra		7–14	okra will turn black if cooked in copper, brass, or tin pots or pans
Onions—green (scallions)		7–14	
Onions—sliced		2–3	
Onions—whole			do not refrigerate whole onions
Parsley		10–15	
Parsnips		7–10	
Peas—blackeye		3–4	
Peas—green		3–4	
Pepper—green bell		2–3	
Pepper—red bell		2–3	
Pepper—yellow bell		2–3	
Potatoes	4–8		potatoes should never be refrigerated after purchasing
Radish		10–14	
Rhubarb		4–7	don't eat leaves—they are poisonous to humans
Rutabaga		3–7	
Salsify—oyster plant		7–14	
Snow peas		4–6	
Spinach		2–3	
Sprouts		7–10	see **Chapter 15** for more details
Squash—acorn, banana, buttercup, butternut, kahoona, Hubbard		4–5	
Squash—crookneck		4–5	
Squash—spaghetti		4–5	
Swiss chard		2–3	
Taro (Dasheen)		2–3	
Tomatoes—ripe or sliced		1–2	
Turnips		5–7	also store well in kitchen or pantry
Zucchini		7–10	

Note: One of the best bags I've used for preserving fruits and vegetables in the refrigerator is a new, high-tech, "anti-fogging" and "breathing," re-useable plastic storage bag. It seems effective in prolonging storage life of many vegetables by absorbing and removing "ethylene" gas released after harvesting. It is available in several different sizes. Contact: **Evert-Fresh Corp.,** P.O. Box 590974, Houston TX 77254.

Local Area Resources

Check with your local County Extension Service or county extension agents for additional information on fumigating techniques, preparation, and other problems with your in-home storage plan.

There are many sources of information and resources for family preparedness and in-home storage. Knowing how to organize and maintain a sensible, continuing, workable, in-home storage program is a matter of constant self-education for each family. The resources found at the back of this book provide supplier information. By having access to a larger selection of vendors, shopping for competitive prices will help combat today's increasing prices and decreasing food availability.

Chapter 4

Water—the Absolute Basic

The most necessary element of your preparedness program is safe drinking water! For all its necessity, water has rather simple beginnings—atoms of hydrogen and oxygen combine. Then, rain and snow fall, snow melts in the high mountains, and water bubbles up from the ground. All together, a network of freshwater creeks is created—streams and rivers, then ponds, lakes, and eventually the great oceans—until water covers 70% of the earth's surface! Then, evaporation occurs, and the cycle repeats itself.

All living things—both plant and animal life—consist mostly of water. In fact, most of the living tissue in the human body—comprising 92% of the blood plasma, 80% of the muscle mass, 60% of red blood cells, and 50% of the rest of the body—is comprised of water! Water is simply the most common substance on earth and is basic to life itself.

However, fresh water, available for human use and management, makes up less than 3% of the earth's total water volume. Most of the fresh water supply—more than 80%, in fact—is in the form of glacial ice and is unavailable for our use. Of the remaining fresh water supply, most is underground, with only 5% present as surface water such as lakes,

> *"Water, water, everywhere... but not a drop to drink."*
>
> from "Rime of the Ancient Mariner," Samuel Taylor Coleridge

ponds, rivers, streams, etc. Total current worldwide water withdrawal[1] from available fresh water supplies is approximately 2400 cubic kilometers (or 1.7 x 1012 gallons) per day. Projections for the middle of the 21st century are almost 10 times as great, nearly 20,000 cubic kilometers (14.5 x 1012 gallons) per day! The volume of fresh water withdrawn for human use is increasing dramatically. At the same time, the major nations are facing increasing problems with pollution of their water supplies.[2]

The clear message: *fresh water is a diminishing resource.* It will require astute management if it is to support us at our accustomed quality of life in the next few decades.

IMPORTANCE OF STORING WATER

Water indeed is a precious commodity, both globally and personally. It is second only in priority to having air to breathe. You could probably live for two weeks—perhaps as long as four weeks—without food, but you can live only a few days without water.

Water is required to digest food; lubricate the body's organs, joints, and membranes; and to maintain the electrical balance in the body's cells. Water also keeps the body cool in summer and warm in winter.

Beyond its life-sustaining function, water is used to wash the body, cook food, and clean cooking utensils. Water is indeed a very important item to have in ready supply!

Therefore, your first priority in preparing for either an emergency situation or for a long-term in-home storage program is to store an adequate reserve of water.

This preparation must be done in a combination of three ways:

1. **Store a subsistence-level or maintenance-level supply of water now!**

2. **Learn how to treat contaminated water so it's safe to drink.**

3. **Learn to identify emergency sources of water to avoid deprivation.**

STORE YOUR EMERGENCY WATER SUPPLY NOW!

Water is probably the cheapest preparedness item to acquire and the easiest to store. It also weighs the most and takes up more space. The difficulties of a water storage program can be easily overlooked when you realize that in times of greatest need, water will be worth its weight in gold!

Usually, the first emergency supply item brought into a disaster area to aid victims is the water wagon. If you've ever been a victim of a hurricane or flood, you understand the mariner's plight when he lamented, *"... water, water, everywhere, ... but not a drop to drink!"*

Acquiring Your Water Reserves

Today, public utilities are distributing household water, as well as the other services, virtually without a hitch—and unappreciated until there's a crisis. A catastrophe can leave

---

[1] **Water Resources Research**, J. L. Napier and Donald Scott.
[2] Americans drank more than 2 billion gallons of bottled water in 1994—it is the beverage industry's fastest-growing segment. That fact alone tells us something about the importance of water.

a community without water resources until repairs are made, the lines are purged, and normal service is restored.

In-home water storage should be implemented now by taking advantage of the existing water system while it's readily available! Because of its preeminence in our very existence, we will spend inordinate amounts of time seeking, locating, and processing water for use in an emergency. Wouldn't it be much better to spend a few minutes now, rather than hours later to have water resources available?

Recommendations for Water Storage

Storing water is as easy as turning the faucet—if only you store it *before* an emergency arises! If you wait until it's critical, then both the frustration factor and the costs increase—in direct proportion to water's availability! The following are some basic recommendations to guide you in completing this fairly simple storage project.

Recommendation #1: *Store water from the source you're currently drinking.* Family members are accustomed to its taste and mineral content, so adjustment to "new" water won't be necessary. There are enough other challenges during emergencies without being frustrated about your water supply.

> **Recommendation #1**
>
> *Store water from the source you're currently drinking.*

Recommendation #2: *Store your water reserves in new, thoroughly cleaned, heavy-duty, plastic containers with tight-fitting lids.* Heavy plastic containers have the major advantage of being shatterproof and lighter than glass bottles or jugs.

The federal government, through the Department of Transportation, has developed a rigid burst test and handling standard (DOT #34) for plastic containers utilized in the interstate hauling industry. Plastic containers in this classification are designed to specifications for strength and transportability when filled with liquids. Plastic containers meeting DOT #34 are available in many sizes, ranging from 5-gallon to 55-gallon models. Water weighs eight pounds per gallon, so the 5-gallon plastic container (at 40 pounds) is about the maximum weight most people can carry—and just the right size for water storage. The 5-gallon container is designed for stacking to conserve space and is easy to handle for rotating your water supply.

> **Recommendation #2**
>
> *Store your water reserves in new, thoroughly cleaned, heavy-duty, plastic containers with tight-fitting lids.*

If you don't have a storage space problem, the larger containers are better for consolidating and organizing water storage. If your storage space is fairly limited, smaller storage containers facilitate stacking and moving them more often. Shipping-grade water containers, when filled with water, are capable of withstanding both outdoor hot and cold temperatures. This is important if some of your volume of water must be stored outside the protected environment of your living space.

There is always a great temptation to "keep it cheap" and store water in used containers. The difference in the price of acquiring and preparing used containers is comparable to acquiring new equipment, all things considered. It's not worth risking loss of your water supply by using containers of unknown origin and quality.

Some of the major reasons for utilizing only new, storage-quality containers are
- water quality is more easily maintained
- storage is neater and easier due to standard sizes
- containers are less likely to break
- supply is more transportable
- supply is more easily rotated

Recommendation #3

Don't re-use plastic containers previously filled with foodstuffs (mustard, ketchup, etc.), fruit or commercial drinks, milk, nonfood products, alkali-based or acid-based products (pickles, vinegar, household cleaners, etc.), or chemicals.

Recommendation #4

Store your water supply away from paint products, all petroleum-based products, acids, or anything releasing objectionable odors.

Recommendation #5

Don't use metal containers for water storage.

Recommendation #6

Rotate water supplies!

Recommendation #3: *Don't re-use lightweight, food-grade, plastic containers previously filled with foodstuffs (mustard, ketchup, etc.), fruit or commercial drinks, milk, nonfood products (pet foods, etc.), alkali-based or acid-based products (pickles, vinegar, household cleaners, etc.), or chemicals.*[3] The residual taste and odor of previous contents is often retained in the plastic, even though not immediately detected by smell or color, and may cause contamination of water storage eventually. Water resources are too important for your survival to risk having a contaminated supply.

The thinner plastic utilized in the commercial food industry is designed to be thrown away after a single use. Many of these lightweight plastic containers meet only minimum standards for bursting strength and durability and are not stable for long-term storage.

Commercial 1-gallon and 2½-gallon plastic water bottles were designed and utilized originally for water-based products and may be re-used for storing water in a protected (in-home) area.

Recommendation #4: *Store your water supply away from paint products, all petroleum-based products, acids, or anything releasing objectionable odors, such as equipment, animal waste, fertilizers, etc.* The composition of plastic containers acts as a permeable membrane which "breathes," allowing contamination of your stored water from strong odors, especially from petroleum-based products.

Recommendation #5: *Don't use metal containers for water storage.* Cans without a special coating of enamel or plastic on the inside tend to impart an unpleasant taste to stored water, especially after lengthy storage. Water makes metal containers rust!

Recommendation #6: *Rotate! Rotate! Rotate!* We can't emphasize this enough! Rotate your water supply as a means of continuously checking its quality and shelf life.

Shelf Life of Stored Water

Water that is bacteria-free when stored in thoroughly clean containers will remain safe for several years. Tests of water quality after long-term storage showed that water stored properly for several years could not be distinguished by appearance, taste, or odor from water recently drawn from the same source. However, the principle of rotation is the best guarantee for monitoring stored water's purity and taste.

Water is not only relatively inexpensive and easy to store, but it also stores indefinitely when a little care is given to its selection and preparation!

---

[3] The only exception to this recommendation is that use can be made of single-use plastic bottles (12-ounce, 16-ounce, 20-ounce, and ½-liter, etc.) and the larger containers (1-liter, 2-liter, and 3-liter bottles) designed and used for soft drinks, fruit juices, and bottled waters.

How Much Water to Store?

Each of us, during the average day, uses approximately 150 gallons of water directly in cooking our food, bathing our bodies, washing our dishes and clothes, flushing our toilets, and watering our lawns.

Each person's need for potable (drinking quality) water will differ, depending upon age, physical condition, level of activity, diet, and climate. Because of its preeminent importance for survival and given the varying levels of need among individuals, it is difficult to determine definitively just how much water should be stored for a given family.

If you used only ½ gallon per day, or 15 gallons per month, you would need approximately 180 gallons per person per year—just for minimal drinking purposes!

At 8 pounds per gallon, that amount of water would weigh more than three-quarters of a ton. It would also occupy approximately 150 cubic feet of valuable living space. Of course, that's space you need for living or for storing food and other preparedness items! Imagine the structural requirements for a large family's water storage, not to mention the cost of the storage equipment. How much more complicated to find storage if you live in an apartment, rent a house, or are away at school!

Since the magnitude of storing hundreds of gallons of water, weighing tons, is overwhelming, consider storing only what is required to provide the amount of water for your family's basic subsistence (drinking water only) or for basic maintenance (drinking water + minimal food preparation, cleaning, etc.) for a defined amount of time, such as 2 weeks.

Basic Subsistence-Level Water Storage Requirements

Basic subsistence-level water storage is defined as the amount of water required to sustain human body functions normally. This is considered a minimum daily amount of drinking water—any less will eventually create physical stress and possible ill effects.

A normally active person needs to drink 2 quarts of water per day—and more is better during emergency periods. To meet the minimum basic subsistence-level storage requirements plus basic personal needs—cooking some food, brushing teeth, washing face, hands, etc.—**store at least 1 gallon for each family member per day for a 2-week period.**

Chart 4–1

Basic Subsistence-Level Water Storage

Number of family members ⟹	
Number of gallons to store for each family member	X 1
Subtotal for family members	=
Multiply by 14 (for 2-week supply)	X 14
Total minimum gallons of water storage required for family ⟹	=

Note the following about the basic subsistence-level quantity of water:

- This amount includes no allowances for washing dishes or the body.

- High-temperature environments require greater water intake.

- Active children, nursing mothers, and sick people will usually need to drink more than 2 quarts of water each day.

Most survival experts agree that when water supplies begin to run low, it should not be rationed (except, perhaps, at sea). The reasoning is there's nothing more demoralizing for the average person than being thirsty when under stress!

The best rationing plan is to drink a reasonable amount of water daily, then find more! Rather than rationing drastically, minimize the amount of water the body needs by reducing activity and staying cool. In the next section you'll discover how to find emergency water sources in and around the house so you won't need to ration water too sharply.

Basic Maintenance-Level Water Storage Requirements

Basic maintenance-level water storage requirements differ from basic subsistence-level requirements by the addition of water reserves to do some of the normally water-intensive chores—cooking and preparing food, cleaning utensils/equipment, and washing the body—without taking a bath! It's only slightly above basic subsistence-level water storage requirements.

The recommended amount of water for basic maintenance-level storage requirements is 2 gallons for each family member per day for a 2-week period.

Chart 4–2

Basic Maintenance-Level Water Storage

Number of family members $\Longrightarrow$	
Number of gallons to store for each family member	X 2
Subtotal for family members	=
Multiply by 14 (for 2-week supply)	X 14
Total minimum gallons of water storage required for family $\Longrightarrow$	=

Not Yet Ready to Begin Water Storage?

If you're not ready to begin your storage program now, at least buy several gallons of purified water at the local grocer. You'll have some water to drink while you look for other water sources should an emergency occur!

Supplies of bottled water are available in a broad range of sizes and prices. Always buy water in plastic bottles, preferably the 16-ounce or 1-liter sizes. All chain grocery stores carry house brands at a fraction of the cost of the familiar brand names. (House brands are usually bottled by name-brand bottling companies!)

Perhaps these ideas will help you overcome your reticence to get a water supply organized:

- Keep a few of the smaller-size, plastic, bottled water containers on hand at all times. They're easy to refill, and they have other practical uses, too. The small plastic bottles are easily tucked into small spaces of your individual and family emergency kits.

- It's a great idea to always have a canteen full of water ready for an emergency. Keep the canteen with your emergency kits. Rotate the water often.

- It's also a good idea to keep some water in a canteen or a strong plastic bottle in the trunk of your car, too. Be sure to rotate water every three months.

CONTAMINATED WATER

As previously mentioned, in emergency situations, you'll need to know how to identify emergency water sources. As you consider locating and using unfamiliar emergency water sources, it is important that you become aware of the dangers of ingesting contaminated water. When normal water supplies are interrupted, you may need to deal with water of unknown quality—if you can find water at all!

Emergency water sources may be muddy, stagnant, brackish, foul-smelling, or otherwise obviously contaminated. Even clear and clean-looking water may be contaminated. In addition to having bad odor and taste, contaminated water usually contains microorganisms that can cause serious diseases.

Using contaminated water for drinking or cooking can lead to problems which range from a minor upset stomach, such as you'd have with the flu, to life-threatening illnesses, such as amebic dysentery, viral infection, cholera, typhoid, hepatitis, or even death.

> **Rule of Thumb**
>
> *Always treat any water before using it if there's any question about its being safe to drink or if it hasn't been tested and approved by the appropriate health authorities.*

Some of the symptoms arising from drinking polluted or contaminated water are

- nausea
- vomiting
- diarrhea
- low-grade fever
- general malaise (vague feelings of discomfort)
- fatigue or weight loss due to above condition(s)

These symptoms appear to be the same as those associated with typical gastrointestinal (GI) problems. They may also be associated with other methods of transmission of "bugs" to the GI system, such as food, viral infections, flu, etc.

TREATING CONTAMINATED WATER

There are many ways to treat contaminated water to make it potable, or drinkable, depending on the severity of contamination. For basic considerations, however, we'll deal only with those pertaining to emergency or subsistence-level needs. These methods for treating contaminated water are boiling and disinfecting.

Boiling Method

Boiling renders water safe to drink by killing the bacteria and all other harmful life. Water must be heated to its vaporization point (212°F or 100°C at sea level) to be effective. This is generally the safest and cheapest method for treating water. It is also the easiest, least technical method for treating almost any volume of water for drinking and cooking.

Boil water at a rolling boil for at least 10 minutes to render it potable!

There are some advantages of boiling water over other methods:

- requires minimum equipment
- simplest process to assure drinking-quality water
- least expensive method to treat drinking water
- requires short amount of time during an emergency
- microbial danger is eliminated by boiling

There are some disadvantages to boiling water as a means of removing contaminants:

- boiled water tastes "flat"[4]
- can consume a large amount of emergency fuel supply
- sometimes a fire is not possible
- pretreatment required to remove debris from water before boiling

Boiling doesn't solve all the contamination problems, but it will make water safe to drink!

Disinfecting Methods

The disinfecting method kills pathogenic organisms in contaminated water. Chlorine and iodine are two chemicals used to kill waterborne microorganisms. Chlorine and iodine are equally easy and effective. There are other chemicals which can be used to treat water.

Effectiveness of disinfecting by either the chlorine or iodine treatment method depends upon:

- chemical concentration—amount of chemical used in water
- exposure—amount of time chemical is in water
- temperature of water—determinant of time required for effect
- pH level—alkalinity/acidity balance
- turbidity—ratio of suspended particles in water, which determines time required for effect

---

[4] All treated and stored water will taste better if it's aerated by pouring water from one clean container to another before drinking.

Basic Bleach Method

For emergency treating of water of unknown quality, use any household bleach containing sodium hypochlorite (5.25% solution) *without* soap additives or phosphates. By using common household bleach as a chemical treatment method, large amounts of safe drinking water can be provided quite inexpensively.

Follow these simple instructions:

- add bleach per **Chart 4–3** to water in container
- thoroughly mix bleach in water by stirring briskly
- let mixture stand for at least 30 minutes[5]

Caution:

Be sure sodium hypochlorite is the only active ingredient in bleach when used for water treatment.

Chart 4–3

Basic Bleach Water Treatment Method

Water Quantity	Water Condition	5.25% Sodium Hypochlorite
1 quart	Clear	2 drops
	Cloudy	4 drops
1/2 gallon	Clear	4 drops
	Cloudy	8 drops
1 gallon	Clear	8 drops
	Cloudy	16 drops
5 gallons	Clear	1/2 teaspoon
	Cloudy	1 teaspoon
120 gallons	Clear	2 ounces
	Cloudy	4 ounces

Mixture should still have a distinct chlorine taste or smell after waiting period. If chlorine smell is not detected, add same dose of the solution to the water and let mixture stand for an additional 15–20 minutes.

Basic Iodine Method

Tincture of iodine (2%) can be used to treat *small* quantities of water. Be sure to stir thoroughly when mixing iodine into the water resource.

Chemical disinfecting by iodine requires these precautions:

- iodine treatment has a peculiar odor and taste some people just cannot tolerate
- water treated with iodine should not be utilized by pregnant or nursing women
- people with thyroid problems should not ingest iodine-treated water

Chart 4–4 on the following page is a guide for the amount of iodine to utilize in treating emergency water supplies.

Note:

The presence of the iodine taste or smell is a sign of safety. If you cannot detect either the taste or smell after water is treated, don't use it! The iodine may have become weakened by either time, heat, or contamination.

---

[5] Conditions requiring longer exposure to the chlorine are cold water and heavy turbidity. The colder the water and the dirtier the water, the longer the time required for the chlorine to kill contaminants. Chemicals do not purify water; they merely render the water potable by neutralizing some of the toxic animal and plant life in the water.

Chart 4–4

Basic Iodine Water Treatment Method

Water Quantity	Water Condition	Quantity of 2% Iodine
1 quart	Clear	3 drops
	Cloudy	6 drops
1/2 gallon	Clear	6 drops
	Cloudy	12 drops
1 gallon	Clear	12 drops
	Cloudy	24 drops

Other Chemical Methods

There are many commercially manufactured chemical combinations which are effective in treating water for emergency use. (Note the term *water treatment*, not *water purification*. The emergency treatments provide emergency-use water quality.) These chemicals are available at sporting good stores and specialty suppliers and come with complete instructions for use.

Water treatment tablets are relatively inexpensive. In tablet, powder, and concentrated liquid form, they are more portable than a bottle of bleach. Some of them render water more drinkable than chlorine-flavored water.

EMERGENCY SOURCES OF WATER

Within a few short hours after an emergency situation arises, drinking-quality water will become a very important personal issue. You may need to be aware of some of the many places where water is found in and around the home. You'll also want to be aware of accessible and available sources off your property, especially if you've failed to prepare enough water storage! You might not think of some of these resources unless you've given water storage a lot of serious planning.

Limited amounts of water for emergency use can generally be found in and around most homes. These "hiding places" are the plumbing system, plumbing fixtures, appliances, and even water beds. A quick review will make you aware of their location(s) and the potential they have for providing an emergency water supply. You may be forced to drink from these water sources.

There are many water sources in and about your home. Suitability of these water sources for human use will depend on the quality of the water, relative ease of access, and intended utilization. Several sources easily located by everyone are identified in **Quick-Guide 4–1** on the following page. The **Guide** will help you review quickly some potential emergency water sources.

Quick-Guide 4–1

Emergency Water Resources Guide

Water Source	Guidelines for Use
Interior Water Sources	
Plumbing system	Best water to use in emergency. Everyone familiar with taste, odor, mineral content & quality of water. Know where to find main water valve for cut-off. Have proper valve key.
water lines	Contain several gallons of water, depending on house size. Easiest water to access. Turn on faucet at lowest point in line. If water doesn't flow, also open the faucet at highest point in line.
hot water heater	Contains 15–40 gallons potable water, depending on size. Open drain faucet at bottom of heater. You may need to screen or filter out sediment before drinking or cooking with it.
tubs & sinks	Fill ahead of time when possible to have additional water on hand.
toilet tanks *(not bowls!)*	Contain 5–7 gallons in tank. Always treat (boiling is preferred method) before using. ***Caution: Not potable if commercial disinfectants or cleaners are used in tank.***
Appliances	Use appliances for emergency water storage.
refrigerator freezer	Consume cooled and frozen drinks & liquid sources (fruits, vegetables, etc.) first—they become less palatable over time during power outage. Ice cubes provide some drinking water; may also be important for first aid or to preserve food longer.
water cooler, clothes washer, tubs, buckets, pots & pans	Fill to capacity for additional reserves.
Water bed	*Controversial storage source.* **To use water bed water for emergency purposes, follow these requirements:** (1) use only a new mattress (2) fill mattress with fresh tap water (3) add 2 ounces bleach per 120 gallons of water *(do not use toxic algae inhibitor solution!)* (4) rotate water at least yearly (5) test 3–4 times yearly for algae & toxins (6) all water bed water must be boiled *before* using it
Exterior Water Sources	
Yard	Water hoses, buckets, barrels of rainwater, puddles, ditches & troughs may contain water.
water hoses	Suspect contamination if hose end is in bucket, barrel, ditch, or puddle. Hoses lying on the ground may have siphoned contaminated water.
hot water spa or swimming pool	*Controversial source.* Could provide both emergency source and long-term storage. Use for nondrinking purposes. If required for drinking or cooking, treat and boil as contaminated.
Precipitation	Rain and snow provide water. If caught in clean containers, may be used without treatment. Otherwise, treat as contaminated water.
rainwater	Collect in bowls, pans, buckets, barrels & storage cisterns. Treat *all* water not caught in clean containers.
snow	First snow to fall contains environmental contaminants. Use only clean-fallen snow as a clean water source. For old snowfall, remove "crust" and use protected snow underneath for clean water use. If not sure of quality, treat as contaminated.
Surface water lakes, streams, ponds, rivers	Collect water and process: (1) find a sandy spot within 1' –6' of water's edge; (2) dig hole 12" below the water level; (3) wait for water to seep into hole; (4) let suspended particles (mud) settle; (5) dip out clear water carefully to avoid transferring mud. Water may be filtered through sand, grass, charcoal, field filtration unit, or use several layers of cloth to remove larger debris. Treat all surface water as contaminated.
Groundwater	Puddles, ditches, and any ground depression can contain water. All groundwater sources must be treated as contaminated.
well water	Unless used as primary water source, test before using. Check for contamination after any unusual disturbance to area.
natural spring	Normally potable unless inundated by flood waters or recharge zone contaminated by oil, chemical spills, dead animals, etc. However, if water is not tested, treat as contaminated.

Chapter 5

Wheat—the Basic Grain

Wheat is referred to as the staff of life because it is the most widely grown and consumed grain in the world. Wheat is utilized in many forms by different cultures, but the form of wheat most widely used is flour, whether for pastas, breads, or other baked goods. Flours are available from the minimally processed whole-wheat flours, such as graham and bread flour, to the highly processed white flours, unbleached or bleached, such as bread, pastry, cake, all-purpose, self-rising, and semolina flour.

Perhaps less known are other types of wheat available for our use. Among them are the unprocessed forms of whole-grain wheat. These include whole or cracked kernels of the *wheat berries*. Slightly more processed forms include bulgur, couscous, wheat germ, wheat bran, rolled and flaked wheat (similar to oatmeal), and the wheat meals. The most recognized forms are the higher processed forms such as farina, semolina, and white flour.

With such a wide range of uses, wheat is considered by many experts to be one of the most basic food storage items. It is certainly easy to store and has high value in the daily diet. Wheat can be prepared easily in an extremely wide variety of dishes—from breakfast cereals to breads to main dishes to desserts.

Wheat is also very nutritious, containing high amounts of protein, calcium, niacin, riboflavin, and thiamin. When sprouted, vitamins A and C are also present in increased amounts.

As interest in wheat storage and in-home storage and use has increased, equipment for in-home processing and food technology for its use and enjoyment have kept pace with the demand. Commercial resources for producing, milling, storing, grinding, and preparing wheat have increased at ever-lower costs. Grinders, grinding mills, storage containers, widespread delivery systems, and availability are working for the wheat devotée.

This chapter contains many helpful ideas for storing and preserving whole-wheat grains. The following chapters have recipes for utilizing wheat from whole kernel to white flour. Virtually every form of preparing wheat in-home is covered.

By the way, here is an early warning message—***don't try to start a whole-wheat diet all at once!*** You would suffer digestive problems an antacid won't resolve! The normal digestive system cannot adapt immediately to the extreme dietary change a diet of whole wheat would cause. Small children would probably have digestive and elimination problems when commencing a high-level wheat consumption diet. A diet with a few ounces per day of processed flour products is a far cry from a diet of *cracked whole-wheat cereal* at breakfast, *whole-wheat bread sandwiches* for lunch, then a *wheat sprout salad*, a *whole-wheat bulgur casserole*, some more *whole-wheat bread,* and a *wheat-based dessert* at dinner! Living on basic foods is a lifestyle unto itself.

Wheat causes allergic reactions in some people, and a whole-wheat diet will be very difficult for them. Many persons who at lower levels of wheat intake may not be aware of their allergy to wheat may discover their latent sensitivity when they ingest more wheat more often.

If you aren't using whole-wheat food daily, start utilizing it at some meal soon. Get accustomed to whole-wheat foods by using some whole-wheat flour in white flour recipes the family already likes. Once you've cleared that hurdle, start on the next one. Eventually you'll be able to utilize whole-wheat flour exclusively when flour is required in a recipe. Then, and only then, are you ready to use only your own wheat flour produced in-home for wonderful dishes, including all those delightful whole-wheat casseroles you'll create!

Let reason prevail—start now in your goal of utilizing wheat in every form. Break into the whole-wheat lifestyle with a gentle, guiding effort. Don't wait for a cataclysm—you'll have more than *one* serious problem with which to deal!

BASIC STORAGE GUIDELINES

Many years ago, Bob Zabriskie outlined the value of wheat storage in his timely publication, *A Family Storage Plan.*[1] His storage plan suggested how much whole wheat to purchase and gave guidelines for storing wheat that are still valid today. Listed below are his suggested criteria for treating and preserving bulk whole wheat:

- **Variety**
- **Protein content**
- **Moisture content**
- **Quantity**
- **Containers**
- **Storage techniques**

Purchasing Whole Wheat

Varieties to buy include Dark Hard Winter, Spring Wheat, Dark Turkey Red, and Montana White Wheat because they store best. Grain should be cleaned for human consumption and free from all foreign matter possible. Buy *Grade #1* for food storage. Always buy the best grade(s) available—the quality of your results in cooking, baking, and realizing the full health benefits whole wheat offers depends on your choice of grain!

Protein content should be 13% or higher. There are wheat varieties available to the consumer with as much as 18% protein.[2]

Moisture content should not exceed 10% in the grain. This will inhibit microbial infiltration and insect infestation.

Quantity to buy varies according to age, weight, size, sex, and appetite of each person. See the **Quick-Guides** in **Chapter 2** for details of suggested quantities for your family.

> *Note:*
>
> *When buying whole-wheat flour from the store, buy it only if it has been refrigerated. Be sure to keep it refrigerated until utilized.*

Containers for Storing Whole Wheat

Use crushproof, waterproof and moisture-proof containers. All food storage products must be protected to prevent infiltration, infestation, and contamination. The better a container meets these requirements, the better condition stored wheat will be in when needed.

Store wheat in round cans. When storing wheat in square cans, allow several inches open space on all sides of the cans to allow air to circulate more freely.

A round, 5-gallon metal bucket, enamel-coated interior, with an airtight lid and waterproof seal is the best option for storing bulk whole wheat. These are generally available from restaurant suppliers, barrel, container, or used-container dealers. This type of container will hold approximately 35 pounds of wheat and is convenient for both transporting and long-term storage purposes. These containers will stack safely, allow better ventilation, protect the contents, and require less storage space.

---

[1] **Family Storage Plan,** Bob R. Zabriskie, publ. Bookcraft Publishers, Inc., 1848 West 2300 South, Salt Lake City UT. His book is a compilation of suggestions for the preparation, preservation, and storage of foods.

[2] Wheat Montana Farms, P.O. Box 647, Three Forks MT 59752 ☎(800) 535-2798. Growers of Montana White Wheat and Golden 86 Hard White Spring wheat with protein in excess of 18%.

A 5-gallon polyethylene bucket with tight-fitting lid and waterproof seal is a good alternative to the metal can. Normally available at the same businesses as metal cans. Same caution as to container's previous contents applies.

Always use a heavy-duty, food-grade, sealable, plastic liner in any container for bulk wheat. With any container, a food-grade plastic liner is necessary to prevent infiltration of contaminants, infestation, and moisture.

Properly processed, treated, prepacked, and factory-sealed wheat can be purchased from reputable mills and food storage dealers. Commercially sealed wheat usually requires neither turning nor aerating when properly stored.

Caution:

Attention to previous contents of any used container is important. Make sure no chemicals, odorous food, or nonfood products were stored in food containers.

Basic Storage Techniques

There are a few critical things about bulk wheat storage we bring to your awareness. Properly stored wheat will store indefinitely. Improperly stored wheat will neither store for very long, due to spoilage, nor have any food value left when used, even if it doesn't spoil.

Temperature Range

Temperature range for storing bulk wheat is 45°–65°F. Edible and sproutable wheat was discovered in the pyramids after centuries of storage. Wheat will keep indefinitely when properly stored. However, since ideal storage conditions are difficult to maintain, always rotate stored wheat. Use older wheat first and replace it annually with new wheat at harvest times, when prices are generally lower.

Moisture Protection

Always store wheat in a dry environment. Bulk wheat must be kept dry to prevent infestation and contamination. Moisture provides an environment for molds, bacteria, and a multitude of bugs to grow.

Wheat draws moisture, so take precautions to protect stored wheat from exposure to high humidity and high temperatures. Use boards or wooden platforms under metal cans to prevent bottoms of cans from touching or being in direct contact with concrete, earth, or any moisture-conducting surface. The bulk wheat draws moisture, so it must be isolated by the wood and air buffer to prevent spoiling.

Ventilation

Leave air space around stored wheat containers. Ventilation is necessary because the ambient air provides a buffer zone for the stored wheat as it gains and loses heat.

When storing wheat in square cans, allow several inches open space on all sides of the cans to allow adequate ventilation. Wheat stored in square cans stacked too closely together does not allow the heat generated to escape. The increased temperatures cause sweating inside the containers.

Use boards or wooden platforms under all storage containers, especially metal cans, to prevent bottoms from rusting.

Light

Avoid storing wheat in bright light. Some light, however, will discourage molds from growing in small containers.

Fumigating Wheat for Storage

Dry-Ice Methods

Carbon dioxide released from evaporating dry ice will kill all animal life in the container. There are two different ways to fumigate wheat with dry ice.

Basic on-top method:
- on top of almost-full 5-gallon container, place $1/4$ pound dry ice on non-conductive (insulating) material such as kraft paper
- press lid down gently so some air can escape
- after 20–30 minutes, check to see if dry ice has completely evaporated
- if not, wait another 5 minutes, then check again
- when dry ice completely evaporated, remove material and seal container

Basic on-bottom method:
- on bottom of 5-gallon metal storage bucket, place $1/4$ pound dry ice under non-conductive (insulating) material, such as kraft paper, that can be left in bucket
- press lid down gently, leaving only a small outlet for escaping air (lid will bulge and will eventually blow off if air can't escape)
- after 20–30 minutes, check to confirm if dry ice has evaporated by closing the lid; if it bulges, loosen lid and wait another 5 minutes, then check again
- when dry ice is completely evaporated, seal container

> **Caution:**
>
> *Do not put dry ice directly on wheat. The wheat will be frozen and becomes useless as food.*

Freezing Method

The freezer will kill all live bugs—but not necessarily the eggs—over an extended period of time. The advantage of the freezer is its simplicity. Its major disadvantage is that the eggs are not usually killed by freezing—that's what makes it difficult to have foolproof storage conditions. It's always best to refreeze the previously frozen wheat after 30 days to assure that any eggs hatched since the last treatment are killed.

Basic freezer method: place small quantities in either chest or upright freezer (*not* freezer section of refrigerator) for 72 hours at 0°F or lower.

Heating Method

The heating method has the advantage of killing all forms of animal life in the wheat. The disadvantage is that it will also kill the wheat when overheated or left in the oven too long!

Basic heating method: pour infested wheat in shallow baking pan to depth of $1/2$ inch. Place in preheated 150°F oven for *only* 15–20 minutes Wheat will scorch if it gets too hot for too long. Oven door may be left open to allow moisture and heat to escape.

Organic Method

Diatomaceous earth is an organic method to eliminate the hungry little critters feeding freely on your storage supply. It will rid the container of all bug and critter life. This organic treatment is not harmful to man or animals. It's also very cheap and simple to use.

Basic organic method: for each 5-gallon container, put in $1\frac{1}{4}$ cup diatomaceous earth, shake vigorously or roll container until all the wheat grains are dusted. To use wheat after treatment, rinse grain before using, then blot dry with towel with massaging action to wipe off powder. Or use it with dust on it—it's treated with an organic compound!

Local Area Guidance

Local County Extension Service agents will have additional information on the best storage techniques and details for your geographical area.

What Not to Do with Storage Wheat

Here's a short list of things to avoid when storing bulk wheat—or when storing any food products:

- Do not pack wheat tightly into any storage space that is not optimal for storage.

- Do not store wheat directly on dirt or cement floors, as wheat draws moisture from these surfaces.

- Do not store wheat in a container which holds more than two bushels or 100 pounds. Large containers are difficult to move and any infiltration, infestation, spoilage, or exposure will contaminate the entire contents.

- Do not store wheat near
      hot or cold water pipes, heating ducts, or steam pipes
      washing machine or clothes dryer (*vented or not*)
      where laundry is hung to dry

- Do not store wheat in any of these locations:
      in an unheated garage or noninsulated space
      in a basement or underground space not completely dry
      in any uninhabitable space

- Do not put salt in wheat when storing it.

- Do not use aluminum garbage cans for wheat storage since an airtight seal is generally impossible to achieve. Even with food-grade plastic liners, garbage cans are not designed for storing edible food.

Grinding Wheat

Note:

Grind only enough wheat for use within one week. Natural whole-wheat flour has practically no food value remaining after 30 days at room temperature.

If you store wheat in bulk, you must have access to a wheat grinder. There are many models on the market, both hand-operated and electric models. The electric models are great but quite expensive. It makes good sense to have a hand-operated or foot- or bicycle-powered model before purchasing an expensive electric model. On an occasional basis, many blender models may have adequate power to produce enough flour for a batch of bread. The more a wheat grinder is utilized, the better it grinds the wheat into flour—the stones literally grind themselves to a perfect fit. All motorized grinders normally ship with instructions, so be sure to follow the operating instructions of the manufacturer for best results. See the resources in the back of this book for manufacturers and vendors.

Storing ground wheat: keep ground whole wheat and all types of fresh-ground or commercially-ground (store-bought) flours in the refrigerator or in an equivalently cool, dry place. Refrigeration at 40°F will extend shelf life of ground wheat by approximately six months. Shelf life of flour is very short at best, and its freshness and effectiveness is compromised by the distribution process.

Chapter 6
Basic Whole-Wheat Bulgur Cookery

One of the most basic and interesting forms of cooked wheat is bulgur. It is used worldwide and ranks as one of the most versatile and utilized whole-wheat foods in many Middle Eastern countries. Bulgur is easily made from whole-wheat kernels as they come naturally from the field, with only the chaff stripped off. Sometimes called *wheat berries,* these whole kernels need soaking or steam cooking to become tender. When cooked, they have a sweet, nutlike flavor and a slightly chewy texture.

Bulgur is probably the easiest whole-wheat food to prepare. None of the measurements are critical, and there's no fussing with stirring, continual watching, etc., as with flour recipes.

Bulgur can be made from whole-wheat kernels and cracked wheat kernels—or many other grains, too. It can be used as a very nutritional breakfast cereal, to replace rice in most dishes, as a substitute for mashed potatoes, or it can be baked with selected seasonings to make a delightful, nutritious, crunchy TV snack, and it is great in stuffing for meats and fowl.

There are many known ways to prepare dishes with wheat bulgur and many ways that haven't been discovered yet.

DIRECTIONS FOR MAKING BASIC BULGUR

Wheat kernels can be made into *Basic Bulgur* quite simply. This recipe is an in-home method for processing the whole-wheat grain—called *wheat berries*—for easy and quick use whenever needed. *Basic Bulgur* exists in two forms, whole grain or cracked.

BASIC BULGUR

1 part whole-wheat kernels	$1/_2$–1 tsp. salt
2–3 parts water	

Basic Bulgur is easy because the measurements are not critical! Cover wheat with water, approximately 2 inches above level of wheat in an appropriately large, heavy pot. Bring ingredients to boil, then turn off heat and let mixture stand for $1^1/_2$–2 hours. Repeat cycle by bringing mixture to rolling boil, adding water if needed. Turn off heat, let stand for 15–30 minutes. Stir in salt to taste. Drain all remaining water from cooked wheat berries. This is a batch of *Basic Bulgur*.

Directions for Making Basic Cracked Bulgur

Cracked bulgur can be made from scratch more quickly and easily than whole-berry bulgur. This is the simple recipe for making *Basic Cracked Bulgur:*

BASIC STEAMED CRACKED BULGUR

Combine 2 cups cracked wheat and 4 cups water in an open-top pan or metal bowl. Elevate pan or bowl (use small bowl or jar lid) inside a larger, covered pan. Add water in the larger pan to 2 inches below the rim of the smaller pan. Cook over high heat, covered, for 15 minutes, then reduce heat to very low. Steam until tender and water in small pan is absorbed, about 3 hours. This is *Basic Cracked Bulgur.*

BULGUR BASICS

These are the additional things you need to know to complete the *Bulgur Basics* course: storage of moist and dried bulgur, drying and rehydrating bulgur, cracking whole-wheat kernels and dried bulgur, and how to make bulgur by alternative methods.

Storing Moist Bulgur

Refrigerator: put moist bulgur in a tightly covered bowl, plastic airtight container, or heavy-duty, self-sealing, plastic freezer bag. This provides storage for about two weeks.

Freezer: for longer-term storage of moist bulgur, package as above. Effective storage period is approximately one year. For longer storage periods, see the following section.

Drying Basic Bulgur

Basic Bulgur can be dried for long-term storage. It dries quickly and easily in either the oven or in an electric dryer. Air drying is not recommended, since bulgur is so water laden it tends to spoil before drying completely. Here are the two best methods for drying *Basic Bulgur.*

Oven drying: spread *Basic Bulgur* in a thin layer on cookie sheet. With oven temperature set at 200°F, allow to slow cook until crispy. Stirring and turning with a spatula decreases drying time. Leave oven door slightly ajar to permit moisture to escape. Allow *Basic Bulgur* to cool completely before packaging.

Electric dryer: cover drying tray with plastic film or kraft paper. Spread cooked bulgur in a thin layer. Dry until crisp and brittle. Cool completely and package for storage.

Cracking Dried Basic Bulgur

Barely crack the dried *Basic Bulgur* in a blender or grain mill. In most *Basic Bulgur* recipes, either cracked wheat or whole berries may be used equally well. However, the *Basic Cracked Bulgur* will be less coarse and have a more delicate wheat taste.

Storing Dried Basic Bulgur

Place dried *Basic Bulgur* in an airtight package. The best packaging for small quantities is the freezer-quality, heavy-duty, food-grade, sealable plastic bag. The large size holds just enough dried bulgur for a meal. Several bags may be placed in a larger metal or glass container to further protect them. Store in a cool, dry, and dark location.

Rehydrating Basic Bulgur

Use the following chart as a guideline for rehydrating *Basic Bulgur.*

Chart 6–1
Basic Bulgur Rehydrating Method

Yield	Ingredients		
1 C. = 1 serving	Water	Salt	Bulgur
1 C.	$3/4$ C.	$1/4$ tsp.	$1/3$ C.
2 C.	2 C.	$1/3$ tsp.	$2/3$ C.
6 C.	4 C.	1 tsp.	2 C.

Rehydrate 15–30 minutes in any liquid, or combination of liquids, until suited to your taste.

> **Note:**
>
> *When a recipe calls for cooked whole wheat, measure equal amount of dried BASIC BULGUR. Add liquid to cover. Bring to a boil until rehydrated to your taste or recipe directions.*

Alternate Methods for Making Basic Bulgur

Use one of the following alternate recipes or methods to make *Basic Bulgur.* With all these choices, there's bound to be one *Basic Bulgur* which will become your favorite.

BASIC MICROWAVE BULGUR

1 C. whole-wheat kernels $1/2$–1 tsp. salt
3 C. water

Put water in a large microwave-safe bowl. Cover with kraft or waxed paper loosely folded over top of bowl. Heat water for 5 minutes on high power setting. Stir in rinsed wheat kernels, cover, and heat again on high power for 5 minutes. Reduce to medium ($1/2$ power), continue covered heat at five-minute intervals until soft and chewy. Allow to stand covered 5 minutes. Remove cover, test for doneness, then stir in salt to taste. This is a batch of *Basic Microwave Bulgur.*

BASIC ALL-NIGHT BULGUR

Combine ingredients for *Basic Microwave Bulgur,* except salt, in a covered pan. Bake about 5 hours or overnight in a warm oven (150°–200°F degrees). Stir in salt to taste.

BASIC BOIL & WAIT BULGUR*

Combine ingredients for *Basic Microwave Bulgur,* except salt, and bring to boil. Then immediately cover and remove from heat. Let stand overnight or at least 10–12 hours. Stir in salt to taste. May be eaten then or warmed later, when desired.

* Some folks make *Basic Bulgur* by this method the night before, warm it in the microwave oven, and eat it on the way to work the next morning.

BASIC BOIL & SIMMER BULGUR

Combine ingredients for *Basic Microwave Bulgur,* except salt. Bring to a boil, reduce heat, and simmer gently for 4–6 hours or until tender. Add water as needed to prevent sticking. Stir in salt to taste.

BASIC STEAM BULGUR

Combine ingredients for *Basic Microwave Bulgur,* except salt, in an open-top pan or metal bowl. Elevate pan or bowl inside a larger, covered pan with water 2 inches below the rim of the smaller pan. Cook over high heat, covered, for 15 minutes, then reduce heat to very low. Steam until tender and water in small pan is absorbed, about 3 hours. Stir in salt and eat.

BASIC SLOWCOOK BULGUR

Cook ingredients, except salt, in a Crockpot or slow cooker. Cover; cook 4–6 hours. Add salt.

BASIC BACHELOR BULGUR

1 C. whole-wheat grain	2 C. boiling water
¹⁄₂ tsp. salt	

Even a bachelor can make this *Basic Bulgur* recipe! Combine ingredients with *boiling water* in 1-quart thermos at night. Screw lid on lightly and leave until morning. Grab it on your way out the door to work! Leave out salt, if you prefer salt-free bulgur.

RECIPES FOR BASIC CRACKED BULGUR

These recipes utilize *Basic Cracked Bulgur.* The whole-wheat berries are cracked in a grinder or blender prior to processing. The cracking process makes a finer, more delicate tasting food than the classic *Basic Bulgur.*

BASIC BULGUR SAUSAGE

1 C. *Basic Cracked Bulgur,* cooked	1 tsp. Worcestershire sauce
1 tsp. sage	1 egg
2 dashes onion salt	1 tsp. brown sugar
2 dashes garlic salt	5 drops liquid smoke
dash cayenne pepper	1 tsp. beef base or bouillon cube

Combine all ingredients, mixing vigorously. Form patties and fry in small amount of oil.

Note:

Basic Cracked Bulgur, as well as many other kinds of grains, may be cooked as described here by decreasing the cooking times.

The only part of the cooking process that could possibly go wrong with making *Basic Bulgur* is to cook it without water!

BASIC BULGUR SEASALAD

5 C. *Basic Cracked Bulgur*, cooked & cooled
¼ C. green pepper, diced
½ C. green onion, diced
1 C. celery, diced

1 C. shrimp (or crab, tuna, etc.)
½–1 C. mayonnaise
2 T. pickle juice or vinegar
salt to taste

Combine and chill. May use cooked and cooled rolled grain instead.

RECIPES FOR BASIC BULGUR

BASIC BULGUR CEREAL

2 C. *Basic Bulgur*   2 C. water

Crack *Basic Bulgur* in grinder or blender. Heat in steam 10–20 minutes or boil 5 minutes in water or other liquid. Serve hot and sweeten to taste.

BASIC SWEET BULGUR

3 C. *Basic Bulgur*
½ C. water

milk
sugar or honey

Heat cooked bulgur in water. Serve hot with milk and sweeten to taste. Makes a chewy breakfast cereal. Add dried fruit for additional flavor and nutrition.

BASIC BULGUR PORRIDGE

6 C. *Basic Bulgur*
¼ C. raisins
1 C. milk

½ C. sugar
honey

Heat bulgur and raisins to boil, reduce heat. Stir in milk and sugar, simmer approximately 3–5 minutes. Serve porridge hot, with additional milk and honey to taste. Brown sugar or maple syrup may also be used to sweeten porridge.

BASIC CRUNCHYSNAX

2 C. *Basic Bulgur*   seasonings of choice

Spread *Basic Bulgur* thinly on cookie sheet. Bake at 325°F, stirring occasionally, until very dry and crunchy. Add seasonings to taste. Serve as snacks.

BASIC BOSTON-BAKED BULGUR

4 C. *Basic Bulgur*
½–1 C. catsup or BBQ sauce
1 onion, sautéed
salt and pepper

1 C. water
½ C. molasses
3–4 tsp. prepared mustard
3 slices bacon, cooked & diced

Mix together and bake 30 minutes at 325°F.

RECIPES FOR BASIC BULGUR SOUPS & SALADS

BASIC BEEF & VEGGIE SOUP

$1^1/_2$ lb. ground beef
1–2 lb. beef knuckle bones
$2^1/_2$ qt. water
1 C. *Basic Bulgur*
1 C. diced or shredded carrots
$^1/_2$ C. chopped onions or leeks
1 C. sliced celery

$^1/_4$ C. chopped parsley
2–3 tsp. pepper
$^1/_8$ tsp. powdered cloves
$^1/_4$ tsp. salt
1 can tomato soup
$^1/_2$ tsp. fresh herbs (*fines herbes[1]*)

Brown ground beef and pour off grease. Remove fat from bones. Simmer together water, ground beef, and bones for 2–3 hours. Add remaining ingredients. Cover and continue cooking until vegetables are tender, 15–20 minutes. Remove meat from bones, dice, and return to soup mixture. Heat to boiling. *Yield: 6–8 servings.*

BASIC BULGUR SALAD

$^1/_2$ C. *Basic Bulgur*
water to cover
4 tomatoes, cubed
1 C. fresh mint (chopped)

1 C. chopped parsley
1 C. chopped green onions
1 green pepper, cut in strips

Cover *Basic Bulgur* in water and soak for 30 minutes. Squeeze out water and transfer to a bowl. Combine remaining ingredients, add salad dressing, and toss. *Yield: 4 servings.*

BASIC SEAFOOD SALAD

1 C. *Basic Bulgur*
2–3 T. mayonnaise
2 T. diced green pepper
$^3/_4$ C. diced celery

1 tomato, cut in wedges
$^1/_4$ C. chopped green pepper
1 C. tuna or cooked shrimp

Marinate *Basic Bulgur* in mayonnaise for 20–30 minutes. Add remaining ingredients. Arrange greens around a bowl, pile seafood mixture on top. Sprinkle paprika over seafood.

RECIPES FOR BASIC BULGUR MAIN DISHES

BASIC BAKED CHICKEN

$^1/_2$ C. *Basic Bulgur*
1 can of mushroom soup
1 C. chicken broth
$^1/_4$ tsp. sage
$^1/_2$ tsp. poultry seasoning

2 T. vegetable oil
1 pkg. chicken thighs
    (skins removed)
1 clove garlic
$^1/_2$ C. chopped onion

---

[1] Fresh herbs (*fines herbes* is the French name) are usually proportionate measures of fresh parsley, chives, tarragon, and chervil—when and where available. Sometimes marjoram and thyme, and even basil, may be added to the mixture. The essence of fresh herbs is achieved by mincing them together with a sharp knife, then adding at the last minute to the pilaf—thus imparting the essential oils to the food.

Put *Basic Bulgur* in casserole dish. In separate bowl combine soup, broth, and seasonings. Pour $1/2$ of the soup mixture into the casserole and mix with the wheat. In a skillet, heat oil and brown chicken. Remove and arrange on top of *Basic Bulgur*. Add garlic and onion to skillet, sauté until tender. Remove with a slotted spoon and stir in remaining soup mixture, then pour over chicken. Bake at 350°F for 1 hour.

BASIC CHEESE CASSEROLE

$2^1/_2$ C. *Basic Bulgur*   2 cans cream of chicken soup*
1 C. milk $1/_2$ tsp. dry mustard
$3/_4$ C. grated cheese

Combine ingredients, reserving $1/_4$ cup cheese to sprinkle on top of mixture. Bake at 375°F for 30–40 minutes.
* Substitute tomato soup and add $1/_4$ tsp. oregano for Mediterranean flavor.

BASIC BEEF CASSEROLE

1 lb. ground beef   1 large onion, diced
1 clove garlic, crushed   1 C. *Basic Bulgur*
1 T. parsley flakes   2 cans tomato soup
1 tsp. celery flakes $1/_2$ C. catsup or tomato sauce
salt and pepper to taste   grated cheese

Sauté meat and seasonings with onion. Combine *Basic Bulgur* with meat mixture, soup, and catsup, then pour into casserole dish. Sprinkle with cheese. Bake at 350°F for 30 minutes. *Yield: 6–8 servings.*

BASIC TOMATO CASSEROLE

3 C. *Basic Bulgur*   3 C. tomato juice
1 tsp. salt $1/_4$ small onion, finely chopped
6 slices bacon, diced & fried   1 C. grated cheese
4 T. flour   bread crumbs (optional)

Place salted *Basic Bulgur* in buttered baking dish. Fry diced bacon; add flour, tomato juice, and onion to make a sauce. Remove from heat and add $1/_2$ cup grated cheese. Pour over *Basic Bulgur*. Top with remaining cheese. Sprinkle bread crumbs or crushed saltine crackers over cheese to add crunch, if desired. Bake 45 minutes at 350°F.

BASIC TUNA CASSEROLE

2 T. chopped onion $1/_8$ tsp. pepper
1 T. butter or margarine   2 eggs, slightly beaten
2 C. *Basic Bulgur* $1/_3$ C. crisp cracker crumbs
1 C. cream of mushroom soup   1 T. butter or margarine
1 can (6 oz.) tuna   paprika
$1/_2$ tsp. salt

Sauté onion in butter over moderate heat until onion is straw colored. Mix in baking dish with *Basic Bulgur*, soup, tuna, salt, pepper, and egg. Top with mixture of crackers and melted butter. Sprinkle with paprika. Bake in moderate oven (350°F) for 30 minutes. *Yield: 6 servings.*

BASIC MUSHROOM CASSEROLE

4 C. *Basic Bulgur*
$1/2$ C. milk or water

1 can cream of mushroom soup
$1/2$ C. chopped onion, sautéed

Mix together in a casserole. Bake at 350°F for 20–30 minutes. For variety add chopped celery, green pepper, or fresh mushrooms. Use in place of rice or potatoes.

BASIC POULTRY CASSEROLE

$1/4$ C. butter or margarine
$1/2$ C. chopped celery
$1/4$ C. finely chopped onion
$1/4$ C. flour
2 C. chicken broth
1 C. milk
1 tsp. salt

$1/8$ tsp. pepper
$1/2$ tsp. poultry seasoning
$1/2$ C. *Basic Bulgur*
5 C. cooked & cubed
    turkey or chicken
1 C. grated cheddar cheese
buttered bread crumbs

Melt butter, add celery and onions. Cook until tender, but not brown. Blend in flour. Stir in chicken broth and milk. Cook over low heat, stirring constantly until thickened. Add seasonings, *Basic Bulgur*, poultry, and cheese. Pour into buttered 2-quart casserole. Sprinkle with buttered bread crumbs and bake 35–40 minutes. in 350°F oven. *Yield: 10–12 servings.*

BASIC BULGUR JAMBALAYA

8 oz. sausage link, cut in $1/2$" rounds
2 lb. ground beef
$11/2$ C. diced ham
$1/2$ C. chopped onion
$1/2$ C. chopped green bell pepper
$3/4$ C. thinly sliced celery
$21/2$ C. *Basic Bulgur*

2 T. chopped parsley
$1/4$ tsp. thyme
$3/4$ C. salt
$1/4$ tsp. pepper
dash of cayenne
$1/8$ tsp. powdered cloves
$1/4$ tsp. chili powder

Sauté sausage, ground beef, ham, onion, bell pepper, and celery in heavy skillet until lightly browned. Drain grease. Add remaining ingredients. Cover and bring to boil; reduce heat and simmer. Stir occasionally until mixture thickens, about 45 minutes. *Yield: 5–6 servings.*

BASIC ITALIAN CASSEROLE

$1/4$ C. salad oil
1 onion, chopped
$1/2$ lb. mushrooms, sliced thin
2 tsp. beef stock base
$1/2$ C. water

$1/2$ tsp. basil leaves
$1/4$ tsp. pepper
3 C. *Basic Bulgur*
2 med. zucchini, sliced thin

Heat salad oil in large frying pan over medium heat. Sauté onion and mushrooms until limp and liquid has evaporated. In a small cup, stir together beef stock base and hot water. Add liquid to the pan with basil leaves, pepper, and cooked, drained *Basic Bulgur*. Cover and bring to simmer. Add zucchini. Cover and simmer until heated throughout and liquid is absorbed, about 10 minutes. *Yield: 6 servings.*

BASIC CHILIBULGUR

1 lb. ground beef (optional)	1 qt. tomatoes, cut up
1 large onion, chopped	1 tsp. Worcestershire sauce
2 tsp. garlic powder	1 T. flour
2 tsp. chili powder	2 beef bouillon cubes
1 tsp. salt	3 C. *Basic Bulgur*

Sauté meat and onions until meat is browned. Add all ingredients except *Basic Bulgur*. Bring to boil, reduce heat, and simmer gently for 30 minutes. Add *Bulgur* and heat thoroughly.

BASIC SPANISH CASSEROLE

4 slices bacon, cut into thin strips	$\frac{1}{2}$ tsp. salt
1 large onion, chopped	1 tsp. seasoned salt
$\frac{1}{2}$ C. chopped celery	$\frac{1}{4}$ tsp. pepper
$\frac{1}{2}$ C. chopped green bell pepper	1 tsp. sugar
1 clove garlic, finely minced	1 tsp. Worcestershire sauce
1 lb. can tomatoes	1 C. *Basic Bulgur*
2 C. water	

Sauté bacon in heavy skillet over moderate heat. Add onion, celery, green pepper, and garlic. Continue cooking until onion is straw colored. Blend in tomatoes, water, salts, pepper, sugar, Worcestershire sauce, and *Basic Bulgur*. Cover and simmer over low heat until most of liquid is absorbed, 20–25 minutes.

RECIPES FOR BASIC BULGUR PILAF

Pilaf is normally prepared as a rice dish. It is made of rice combined with seasonings, vegetables, meat, fish, or poultry. There are as many variations of rice pilaf as there are cooks. Pilaf made from wheat is economical and certainly more nutritious than rice pilaf. These pilaf recipes demonstrate the usefulness of wheat as *Basic Bulgur Pilaf*.

BASIC PILAF MIX

2 T. butter (margarine or oil)	$\frac{1}{4}$ C. water
3 T. chopped onion	$\frac{1}{2}$ tsp. salt
1 C. *Basic Bulgur*	$\frac{1}{8}$ tsp. pepper

Heat butter in heavy skillet; add onion and sauté until straw colored. Add *Basic Bulgur*, water, salt, and pepper. Cover and simmer over low heat until all liquid is absorbed. Use this *Basic Pilaf Mix* to make flavored variations described below. *Yield: 4 servings.*

BASIC CHICKEN-FLAVORED PILAF

1 batch *Basic Pilaf Mix*	2 C. chicken bouillon or stock

Prepare *Basic Pilaf Mix*. Add *Mix* to boiling bouillon or stock. Cover and simmer over low heat until added liquid is absorbed. To save cooking time, use less liquid. *Yield: 4–6 servings.*

BASIC FRESH HERBS PILAF

1 batch *Basic Chicken-Flavored Pilaf*   1 T. fresh herbs *(fines herbes)*

Prepare *Basic Chicken-Flavored Pilaf.* Stir fresh herbs into bowl just before serving for a fresh taste. *Yield: 4–6 servings.*

BASIC BEEF-FLAVORED PILAF

1 batch *Basic Pilaf Mix*   1 T. Worcestershire sauce
2 C. beef bouillon or stock

Prepare *Basic Pilaf Mix.* Add *Mix* to boiling bouillon or stock, then add Worcestershire sauce. Cover and simmer over low heat until added liquid is absorbed. To shorten cooking time, use less liquid. *Yield: 4–6 servings.*

BASIC MEDITERRANEAN PILAF

1 batch *Basic Pilaf Mix*   1 C. tomato juice
1 C. chicken bouillon or stock

Prepare *Basic Pilaf Mix.* Add *Mix* to boiling bouillon or stock and tomato juice. Cover and simmer over low heat until added liquid is absorbed. To save cooking time, use less liquid. *Yield: 4–6 servings.*

BASIC PARMESAN PILAF

1 batch *Basic Chicken-Flavored Pilaf* $^1/_3$ C. Parmesan cheese
$^1/_4$ C. chopped onion   1 T. chopped parsley flakes
$^1/_4$ tsp. garlic salt

Prepare *Basic Chicken-Flavored Pilaf.* Add onion and garlic salt. After cooking, stir in cheese and parsley. *Yield: 4–6 servings.*

BASIC TAIWAN PILAF

1 batch *Basic Chicken-Flavored Pilaf*   2 T. soy sauce

Prepare *Basic Chicken-Flavored Pilaf.* Add soy sauce just before serving. *Yield: 4–6 servings.*

BASIC CANTONESE CHICKEN & TAIWAN PILAF

1 batch *Basic Taiwan Pilaf* $1^1/_2$ C. chicken stock
3 T. oil $^1/_2$ tsp. salt
1 C. Chinese pea pods, cut $^1/_2$" $1^1/_8$ tsp. white pepper
$^1/_2$ C. sliced water chestnuts   2 T. cornstarch
$1^1/_2$ C. sliced mushrooms $^1/_2$ C. water
$^1/_3$ C. slivered almonds   2 C. sliced cooked chicken

Prepare *Basic Taiwan Pilaf.* In another heavy skillet, heat oil, then add pea pods, chestnuts, mushrooms, and almonds. Sauté over moderate heat 2 minutes, then add chicken stock, salt, and pepper. Cover and cook 6 minutes. Make a paste of cornstarch and water. Stir into pea pod mixture. Add chicken and return to heat. Stir frequently until mixture thickens and reaches boiling for 2–3 minutes. Serve over *Basic Taiwan Pilaf. Yield: 4–6 servings.*

Chapter 7

Basic Whole-Wheat Flour Cookery

Versatility is one of the most important benefits of storing whole wheat. What makes wheat an essential storage food is that its range of applications increases beyond *Basic Bulgur* by processing the whole-wheat berries to whole-wheat flour. This processing requires merely grinding the berries with a hand-operated grinder, an electric grinding mill, or a blender. The necessity of such equipment becomes apparent if you store whole wheat. An alternative is to store purchased whole-wheat flour.

The obvious advantage of the home grinder is freshness—you make it when you need it—there are no date codes or possible contamination due to distribution problems. The entire wheat kernel is ground into flour, allowing the freshness—as well as the health benefits—to really come through!

By using your own home-ground whole-wheat flour and supplemental storage foods you can make pancakes, waffles, snacks, pretzels, pasta, tortillas, pie crusts, muffins, cakes, and cookies. This adds tremendous variety to your basic diet. Recipes are included in this chapter for these wheat-based foods.

Of course with whole-wheat flour you can also make bread and bread stuffing. Directions for basic breadmaking are provided in this chapter. This is a more advanced use of wheat flour and requires a little more effort than the previously mentioned foods, but certainly bread is a significant addition to a basic diet. As an extra in this chapter, there is a recipe for making "wheat sugar" which can be used in bread recipes.

A few of the recipes call for *stone-ground* whole-wheat flour. In-home ground flour is usually equal to coarser stone-ground flour. Both home-ground and stone-ground are coarser than whole-wheat flour bought at the grocery store. Almost always you may substitute one for the other without problems.

RECIPES FOR PANCAKES, WAFFLES & MORE

BASIC QUIXMIX

This recipe introduces *Basic QuixMix,* a simple and easy basic mix for quick-to-fix recipes to help you enjoy whole-wheat flour products. It's a quick mix to have on hand for preparing whole-wheat biscuits, pancakes, waffles, crackers, sweet breads, loaf breads, pretzels, and a number of other home-baked items.

You can use *Basic QuixMix* in most recipes calling for "biscuit mix."

8 C. whole-wheat flour	$1/2$ C. sugar
$1/3$ C. baking powder	2 C. powdered milk
4 tsp. salt	2 C. shortening or margarine

Mix dry ingredients well. Cut in shortening until texture resembles cornmeal. A mixer may be used. Store *Basic QuixMix* in an airtight container in the refrigerator or freezer.

BASIC QUIXMIX BISCUITS

1 C. *Basic QuixMix*	$1/2$ C. water

Rolled method: prepare *Basic QuixMix*. Mix with water until soft dough forms. Add additional dry mix if necessary. Keep it easy to handle, then roll it into a ball. Knead gently for 30 seconds. Roll out to $1/2$ inch thick. Cut biscuits with 2-inch round biscuit cutter. Bake on ungreased cookie sheet 8–10 minutes at 450°F.

Drop method: prepare *Basic QuixMix*. Combine with water. Drop onto greased baking sheet. Bake 12–15 minutes at 375°–400°F. *Yield: 8–12 biscuits.*

BASIC QUIXMIX PANCAKES

$1 1/3$ C. *Basic QuixMix* 1 egg	1 C. water

Prepare *Basic QuixMix*. Mix ingredients, let stand for 5–10 minutes. Cook on hot griddle until brown, then turn and brown on other side.

Variation #1: use milk instead of water for better-tasting pancakes.

Variation #2: add 1 egg, thoroughly beaten into batter for richer pancakes.

BASIC QUIXMIX BREAKFAST BREAD

2 C. *Basic QuixMix*
1/4 C. brown sugar
2 eggs, slightly beaten

3/4 C. water
1/2 C. raisins

Prepare *Basic QuixMix*. Blend in sugar. Combine eggs and water in separate bowl and stir into *Mix*. Add raisins.[1] Pour into greased 9-inch pan. Bake at 350°F for 35–40 minutes.

BASIC QUIXMIX CINNABREAD

CinnaBread ingredients:
2 C. *Basic QuixMix*
1/4 C. brown sugar
2 eggs, slightly beaten

3/4 C. water
1/2 C. raisins

CinnaBread topping ingredients:
1/2 C. brown sugar
1/2 C. chopped nuts

1/2 tsp. cinnamon

Prepare *Basic QuixMix*. Blend in sugar. Combine eggs and water in separate bowl; stir into *Mix*. Add raisins. Pour into greased 9-inch pan. In separate bowl, combine sugar, cinnamon, and nuts. Sprinkle over top of *Bread*. Bake at 350°F for 35–40 minutes. Serve hot. Check bread during last 5 minutes to make sure topping doesn't burn.

BASIC "SCRATCH" BATTER

1 1/4 C. sifted whole-wheat flour
3 tsp. baking powder
3 T. brown sugar
3/4 tsp. salt

2–3 eggs, well beaten
1 1/4 C. milk
3 T. oil

Sift together dry ingredients (flour, baking powder, sugar, salt). Combine liquid ingredients (eggs, milk, oil) in separate bowl. Stir liquid mixture into flour mixture. Bake on greased hot griddle until golden brown.

> **Note:**
> *Experiment with* BASIC "SCRATCH" BATTER *to determine which kind your family likes best. Then, add bananas, nuts, apple cubes, or any other fruit or flavoring for a taste treat.*

BASIC OATCAKES

1 C. oats
1 C. whole-wheat flour
1/4 tsp. baking soda
1/4 tsp. salt

1 T. honey
2 eggs
2 C. buttermilk
1/4 C. melted butter

Stir dry ingredients (oats, flour, soda, salt) to mix well. Add remaining ingredients and stir. Aging several hours or overnight in refrigerator improves flavor. Add 1/4 cup wheat germ to dry ingredients for extra nutrition and flavor. Cook on greased, hot griddle until brown.

---

[1] To prevent raisins and other fruits from going to the bottom of the pan during baking, dust fruits with flour before stirring them into the batter or dough.

BASIC BLENDER PANCAKES

1¹/₂ C. buttermilk*	2 eggs
³/₄ C. whole-wheat flour	¹/₄ C. margarine
2 T. cornmeal	¹/₂ tsp. baking soda
2 T. brown sugar	1 T. baking powder

Blend buttermilk and whole-wheat flour on high speed for 3–4 minutes. Add cornmeal, brown sugar, eggs, and margarine and blend till combined. Add soda and baking powder, blend briefly. Using large spoon or small measuring cup, pour batter onto hot griddle. Turn when steam no longer rises from pancakes. Brown on both sides. Serve hot with favorite syrup.

* Substitute: 1 C. yogurt and ¹/₂ C. milk.

RECIPES FOR BASIC SNACKS

BASIC WHEATNUTS

3 C. whole-wheat flour	2 T. baking powder
2 T. malted milk powder	1 C. brown sugar
¹/₂ tsp. salt	1 C. buttermilk or sour milk
¹/₂ C. wheat germ	

Combine all ingredients and mix. Dough should be sticky. Press onto greased cookie sheet to ¹/₂ inch thickness. Bake at 350°F for 30–35 minutes. Cut into strips and put through a meat grinder. Return to oven and dry.

BASIC GRAINOLA

4 C. rolled oats (uncooked)	¹/₂ tsp. salt
1 C. wheat germ	³/₄ C. honey
1 C. coconut (shredded)	1 C. vegetable oil
¹/₄ C. sesame seeds	2 C. dried fruit and nuts, mixed

Combine dry ingredients (oats, wheat germ, coconut, sesame seeds, salt) in a large bowl. Mix honey and oil together and heat until honey is thinned. Stir into dry mixture. Spread on 2 greased cookie sheets or 2 cake pans. Bake at 300°F until lightly browned (15–20 minutes). Stir every 5 minutes during baking and several times while cooling.

Add mixed dried fruits and nuts using any of the following: raisins, dried apples, dried bananas, dried apricots, toasted sunflower nuts, walnuts, pecans, almonds, etc.

BASIC GRAINOLA #2

1 C. soy flour	1 C. sunflower seeds
1 C. dry powdered milk	1 C. wheat germ
5 C. rolled oats	1 C. shredded coconut
1 C. sliced almonds	1¹/₄ C. honey
1 C. sesame seeds	1 C. warm vegetable oil

Combine dry ingredients (flour, milk, oatmeal, almonds, seeds, wheat germ, coconut) in large bowl. Mix honey and oil together and heat until honey is thinned. Stir into dry mixture. Spread on 2 greased cookie sheets or 2 cake pans. Bake at 300°F until lightly browned (15–20 minutes). Stir every 5 minutes during baking and several times while cooling.

BASIC GRAINOLA #3

4 C. oatmeal	$^3/_4$ C. honey
1 C. coconut	1 tsp. vanilla
1 C. wheat germ	$^1/_2$ C. chopped nuts
1 C. sesame seeds	$^1/_2$ C. raisins
1 C. vegetable oil	

Mix all ingredients together, except nuts and raisins; spread thin on 2 cookie sheets. Bake at 300°F for 20 minutes. Stir every 5 minutes to avoid burning. When cool, add chopped nuts and raisins. Cool before taking off cookie sheet.

BASIC GRAINOLA #4

8 C. rolled oats	$^1/_2$ tsp. salt
1 C. nuts (pieces)	1 C. vegetable oil
1 C. wheat germ	$^1/_2$ C. water
1 C. shredded coconut	$^1/_2$ C. date nuggets
$^1/_2$ C. brown sugar	

Mix all ingredients together and place on large tray. Bake at 250°F for 2 hours, stirring approximately every 30 minutes.

BASIC HAWAIIAN GRAINOLA

$^1/_3$ C. margarine or vegetable oil	$^1/_4$ C. wheat germ
$^1/_2$ C. brown sugar	$^1/_4$ C. sesame seeds
$^1/_4$ tsp. salt	1 C. sunflower seeds
$^1/_4$ C. water	$^1/_2$ C. coconut
$^1/_4$ C. honey	1 C. chopped nuts
1 tsp. cinnamon	1 C. dried fruit bits
3 C. rolled grain	

Melt margarine; add brown sugar, salt, water, honey, and cinnamon. Mix remaining ingredients except dried fruit. Pour margarine mixture over dry ingredients. Mix well and spread in a 9 x 13-inch baking pan. Bake at 350°F for 15–20 minutes, stirring occasionally. Cool; add dried fruit. Store in an airtight container.

Low-fat, low-sugar variation: omit margarine/vegetable oil, brown sugar, and honey. Add $1^1/_4$ C. apple juice concentrate.

BASIC GRAINOLA COOKEES

3 C. *Basic Grainola*	1 tsp. baking soda
1 C. butter (margarine)	1 tsp. salt
1 C. brown sugar	2 tsp. vanilla
2 eggs	12 oz. chocolate morsels
2 T. water	1 C. chopped nuts or coconut
$1^3/_4$ C. flour	

Prepare *Basic Grainola*. Cream butter, brown sugar, and eggs until fluffy. Add water and blend well. Sift flour, soda, and salt together and add to creamed mixture. Stir in *Basic Grainola*, vanilla, chocolate morsels, nuts, or coconut. Mix until well blended. Drop by teaspoon onto greased cookie sheet and bake at 350°F for 12 minutes.

RECIPES FOR BASIC PRETZELS

Pretzels are usually made from regular white flour, but the following recipes use whole-wheat and wholesome rye flours. Before baking, dip each pretzel in boiling salted water, to give the familiar shiny crust to the pretzel, then sprinkle with coarse salt. Soft pretzels are delicious with a soup or salad lunch, or with sausages and cheese for a late supper. Serve them hot, warm, or at room temperature, spread with butter. Or, my favorite, the hot pretzel with cold mustard! Pretzels can be refrigerated or frozen, then reheated for serving.

BASIC SOFTWHEAT PRETZELS

1 T. active dry yeast	3 C. stone-ground whole-wheat
$1/2$ C. warm water	flour (approx.)
$1/2$ C. sugar	3 C. all-purpose flour, unsifted
$1^1/_2$ tsp. salt	$3/_4$ tsp. baking powder
2 C. milk, scalded, cooled to room temperature	4 T. coarse salt, kosher style
2 qt. boiling water	$1/_4$ C. vegetable oil
1 egg white, slightly beaten	

In a large bowl, dissolve yeast in the warm water. Then stir in sugar, $1^1/_2$ teaspoons salt, milk, and vegetable oil. With a wooden spoon gradually mix in $1^1/_2$ cups stone-ground whole-wheat flour and 1 cup of the all-purpose flour.

Cover and let rise in a warm place until bubbly, about 40 minutes. Sift $1^1/_2$ cups more of the all-purpose flour with baking powder; add to dough with remaining $1^1/_2$ cups of stone-ground whole-wheat flour. Mix with wooden spoon, then turn out dough on a lightly floured board.

Knead for about 5 minutes or until dough is no longer sticky, adding a little more all-purpose flour if necessary. Roll out and pat dough into a 9 x 15-inch rectangle. Press a long-blade knife straight down through dough to cut into strips $1/_2$ inch wide and 15 inches long. With your palms, roll each strip back and forth on the board into a strand about 20 inches long; twist each into pretzel shape. Let rise, uncovered, for 30 minutes.

Dissolve 3 tablespoons coarse salt in boiling water. With a slotted spoon, lower 1 pretzel at a time into boiling water; after about 2 seconds, lift out, wipe the bottom of the spoon on paper towels to drain briefly. Set pretzels on a liberally greased baking sheet, arrange $1/_2$ inch apart. Brush with egg white and sprinkle lightly with remaining coarse salt.

Bake at 400°F for 20 minutes or until crust is golden brown. Serve warm or transfer to a rack to cool. Wrap airtight for storage. To reheat, set pretzels directly on oven rack at 350°F for about 5 minutes (8 minutes if frozen) or until crusty. *Yield: approximately 18 pretzels.*

BASIC SOFTRYE PRETZELS

Follow directions for *Basic SoftWheat Pretzels*, substituting rye flour for whole-wheat flour. Add 3 tablespoons. crushed dill seed for extra good taste, if desired.

RECIPES FOR BASIC CRACKERS

BASIC SALTCRAX

4 C. whole-wheat flour   1 T. honey
2 tsp. salt   1 T. active dry yeast
$2/_3$ C. dry powdered milk $1/_3$ C. vegetable oil
$1^1/_2$ C. warm water

Mix together flour, salt, and powdered milk. In 1 cup warm water dissolve honey and
yeast. Add to the dry ingredients along with vegetable oil. Add remaining (or a little more)
warm water. Form into a ball. Place in a greased bowl, cover, and let rise $1/_2$–1 hour.

Knead for a few minutes. Return to bowl. Take a lemon-sized piece of dough at a time,
keeping the remaining dough covered. Roll out the dough on a lightly floured board.
Roll each piece as thin as possible. Bake on ungreased cookie sheet in 350°F oven about
6 minutes. Turn pan around, turn crackers over and bake 2–3 minutes more. Watch
browning very carefully. Cool slowly. Break by hand into irregular shaped crackers.

BASIC GRAMMACRAX

$1/_2$ C. butter or margarine $1/_2$ tsp. baking powder
$2/_3$ C. dark brown sugar, firmly packed $1/_4$ tsp. ground cinnamon
$2^3/_4$ C. whole-wheat flour $1/_2$ C. water

Cream butter or margarine and sugar well. Mix remaining ingredients and add to
creamed mixture, alternating with $1/_2$ cup water. Mix well. Let stand 30 minutes. Roll
out dough on floured board to $1/_8$-inch thickness, cut in 1-inch squares, and put on oiled
cookie sheet. Bake in preheated 350°F oven for 20 minutes or until slightly browned.

BASIC HONEY GRAMMACRAX

$2^1/_4$ C. whole-wheat or graham flour $1/_3$ C. margarine or shortening
$1/_2$ tsp. salt $1/_4$ C. warmed honey
1 tsp. baking soda   3 T. water
$1/_3$ C. brown sugar

Combine dry ingredients (flour, salt, soda, sugar) and cut in margarine or shortening.
Combine honey and water and add to dry ingredients. Blend well. Roll out half the
dough on an ungreased cookie sheet to $1/_4$-inch thickness. Prick dough with a fork.
Repeat with remaining dough. Bake at 375°F for 8–10 minutes or until golden brown.
Remove from oven and cut into squares. Cool.

BASIC SESAME WHEATCRAX

$1^1/_2$ C. whole-wheat flour   4 T. sugar
$1^1/_2$ C. all-purpose flour $1/_2$ C. vegetable oil or shortening
$1/_4$ C. wheat germ $1^1/_2$ C. milk or water
$1^1/_2$ tsp. salt $1/_4$ C. sesame seeds
2 C. rolled oats

Mix dry ingredients (flours, wheat germ, salt, oats, sugar) with oil and milk or water. Add
sesame seeds and knead until a smooth dough is formed. Roll out thin and cut into desired
shape. Put on lightly greased cookie sheet. Bake at 375°F until golden with brown spots.

RECIPES FOR BASIC PASTA

Everyone loves pasta, and everyone will love whole-wheat pasta even more! Use the following recipe to make *Basic Pasta Mix*, then expand your pasta skills and meals with it.

BASIC PASTA MIX

$3/_4$ C. egg (measure exactly)	2 T. vegetable oil
2 T. + 1 tsp. water	$3^3/_4$ C. whole-wheat flour

Mix ingredients together until the size of popped corn. Shape according to pasta maker directions or roll $1/_8$ inch thick and cut into thin noodles and hang or lay flat to dry. Use *Basic Pasta Mix* for any pasta, noodles, lasagna—even dumplings!

BASIC NOODLES

6 eggs	2 C. whole-wheat flour
$1/_2$ tsp. salt	boiling broth or salted water
1 tsp. vegetable oil	

Beat eggs thoroughly, add salt, oil and flour. Mix well. Roll mixture out on floured board with wax paper between rolling pin and dough. When $1/_8$ inch thick, cut with sharp knife, large needle, or cutter, roll up, and put into boiling broth or salted water.

BASIC NOODLE CASSEROLE

1 batch *Basic Noodles*	1 can tuna
1 can peas, #303	$1/_4$ tsp. salt
1 can mushroom soup, undiluted	

Mix ingredients in greased casserole dish. Bake at 350°F for 30 minutes. *Yield: 6 servings.*

RECIPES FOR BASIC TORTILLAS

BASIC WHEATORTILLAS

4 C. whole-wheat flour	$1/_2$ C. shortening
$1^1/_2$ tsp. salt	water

Mix flour and salt. Cut in shortening. Mix in enough water to make a pliable dough. Knead until soft and stretchy. Form balls, cover with a cloth. Let rest 30 minutes. Roll paper thin. Cook in ungreased, medium-hot, cast-iron skillet until high spots turn dark brown.

BASIC CORNY WHEATORTILLAS

$1^1/_2$ C. cornmeal	$3/_4$ tsp. salt
$1^1/_2$ C. whole-wheat flour	6 T. shortening
$1/_2$ tsp. baking powder	$3/_4$ C. water

Combine cornmeal, flour, baking powder, and salt. Cut in shortening. Add warm water and stir until mixture is moistened. (A teaspoon or more additional water may be added if dough is too stiff.) Turn out onto a floured surface and knead 5 minutes or until mixture is no longer sticky. Shape into 14 balls. Roll each into a thin 6-inch circle. Bake on a hot, ungreased griddle for 1 minute each side.

RECIPES FOR BASIC PIE CRUSTS

BASIC PIE CRUST MIX

2 C. whole-wheat flour
1 tsp. salt

$^3/_4$ C. vegetable shortening
4–8 tsp. ice water

Mix whole-wheat flour and salt. Cut $^1/_2$ cup of the shortening into flour mixture until fine as meal. Cut remaining shortening into mix until mixture resembles the size of green peas. Sprinkle 4–8 teaspoons ice water on mixture, stirring in lightly with a fork. Then mix well, shaping into a ball. Roll out to fit pan. Bake at 400°F for 8–12 minutes.

BASIC PIE SHELL

1 C. stone-ground whole-wheat flour
$^1/_4$ tsp. salt

$^1/_3$ C. vegetable shortening
cold water

Mix stone-ground whole-wheat flour and salt in bowl. Cut in vegetable shortening until mixture resembles coarse meal. Mixing with fork, add enough cold water to hold ingredients together. Gather into ball and roll on floured board to fit pie pan. Trim edges and flute. Bake at 400°F for 8–12 minutes.

RECIPES FOR BASIC MUFFINS & QUIXBREAD

BASIC WHEATBRAN MUFFINS

3 C. wheat bran*
1 C. boiling water
1 C. brown sugar
$^1/_2$ C. margarine
2 eggs

$2^1/_2$ C. whole-wheat flour
$2^1/_2$ tsp. baking soda
1 tsp. salt
1 pint buttermilk

Combine 1 cup wheat bran and 1 cup boiling water, stir, and let steep. In a separate bowl, cream sugar and margarine. Beat eggs. Combine flour, soda, salt. Combine the 1 cup of steeped bran with remaining 2 cups bran, eggs, flour mixture, buttermilk, margarine, and sugar. Mix. Store in tightly covered plastic container. Let stand at least 12 hours before baking. Batter will keep in refrigerator for 6 weeks. When preparing to bake, preheat oven to 400°F. Stir batter well and spoon into lined muffin tins, $^2/_3$ full. Bake 20–22 minutes.

* Substitute oat bran, if preferred.

BASIC OATBRAN MUFFIN MIX

1 C. dry buttermilk powder
   or powdered milk
3 C. whole-wheat flour
2 T. baking soda

1 T. salt
1 C. brown sugar
6 C. oat bran*
6 T. molasses

In a large bowl, combine buttermilk powder, flour, baking soda, and salt. Stir to blend. Add brown sugar, making sure there are no lumps. Add oat bran whole or process dry in a blender. Stir into flour mixture. Slowly pour molasses over mixture while mixing until evenly distributed. Keep in an airtight container in the refrigerator or freezer.

* Use all or part of the oat bran.

BASIC OATBRAN MUFFINS

3 C. *Basic OatBran Muffin Mix*
$3/_4$ C. water

$1/_4$ C. vegetable oil
4 egg whites (or equivalent)

Prepare *Basic OatBran Muffin Mix*. Combine egg white, oil, and water in separate bowl. Add *Mix* and stir just until moistened. Bake in paper-lined muffin tins for 15–20 minutes at 400°F or until wooden pick inserted in the middle comes out dry. *Yield: 12 large muffins.*

Variation: Omit 2 egg whites and add 1 cup mashed or shredded fruit such as bananas, apples, pineapple, carrots, etc.

BASIC ZUCCHINI BREAD

2 C. sugar
1 C. vegetable oil
3 eggs, beaten
2 zucchini (unpeeled and grated)
3 tsp. vanilla
3 C. whole-wheat flour

1 tsp. salt
1 tsp. baking soda
3 tsp. cinnamon
$1/_4$ tsp. baking powder
$1/_2$ C. chopped nuts

Mix sugar, oil, eggs, zucchini, and vanilla in large bowl. Sift together in separate bowl flour, salt, soda, cinnamon, and baking powder. Add dry ingredients to first bowl, stirring to combine well. Add chopped nuts. Bake at 350°F for 45–60 minutes. *Yield: 2 loaves.*

RECIPES FOR BASIC CAKES

BASIC WHEATCAKE MIX

$2/_3$ C. vegetable shortening (margarine)
$1^1/_2$ C. brown sugar (packed tightly)
$4^1/_2$ tsp. baking powder
1 tsp. salt

3 C. whole-wheat flour, sifted
$1^1/_2$ tsp. vanilla
3 eggs
$1^1/_2$ C. milk

Cream together shortening, brown sugar, and vanilla. Add eggs and beat thoroughly. Sift together whole-wheat flour, baking powder, and salt. Combine wet and dry mixtures, adding milk. After thorough mixing, pour into greased 11 x 17-inch pan. Bake at 350°F for 25–30 minutes. (In 9 x 9-inch pans or for cupcakes, bake 20–25 minutes. *Yield: 24–28 cupcakes.*)

BASIC SPONGE WHEATCAKE

6 eggs, separated
$1/_2$ C. water
$1^1/_2$ C. sugar
$1/_4$ tsp. almond extract

$1/_2$ tsp. salt
$1/_2$ tsp. lemon juice or extract
1 tsp. cream of tartar
$1^1/_2$ C. stone-ground whole-wheat flour

Use mixer to beat yolks, water, sugar, and flavoring 5–7 minutes until very thick and creamy. Sift flour and salt twice, then add to bowl of liquid. Beat egg whites until stiff and fold into batter. Add remaining ingredients gradually, continuing to beat. Pour into cake pans. Bake at 325°–350°F for approximately 1 hour until top springs back from touch.

BASIC APPLECAKE

4 fresh, diced apples	2 eggs
2 C. sugar	2 C. whole-wheat flour
$^1/_2$ C. vegetable oil	2 tsp. cinnamon
2 tsp. vanilla	1 C. nuts (optional)
2 tsp. baking soda	1 C. raisins (optional)
1 tsp. salt	

Place diced apples (not grated) in bowl. Add sugar, oil, vanilla, soda, salt, and eggs and mix thoroughly. Sift dry ingredients (flour, cinnamon, nuts, raisins) together, then add to wet mixture. Pour into greased 9 x 13-inch pan. Bake in 350°F oven for 60 minutes or until cake shrinks from sides of pan. Frost with frosting recipe.

Frosting:

2 C. powdered sugar	4 oz. cream cheese
$^1/_2$ C. butter	1 tsp. vanilla

Combine ingredients and beat well. Spread topping with knife or spatula.

BASIC APPLESAUCE CAKE

$^1/_2$ C. shortening	$^1/_2$ tsp. cloves
1 C. sugar	1 tsp. cinnamon
1 egg	1 C. chopped nuts
2 C. sifted whole-wheat flour	1 C. raisins
$^1/_4$ tsp. salt	1 C. thick unsweetened
$^3/_4$ tsp. baking soda	applesauce (warmed)

Cream shortening and sugar until light and fluffy. Add egg and beat thoroughly. Add sifted dry ingredients (flour, salt, soda, cloves, cinnamon), then nuts and raisins. Warm applesauce and stir into batter. Pour into well-greased and floured 8 x 8-inch pans. Bake 50 minutes at 350°F.

BASIC ANGELCAKE

1 C. + 2 T. whole-wheat pastry flour*	$1^1/_2$ tsp. cream of tartar
12 large egg whites ($1^1/_2$ C.)	$1^1/_2$ C. sugar
1 tsp. vanilla or almond extract	$^1/_2$ tsp. salt

Combine flour and $^3/_4$ cup sugar and stir. Set aside. Combine salt and cream of tartar with egg whites and whip until whites stand in peaks. With mixer on low speed, gradually add the remaining $^3/_4$ cup sugar and flavoring. When sugar blends, stop mixer and sprinkle $^1/_3$ of the flour mixture over the beaten egg whites and blend briefly. Add another $^1/_3$ of flour mixture and blend briefly. Add final $^1/_3$ of flour and *blend only until mixed.*

Pour into ungreased angel food cake pan. Bake for 1 hour at 350°F. Invert pan to cool. *Do not remove cake until cool.*

* Substitute: $^3/_4$ C. flour and $^1/_4$ C. cornstarch for pastry flour.

BASIC FRUIT COCKTAIL CAKE

1 egg	1/4 tsp. salt
1 C. sugar	1 tsp. baking soda
2 C. fruit cocktail, not drained	1/2 C. brown sugar
1 C. whole-wheat flour	1/2 C. chopped nuts

Beat egg and add sugar; beat together well. Stir in fruit cocktail along with the juice—*do not drain.* Mix flour, salt, and soda together. Combine mixtures. Put in greased 7 x 12-inch or 8 x 13-inch pan and sprinkle with brown sugar and nuts. Bake at 350°F for 50–60 minutes. *Yield: approximately 8 servings.*

BASIC QUIKCAKE

1 1/2 C. whole-wheat flour	5 T. vegetable oil
3 T. cocoa or chocolate	1 T. vinegar
1 tsp. baking soda	1 T. vanilla
1 C. sugar	1 C. cold water
1/2 tsp. salt	

Sift together first five items into a greased 9 x 9 x 12-inch pan. Pour next three ingredients into hollow of dry ingredients. Pour cold water over all ingredients and mix with spoon until nearly smooth and flour is not visible in mixture. Bake at 350°F for 30 minutes.

BASIC CARROTCAKE

3 C. finely shredded carrots	1/2 tsp. salt
1 C. vegetable oil	2 tsp. baking powder
4 eggs	1/2 tsp. baking soda
2 C. sugar	2 C. whole-wheat flour
1 tsp. cinnamon	

Mix together carrots, oil, and eggs. Mix in sugar, cinnamon, salt, baking powder, and soda. Mix on medium speed for 2 minutes. Add whole-wheat flour and mix just until moistened. Bake in a 350°F oven for 35–40 minutes.

Cream Cheese Frosting:
Combine 8 ounces cream cheese, softened, 2 tablespoons milk and 4 cups powdered sugar. Add 1 teaspoon vanilla. Beat until smooth.

RECIPES FOR BASIC COOKEES

These "cookee" treats made with whole-wheat flour are as nutritious as they are delicious. They are good for quick energy and help children adapt to whole-wheat cookery. These particular *Basic Cookees* recipes have proven to be favorites for children of all ages. These are classified as *s'more* cookies—that's short for "I want some more *Cookees, Mom.*"

BASIC YOGURT COOKEES

1 C. margarine	1 tsp. baking powder
1 C. white sugar	$1/4$ tsp. salt
1 C. brown sugar	$1/2$ tsp. nutmeg
1 tsp. vanilla	4 C. sifted whole-wheat flour
2 eggs, beaten	1 C. yogurt

Cream margarine and sugars. Add vanilla and beaten eggs. Sift dry ingredients (baking powder, salt, nutmeg, flour) together twice and add, alternately with yogurt, to the egg mixture. Working with half the dough at a time, roll out on floured board to $1/8$ inch thickness. Cut in small rounds with cookie cutter. Place on greased cookie sheet and bake at 400°F for 8–10 minutes *Yield: 24–30 cookies.*

BASIC MOLASSES COOKEES

$1/4$ C. butter or margarine	1 tsp. cinnamon
$1/4$ C. sugar	1 tsp. ground ginger
$1/2$ C. molasses	$1/4$ tsp. cloves
$1/2$ tsp. salt	$11/2$ C. whole-wheat flour
2 tsp. baking soda	2 T. vinegar

Melt butter or margarine with sugar and molasses in small saucepan over low heat, then cool. Combine salt, baking soda, cinnamon, ginger, and cloves with whole-wheat flour in mixing bowl. Stir in molasses mixture. Add vinegar and stir in. Drop by teaspoon onto greased cookie sheets. Bake in moderate oven (350°F) for 7 minutes or until cookies are set. Remove carefully with spatula. *Store in covered jar.*

BASIC CHOCKEES

$1/2$ C. Nestle's Quik Cocoa	$1/2$ tsp. baking soda
$1/4$ C. warm water	2 C. milk
$11/2$ C. margarine	2 tsp. vanilla
2 C. sugar	2 C. raisins
2 tsp. salt	1 C. chopped nuts
6 C. whole-wheat flour	

Mix cocoa with enough warm water to make a medium-thick paste. Cream margarine and sugar together in separate bowl. Sift together all dry ingredients (salt, flour, soda). Add to sugar mixture alternately with milk. Finally, add cocoa mixture, vanilla, raisins, and nuts. Drop onto greased cookie sheets. Bake at 350°F for 10 minutes.

As an added treat and to heighten eye appeal, dust with powdered sugar.

BASIC SUGAR COOKEES

1 C. shortening	3½ C. whole-wheat flour
2 C. powdered sugar	1 tsp. baking soda
2 eggs	1 tsp. salt
½ C. buttermilk	

Mix shortening, powdered sugar, and eggs together thoroughly. Stir in remaining ingredients. Drop rounded teaspoonfuls about 2 inches apart on lightly greased baking sheet. Bake at 400°F for 8–10 minutes. *Yield: approximately 6 dozen cookies.*

BASIC CHOCOCHIP COOKEES

2¼ C. whole-wheat flour	1 tsp. vanilla
1 tsp. baking soda	4½ T. powdered dry milk
1 tsp. salt	1 T. water
½ C. soft butter or margarine	1 pkg. chocolate or carob chips
1½ C. brown sugar (packed)	¾ C. chopped peanuts
3 eggs, beaten	1 C. sunflower seeds, unsalted

Stir together dry ingredients (flour, soda, salt). Cream the butter and sugar. Add to eggs, vanilla, powdered milk, and water. Beat until fluffy. Add flour and blend well. Stir in chocolate chips and nuts. Drop onto greased cookie sheet. Bake at 375°F for 10–15 minutes.

BASIC APPLESAUCE COOKEES

1 C. brown sugar	½ tsp. salt
½ C. vegetable shortening	½ tsp. nutmeg
1 egg, beaten well	½ tsp. cinnamon
1 C. applesauce	¼ tsp. cloves
1 tsp. baking soda	1 C. raisins
2 C. whole-wheat flour	½ C. chopped nuts

Cream brown sugar and vegetable shortening. Add beaten egg; mix well. Add applesauce and soda, mixing thoroughly. Add remaining ingredients, mixing well. Drop spoonfuls onto greased cookie sheet. Bake at 375°F for 15–20 minutes.

BASIC WHOLE-WHEAT BREAD COOKERY

The whole breadmaking scene these days is made more attractive by the use of a commercial bread mixer. There are many on the market, and we suggest every family eventually buy one—but only after the basic food items are in the larder!

If you already have one of these new countertop, automatic loaf breadmakers and don't want more than a really basic 1–1½-pound loaf when you bake, your worries are probably over. The rest of this section on breadmaking is superfluous for you—just read the instructions with your breadmaker. If you don't have a bread baking machine or a bread mixer yet, read on!

Don't let the prospect of making homemade bread by hand deter you from enjoying a wonderful and rewarding experience in creativity. Added to the personal growth is the money saved by making bread from your stored wheat. It does take extra time to make your own fresh-baked bread—what accomplishment doesn't have its price or skill its apprenticeship?

In this chapter, you'll discover why it takes more time to make whole-wheat bread than bread made with all-purpose flour. You'll learn that whole-wheat flour is coarser and heavier. You'll understand why whole-wheat dough must be kneaded for 10–15 minutes to produce loaves with an even texture and that each rising also takes longer.

In the following paragraphs you will find what you need to know about basic breadmaking—the how-tos, the whys, and the wherefores of certain breadmaking steps—to succeed in making every bread recipe in this section.

Directions for Basic Breadmaking

Mixing

The yeast and flour manufacturers have discovered that equally consistent quality and even quicker preparation will result when half the flour and all the undissolved yeast are stirred together in the mixer bowl. By eliminating the additional step of dissolving the yeast in warm water separately, the preparation time is significantly shortened.

Most basic recipes work either way, though. If you prefer the separate steps method, then continue. Only a few recipes in this *Handbook* are not modified to mixing yeast and flour initially—but you can convert them easily; merely choose the better way for you.

Next, add the warm liquid ingredients and beat with an electric mixer. This beating stage begins the important process of developing the gluten—the bread's framework. Now stir in as much flour as necessary, by hand, to make a moderately stiff dough that comes out of the bowl in a mass. There should be some flour left over for the next step.

Kneading

Turn the dough out on a lightly floured surface. The flour used for kneading is part of the measured amount. You will want to flour your hands, since a moderately stiff dough is still rather sticky.

To knead dough, curve your fingers over the dough, pull it toward you, then push it down and away from you with the heel of your hand. Then give the dough a quarter turn, fold the dough toward you, and push it down again. Add flour till the dough loses its stickiness.

Notes:

When a recipe gives a range for the amount of flour needed, start with the smaller amount, adding only enough extra flour to make the dough easy to handle. Using more flour than necessary makes the dough stiff and less manageable during kneading and shaping, thus producing heavier bread.

Kneading is the key step to a good loaf of bread. This process develops the gluten in the flour into long, thin strands. In the dough, firm kneading strokes develop long strands of gluten, giving bread small uniform holes and a fine texture. Rough or too vigorous kneading breaks and shortens the gluten strands, causing large holes in the bread. This results in poor rising.

Knead till the dough develops a "life" of its own. It will feel elastic and respond to your touch. Kneading usually takes about 8–10 minutes. Don't worry about too much kneading; you won't knead dough too long—it'll wear you out long before you overdo the kneading.

Rising

A constant temperature of 80°F is ideal for the rising of yeast bread. During rising, the yeast grows and gives off carbon dioxide which is trapped in the gluten strands, causing the mass of dough to stretch. This gives the bread its fine texture.

Place dough in a warm place for rising. Place it on the top rack of a cold oven and put a pan of hot water on the lower rack. Or, if you prefer, just set the bowl of dough on your kitchen counter, making sure the rising dough is protected from drafts. Rising times given in recipes are approximate—actual rising time depends upon temperature and humidity in your kitchen.

To prevent the surface of the dough from becoming dry and hard as it rises, place dough in a lightly greased bowl, turning once to completely coat its surface. Cover the coated dough loosely with waxed paper or a dampened kitchen towel.

Rising is completed and the dough is ready for shaping when it has doubled in bulk and two fingers pressed lightly $1/2$ inch into the dough leave an indentation. Punch the dough down by pushing your fist into the center once. Then, pull the edges of the dough to the center, turn the dough over, and place it on a lightly-floured surface.

Shaping

Various methods can be used to shape dough, but first let the dough rest covered for about 10 minutes after it has been punched down and divided into manageable portions. This resting period allows the gluten strands to relax, making the dough less elastic and much easier to handle.

Handling the dough during shaping bursts the large air bubbles and produces bread with a smooth, even exterior. To shape dough into a loaf, roll into a 12 x 8-inch rectangle. Be sure to roll to outer edges to pop any air bubbles. Roll rectangle up tightly, starting with the 8-inch edge. As you roll, seal with fingertips. Seal the seam completely by pinching the dough together. Also seal the ends by pinching each into a thin sealed strip. Fold strips under the loaf into the seam side.

Place loaf seam-side down into a greased baking pan. Grease and cover the surface and let rise again till it's almost doubled in size. When checking the second rising, press fingers lightly against the edge of the loaf. The dough should feel light and spongy. It will have lost its elasticity and won't bounce back.

If you prefer, you can shape loaves into empty fruit juice cans or bake them in layer cake pans or on cookie sheets—or make great dinner rolls. Braided bread is popular, but be sure to braid the bread very loosely so the interwoven effect is not lost as the bread doubles in bulk while rising again.

Making Sugar from Whole-Wheat Berries

Diastatic malt is the European bread bakers' secret ingredient. It's made from sprouted and roasted grain, usually barley. Fortunately for us, sprouted wheat berries work equally well. The malt's enzymes mellow and soften the gluten in flour, converting some of the flour's starch into sugar. This helps create bread with a better flavor, delicate and slightly nutty. Bread texture is improved, also. Wherever diastatic malt is found, both powdered and liquid forms are usually available.

Diastatic malt is very easy to make at home by drying sprouted wheat berries. When sprout is about the same length as the wheat berry, rinse and dry on a cloth towel. Spread $1/2$ inch thick on dryer tray, or on cookie sheet if you're using the oven as a dryer, and allow to dry until crispy. Then, grind dried sprouts in a grain mill or pulverize in a blender until powdered.

Stored in the refrigerator, diastatic malt will retain its enzymes for up to two years. When properly stored in freezer, it will last as long as stored wheat.

BASIC WHEAT SUGAR

(Diastatic Malt or Malt Extract)

2 C. sprouted wheat or barley

Sprout wheat berries or barley seed until sprout is same length as grain. (See chapter on **Basic Sprouting**.) Dry wheat sprouts at 140°–150°F until crispy. Do not allow temperature to exceed 170°F, or the enzymatic action will be killed. Grind or pulverize in blender at high speed until powdered. May be used to replace up to one-fourth of the sugar called for in most bread recipes.

Recommendation for use:

Use 1 teaspoon per batter for 2–4 loaves of bread.

Note: using a little diastatic malt is good, but using too much is bad—too much always makes breads dark and sticky, and sometimes either too sweet or just plain bitter!

Baking

Bake bread at the temperature specified in the particular recipe. During the first few minutes of baking, the leavening gas in the dough expands rapidly, giving the bread its greatest volume. This is the reason the oven should be preheated to the correct temperature before putting the raised loaf in to bake. As bread bakes, the gluten framework is set, the yeast is destroyed, and this in turn stops the rising action. At this point, the flavor of the bread is fully developed. That's also when the family starts hanging around the kitchen!

After the suggested time for baking has elapsed, test the bread for doneness by tapping the top crust with your finger. When there is a hollow sound, the bread is thoroughly baked, and the crust should be nicely browned. If the bread browns too quickly, cover the loaf with aluminum foil while baking to prevent the crust from burning. Use the foil cover also after the top has browned but sides are still light.

Remove yeast breads from baking pans immediately after taking them from the oven. This prevents the crust from being "steamed" in the pan. Place bread on a wire rack to cool, or be devoured, whichever comes first.

Note:

If you consistently have problems with crusts browning too quickly, check oven temperature with an oven thermometer to make sure the oven reading is correct.

How to Keep Bread Fresh

Hopefully, the instructions and guidelines in the previous paragraphs will help elevate you above the level of a basic breadmaker. Now that you're on your way to homemade breads, rolls, and other treats, here are some suggestions for storing homemade bread dough and breads:

- Wrap cooled breads in foil or clear plastic wrap. Store in a well-ventilated bread box.

- Do not unnecessarily refrigerate baked yeast breads or rolls—refrigerator temperatures cause breads to go stale.

- Refrigeration prevents mold from forming in the short range. During hot weather, it may be the better choice, depending on how fast bread disappears in your house.

- Store crisp-crusted bread and rolls unwrapped. Try to use them the same day.

- For "just-baked" freshness when life is hectic, freeze your baked bread. The fresh quality is retained up to 3 months in fully baked products.

- To use frozen bread, thaw first, then unwrap.

- Unbaked homemade dough will freeze well for only a few weeks.

- Slice bread before freezing—it's not convenient to use if entire bread must be thawed.

- There's no need to thaw bread before toasting or when making sandwiches to eat later in the day.

- Reheat bread and rolls to restore their crispness.

- Dinner rolls and sweet rolls will freeze for up to three months satisfactorily.

- Apply toppings after breads or rolls are thawed. Glazes, icings, and frostings with powdered sugar do not freeze well.

RECIPES FOR BASIC BREADSTUFFS

The previous section provided suggestions for basic breadmaking techniques. These recipes will help you bake some basic breads, as well as our favorite advanced basic breads.

BASIC ONE-RISE WHEATBREAD

2 T. active dry yeast	3 T. shortening
$1/2$ C. warm water	$3^1/_2$ C. scalded milk (powdered,
$1/4$ tsp. sugar	2%, or diluted canned)
$1^1/_2$ T. salt	$5^1/_2$–6 C. whole-wheat flour
4 T. honey	$2^1/_2$ C. white flour
2 T. molasses	

Dissolve yeast in warm water and sugar. Add salt, honey, molasses, and shortening to scalded milk and allow mixture to cool to lukewarm. Stir 2 cups flour into liquid and beat with mixer until thin batter stage. Add yeast and beat well. Add remaining flour, 1 cup at a time, mixing or stirring until dough will not absorb more flour. Knead 15 minutes. Put into pans and let rise 45 minutes (doesn't need to rise twice). Bake at 425°F for 15 minutes, then reduce to 325°F for 45 minutes. *Yield: 3 small loaves.*

BASIC WHEATBREAD

$3^1/_4$ C. warm water	1 T. salt
2 T. brown sugar	1 C. powdered milk
2 T. active dry yeast	1 to 2 C. white flour
2 T. honey	6 to 8 C. whole-wheat flour
2 T. molasses	2 T. vegetable oil
2 tsp. butter or margarine	

In a large bowl, mix $1/2$ cup warm water with sugar, add yeast, and let stand about 5 minutes. Add honey, molasses, butter or margarine, salt, powdered milk, and $2^3/_4$ cups warm water. Stir in white flour, then stir in wheat flour until dough is easy to knead—not too stiff and not too sticky. Knead 10 minutes, using oil.

Divide into loaves, shape, and place in greased pans. Let rise 45–60 minutes, then bake 45 minutes in 350°F oven. Let cool slightly, then brush tops of loaves with butter or margarine. *Yield: 2 large loaves.*

BASIC WHEATROLLS

2 T. yeast	2 eggs, beaten
$1/2$ C. warm water	$1/2$ tsp. salt
$1/3$ C. vegetable oil	$1/2$ C. dry powdered milk
$1/3$ C. brown sugar	$4^1/_2$–5 C. whole-wheat flour

Mix yeast and warm water, set aside for 5 minutes. Mix together oil, brown sugar, eggs, and salt. Then add powdered milk, mixing well. Add enough flour to make a soft dough which leaves the side of the bowl. Turn onto well-floured board. Turn dough over to coat with flour and knead 10 minutes or until smooth and satiny. Place in a greased bowl, cover, and allow to rise until almost double in bulk (1–2 hours). Shape as desired and place in greased pans. Let rise again. Bake at 400°F for 15 minutes.

BASIC ONION BUNS

3 T. butter or margarine	$^3/_4$ C. finely chopped onion
3 C. all purpose flour (unsifted)	3 T. sugar
3 C. whole-wheat flour	$1^1/_2$ tsp. salt
2 T. active dry yeast	2 C. hot water

In fry pan, sauté onion in butter until golden. Set aside. In large mixer bowl, blend 1 cup regular flour, 1 cup whole-wheat flour, sugar, salt, and yeast. Add onion mixture (saving 2 tablespoons for topping buns) and the hot water. Beat at low speed for 2 minutes. Add 1 cup whole-wheat flour and beat at high speed for 2 minutes. Stir in remaining whole-wheat flour and enough regular flour to make a soft dough. Sprinkle $^1/_3$ cup regular flour on a board; turn dough out and knead until smooth and elastic, about 5 minutes, adding more flour as needed.

Place in greased bowl, turning over to grease top. Cover. Let rise in warm place until double, about 1 hour. Punch down and divide into 2 equal pieces. Roll each into a ball and place 4 inches apart on greased baking sheets. With greased fingers flatten each into a 4-inch circle. Spread some of the reserved onion mixture on each. Let rise until double, about 50 minutes. Bake at 375°F for 20–25 minutes.

BASIC TOMATOBREAD

3 T. active dry yeast	1 C. honey
1 T. sugar	$^1/_2$ C. molasses
1 C. lukewarm water	$^1/_2$ C. shortening
$1^1/_2$ qt. tap water	18–20 C. whole-wheat flour
1 C. tomato juice	butter or margarine
4 T. salt	

Add yeast and sugar to lukewarm water. Set aside while mixing the other ingredients. In a large mixing bowl beat together water, tomato juice, salt, honey, molasses, and shortening. Add yeast mixture. Beat in 10 cups whole-wheat flour.

Knead in 8–10 more cups whole-wheat flour. Cover and let rise until double in size. Knead down again and shape into loaves.

Place in well-greased loaf tins. Let dough rise to top of pans. Bake at 350°F for 40 minutes. Cool slightly and grease tops of loaves with butter, then turn loaves on sides to cool. *Yield: 7 medium loaves.*

BASIC PUMPERNICKEL BREAD

4 T. active dry yeast	$^3/_4$ C. cornmeal
$3^1/_2$ C. warm water	2 tsp. caraway seeds
$^1/_2$ C. molasses or honey	$^1/_2$ C. sunflower seeds
1 T. oil	2 T. carob or cocoa powder
2 T. salt	3 C. rye flour
2 C. mashed potatoes	9–10 C. whole-wheat flour

Sprinkle yeast over water and allow to activate. Add the remaining ingredients and mix well. Knead 10–12 minutes. Let rise until double. Shape into 4 loaves. Let rise to double again. Bake in a 350°F oven for 50 minutes. *Yield: 4 small loaves.*

BASIC DILLYBREAD

1 T. active dry yeast	1 T. dehydrated onion flakes
4 tsp. sugar	2 tsp. dill seed
$1/4$ C. warm water	2 C. whole-wheat flour
$1/3$ C. powdered milk	$1/8$ tsp. baking soda
$1/2$ C. water	1 tsp. margarine
1 egg, unbeaten	1 tsp. salt

Dissolve yeast and sugar in warm water. Combine powdered milk and water to make thick milk. (*Basic Cottage Cheese* may be substituted.) Add egg, onion flakes, dill seed, and yeast; beat well. Mix flour and soda. Add flour $1/3$ at a time, beating well after each addition. Cover. Let rise in warm place until doubled in bulk.

Stir down dough. Turn into well greased $1 1/2$-quart casserole dish. Let rise in warm place until light, about 30–40 minutes. Brush with butter, sprinkle with salt. Bake at 350°–400°F for 50–60 minutes. *Yield: 1 loaf.*

BASIC CARROTRAISIN BREAD

1 T. active dry yeast	$1/2$ C. honey
$1/3$ C. warm water	$6 1/2$ C. stone-ground whole-
2 C. milk, scalded and cooled	wheat flour (approx.)
5 T. melted butter or margarine	1 C. finely shredded carrots
1 tsp. salt	1 C. raisins

Dissolve yeast in water in large bowl. Add milk, 3 tablespoons of butter, salt, honey, and gradually stir in 5 cups flour to make a soft dough. Stir in carrots and raisins. Spread about $3/4$ cup of the remaining flour on breadboard.

Turn out the dough, and knead until dough is elastic and not sticky, for 10–15 minutes. Sprinkle additional flour on the board and hands as needed to prevent sticking. Place dough in a greased bowl. Turn dough over to grease the top, cover with a towel, and let rise in a warm place until almost doubled. Let rise another 45 minutes more, then punch down. Let rise another 20 minutes, then punch down; let rise 10 minutes, then punch down. Squeeze dough to release air bubbles. Divide dough in 2 equal portions. Knead each for about 30 seconds on a lightly floured board and shape into a smooth round loaf. Place each loaf on a greased cookie sheet. Cover and let rise until almost doubled—about 1 hour.

Brush tops with the remaining butter. Bake at 350°F for about 30 minutes or until browned and the loaves sound hollow when tapped. Let cool on racks. Wrap airtight. Can be stored at room temperature for up to three days. Freeze for longer storage. *Yield: 2 loaves.*

BASIC SPROUTBREAD

1 C. scalded milk	1 C. wheat sprouts
$1/2$ C. warm water	1 tsp. salt
2 T. oil	4 C. whole-wheat flour
2 T. honey	1 T. active dry yeast
1 egg	

Put scalded milk, water, cooking oil, honey, egg, and sprouts in blender and blend. Pour into mixer bowl, add salt and 2 cups flour, then blend. Add yeast and 2 cups flour and knead for 10 minutes. Form dough into a loaf and place in a greased 5 x 9-inch bread pan. Let rise until double. Bake at 350°F for 60 minutes. *Yield: 1 loaf.*

BASIC STONEBREAD MIX

2 T. dry active dry yeast	2 T. salt
5–6 C. lukewarm water	5 C. dry powdered milk
1/2 C. honey	1/3 C. shortening or margarine
20 C. stone-ground whole-wheat flour	

Make yeast mixture with yeast, 1/2 cup warm water, and 1 teaspoon honey and let stand for 10 minutes. Mix dry ingredients (flour, salt, milk) in large mixing bowl, making a well in the center. Pour in remaining liquids and yeast mixture. Stir with spoon as long as possible, then continue mixing with hands. Mix until stickiness begins to leave the dough.

Grease the sides of the bowl and your hands with shortening or margarine and continue to work the dough, kneading it very thoroughly. Use considerable pressure when forming the loaves in order to remove all air bubbles. Place loaves in well greased pans and cover with wax paper. Allow to rise until almost double in size.

Place in a preheated oven at 300°F and bake for 1 1/4 hours. Remove loaves from pans and leave uncovered for 15 minutes, then cover with wax paper and a heavy towel to finish cooling. *Yield: 5 loaves.*

BASIC RAISINBREAD

1 batch *Basic StoneBread Mix*	1 1/2 C. raisins
1 tsp. ginger	

Prepare *Basic StoneBread Mix.* Add raisins and spices to *Mix* before first mixing of dough. Then follow remaining directions in *Basic StoneBread Mix* above.

BASIC CINNAROLLS

1 batch *Basic StoneBread Mix*	1/2 C. brown sugar
1 tsp. ginger	1 T. cinnamon
1 tsp. grated orange peel	1 T. soft butter

Prepare *Basic StoneBread Mix.* Add ginger and grated orange peel to batter before first mixing of dough.

When shaping rolls, sprinkle surface of dough with mixture of sugar, cinnamon, and soft butter before rolling. Place on greased baking pans. Bake at 400°F for 30–40 minutes. Serve piping hot.

BASIC STUFFING & DRESSING COOKERY

Perhaps your family enjoys stuffing or dressing with their favorite entrées. Stuffing is a great taste addition to any meal. It's a good way to utilize all those bits and pieces of vegetables, meats, seasonings—whatever's on hand. When you're really hungry for some stuffing, the *Basic EasyBread* recipe is designed to provide a homemade bread for the stuffing base. It is also a great bread for slicing, too!

Directions for Making Basic EasyBread

BASIC EASYBREAD

1 T. dry active dry yeast	1 T. salt
3 C. warm water	9+ C. whole-wheat flour
¹/₄ C. honey	

Dissolve yeast in ¹/₄ cup of the warm water and 1 tsp. of the honey. Let stand 5 minutes. Stir in remaining water, honey, and salt. Add flour. Knead 10 minutes. Put dough in lightly greased bowl. Cover with damp cloth and place in unheated oven over large pan of hot water until double in bulk. Divide and form into loaves. Place in greased pans. Let rise until double. Bake at 350°F for 1 hour. After allowing to cool fully, cut into ¹/₂-inch slices, then cut into cubes. Dry bread thoroughly in oven, let cool. Then, place dried bread cubes and crumbs into sealed plastic bags. Store in refrigerator or freezer until needed.

Basic EasyBread is the base for *Basic StuffMix*. The following chart provides information to help mix and match ingredients to have the most taste variations with the least ingredients. It should be helpful in determining the amount of stuffing or dressing needed to fill the poultry neck and body cavities. Measurements are not particularly critical; consider them guidelines in developing creativity. Any of the ingredients or all of them may be used interchangeably. No two stuffings or dressings should ever be made the same. Stuffings should be a pleasure to prepare and a joy to eat!

> **Note:**
>
> This is *BASIC EASYBREAD*—it's easy to make and economical besides.
>
> *BASIC EASYBREAD* is used as the filler base for stuffing & dressing recipes.

Chart 7–1

Basic StuffMix Ingredient Measures

Ingredients for *Basic StuffMix*	Poultry Weight (Uncooked)			
	3–6 lb.	**10–12 lb.**	**16–18 lb.**	**22–24 lb.**
Basic EasyBread, cubed and dried (see recipe above)	4 C.	6 C.	12 C.	16 C.
stock: broth, milk, or water	³/₄ C.	1¹/₂ C.	2¹/₄ C.	3 C.
egg(s), beaten	1	2	3	4
butter (margarine)	¹/₂ C.	¹/₂ C.	1 C.	1¹/₂ C.
celery, chopped	¹/₂ C.	1 C.	1¹/₂ C.	2 C.
onion, chopped	¹/₂ C.	1 C.	1¹/₂ C.	2 C.
salt	1 tsp.	2 tsp.	3 tsp.	4 tsp.
pepper	1 tsp.	2 tsp.	3 tsp.	4 tsp.
thyme	¹/₈ tsp.	¹/₄ tsp.	¹/₂ tsp.	1 tsp.
sage	¹/₈ tsp.	¹/₄ tsp.	¹/₂ tsp.	1 tsp.
parsley flakes	¹/₂ tsp.	1 T.	1¹/₂ tsp.	2 T.

RECIPES FOR BASIC EASYBREAD STUFFING

BASIC STUFFMIX
(3–6 lb. poultry or fowl)

4 C. *Basic EasyBread*, cubed and dried   ½ C. celery
1 tsp. pepper   ½ C. chopped onion
⅛ tsp. thyme   ½ C. butter (margarine)
⅛ tsp. sage   ¾ C. stock
½ T. parsley flakes   1 egg, beaten
1 tsp. salt

Prepare *Basic EasyBread* in advance. Slice, then cube and dry in oven. Mix lightly all dry ingredients (bread, pepper, thyme, sage, parsley, salt). Sauté celery and onion in butter, pour over dry mix. Add stock and egg, tossing lightly to prevent crushing bread cubes.

Spoon *Basic StuffMix* into salted body cavity of any fowl. Do not overstuff. Close openings, bake according to poultry roasting directions. *Yield: approximately 1 quart stuffing or dressing.* (See **Chart 7–1** above for other amounts.)

Basic StuffMix Variations

Basic StuffMix can be used to stuff wild poultry (duck, goose, Cornish hen, rock hen, etc.), as well as pork chops, ham slices, leg of lamb, lamb chops, fish, or even bell peppers. By varying the liquid and dry ingredients, there are literally thousands of possible stuffings for any conceivable purpose.

Liquid ingredients: use poultry or fowl drippings or giblet stock, diluted with water, milk, or dry powdered milk to change the flavor.

Dry ingredients: heighten flavor of *Basic StuffMix* and embellish the stuffing by adding chopped nuts, sliced raw apples, sausage (cooked and crumbled), chopped green or red bell peppers (sautéed), chopped pineapple, canned or frozen oysters, mushrooms, dried prunes or apricots (chopped or sliced), wild rice, and of course giblets (cooked and chopped).

Try these variations for *Basic StuffMix:*

BASIC STUFFMIX DRESSING

Spoon *Basic StuffMix* into greased covered dish. Bake at 350°F for 30–40 minutes. To crispen top, remove cover during final 5 minutes of cooking.

BASIC STUFFMIX MEATLOAF

Crush dried bread in the ingredients before making *Basic StuffMix*. Then substitute mixture for bread crumbs and herbs in your favorite meat loaf recipe.

Chapter 8

Basic "WheatMeat" Cookery

Grains of wheat add another menu dimension to your food storage when ground into whole-wheat flour and used to prepare a meat substitute. Whole-wheat flour combined with water in a three-step process results in *Basic Gluten*, a gluey vegetable protein substance that causes the whole-wheat dough to become sticky and dense. When gluten is dried, cooked, and flavored with meat, meat juices, bouillon, or other seasonings, it can be used as a meat replacement.

Basic Gluten is fairly easy to make, and the task can be delegated to a younger member of the family, since no subtle or delicate handling is required. In fact, the success of a gluten batch depends on the thoroughness of the beating it gets—the rougher the better.

Experimentation is the key to gluten's success. There are many ways to use it in the family's diet. Try the recipes for *Basic Flavorings* and *Basic Gluten Beef Flavoring* included in this chapter. Then create your own "wheatmeat" specialties.

DIRECTIONS FOR BASIC 3-STEP GLUTEN

This is a simplified and improved *Basic Gluten* recipe. Instructions are designed for beginning gluten making. The best gluten is made from freshly-ground, hard, whole-wheat flour.[1] Merely add some water to stone-ground wheat flour to make the glutinous mass. Then rinse the dense, gooey mass under hot running water for a batch of *Basic 3-Step Gluten*. Simple!

BASIC 3-STEP GLUTEN

16 C. stone-ground whole-wheat flour	3 C. water (approx.)

> **Note:**
>
> *Successful gluten-making depends upon a very thorough beating of the dough mass.*

1. Combine flour and water into a ball-like mass. Then knead, pound, or beat the ball (or mix in bread mixer if you have one) for 10–15 minutes.

2. Cover glutinous mass with cold water and let it set for 1 hour. Then, wash out the starch by holding the soft dough in your hands under water as hot as your hands can tolerate. When the dough is firm, starch has been removed. Continue rinsing until the bran, which feels like sand, has been washed out. Drain in a colander or straining basket 30 minutes more for easier handling. If too wet, dry in 200°F oven approximately 30 minutes.

3. The final step cooks and flavors the *Basic Gluten*. If you've decided what you'll make with the gluten, both can be done simultaneously. Any seasoning may be used.

FLAVORING BASIC GLUTEN

Basic Gluten can be flavored by either of two easy methods. Flavoring can be done in small batches or as needed when you're at the stove preparing a meal.

"Frying-in" flavoring: cut *Basic Gluten* into strips or rolls, or shape into patties. Fry in bacon, sausage, or beef juices until enough flavor for your taste is absorbed.

"Boiling-in" flavoring: cut *Basic Gluten* into strips, rolls, or patties as above. Drop shaped gluten into simmering stock, juices, or any flavoring of your choice.

After flavoring, allow to drain in a colander. May be stored in refrigerator for up to 2 weeks.

---

[1] The best available book about preparing gluten I know is **The New Gluten Book,** by LeArta Moulton, publ. The Food Place, PO Box 482, Provo UT 84603 ☎(801) 374-1858. She also has a 60-minute "how-to" video in VHS format, **The Quick Wholesome Foods Video,** by Rita Bingham & LeArta Moulton. It's great for teaching beginners the skills for making 100% whole-wheat breads and working with gluten and seasonings for meat substitutes.

The following flavoring recipes will help make *Basic Gluten* a tasty menu addition.

BASIC GLUTEN "LITE" FLAVORING

7 C. water
1 #303 can consommé or beef broth

$^1/_2$ C. lite soy sauce
salt and pepper to taste

Bring water to boil, reduce heat, then add soup and soy sauce. Roll out *Basic Gluten* and cut into $^1/_2$-inch strips with sharp knife or heavy scissors. Drop strips into broth. Simmer 30 minutes. Use chicken, ham, turkey, onion, garlic, mixed vegetable—any flavoring of your choice—in lieu of the consommé in the ingredients above. The flavoring can be as subtle or intense as you'd like. Perhaps you'll get some ideas from these basic recipes:

BASIC GLUTEN BEEF FLAVORING

2 T. beef base granules*
1 T. soy sauce
$^1/_2$ C. chopped onion

7 C. water
$^1/_4$ T. pepper
4 tsp. seasoned salt

Mix all ingredients and bring to a boil. Add *Basic Gluten* strips and simmer 30 minutes.
* Substitute 12 beef bouillon cubes.

RECIPES FOR BEEF-FLAVORED BASIC GLUTEN

BASIC STEAKETTES

Form *Basic Gluten* into steak-shaped forms and season with *Basic Gluten Beef Flavoring*. Then follow these directions for delicious meat substitutes.

BASIC PAN-FRIED STEAKETTES

Basic Steakettes
$^1/_2$ C. butter (margarine)

1 C. sliced mushrooms
salt and pepper to taste

Prepare *Basic Steakettes*. Sauté *Steakettes* in butter. Reduce heat to low. Sprinkle sliced or rehydrated mushrooms over *Steakettes* and cover with lid for 5 minutes. Serve hot.

BASIC SKILLET STEAKETTES

Basic Steakettes
1 egg, beaten
2 C. bread crumbs, crushed fine

6 slices bacon
1 C. butter (margarine)
1 can mushroom soup, undiluted

Prepare *Basic Steakettes*. Dip *Steakettes* in egg, then roll in bread crumbs. Fry bacon in pan, remove, and chop fine. Return bacon to pan, add butter. Brown *Steakettes* in bacon grease. Pour mushroom soup over *Steakettes* until simmering. Serve hot over rice or noodles. (This dish may be baked in the oven for 15 minutes at 425°F.)

BASIC GROUND BEEF

After simmering or frying *Basic Gluten* in beef flavoring, grind gluten in meat grinder and substitute in recipes calling for ground beef. See following recipe for using *Basic Gluten Ground Beef* in a burger.

BASIC GLUTENBURGER

1 batch *Basic Ground Beef*
1 egg
1 medium onion, chopped fine

all-purpose flour
1/2 C. butter (margarine)
salt and pepper to taste

Prepare *Basic Ground Beef*. Stir egg and chopped onion into *Ground Beef*. Add just enough flour to make patties. Fry in butter, browning both sides. Cover and steam 5 minutes to bring out full flavor.

BASIC PATTIES IN MUSHROOM SAUCE

2 C. *Basic Ground Beef*
2 eggs
1 medium onion, chopped
1/2 C. soy sauce

dash garlic salt
2 tsp. sage
2 C. cooked rice
1 can mushroom soup, undiluted

Prepare *Basic Ground Beef*. Mix egg, onion, soy sauce, garlic salt, and sage together, then add *Ground Beef* and rice. Form into patties. Fry in oil slowly until browned. Add undiluted mushroom soup, simmering 10–15 minutes.

BASIC SAUSAGE

1 batch *Basic Ground Beef*
sausage seasoning to taste
1 egg

1 T. flour
1/2 C. butter (margarine)

Season *Basic Gluten Ground Beef* with sausage seasoning until the flavor suits you. Then stir in egg and flour. Form into patties and fry in butter, browning both sides.

Chapter 9
Basic Sourdough Cookery

Sourdough is mentioned in Egyptian history more than 4,000 years ago. Its history is replete with the salvation of generations. What could be simpler than mixing flour with water, then leaving it covered in a warm place overnight? The wild yeast spores in the air will find a home in the mixture, and they start working their magic to form a sourdough—talk about your first "convenience" food! It's difficult to feel sorry for the ancient civilizations when you realize how easy it was for them to earn their bread!

More recently, when America was in its formative and early growth years out in the Old West, sourdough was known as the frontiersmen's survival kit. Later, it was such a major part of prospectors' diets that the nickname "Sourdough" became a complimentary and hard-won title for the hardy souls who "won the West."

Sourdough cookery is yet another way to use the whole wheat in your food storage. Sourdough starter, a form of leavening like yeast, when added to whole-wheat flour and water, makes a batter which can be used to prepare pancakes, breads, rolls, cookies, and cakes. To help you use your stored wheat in sourdough cookery, this chapter offers you recipes for *Basic Sourdough Starters* and a *Basic SourBatter Mix* which are used to make breads and other sourdough delights. Directions for sourdough breadmaking and a yeast recipe conversion table are included.

HINTS FOR SUCCESSFUL BASIC SOURDOUGH COOKERY

Basic Sourdough Cookery can be fun and often provides more satisfaction than any other type of baking. The only limits to the use of sourdough are the limits of your imagination. Keep these points in mind when cooking with sourdough:

- Sourdough is a form of yeast, reacting to the same conditions as all other yeast.

- Sourdough is slower-acting and always needs more warmth for a longer period of time to ensure best results. With reasonable care to prevent contamination of the starter, and allowing enough time and warmth to provide proper fermentation, there are no mysteries to sourdough cookery.

- Allow sufficient time for preparation and follow directions until you feel comfortable with the difference in sourdough leavening.

- By saving a cup of sourdough from each batch, you have your "starter" for the next time. *(Remember: take out a cup, put in a cup!)* If you protect your *Basic Sourdough Starter*, it will become your true kitchen friend and could ultimately make a billion pancakes—if you have the time and patience.

- Most flour in grocery stores today is all-purpose flour—good enough for ordinary pancakes, cookies, and cakes, but not good enough flour for *Basic Sourdough Cookery*. Grind fresh flour from your wheat storage to get the best results. If you must buy flour, you'll get better results using *unbleached hard winter wheat flour*. It makes a better-tasting and more nutritious loaf of bread. This flour may not be available at your local grocery stores. However, whole-food, health, and natural food stores may have a better selection of flours for *Basic Sourdough Cookery*.

Note:

Most beginner failures are the result of the starter being too cool at night, preventing the sourdough leavening action from occurring normally.

BASIC SOURDOUGH STARTER

There are a variety of *Basic Sourdough Starters* for *Basic Sourdough Cookery*. On the following pages are a number of ways to initiate your own *Basic Sourdough Starter*. One of the easiest things about all sourdough recipes is that *any* sourdough item can be prepared with *any* sourdough starter.

Obtain a starter from someone who has one "going"—in fact, the genealogy of an aged starter can be as prestigious to the cook as the prepared food is to the delight of the person eating it! If you don't have an acquaintance who has a starter, there are 5 different *Basic Sourdough Starter* recipes on the following pages—now you can have it all!

If you're just beginning with sourdough cookery, here are a few bits of information you might want to know when you're utilizing *Basic Sourdough Starters*:

- Storing sourdough starters at room temperature invites the growth of undesirable bacteria and molds.
- Get a crockery pot (ceramic cheese pots are perfect) for your sourdough starter. Scald the pot before adding the starter. Always keep some sourdough starter "going" in your sourdough pot in the refrigerator.

- Storing sourdough starter at cold temperatures is important because the starter is not a sterile yeast culture. The cold temperature does not harm the yeast, it merely reduces its reproduction rate.
- If your starter becomes too sour, add just a pinch of baking soda to sweeten it.
- A good sourdough starter has a strong, sour milk odor. The sour smell is a part of normal "aging."
- Sourdough starter is most effective for mixing and rising when between 78°–85°F.
- Liquid separates from sourdough starter that goes too long without being used and replenished. To restore the sourdough starter, just use it and replenish it with a cup of batter, or "sweeten" it by stirring in a teaspoon of sugar.
- If starter develops any abnormal discoloration or odor or has mold growing in it, discard it immediately. The presence of fuzzy mold indicates the starter should be discarded.
- If replenished (by using) regularly, sourdough starter stays fresh. If starter is not to be used for several weeks, freeze or dry it to keep it from spoiling.
- Avoid spoilage by washing starter crock weekly. Wash it with detergent in hot, soapy water. Rinse and dry carefully before returning sourdough starter to starter crock.
- To carry sourdough starter to camp or for backpacking, add enough flour to shape the starter into a ball and place it in a sealable, heavy-duty, food-grade plastic bag with flour.
- Starter can be dried by following directions in the next section. Just mix the dried starter with the appropriate amount of liquid the night before you intend to use it so it can reactivate. Combine with recipe ingredients the following morning for great sourdough cooking—like the prospectors and pioneers of the Old West did!

RECIPES FOR BASIC SOURDOUGH STARTER

Make your own *Basic Sourdough Starter* by preparing one of the following recipes:

BASIC WATER-BASE SOURDOUGH STARTER

2 C. flour of your choice	1 pkg. active dry yeast
2 C. water	

Mix ingredients well. Keep in a warm place overnight. Next morning, you have *Basic Sourdough Starter.* If you prefer, allow to "age" up to 48 hours for a stronger, more robust sourdough taste.

Put 1 cup of this *Starter* mixture in a scalded (but cooled) container with a tight cover. Store in the refrigerator for future use. The remaining batter can be used immediately for pancakes, muffins, bread, or cake.

When replenished every week with flour and water in equal amounts, *Basic Sourdough Starter* will last years—if not a lifetime.

BASIC MILK-BASE SOURDOUGH STARTER

1 C. buttermilk   1 C. flour of choice

After mixing ingredients, let stand for 48 hours or until fermentation begins. To expand the *Basic Milk-Base Sourdough Starter*, add equal amounts of flour of your choice and condensed milk. Be sure to save 1 cup of the mixture in a ceramic cheese pot for future use.

BASIC RYE SOURDOUGH STARTER

$1^1/_2$ C. rye flour $^1/_2$ T. active dry yeast
$^1/_2$ C. water

Mix ingredients together well. Place in warm spot for 24 hours to ferment.

Place 1 cup *Basic Rye Sourdough Starter* in ceramic cheese pot and refrigerate for future use.

BASIC SAN FRANCISCO SOURDOUGH STARTER

$3^1/_2$ C. unsifted whole-wheat flour   1 package active dry yeast
1 T. sugar   2 C. warm water

Combine flour, sugar, and undissolved yeast in a large bowl. Gradually add warm water to dry ingredients and beat until smooth. Cover with transparent wrap and let stand in warm place for 2 days. *Basic San Francisco Sourdough Starter* is usually somewhat more sour than other *Basic Sourdough Starters*.

Put 1 cup *Basic San Francisco Sourdough Starter* in ceramic cheese pot and refrigerate for future use.

To replenish *Basic San Francisco Sourdough Starter*, add $1^1/_2$ cups whole-wheat flour and 1 cup warm water. Beat until smooth, then place in warm spot to ferment. Stir before using. Remember to save 1 cup for future use.

BASIC HONEY SOURDOUGH STARTER

3 C. water   1 tsp. honey
3 C. flour

Mix ingredients in blender or stir very well. Let stand in warm room in open crock-pot or large bowl for 3 days or until it smells yeasty and is full of bubbles. Stir often during aging process.

Save 1 cup *Basic Honey Sourdough Starter* in a tightly covered ceramic cheese pot in the refrigerator. This *Starter* will keep for several weeks.

Freeze *Basic Honey Sourdough Starter* if not used often. Reactivation requires 24 hours after freezing.

To activate refrigerated *Starter,* add 3 cups water and 3 cups flour (for making up 2 loaves of bread). Stir often and keep in warm room. It will be ready to use in about 6 hours.

Drying Basic Sourdough Starter

If you're not going to use your prized *Basic Sourdough Starter* immediately, or if you want to preserve it for posterity, you can dry it just as vegetables are dried for storage. In the dried form, the yeast goes into a spore stage, with the ability to stay inert for a lengthy period of time.

Here are instructions for drying *Basic Sourdough Starter:*

- Spread *Basic Sourdough Starter* in a thin layer on plastic wrap or kraft or butcher paper (not wax-coated paper!).

- Set electric dryer or oven at 120°–130°F. *Never allow temperatures to exceed 140°F.* Temperature control is critical. *Basic Sourdough Starter* yeast culture is destroyed for baking purposes at temperatures in excess of 143°F. Open-air drying is a possibility in climates where sun drying is successful, but the problem of unfriendly mold and bacteria is too great for my personal gambling instincts.

- Dry until thoroughly dry on top. Peel from sheet of plastic or paper, turn over and dry the other side thoroughly. Continue turning and drying until extremely dry and brittle.

- Break into pieces and pulverize in blender.

- Pack in heavy-duty, food-grade, sealable, waterproof plastic bags. Mark on package the original liquid amount of the now-dry starter. You'll need that information when you rehydrate it for use later or to inform anyone receiving it as a gift. Store in refrigerator or freezer.

- *Basic Sourdough Starter* properly dried and sealed in an airtight, heavy-duty, food-grade, sealable plastic bag will store for up to 6 months. Always store in a dark, dry, and cool location. *Starters* will keep up to 2 years in the refrigerator and indefinitely in the freezer.

- To reactivate dried *Basic Sourdough Starter*, merely add enough water or milk to obtain the original consistency of the starter. Enzyme reactivation begins at 50°F. Water and warmth bring the yeast in the *Starter* back to the active stage. *Starter* mixture should remain at room temperature for 8–12 hours to allow cultures to activate fully.

Yeast Recipe Conversion for Basic Sourdough Cookery

Virtually every regular yeast recipe can be converted to *Basic Sourdough Starter* leavening. To accomplish this, **two** factors must be kept constant in the recipe conversion:

- **leavening quality and quantity**

- **moisture and dough consistency**

Recipe conversion is tricky, requiring practice, patience, and effort—not to mention a good bit of luck, sometimes! The results are worth the effort in taste alone, if you're a true devotée of sourdough cookery.

The following chart interprets some of the ground rules for conversion from regular yeast recipes to *Basic Sourdough Cookery*:

Chart 9–1

Exchanges for Converting Yeast Recipes to Basic Sourdough

Yeast Recipe	Exchanges for Conversion to *Basic Sourdough*		
If Ingredients Require:	**Add**	**&**	**Delete**
yeast*	1 C. starter		yeast
baking soda	1 tsp.		
baking powder (if required)			1 tsp
baking powder (if not required)	¹/₄ tsp. (if bread is too *heavy*)		
flour			¹/₂ C.
milk	may substitute equal buttermilk		
rising time	more time—rises more slowly & requires slightly more warmth		

* 1 teaspoon active dry yeast or ¹/₃ ounce compressed dry yeast in regular yeast recipe requires 1 cup *Basic Sourdough Starter.*

DIRECTIONS FOR BASIC SOURBATTER

Basic SourBatter is used in almost every *Basic Sourdough Cookery* recipe. Each recipe can be made from your choice of sourdough starter. You can add water or milk to water-base starter and milk or water to milk-base starter to affect the taste.

Basic SourBatter should be prepared at least the evening before it's needed. That means if you want pancakes for breakfast in the morning or to make bread tomorrow, prepare the starter today or tonight.

BASIC SOURBATTER MIX

1 C. *Basic Sourdough Starter* (your choice)   2 C. flour (wheat, rye, etc.)
2 C. warm water or milk

> **Note:**
>
> Don't use a metal container or leave a metal spoon in the batter. The chemical reaction could kill the starter's leavening action.

Place *Basic Sourdough Starter* of choice in a large mixing bowl (large enough to allow for any expansion that may take place, depending on how warm it is), preferably of glass, pottery, wood, or plastic.

Add the water, milk, and flour. Mix thoroughly. The mixture will be thick and lumpy, but will become thin while fermenting and be lively by morning.

Cover the bowl and put in warm spot overnight. Allow 10–12 hours during the night in a warm spot in the kitchen for complete fermentation. In the morning, return 1 cup of the *Basic SourBatter Mix* to the sourdough pot to replenish your starter and keep in the refrigerator until next use. The remaining *Basic SourBatter Mix* is what you use in your recipe.

> **Note:**
>
> BASIC SOURBATTER is just starter until the other ingredients of the recipe are added.

To increase the amounts of *Basic SourBatter Mix* for pancakes or waffles to serve a larger number of people, the *Basic Sourdough Starter* (leaven) should be increased proportionally to the amount of flour and water you use. Be sure to increase other recipe ingredients proportionally, too!

Alternate directions: there is an improved way to use sourdough which does not require night-before preparation as when using the traditional method. Make up *Basic SourBatter* as much as a week before need. Allow it to become leavened for a day or so. Store *Mix* in a tightly sealed ceramic pot.

Then, when *Basic SourBatter Mix* is needed for a favorite sourdough recipe, take the batter from the refrigerator and allow it to stand at room temperature for 30–60 minutes. The *Mix* is now ready to use at your convenience without night-before planning.

DIRECTIONS FOR BASIC SOURBREADMAKING

Flour quantities, especially in *Basic Sourdough Cookery* recipes, are approximate because of the many differences in liquid absorption, compactness, and the amount of liquid alcohol present in the batter. The variation in liquid is peculiar to sourdough since the yeast breaks the flour starch down into alcohol and carbon dioxide gas during fermentation. Although this occurs in all yeast breads, the long and variable fermentation period of any sourdough starter produces substantially more liquid alcohol, depending on the starter's strength.

Here are the 10 steps for simplified *Basic SourBreadmaking:*

1. Place *Basic SourBatter Mix* in nonmetal bowl. Stir in required sugar, salt, and flavorings gently. The yeast enzymes are already active and in suspension in the *Mix.*

2. Add the flour a little at a time and stir until the dough pulls away from the sides of the bowl.

3. Turn out dough onto floured board and knead until it feels smooth and elastic. When properly kneaded, dough should not be sticky and should spring back when pressed with the finger.

4. Dough may be given one or two risings. Two risings produce a finer texture in the loaf, but one rising produces a highly satisfactory bread, especially when it is well kneaded. If one rising is preferred, skip now to *Step #7.*

5. To let rise twice, shape the dough into a ball and place in a greased bowl. Roll the dough in the bowl to coat entire surface. Cover with clean dishtowel and place in a warm place to rise until dough doubles. Sourdough usually takes $1^1/_2$–2 times longer to rise than other yeast dough.

6. Punch the dough down and turn out onto lightly floured board. Knead gently.

7. When a double recipe or a recipe for two loaves is used, divide the dough into two equal parts. Shape the dough and place in a greased loaf pan.

8. Cover dough with clean dishtowel and put in warm spot to rise. Allow dough to rise until about double in bulk or until top of the dough reaches $^1/_2$–1 inch above the rim of the pan. The bread will rise slightly more during baking. Preheat oven while dough rises.

9. Brush dough with a glaze of oil or butter just before placing in the oven.

10. Bake at appropriate temperature until done. The loaves will sound hollow when tapped on top crust.

RECIPES FOR BASIC SOURDOUGH BREAD

BASIC SOURBREAD

2 C. *Basic SourBatter Mix*
4 C. sifted flour (more if needed)
2 T. sugar

1 tsp. salt
2 T. vegetable oil or shortening

Prepare *Basic SourBatter Mix*. Sift dry ingredients (flour, sugar, salt) into a bowl, making a well in the center. Add oil to *Mix* and mix well. Pour *Mix* and oil into the well of flour. Add enough flour to make a soft dough for kneading.

Knead on a floured board for 10–15 minutes. Place in a greased loaf pan. Cover and let rise until doubled in size. Bake at 375°F for 1 hour. *Yield: 1 loaf.*

Variations:

Basic Whole-Wheat SourBread: substitute 1 cup whole-wheat flour for 1 cup white flour.

Basic Sourdough Sweet Bread: use honey, brown sugar, or molasses instead of sugar.

Basic Orange SourBread: add juice of 1 orange and grated orange rind.

BASIC SOURBREAD #2

$1^1/_2$ C. *Basic SourBatter Mix*
$^3/_4$ C. milk
3 T. sugar
1 tsp. salt

2 T. margarine
$^1/_4$ C. warm water, 105°–115°F
1 package active dry yeast
5–6 C. unsifted flour

Prepare *Basic SourBatter Mix*. Scald milk. Stir in sugar, salt, and margarine; cool to lukewarm. Measure warm water into large warm bowl. Sprinkle in yeast; stir until dissolved. Add lukewarm milk mixture, *Mix,* and $2^1/_2$ cups flour. Add the remaining flour slowly and mix thoroughly. Turn out onto lightly floured board; knead until smooth and elastic, about 8–10 minutes. Place in greased bowl, turning to grease top. Cover; let rise in warm, draft-free location until doubled in bulk.

Punch dough down; divide into three equal pieces. Form each piece into a smooth round ball or a 14-inch tapered roll. Place on greased baking sheets. With a sharp knife make several crisscross cuts on tops of round loaves or make several diagonal cuts on tops of long loaves. Cover; let rise in warm, draft-free location until doubled in bulk again.

Bake at 400°F about 25 minutes or until done. Remove from baking pans and cool on wire racks.

BASIC SOURHONEY BREAD

4 C. *Basic SourBatter Mix*
2 C. milk
2 T. butter
2 tsp. salt
2 T. sugar
$^1/_4$ C. honey

2 tsp. baking soda
$^1/_4$ C. wheat germ
2 C. wheat flour
4 C. white flour
1 package active dry yeast

Prepare *Basic SourBatter Mix*. Scald milk, then melt butter and honey in milk. Allow to cool to lukewarm, mix yeast in milk, and stir to dissolve. Add to *Mix*. Sift wheat flour and wheat germ into dough. Blend sugar, salt, and soda in another bowl until smooth, then sprinkle over top of dough, stirring in gently.

Set dough in warm spot for 30 minutes, covered with cloth. Punch down and sift in white flour until the dough is too stiff to stir with spoon. Turn out on floured board and begin to knead with hands.

Work in the remaining flour, kneading with heels of hands 100 times until the dough is light and satiny to the touch. (*Caution*: *Do not knead too long or include too much flour.*)

Separate into loaves. Flour lightly, fold over, seal, and place in greased pans. Pans should be half full. Grease tops, set in warm spot, and let double in bulk again.

Preheat oven to 400°F, bake for 20 minutes, then reduce to 325°F and continue to bake until bread shrinks from sides of pans. If done, bread will give a hollow sound when thumped on top. Remove from oven, turn out onto rack or towel, and butter top and sides.

> **Note:**
>
> *Flour required may vary from quantity indicated—gauge the feel.*
>
> *Rather too little than too much.*

BASIC SOURHONEY BREAD #2

3 C. *Basic SourBatter Mix*	2 T. dry milk
$1/_2$ C. warm water	1 T. honey
$3^1/_2$ C. whole-wheat flour	2 T. vegetable oil
2 tsp. salt	

Prepare *Basic SourBatter Mix*. Mix ingredients together until satiny and smooth, reserving the oil for the final mixing. Let rise for 1 hour. Mold two loaves or use 46-ounce juice cans. Let dough rise again until double in bulk. Bake 30 minutes at 400°F, then 30 minutes more at 325°F.

BASIC SOURDOUGH BANANANUT BREAD

1 C. *Basic SourBatter Mix*	2 C. flour
$1/_3$ C. shortening	1 tsp. salt
1 C. sugar	1 tsp. baking powder
1 egg	$1/_2$ tsp. baking soda
1 C. mashed bananas	$3/_4$ C. chopped walnuts

Prepare *Basic SourBatter Mix*. Cream together shortening and sugar; add egg, mixing until blended. Stir in banana and *Mix*. Sift flour, measure, and sift again with salt, baking powder, and soda. Add flour mix to batter, then add walnuts, stirring until blended. Pour into greased loaf pan. Bake at 350°F for 1 hour or until toothpick comes out clean.

BASIC SOUR-RYE BUNS

1 C. *Basic SourBatter Mix*	$1/_2$ C. vegetable oil
$3^3/_4$ C. warm water	1 tsp. salt
$1/_4$ C. all-purpose flour	1 egg white, beaten
4 C. rye flour	coarse salt or caraway seed

Prepare *Basic SourBatter Mix*. In large bowl, combine *Mix* and warm water. Stir in flour. Beat well. Cover and let stand several hours or refrigerate overnight. Add rye flour, oil, and salt. Mix well. Dough will be a bit sticky. (*continued on next page*)

Knead on lightly floured surface about 5 minutes, adding more all-purpose flour as necessary to make a soft dough. Place in greased bowl; turn once to grease surface. Cover and let rise till double. Punch dough down; divide dough into three portions. Cover, let rest 5 minutes.

Divide each portion into 8 balls. Turn each ball in hands, folding edges under to make circle. Press ball flat between hands. Place on greased baking sheet, pressing into 3–4-inch circles. Brush with egg white; sprinkle with coarse salt or caraway seed. Let rise till double. Bake in 375°F oven 25–30 minutes. *Yield: 18–24 buns.*

RECIPES FOR BASIC SOURDOUGH BISCUITS, MUFFINS & PANCAKES

BASIC SOURBISCUITS

¹/₂ C. *Basic SourBatter Mix*	¹/₄ tsp. baking powder
1 C. milk	¹/₂ tsp. baking soda
2¹/₂ C. sifted flour	2 T. yellow cornmeal
1 T. sugar	2 T. salad oil
³/₄ tsp. salt	3 T. melted butter or margarine

Night before: prepare *Basic SourBatter Mix,* then measure ¹/₂ cup into large bowl. Add milk and 1 cup flour; mix well. Let stand covered overnight.

Next morning: beat in 1 cup flour; mix well. Add sugar, salt, baking powder, baking soda, and remaining ¹/₂ cup flour in sifter. Sift evenly over dough. With wooden spoon, beat into dough to mix well; beat until dough is stiff enough to clean side of bowl. On lightly floured surface, knead dough about 15 times until light (dough will be soft). Let dough rest, covered with inverted bowl for 10 minutes.

Roll dough ¹/₂ inch thick. Cut biscuits with lightly floured cutter. Sprinkle bottom of 9 x 9 x 2-inch pan with 1 tablespoon cornmeal. Dip each biscuit into combined oil and butter. Arrange close together in prepared pan. Sprinkle tops of biscuits with remaining cornmeal. Let rise in warm place. When almost doubled, bake in 375°F oven until browned.

BASIC SOURBERRY MUFFINS

³/₄ C. *Basic SourBatter Mix*	1 egg
¹/₂ C. whole-wheat flour	1 C. drained blueberries
1¹/₂ C. white flour	³/₄ tsp. baking soda
¹/₂ C. cooking oil	¹/₂ C. undiluted canned milk
¹/₂ C. sugar	

Prepare *Basic SourBatter Mix.* Stir the above ingredients into *Mix* in the order of listing, to make the mixture moist and hold together nicely. *Do not beat vigorously.* If necessary, add more *SourBatter Mix.* Bake in greased muffin tins at 375°F for 30–35 minutes.

Note: this recipe cooks more slowly than other sourdough muffins, so be sure they are done before you remove them from the oven.

BASIC SOURGRIDDLE MUFFINS

1 C. *Basic SourBatter Mix*	6 T. yellow cornmeal
³/₄ C. buttermilk	1 tsp. baking soda
2³/₄ to 3 C. flour	¹/₄ tsp. salt

Prepare *Basic SourBatter Mix.* Mix together *Mix* and buttermilk. Combine flour, 4 table-spoons cornmeal, soda, salt and add to buttermilk mix. Stir to combine, using hands when necessary. Turn out and knead until smooth. Roll $^3/_8$ inch thick. Cover and let rise a few minutes.

Cut muffins with 3-inch cutter. Sprinkle sheet of waxed paper with 1 tablespoon corn-meal. Place muffins on paper and sprinkle with remaining cornmeal. Cover and let rise 45 minutes. Cook on medium hot griddle for 30 minutes, turning often. Cool and split. *Yield: 12–14 muffins.*

BASIC SOUROAT MUFFINS

$^3/_4$ C. *Basic SourBatter Mix*	1 egg, slightly beaten
$1^1/_2$ C. sifted flour	$^1/_2$ C. buttermilk
$^1/_2$ C. brown sugar, firmly packed	1 C. rolled oats
1 tsp. salt	$^1/_2$ C. salad oil
1 tsp. baking soda	

Prepare *Basic SourBatter Mix.* Mix together flour, brown sugar, salt, and soda. Make a well in the center. Blend egg, buttermilk, rolled oats, and oil together; stir in *Mix.* Pour this mixture all at once into the flour well. Stir lightly to moisten ingredients. Batter will be lumpy. Grease muffin cups or line with baking cup liners; fill about $^2/_3$ full. Bake at 375°F for 30–35 minutes. *Yield: 12–15 muffins.*

BASIC SOUR-RAISIN MUFFINS

1 C. *Basic SourBatter Mix*	$^1/_2$ C. cooking oil
$^1/_2$ C. whole-wheat flour	$^1/_2$ C. undiluted canned milk
$^1/_2$ C. white flour	1 egg
$^1/_2$ C. sugar	1 C. raisins
$^3/_4$ tsp. baking soda	

Prepare *Basic SourBatter Mix.* Combine dry ingredients (wheat flour, white flour, sugar, soda) in bowl. Make a well in the center and add all of the liquids at once. Stir just to moisten. Add raisins and enough *Mix* to make the mixture moist and hold together nicely.

Stir gently till combined. Bake in greased muffin tins at 375°F for 30–35 minutes. *Yield: 16–18 muffins.*

Note: these muffins seem to take a long time to bake completely, so check to be sure they are done.

BASIC SOURWAFFLES

4 C. *Basic SourBatter Mix*	$^1/_4$ C. milk
1 egg	1 tsp. baking soda
4 T. oil or shortening	1 tsp. salt

Prepare *Basic SourBatter Mix.* Add egg, oil, and milk to *Mix,* stirring in well. Blend dry ingredients (soda, salt) in small bowl; sprinkle over wet mixture and stir in gently. Let rest 5 minutes, then drop or pour onto a hotter-than-normal waffle iron. If mixture appears too thick, add more milk. *Yield: 10–12 waffles.*

Basic Griddle SourCakes

3 C. *Basic SourBatter Mix*
1 or 2 eggs
1 tsp. baking soda

1 tsp. salt
1 T. sugar
2 T. bacon grease or salad oil

Prepare *Basic SourBatter Mix*. Add eggs, soda, salt, and sugar. Beat with a fork until blended. Add melted grease. Cook pancakes on griddle; serve with butter and syrup or honey. Molasses, jelly, or honey from your storage are also good. *Yield: 10–12 servings.*

Basic Corny SourBread Mix

1 C. *Basic SourBatter Mix*
$1^1/_2$ C. yellow cornmeal
$1^1/_2$ C. evaporated milk
2 eggs, beaten

2 T. sugar
$^1/_4$ C. melted butter
$^1/_2$ tsp. salt
$^3/_4$ tsp. baking soda

Prepare *Basic SourBatter Mix*. Thoroughly mix the *Mix*, cornmeal, milk, eggs, and sugar in large bowl. Stir in melted butter, salt, and soda. Turn into a 10-inch greased pan and bake 450°F for 25 minutes. Serve hot with butter and honey.

Basic Corny SourSticks

Prepare *Basic Corny SourBread Mix* according to directions. Spoon *Mix* into a buttered cornbread stick pan, filling each cup $^2/_3$ full. Bake at 425°F for 20 minutes or until done.

Basic SourScones

1 C. *Basic SourBatter Mix*
1 C. flour
2 tsp. baking powder
1 tsp. baking soda

$^1/_2$ tsp. salt
1 T. sugar
$^1/_4$ C. melted shortening
2 eggs, slightly beaten

Prepare *Basic SourBatter Mix*. Combine dry ingredients (flour, baking powder, soda, sugar) and make a hole in center. Combine shortening, beaten eggs, and *Mix,* then pour into dry ingredients. Mix and add additional flour, kneading until dough leaves fingers and is no longer sticky. Tear off pieces of dough, flatten in hand, and pull to thin patty. Fry in deep hot oil (375°F) until golden on each side. Drain on paper towels. Serve piping hot with butter, honey, or jam.

Basic SourLoaf

$^1/_2$ C. *Basic SourBatter Mix*
$1^1/_2$ C. unsifted flour

1 C. undiluted evaporated milk
2 T. sugar

Night before: prepare *Basic SourBatter Mix*. Combine *Mix*, flour, evaporated milk, and sugar. Set in warm spot to ferment.

Next morning: add the following ingredients to *Mix*.

$^3/_4$ C. brown sugar, packed
$^1/_4$ C. butter
1 C. chopped dates
$^1/_2$ C. chopped walnuts
2 eggs, beaten

$^1/_2$ C. quick-cooking rolled oats
1 tsp. baking powder
$^1/_2$ tsp. baking soda
$^1/_2$ tsp. salt

Cream brown sugar and butter, add dates and nuts; set aside. Combine eggs, rolled oats, baking powder, soda, and salt. Stir date mixture into the *Mix*. Turn into a greased loaf pan (5 x 9-inch) and let rise about 1 hour. Bake at 375°F for 1 hour. Cool for 10 minutes in pan, then remove to cooling rack. *Yield: 1 loaf.*

RECIPES FOR SOURDOUGH CAKES, ROLLS, AND DOUGHNUTS

BASIC SOURDOUGH CINNAROLLS

$^1/_2$ C. *Basic SourBatter Mix*
1 C. undiluted evaporated milk

2 C. unsifted flour

Night before: prepare *Basic SourBatter Mix*. Combine *Mix*, evaporated milk, and flour in large bowl; leave in warm spot overnight.

Next morning: add following ingredients to *Mix*.

$^1/_4$ C. soft butter
3 T. sugar
1 egg
$1^1/_2$ C. unsifted flour (or more)
$^1/_2$ tsp. baking soda
1 tsp. baking powder

1 tsp. salt
2 T. butter, melted
$^1/_4$ C. brown sugar
$1^1/_2$ tsp. cinnamon
$^1/_4$ C. raisins (optional)
melted butter

Beat together butter, sugar, and egg; blend into *Mix*. Combine the dry ingredients (flour, soda, baking powder, and salt); mix with batter. Turn onto a floured board and knead until the surface is satiny and doesn't stick to board (add flour if necessary). Place ball of dough in the center of board and roll out to a rectangle 8 x 16 inches. Brush surface with melted butter and sprinkle with a mixture of brown sugar and cinnamon (and raisins, if you wish).

Roll up dough, starting on one of the long sides; cut roll at $^3/_4$-inch intervals. Dip top and bottom of each roll in melted butter. Place in a square 9-inch pan, cover loosely, and let rise in a warm spot for about 1 hour or until nearly doubled. Bake at 375°F for 30–35 minutes or until crust is golden brown. *Yield: 9 large rolls.*

BASIC SOURDOUGH CHOCOCAKE

$^1/_2$ C. thick *Basic SourBatter Mix*
1 C. water
$1^1/_2$ C. flour
$^1/_4$ C. nonfat dry milk
$^1/_2$ C. shortening
1 C. sugar

1 tsp. vanilla
1 tsp. cinnamon
3 squares melted chocolate
$^1/_2$ tsp. salt
$1^1/_2$ tsp. baking soda
2 eggs

Prepare *Basic SourBatter Mix*. Combine *Mix*, water, flour, and dry milk; allow to ferment 2–3 hours in a warm spot until bubbly and has strong sour milk odor. Cream shortening, sugar, flavorings, chocolate, salt, and soda. Add eggs one at a time, beating well after each addition. Combine with *Mix*. Beat well. Pour mixture into deep cake pan. Bake at 350°F for 25–30 minutes.

BASIC SOURDOUGHNUTS

$1/2$ C. *Basic SourBatter Mix*	$1/2$ tsp. salt
1 C. lukewarm water	1 tsp. baking powder
1 C. flour	$1/2$ tsp. nutmeg
2 T. sugar	1 egg
2 T. brown sugar	2 T. melted shortening
1 tsp. baking soda dissolved in 1 T. water	$1^1/2$ C. flour

Night before: prepare *Basic SourBatter Mix* and combine with water, flour, and sugar in bowl and let stand at least 6 hours or overnight.

Next morning: add remaining ingredients to *Mix*. Knead on lightly floured board 25 times. Roll $1/2$ inch thick and cut with doughnut cutter. Drop in hot fat, 380°F, fry until golden brown, then turn on other side.

Drain on paper towels spread over newspaper or paper bag. Roll in powdered or granulated sugar. Serve warm. *Yield: 10–12 doughnuts.*

BASIC SOURDOUGH GLAZED APRICAKE

1 C. *Basic SourBatter Mix*	1 tsp. baking soda
$1/2$ C. shortening	$1/8$ tsp. nutmeg
$1^1/2$ C. sugar	$1/2$ C. milk
2 eggs	$1/2$ C. apricots, finely chopped
$1^1/2$ C. unsifted flour	1 tsp. salt
$1^1/2$ tsp. baking powder	3 T. apricot jam
powdered sugar	

Prepare *Basic SourBatter Mix*. In large bowl, cream shortening and sugar. Add eggs, one at a time, beating well. Add dry ingredients (flour, salt, baking powder, soda, nutmeg) to *Mix* alternately with milk, mixing after each addition. Add chopped apricots, lightly floured, stirring until well blended. Turn into greased and floured $1^1/2$-quart tube mold. Bake at 350°F, 50–60 minutes. Allow cake to cool 10 minutes, then invert on cooling rack, removing the mold carefully. Allow to cool completely. Brush on apricot glaze made from 3 tablespoons apricot jam warmed over low heat until soft enough to spread, then dust with powdered sugar.

BASIC SOURALMOND SPICECAKE

1 C. *Basic SourBatter Mix*	1 tsp. baking soda
$1/2$ C. shortening	$1/2$ tsp. cinnamon
$1^1/2$ C. sugar	$1/4$ tsp. nutmeg
2 eggs	$1/8$ tsp. cloves
$1^1/2$ C. unsifted flour	$1/2$ C. milk
$1^1/2$ tsp. baking powder	$1/2$ C. ground almonds
1 tsp. salt	powdered sugar

Prepare *Basic SourBatter Mix*. In large bowl cream shortening and sugar. Add eggs, one at a time, beating well after each addition. Blend in *Mix*. Combine flour, baking powder, salt, soda, cinnamon, nutmeg, and cloves. Add dry ingredients to batter alternately with milk, mixing after each addition until well blended. Add ground almonds and mix until well blended. Turn into a greased and floured $1^1/2$-quart tube mold. Bake at 350°F for 50–60 minutes or until done. Allow cake to cool for 10 minutes, then invert on cooling rack, removing mold carefully. Cool until slightly warm to touch and sprinkle with powdered sugar.

Chapter 10

Basic White Flour Cookery

Estimates indicate that at least one-third of all the food we eat is made with white bleached flour. In the grocery store, the baked goods department and the bread aisle have a fairly large percentage of the store's total area. Most commercial bakery products are made from white bleached flour. Check the bread, pasta, and prepared mixes aisles for all the loaves of bread, cake, pancake, and biscuit mixes—all clearly made from white flour. Anyone can see that white flour is a significant part of the American diet.

This section on white flour cookery is included in the *Handbook* because we recognize the broadscale use of white flour. As long as there's wheat, there will be those who will demand white flour.

One of my college professors told us in class, "Minds are like parachutes—neither functions if it isn't opened." The following information about white flour is presented so anyone with an open mind can evaluate the value of white flour in an in-home storage program. Some of the readily apparent problems with white flour are that it cannot be made in-home, it costs more to buy at the store than to make home-ground whole-wheat flour, it doesn't store very well, and it has very little nutritional value in and of itself.

THE CASE AGAINST WHITE FLOUR

Whole wheat contains 26 minerals and vitamins, plus other trace minerals. These vitamins and minerals are locked in until the outer shell is broken. As wheat is processed at the typical milling operation, the first step in processing is a hot steam wash to soften the outer shell, or bran. This bran layer is a rich source of food fiber, the roughage to help with the body's normal digestive process.

The outside layer is then scarified by tiny, sharp, razorlike blades until it is totally removed. These hull shavings are pieces of bran and are normally sold separately, often to health food stores so they can sell it to people who want to be healthy!

The next layer is called the endosperm, or middling, at the mill. It is taken off by the same method as the bran. Middlings are generally sold to farmers to keep their pigs and cows healthy. Finally, the wheat germ and oil are removed. More than 72% of all the nutrition in wheat is in the germ and oil. Wheat germ is the concentrated source of the wheat nutrient—the vitamins, minerals, and proteins. This is the living part of the grain that can reproduce itself when the seed is planted. When the germ and oil are left in the flour, it soon turns rancid. Flour that turns rancid quickly is a bad commercial product, so germ and oil are removed. Removal of the bran, the endosperm or middling, the wheat germ, and the wheat oil decreases the nutritional value of wheat by as much as 85%.

The residue of powder left after milling is called unbleached flour. Consumers want white flour, so bleaching agents (chemicals) are added. The bright white color makes us think we have the best quality product—in reality, there is virtually little food value remaining in the flour; it's merely stripped wheat kernels.

The white flour purchased at the grocery store is merely white dust—highly processed, chemically treated, with added synthetic compounds—and it's called enriched white flour! More than fifty years ago the Food and Drug Administration knew there was no nutritive value left in the processed white flour, so a law was passed that assured all white flour would be enriched with three vitamin Bs—*thiamin, niacin, and riboflavin*—and iron. Perhaps that ruling is a major indicator as to why we should consider the whole-wheat alternative instead of commercial bleached white flour.

The Endosperm

The Bran

The Wheat Germ

A WHITE FLOUR EXPERIMENT

Let me relate a story told me by Delsa Wilson:[1]

Have you ever seen a trail of ants? The next time you see such a trail, gather some children or curious adults and do this scientific experiment. Merely take a quarter cup of white bleached flour from the sack in your kitchen and make or lay a strip barrier across the ants' trail. As the ants march along their trail, you'll notice they move with great speed. However, when they reach the flour barrier, they'll begin to make crazy little circles in a seeming fit of confusion. Ultimately, an ant scout will find the outer edge of the flour barrier and all the ants will follow the scout back to the other side of the flour strip. They resume their orderly trail speed and continue on their path.

---

[1] Delsa Wilson, 3686 South 2455 East, Salt Lake City UT 84109 ☎(801) 278-6950. Delsa is a twenty-year "veteran" in the industry. She is an active food storage consultant. She is a provider of preparedness products. She will teach and train. She practices what she preaches—even the choir listens to her sermons!

To finish the experiment, use the same amount of fresh-ground whole-wheat flour and make a similar barrier strip 3–4 feet away from the white flour strip. With a magnifying glass, you should be able to see the ants within 12 to 18 inches turn their heads toward the whole wheat. They'll literally stop in their tracks, turn around, and go back to the whole-wheat flour and devour it!

This experiment indicates that ants, being both industrious and intelligent, dismiss white flour from their diet. Another case in point—it has been proven that no self-respecting cockroach will eat anything made with white bleached flour. If the insect world won't eat white bleached flour, why do humans insist on consuming tons of it?

My son lives in Texas where garden pests are a problem. He told me how proud he was of his organic garden because it had no insect problems. He said they only buy white bleached flour to put in his dust gun to dust his vegetables—and it's the most effective treatment he's found for keeping the pests at bay!

THE CASE FOR WHOLE WHEAT

Our society is so accustomed to the processed, quick-fix, convenience-foods environment that it is taking a toll on our individual and collective well-being and longevity. If one-third of all the food we eat is made with bleached white flour, is it any wonder our population has so many health problems?

At the University of Utah, a test was done with computer technology which identified all the vitamins, minerals, amino acids, and calories of any substance. Equal-sized slices of white bakery bread and homemade wheat bread were analyzed based on the same criteria by the system. The results of the calculations indicated it would require 150 slices of white bread to equal the nutrition of 1 slice of homemade whole-wheat bread.

The Cancer Society has stated that we could prevent most of the lower tract cancers, diverticulitis, and infections in the colon if we ingested enough soluble and insoluble fibers which come from vegetables, fruits, *grains*, legumes, nuts, and seeds. Perhaps this is another important argument for the use of whole-wheat flour in a food storage program.

Now that we've completed the treatise on the evils of white flour, here are some white flour recipes for your in-home storage program.

RECIPES FOR WHITE FLOUR

BASIC WHITE FLOUR BISCUIT MIX

8 C. sifted white flour
1 C. nonfat dry milk
1/4 C. baking powder
4 tsp. salt
1 1/3 C. shortening
1/3–1/2 C. water or milk

Sift together dry ingredients (flour, milk, baking powder, salt). Cut in shortening with two knives until fine as flour, then add water or milk.

Drop onto greased baking sheet. Bake at 450°F for 12–15 minutes.

BASIC DUMPLINGS

Use *Basic White Flour Biscuit Mix* for excellent dumplings. Drop 'em by spoonfuls into 2 quarts boiling water with 1 teaspoon salt. Or, add to boiling liquid in stews, soups, etc.

BASIC VEGGIE-FILLED BISCUITS

Basic White Flour Biscuit Mix
2 C. chopped celery
2 C. coarsely grated carrots
1 large onion, finely chopped

$^1/_2$ tsp. salt
2 T. margarine
$^1/_2$ tsp. melted margarine

Prepare *Basic White Flour Biscuit Mix*. In covered pan, cook celery, carrots, onion, salt, and margarine for 10 minutes, stirring occasionally. Roll *Mix* into a square or rectangle and cut in 5-inch squares. Fill each square with $^1/_3$ cup cooked vegetables. Fold up the corners to meet in the center and pinch edges together to seal. Place biscuits on greased baking sheet. Brush with melted margarine and bake at 400°F for 15 minutes or until lightly browned. *Yield: 9 to 12 biscuits.*

BASIC BEEF PIE

Basic White Flour Biscuit Mix
1 lb. lean ground beef
$^1/_2$ C. chopped onion
8 oz. tomato sauce

8 oz. sliced mushrooms
1 tsp. salt
$^1/_8$ tsp. garlic salt
1 tsp. chili powder

Prepare *Basic White Flour Biscuit Mix*. In separate pan or skillet, brown beef, then add onion and cook until tender. Add half of the tomato sauce and mushrooms; then add salt, garlic salt, and chili powder; heat until bubbly. While meat mix cooks, knead *Mix* 8–10 times on floured board. Divide dough in half. Roll out half the dough to fit a 9-inch pie pan.

Line pan, pour in hot filling. Roll out remaining dough and place over filling. Crimp edge; slit top. Bake at 425°F for 15–20 minutes or until done.

Heat remaining tomato sauce and mushrooms in saucepan. Serve sauce over wedges of beef pie. *Yield: 4–6 servings.*

BASIC PIZZA CRUST

2 T. active dry yeast
$3^1/_2$ C. flour
$^1/_4$ C. oil

pinch sugar
1 tsp. salt
$1^1/_4$ C. lukewarm water

Crust: mix all ingredients well. Knead until smooth and shiny. Let rise $1^1/_2$ hours.

Pizza: brush top side with olive oil. Spread tomato sauce or prepared pizza sauce to within $^1/_4$ inch of crust edge, cover with grated mozzarella cheese, then sprinkle parmesan cheese on top. Add any meats or vegetables of your choice. Bake at 425°F for 15–20 minutes.

BASIC FRENCH BREAD

2 T. active dry yeast
2$^1/_2$ C. warm water
2 T. shortening
3 tsp. salt

6–7 C. flour
cornmeal
1 egg white

Dissolve yeast in $^1/_2$ cup warm water. While yeast is rising, put shortening, salt, and remaining water into bowl and mix. Add yeast mixture. Gradually add flour to form stiff dough. Knead 5–10 minutes. Cover and let rise until double in bulk (about 1 hour).

Punch down and let rise again in bowl until double in bulk (about $^3/_4$ hour longer). Punch down again. Remove from bowl and form into loaves as follows: divide dough in two parts and roll each part into a rectangle about 10 x 14 inches. Roll dough jelly roll fashion to form a loaf about 14 inches long.

Slash top of bread and place on cookie sheets which have been sprinkled with cornmeal. Cover and let rise until double in bulk.

Bake at 400°F for 15 minutes and 350°F for about 45 minutes longer. Brush loaves with egg white while baking for a golden brown crust.

BASIC RAISIN BREAD

1 box raisins (6 oz.)
2 C. cold water
2 T. active dry yeast
$^1/_4$ C. warm water
2 T. butter or margarine
2 T. sugar
$^1/_8$ tsp. mace

1 tsp. salt
1 tsp. lemon extract
2 C. scalded milk
2 eggs, beaten
6 C. flour (approx.)
melted butter

Soak raisins 1 hour in 2 cups cold water. Drain well. Dissolve yeast in warm water. Put butter, sugar, spice, salt, and flavoring into a bowl. Pour scalded milk over all. When cooled to lukewarm, add eggs, yeast mixture, and raisins. Gradually, add flour, kneading to make a smooth ball. Cover and let rise until double in bulk. Punch down and form into two loaves.

Put into greased bread pans and let rise until double in bulk. Bake at 400°F for 15 minutes, then 350°F for 35 minutes longer. Remove from pans, brush with melted butter. Cool on racks.

BASIC SWEETROLL DOUGH MIX

2 T. (pkg.) active dry yeast
$^1/_2$ C. lukewarm water
$^1/_2$ C. scalded milk
$^1/_2$ C. sugar

1 tsp. salt
$^1/_2$ C. butter or margarine
4$^1/_2$–5$^1/_2$ C. flour
2 eggs, slightly beaten

Dissolve yeast in warm water. Put scalded milk, sugar, salt, and butter into separate bowl and mix. When cooled to lukewarm, add yeast. Add 1 cup flour and eggs. Slightly mix. Continue adding flour until a firm ball is formed. Cover and let rise until double in bulk. Punch down and let rise 1 hour. Punch down once again and turn out onto floured board and form as desired. Bake at 400°F for 25 minutes.

BASIC CINNAMON-NUT COFFEE CAKE

Basic Sweet Roll Dough Mix	2 tsp. cinnamon
1/3 C. flour	3 T. soft butter
1/3 C. sugar	1/4 C. chopped nuts

Prepare *Basic Sweet Roll Dough Mix*. After second rising of *Dough Mix*, roll 1/3 of it into circle to fit a 9-inch pan. Sprinkle top with mixture of flour, sugar, cinnamon, butter, and chopped nuts. Cover and let rise until double in bulk. Bake at 400°F for approximately 25 minutes. Serve warm. *Yield: 3 pans of 9-inch round cakes.*

BASIC HONEY TWIST

Basic Sweet Roll Dough Mix	1 egg white
1/4 C. butter, creamed	1 C. confectioners' sugar
2 T. honey	

After second rising of *Basic Sweet Roll Dough Mix*, roll into a long cylinder 1 inch in diameter. Coil into buttered 9-inch layer pan beginning at outer edge and covering the bottom. Cover and let rise until double in bulk. Bake at 375°F for 20–25 minutes.

While hot, spread with mixture of butter, honey, egg white, and sugar.

Chapter 11

Basic Triticale Flour Cookery

Triticale is a grain derived from crossing wheat and rye genetically and has been touted as an equal or better grain than wheat. As an alternative grain for in-home storage, triticale has good storage qualities. It is a larger kernel, or berry, than wheat, has a higher protein efficiency ratio (P.E.R.) than wheat, and a higher percentage of protein. Triticale flour also makes an excellent replacement for wheat pastry flour—and does not taste like rye at all! Gluten strands do not form as in whole-wheat batters; therefore, *wheat flour must be mixed in with any triticale bread recipe to make a high-rising bread.*

Since most cooks haven't developed recipes for triticale in their cookbooks, there are two cautions of which you should take note when substituting triticale in wheat recipes:

- *Triticale cannot be substituted measure-for-measure for wheat because it has lower elasticity.*

- *Substitution of triticale for wheat should not exceed $^1/_2$ the wheat flour required.*

The following recipes have been specially formulated for triticale flour.

RECIPES FOR BASIC TRITICALE BREADS, BISCUITS & MUFFINS

BASIC TRITIQUIX BREAD (2-HOUR BREAD RECIPE)

3 T. active dry yeast   6 T. safflower oil
5 C. lukewarm water $1/2$ C. honey
1 tsp. sugar   11 C. triticale flour
1 heaping T. salt   1 C. regular wheat flour

Mix dry yeast and $1/2$ cup warm water, sprinkle sugar on top, and stir. Mix salt, safflower oil, and honey into $41/2$ cups warm water, mix well, and stir in yeast mixture. Stir in 4 cups triticale flour and $1/2$ cup regular wheat flour, mixing well. Add 4 more cups triticale flour and $1/2$ cup regular wheat flour, mix well; add remaining triticale flour, mix well.

Knead well for about 5 minutes, place in pan, and let rise for $1/2$ hour.

Cut batter into four even parts and knead each several minutes. Place in greased loaf pans and let rise to level of rim for approximately 25 minutes. When bread is ready to bake, place in preheated 350°F oven for 45 minutes. Remove from oven, take bread from pans, and allow to cool. Brush tops of loaves with warm butter. *Yield: 4 medium loaves.*

> **Notes:**
>
> *Triticale cannot be substituted measure-for-measure for wheat because it has lower elasticity.*
>
> *Substitution of triticale in wheat flour recipes should not exceed $1/2$ the wheat flour required.*

BASIC BUTTERMILK BREAD

$21/2$ C. triticale flour $1/2$ C. raisins (optional)
1 tsp. salt $1/2$ C. molasses
$1/2$ C. cornmeal $1/2$ C. sour cream
$11/2$ tsp. baking soda $11/3$ C. buttermilk

Combine dry ingredients (flour, salt, cornmeal, soda) with raisins, if used. Mix molasses with sour cream and buttermilk. Combine the two mixtures.

Bake in greased bread pan 1 hour at 350°F.

BASIC CHERRYANA BREAD

$1/2$ C. shortening $1/2$ tsp. baking powder
1 C. sugar $1/4$ tsp. salt
3 eggs $1/3$ C. maraschino cherries
1 tsp. baking soda   1 C. banana pulp
$1/2$ C. chopped nuts   2 C. triticale flour

Cream shortening and sugar until light and fluffy. Add eggs one at a time and beat well after each addition. Dissolve soda in mashed bananas, add to creamed mixture. Add dry ingredients (baking powder, soda, salt). Fold in cherries that have been chopped and well drained, then stir in nuts. Pour into greased loaf pan and bake for 1 hour at 350°F.

Variation: replace cherries with chopped dried apricots for *Basic TritiCotana Bread.*

Basic TritiBiscuits

2 C. triticale flour	6 T. shortening
1½ tsp. salt	⅔ C. milk
4 tsp. baking powder	

Mix dry ingredients (flour, salt, baking powder); cut in lard or vegetable shortening with a wire pastry blender. Stir in milk, adding just enough to make a soft, light dough, stirring as little as possible. Drop from spoon onto a greased, floured baking sheet. Let stand 3 minutes, then bake at 375°F approximately 10 minutes. *Yield: 12–16 biscuits.*

Basic TritiBran Muffins

2 C. boiling water	4 beaten eggs
3 C. bran flakes (cereal)	3 C. triticale flour
1 qt. buttermilk	7 C. flour
1 C. shortening	5 tsp. baking soda
3 C. sugar	1 tsp. salt

Pour water over bran cereal, add buttermilk. Cream shortening and sugar; add eggs and mix well. Add mixture to cereal. Sift in flours, soda, salt. *Do not mix too long.* (Batter can be stored in the refrigerator and will keep approximately 3 weeks.) Spoon mixture into greased muffin pans, filling about ¾ full. Bake for 15–20 minutes at 350°F. *Yield: 4–5 dozen.*

Basic TritiCot Bran Muffins

boiling water	¾ tsp. salt
⅔ C. finely cut dried apricots	1 C. whole bran
2 T. sugar	¾ C. milk
1 C. triticale flour	1 egg, beaten
2½ tsp. baking powder	¼ C. salad oil
⅓ C. sugar	

Pour boiling water over apricots to cover, let stand 10 minutes. Drain well; mix with 2 tablespoons sugar. Sift together dry ingredients (flour, baking powder, sugar, salt). Mix bran, milk, egg, and oil; add to flour mixture, stirring just till moistened.

Gently stir in apricots, fill greased muffin pans ⅔ full. Sprinkle tops with additional sugar. Bake in 400°F oven about 25 minutes. *Yield: 1 dozen muffins.*

RECIPE FOR TRITICALE MAIN DISH

Basic TritiMeat Loaf

1 lb. ground beef	1 C. triticale flour
¼ tsp. oregano	½ tsp. dry mustard
1 tsp. sugar	1 T. Worcestershire sauce
¼ C. chopped onion	¼ C. green pepper, chopped
1½ C. tomato juice	1 egg

Mix all ingredients well. Place in loaf pan. Bake 350°F for 60 minutes. *Yield: 6–8 servings.*

RECIPES FOR TRITICALE DESSERTS

BASIC APPLECAKE

3 T. butter

1 C. sugar

1 egg, beaten

$1/2$ tsp. nutmeg

1 C. triticale flour

$1/2$ tsp. cinnamon

$1/2$ tsp. salt

1 tsp. baking soda

3 C. chopped apples

1 tsp. vanilla

$1/2$ C. chopped nuts

Cream butter and sugar; add egg and mix well. Sift dry ingredients (nutmeg, flour, cinnamon, salt, soda) together. Add to creamed mixture. Stir in chopped apples, vanilla, and nuts. Pour in greased 8 x 8-inch pan, bake in 350°F oven about 45 minutes. Serve warm with whipped cream or ice cream. *Yield: 10–12 servings.*

BASIC APPLESPICE CAKE

$1/3$ C. oil

1 C. sugar

1 egg

1 C. sweetened applesauce

$1^3/4$ C. triticale flour

1 tsp. baking soda

1 tsp. ground cloves

1 tsp. salt

1 tsp. cinnamon

1 C. raisins

1 C. currants

In a large bowl combine oil, sugar, and egg with electric mixer. Then beat in applesauce. Sift together dry ingredients (flour, soda, cloves, salt, cinnamon). Add flour mixture to the batter gradually, continuing to beat batter until smooth. Stir in raisins and currants. Transfer to greased and floured 9 x 13-inch cake pan. Bake in 350°F oven for 40 minutes.

BASIC GINGER QUIXBREAD

2 C. triticale flour

1 tsp. salt

1 C. molasses

$1/2$ C. sugar

4 T. melted shortening

$1^1/2$ tsp. baking soda

2 tsp. ginger

2 eggs

1 C. sour milk

Combine all ingredients and beat for 2 minutes. Bake 35–40 minutes at 350°F. Serve warm or cold, topped with whipping cream.

BASIC FRUITORTE

1 C. sugar

1 egg, beaten

1 can fruit cocktail, drained

1 C. triticale flour

$1/2$ tsp. salt

$3/4$ tsp. baking soda

4 T. brown sugar

$1/4$ C. chopped walnuts

Blend sugar and beaten egg; add the drained cocktail mix and the sifted dry ingredients (flour, salt, soda). Spread in square 9-inch pan. Mix the brown sugar and nuts and sprinkle on top. Bake at 325°F for 15 minutes, then reduce to 300°F and bake another 45 minutes. Serve with whipped cream or ice cream.

BASIC NO-CRUST APPLE PIE

8 C. apples, peeled, cored & cut
    in thin wedges
$1/_2$ C. sugar
1 tsp. cinnamon or nutmeg

$1/_2$ C. brown sugar
$1/_2$ C. triticale flour
$1/_4$ C. butter
pinch of salt

Toss together first three ingredients and put in shallow 2-quart baking dish. Mix remaining ingredients until crumbly. Sprinkle over apples and bake in preheated 400°F oven about 30 minutes. Serve with whipped cream or ice cream. *Yield: 6 servings.*

BASIC TRITIBROWNEES

4 squares unsweetened chocolate
$2/_3$ C. shortening
2 C. sugar
4 eggs
1 tsp. vanilla

1 tsp. baking powder
$11/_4$ C. triticale flour
1 C. nuts
1 tsp. salt

Heat oven to 350°F. Grease oblong pan, 13 x 9 x 2 inches. In large saucepan, melt chocolate and shortening over low heat. Remove from heat. Blend in sugar, eggs, and vanilla. Mix in remaining ingredients. Spread in prepared pan. Bake 30 minutes or until brownees pull away from sides of pan. Do not over bake. Cool slightly; cut into bars about 2 x $11/_2$ inches. *Yield: 24–32 brownees.*

BASIC PEANUTTY COOKEES

1 C. raw or brown sugar
$1/_2$ C. shortening
1 egg, well beaten
$1/_2$ C. peanut butter

2 T. evaporated milk or cream
$11/_2$ C. triticale flour
1 tsp. baking soda

Cream sugar and shortening, add egg and peanut butter. Add cream and dry ingredients (flour, soda). Form into small balls, about 1 inch in diameter. Place on greased cookie sheet and bake at 350°F. for 8–10 minutes.

BASIC CHOCOCHIP COOKEES

$11/_2$ C. sugar
$11/_2$ C. brown sugar (packed)
2 C. shortening
2 tsp. vanilla
1 tsp. water
4 eggs

6 C. triticale flour
2 tsp. baking soda
1 tsp. salt
12 oz. pkg. chocolate chips
1 C. chopped nuts

Cream together sugars, shortening, vanilla, water, and eggs. Add dry ingredients (flour, soda, salt, chocolate chips, and nuts), mixing thoroughly. Spoon onto greased cookie sheet. Bake 375°F for 10–12 minutes or until golden brown.

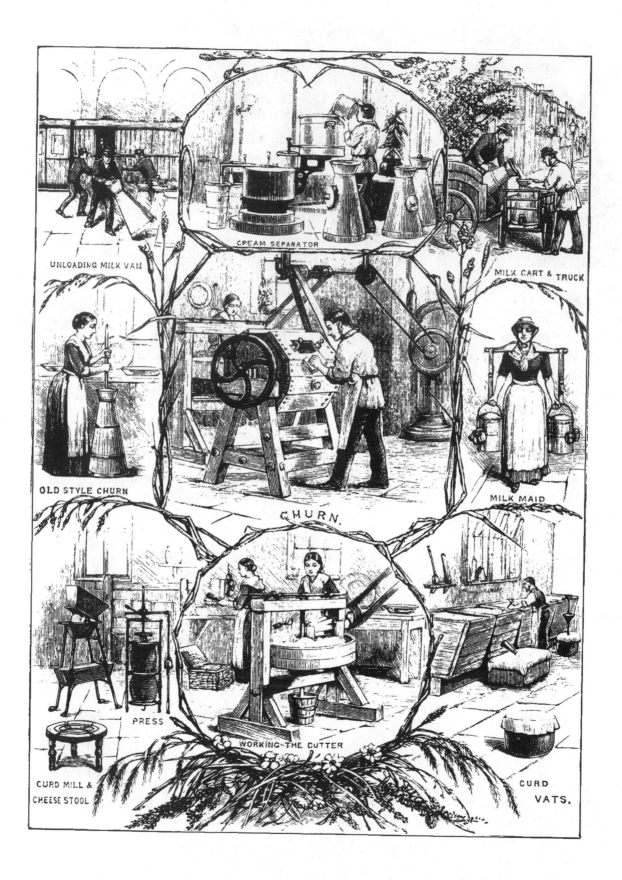

CREAM SEPARATOR

UNLOADING MILK VAN

MILK CART & TRUCK

OLD STYLE CHURN

CHURN.

MILK MAID

PRESS

WORKING THE BUTTER

CURD MILL &
CHEESE STOOL

CURD
VATS.

Chapter 12

Basic Dairy Products from Powdered Milk

Few foods are as valuable as milk and milk products. For food storage purposes, powdered milk is a versatile milk derivative with numerous applications. Most dairy products can be made from rehydrated powdered milk: cottage cheese, yogurt, cream cheese and even hard cheeses. For those who really want to get into cheesemaking, you can even try homemade farmer, cheddar, or European-style cheeses. This chapter provides instructions for making these basic dairy products and has additional main meal recipes for use with your stored powdered milk.

POWDERED MILK NUTRITION

Dry powdered milk, whether whole or skim (nonfat), provides many of the USRDA (United States Recommended Daily Allowance) minerals and vitamins—most notably calcium. Realize, however, that rehydrated dry milk is not the equivalent of raw milk. The heating, pasteurizing, and drying processes destroy not only the bacteria but also some of the essential enzymes. Therefore, if you use powdered milk exclusively for an extended period of time, you should supplement your diet with an appropriate selection of vitamins and minerals your body needs. (See **Chapter 14, Basic Self-Health with Supplementation** for more details.)

Within several months after processing, all processed foods, including powdered milk, begin to lose nutritional value. The nutritional shelf life of powdered milk is relatively short when compared to its useful shelf life. Powdered milk can still be utilized in recipes and will act acceptably as an ingredient even when no longer nutritious. Since that's true for virtually all stored foods, two things become evident: the need for a nutritional supplement program and rotation through utilization.

PURCHASING POWDERED MILK

Use the following guidelines in purchasing powdered milk for your home storage program:

- non-instant, nonfat powdered milk (made from skim milk)
- less than 4% moisture
- "extra" grade, low-heat, spray-processed
- no artificial color, flavor, or preservatives added
- fortified with vitamins A and D

It is important to select the best quality product for storage because it will be more nutritious and actually store longer. The best grade is labeled "extra" and should contain no more than 4% moisture. Low moisture content is very important, as the moisture factor determines the period of time powdered milk may be stored and still remain nutritious.

Be aware that some brands of dry milk are made from *grade B* milk sources. That is one reason they are cheaper than the "extra" grade powdered milk. "Instantized" powdered milk has been processed further than non-instant and therefore has a shorter shelf life.

When buying powdered milk for storage, check quality, age, moisture content, warranty provisions, and whether the product is being sold by reputable persons and companies. Always check expiration dates when buying at all grocery, retail, or health food stores.

POWDERED MILK STORAGE

The "extra" grade dry skim milk should be purchased in double-sealed 5-pound cans or in double-wrapped, foil-lined and paper- or mylar-reinforced bags. This higher-grade powdered milk will store for up to 60 months if kept dry and cold (40°F).

Storage at temperatures of 60°–70°F will reduce effective (nutritional) storage time to 12–24 months. However, it is possible to use it in recipes and benefit from the stored milk.

REHYDRATING POWDERED MILK

There are many brands of powdered skim milk on the market. Each brand has instructions on the package indicating how much water and milk powder to use for rehydration.

The following recipe is a general guideline for rehydration—don't be afraid to experiment with quantities to formulate the best mixture for your own palate. Improve the flavor of powdered milk by mixing it half-and-half with whole milk. Add honey, nondairy creamers, fruit juices, sugar, powdered sugar, vanilla flavoring, or any flavoring of choice the family likes to improve the somewhat flat taste of rehydrated dry milk.

RECIPES FOR BASIC POWDERED MILK

BASIC REHYDRATED POWDERED MILK

4 C. cold water $1^2/_3$ C. powdered milk

Beat ingredients with beater or mixer until smooth. *Yield: 1 quart milk.*

BASIC VITALITY COOLER

1 C. *Basic Rehydrated Milk* 2 C. water
$1/_2$ C. sugar (or honey) ice
6 oz. frozen orange juice concentrate

Put milk, sugar, and orange juice in blender; blend until mixed. Add water and ice, blending until mushy. Serve with snacks or for breakfast. May be thinned with additional water and ice, then sweetened to taste. *Yield: approximately 1 quart.*

BASIC SOFT ICE CREAM

1 C. non-instant dry milk 3 T. honey
3 C. water

Mix in blender, put in shallow tray and freeze until solid. To serve, break into small chunks and stir with whip or beat with mixer at slow speed until soft. Serve with chocolate syrup, jams, jellies, or other flavorings.

BASIC YOGURT FROM POWDERED MILK

Yogurt is a very flexible food—it can be a drink when thinned with milk, buttermilk, fruit juice, or water; mixed with fruit for a dessert; set in Jell-O®; or used in place of sour cream in stroganoff, sauces, chip dips, and fruit salads. *Basic Yogurt* is a tasty, healthful food with all the advantages of milk. However, it is lower in lactose for those who don't tolerate milk products. It has proven helpful to children and adults with diarrhea. Yogurt is a great way to vary the daily diet and adds a gourmet touch to many recipes.

In-Home Basic Yogurt Production

Yogurt is a cultured milk product made from enriched milk to which a yogurt culture, or *starter,* has been added. The milk must be concentrated from one-half to two-thirds of its original volume. Since powdered milk is already concentrated, it is particularly easy to use in making *Basic Yogurt* at home.

Basic Yogurt is very simple to make. All that is required is some warm water, powdered milk, and a little yogurt starter—which is available in the grocery store! The milk with yogurt culture added is kept at a temperature of 100°–120°F for approximately 3–4 hours. When the *Basic Yogurt* sets up, it can be eaten immediately while warm or refrigerated for later consumption when it's cold. Remember to save a little bit of the *Basic Yogurt* as the starter for the next batch, and you are literally set for life!

To maximize storage of fresh-made *Basic Yogurt,* chill immediately when set-up occurs. *Basic Yogurt* may be stored in refrigerator up to one week. (Then you make it into cheese!)

In France and Switzerland, I knew families who had inherited yogurt starter from their grandparents.

Suggestions for Making Basic Yogurt Successfully

Ingredients

The most important advice relative to ingredients for *Basic Yogurt* are
  • Use the best grade powdered milk available.
  • Procure a yogurt starter from a reliable source.

Rehydrating powdered milk: when using any powdered milk, whether instant or non-instant, *rehydrate it just a little short of being double in strength.*

Yogurt starter: in *Basic Yogurt* recipes, use unflavored commercial yogurt for the starter or use yogurt from the last batch (it shouldn't be more than a week old). Pure yogurt culture can be obtained from health food stores. Most authorities recommend a fresh start every month or two if you are not using it at least weekly. Use 2 tablespoons yogurt starter for every 3 cups of doubly-rehydrated milk. Using this rule of thumb, make as much or as little *Basic Yogurt* desired.

Temperature

The lower the set-up temperature, the longer *Basic Yogurt* takes to set. Temperatures of 110F°–120°F will produce firm yogurt in approximately three hours. There are several methods for keeping the *Basic Yogurt* mixture at the correct temperature. Perhaps the easiest way to maintain the proper temperature is to buy a commercial yogurt maker, available at most grocery, retail, and health food stores. Alternatively, the yogurt mixture can be placed over a heat register, pilot light, or hot plate—we've even used a heating pad! In using any of these methods, test the temperature by setting a covered pan of warm water over the heat source for several hours, checking the temperature periodically to assure maintenance of temperature in the 110°–120°F range.

Storage

Yogurt will keep in the refrigerator for a week or longer. However, *the longer yogurt sits in the refrigerator the more pronounced the flavor becomes.* Make a batch of yogurt at least once a week to keep the starter fresh.

RECIPES FOR MAKING BASIC YOGURT

The recipes on the following pages will get you started with in-home production of yogurt, utilizing either powdered, commercial, or whole milk. The best part about home-made *Basic Yogurt* is that the flavor can be varied from very mild to quite strong. Customize *Basic Yogurt* to your individual taste as you experiment with homemade products. This is a distinct advantage over buying commercial yogurt, and it's cheaper than store-bought, too. Should a batch fail to set up, there is a section later in this chapter titled **"If Yogurt Fails" Check-List** to help resolve *Basic Yogurt* production problems.

BASIC YOGURT FROM POWDERED MILK

2 C. warm water	2 T. yogurt starter (unflavored)
1 C. non-instant powdered milk	

Pour warm water (100°F) in the blender and turn on low speed; add powdered milk slowly. Blend until smooth. Add yogurt and blend a few more seconds. (This whole process can be done by hand, but be sure to beat until all the lumps are out.) Pour into jars or glasses. Place jars neck-deep in a pan in warm (100°F) water. Cover pan with lid.

Place on yogurt maker (or any place a temperature of 100°–200°F can be maintained) for 3–4 hours. Check after 3 hours to see if *Basic Yogurt* mixture has set up. If not set up, check each 20 minutes until set. *(If not set up in 4 hours, you probably have a failure.)*

BASIC YOGURT FROM FRESH MILK

4 C. fresh raw milk   2 T. yogurt starter (unflavored)
$^1/_2$ C. non-instant powdered milk

Boil (180°F) fresh, raw milk in a saucepan for five seconds. Cool until warm (100°F). Stir in powdered milk. Thoroughly mix yogurt starter with a little warm milk in a small bowl, then add to the rest of the warm milk, stirring in well. Pour mixture into jars or glasses and let stand neck-deep in yogurt maker at 110°F until set (usually about 3 hours). Chill immediately after yogurt sets. Keeps in refrigerator approximately one week.

> **Note:**
> *At first you might forget to use yogurt freely, but in time you'll find uses for it every day. And remember, if at first you don't succeed in getting the family to use yogurt readily, keep trying. It's certainly worth the effort.*

"If Basic Yogurt Fails" Checklist

If yogurt doesn't set up properly, check the following indicators to ascertain what may have caused the failure:

- ❏ Yogurt was disturbed or stirred while setting up.
- ❏ The start was added to hot instead of warm milk.
- ❏ Temperature was too hot (kills yogurt bacteria) or too cool (causes ordinary sour milk bacteria to develop).
- ❏ Yogurt start was too old or was inactive for some other reason.
- ❏ Jars or other equipment were not clean.
- ❏ Fresh, raw milk was not boiled.
- ❏ Yogurt was in yogurt maker too long (indicated when yogurt is bubbly and starts to separate).

Constructing a Basic Yogurt Maker

If you are truly converted to in-home yogurt production, you can make your own yogurt maker for a few nickels and dimes. On the following page is **Illustration 12–1**, detailing how to make the *Basic Yogurt Maker* from a #10 can, a light socket, and a light bulb:

- Completely remove one end of the can.
- Punch a hole in the remaining end of the can.
- Secure the lamp socket.
- Punch holes in the base and top to provide a draft to heat the pan of water.
- Vary the wattage of the light bulb and its distance from the bottom of the pan to stabilize temperature between 110°–120°F. Generally, 25W to 50W bulbs will maintain the proper temperature. An in-line dimmer provides additional heat control.

Illustration 12–2 shows how to use the *Basic Yogurt Maker*.

Illustration 12–1

Basic Yogurt Maker

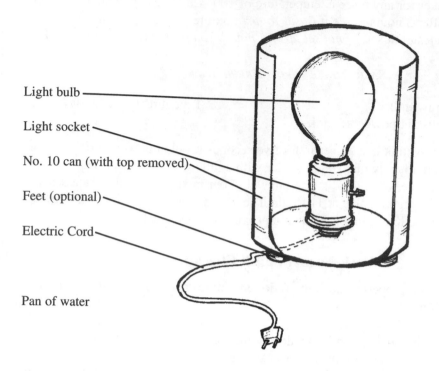

Light bulb

Light socket

No. 10 can (with top removed)

Feet (optional)

Electric Cord

Pan of water

Illustration 12–2

Using the *Basic Yogurt Maker*

Jars in water

RECIPES FOR BASIC YOGURT

FLAVORED BASIC YOGURT

Use jams, honey and vanilla, maple syrup, molasses, etc., for flavoring *Basic Yogurt*. Flavorings should always be added after the yogurt is set.

> When adding any flavoring to yogurt, stir lightly; the more yogurt is stirred, the thinner it becomes.

BASIC YOGURT FLIP

Basic Yogurt   Fruit juice

Mix small amount of *Basic Yogurt* in fruit juice of choice. With each successive serving, increase yogurt, gradually working up to more yogurt than juice.

BASIC FRUIT YOGURT

Use fresh, canned, dried, or strained fruit to flavor plain *Basic Yogurt*.

> These recipes will help reluctant children learn to like yogurt.

BASIC YOGURT POPSICLE

2 C. *Basic Yogurt*   6 oz. frozen orange juice
2 tsp. vanilla

Mix ingredients together until smooth. Pour into Popsicle molds or paper cups and insert ice cream sticks. Freeze until firm.

BASIC YOGURT PARFAIT

1 C. *Basic Yogurt*   1 C. fruit

Cover bottom of dessert dish with fruit, then add layer of *Basic Yogurt*. Repeat layers, topping with fruit. Chill and serve.

BASIC YOGURT BUTTERMILK

1 C. *Basic Yogurt*   1 C. water

Mix equal parts *Basic Yogurt* and water in blender. *Basic Yogurt* mixed in this manner will replace buttermilk in most recipes. Makes a good drink, too!

BASIC YOGURT JELL-O

Jell-O®, partially set   1 C. *Basic Yogurt*

When mixing Jell-O®, leave out 1/4 cup water. Add 1 cup *Basic Yogurt* to partially set Jell-O®. Fruit may be added. Lemon-lime and orange Jell-O® are especially good with yogurt added.

BASIC YOGURT CREAM SAUCE

Warm (115°–120°F) *Basic Yogurt* and use as a cream sauce on vegetables or in stroganoff recipes. *Do not heat Basic Yogurt above 120°F.* Heat will kill the yogurt bacteria that are beneficial to good health.

BASIC YOGURT SOUR CREAM

Basic Yogurt can be used to replace commercial sour cream in most recipes. Use plain, or add chives, bacon bits, onion flakes, onion or garlic salt, seasoning salt, or ground pepper to flavor *Basic Yogurt*. Use as a base for chip dips or gourmet dressings by adding herbs and spices.

BASIC YOGURT AVOCADO DIP

½ C. *Basic Yogurt*	garlic powder
1 large avocado	salt to taste
3 T. lemon juice	

Mash avocado, add lemon juice and seasonings; add *Basic Yogurt* and beat well. Serve with fresh crisp vegetables. (Cauliflower, carrots, turnips, celery, green peppers, jicama, broccoli, etc., are excellent.)

BASIC YOGURT HEALTH DIP

2 C. unflavored *Basic Yogurt*	½ tsp. celery salt
2 C. skim milk cottage cheese	garlic powder
¼ tsp. garlic powder	salt
¼ C. toasted sesame seeds	¼ C. wheat germ

In a medium bowl blend *Basic Yogurt* and cottage cheese thoroughly. Sprinkle in sesame seeds, wheat germ, celery salt, and garlic powder. Blend well. Salt to taste. Chill. *Yield: 4 cups.*

Serve as a dip accompanied by vegetable relishes or crisp crackers.

Vegetable relishes: Raw cauliflowerettes, carrot and celery sticks, jicama, sliced cucumber, and green, red, and sweet pepper chunks.

BASIC YOGURT ROQUEFORT DRESSING

1 C. *Basic Yogurt*	ground pepper
½ C. cottage cheese, fine curd	garlic salt
4 oz. Roquefort cheese	

Mix *Basic Yogurt* and cottage cheese, adding crumbled cheese. Season to taste, then chill to allow seasonings to mingle. Serve cold. (See *Basic Cottage Cheese* information in the following section for directions for your own homemade cottage cheese!)

BASIC YOGURT & HONEY DRESSING

dash salt	1 T. sugar
dash pepper	2 T. honey
dash dry mustard	1 C. *Basic Yogurt*
1 T. lemon juice	

Blend salt, pepper, dry mustard, and sugar into a bowl with honey. Add *Basic Yogurt*, stirring lightly. Then gently stir in lemon juice. Goes well with crisp salads, grilled chicken and turkey strips, and any of the popular salad greens.

Basic Yogurt Green Goddess Dressing

soft, ripe avocado
1 C. *Basic Yogurt*
1 T. parsley flakes
2 tsp. instant minced onion

$\frac{1}{2}$ tsp. salt
$\frac{1}{2}$ tsp. seasoned salt
$\frac{1}{4}$ C. mayonnaise

Put all ingredients into mixing bowl. Blend ingredients with wire whip. Mix thoroughly. *Yield: approximately 2 cups.*

Basic Yogurt Beef Stroganoff

1 lb. ground beef
5 slices of bacon, diced
$\frac{1}{2}$ C. chopped onion
$\frac{1}{2}$ tsp. salt
1 #303 can cream of mushroom soup
hot buttered noodles of choice

dash of pepper
$\frac{1}{2}$ tsp. sweet basil
1 tsp. garlic salt
$\frac{1}{4}$ tsp. paprika
1 C. *Basic Yogurt*

In skillet, brown ground beef with bacon. Add onion and cook until tender but not brown. Drain off excess fat. Add salt, basil, paprika, garlic, and pepper. Stir in cream of mushroom soup and cook slowly, uncovered, 20 minutes, stirring frequently. Stir in *Basic Yogurt*. Keep hot, but *do not boil*. Serve meat sauce over hot buttered noodles. *Yield: 4–6 servings.*

Basic Yogurt Wheat Germ Rolls

1 C. warm *Basic Yogurt*
1 envelope active dry yeast
$\frac{1}{4}$ C. butter or margarine
$1\frac{1}{2}$ tsp. salt
3 T. blackstrap molasses

1 egg
$\frac{3}{4}$ C. wheat germ
$2\frac{1}{2}$ C. whole-wheat flour
$\frac{1}{3}$ C. powdered milk

Before preparing other ingredients, stir dry yeast into *Basic Yogurt*. Add butter, salt, egg, molasses, and wheat germ and stir briskly. Sift in flour and powdered milk. Stir until all ingredients are combined, then beat 200 strokes (10 minutes in electric mixer). Cover bowl and set in warm place until double (about 1 hour). Make into rolls at once or stir and chill in refrigerator 1–8 hours before using. Bake at 350°F for 20 minutes. *Yield: 20 2-inch rolls.*

Basic Yogurt Rye Bread

1 envelope active dry yeast
2 C. warm water
2 T. honey
1 C. plain *Basic Yogurt*

2 tsp. salt
$1\frac{1}{2}$ C. rye flour
7–9 C. whole-wheat flour

In a large mixing bowl combine the yeast and water and allow the yeast to dissolve (takes about 5 minutes). Stir in the honey, yogurt, salt, and rye flour. Slowly add wheat flour until the dough pulls away from the sides of the bowl. Turn dough onto a floured breadboard and knead until it feels smooth and elastic, about 5–7 minutes. Divide the dough into 2 equal parts; shape and place in greased 9 x 5 x 3-inch pans. Cover with a clean dishtowel and set in a warm place (85°F) to rise. Preheat oven to 350°F. Bake for 45–50 minutes or until done. *Yield: 2 loaves.*

Basic Yogurt Cream Cheeses

Basic Yogurt Cream Cheese

Simply pour *Basic Yogurt* into a cheese bag and let drain for an hour or two. A thicker consistency than ordinary yogurt is obtained by draining off the excess water. This drained yogurt can be used in recipes for dips, spreads, sauces, and dressings. This is perhaps the simplest cream cheese method. The result is tangy and delicious.

Alternate Method for Basic Yogurt Cream Cheese

Dump a cup of *Basic Yogurt* into a piece of sheeting or fine cheesecloth and hang it above the sink to drain overnight. The following morning there will be a white ball of the most tender, creamiest cream cheese with no fat. To give this cheese more flavor, season with salt and a little brown sugar. Make a delicious sandwich spread by mixing chopped olives or nuts into cheese. Let your imagination run a little wild!

Sharp Basic Yogurt Cream Cheese

For sharper cream cheese, use *Basic Yogurt* that has aged in the refrigerator for several days. Add some kelp powder or salt to taste. Mix with either minced green onions, chives, caraway seeds, pimentos, olives, or crushed pineapple to make tantalizing spreads and sandwich fillings.

Ricotta Basic Yogurt Cream Cheese

Squeeze *Basic Yogurt* until whey (liquid) is expelled, and the result is a cheese much like ricotta. It can be used as cream cheese in most creamed cheese recipes—try these recipes made with *Basic Yogurt Cream Cheese:*

BASIC YOGURT LEMON CREAM CHEESECAKE

Filling:
- 12 oz. *Basic Yogurt Cream Cheese*
- 2 eggs, beaten
- $1/_2$ C. lemon juice
- $1/_2$ C. sugar

Vanilla Wafer Crust:
- 1 C. vanilla wafer crumbs
- 1 T. sugar
- 2 T. melted butter or margarine
- pinch salt

Topping:
- 1 C. sour cream
- 1 T. grated lemon rind
- 1 T. sugar

Filling: blend *Basic Yogurt Cream Cheese* and lemon juice thoroughly. Add eggs and sugar and beat until smooth. Pour into vanilla wafer crust. Bake at 350°F for 15–20 minutes or until firm. Remove from oven and cool 5 minutes.

Crust: mix ingredients until butter is absorbed; place crumbs in round 9-inch baking pan and spread in even layer.

Topping: mix topping ingredients and pour over pie filling. Bake 10 minutes longer. Cool. Chill in refrigerator 5 hours before serving. *Yield: 6 to 8 servings.*

BASIC YOGURT BLEU CREAM CHEESE DRESSING

¹/₂ –1 C. buttermilk	1 T. chives
1 C. *Basic Yogurt Cream Cheese*	1 T. Worcestershire sauce
4 oz. bleu cheese, crumbled	

Put ¹/₂ cup buttermilk and all other ingredients in bowl. Mix well, adding more buttermilk until desired consistency is attained. Chill in refrigerator. Serve cold with vegetable slices or strips. *Yield: approximately 2 cups.*

BASIC COTTAGE CHEESE FROM POWDERED MILK

Cottage cheese is made commercially from skim milk, rehydrated concentrated skim milk, or nonfat dry milk solids. The only reason it's not made from whole milk is the cost. However, you can make cottage cheese at home from any type of milk available.

Cottage cheese is full of body-building protein and calcium, but low in butterfat. This makes it filling without the attendant high-calorie intake problems. Cottage cheese makes food taste rich and fattening—without being either.

Cottage cheese is generally interchangeable with yogurt in most recipes and "softens" the taste of the recipe.

BASIC COTTAGE CHEESE

To make your own delicious and nutritious *Basic Cottage Cheese*, use the easy directions which follow. This recipe utilizes rennet or Junket tablets to help produce low-acid cottage cheese with minimal effort:

1 rennet tablet (or Junket tablet)	1 pt. buttermilk or *Basic Yogurt*
1 gal. *Basic Rehydrated Powdered Milk*	

❏ Dissolve rennet tablet in warm water.

❏ Pour *Basic Rehydrated Powdered Milk* into a large heavy pot and heat to 90°F.

❏ Add buttermilk or *Basic Yogurt*, stirring to mix. Then add dissolved rennet. Cover pot and leave overnight in a warm place.

❏ Next day, a gelatinous, almost solid mass, like firm yogurt, has formed in the pot. This is the curd. With a silver knife cut through this curd to break it into small pieces.

❏ Set the bowl with the curd into a pan of warm water and bring the curd up to 110°F. Shake the bowl gently while it is being heated to help distribute the heat more evenly throughout the curd.

❏ When the curd temperature reaches 110°F, turn off the heat, leaving the cheese bowl in the water for about 30 minutes. Then pour the cheese into a cloth bag or several layers of cheesecloth and hang it up to drain.

❏ When the curds have drained, mash the cheese with a fork, work in a little sweet or sour cream if you used skim milk, or moisten it with a little *Basic Yogurt* if you don't want the extra fat. You now have a delicious *Basic Cottage Cheese*!

Seasoning alternatives: season *Basic Cottage Cheese* with a little (or lots!) kelp, salt, caraway seeds, chopped chives, dill, or parsley to vary the flavor and taste.

Alternate Basic Cream Cheese method: put *Basic Cottage Cheese* in a blender, chop for a few seconds, and it makes a delicious cream cheese—with or without seasonings.

RECIPES FOR BASIC COTTAGE CHEESE

BASIC COTTAGE CHEESE CORNBREAD

1 C. cornmeal (yellow or white)	1 tsp. salt
$1/2$ C. skim milk	1 tsp. baking powder
$1/2$ C. *Basic Cottage Cheese,* creamed	$1/2$ tsp. baking soda
1 egg	1 T. sugar

Stir together well all ingredients and spoon into an 8-inch square greased cake pan. Bake in preheated 425°F oven for 20–25 minutes. Cut into squares.

BASIC COTTAGE CHEESE CLAM DIP

1 C. *Basic Cottage Cheese*	1 T. grated onion
1 tsp. lemon juice	dash of garlic salt
$3/4$ tsp. horseradish	paprika
1 can ($7^1/2$ oz.) minced clams, drained	parsley
1 T. cream	

Combine *Basic Cottage Cheese*, lemon juice, horseradish, clams, cream, onion, and garlic salt. Mix well; whip. Pour into serving bowl, sprinkle with paprika. Garnish with parsley.

BASIC COTTAGE CHEESE CORNCAKES

$1/2$ C. flour	$1/2$ tsp. baking soda
$1/2$ C. cornmeal	1 egg
1 tsp. baking powder	1 tsp. salt
$1/2$ C. *Basic Cottage Cheese,* creamed	$3/4$ C. water

Stir all ingredients together; add more water if needed. Use a Teflon®-coated fry pan or griddle for cooking. Preheat griddle until a drop of water "dances."

Pour batter to make 4-inch diameter hot cakes. Turn with a spatula when bubbly. Serve with syrup, jam, or powdered sugar topping. *Yield: 10–12 hotcakes.*

BASIC CHEESE FROM POWDERED MILK

Heating milk and adding rennet, an enzyme found in the stomach of suckling calves, is virtually all that is required to produce cheese. The heat and enzyme application result in the milk's separation into a liquid portion, the whey, and a solid portion, the curd. The milk "curdles" when the lactic acid level is raised.

This section describes how to make *Basic Cheese* from powdered milk in 25 simple steps. This *Basic Cheese Making* method utilizes buttermilk to achieve the higher acid level required to produce cheese. Heat is applied to cause coagulation. The coagulate is cut into small pieces, causing the curd to separate from the whey. The heat is then raised to cook the curd. This process, called *cheddaring*, reduces the curd to a consistency which allows for compression into familiar balls or blocks of cheese.

If you're stumped for ways to get highly nutritional foods into the family's diet, try the following recipes using BASIC COTTAGE CHEESE. Substitute BASIC COTTAGE CHEESE for BASIC YOGURT in any of the recipes prior to this section.

Basic Cheese Making Requirements

Equipment

This equipment is necessary to make *Basic Cheese* with powdered milk:

❏ 4-quart pan (for 1 batch)   ❏ thin spatula or long knife
❏ cheesecloth, fine mesh   ❏ thermometer, dairy
❏ large strainer or colander   ❏ press for cheese
❏ clock for timing   ❏ wooden spoon for stirring
❏ plastic wrap

Temperature control is critical in *Basic Cheese Making*. This *Basic Cheese* method requires a thermometer—be sure to have one. Accurate temperature control can be enhanced by using a double boiler. If you don't have a large double boiler, place the pan with the milk mixture in a cake or biscuit pan partially filled with water. You may have difficulty finding a cheese press, but you can make a *Basic Cheese Press* by assembling the parts detailed in **Illustration 12–3**.

Ingredients

These ingredients are necessary to make one batch of *Basic Cheese:*

❏ 1 gal. milk   ❏ 1 rennet tablet
❏ 3 T. buttermilk   ❏ 3 tsp. salt
❏ 6–12 drops yellow coloring (optional)

Nonfat dried, regular homogenized, or fresh raw milk may be used. However, when using powdered milk, you must add 1 cup whipping cream to bring the butterfat content to the required level. Also, nonfat dried milk coagulates faster when mixed several days before using in the *Basic Cheese Making* process. Keep it refrigerated until ready to use.

Coagulation times differ, based on which type milk is used. Homogenized and fresh raw milk coagulate in approximately 30 minutes. Nonfat dried milk may take up to 3–4 times longer and must be kept at 88°–90°F during the coagulation period.

Directions for Basic Cheese Making

Check off the steps as they are completed, and it should be simple to make some of the best cheese you've ever tasted! Season, color, and shape cheese to your personal taste.

❏ 1. Pour 1 gallon of milk into the 4-quart pan.

❏ 2. Add and stir in 3 tablespoons. buttermilk.

❏ 3. Cover and leave at room temperature at least 4 hours. Mixture can safely remain at room temperature as long as 12 hours. *Keep out of direct sunlight.*

❏ 4. Place pan of prepared milk mixture over low to medium heat. Slowly raise the temperature of the mixture to 86°F.

❏ 5. Add coloring to obtain desired tint. *(This coloring is optional—if you desire white cheese, omit this step.)*

❏ 6. Place rennet tablet in 2 tablespoons cold water. Dissolve by stirring. (Hot water will destroy the rennet's enzymatic action.)

❏ 7. Raise the temperature of the milk mixture to 88°–90°F.

❏ 8. While stirring mixture, add the rennet solution. Continue stirring 1–2 minutes.

❏ 9. Cover the pan, remove from heat, and allow to stand undisturbed for at least 30 minutes. (If you use nonfat dried milk in this recipe, you must leave the mixture on the heat, maintaining 88°–90°F, to facilitate coagulation.)

❏ 10. When coagulation is completed, use the thin spatula to cut curd to bottom of pan in parallel lines approximately $1/2$ inch apart.

❏ 11. Turn pan 90° and repeat cutting of parallel lines, forming $1/2$-inch squares.

❏ 12. Turn pan 45° and cut diagonally through the curd, intersecting the cuts previously made.

❏ 13. Turn pan 90° and repeat cutting procedure.

> *Cooking is complete when the curd holds its shape and readily falls apart on your hand without squeezing. The curd will look like scrambled eggs. Curd will be about the size of small-curd cottage cheese.*

❏ 14. Stir the curd gently with your hand, using long slow movements around and up through the curd. Stir and sift the curd by hand for 15 minutes. Carefully cut up any larger pieces that come up from the bottom, but do not squeeze the curd. You will see and feel the curd begin to separate from the whey. The curd will begin to shrink in size. Stirring keeps the curd from sticking together too soon in the cheese making process.

❏ 15. To cook the curd, slowly apply heat over a 20–30 minutes. period to raise the temperature of the developing curds and whey to 102°F. Hold at 102°F for another 30–40 minutes. Continue to gently stir with a spoon every 3–5 minutes.

❏ 16. To firm the curd, remove from heat and let the curds and whey stand for 1 hour, stirring every 5–10 minutes.

❏ 17. To drain the curd, line a large strainer with a doubled piece of cheesecloth. Pour curds and whey into the cheesecloth. Thoroughly drain off the whey.

❏ 18. Flavor the cheese by sprinkling salt over the curd.

❏ 19. Wrap the cheesecloth around the curd, making a ball. Squeeze out as much whey as possible and drain for 10 minutes over bowl or sink.

❏ 20. Put ball of cheese into cheese press, pressing firmly. Apply pressure until curds begin to show through drain holes.

❏ 21. Increase pressure about every 5 minutes for the next 30 minutes. The harder the cheese is pressed, the firmer it will be when removed from the press.

❏ 22. Remove cheesecloth and allow cheese to remain at room temperature until the surface is dry. Drying usually takes 4–8 hours.

> **Note:**
>
> *Wrapping the fresh cheese is necessary to prevent drying out or bacterial and odor contamination. Wrapping will prevent mold from forming for a considerable length of time.*

❏ 23. Cheese is ready to eat or store. The "green" cheese is rather bland and approximates pot cheese in consistency. Cheese spreads can be made at this point.

❏ 24. To "age" the cheese, wrap the cheese tightly in plastic wrap. Be sure to mark the production date on wrapper.

❏ 25. Store cheese in the crisper section of the refrigerator at 35°–40°F. The flavor will strengthen as the cheese ages. *Yield: 1–2 pounds, depending on butterfat content of milk ingredients.*

How to Vary Basic Cheese Flavor

Once you've acquired the knack for making *Basic Cheese*, the challenge and thrill of flavor variation lies ahead. The fun begins as you learn to make creative changes to achieve the taste and consistency you want. Sometimes, even minor variations will produce rather significant results in flavor, texture, moistness, and consistency.

The following paragraphs detail how the *Basic Cheese Making* method may be altered to produce different kinds of cheeses. Basically, flavor and appearance variations result from variations in two general areas—ingredients and techniques.

Ingredient Variations

The resulting taste will depend on the ingredients and the mixture of these variables:

Milk base: one of the first ways to change the end result is by changing the milk base. Milk base for cheese comes from fresh raw milk, regular milk, 2% milk, evaporated milk, powdered milk, cream, or even goat's milk. By combining any two or more of the milk base possibilities, there will be a resultant taste difference in the final product.

Starter: there are two starters for *Basic Cheese Making,* either buttermilk or yogurt. By increasing the percent of starter, or by combining them, there will be some change in the coagulation time and also the final taste.

Seasoning: perhaps the most startling taste differences may be achieved by adding salt, herbs, spices, and molding agents to the *Basic Cheese* method. Salt, onion and garlic salt, seasoning salt, parsley, chives, caraway or sesame seeds, hot pepper, olives, pimento, or Roquefort, bleu, or other cheese molds heighten flavor and give each cheese "personality." The flavor determines the range of each cheese's use.

Coloration: even though coloring will not generally affect the final taste, it will heighten the visual appeal of the final product.

Technique Variations

If any one or a combination of these is varied, a different consistency will result:

Curd development: consistency and compression of the final cheese product is determined by

   •how the reduction of the gelatinous curd is handled
   •temperature level of the curd while cooking
   •amount of time the curd cooks

Pressure: the amount of pressure applied while the cheese is in the press determines whether a cheese will be moist or dry, soft or hard. Again, these variables, in tandem with other technique variations, will produce different results, depending on the combination used.

Aging: the "tang" or "bite" of a cheese may be enhanced by longer aging periods. The molds which create the strong-flavored cheeses require weeks to expand throughout the cheese. Storage temperature of aging cheese will determine the "curing time" of cheese. The higher the temperature, the faster the cheese ages. However, the cheese will sour or spoil in temperatures in excess of 50°F. As in all other phases of cheese production, you decide what you like—then produce your own favorite cheeses.

Experimentation is the key to full enjoyment of this fascinating and money-saving facet of home storage basics. The following sections explain how to produce two favorite types of cheeses.

Directions for Basic Cheddar Cheese

Basic Cheddar Cheese is different from *Basic Cheese* in the method of firming the curd. Follow the steps in the *Basic Cheese* method through step 15, then follow these directions:

❏ A. Drain whey from curd by straining through double layers of cheesecloth in a sieve, colander, or strainer. Save the whey for later use, if desired.

❏ B. Spread cheesecloth on broiler pan rack, spreading pile of curd on the cheesecloth about $3/4$–1-inch thick.

❏ C. Place rack over broiler pan on stove top burner, maintaining 98°–100°F temperature. Curd will mat into a rather solid, rubbery mass within 30 minutes.

❏ D. Slice curd mass into $3/4$–1-inch strips.

❏ E. After 15 minutes, turn the strips over once, then once again each 15 minutes for 1 hour, maintaining 98°–100°F constant temperature.

❏ F. Remove cheddar from heat and cut into cubes. Sprinkle salt lightly over cheddar cheese, allowing to cool to room temperature.

❏ G. Press cheddar cheese into mold or press into a ball or block with hands.

❏ H. Cheese may be eaten immediately or aged, according to your taste.

Directions for Basic White Cheese

To make a smooth *Basic White Cheese*, much like Italian mozzarella, vary the *Basic Cheese* method as follows:

❏ A. Prepare milk mixture, doubling buttermilk starter. (Steps 1, 2, 3, 4)

❏ B. Do not add coloring. (Step 5)

❏ C. Continue with directions. (Steps 6, 7, 8, 9)

❏ D. After the curd forms, use your *hands* to break up the mass, squeezing firmly.

❏ E. Add 1–2 teaspoons salt to curds while squeezing through hands. (If you want a sweet, bland cheese, leave out salt.)

❏ F. While squeezing curds in whey, raise temperature until hot as your hands can tolerate. Then, gather curds, pressing them in cupped hands until a large firm ball is formed. Line the interior of the cheese press with cheesecloth.

❏ G. Remove cheese ball from whey and place in cheese press. Press firmly to tighten the ball. You may want to pour whey over ball to get remaining curds, but capture whey in a container for use later in soups and gravies.

❏ H. Put pressed cheese back into whey, bringing temperature to approximately 200°F (just below the boiling point).

❏ I. Remove pan from heat and let cheese stand in whey until cool. Take pressed cheese from whey, hang to dry for 8–24 hours in cheesecloth, then it's ready to eat.

RECIPES FOR BASIC CHEESES

BASIC CHEDDAR CHEEZ-O-LETS

Basic Cheez-O-Lets are a cross between a pancake and a cheese omelet.

4 oz. *Basic Cheddar Cheese*, grated
3 eggs
2 heaping T. whole-wheat flour
1/2 tsp. baking powder

1 T. grated onion
1 T. dried parsley
salt and pepper
vegetable oil for frying

Blend all ingredients together. Heat oil in skillet and drop mixture in by spoonful. Fry until crisp and golden brown. Turn to brown other side. Drain well on absorbent paper. Serve hot. *Yield: serves 2–3.*

BASIC WHITE CHEESE LASAGNA

18 oz. pkg. lasagna noodles, cooked per directions

Meat Sauce:

1/4 tsp. sweet basil
1 lb. ground beef
1 clove garlic, minced
1 med. onion, finely chopped

2 cans pizza topping mix
1 can (6 oz.) tomato paste
salt and pepper

Brown beef in saucepan with lid. Add garlic, onion, basil, pizza topping, tomato paste, salt and pepper to taste. Simmer for 20 minutes, stirring occasionally till done.

Cheese Filling:

2 lb. *Basic White Cheese*, grated
1 tsp. parsley flakes

2 eggs
salt and pepper

Mix all ingredients together, salt and pepper to taste.

Topping:

6 oz. mozzarella, grated or slices
(or use more *Basic White Cheese*)

1/2 C. Parmesan cheese

Lightly grease baking dish and spoon in enough meat sauce to cover the bottom. Top with strips of noodles, then spread layer of cheese with part of the cheese filling mixture. Repeat layers, with meat sauce on top.

Sprinkle with Parmesan cheese and top with mozzarella cheese, grated or sliced. Bake in oven at 350°F for 30 minutes. Let stand 5–10 minutes so all layers set before serving. *Yield: 6 servings.*

Illustration 12–3

Basic Cheese Press

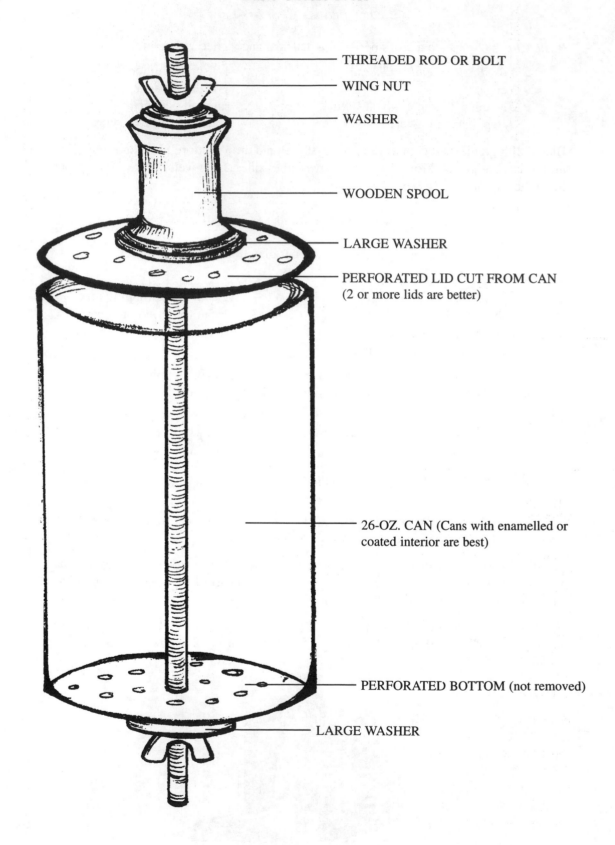

THREADED ROD OR BOLT

WING NUT

WASHER

WOODEN SPOOL

LARGE WASHER

PERFORATED LID CUT FROM CAN
(2 or more lids are better)

26-OZ. CAN (Cans with enamelled or
coated interior are best)

PERFORATED BOTTOM (not removed)

LARGE WASHER

Chapter 13
Basic Honey Use

The history of mankind's relationship to honey is an indicator of its importance in food storage. References to honey are recorded on the walls of post-Ice Age cave-dwellers, depicting their honey-gathering expeditions. The Old Testament mentions the Promised Land flowing with milk and honey—symbols of abundance. Honey was discovered in the Egyptian tombs unspoiled—even after being in storage for more than 2,000 years!

The Egyptians held honey in high esteem and approached its use reverently, feeling it had almost magical properties. Jars of honey found in the Pharaohs' tombs date from as early as 1400 BC.

It was also used to preserve and embalm—Alexander the Great was embalmed in a large jar of honey!

Besides being used as food, it was used as medicine—more than half the remedies prescribed by Egyptian doctors contained honey. Ancient Egyptians, Greeks, and Romans spread honey on wounds to hasten their healing—so did the German field medical personnel during World War I! Even as late as 1970 in England, a surgeon announced he was using honey on open wounds after surgery—and had fewer bacterial infections than similar wounds treated with antibiotics. Honey proved to be an effective disinfectant; it hastened healing; and bacteria did not develop resistance to it, as often happens with antibiotics.

"For he on honey-dew hath fed, And drunk the milk of Paradise."

from "Kubla Kahn," Samuel Taylor Coleridge

When the early settlers brought bees to America, the Indians called them *"White Man's flies."* The white-blossomed clover which was provided for the bees was called *"white foot."* During the settlement of America, until the development of the maple syrup industry, honey was the only source of sweetening for the hardy pioneers.

Honey is the oldest known sweetener. Concentrated from the natural nectar of flowers, honey usually tastes like its major source of nectars. Bees in orange-grove country produce orange-flavored honey; bees in garden areas produce honey with a more complicated array of flavors, depending on the mixture of flower types. The most common sources of honey are clover and alfalfa crops.

Since the early settlers arrived, generations of Americans have grown up on mild-tasting and light-colored honey. Today, blended honey is typically what we find in retail stores. Though blended honey is not necessarily any lower in quality, it does provide the sameness we've come to expect when we buy processed foods.

Unfortunately, honey has 64 calories per tablespoon—18 more calories per tablespoon than table sugar. However, depending on its source, honey may also have as much as 25%–40% more sweetening power. This usually means smaller amounts of honey than sugar are required to achieve the same level of sweetness. Honey contains very small amounts of trace minerals and vitamin nutrients, making it a better choice than sugar. Honey is a whole food, and since no chemicals are utilized in its production, honey is an organic choice, also. Whether honey is a *better* sweetener than sugar is your choice.

BUYING HONEY

Caution:

When buying honey directly from the farm, always ask about the processing method used—if the answers don't make sense, don't buy large amounts.

Buy and store honey labeled **U.S. Grade A** or **U.S. Fancy** if buying in retail outlets. Be apprised, however, there are no federal labeling laws governing the sale of honey, so only honey labeled "pure" is entirely honey and not a blend. Unfortunately for the consumer, honey grading is currently a matter of voluntary compliance—with very lax interpretations by some producers. This lack of standardization causes consumers particular grief when manufacturers selectively use misleading words such as *organic, raw, uncooked,* or *unfiltered* on labels. However, the FDA[1] investigates producers and distributors engaged in fraud or acts which put the honey consumer at risk.

Local honey producers normally are very careful about the quality of their products, and their supplies are usually safe. However, always use caution when purchasing any farm product from unknown sources.

HONEY SELECTION CRITERIA

Commercial honey quality is judged by these **4** factors:

1. mild flavor
2. clean aroma
3. absence of defects (bits of honeycomb, critter body parts, etc.)
4. light to clear color

[1] The FDA takes a great deal of interest in "sticky" problems related to honey purity. Adulteration of honey by adding syrups from cheaper sugar sources are investigated rigorously by the FDA. More proof that nothing's perfect, however—the FDA does not regulate the drugs used in raising bees. Drugs are used because bees are susceptible to a number of diseases. *Fumagillin* is the drug of choice for a parasite that attacks the digestive tract of the bees; *oxytetracycline* is used to control European foulbrood disease which destroys the young bees in the hive.

Honey ranges in color from almost clear, to nearly white, to nearly black. Honey can have tints of yellow, amber, orange, green, and even blue. Honey is considered more valuable when its color is lighter and costs even more when it's almost colorless. The lighter-colored honey usually has a more delicate flavor and aroma. In fact, honey grading, and therefore its pricing structure, is based on its appearance relative to color and clarity.

Use these parameters of quality when selecting honey for long-term in-home storage:

- **whole-comb honey** is the least processed form of honey, but be sure to verify it came from the hive without going through some processing.

- **unfiltered** honey is usually heated some to allow the impurities to be removed by a screening process, but most of the nutrients remain in the honey.

- **raw (uncooked)** honey may contain some spores of botulism,[2] generally harmful only to children less than 1 year old.

- **liquid** honey is heated to higher temperatures to allow it to be filtered more easily and to remove bee parts, hive intruders (dead, of course!), bits of honeycomb, etc.; liquid honey is usually lighter in color, has greater clarity, is easier to package, resists crystallization longer—but destroys many or most of the beneficial nutrients inherent in natural whole-comb honey.

- **crystallized honey** is a creamy, smooth spread, often used for spun, creamed, or aerated forms of retail honey. The honey crystals are mixed in or blended in to give body to the liquid honey base.

STORING HONEY

For best storage capability, store pure, unprocessed honey. It does not normally support growth of bacteria and requires no refrigeration to prevent yeast and mold populations.

Store all forms and varieties of honey in containers with tight-fitting lids to prevent

- absorption of moisture, which could alter the texture

- environmental exposure, which could alter the taste.

Pure honey stores extremely well—it is the only storage food that will not spoil!

As with all stored products, honey should be rotated, even in view of its seeming long life. The secret to storage and use is to store it in small quantities. Even though stored honey usually gets darker in color and stronger in flavor, it's still effective as ever in sweetening foods.

---

[2] According to the Center for Disease Control in Atlanta, GA, infants less than a year old should not be fed raw honey because of the danger of *clostridium botulinum*, which transmits "infant botulism." An adult's immune system would kill the botulism bacterial spores before infection set in.

Storage Considerations

There are many different kinds of honey available. However, there are only **3** considerations for its storage—that's what makes it such a favorite sweetener in food storage:

1. **Contamination**

2. **Temperature**

3. **Length of storage**

Contamination

As long as honey is kept sealed in a cool, dry, and dark place, it has virtually no storage limitations, as proven by the ancients. Avoid storing honey in plastic buckets or pails near petroleum products (including the power lawnmower), chemicals, or any other fume- or gaseous odor-producing product.

Temperature

Both high and low temperatures affect honey storage, though neither will destroy its usefulness. Lower temperatures cause honey to become very dense. Higher temperatures will cause honey to be runny. However, in either case, as long as the honey is tightly covered, no damage should result.

Length of Storage

Usually the worst thing that happens to older honey is *crystallization*—which is easily cured by warming the honey container gently in warm water. Crystallization is a natural aging process and does not affect the honey's food value, although it darkens the color and intensifies the flavor.

How to decrystallize honey: Simply place the container of honey in a pan of warm water until the crystals disappear. If more heat is required, keep the container from touching the bottom of the pan by putting a rack under it and set the pan over low heat, at approximately 150°F. Be careful not to overheat crystallized honey, since too much heat causes the honey to change color and flavor. It's easier and less frustrating to decrystallize small containers of honey.

Storage Differences

Pure, unprocessed comb honey: keeps best in covered containers in a cool, dark, and dry place. It is the purest form of honey and requires no preservatives. Pure honey usually becomes crystallized as it ages or if stored at cold temperatures.

Creamed honey: may be stored at room temperature or in the refrigerator. Freezing or refrigeration will not harm creamed honey, but may speed its crystallization. This crystallization can be "cured" by warming as explained in the previous section. Creamed honey may partially liquefy if stored at too high a temperature. There are a number of creamed mixtures made from honey. These mixtures are created by adding water, air, and / or flavorings and are generally "spreads" used as toppings or desserts. You can make your own with a blender or mixer, some butter or margarine, a little peanut, almond, or cashew butter—the combinations are endless!

Diluted honey: when diluted with water or any other liquid, honey should be kept tightly covered in the refrigerator. As with other syrups, diluted honey may ferment or mold quickly if not kept cold. Usually the label on the honey container will indicate the best means of storage.

USING HONEY

Honey has several advantages over sugar:

- Honey is sweeter, measure-for-measure, than sugar. Honey weighs 12 ounces per cup, but 1 cup of sugar weighs only 7 ounces—that's why honey has more sweetening power than sugar.

- Honey is a natural food—it's much better for your health than refined sugars.

- Baked products stay fresher longer when honey is used. Honey absorbs and retains moisture, thus retarding the drying out and staleness associated with home-baked items. This is especially important when you want to bake in advance or save baked goods for any length of time.

When honey is utilized even in small amounts, it adds a slightly heightened flavor to the recipe. Adding too much honey, on the other hand, will make the recipe too sweet, and the possibility of recipe failure is increased. You'll have new tastes to surprise and delight you as the experimentation process of substituting sugar with honey develops.

Substituting Honey for Sugar

Honey may be used, measure-for-measure, in place of sugar in the following preparations:

- baked apples
- baked ham
- candied vegetables
- cinnamon toast
- custards
- dressings for salads
- glazes
- lemonade
- pie fillings
- puddings
- punch drinks
- sweet & sour dishes

When baking with honey as a substitute in regular recipes, these are *3 steps you must take* to make the substitution of honey work:

1. *Use only 75% liquid honey for sugar—³/₄ cup honey* for each *1 cup sugar* required.

2. *Reduce the total liquid ingredients by 25%*—eliminate ¹/₄ cup liquid for each cup of sugar replaced by honey.

3. *Reduce oven heat approximately 25°–35°F.* Honey caramelizes, becoming darker and/or burning at a lower temperature than sugar.

Note:

Honey does not replace sugar, measure-for-measure in standard recipes.

The following chart illustrates a formula for substituting honey for sugar in most recipes:

Chart 13–1

Sugar-to-Honey Recipe Conversion Chart

Sugar to be Replaced	Honey Amount Substituted	&	Recipe Liquid Decreased		Option: instead of decreasing liquid, add following ingredients with honey:		
					Flour	+	Soda
1 C.	$3/4$ C.	&	$1/4$ C.	or	4 T.	+	$1/4$ tsp.
$1/2$ C.	6 T.	&	2 T.	or	2 T.	+	$1/8$ tsp.
$1/3$ C.	$1/4$ C.	&	$1 1/2$ T.	or	$1 1/2$ T.	+	$1/12$ tsp.
$1/4$ C.	3 T.	&	1 T.	or	1 T.	+	$1/16$ tsp.

Basic Hints for Honey Use

General

These tidbits of kitchen wisdom about using honey in the place of sugar have evolved over the years:

- Measure all ingredients carefully—accuracy is very important when using honey. All measurements are level—*do not overfill measuring utensils.*
- Unless noted specifically in the recipe, use liquid honey *only.*
- Use mild flavors of clover-type honey in most recipes.
- Stronger-flavored honey is best utilized in spice cakes, gingerbread, brownies, fruit punches, and oven-baked ham where its pronounced flavor is not overpowering.
- Honey should always be used at room temperature, or even slightly warmer, so it will flow easier and combine better with the other ingredients.
- When preparing oven-baked recipes, mix honey thoroughly with other ingredients before pouring mixture into baking pans. This prevents a too-moist, oversweetened layer from collecting on the top of the baked item.
- Combine honey with liquid ingredients to assure complete distribution in the mixture.
- Sauces will be smoother when made with honey instead of processed sugar.
- Honey will come out of a measuring utensil much better when a coating of oil is placed on the utensil prior to putting honey in it.
- A rubber or flexible plastic spatula is useful in getting all the honey out of the bowl or off the utensil.

Cakes

Honey can generally replace up to one-half of the required sugar required in standard recipes without changing the proportions of the other ingredients in the recipe.

Cookies

The amount of honey used to substitute for sugar in standard cookie recipes is directly related to the hardness or crispness desired in the final product.

For hard cookies: substitute no more than $^1/_3$ of the required sugar. Keep in mind that hard cookies will probably lose their crispness if not eaten in a short time. Most honey cookies, candies, and frostings become too soft during high-humidity weather.

For soft cookies: substitute up to $^1/_2$ the required sugar with honey.

For moist-type fruit bars and soft, "gooey" mixtures: substitute up to $^2/_3$ of the required sugar with honey.

Bread

Freezing bread with honey as sweetening is not advised, since honey deteriorates when frozen, causing the thawed bread to be "mushy."

RECIPES FOR HONEY

BASIC HONEY-BUTTER MIX

$^1/_2$ C. butter	1 C. bland honey

Combine ingredients with electric mixer until creamy and smooth. Store in refrigerator in tightly closed container.

BASIC CINNAMON BUTTER

1 C. *Basic Honey-Butter Mix*	1 tsp. cinnamon

Combine ingredients with electric mixer on high speed. Store in tightly closed glass or plastic container with tight-fitting lid.

> **Note:**
>
> *Some honey-flavored cakes and other baked goods improve in flavor and texture when aged a few days.*

BASIC HONEY-BUTTER CINNAMON BUNS

$^2/_3$ C. very warm water	2 T. nonfat dry milk
1 T. yeast	$^1/_4$ C. raisins
$^1/_2$ C. *Basic Cinnamon Butter*	$^1/_4$ C. chopped pecans
1 egg	2 C. sifted flour
$^1/_2$ tsp. salt	additional cinnamon, if desired

Measure very warm water into large mixing bowl. Sprinkle or crumble yeast over water; stir until dissolved. Combine *Basic Cinnamon Butter*, egg, salt, and dry milk. Add to yeast mixture; blend well. Add fruit, nuts, and flour. Stir to mix; then beat until batter is shiny and smooth, about 2 minutes. Scrape sides of bowl. Let rise in warm place, free from draft until doubled, about 30 minutes. Roll out in long "snakes" and coil into 3- to 6-inch circles. Bake at 350°F for 20–25 minutes. Remove from pan, serve warm. *Yield: 12 buns.*

BASIC FRENCH TOAST

2 eggs, slightly beaten	8 slices bread
$^1/_4$ C. milk	butter or oil for frying
$1^1/_4$ C. *Basic Honey-Butter Mix*	2 T. lemon juice
$^1/_4$ tsp. salt	

Combine beaten eggs, milk, $^1/_4$ cup *Basic Honey-Butter Mix* and salt. Dip bread in mixture and fry in butter until golden brown. Combine remaining *Mix* and lemon juice. Heat and serve over toast. *Yield: 4–6 servings.*

BASIC HONEY CHIPPEES

$1/2$ C. butter	$1/2$ tsp. baking soda
$1/2$ C. honey	$1/2$ tsp. salt
1 egg	1 C. chocolate chips
$1^1/_4$ C. sifted flour	$1/2$ C. chopped pecans

Cream butter and honey together; add egg and beat well. Sift together dry ingredients and add to creamed mixture. Stir in chocolate chips and pecans. Drop by rounded teaspoons onto greased cookie sheet. Bake at 375°F for 12–15 minutes. *Yield: 3 dozen cookies.*

BASIC HONEYOAT BREAD

1 C. rolled oats (regular)	$1/4$ C. vegetable oil
2 C. boiling water	$1/2$ C. dry milk
2 T. yeast	6–$6^1/_2$ C. sifted wheat flour
$1/3$ C. lukewarm water	$2^1/_2$ tsp. salt
$1/2$ C. honey	

Place rolled oats in large bowl or pan and add boiling water. Let stand until lukewarm (about 20 minutes). Dissolve yeast in lukewarm water and let stand 5 minutes, then add to mixture. Add honey and oil. Sift together dry ingredients twice and then add to mixture. Knead well for 5 minutes.

Let rise until double in bulk, then knead again. Shape into two loaves. Let rise 10 minutes and bake in well-greased loaf pans at 325°F for 1 hour. Turn out and brush tops with butter.

BASIC HONEY-BUTTER COOKEES

2 C. butter	8 C. sifted flour
1 C. honey	$1^1/_4$ tsp. baking powder
2 eggs, separated	2 T. lemon juice
1 T. grated lemon peel	1 C. almonds, chopped

Cream butter and gradually add honey. Beat in egg yolks and lemon peel, flour, baking powder, and lemon juice. Stir well and chill.

Shape into small balls and flatten. Brush with beaten egg whites and sprinkle with almonds. Bake at 350°F for 10–15 minutes. *Yield: 7–8 dozen cookies.*

BASIC HONEY CRISPEES

$1/2$ C. butter	$1/4$ tsp. salt
2 T. milk	1 C. coconut
1 C. flour	1 tsp. vanilla
$3/4$ C. honey	2 C. Rice Krispies® cereal

Combine all ingredients except vanilla and cereal in saucepan. Cook over medium heat, stirring constantly until dough leaves sides of pan and forms a ball. Remove from heat. Cool. Add vanilla and cereal. Shape into balls; roll in additional coconut. If not eaten at once, store in refrigerator.

BASIC BUTTER PECAN COOKEES

1 C. butter
1/4 C. honey
2 C. sifted flour
1/2 tsp. salt

2 tsp. vanilla extract
2 C. finely chopped pecans
confectioners' sugar

Cream butter; gradually add honey and beat well. Stir in flour, salt, and vanilla. Mix well. Add chopped nuts. Form into very small balls and place on greased baking sheet. Bake at 300°F for 40–45 minutes. Roll in confectioners' sugar while still hot. *Yield: 6 dozen cookies.*

BASIC HONEY CUSTARD

2 eggs
2 C. milk

1/4 C. honey
1/8 tsp. salt

Beat eggs slightly. Add milk, honey, and salt. Pour into individual molds and set in a pan of water.

Bake at 350°F for 30 minutes. Allow to cool and chill in refrigerator. *Yield: 6 (4-ounce) cups.*

BASIC PEANUTTY CHOMPERS

1 C. honey
1 C. peanut butter

1–1 1/2 C. nonfat dry milk
(non-instant)

Add peanut butter to warm honey and mix well. Stir in 1–1 1/2 cups dry milk. (The amount of powdered milk depends on the peanut butter's oiliness.) Form into small balls.

BASIC FRUIT CUP MIX

4 C. mixed fruit
1/2 C. honey

1 T. chopped candied ginger
1 T. lemon juice

Place fruit in serving bowl or refrigerator dish. Combine honey, candied ginger, and lemon juice; pour mixture over fruit and chill for 2 hours before serving. *Yield: 4–6 servings.*

A typical winter mix could include grapefruit and orange sections, fresh pineapple, bananas, red grapes, etc. A summer mix might include melon, berries, peaches, pears, etc.

BASIC SWEET PEARALILLI

7 C. firm ripe pears
1/2 C. diced green pepper
1 can (4 oz.) diced pimento
2 C. golden raisins
4 C. mild-flavored honey
1/2 C. lemon juice

1 T. grated lemon peel
1 tsp. salt
1/4 tsp. ground ginger
1/4 tsp. whole cloves
1/2 tsp. ground allspice
4 sticks cinnamon

Put unpeeled, cored pears through food grinder, using coarse blade (or use food processor). Combine with balance of ingredients in a pot. Tie whole spices in a cloth so they may be easily removed. Stir well to blend. Over medium heat, bring to boil, stirring continually. When rolling boil is reached, reduce heat and simmer, stirring often to prevent sticking, until relish is thick enough to spoon into sterilized pint jars. Remove spice bag. Seal lids at once. *Yield: approximately 4 pints.*

Chapter 14

Basic Self-Health with Supplementation

Your body requires vitamins and minerals for its normal functions of growth and maintenance. You may expect that the food you eat supplies those essential nutrients. Today, however, the nutritional value of food diminishes as it is processed, packed, distributed and warehoused, then placed in a retail outlet for the consumer's selection and purchase. This means even a routine diet requires nutritional supplementation.

Most Americans are missing at least one essential nutrient in their bodies. Many are deficient in more than one vitamin or mineral nutrient. A recent nationwide survey conducted by the University of California at Berkeley confirmed that 70% of the men and 80% of the women reported eating foods containing less than two-thirds of the recommended level of one or more of the 15 vitamins and minerals considered essential for good health. On top of that, when the excess fat being consumed was added to their food consumption habits, 98% of those surveyed were inadequately nourished. The study reveals the nutrients most often missing are calcium, zinc, folic acid, magnesium, and vitamins A, C, E, and B_6.

This chapter will provide you with guidelines for a supplementation program that will help you maintain good health under normal circumstances and during more stressful times,

No statements made in this chapter shall be construed as claims or representations that any of these nutritional food supplements for special dietary use are offered for the diagnosis, cure, mitigation, treatment or prevention of disease.

whether caused by disasters or by a permanent lifestyle change. When your body is under stress due to any changes, you will have an even greater need to support your physical and mental health with the appropriate vitamin, mineral, and herb supplementation.

Supplementation is just what the word means—*supplements* to be taken in addition to an intelligent diet combined with a health/fitness and body maintenance program. There are optimum amounts of each nutrient that one should take. Levels in excess of the optimum daily allowance levels have minimal or even nonexistent benefits—except for the product vendors!

This is the first edition of the ***Handbook*** in which a preeminent doctor, with great holistic medical and research credentials combined with clinical experience, has suggested a specific supplementation program and explains why each supplement should be a part of your in-home storage program—not to mention its utilization in your daily diet.

ABOUT DR. ZOLTAN RONA

In my efforts to provide the best recommendation possible for this important food storage and emergency preparedness category, I asked Zoltan P. Rona, M.D., M.S., to give his guidance for a valid vitamin, mineral, and herb supplementation selection for a "typical" in-home storage program. Dr. Rona is eminently qualified to provide such guidelines. He graduated from McGill University Medical School, and he also earned master's degrees in biochemistry and clinical nutrition from the University of Bridgeport in Connecticut.

Dr. Rona is currently a general medicine practitioner with an emphasis on preventive medical counseling, particularly in the field of nutrition and holistic medicine.[1] He has excellent credentials as a recognized expert in holistic medicine, having recently served as President of the Canadian Holistic Medical Association.

DR. RONA: WHY SUPPLEMENTATION?

In one of my early conversations with Dr. Rona, I asked which question was the one most commonly asked of him as a healthcare practitioner. He indicated the question most asked was, "Does everyone need to take vitamin, mineral, and herbal supplements?"

His response to this question is an unequivocal **"Yes!"** I asked him to explain why he recommends supplementation so strongly. The following pages are the result of his discussions with us about the need for supplementation for short-term emergency preparedness, longer-term food storage, and on an daily basis.

Vitamin and Mineral Needs Not Met by Food Alone

The quality of our food grown in mineral-depleted soils is not what the agribusiness industry wants us to believe. With over 70,000 new chemicals added to our environment since the 1940s, how could anyone say that our food supply is the best it's ever been? Studies indicate that our daily vitamin and mineral needs are not met by food alone. Up

---

[1] Dr. Rona regularly contributes to magazines in the medical field, including his columns in *Alive Magazine*, *Health Naturally*, and *The Toronto Star*. He is known for his many public lectures and media appearances in Canada and the U.S. He is the author of the international best-seller, **The Joy of Health—A Doctor's Guide to Nutrition and Alternative Medicine,** as well as **Fertility Control—The Natural Approach,** and numerous articles and columns for magazines and medical journals. His second book about natural health and nutrition, **Return to the Joy of Health—A Doctor's Guide to Nutrition and Herbal Medicine,** was released in the summer of l995.

to 80% of our food's value is lost through spraying crops, processing, transporting, freezing, storing, cooking, and adding chemicals for preservation.

Have you noticed over the years you've been shopping that the food found in stores tastes less and less like real food? Since there is a taste difference—what makes you think there isn't a corresponding difference in nutritive values?

According to some experts, at the present rate of extinction, as many as one-fourth of the world's plant species will be lost within the next 50 years! If you were really aware of the content of the food you buy in any supermarket in the U.S., you'd be surprised to know that almost 90% of our food is now provided by *only* 20 major botanical plants—where would we be if another blight such as caused the Irish potato famine were to happen?

It's indeed fortunate that we see more farmland being diversified, crop rotating, and rebuilding of soil without chemicals. However, based on current chemical agricultural practices, eventually there won't be enough topsoil left to grow the food from the plant species remaining!

Leonardo da Vinci said, "We know more about the movement of celestial bodies than about the soil underfoot." The soil is the crucible of plant life, and in it is the hope and reality of matter and energy for growing food that will not only sustain us but give us both better health and longer lives.

To derive the same amounts of vitamins and minerals your grandparents did from food alone in the early part of the 20th century, you would need to consume six large meals per day. Since this would overload you with calories, it's far better to take vitamin and mineral supplements. The apparent lack of adequate vitamins and minerals in the average diet has prompted some health professionals to conclude that one of the reasons for today's epidemic-like levels of obesity, fatigue, and mental illness is micronutrient deficiency.

> *"... everything man needs to maintain good health can be found in nature...*
>
> *The true task of science is to find those things..."*
>
> Paracelsus, the father of pharmacology

Protection for the Body

A primary reason for taking supplemental vitamins and minerals is to protect our bodies against the toxic effects of a polluted environment. Over the past decade, extensive research has been done on the subject of *free radical pathology.* Many reputable scientists and medical doctors believe that free radical pathology is at the root of immune system disorders such as cancer, heart disease, and a long list of degenerative diseases, including aging.

Free radicals are highly reactive molecules (containing an unpaired electron) which can cause damage to the body. They can be offset by antioxidants—vitamins, minerals, and enzymes. Free radicals contribute to the degradation of any organ or system, leading to such symptoms as hardening of blood vessels, plaque, wrinkles in skin, etc. By the way, *free radicals have been damaging our bodies since our first breath!*

Free radicals come from radiation, hydrocarbons from car exhaust, cigarette smoke, drugs, pesticides, herbicides, food additives, industrial waste products, and many other sources. The gradual deterioration of the ozone layer plays a part. All of this necessitates even greater protection with antioxidant nutrients like beta carotene, vitamin A, B vitamins (especially B_3 and B_6), vitamins C and E, bioflavonoids, selenium, zinc, silicon, amino acids, enzymes such as S.O.D. (*superoxide dismutase*), coenzymes, and essential fatty acids.

Basic Self-Health Improvement

Dr. Rona suggests two very easily implemented steps we can take immediately to improve our health:

1. Eat Healthier Food.[2] Even in the face of less than ideal food quality, eating a healthier diet is possible. Follow these general guidelines to improve your diet:

- most importantly, decrease the intake of saturated fat and cholesterol by eliminating red meats
- keep high-fat dairy products, especially cheeses, to a minimum
- eating cultured dairy products, such as yogurt or buttermilk in small amounts, is fine if they are low-fat products
- avoid coffee and regular tea
- consume no alcohol
- eliminate refined sugars
- drastically reduce use of white flour products.

In essence, the more vegetarian your food selection...

the better for your overall health and well-being.

2. Take Antioxidants.[3] Take some broad-spectrum antioxidant supplements. The two worry-free supplements Dr. Rona recommends, for a variety of reasons, are

- **bee pollen**

    and

- **a green supplement**, such as blue green algae or chlorella

This antioxidant combination provides a perfect mixture of maximum-spectrum antioxidants, the richest available in tablet or capsule form. Some scientists have called both bee pollen and green food concentrates nature's most perfect foods. Together they contain a very well-balanced supply of all the essential amino acids, vitamins, trace minerals, essential fatty acids, RNA, DNA, plant enzymes, coenzymes, and prostaglandin precursors.

---

[2] Authoritative governmental and public service agencies recommend eating a balanced diet containing at least five servings daily of fruits and vegetables rich in antioxidant vitamins. Other self-protective health measures should be included, such as decreasing the intake of fats and salt, not smoking, exercising reasonably, and having regular checkups.

[3] The antioxidants discussed here are the vitamins C, E, and the provitamin beta carotene. They are important to the body's cell-protection systems. Antioxidants have the ability to neutralize free radicals, those highly-reactive and unstable molecules that can cause cell damage. The body's billions of cells are continually exposed to these free radicals, which are produced through normal bodily processes as well as external sources, such as air pollution. (And how do we avoid air pollution?) Many scientists believe this cellular damage, along with other factors, may lead to the development of chronic diseases such as cancer, cataracts, and even heart disease.

Many physicians and other scientists now believe vitamin supplements or eating foods that are fortified with vitamins and minerals is a sound health practice—especially for people who don't eat a wholesome diet and for those with special dietary needs, such as pregnant and lactating women and the elderly. The antioxidant vitamins themselves can be obtained through a wide variety of supplements and food products, including breakfast cereals and real juice drinks. (The nutrient contents of foods and supplements can be determined by checking the labels.)

Overwhelming scientific evidence indicates there are virtually no inordinate risks of health problems or reactions to reasonably elevated levels of the antioxidant vitamins C, E and beta carotene. (In fact, all three of these vitamins are officially classified as *Generally Recognized as Safe* (**GRAS**)—but it's always prudent to follow label instructions or the advice of a healthcare professional.)

Blue green algae and chlorella are vegetarian sources of vitamin B_{12}. These superfoods fulfill daily essential vitamin and mineral needs and provide antioxidant protection. Both these products can be used to enhance work and sports performance. The use of bee pollen by professional and Olympic athletes for physical endurance and power is well documented. The world medical literature reports benefits from bee pollen extract in a long list of chronic conditions:

- anemia
- depression
- obesity
- prostatitis

- arthritis
- insomnia
- poor memory and concentration

- chronic fatigue
- menopause
- premature aging
- senility

Blue green algae, on the other hand, has been demonstrated to help in both the prevention and treatment of all viral conditions. Side effects and toxicity from overdoses of either blue green algae or bee pollen, even in children, have never been reported in more than thirty years of broad-scale use. For those who want a safe and effective way of optimizing health, preventing illness, and living longer, these whole food supplements may very well be the answer.

BASIC SUPPLEMENTATION FOR IN-HOME STORAGE

After discussing the concept of food storage with its concomitant food quality and nutritional deficiency problems, Dr. Rona and I both felt a vitamin, mineral, and herbal supplementation program would be needed in a basic food storage program. These are the major reasons supplementation is recommended for your in-home storage program:

- difficulty of determining the nutritional value remaining in stored foods
- continuing loss of food value, including vitamin and mineral potency
- additional food value losses occurring when food storage items are improperly stored and/or prepared

You are urged to do the following **three** things, in consultation with qualified healthcare providers:

1. **Examine your own diet, lifestyle and potential supplementation requirements.**
2. **Determine your specific needs for supplementation.**
3. **Plan and execute your own personal supplemental nutritional program.**

After your own careful examination of the information presented in this chapter, search other sources to guide your efforts in deriving the best plan for you and your loved ones. Use the information contained in both the text and the four **Intake Guides** to plan adequate protection for your biggest investment—your health and personal well-being. Take the time to establish a supplementation program for your family as you implement your in-home storage plan.

No plan is perfect for everyone, so your personal homework is essential. Be sure to assess this area of your life as rigorously as any other in preparation for a long-term program of good health maintenance.

"Dr. Rona, what vitamin, mineral, and herbal supplements are applicable for a home storage program?"

Here is a listing of possible supplements for in-home storage that are easy and inexpensive to have on hand. They are apple cider vinegar, aloe vera, bee products, beet root powder, beta carotene, bioflavonoids, bladderwrack (a seaweed, *kelp*), blue green algae and other green foods, boron, chromium picolinate, copper, fo-ti, ginger, ginkgo biloba, hawthorne berries, kola nut, live whole food concentrates, ma huang, parsley, saw palmetto, selenium, Siberian ginseng, vitamins C and E, white willow, yerba maté and zinc. These supplemental nutrients can be taken without side effects by most people. The primary reason for the effectiveness of supplementation is due to the deficiency in one or more of these vitamins or minerals. These supplemental items are available at most natural food stores. Sections following provide more details.

Purchasing Supplementation

Be an informed buyer. Study carefully every supplement you plan to purchase. Compare labels from suppliers. Supplemental product forms include caplets, capsules, gels, liquids, powders, time-release and non-time-release forms, gelled capsules, lotions, ointments, and other forms, such as creams, injections, and patches. Some forms of these supplements provide better bioavailability (absorption in the body) than others, even with the same dosage. Some will be buffered, others chelated—there are many names for processes to enhance absorption into the body with increased effectiveness. However, *no form of supplement provides 100% absorption.*

Generally, except for some of the fat-soluble vitamins, it doesn't matter whether you buy "natural" or "synthetic" vitamins. Buy with knowledge about which forms of supplements are best suited to your own body's chemistry. Study the products from various companies before investing either your money or your health in *any* supplements plan or program.

The *Yellow Pages* in virtually every phone book will have local listings for retailers of vitamins, minerals, and herbal supplements. Ask holistic health professionals for their recommendations.

> **Quality is foremost in buying and utilizing vitamin, mineral, and herbal supplements—as it is in all items on which you're betting your health or your life!**

Storing Supplements

Store vitamins, minerals, and herbs in a dry, cool, and dark environment. Supplements will not store for long periods. Potency and flavor diminish when stored too long, in high temperature locations, or in bright light. Supplements must be rotated as other storage items.

Refrigeration for vitamins, minerals, and herbs is neither normally required nor is it recommended—unless such storage is recommended by the manufacturer. When transferring products from a large container to a smaller one for convenience, be sure caps are tightly closed and the containers are opaque to protect products from diminished potency.

LIVE WHOLE FOOD CONCENTRATES

Live whole food concentrates might well be the most logical and convenient answer to the deteriorated quality of foods available from supermarkets today. Whenever possible, use whole food concentrates rather than single nutrient tablets or capsules. That's because when one isolates a single component from a given food, a lot of the benefits of the complete food are lost. Supplemental vitamins and minerals cannot duplicate the mixture of nutrients and many yet-to-be-identified substances of value to health found in natural foods. Whole foods contain what are called *"phytochemicals"* which are linked to both the prevention and treatment of such major degenerative diseases as heart disease, strokes, high blood pressure, and cancer. ***The only way to get these phytochemicals is by eating whole foods or live whole food concentrates.***

Some of the best-known phytochemicals are
- *Indoles* and *isothiocyanates*: found in cruciferous vegetables like broccoli, Brussels sprouts, cabbage, cauliflower, kale, bok choy, rutabagas, and turnips. They help protect against colon cancer. Evidence is also mounting that these phytochemicals help in both the prevention and treatment of other cancers, most notably breast cancer.
- *Isoflavones,* such as *genistein:* found in soybean products like tofu and soy milk. Isoflavones offset the negative effects of excessive estrogen in breast and ovarian cancers.
- *Limonene*: found in citrus fruits, produce enzymes that eliminate cancer-causing substances from the body. Citrus fruits are mostly known for their high content of vitamin C and bioflavonoids, both of which are also vital for optimal immune system function.
- *Phytosterols:* found in soybeans, can lower the absorption of cholesterol from the diet and help prevent colon cancer.

Under emergency or survival conditions, when people do not have access to live whole foods, the only option may be live whole food concentrates. Live whole food concentrates are processed and converted from live whole food at temperatures less than 100°F, thereby maintaining the "life" within the food. Temperature during the conversion process is the crucial deciding factor distinguishing a "live" from a "dead" food. Shelf life of live whole food concentrates can be at least 10 years.

The major advantages of live whole food concentrates are
- naturally occurring high vitamin and mineral content with highly bioavailable antioxidants
- naturally occurring, highly concentrated phytochemicals
- naturally low in calories, fats, salts, and sugar
- naturally occurring live active enzymes and soluble fiber
- a rapid and convenient way of supplying the vital 5+ daily servings of fruits and vegetables that is pesticide- and herbicide-free

VITAMINS

Beta Carotene

Beta carotene is a fat-soluble nutrient that the liver can convert to vitamin A in the body slowly—and only when the body needs it. Beta carotene is nontoxic in nature, so it is an alternative or substitute for traditional forms of vitamin A. The best source of beta carotene is whole carrots. Equally good is a live whole food concentrate of carrots. Eating carrots or swallowing live whole food carrot concentrate capsules is therefore better than just drinking carrot juice—which in turn is better than just taking a beta carotene supplement.

Carrots and carrot juice are alkaline-forming foods. They lower the risk of cancer, especially smoking-related cancers like lung cancer. They help lower blood cholesterol and are excellent complementary treatments for all skin disorders and respiratory problems like asthma and bronchitis. They may also be of help for gastrointestinal problems like colitis, enteritis, and ulcers. Fruits and vegetables are rich in beta carotene as well as other carotenoids, which all help boost the immune system against bacterial, viral, fungal, and parasitic diseases as well as cancer. It's far better to eat the whole food and/or its juice—the whole food has much more nutritional value.

Bioflavonoids

Bioflavonoids are special antioxidant compounds found in many fruits, especially berries, vegetables, green tea, and wine. Some better known bioflavonoids include *catechin, hesperidin, rutin, quercetin, pycnogenol, pronogenol,* and *polyphenols.* Bioflavonoids can lower LDL-cholesterol levels and inhibit platelet stickiness. Together with vitamin C in large doses, bioflavonoids are very effective in the treatment of allergies. They also help prevent the rapid deterioration of vitamin C by oxidation. Bioflavonoids are considered essential in the human body because they strengthen the walls of the capillaries and are known to help build resistance to infections. They help increase the effectiveness of vitamin C and aid in prevention of bleeding gums.

Vitamin C

Vitamin C is an antioxidant which helps prevent all degenerative diseases. It lowers high blood cholesterol levels and helps prevent atherosclerosis by directly promoting the breakdown of triglycerides. By regulating arterial wall integrity, vitamin C performs an essential role in collagen formation. Vitamin C regenerates and reactivates the vitamin E used in the body to block oxidation of LDL-cholesterol. It helps resist infection, aid healing, and maintain healthy gums and teeth. Because vitamin C is water soluble, it is flushed away every day by our bodies and must be replenished.

People who smoke, drink alcohol, are under stress, or are elderly may need higher levels of vitamin C. It is also important for the following reasons:
- formation of collagen and the health of bones, teeth, gums, nails, muscles, ligaments, and all other connective tissue
- strengthens blood vessels; prevents bleeding and plaque formation in the arteries
- promotes healing of all body cells
- increases resistance to infection
- aids iron absorption and utilization
- antioxidant which helps prevent cancer and heart disease
- natural antihistamine in high doses

Get your vitamin C from whole food sources. If you don't tolerate citrus, try eating more peppers, garlic, onions, cantaloupe, kale, parsley, turnip greens, broccoli, rose hips, black currants, strawberries, apples, persimmons, guavas, acerola cherries, potatoes, cabbage, and tomatoes. All fresh fruits and vegetables contain vitamin C and variable amounts of bioflavonoids.

Some people have bad reactions to vitamin C, including headaches, gas, nausea, and lightheadedness. Often these symptoms can be overcome by using buffered forms of vitamin C like sodium ascorbate, calcium ascorbate, ester C, and others. In general, vitamin C is a weak acid. Candida, bacteria, fungi, and parasites are often killed off by high-dose vitamin C, and this releases toxins into the system. Stomach gas, headache, nausea, and lightheadedness sometimes result—but this is just a sign of a temporary cleansing or detoxification reaction. These problems can be eliminated by doing a vitamin C flush.[4]

If stomach gas is a problem with a vitamin C supplement and you don't wish to do a vitamin C flush, consider adding sodium bicarbonate to your ester C, sodium ascorbate or calcium ascorbate supplement. This is available in powdered form and can be taken immediately after taking the vitamin C. Start with low doses of vitamin C and increase gradually as tolerated. Additionally, use a good *lactobacillus acidophilus* and *bifidus* supplement to help control the bowel flora, reducing gastrointestinal toxins and improving digestion.

Worsening hay fever and bleeding gums are signs of vitamin C deficiency. They are also a sign of a greater need for bioflavonoids. These can be taken in high doses without side effects and might also help you tolerate vitamin C supplements better.

If you are having trouble tolerating even the buffered forms of vitamin C, consider getting yourself checked out for chronic gastrointestinal dysbiosis. It is possible that you are suffering from a bacterial flora imbalance, candida overgrowth, bacterial infection, or parasites. A natural healthcare practitioner can order a comprehensive stool and digestive analysis with a comprehensive parasitology evaluation to rule out this potential problem.

Vitamin E

Vitamin E is otherwise known as *alpha-tocopherol*. Studies indicate that supplementation of as little as 200 IU daily in men can reduce the risk of a heart attack by 46%; in women the risk reduction is by 26%.

*Whether natural source or synthetic source, **all** forms supply the body with at least some vitamin E activity.*

- The natural forms of vitamin E are *d-alpha-tocopherol, d-alpha-tocopheryl acetate, d-alpha-tocopheryl succinate* and *mixed tocopherols.*

- The synthetic forms are *dl-alpha-tocopherol, dl-alpha-tocopheryl acetate* or *dl-alpha-tocopheryl succinate.*

Studies indicate that the most biologically active are the esterified natural forms: *d-alpha-tocopheryl acetate* and *d-alpha-tocopheryl succinate*. Both have been found to

---

[4] ***Vitamin C flush***: This is done by increasing the dose of vitamin C to the point of clear, watery diarrhea which usually results in an effective purge of the majority of these toxins. The vitamin C flush is best done with buffered vitamin C powder. Take 1 teaspoon in juice every $1/2$ hour until watery diarrhea is reached. After this bowel tolerance level is attained, adjust dosage to where the bowels feel comfortable. The gas and other detoxification reactions should disappear when the bowel movements are again normal.

provide full antioxidant activity in the body and are the ones recommended by the top authorities on vitamin E at the Shute Institute and Medical Clinic in London, Ontario.

Recent studies indicate that high levels of stored iron in the body (ferritin) are associated with a greater risk of heart disease and diabetes. High-dose vitamin E supplements can interfere with iron absorption. If you have been prescribed iron to correct iron deficiency, take your iron supplement about 12 hours apart from vitamin E. Iron destroys vitamin E in the body. Iron absorption is enhanced by sufficient acid in the stomach. A supplement of vitamin C (500–1000 mg.) can increase iron absorption by up to 30%. Other good absorption aids include Swedish bitters, betaine or glutamic acid hydrochloride, apple cider vinegar, and lemon juice.

Birth control pills, mineral oils, alcohol, pollution, and chlorinated drinking water can also possibly deplete vitamin E in the body.

VITAMIN SUPPLEMENTS INTAKE GUIDE

Vitamins are indispensable to our general nutrition and good health. However, they do not directly contribute to energy or body-building materials. Their important work is to form complex chemical compounds that have enzymatic activity necessary to convert food to energy and to build tissue. A prolonged lack of vitamins results in serious health problems.

Most people assume all vitamins are supplied by a well-balanced diet. However, it is difficult under current conditions to eat either the necessary variety, quality, or quantity of foods to get all the essential vitamins. Adequate research has been done to prove the normal consumption of foods detailed in the *four food groups* does not supply these necessary vitamins. This is due mainly to the inadequate processing, distribution, handling, storage, and preparation of food. Pollutants (oxidants) also put tremendous stress on our immune systems, thereby requiring more vitamins to rid the body of unwanted toxins. The standard three-meals-a-day diet is lacking in some of the vitamins we need for our body's metabolic competence. The lack of vitamins allows our body's defenses to be more vulnerable to disease. Also, some of the foods we eat are in reality "antinutrient" foods, thus robbing our body of nutrients necessary for digestion and assimilation.

The **Vitamin Supplement Intake Guide (Quick-Guide 14–1)** on the following pages details this specific information:

1. The current United States Recommended Daily Allowance (USRDA) for selected vitamins.
2. A recommendation for the corresponding *Basic Optimal Health Daily Allowance* (BOHDA), based on major studies which differ from the USRDA's published information.
3. Whether the selected vitamins are fat or water soluble.
4. The known function of the vitamins in the body.
5. Food sources which provide the vitamins.

Quick-Guide 14–1

Vitamin Supplements Intake Guide[1]

Dietary Supplement & Solubility	USRDA[2] Ch = 12 mo.- 4 yr. Ad = 4 yr.-Adults Fe = Adult Female PL = Pregnant/Lactating	Corresponding Basic Optimal Health Daily Allowance[3]	Function in Body	Selected Food Sources[4]
Beta carotene	no USRDA established	• Ch @ • Ad @ 5,000–25,000 IU • Fe @ • PL @	• decreases free radical damage to lipoprotein • decreases risk of heart attacks • converted in liver & intestines to preformed vitamin A	blue green algae, spirulina, chlorella, yellow, orange & dark green vegetables, fish liver oil, green leafy vegetables, peach, alfalfa sprouts, sweet potato, papaya
Biotin *B-complex vitamin*	no USRDA established	• Ch @ 25 mcg • Ad @ 50–300 mcg • Fe @ 25–300 mcg • PL @	• *water-soluble* coenzyme aids metabolism of carbohydrates-fats-proteins • aids in prevention of nervous system disorders • not a true vitamin (made in intestines)	unrefined whole grains: oats, rice, rye, wheat; all meats, liver, leafy green vegetables, poultry, saltwater fish, eggs, nuts, beans
Bioflavonoids* *(see Vitamin P)*				
Folic acid *(folacin)* *B-complex vitamin*	• Ch @ 200 mcg • Ad @ 400 mcg • Fe @ • PL @ 800 mcg	• Ch @ 400 mcg • Ad @ 400–1200 mcg • Fe @ 400–800 mcg • PL @ 800 mcg / pregnant • PL @ 500 mcg / lactating	• *water-soluble* vitamin helps in formation of hemoglobin and red blood cells • normal growth & reproduction • enhances protein metabolism • treats pernicious anemia & sprue	green leafy vegetables, broccoli, asparagus, okra, parsnips, cauliflower, cantaloupe, nuts, legumes, Brussels sprouts, whole-grain cereals, yeast, oranges, carrots
Niacin *(see Vitamin B₃)*				
Pantothenic acid *(see Vitamin B₅)*				
Vitamin A[5] *(retinol)*	• Ch @ 2,500 IU • Ad @ 5,000 IU • Fe @ • PL @ 8,000 IU	• Ch @ 15,000 IU • Ad @ 10,000–50,000 IU • Fe @ • PL @	• essential *fat-soluble*[6] nutrient & antioxidant • aids in growth & repair of body tissues • necessary for night vision • essential for the formation of visual purple	eggs, colored fruits & vegetables, fish liver oil, milk & dairy products, beef liver

[1] The FDA requires disclosure of certain nutritional values in food products. Shaded rows of the chart indicate which values *must* appear on nutrition labels of foods and drugs—all other ingredients *may* be listed.
[2] The U.S. government's evaluation of the minimum daily requirements of a substance to prevent a deficiency disease or condition.
[3] Where there is a distinct difference between the USRDA and other major studies.
[4] Complete listings available from published literature. Amounts of nutrients and vitamins vary among producers and their respective products. Always check labels of foods to verify contents.
[5] Recommended one-half of the requirement be in the form of beta carotene.
[6] *Fat-soluble vitamins* are stored in either the fat (lipid) tissues or body organs for longer periods and can cause toxicity only at very large doses. Likewise, minerals, which are stored primarily in the bones and muscle tissue, require extremely large doses to cause toxicity in the body.

Vitamin Supplements Intake Guide (continued)

Dietary Supplement	USRDA Ch = 12 mo.- 4 yr. Ad = 4 yr.-Adults Fe = Adult Female PL = Pregnant/ Lactating	Corresponding Basic Optimal Health Daily Allowance	Function in Body	Selected Food Sources
Vitamin B₁ *(thiamin)*	• Ch @ 0.7 mg • Ad @ 1.5 mg • PL @ 2 mg	• Ch @ 25 mg • Ad @ 50–300 mg • Fe @ 25–300 mg • PL @	• maintains healthy skin, mouth, eyes, hair • helps stabilize appetite • essential for carbohydrate metabolism • essential for normal function of heart, nervous system, digestion, growth, learning capacity	organ meats, pork, nuts, whole wheat, wheat germ, poultry, fish, brown rice, egg yolks, legumes, whole grains, blackstrap molasses, brewer's yeast
Vitamin B₂ *(riboflavin)*	• Ch @ 0.8 mg • Ad @ 1.7 mg • PL @ 2 mg	• Ch @ 25 mg • Ad @ 50–300 mg • Fe @ 25–300 mg • PL @	• *water-soluble* vitamin prevents inflammations • helps carbohydrate-fat-protein metabolism • produces antibody & red blood cells • essential for healthy eyes, hair, skin, nails	cheese, milk & milk products, egg yolks, peanuts, brewer's yeast, nuts, organ meats, whole grains, blackstrap molasses
Vitamin B₃ *(niacin & niacinamide)*	• Ch @ 9–16 mg • Ad @ 8 mg • Fe @ 13 mg • PL @ 15 mg	• Ch @ 25 mg • Ad @ 50–500 mg • Fe @ 25–300 mg • PL @	• *water-soluble* coenzyme essential in digestion • dilates blood vessels & helps blood circulation • reduces cholesterol in blood • needed for healthy skin, nervous system & production of sex hormones	lean meats, poultry, fish, peanuts, wheat germ, brewer's yeast
Vitamin B₅ *(pantothenic acid)*	• Ch @ 5 mg • Ad @ 10 mg • Fe @ • PL @ 10 mg	• Ch @ 25 g • Ad @ 25–500 g • Fe @ 25–300 g • PL @	• *water-soluble* vitamin aids in resisting stress • aids in formation of fats & provides energy • stimulates growth	eggs, orange juice, brewer's yeast, legumes, liver, whole grains, wheat germ, mushrooms, salmon
Vitamin B₆ *(pyridoxine)*	• Ch @ 700 mcg • Ad @ 2 mg • Fe @ • PL @ 250 mg	• Ch @ 25 g • Ad @ 50–500 mg • Fe @ 50–300 mg • PL @	• essential *water-soluble enzyme* factor for carbohydrate-fat-protein metabolism • helps in digestion & weight control • enhances healthy skin, nerves & muscles • forms antioxidants	milk, cabbage, cantaloupe, legumes, blackstrap molasses, meats, organ meats, peas, wheat germ, whole grains, brown rice, prunes, leafy green vegetables, brewer's yeast
Vitamin B₁₂ *(cobalamin)*	• Ch @ 3 mcg • Ad @ 6 mcg • Fe @ • PL @ 8 mcg	• Ch @ 25 g • Ad @ 50–500 mcg • Fe @ 25–300 mcg • PL @	• *water-soluble* vitamin essential to formation & maintenance of red blood cells • enhances carbohydrate-fat-protein metabolism • promotes healthy nervous system	pork, beef, organ meats, cheese, milk & milk products, eggs, fish
Vitamin C *(ascorbic acid)*	• Ch @ 40 mg • Ad @ 60 mg • Fe @ 60 mg • PL @ 60 mg	• Ch @ 1,000 mcg • Ad @ 1,000–10,000 mg • Fe @ 500–10,000 mg • PL @	• *water-soluble* nutrient & antioxidant • essential in formation of skin connective tissue • strengthens body's immune system • helps in wound healing	tomatoes, acerola cherries, sprouted alfalfa seeds, peppers, citrus fruits, papaya, cantaloupe, broccoli, strawberries

Vitamin D (cholecalciferol)	• Ch @ 400 IU • Ad @ 400 IU • PL @ 400 IU	• Ch @ 400 IU • Ad @ 400–600 IU • Fe @ 600–800 (age 60+) • PL @	• *fat-soluble* nutrient essential for proper function of nervous system, heart & normal clotting • aids in calcium & phosphorous absorption to prevent osteoporosis in elderly persons	fat, butter, fish liver oil, oily fish (herring, sardines), egg yolks, salmon, tuna, organ meats, bonemeal
Vitamin E (tocopherol)	• Ch @ 10 IU • Ad @ 30 IU • PL @ 30 IU	• Ch @ 200 IU • Ad @ 200–800 IU • Fe @ 100–800 IU • PL @	• *fat-soluble* powerful antioxidant & free radical scavenger • essential for cell respiration & sustains the efficiency of blood flow • composed of several tocopherols of which the alpha form is most active	margarine, cold-pressed oil, whole wheat & wheat germ, sweet potatoes, molasses, nuts, dark green vegetables, eggs, organ meats, oatmeal, liver, desiccated liver
Vitamin F (lineolic acid)	**no USRDA established**	• Ch @ • Ad @ • Fe @ • PL @	• unsaturated fatty acid essential to growth • necessary for healthy skin & hair • makes calcium available to body cells • enhances normal glandular activity • destroys cholestrol	butter, wheat germ, vegetable oils, sunflower seed
Vitamin K (phylloquinone)	**no USRDA established**	• Ch @ • Ad @ 80 mcg males • Fe @ 65 mcg females • PL @	• *fat-soluble* group of similar compounds including: **K-1** from plants; **K-2** made in the intestines by bacteria; **K-3**, a synthetic form • produces blood-clotting factors • helps prevent osteoporosis • not a true vitamin, developed in intestines	widely available in foods such as spinach, green cabbage, tomatoes, liver, lean meats, egg yolk, whole wheat, strawberries
Vitamin P (bioflavonoids)	**no USRDA established** *(take with equivalent amount of vitamin C)*	• Ch @ • Ad @ 500–10,000 mg • Fe @ 500–5,000 mg • PL @	• *water-soluble* vitamin prevents colds & flu • promotes healthy capillary walls • enhances growth of connective tissue • helps prevent bruising	buckwheat, black currants, cherries, grapes, fruits

Notes on Vitamins

Notes on Vitamins

MINERALS

Boron

Boron is a trace mineral which is essential in the prevention of osteoporosis and arthritis. Many people are deficient in this mineral simply because of poor soil quality. Lack of boron in soils may be one of the reasons for the failure of medical therapies in the treatment of both osteoporosis and osteoarthritis. Boron is a *helper* mineral that helps the body maximize its use of calcium, magnesium, and phosphorous.

Chromium Picolinate

Chromium picolinate is the most bioavailable (best absorbed) form of chromium. It is essential for the prevention and the complementary medical treatment of diabetes, heart disease, atherosclerosis, high blood cholesterol, obesity and other eating disorders. Chromium picolinate is a general tonic which improves energy, cuts the cravings for sweets, and normalizes blood sugar levels by helping in the production of insulin. It plays a vital role in the breaking down of simple sugars in the body. It is also important to the body's enzymes and hormones.

Copper

Copper is an important trace mineral stored in the liver. This vital component of enzymes is necessary to the breaking down of proteins for rebuilding body tissue. It is also required to convert the body's iron into hemoglobin—and is essential in the utilization of vitamin C.

Copper is essential to optimal operation of brain nerves and connective tissues. Copper in the optimal doses controls cholesterol and is vital in the prevention of aortic aneurysms. The zinc-to-copper ratio must be balanced in the body (*8:1 zinc:copper is ideal*) and can be determined through a combination of blood, urine, and hair tests. If testing is not possible, make sure that supplemental zinc and copper are taken in the optimal ratio.

Selenium

Low selenium levels are associated with an increased risk of atherosclerosis. Approximately 80% of selenium content in foods is lost in the processing of food. Selenium is an antioxidant which works in conjunction with vitamin E to protect vascular tissue from damage by toxins. Besides preventing cardiovascular disease, selenium helps in both the prevention and complementary medical treatment of cancer, arthritis, and a long list of degenerative diseases, among which are premature aging and hardening of the tissues. It is generally conceded that men need more selenium than women. Almost half the selenium found in the male body is in the reproductive organs.

Zinc

This essential mineral is needed by everyone! It is found in every cell of the body. Zinc performs many important functions in the body such as converting proteins into energy, RNA/DNA formation, male prostate gland protection, and, in conjunction with calcium, increasing bone formation.

Zinc is becoming the most frequently prescribed supplement in holistic health centers—and with good reason. It can have a wide range of beneficial effects that include enhancement of wound healing, promotion of a healthy immune system, optimizing sexual performance, and balancing thyroid function.

Zinc is believed to play a vital role in mental functions, the healing process, blood stability, and in keeping a proper alkaline balance in the body. The wound-healing effects of zinc supplementation have been known since 1955. Many double-blind studies since that time have demonstrated zinc's ability to accelerate healing in post-surgical cases, leg ulcers, and gastric ulcers.

Zinc deficiency signs and symptoms are similar to the general signs of malnutrition and include growth retardation, infertility, delayed sexual maturation, low sperm count, hair loss, various skin conditions, diarrhea, weakened immune response, behavioral and sleep disturbances, vitamin A nonresponsive night blindness, impaired taste or smell perception, impaired wound healing, and white spots or horizontal ridges on the fingernails.

A recent study showed that taking about 10 zinc lozenges (containing 23 mg. of zinc) per day reduced the length of recovery from the common cold from an average of 10.8 days to 3.9 days. One of the reasons for this may be because zinc is a cofactor for a number of enzymes involved in the immune response. Zinc deficiency is associated with compromised immune response and is normalized by zinc replacement therapy.

Many skin problems, including acne, boils, some forms of hair loss, and severe body odor, respond favorably to zinc supplementation of 100–150 mg. per day. Topical application of zinc sulfate solution can reduce the length of healing of cold sores caused by both Type 1 and Type 2 herpes virus from 17 days to 5.3 days.

Many over-the-counter ointments advertised for the relief of cold sores, diaper rashes, and hemorrhoids have zinc as one of their ingredients. At least one mouthwash advocated for periodontal disease prevention and halitosis contains therapeutic amounts of zinc. Corticosteroid therapy used for a variety of reasons rapidly depletes zinc stores and causes retardation of tissue healing. A variety of other drugs, alcohol, and tobacco smoke also deplete zinc body stores and require supplementation to prevent skin and immune system problems.

Growth in children, healthy hair, taste perception, and the sense of smell are all related to zinc status. Anorexia nervosa, bulimia, and other eating disorders respond positively to zinc supplementation.

Most recently, ophthalmologic studies have demonstrated that zinc supplementation can prevent macular degeneration, a common cause of blindness that occurs with aging. Memory problems (*"no zinc, no think"*), behavioral disorders, insomnia, depression, and many other nervous system abnormalities have been associated with zinc insufficiency. Processed foods, stress, diuretics, alcohol, and other factors deplete the body of zinc. The nearly 200 signs and symptoms of the "candidiasis syndrome," popularized by a rash of sensationalized books, all recommend the use of zinc supplementation as a part of both its treatment and prevention. Many authors wonder whether candidiasis is really a zinc deficiency problem in disguise. Zinc and copper are both involved in optimal thyroid function, liver function, and cholesterol control. This balance is also essential for the correct metabolism of essential fatty acids and their conversion into various hormones. Balancing these two minerals may be crucial to the prevention of many common diseases, including cardiovascular disease, hypothyroidism, prostatitis, and different forms of arthritis.

Dr. Rona does not recommend the long-term use of zinc supplementation without supervision by a healthcare practitioner. Aside from the potential heart and circulatory problems caused by copper depletion with high zinc supplementation, some individuals have problems with absorption of one or both of these minerals.

For those concerned about being adequately nourished in zinc the safest thing to do is to optimize the diet. The most recently published RDA (Recommended Dietary Allowance) for adults is 15 mg. per day. In approximately 1,000 nutritional intake assessments done in Dr. Rona's practice over the past five years, less than 10% get the minimum RDA zinc intake levels from their diets. The richest sources of zinc are generally the high-protein foods such as organ meat, seafood (especially shellfish), oysters, whole grains, and legumes (especially beans and peas). Beyond ensuring zinc adequacy from the diet, the best thing to do is see a holistic healthcare practitioner to decide whether or not supplementation for specific therapy is worth trying.

Mineral Supplements Intake Guide

Essential mineral elements normally found in the body are supplied in natural foods. Often, they are lost or destroyed in production, distribution, delivery, storage, and/or during meal preparation. These natural minerals are needed for the body's purifying and cleansing processes. The essential minerals are divided into two categories, *macrominerals* and *microminerals*. The listings in the chart below differentiate these two types of essential minerals. Those noted in the listing here are detailed in the chart on the following pages.

Macrominerals	Microminerals	
• Calcium	• Boron	• Molybdenum
Chlorine	Cobalt	• Nickel
• Magnesium	• Chromium	• Selenium
• Phosphorous	• Copper	• Silicon
Potassium	Fluorine	• Tin
Sodium	• Iodine	• Vanadium
Sulfur	• Iron	• Zinc
	Manganese	

Macrominerals are needed in the diet in amounts exceeding 100 mg. per day. Of all the macromineral nutrients, only calcium tends to be low in the American diet.

Microminerals are also known as "trace elements" and are needed in the body in extremely small units. Many of the micronutrients are needed in such minute amounts, they are rarely a problem, with the exception of iron and zinc.

The **Mineral Supplements Intake Guide (Quick-Guide 14–2)** details the following information for the macrominerals and microminerals indicated above:
1. The current United States Recommended Daily Allowance (USRDA) for the selected minerals mentioned in the chapter.
2. A recommendation for the corresponding *Basic Optimal Health Daily Allowance* (BOHDA), based on major studies which differ from the USRDA's published information.
3. The known function of the mineral in the body.
4. Food sources which provide the mineral.

Quick-Guide 14–2

Mineral Supplements Intake Guide

Dietary Supplement	USRDA[1] Ch = 12 mo.- 4 yr. Ad = 4 yr.-Adults Fe = Adult Female PL = preg-nant/lactating	Corresponding Basic Optimal Health Daily Allowance[2]	Function in Body	Selected Food Sources[3]
Boron*	**no USRDA established**	• Ch @ • Ad @ 3–6 mg • Fe @ 2–5 mg • PL @	• *micromineral* modulates calcium & magnesium retention in bones & lessens fibromyalgia • helps prevent osteoporosis, rheumatism & arthritis • treats tendinitis, joints & joint deterioration, sciatica, heel & bone spurs • treats skin disease & scleroderma • treats hormone imbalance & raises serum estrogen levels • lessens progression of Alzheimer's disease	fruits, vegetables
Calcium *(highest mineral content in body)*	• Ch @ 800 mg • Ad @ 1000 mg • PL @ 1300 mg	• Ch @ 800–1000 mg • Ad @ 1000–2000 mg • Fe @ 1000–1500 mg • Fe @ 1200–2000 mg (over 52 yr.) • PL @ 1500–2000 mg	• *macromineral* essential to body synthesis • develops and maintains strong bones & teeth • protects against osteoporosis • ensures proper blood clotting • aids vitality & endurance	dairy prod. (8 oz. nonfat milk = 300 mg; 1 C. yogurt = 400+ mg); goat's milk, tofu, oats, brewer's yeast, legumes & dark green vegetables, enriched cereals, citrus fruits, figs, shellfish, liver, nuts, antacids w/o aluminum (Tums® = 200+ mg)
Chromium* *(in picolinate form)*	**no USRDA established**	• Ch @ 200 mcg • Ad @ 200–600 mcg • Fe @ 200–600 mcg • PL @	• *micromineral* essential for maximization of glucose • for synthesis of cholesterol & fatty acids • essential part of enzyme systems	whole grains & whole-grain cereals, brewer's yeast, beer, clams, corn oil, dried beans, cheese, potato, brown rice, meats
Copper	• Ch @ 1 mg • Ad @ 2 mg • Fe @ 2 mg • PL @ 2 mg	• Ch @ 1 mg • Ad @ 0.5–2 mg • Fe @ 0.5–2 mg • PL @	• *micromineral* prevents anemia by controlling storage & release of iron to form hemoglobin • promotes energy and connective tissue metabolism • essential part of tissue covering nerves	nuts, dried peas & beans, dried fruit, raisins, whole grains, leafy vegetables, molasses, organ meats, fish, shell fish, legumes—widely available in most foods

[1] The U.S. government's evaluation of the minimum daily requirements of a substance to prevent a deficiency disease or condition.
[2] Where there is a distinct difference between the USRDA and other major studies.
[3] Complete listings available from published literature. Amounts of nutrients and minerals vary among producers and their respective products. Always check labels to verify contents.
* Essential for human nutrition, but no USRDA has been established.

Mineral Supplements Intake Guide (continued)

Dietary Supplement	USRDA Ch = 12 mo.- 4 yr. Ad = 4 yr.-Adults Fe = Adult Female PL = preg- nant/lactating	Corresponding Basic Optimal Health Daily Allowance	Function in Body	Selected Food Sources
Iodine	• Ch @ 70 mcg • Ad @ 150 mcg • Fe @ 150 mcg • PL @ 150 mcg	• Ch @ 100 mcg / from iodized table salt • Ad @ 150–300 mcg • Fe @ 150–300 mcg • PL @	• *micromineral* essential for total body metabolism • essential for normal function of thyroid gland • prevents goiter	iodized table salt, food grown near the ocean, kelp (bladderwrack), mushrooms
Iron	• Ch @ 10 gm • Ad @ 10 gm • PL @ 18 mg	• Ch @ • Ad @ 15–30 gm • Fe @ 15–30 gm • PL @ 20–30 gm	• *micromineral*, essential part of hemoglobin carrying oxygen to tissues • part of enzyme system of all cells for energy production • important to muscle tone	whole-grain cereal products, nuts, legumes, raisins, molasses, green leafy vegetables, potatoes, yellow vegetables, dried fruits, boiled lentils or kidney beans
Magnesium	• Ch @ 200 mg • Ad @ 400 mg • PL @ 450 mg	• Ch @ 250–500 mg • Ad @ 500–1,000 mg • Fe @ 500–750 mg	• *macromineral* helps develop strong bones & teeth • helps regulate muscle tone • aids in proper functioning of nerves	green leafy vegetables, nuts, seeds, whole-grain cereals, legumes, apples, cherries, figs, raisins, prunes, lemons, alfalfa, celery, cherry juice
Phosphorous (2nd highest mineral content in body)	• Ch @ 800 mg • Ad @ 1 gm • PL @ 1.3 gm	• Ch @ • Ad @ 200–400 mg • Fe @ 200–400 mg • PL @	• *macromineral* essential for development of strong bones & teeth • essential to development of enzymes in cells that control storage & release of energy • transports fatty acids in body	whole-wheat grains, nuts, legumes, dairy products, eggs, phosphate additives/carbonated drinks, yellow cheese, glandular meats, poultry, seeds: sesame, sunflower
Selenium*	**no USRDA established**	• Ch @ 100 mcg • Ad @ 100–400 mcg • Fe @ 150–300 mcg • PL @	• *micromineral* required to activate enzyme to combat cell membrane oxidation • preserves tissue elasticity for body's maximum immune response & helps prevent cancer • protects normal cells against radiation damage	broccoli, onions, tomatoes, tuna, nuts, brown rice, grains, nuts, cereals (especially those grown in ND, SD, MT, WY), chicken, turkey, brewer's yeast
Zinc	• Ch @ 8 mg • Ad @ 15 mg • Fe @ 12 mg • PL @ 20/25 mg	• Ch @ 15 mg • Ad @ 30–100 mg • Fe @ 20–50 mg • PL @	• *micromineral* aiding digestion & metabolism of phosphorous, carbohydrates & proteins • component of body synthesis for normal growth & development; enhances wound healing • promotes healthy immune system • part of insulin & reproductive processes • increases male sexual potency; elevates testosterone; reduces prostate swelling	organ meats, poultry dark meat, fish, seafood (especially oysters), liver, eggs, legumes (soybeans & peanuts), whole grains, spinach, mushrooms, sunflower seeds

HERBS AND WHOLE FOOD SUPPLEMENTS

Aloe Vera

Many of you know that aloe vera is an ingredient in cosmetics, pharmaceuticals, gels, lotions, shampoos, juices, creams, toothpastes, and nutritional supplements. Some people use aloe topically for its antibiotic properties, others internally for its bowel cleansing action, antioxidant, or anti-aging effects.

Aloe vera contains many free radical scavengers and immune system enhancers. These include beta carotene, vitamin B complex, vitamin C, selenium, silicon, zinc, boron, calcium, chromium, magnesium, manganese, potassium, polyphenols, essential fatty acids, saponins, and large molecular weight polymeric sugars (e.g., acemannan).

Aloe is very effective in the treatment of digestive disorders. One of the many reasons why aloe vera is so effective for digestive problems is its content of natural digestive enzymes and cofactors. Aloe contains amylase, lipase, oxidase, catalase, bradykinase, glucomannan, and fiber. All reduce inflammation; stimulate better digestion of protein, carbohydrate, and fat; and soothe ulcers.

Medical and scientific literature supports aloe vera's primary or complementary use for a long list of conditions. The following chart indicates a partial listing of conditions known to benefit from aloe vera:

Chart 14–1
Selected Conditions Known to Benefit from Aloe Vera Treatment

- Acne
- Allergies
- Amenorrhea (no menses)
- Asthma
- Bites (bee stings/insect bites)
- Bleeding/hemorrhage (anywhere)
- Boils
- Burns
- Bruises
- Cancer[5]
- Canker sores (mouth ulcers)
- Chemical burns
- Chicken pox itch
- Colds and flu
- Colitis and Crohn's Disease
- Constipation[6]
- Coughs
- Denture sores
- Diaper rashes
- Eczema
- Fatigue (often used as a tonic)

- Fever
- Food poisoning
- Headache
- Heartburn/indigestion (from any cause)
- Hemorrhoids
- Hepatitis and jaundice
- Herpes
- Inflammation and infections (anywhere)
- Menopause
- PMS (Pre-Menstrual Syndrome)
- Pain
- Psoriasis
- Scars
- Sunburns
- Stomach problems
- Thinning hair
- Tinnitus (ringing in the ears)
- Ulcers (anywhere)
- Venereal diseases
- Warts
- Wounds (anywhere)

---

[5] Aloe contains several anticarcinogenic compounds.
[6] Avoid as a laxative during pregnancy unless anthraquinone content of the aloe vera being consumed is known to be low.

Dr. Rona has often recommended aloe vera be taken internally in juice form. Most patients love the results but hate the taste of different brands of aloe vera juice. Many either try to disguise the taste by diluting it with sweet juices, thus reducing its potency, or just give up because nothing neutralizes the sour/bitter aftertaste. One option may be to swallow capsules containing live aloe vera concentrate.

The whole leaf cold processing method maximizes the desirable constituents of aloe vera juice, increases the pleasant polysaccharide concentration, eliminates the undesirable anthraquinones, and improves its penetration into the body.

"Dr. Rona, how can aloe vera be effective for so many different conditions?"

The answer lies in the nearly 100 ingredients contained in the leaf of the healthy aloe plant. These include numerous antioxidant vitamins and minerals. A closer look at the listing of reported and suggested uses will give you confidence that aloe vera has withstood the test of time and the scrutiny of cynical investigations.

It is difficult to know how aloe vera works—it has very complex properties:
- It is an excellent nutrient with important proteins, vitamins, minerals, and some substances that are essential to the release of energy in the body of humans and animals alike.
- Its chemical properties allow it to penetrate the skin and body membranes, thus carrying essential nutrients to the living cells of both the skin and internal organs.
- It contains several enzymes necessary to the body but not yet fully understood by science.

Apple Cider Vinegar

Apple cider vinegar is a fundamental health aid that has a multitude of uses and is especially useful in both short- and long-term storage scenarios, whether for cooking or for its medicinal properties. It's made by fermenting the juice of whole, fresh apples. It's high in calcium, potassium, sodium, phosphorus, and other trace minerals. It has an average acetic acid content of 5% and has been used as both a food and a medicine.

A long list of medical conditions can benefit from apple cider vinegar supplementation, including obesity, infections, allergies, arthritis, fatigue, circulatory disorders, and thinning hair. It is true that apple cider vinegar can increase the body's acidity, but in many individuals this produces a beneficial effect. In others, the excess acidity makes their symptoms worse. Some people are allergic to it—in other cases apple cider vinegar has no effect whatsoever. Published research indicates that apple cider vinegar inhibits diarrhea due to its astringent property, helps oxygenate the blood, increases metabolic rate, improves digestion, fights tooth decay and intestinal parasites, and improves blood clotting ability.

Many people over age 60 suffer from a lack of stomach acid. Supplementation of 1 to 2 tablespoons of apple cider vinegar with each meal aids in protein digestion and prevents many vitamin and mineral deficiencies. Add some honey to sweeten vinegar's taste, if necessary. Apple cider vinegar can also be used as a mouthwash and throat gargle for antiseptic purposes. It has no significant side effects and is safe for diabetics. Also, despite its sodium content, apple cider vinegar is suitable for low-sodium diets.

Bee Supplements

Most of you are familiar with bee supplements like bee pollen, royal jelly, and propolis. If not, here is basic information about these bee-produced supplements:

- *Propolis* is a rather strong-tasting bee product well known by health advocates for its natural antibiotic properties.
- *Royal jelly* is a supplement which must be combined with honey to preserve its potency. Royal jelly has been touted as a natural substance which benefits a wide range of health conditions. This is because it contains all the B complex vitamins, high concentrations of vitamin B_5 (pantothenic acid), vitamin B_6, acetylcholine, minerals, vitamins A, C, D, and E, enzymes, hormones, amino acids and immune-boosting substances. Most healthy people tolerate it well without any side effects.
- *Bee pollen* contains simple sugars, amino acids, calcium, carotene, copper, enzymes, iron, magnesium, manganese, polyunsaturated fatty acids, sodium, potassium, vitamin C, and plant sterols.

There is no known toxicity, but the rare individual may be allergic to pollen and experience hay-feverlike symptoms. If you are a well-controlled diabetic or have hypoglycemia (low blood sugar), taking any bee supplement should not affect your blood sugars noticeably. If, on the other hand, your sugar level is poorly controlled, these supplements might upset the apple cart for you. Check the label or check with the manufacturer concerning the amount of glucose and fructose in each capsule or tablet before taking bee-produced supplements.

Beet Root Powder

Beet root powder is particularly high in carotenes, iron, calcium, potassium, niacin, copper, vitamin C, folic acid, zinc, manganese, magnesium, and phosphorus. Beet root powder enriches the blood and is also a good general tonic. The most optimal way of deriving the benefits of beet root aside from eating the real thing is to swallow capsules of beet root live food concentrate.

Bladderwrack

Also known as *fucus vesiculosus,* or *kelp,* bladderwrack is high in sodium alginate, calcium, phosphorus, magnesium, iron, sodium, selenium, potassium, iodine, sulfur, vitamins C and B_{12}. It's an alkaline-forming food, replenishing glands and nerves, particularly the thyroid. Bladderwrack is a good source of trace minerals and has traditionally been used in the complementary medical treatment of obesity, goiter, hypothyroidism, anemia, emaciation, impotence, nervousness, a weakened immune system, and hair loss.

Blue Green Algae & Other Green Foods

Blue green algae, spirulina, chlorella, barley green, green kamut, and other concentrated green foods are all excellent sources of high-quality vegetable protein, complex carbohydrates, essential fatty acids, essential amino acids, phytochemicals, chlorophyll, vitamins, minerals and fiber. *These whole foods plus water provide enough nutrition to help sustain life for years.*

Although there are only minor differences among all these "green food" products, blue green algae seems to have a bit of an edge in some areas, especially with respect to a higher vitamin B_{12} and beta carotene content. All green foods have these qualities:

- natural appetite suppressants
- rich in beta carotene and other carotenoids

- high bioavailability (easily digested and absorbed compared to synthetic vitamins and minerals)
- strong antioxidant properties

Some of the many beneficial effects of green foods include higher energy, greater physical stamina, improved digestion and elimination, allergy relief, and immune system boosting. All green foods are compatible with each other as well as all other supplements on this list.

Fo-Ti

Fo-ti is a Chinese herb useful for improving deleterious effects of aging, arthritis, rheumatism, atherosclerosis, constipation, senility, gray hair, impotency, and insomnia. Effective in increasing blood circulation and energy.

Ginger

Also known as *zingiber officinale*, this herb is best known for its soothing qualities for the gastrointestinal tract. It is particularly effective for nausea associated with pregnancy (morning sickness), anorexia, gas and flatulence, gastric and intestinal spasms, acute colds, painful menstruation, joint stiffness, and cold extremities. Ginger is a cardiac tonic, eases uterine pain, decreases serum cholesterol, and helps poor circulation.

Ginkgo Biloba

Also known as *maidenhair*, ginkgo is a strong antioxidant which can produce relaxation of blood vessels, inhibit platelet aggregation, increase peripheral and cerebral blood flow, and act in general as a cardiovascular and brain tonic. Ginkgo biloba has traditionally been used in the complementary medical treatment of arterial insufficiency, ischemic heart disease, peripheral vascular disease (it affects both arteries and veins), memory loss, other failing mental faculties, almost any neurological condition, tinnitus (ringing in the ears), and high blood pressure.

Hawthorne Berries

Also known as *crataegus oxyacantha*, this herb is best known for its use in cardiac weakness, valvular murmurs, shortness of breath, mitral valve regurgitation, chest/angina pain, anemia associated with heart irregularity, and nervous exhaustion. Hawthorne is high in bioflavonoids which can help heal chronic muscle, tendon, and ligament inflammations. It has traditionally been used in the complementary medical treatment of coronary artery disease, angina pectoris, arrhythmias, arteriosclerosis, and other circulatory weaknesses. Hawthorne berries have a potent synergistic effect with the digitalis cardiac glycosides and should be used with caution by people taking prescription cardiac drugs.

Kola Nut

Also known as *cola acuminata, cola sitida,* and *cola vera*, this herb is a natural antidepressant, gastrointestinal stimulant, astringent, diuretic, and pain reliever. Kola nut has traditionally been used in the complementary medical treatment of depression, nervous irritability of the stomach, chronic diarrhea, obesity, migraines, tremors, insomnia, and constipation.

Ma Huang

Also known as *ephedra, Brigham, desert, or Mormon tea.*[7] It stimulates the sympathetic nervous system, decreases bronchial spasms, works as a natural decongestant, increases energy, and helps curb appetite. It has traditionally been used in the complementary medical treatment of asthma, allergies, fatigue, colds, the flu, eating disorders, and obesity. Studies also indicate that it boosts *thermogenesis*—the body's natural ability to burn fat. Ma huang works synergistically with white willow bark and seaweeds such as bladderwrack (kelp) and dulse for the treatment of fatigue, colds, flu, and obesity.

Parsley

Also known as *ligusticum porterii*, this common herb has natural anti-viral, anti-bacterial, expectorant, and diuretic effects. It has traditionally been used in the complementary medical treatment of viral infections, sore throats, bronchitis, coughs, infected cuts and wounds, enlarged prostates, and fluid retention. Parsley works well to disguise the odor of garlic and synergistically with other herbal antibiotics like echinacea, goldenseal, and chaparral.

Saw Palmetto

Also known as *serenoa serrulata, serenoa repens,* or *sagal serrulata*, this herb works as a diuretic, nerve sedative, expectorant, general nutritive tonic, urinary antiseptic, gastrointestinal stimulant, muscle builder, and circulatory stimulant. Saw palmetto has traditionally been used in the complementary medical treatment of prostate conditions (benign prostatic hypertrophy, prostatitis), enuresis (bed wetting), stress incontinence, infections of the genitourinary tract, and muscle-wasting diseases of any kind.

Siberian Ginseng

Also known as *eleutherococcus senticosus*, this general tonic is a circulatory stimulant which fights stress, debility, exhaustion, depression, obesity, poor memory, and low sex drive. Studies show that long-term use may increase both physical stamina and IQ.

White Willow

Also known as *salix nigra, salix alba,* or *salix discolor*, this herb is powerful because of its content of salicin and tannins. It has anti-inflammatory, antipyretic, analgesic, antiseptic, and astringent properties. Studies also indicate that it can boost thermogenesis—the body's natural ability to burn fat. White willow has traditionally been used in the complementary medical treatment of pain, obesity, arthritis and rheumatism, connective tissue inflammation, headaches, muscle aches, fevers, and infections of all types.

---

[7] A great deal of confusion surrounds the purported toxicity of this herb. If you isolate one of the dozens of chemical compounds found in any herb, concentrate it, and use it as a drug, there could indeed be toxicity. Herbs were not meant to be used in this fashion. Only pharmaceutical manufacturers use herbs in this way and as a result, get toxic effects. When one uses the whole herb, balanced by nature or synergistically with other herbs, toxicity is extremely rare. Ma huang (*ephedra*) is a whole herb. Ephedrine is simply one of the many components of ma huang and is synthesized by drug companies and sold as a drug. Ephedrine is the chemical responsible for the side effects frequently complained about by the critics of herbal medicine. *Ephedrine does not have the same properties as ma huang*—any claim to the contrary is false.

Yerba Maté

Also known as *ilex paraguayensis*, this herb is used as a stimulating beverage throughout much of Latin America.

Yerba maté is a central nervous system stimulant but has some calming properties. It is an antispasmodic, helps control excessive appetite, and, if taken only during daytime hours, helps induce a restful sleep at night. Yerba maté contains caffeine (0.2%–2%), but significantly less than coffee or tea. It also contains iron and may help with alertness and iron deficiency. It has diuretic properties but is nontoxic if used in moderation. Excessive consumption or caffeine sensitivity may be problematic (diarrhea, insomnia, anxiety) in sensitive individuals but far less so than coffee, tea, or soft drinks and well worth using in small amounts for its health-promoting qualities.

Herbal and Whole Food Supplements Guides

There are more than 400 herbs in commerce in the U.S. today.[8] It is neither possible nor needful to review all of them here. However, the next two **Guides** will further explicate those herbs and whole food supplements discussed earlier in this section. The **Basic Herbal Supplement Efficacy Guide (Quick-Guide 14–3)** on the following page lists the herbs referenced in this chapter, classifying them according to the **body system(s) benefited** and **identifying which vitamins and minerals they supply.** The body systems categories are

1. **Stimulants:** increase system stimulus and increase blood circulation
2. **Diuretics:** increase the urine output to remove harmful substances
3. **Expectorants:** cause the expulsion of mucus and break up congestion
4. **Astringents:** cleansers acting as natural "antibiotics"
5. **Nervines:** relieve nervous irritation caused by strain and tension
6. **Tonics:** strengthen all organs affected by the action of digestion

Some herbs may be listed under more than one category. Most botanical plants contain vitamins and minerals the human body can digest more easily than those from animals or fish. This makes herbs excellent sources of vitamins and minerals our bodies need.

The **Basic Herbal and Whole Food Supplement Intake Guide (Quick-Guide 14–4)** identifies the major function(s) of these herbs in the body, their sources, and the forms available for their utilization. Every family's medicine chest should contain herbal remedies to alleviate the symptoms of simple, everyday health problems. Recommendations for *Basic Optimal Health Daily Allowance* (BOHDA) are made for selected herbs, based on major efficacy studies.

> **Caution:**
>
> Any substance, including the mildest of herbs, can be toxic when used without intelligent and reasonable care.
>
> Toxicity and consumer safety are relative—any herb is safe when consumed in reasonable amounts by reasonable consumers.

---

[8] As of late fall 1995, approximately 280 herbal supplements have been approved by the Food and Drug Administration (FDA). Sales of herbs have more than doubled in the past 10 years. During the past 30-year period, medical records and poison control center reports regarding herb-related toxicity incidents have provided no substantial evidence that herbs are hazardous to the health of consumers. Most herbs have been used for generations—evidence of their efficacy for treating humans.

Quick-Guide 14–3

Basic Herbal Supplement Efficacy Guide

The selected body systems categories affected by these herbs are: **Stimulants, Diuretics, Expectorants, Astringents, Nervines, and Tonics.**

Herb	S	D	E	A	N	T	Available Vitamin & Mineral Nutrients
Aloe vera	X	X	X			X	beta carotene, B complex, C, selenium, silicon, zinc, boron, calcium, chromium, magnesium, manganese, niacin, phosphorous, potassium, polyphenols, essential fatty acids, saponins, polymeric sugars (acemannan), amylase, lipase, oxidase, catalase, bradykinase, glucomannan, crude & dietary fibers, zinc, natural digestive enzymes & cofactors
Apple cider vinegar	X			X	X		calcium, potassium, sodium, phosphorus, other trace minerals (*more than 90 compounds in all*), crude fiber, niacin, riboflavin, thiamin, vitamins A & C
Bee supplements (Of the 22 elements in the body needing renewal by nutrient intake—enzymes, hormones, amino acids, etc.—only bee pollen contains them all!)	X			X	X	X	**Vitamins:** provitamins A, B$_1$, B$_2$, B$_3$, B$_6$ group, B$_{12}$, pantothenic acid, biotin, folic acid, choline, inositol, C, D, E, K, rutin **Minerals:** calcium, phosphorous, potassium, sulfur, sodium, chlorine, iron, manganese, copper, iodine, zinc, silicon, molybdenum, boron, titanium **Enzymes:** amylase, diastase, saccharase, pectase, phosphatase, catalase, disphorase, cozymase, cytochrome, lactic, dehydrogenase, succinic, hydrogenase, 24 oxidoreductases, 21 transferases, 33 hydrolases, 11 lyases, 5 isomerases, pepsin, trypsin **Amino Acids:** isoleucine, leucine, lysine, methionine, phenylaline, theonine, alanine, valine, histidine, arginine, cystine, tyrosine, aspartic acid, glutamic acid, hydroxyproline, proline, serine **Other:** nucleic acids, flavonoids, phenolic acids, tarpenes, nucleosides, glucose, fructose, gibberellins **Propolis:** potent natural antibiotic properties kills all types of bacteria, viruses, yeasts, fungi & parasites; natural sterilizer **Royal jelly:** benefits a wide range of health conditions; contains all B complex, high concentrations of B$_5$ (pantothenic acid), B$_6$ acetylcholine, minerals, A, C, D, and E, enzymes, hormones, amino acids & immune-boosting substances **Bee pollen:** contains simple sugars, amino acids, calcium, carotene, copper, enzymes, iron, magnesium, manganese, polyunsaturated fatty acids, sodium, potassium, C & plant sterols
Beet root powder						X	B$_6$, carotenes, highest iron available, calcium, potassium, niacin, copper, C, folic acid, zinc, manganese, magnesium, phosphorous
Bladderwrack	X	X				X	calcium, phosphorus magnesium, iron, sodium, selenium, potassium, iodine, sulfur, vitamin A, C, B$_{12}$, high in sodium alginate, good source of trace minerals, zinc, crude & dietary fibers, protein
Blue green algae						X	
Fo-ti	X					X	magnesium, cobalt, dietary & crude fibers, iron, manganese, niacin, phosphorous, potassium, protein, riboflavin, selenium, sodium, thiamin, tin, vitamin C
Ginger root	X	X				X	magnesium
Ginkgo biloba						X	trace minerals, zinc
Hawthorne						X	3.5% caffeine
Kola nut	X				X	X	vitamin A, C, thiamin riboflavin, phosphorous, iron, manganese, niacin, phosphorous, potassium, protein, thiamin
Ma huang	X	X					A & C, trace minerals, zinc, calcium, crude & dietary fibers, magnesium, manganese, niacin, phosphorous, potassium, protein
Parsley	X	X		X		X	vitamin A
Saw palmetto	X	X		X		X	B, copper, zinc, calcium, iron, chromium, manganese, niacin, potassium, riboflavin, thiamin
Siberian ginseng	X					X	calcium, trace minerals, cobalt, crude & dietary fiber, iron, magnesium, manganese, niacin, phosphorous, potassium, protein, riboflavin, selenium, silicon, sodium, tin, vitamin C, zinc
White willow		X		X			flavin, selenium, silicon, sodium, tin, vitamin C, zinc
Yerba maté	X					X	0.2%–2% caffeine, significantly less than coffee or tea, iron

Quick-Guide 14–4

Basic Herbal and Whole Food Supplements Intake Guide

Dietary Supplement (no USRDA established)	Basic Optimal Health Daily Allowance Ch = 12 mo.– 4 yr. Ad = 4 yr.–Adults Fe = Adult Female PL = Pregnant/Lactating	Complementary Medicinal Properties (Functions in Body)	Plant Source & Forms
Aloe vera	*external use:* apply to all areas generously • Ch @ apply 3X–4X • Ad @ apply 3X–4X • Fe @ apply 3X–4X • PL @ apply 3X–4X *internal use:* • Ch @ ½ adult dosage • Ad @ 2–4 fl oz 2X • Fe @ 2–4 fl oz 2X • PL @ use not advised	• *externally:* excellent tissue-healing agent: stimulates cell renewal, deters wrinkles, soothes sunburn, burns & cuts, minimizes scarring & relieves pain; radiation burn treatment without equal; hemorrhoid remedy • *internally:* excellent anti-inflammatory, antiviral & immune-enhancing properties • effective treatment of digestive system, promotes regularity & soothes stomach ulcers; reduces bowel transit time • reduces mucous membranes infection; reduces allergies • helps facilitate & regulate menstrual flow • antioxidant combats damage by free radicals • combats effects of airborne chemical pollutants & radiation • reduces inflammation; relieves diaper rash	**Source:** 200 varieties, only *Barbadensia Miller* species considered the "true aloe" plant; leaves provide the juice (whole-leaf, cold-processed is most effective liquid form and is 99.5% water) **Forms:** *external use:* cream, gel, lotion *internal use:* gel, liquid, flavored juice, capsules of live whole food concentrate, freeze-dried
Apple cider vinegar	• Ch @ 1 tsp. 2X daily • Ad @ 1–2 T. 2X daily • Fe @ 1 T. 2X daily • PL @ 1 T. mealtime • Adults 60+ 1–2 T at mealtime	• *externally:* conditions skin & relieves itching; soothes sprained muscles; relieves foot corns, calluses & athlete's foot • *internally:* beneficial in treating obesity, infection, allergies, fatigue, circulatory disorders, stomach disorders, diarrhea & thinning hair • improves digestion; combats intestinal parasites; helps sweeten bad breath; effectively aids protein digestion & prevents many vitamin and mineral deficiencies; fights tooth decay • eases arthritis, aches & pains; relieves nighttime leg cramps • helps lower cholesterol • helps oxygenate the blood; improves blood-clotting ability • increases metabolic rate	**Source:** fermented juice of whole, fresh apples; usually available in 5% acetic acid content **Forms:** organic liquid form @ 5% acidity recommended **Caution:** *Do not use distilled white vinegar as a substitute for apple cider vinegar.*
Bee supplements, including bee propolis	• Ch @ 2–4 gm 3X • Ad @ 3–6 gm 3X • Fe @ 3–6 gm 3X • PL @ 3–6 gm 3X	• completely fulfills essential vitamin & mineral needs • provides antioxidant protection for life extension • enhances work & sports performance • used by professional & Olympic athletes to increase physical endurance • effective in treatment of multiple sclerosis, infections, cancer, bowel disorders, prostate problems, depression, anemia, arthritis, chronic fatigue, depression, insomnia, menopause, obesity, poor memory and concentration, premature aging, prostatitis, senility, helps allergies & allergic conditions • high dosages used to treat coronary artery disease, high blood fats & nocturia (need to urinate at night caused by an enlarged prostate)	**Source:** plant pollen collected by bees **bee pollen**—male germinating cell of plants, collected & used for food & making royal jelly **propolis**—sticky resin gathered by bees for structural components of hive, sealant & microbial inhibitor **royal jelly**—made by worker bees & fed to all bees for first 3 days, then only to queen bee; super-nutrient & whole food **Forms:** granule, liquid, capsule, tablet, extract, tincture, honey-preserved

	Dosage	Benefits	Source / Forms
Beet root powder	• Ch @ ½ adult dose • Ad @ • Fe @ • PL @	• enriches blood • good general tonic	**Source:** beet root **Forms:** powder of live whole food concentrate, capsule
Bladderwrack (kelp)	• Ch @ ½ adult dose • Ad @ 5–10 gm 3X • Fe @ 5–10 gm 3X • PL @ 5–10 gm 3X	• treatment of immune system & anti-aging • replenishes glands & nerves; treatment of hypothyroidism & goiter • treatment of obesity, anemia, emaciation, hair loss, impotence & nervousness • toxin scavenger for digestive tract	**Source:** *fucus vesiculosus*, or kelp, an ocean plant; whole herb used **Forms:** cut & sifted, powder, capsule, extract
Blue green algae & other green foods	• Ch @ 1–6 gm 3X • Ad @ 4–6 gm 3X • Fe @ 3–6 gm 3X • PL @ 3–6 gm 3X	• nutri-dense concentrated green superfoods strengthen immune system; superior antioxidant source • increases energy, stamina, physical endurance & power of athletes • adds alkalinity to system • cleans cells & tissues of toxins • enhances work and sports performance • prevention & treatment of all viral conditions including Chronic Fatigue Syndrome and AIDS	**Sources:** whole plant of blue green algae, chlorella, spirulina; leaves or sprouts of barley grass, wheat grass, green kamut, spinach, alfalfa; leaves and flowers of broccoli **Forms:** powder, capsule, tablet
Fo-ti	• Ch @ ½ adult dose • Ad @ • Fe @ • PL @	• improves blood circulation; increases energy & stamina, resistance to disease • strong antioxidant & anti-aging properties for arthritis, rheumatism, atherosclerosis, senility, premature gray hair & impotency • stimulates kidneys; diuretic • reduces pain of sciatica & knee joint pain • reduces constipation; detoxifies liver; tonic	**Source:** Chinese herb *Ho Shou-Wu*, tuberous root of *Polygonum multiflorum* **Forms:** powder, extract
Ginger root	• Ch @ ½ adult dose • Ad @ 1–3 gm 3X • Fe @ 1–3 gm 3X • PL @ 1–3 gm 3X	• cardiac tonic stimulates circulatory system, lowers serum cholesterol & lessens joint stiffness & cold extremities • relieves sore throat & reduces effect of acute colds • cleansing of kidneys & bowels • soothes gastrointestinal tract & reduces gas & flatulence, gastric & intestinal spasms • effective for nausea associated with pregnancy (morning sickness) & motion sickness • lessens effects of anorexia • relieves painful menstruation & uterine pain	**Source:** rhizome (underground stalks) of ginger plant; has good storage qualities due to covering on root **Forms:** fresh juice or minced for tea, cut & sifted, powder, capsule, extract
Ginkgo biloba	• Ch @ ½ adult dose • Ad @ 40 mg 3X • Fe @ 40 mg 3X • PL @ 40 mg 3X	• cardiac vasodilator helps heart muscle to reduce heart attack risk • increases peripheral circulation in heart & cold extremities • prevents free radical damage; strong antioxidant • enhances brain's ability to metabolize glucose, increases neurotransmission by improving brain function • improves short-term memory & improves mental alertness; improves brain function by increasing blood supply to the brain • relieves impotency when caused by arterial deficiency • improves memory, failing mental faculties, and other neurological conditions • improves alertness & concentration • aids in proper eye & ear function, effective in treating tinnitus & vertigo	**Source:** fruit of oldest tree on earth, tree leaf extract, also known as *maidenhair* **Forms:** powder, extract

Basic Herbal and Whole Food Supplements Intake Guide (continued)

Dietary Supplement (no USRDA established)	Basic Optimal Health Daily Allowance Ch = 12 mo.- 4 yr. Ad = 4 yr.-Adults Fe = Adult Female PL = Pregnant/Lactating	Complementary Medicinal Properties (Functions in Body)	Plant Source & Forms
Hawthorne berries	• Ch @ ½ adult dose • Ad @ 250 mg 2X • Fe @ 250 mg 2X • PL @ 250 mg 2X	• complementary medical treatment of coronary artery disease, angina pectoris, arrhythmias, arteriosclerosis, and other circulatory weaknesses; potent synergistic effect with digitalis cardiac glycosides (should be used with caution when taking prescription cardiac drugs), used in treatment of cardiac weakness, valvular murmurs, shortness of breath, mitral valve regurgitation, chest/angina pain & anemia associated with heart irregularity and nervous exhaustion • high level of bioflavonoids helps heal chronic muscle, tendon, and ligament inflammations; stabilizes collagen in joints to reduce arthritis suffering • relieves irregularity • aids in insomnia • prevents "little" heart attacks; works best when taken over long period of time	**Source:** made from berries, flowers & leaves of *crataegus oxyacantha* plant, thorny shrub native to Europe **Forms:** powder, cut & sifted, capsule, tea, extract
Kola nut	• Ch @ ½ adult dose • Ad @ • Fe @ • PL @ use not advised	• natural anti-depressant used in complementary medical treatment of depression, nervous irritability of the stomach, chronic diarrhea, obesity, migraines, tremors, insomnia & constipation • gastrointestinal stimulant; natural diuretic • pain reliever • stimulates brain • increases performance & endurance	**Source:** nut of *cola acuminata, cola sitida,* and *cola vera* **Forms:** powder, tea
Ma huang	• Ch @ use not advised • Ad @ 1–4 gm 3X • Fe @ 1–4 gm 3X • PL @ use not advised	• effective bronchodilator to clear respiratory system • suppresses appetite • gives energy to lungs & kidneys; diuretic action • stimulates heart & increases blood pressure • promotes circulation & warms skin • not for persons with hypertension, heart conditions, or weak internal organs	**Source:** common Chinese name for *ephedra sinica*, most popular Chinese herb, made from the whole herb **Forms:** powder, tea, extract
Parsley	• Ch @ ½ adult dose • Ad @ 2–4 gm 3X • Fe @ 2–4 gm 3X • PL @ 2–4 gm 3X	• removes kidney & gall stones • relieves liver ailments • natural antiviral, antibacterial, expectorant, and diuretic effects • used in complementary medical treatment of viral infections, sore throats, bronchitis, coughs, infected cuts & wounds • reduces enlarged prostate • reduces fluid retention • works synergistically with other herbal antibiotics: echinacea, goldenseal & chaparral	**Source:** leaves & seeds of *ligusticum porterii* plant—leaves have more iron than any other green vegetable; uses whole herb **Forms:** powder, flakes, capsule, tea, extract

	Benefits	Dosage	Source & Forms
Saw palmetto	• relieves mucus in head & nose • prevents progression of prostate disease & wasting diseases; relief for male & female reproductive systems • works as a diuretic, nerve sedative, expectorant, general nutritive tonic, urinary antiseptic, gastrointestinal stimulant, muscle builder, and circulatory stimulant • complementary medical treatment of prostate conditions: benign prostatic hypertrophy & prostatitis; treatment for genitourinary tract conditions: enuresis (bed wetting) & stress incontinence • treatment of infections of all muscle-wasting diseases	• Ch @ $1/2$ adult dose • Ad @ 160 mg 2X • Fe @ use not advised • PL @ use not advised	**Source:** berries (fruit) of *serenoa serrulata, serenoa repens* or *sagal serrulata* **Forms:** whole, powder, capsule, tea, extract, concentrate
Siberian ginseng	• builds resistance to mental & physical stress • helps in adapting to extreme temperatures • increases efficiency of mental & physical work • enhances cognitive & memory functions by increasing level of neurotransmitters in brain, improving brain cell metabolism, optimizing action of certain enzymes & increasing supply of oxygen to brain cells • slows aging process • stimulates circulatory system & normalizes heart • regulates & normalizes blood sugar levels • helps increase sex drive • increases stamina & endurance • lowers blood pressure & blood fat levels • combats stress, debility, exhaustion, depression, obesity • long-term use increases physical stamina • hair stimulant	*Short-term stress (30 days or less duration):* • Ch @ $1/2$ adult dose • Ad @ 1–2 gm 3X • Fe @ 1–2 gm 3X • PL @ use not advised *Long-term stress (more than 30-day duration):* • Ch @ $1/2$ adult dose • Ad @ 250–500 mg • Fe @ 250–500 mg • PL @ use not advised	**Source:** root of *eleutherococcus senticosus*, shrub up to 9' tall **Forms:** powder, cut & sifted, capsule, tea, extracted powder
White willow	• effective aspirin substitute • powerful pain reliever due to content of salicin & tannins • used in the complementary medical treatment of pain, obesity, arthritis and rheumatism, connective tissue inflammation, headaches, muscle aches, fevers & infections of all types • can boost thermogenesis—the body's natural ability to burn fat	• Ch @ $1/2$ adult dose • Ad @ 1–3 gm 3X • Fe @ 1–3 gm 3X • PL @ use not advised	**Source:** bark of *salix nigra, salix alba,* or *salix discolor,* or white willow tree **Forms:** cut & sifted, powder, capsule
Yerba maté	• stimulates central nervous system; helps maintain alertness • antispasmodic; calming effect on nerves • helps control excessive appetite • helps induce a restful sleep (if taken only during daytime hours) • combats iron deficiency • nontoxic if used moderately (*contains less caffeine than coffee, tea, or sodas*)	• Ch @ use not advised • Ad @ 1 cup 2X • Fe @ 1 cup 2X • PL @ use not advised	**Source:** *ilex paraguayensis* **Forms:** tea (*a stimulating beverage throughout much of Latin America*)

PROFESSIONAL REFERENCES FOR SUPPLEMENTATION

The following listing provides additional information from recognized professional, medical, and botanical specialists, including their published literature. These writings report the results of their studies regarding the benefits of supplementation.

Goldstrich, Joe D., *The Cardiologist's Painless Prescription for a Healthy Heart and a Longer Life.* Dallas TX: 9-HEART-9 Publishing, 1994. N.B.

Goldstrich, Joe D., *The Cardiologist's Painless Prescription for a Healthy Heart and a Longer Life.* Dallas TX: 9-HEART-9 Publishing, 1994. N.B.

Haas, Elson M., *Staying Healthy with Nutrition. The Complete Guide to Diet & Nutritional Medicine.* Berkeley CA: Celestial Arts, 1992.

Hamilton, Kirk, *Clinical Pearls in Nutrition and Preventive Medicine. 1990–1995.* Sacramento CA: IT Services, 1995. For subscriptions, contact IT Svcs., 3301 Alta Arden #3, Sacramento CA 95825.

Hamilton, Kirk., *CP Currents. 1990–1995.* Sacramento CA: IT Services, 1995. ☎ (916) 489-4400 (in CA) or (800) 422-9887 🖨 (916) 489-1710.

Rona, Zoltan P., *The Joy of Health, A Doctor's Guide to Nutrition and Alternative Medicine.* Toronto, ON Canada: Hounslow Press, 1991.

Rona, Zoltan P., *Return to The Joy of Health.* Vancouver, BC Canada: Alive Books, 1995.

Werbach, Melvyn R., *Nutritional Influences on Illness.* Northhamptonshire England: Thorsons, 1989.

Werbach, Melvyn R., *Nutritional Influences on Illness.* 2d Ed. Tarzana CA: Third Line Press, 1993.

Werbach, Melvyn R., *Nutritional Influences on Mental Illness.* Northamptonshire England: Thorsons, 1991.

Werbach, Melvyn R. and Murray, Michael T., *Botanical Influences on Illness.* Tarzana, CA: Third Line Press, 1994.

Chapter 15

Basic Sprouting & Kitchen Gardening

My friend Richard tells this story[1] from his youth: "*I remember when I was a very young boy, and during all my growing-up years, each year Dad would buy one hundred baby chicks. Like all the other farmers in the area, he fed them starter mash and then growing mash until they reached their mature stage. Then most of them would be killed, dressed, and put into the freezer for our winter meat, leaving a few of the best layers to provide fresh eggs for the winter.*

I distinctly remember my dad putting those chickens on the scales, one at a time. He'd say, 'Yep, this one's five pounds! Yep, five pounds!' Occasionally he'd say, 'OOPS! this one didn't eat enough, it's not five pounds.' I also remember the large streaks of yellow fat on the fatter chickens when they were being dressed and wrapped before freezing.

---

[1] This story was told to me by Delsa Wilson, a long-time food storage consultant. Richard is currently president and owner of one of the largest sprouting equipment and seed businesses in the Intermountain West—he's certainly committed to the concept of sprouting! Richard can be contacted at **Life Sprouts**, P.O. Box 150, Paradise UT 84328-0150 ☎(800) 241-1516. Be sure to ask about his organic honey! See next footnote for more about Delsa.

Now I have a large family of my own. We've also raised our hundred baby chicks to five pounds with lots of fat on their bodies, too. A few of years ago, my then eight-year old son and I decided to experiment on a recommendation from a friend. He said we could increase the chickens' growth with sprouts, so we decided to feed at least half of our chickens a diet of three-day sprouted wheat and other sprouts.

That year our chickens reached 6–6½ pounds with very little fat! The next year we decided to go all the way and feed all the chickens a sprout diet uniquely. Every bite of food we fed them was 'live food,' as opposed to 'dead food' of dried ground grains. Much to our surprise, not one chicken was under 8 pounds, and some were as much as 8½ pounds—with absolutely no fat at all!

We had kept track of how many hundreds of pounds of grain it normally took to raise those chickens. The big surprise was that with the live sprouts, we used 25% less food by sprouting the same amount of grain—and yet those chickens were much bigger, heartier and had less fat!"

> *Sprouts are live whole food, providing great nutritional value to the diet.*

When we tell people about Richard's experiment, sometimes we hear older folks say they don't want to grow that much bigger! They're missing the point: *the importance of sprouts has nothing to do with adults growing to be giants, but being healthier and having less body fat at any age!*

Live sprouts have live enzymes, vitamins, minerals, and amino acids we need for everyday healthy living. The truth is we could live on "live" sprouts for a very long time and remain very healthy. It doesn't take too much effort to sprout seeds for food—*Quinoa seeds sprout in as little time as twelve hours!*

WHY USE SPROUTS?

The reasons for using sprouts are so plentiful and so important it's probably merely a matter of listing them to convince you to try this very special kind of gardening. Increasing numbers of families find seed sprouts nutritious and delicious.

Nutritional Advantages

> **Watching your weight?**
>
> *One additional benefit of sprouts is the low carbohydrate, fat, and cholesterol content—a real plus for weight-watchers.*

Nutritionally, dried seeds, grains, and legumes provide only a small portion of the total nutrients the body requires. However, once they are sprouted, seeds provide the largest relative amount of nutrients per unit of intake compared to other food sources. Sprouting multiplies the content of minerals and vitamins in the seed many times because a wealth of nutrients are released to aid the development of the seed during its growth process.[2]

There is no doubt more nourishment contained in a plant's sprout than at any other time in its life cycle. Often, new nutrients occur where there were none before. Vitamins A, B complex, C, and E are increased sometimes as much as ten times!

Both the quantity and quality of the protein of most sprouts are dramatically increased. New amino acids form as the seeds sprout, resulting in increased digestibility.

[2] Some of the information in this chapter contributed by Delsa Wilson, 3686 South 2455 East, Salt Lake City UT 84109 ☎(801) 278-6950. Delsa is a long-time "sprouter" and expert food storage consultant. For 20+ years, she's been developing her experience in both teaching and training other food storage experts, giving seminars to thousands and classes to nonprofit groups by the scores. She operates her own mail-order business for people seeking not only quality food storage products and supplies but also the knowledge to use them wisely and well.

Sprouts are biogenic—alive and capable of transferring their life energy to your body. They contain enzymes which aid in digestion of foods, provide a good source of fiber, and slow the aging process. They are also an excellent multipurpose vegetable. Using sprouts greatly increases vitamin content of dishes, provides a "live" food, and in general supports better health for the body. To add to all of their nutritional plusses, untreated and organic sprouts are free of pesticides (and are pest-free, too).

Food Preparation Advantages

Using sprouts varies the menu, adds bulk, and improves the flavor of many dishes. Sprouts are versatile. They can be used in so many ways—alone; in salads, teas, sandwiches, soups, gourmet entrées, casseroles, pancakes or breads; raw, boiled, sautéed, steamed, or stir-fried—you're limited only by your imagination! In fact, you can create your own *designer* or *gourmet* sprout combination by mixing and matching your favorite grains, seeds, and beans in the same batch. This allows customization for your eating pleasure and maximizes your inventory of sproutables, too.

There is no waste in preparation, no fuel required to prepare them, and once you get the hang of it, practically no failures. Sprouting is not only one of the keys to nutritional stability—a potential life-saver—but is also a great money-saver. Children especially like to help with this kitchen duty. In fact, most elementary schools teach sprouting as part of the curriculum. A child's natural inquisitiveness will help him master sprouting in a short time, leaving more of your time for the more complicated and time-consuming household and kitchen duties.

Storage Advantages

It really doesn't matter how sprouts are utilized in food preparation, they will sustain good health and stamina. If you had only a supply of sprouting seeds in your food storage, you could live a full year or more, eating only from your kitchen garden. The best part is that sprouts are also the least expensive fresh vegetables you can procure!

It is virtually impossible for a family to store enough fresh vegetables to last a long period of time—or to have them available in times of extreme duress, whether due to man-made or natural disasters. By sprouting seeds, fresh vegetables are only 2–3 days away, year-round! Sprouts substitute for green vegetables and replace lettuce and other greens if they become expensive or unavailable. Get a variety of seeds and learn to use them and you will have fresh green vegetables year-round, even when there is no way to grow vegetables in the soil. This makes sprouting seeds a high-priority acquisition item.

The amount of food value stored in such a small space is a boon to a home storage program. Sprouting is a very easy way to increase the utility of many types of grains, seeds, and legumes or beans. Sprouts are easy to prepare and utilize. Both equipment and supplies are easily found and readily available almost anywhere. The effort required for a batch of sprouts is minimal. Bringing sprouts to the table ready to eat *takes less than 10 minutes* during the entire 3-day growth period. Compared to vegetable gardening, kitchen gardening with sprouts is *easy*. There is little fuss and bother. Sprouts require no fertilizer. In fact, all that's required is some moisture, a little air, and a small nook where they can grow. Sprouts conserve energy, too. You can eat sprouts without cooking them, and any sprouted beans or grains cook much quicker. Sprouts save money—all of the above, and this, too! Sprouting inexpensive seeds can help support any family's over-worked budget!

Note:

Untreated and organic sprouts are free of pesticides but also free of pests.

BASIC SPROUTING

This chapter is designed solely to help readers realize the importance of sprouting in their food storage program—and now is the time to start learning how to sprout! On subsequent pages are found the expanded **Basic Sprouting Guide (Quick-Guide 15–1).** It summarizes the basic information needed to either become an accomplished sprouter or to improve your sprouting acumen.

Experiment! Don't be afraid to try something new—there's not much you can do to hurt sprouts! After a few tries, you'll discover at which stage of sprout development your family prefers different sprouted seeds. Some like sprouted seeds best after they have sprouted just 48 hours, others when 4–5 days old, when the sprout has more "chewiness" and has a more substantially developed flavor. Past this point, as the sprout is actually becoming a plant, they tend to become bitter. Actually, sprouts may be used any time after the shoot emerges from the seed, but with some seeds, it's better to wait until the shoot is longer. *Sprouts are best when they taste best to you!*

> *Sprouts require no fertilizer. All that's required is some moisture, some air, a small place in a kitchen cabinet and a small spot on the window sill.*

Basic Sprouting Equipment

Generally, the only equipment needed for sprouting can easily be found in your house. Here's the short list:

- a quart jar
- a piece of cotton gauze, nylon net, or pantyhose top—any durable fabric
- a strong rubber band (or sealing ring for quart jar)

Voilà—simple and inexpensive sprouting equipment for a *basic sprouting system*!

Of course, a number of companies have developed easy-to-use, manufactured sprouting systems. I use several different ones to speed up my personal production when large quantities are needed. There are several kinds, some better than others, depending on your needs and the type of seeds, beans, or grains you choose to sprout.

Make your own BASIC SEED SPROUTER with a quart jar and a small piece of nylon net (or gauze) held in place at the jar neck with a strong rubber band.

Step-by-Step Basic Sprouting Method

There are only a few general rules for sprouting—it's practically foolproof! Almost all seeds are sprouted the same way, with a few exceptions. The **Basic Sprouting Guide** points out some special handling requirements for particular seeds, grains, and beans. Check the **Guide** for specifics when sprouting.

To utilize the basic sprouting method, follow these general directions:

- Measure the appropriate amount of beans, grain, or seeds for a batch, picking out broken seeds and foreign objects.

- Place measured amount of seeds in jar half-full of warm water. Cull out "floaters" or "sinkers" ("floaters" when majority of seeds rest on bottom—when majority float, pick out the "sinkers").

- Secure gauze (or nylon fabric) over the mouth of the jar with the rubber band (or jar ring).

- Soak 6–8 hours, or as directed in the **Quick-Guide 15–1,** in a warm location in the kitchen.

- Then drain seeds well by turning bottle upside-down. Leave it angled to one side in the sink or dish drainer for a few minutes. Rinse them again gently in warm water to remove contaminants. Allow to drain once more, then place in kitchen cabinet, on the counter, or in the window covered with a dark towel so germination may begin. (Be sure to place jar where it's warm.)

- Drain and rinse seeds 2–3 times each day (or as directed by **Guide,** always draining well to prevent souring of sprouts.

- When sprouts attain desired length, eat the whole thing—seed, sprout, and roots—for a healthier meal or snack.

- Store unused sprouts in refrigerator to retard further growth. The **Guide,** gives the recommended sprout length for each seed. Sprouts generally achieve peak palatability, highest vitamin content, and potency within 2–3 days.

What Not to Do

- Don't sprout seeds *intended for agricultural use.* They are generally treated with poisonous insecticides and may not be safe for human consumption.

- Don't sprout *tomato* or *potato* seeds—they are generally poisonous to humans.

> **Caution!**
>
> Here are the two most important things **not to do** when sprouting.

There are many commercial sprouters. The stacking models allow sprouting of different types of seeds at one time.

QUICK-GUIDE 15–1

BASIC SPROUTING GUIDE

Step 1	Step 2	Step 3	Step 4	Step 5	Step 6
Selecting Sprouting Seed	Measuring Quantity	Soaking Hours	Sprouting Days	Recommended Daily Rinsing & Special Handling Requirements	Recommended Length
use only untreated or organic grains, seeds & beans	measure for 1 qt. harvest	thoroughly wash, cull, soak & drain	average days required to mature	• daily rinses under cool, clean, running water; always drain thoroughly after rinsing • special treatment required for selected seeds • some precautions when using sprouts	mature length range for best eating flavor
Adzuki	1 C.	8–12	4–5	• rinse 3–4 times	$\frac{1}{2}$"–1"
Alfalfa	3 T.	4–8	3–5	• rinse 2–3 times; *also sprout in kitchen window* • rinse vigorously on last day to remove hulls	1"–2"
Almond—shelled	$\frac{1}{2}$ C.	8–12	3–5	• rinse 2–3 times; can be difficult; sprinkle method	when split
Amaranth	12 T.	none	2–3	• rinse 3–4 times	$\frac{1}{4}$"
Anise	6 T.	8–12	2–3	• rinse 5–6 times	1"
Barley—unhulled	2 C.	4–8	3–4	• rinse 3–4 times; can be difficult to sprout • make diastatic malt for baking (*see chapter 7*) • steam prior to eating	seed length
Beans—general, see listings	1 C.	8–24	3–5	• rinse 3–5 times, depending on bean • *larger bean + shorter sprout = sweeter taste* • steam prior to eating to destroy antinutrients & toxins present in raw beans	$\frac{1}{4}$"–1$\frac{1}{2}$"
Black-eyed Peas	1 C.	12–18	3–5	• rinse 3–4 times • steam prior to eating to destroy toxins	$\frac{1}{2}$"–1"
Buckwheat— unhulled hulled	1 C. 1$\frac{1}{2}$ C.	15–30 min. 8–12	2–3 3–5	• rinse both 4—5 times 1ˢᵗ day; 2–3 times thereafter • unhulled seed somewhat difficult to sprout • hulled seeds are easier to sprout	$\frac{1}{4}$"–$\frac{1}{2}$" 1"–3"
Cabbage— Savoy Chinese	3 T.	8–12 6–8	3–4 4–5	• rinse 2–3 times; *also sprouts in kitchen window* • stronger flavor when longer & older • use soon after sprouting	$\frac{1}{2}$"–$\frac{3}{4}$" 1"–1$\frac{1}{2}$"
Canola	3 T.	6–8	2–3	• rinse 2–3 times; *also sprouts in kitchen window*	1"–1$\frac{1}{2}$"
Chia	2 T.	none	1–4	• mucilaginous seed—must use sprinkle method • usually very difficult to sprout	$\frac{1}{4}$"–1"
Clover—red	1$\frac{1}{2}$ T.	8–12	3–5	• rinse 2–3 times; *also sprouts in kitchen window*	1"–2"
Corn— regular popcorn	2 C. 1$\frac{1}{2}$ C.	4–8 8–12	2–3	• rinse 2–3 times • *longer sprouts have stronger flavor* • best when steamed; may be eaten raw	$\frac{1}{4}$"–$\frac{1}{2}$"
Fenugreek	1 C.	4–8	3–5	• rinse 1–2 times; *longer sprouts = bitter taste*	1"–2"
Flax	4 T.	none	4–5	• mucilaginous seed—use sprinkle method • usually very difficult to sprout	1"–1$\frac{1}{2}$"
Garbanzo *(chickpea)*	1$\frac{1}{2}$ C.	8–12	3–4	• rinse 4 times; can be difficult to sprout • lightly steam prior to eating to destroy toxins found in all raw beans	$\frac{1}{2}$"
Kidney Bean	$\frac{3}{4}$ C.	8–12	2–4	• rinse 3–4 times • lightly steam before eating to destroy toxins	$\frac{1}{2}$"–1"
Lentil	$\frac{2}{3}$ C.	6–12	2–4	• rinse 2–4 times; eat when sprout is visible • lightly steam before eating to destroy toxins	$\frac{1}{4}$"–1"
Lettuce	3 T.	4–8	3–5	• rinse 2–3 times; *also sprouts in kitchen window* • longer sprouts have stronger flavor	1"–1$\frac{1}{2}$"

Step 1	Step 2	Step 3	Step 4	Step 5	Step 6
Selecting Sprouting Seed	Measuring Quantity	Soaking Hours	Sprouting Days	Recommended Daily Rinsing & Special Handling Requirements	Recommended Length
use only untreated or organic grains, seeds & beans	*measure for 1 qt. harvest*	*thoroughly wash, cull, soak & drain*	*average days required to mature*	• *daily rinses under cool, clean, running water; always drain thoroughly after rinsing* • *special treatment required for selected seeds* • *some precautions when using sprouts*	*mature length range for best eating flavor*
Millet, hulled	2 C.	4–8	3–4	• rinse 2–3 times • tastes like barley • best when steamed before using	$1/4$"
Mung	1 C.	8–12	3–5	• rinse 3–4 times vigorously to remove hulls • steam prior to eating to destroy antinutrients & toxins present in raw beans	1"–2"
Mustard	$2^1/2$ C.	8–12	3–4	• rinse 2–3 times; *also sprouts in kitchen window*	1"–$1^1/2$"
Oats, unhulled	2 C.	2–6	1–2	• rinse 1–2 times—excess water causes souring • use sprinkle method	seed length
Peanut	$1/2$ C.	8–12	2–3	• rinse 2–3 times • steam 10–15 min. prior to eating to destroy toxins (peanuts are beans!)	$1/4$" – 1"
Peas—general, see listings	3 C.	8–12	2–3	• rinse 2–3 times; split peas will not sprout • steam 10–15 min. prior to eating to destroy toxins in raw beans (peas are beans!)	seed length
Pinto Bean	1 C.	8–12	3–4	• rinse 3–4 times; steam 10–15 min. prior to eating to destroy toxins present in raw beans	$1/2$"–$1^1/4$"
Pumpkin—hulled	2 C.	8–12	3	• rinse 2–3 times • *light toasting = better-tasting sprouts*	$1/4$"
Quinoa	$1/4$ C.	4–6	1–2	• rinse 2–3 times; sprouts very quickly	$1/4$"–$1^1/2$"
Radish	3 T.	6–8	3–6	• rinse 2–3 times; *also sprouts in kitchen window* • gets "hotter" with increasing length	$1/8$"–$1^1/2$"
Rice—brown, whole grain	$1^1/2$ C.	8–24	3–4	• rinse 2–3 times • short-grain brown rice will sprout best • best when steamed before using	seed length
Rye	1 C.	8–12	2–3	• rinse 3–4 times; eat within 3 days	$1/4$"–$1/2$"
Sesame	$1^1/2$ C.	8–12	$1^1/2$–2	• rinse 3–4 times; only unhulled seeds will sprout	seed length
Soybean	1 C.	18–24	4–6	• rinse 5–6 times; difficult to sprout; don't keep too long after sprouting, ferments very easily • steam prior to eating to destroy antinutrients & toxins present in raw soybeans	$1/2$"–2"
Spinach	2 T.	6–8	3–5	• rinse 2–3 times; *also sprouts in kitchen window*	$1/2$"–2"
Sunflower—shelled	1 C.	2–8	1–2	• rinse 2–3 times; edible in 12–36 hours • sprouts taste bitter when more than 2"	1"–2"
Triticale	2 C.	8–12	2–3	• rinse 3–4 times; eat within 3 days • use same as wheat sprouts • use quickly, ferments easily—even in refrigerator	seed length
Vegetable seeds *(see listings)*	2–3 T.	6–12	2–3	• rinse at least 2 times • best when eaten raw • use soon after sprouts reach maximum length	1"–2"
Watercress	2 T.	none	3–5	• mucilaginous seed—use sprinkle method • usually very difficult to sprout	$1/2$"
Wheat	1 C.	8–12	3–6	• rinse 2–3 times; *long & old sprouts = bitter taste*	seed length

Special Treatment for "Reluctant" Sprouting Seeds

There are some seeds that need special treatment to achieve sprouting. Here's how to deal with these reluctant sproutables.

"Paper-Towel" Sprouting Method

Use this method when the seeds are large or have thick skins, such as nuts.

- Use a large glass baking dish or metal pan that won't rust.
- Place a baking or cooling rack in the dish or pan.
- Spread two layers of *dampened* paper towels on the raised rack to make a sprouting "bed."
- Place presoaked seeds on moist—not sopping wet—towels.
- Cover seeds with another two layers of moist (with all excess water squeezed out) paper towels, leaving ends and sides open so air can circulate.
- Rinse frequently as indicated in the **Basic Sprouting Guide.** Remove seeds from between damp towels when rinsing. Use a sieve, strainer or colander to contain them while rinsing in running water, then return seeds to the damp paper towels. Thoroughly moisten paper towels by re-soaking, then wringing them out during each rinsing cycle.
- Keep the seeds moist between rinses by sprinkling *only* the top layer of paper towels.
- Remove sprouted seeds from sprouting bed when ready to eat. Store sprouts tightly covered in refrigerator to preserve their freshness.

"Sprinkle" Sprouting Method

This method of sprouting reluctant seeds is for mucilaginous seeds such as chia, flax, and watercress. Here's how to deal with these seeds:

- Eliminate the normal presoaking of these seeds. Instead, cover with just enough water to wet seeds. Pour off excess water. Allow seeds to sit for an hour. (If seeds seem to dry out during this time, add water by sprinkling them lightly.)
- Seeds will form a jelly-like, gelatinous mass. Do not remove the "jelly." The seeds will sprout in the jelly, and there is no need to rinse them if you keep the jelly moist by sprinkling the seed mass regularly.
- When the seeds have reached the edible stage, rinse the seeds in cold running water until the jelly is washed away. Use soon, as these seeds are prone to drying out and/or molding quickly.

Should you need additional information about advanced sprouting techniques, check the supplemental materials at the end of the book for listings of many sprouting seed and equipment suppliers.

TIPS FOR USING SPROUTS IN RECIPES

There are so many ways to utilize sprouts, they would fill many cookbooks! Before going to the cost and effort to buy other books, try some of the following ideas first.

General Use

Stir-fry: Add to other vegetables alfalfa, clover, mung, or radish sprouts—or all at the same time!

Mashed potatoes: Grind or chop very fine either alfalfa, chia, or clover sprouts—for taste and color, too!

Vegetable juice: Make your own *Basic Sprout-8* with tomato juice and ground chia, barley, cabbage, clover, lettuce, radish, and/or watercress sprouts! This one will become a favorite! If too much flavor, start with any one sprout, adding more until you get the taste you like.

Sautéed vegetables: Add cabbage, corn, garbanzo, lentil, mung, pea, radish, or watercress sprouts for *zingggg*! These sprouts are especially good with sliced onion, clove of garlic, and some green peppers—try it with a game-time snack bowl over white rice steamed to perfection!

Steamed vegetables: Add whole alfalfa, chia, clover, corn, garbanzo, lentil, mung, pea, radish, or wheat sprouts to last 2 minutes of steaming time.

Rice: Add chopped almond or finely chopped or whole alfalfa, barley, chia, pea, radish, or watercress sprouts to rice dishes and to steamed rice after cooking—and just before serving!

Soups: Add chopped or whole corn, garbanzo, lentil, mung, pea, radish, or wheat sprouts for flavor and thickener.

Baking

Home-baked goods: Enhance by adding whole or chopped sprouts.

Baked beans: Add any sprouted bean with short sprout—*best when bean has just split open by growth*— try lentil, mung, lima, pinto, or navy bean sprouts.

Breadmaking

Breads: Ordinary homemade breads become more eye-appealing with sprouts peeking through the crust and seen throughout the loaf. Sprouts add great taste and greater nourishment in each delicious slice! Some care is required when adding or substituting sprouts in bread recipes. The rule for substituting sprouts in any recipe is:

> **Substitute 1 cup sprouts in any bread or flour recipe for $1/2$ cup flour and $1/2$ cup liquid.**

Note: for substituting sprouts in bread recipes, be aware of these potential problems:
- *If the yeast does not fully react in the dough, the dough will produce heavy bread.*
- *When adding sprouts to yeast goods, add them as late as possible in the mixing process, then be sure dough is warm and working.*
- *Do not allow dough to sit too long with sprouts added—the dough may sour.*

> **Note:**
>
> *Exercise care when using sprouts in breadmaking. Sprouts are an abundantly rich source of enzymes. Some of these enzymes have the ability to digest protein, so yeast action will be inhibited and will result in heavy bread.*

Breakfast Treats

Try some of the following to add zest and nutrition to a sedate breakfast:

Omelets & scrambled eggs: Add chopped or whole alfalfa, chia, clover, mustard, or radish sprouts for a bright-eyed start to your day.

Pancakes and waffles: Ground or finely chopped buckwheat sprouts enhance nutritional value of an ordinary breakfast.

Casseroles

When using sprouts in casseroles, add them just a few minutes before serving, either in the pan or sprinkled on top. Sprouts add vitality and flavor to any casserole. Add $1/_2$ cup to 1 cup whole or chopped sprouts—adzuki, barley, cabbage, chia, clover, corn, lentil, mung, spinach, or wheat—to your favorite casserole.

Salads

Eat sprouts fresh and uncooked for a taste treat. Create your own combinations. Get creative with sprouts, and you'll certainly be healthier and less harassed in preparing nutritious meals.

Basic sprout salad: Perhaps the easiest salad to make: mix a handful of chilled sprouts, whether one kind or a combination, in a bowl. Then pour French, Italian, Russian, bleu cheese, or plain homemade mayonnaise over them and stir until sprouts are lightly covered.

Deluxe salad: Add to a regular lettuce salad sprouts of alfalfa, mung, chia, radish, wheat—you get the idea.

Lettuce substitute: Use sprouts as a complete substitute for lettuce in your favorite salad.

Coleslaw: Substitute chopped cabbage sprouts for cabbage. For a different taste, add radish sprouts!

Potato salad: Add alfalfa, lentil, mung, or radish sprouts to "liven up" a dead potato salad.

Sandwiches

Improve the flavor and nutrition of your favorite sandwich by adding sprouts. Try these additions to your diet:

Chicken salad or tuna salad: Alfalfa sprouts are better than lettuce, cheaper, and more easily available!

Lettuce substitute: Use any sprout or combination of sprouts to replace lettuce (alfalfa, chia, clover, lentil, mung, or radish).

Avocado (mashed): Spread thickly on fresh, home-baked whole-wheat bread. Top with alfalfa, barley, clover, or chia sprouts.

Super sandwich spread: Add to salad spread mixture chopped or ground alfalfa, chia, clover, lentil, mung, and/or radish sprouts.

Sprout cheese filling (or dip): Add ground or chopped alfalfa, clover, lentil, mung, or radish sprouts to softened cream or Neufchatel cheese.

Grilled cheese: Top hot sandwiches with alfalfa, chia, clover, lentil, lettuce, mung, sesame, or watercress sprouts for added flavor.

Soups

If you like the flavor of any particular bean, seed, or grain, you can make it into a sprout soup. Simply sprout your selection, add one cup of sprouts into boiling water slowly, then cover and simmer. Cook till tender or to your preference. Season to taste and serve hot. That's all there is to making sprout soup. Bean sprouts are even more palatable and digestible when cooked before eating. The antinutrients in the bean family are nullified when cooked.

BASIC SPROUT SOUP

1 C. sprouts (your choice)	$^1/_2$ C. sour cream
1 C. water	1 tsp. soy sauce
pinch of parsley	salt & pepper to taste

Add sprouts to boiling water. Reduce heat, simmer 3–5 minutes, then stir in sour cream. Season to taste with soy sauce. Sprinkle parsley on top just before serving.

EGG-SPROUT SOUP

2 C. bean sprouts	1 T. soy sauce
4 C. vegetable broth or soup	salt
2 eggs, beaten	

Add sprouts to broth. Simmer 8–10 minutes. Remove from heat and stir in beaten eggs. Season to taste with soy sauce.

> **Note:**
>
> The BASIC SPROUT VEGETABLE recipe may be used as a basic ingredient for many recipes.

Vegetables

Sprouts are vegetables. They may be boiled, baked, or sautéed as any other vegetable, served alone, or in combination with other vegetables. The number of recipes for sprouts is endless because they can be added to almost any vegetable or meat dish to improve taste and nutritional value. The secret to gaining the most nutritional value from sprouts is to cook them as little as possible. The following recipes will guide you in utilizing sprouts as vegetables.

BASIC SPROUT VEGETABLE

1 C. sprouts of choice	pinch salt
2 C. water	$^1/_2$ T. butter

Add sprouts to boiling salted water, reduce heat, and simmer 3–5 minutes. Remove from heat, add butter, and cover for 20 minutes. Serve hot. Serve alone or with bacon, cheese—whatever!

Chapter 16

Basic In-Home Drying of Fruits & Vegetables

Frying, bottling, canning, pickling, brining, smoking, fermenting, and root-cellaring are different approaches our forebears used to save and have food for the future. Not having these methods to slow or stop food deterioration would have meant hunger, starvation, and ultimately death. To this already substantial list, we can add more recently developed preservation methods that have proven commercially and economically effective, such as refrigeration, freezing, dehydrating, and freeze-drying.

Today, for most of us city-dwellers, preservation methods such as *curing, smoking*, and *root-cellaring* require more time, space, equipment, etc., than we have available. There's already plenty of stress on our limited resources. In fact, many of us are barely competent in *refrigerating* or *freezing* our food to have for future use!

Fermenting sauerkraut, *brining* and *pickling* tasty relishes, maybe some *canning* ("putting up") jam and jelly in bottles are methods likely to be within our capability and interests. But the time required and expenses involved in *drying* make it an even more practical preservation method for our times. In-home drying of fruits and vegetables is the oldest method of food preservation—it's been around several centuries longer than any other.

See how many of these food preservation methods meet your resource capabilities and skill levels:

- *Canning* and *bottling* methods use extremely high temperatures to kill all biological activity. They also require some special equipment and lots of preparation time, a great deal of storage space, and heavy stuff to handle.

- *Freezing* uses extremely cold temperatures to slow the spoilage factor through a type of suspended animation. Again, a great deal of time required for processing, cost of the freezer(s) required for adequate storage, energy costs, and the space needed.

- *Fermenting, pickling, brining,* and *salting* use chemical solutions to achieve preservation—not good for our health, given what we understand now.

- *Dehydration* is commercial food drying with special equipment to remove water from food at temperatures below cooking level. Most in-home storage programs are built around storing dehydrated foods. Purchased thoughtfully and used properly, dehydrated foods are an excellent method for economical in-home storage.

- *Freeze-drying* entails freezing fresh or fresh-cooked foods, then dehydrating them by vacuuming off the moisture at sub-zero temperatures.[1] Commercial freeze-dried food is perhaps the ultimate food storage medium. Unfortunately, for most budgets, its higher quality is reflected in its price.

- *Curing* and *smoking* are not particularly difficult, but again there are serious health questions about the curing agents utilized. There are also limited fruits and vegetables that can be appropriately cured or smoked in the typical household.

- *Root-cellaring* of fruits and vegetables requires a good-sized, below-ground level, indoor or outdoor space. Digging a pit or mounding earth and using insulating straw to extend storage of root crops and tree fruits just isn't within the reach of most of us. Experience indicates the urban dweller can use drying much more effectively and economically. If you have the space and the inclination to construct or improvise a root cellar, there are resources available to help you utilize this method of storage.

Even without a complete analysis of all the food preservation systems, it's fairly easy to conclude that most food preservation methods are neither affordable nor effective in-home methods for the majority of us.

If you're like me, however, you might get passionate about basic in-home drying. It is the simplest and most fascinating method for preparing food today for use tomorrow. In-home drying is technologically nonthreatening and low stress—it can be done while watching your favorite TV show. Storing dried foods is easy and fairly uncomplicated. Another advantage of this method is that some of the dried food can be eaten like snacks now or later, without cooking them before enjoying them.

Dried food products keep longer, cost less to prepare, and take less storage space. Most people agree the taste is better, too, when compared to other methods of preservation. The real bonus is the ease of preparation and quick turn-around time from both the fresh-to-dried state and back from dried to the ready-to-eat state.

---

[1] Contrary to what some may believe, in-home freeze-drying is not a possibility, even though some of the foods found in the bottom of home freezers are so badly freezer burned they appear freeze-dried!

DRYING METHODS

Drying removes the moisture from the food that microorganisms need to remain biologically active. Food deterioration is slowed tremendously by drying. The differences[2] among drying methods are determined by the sophistication of the equipment and technology involved:

- **In-home food drying** removes 80%–90% of moisture.
- **Commercial food dehydrating** removes 96%–97.5% of moisture.
- **Commercial food freeze-drying** removes 98%+ of moisture.

In-home drying is fairly unsophisticated when compared to the commercial facilities specializing in food dehydration and freeze-drying and cannot approach the low levels of moisture attained by commercial establishments. On the other hand, there is a greater loss of nutritional values from commercial methods, as shown in **Chart 16–1**. In-home drying compares more than favorably with all of the other drying preservation processes in relationship to nutritional losses.

Chart 16–1

Nutritional Losses by Selected Preservation Processes

Preservation process	Normal loss of nutrition	Processing method
Canning	60–80%	high temperatures and water-logging
Freezing	40–60%	rupturing of cells
Comm'l Dehydrating	5–15%	moderate heat and moderate air flow
In-home Drying	3–5%	low heat and gentle air flow

IN-HOME DRYING

Advantages of In-Home Drying

In-home dried foods retain more of their nutritive values than hot or cold packing, freezing, or pickling. When compared to *canning,* the most common method of preservation in the United States, *drying* is outstanding in keeping the food values in foods after processing. Drying foods in-home is the least expensive, most nutritious, and most realizable method of preserving foods for most of us. Since time is our most precious and least available resource, in-home drying is the best investment we can make to facilitate an effective method of preserving food.

Because in-home drying does not use extremely high temperatures, almost all the vitamins, minerals, and enzymes are retained intact. The flavors of fruits and vegetables are retained much better because rehydrated dried foods have a concentration of wholesome, real-flavor sweetness and taste that is intensely, delightfully delicious. As a bonus, dried foods are full of fiber, have no refined sugars added, and have concentrated amounts of naturally occurring nutrients, sugars, and flavors.

---

[2] See the USDA Agriculture *Family Preparedness Handbook No. 8, Composition of Foods: Raw, Processed, Prepared.* If not available from USDA, try the library or your County Extension Agent.

Basic Reasons for In-Home Drying

Drying foods in-home is one of the best and most basic methods of home storage for these reasons:

Saves space: dried foods can be stored in 40%–50% less space. With such a high percentage of their water removed, dried foods are smaller.

Saves weight: dried foods weigh up to 75% less than their fresh equivalents.

Convenient: reconstitute in minutes by simply soaking in water.

Economical:
- allows you to take advantage of seasonal prices of produce
- saves losses from excess production—both market and home (leftovers)
- costs only pennies per hour to operate dryer
- packaging supplies are inexpensive and readily available

Nutritious:
- retains greater percentage of nutrients than other methods of preservation
- food tastes better than when processed by other methods
- dried food is edible as is or can be reconstituted to its natural state by simply soaking in plain water
- there are no synthetic or unnatural preservatives required in the drying process

Secrets to Successful In-Home Drying

The secrets to successful in-home drying are
- choosing the highest quality foods available
- handling foods in each step of the process quickly to prevent deterioration of quality
- keeping all equipment and working surfaces hygienic
- deactivating the enzymatic action in foods
- treating appropriately to preserve color, nutrients, taste, and food quality
- ensuring even drying to extend storage life and reduce decomposition
- drying in the shortest time possible without actually cooking or burning foods
- removing enough moisture from foods to prevent spoilage from growth of organisms and molds:
  - —vegetables should contain less than 10% moisture
  - —fruits should contain less than 20% moisture

BASIC IN-HOME DRYING METHOD

There are only **6** steps to in-home drying of fruits and vegetables, storage, and rehydration for use. A full explanation of each of these steps is found in the following sections. These steps are

1. **Selection of fruits and vegetables**
2. **Preparation for drying**
3. **Preservation treatment prior to drying**
4. **Drying (including doneness testing)**
5. **Post-drying handling to extend shelf life**
6. **Rehydration for use**

The **Basic In-Home Fruit Drying Quick-Guide 16–1** and the **Basic In-Home Vegetable Drying Quick-Guide 16–2** at the end of this chapter detail the requirements for in-home drying of fruits and vegetables. Preparation, treatment prior to drying, testing for doneness, estimated shelf life, and rehydration use details are also included. Specific instructions and suggested alternatives for each step are noted. These **Quick-Guides** serve as quick references and summaries for drying the most common fruits and vegetables.

Step 1: Selection of Fruits & Vegetables

Always use fruits and vegetables in their "prime." Select sound, fresh, ripe but firm fruits and vegetables at their maturity. Keep in mind the axiom used in modern-day parlance, "the best beginning makes the best finish." A low-quality product at the beginning will produce a low-quality product when dried, or prepared in any manner.

The best dried produce will normally come from your own family garden, mainly due to its freshness and your careful handling.[3] When shopping at your grocer's for drying produce, sort out the bruised, overripe, and immature products. Wash all produce carefully, whether homegrown or store-bought, as part of the preparation step.

Step 2: Preparation of Fruits & Vegetables for Drying

Preparation involves washing, drying, peeling, cutting, slicing, pitting, removing seeds, coring, chopping or dicing, mashing, or blending. Do this before treating. The following general suggestions will help you prepare fruits and vegetables for drying:

- Wash all produce to remove dirt, germs, or pesticides that might be on the surface. Put a drop of mild, liquid dishwashing detergent in a clean sink full of warm water. This will remove most pesticides, waxes, dirt, and germs without damage to foods.

- Use a vegetable brush for all root crops or other hard-surfaced produce.

- When produce is to be chopped or diced, wash before *and* after cutting.

- Discard all outer leaves of leafy produce before washing.

- Always wash exterior of fruits and vegetables prior to peeling or cutting. Remove all possible contaminants prior to exposing "flesh" of all fruits and vegetables. This prevents cross-contamination while cutting and slicing, putting pieces on trays, etc.

- Always use a stainless steel knife to prevent discoloration of the fruit or vegetables.

- Turn pitted fruits "inside out" to aid treating and drying.

- Cut all pieces approximately the same size. Obviously, the larger the pieces of food, the longer they'll take to treat, dry, and rehydrate. Larger pieces are also a greater risk for spoilage, particularly if careful attention is not given them in the dryer. When all pieces are the same size during drying, the overall quality of the batch will be higher.

---

[3] My personal observation of produce departments in today's markets is that they lack care in handling our already vitamin-depleted, over-processed, and mechanically-handled foods. I've watched many produce clerks slam-dunk fruits and vegetables into bins and slam fruits and vegetables together so they'd stack without rolling. If the produce weren't already damaged or beginning to rot in the bins or on the display counters, the checker would roll, drop, bang, and otherwise bruise it while handling it through the checkout lane. If anything got past the checker, then the grocery bagger made sure it would be bruised when double-dribbled into the grocery sack—or into the vehicle! Lately, I've asked them to handle my selections as if they were taking them home themselves, and it helps.

Step 3: Pretreatment for Fruits & Vegetables

Blanching Pretreatment

Blanching is a pretreatment for some fruits and all vegetables. It was one of the secrets of Clarence Birdseye, as part of his discovery for freezing foods successfully, introduced in 1924. Blanching foods can be achieved in two ways. Foods can either be steamed in a basket over boiling water or be put directly into the boiling water.

Foods being processed for in-home drying must be blanched—*but not completely cooked!* Successful blanching doesn't cook foods fully but brings them to the point of just being tender. However, if foods are mistakenly left in the steam or water too long, *over-blanching is better than under-blanching.* Most of the vitamin loss in the drying process occurs while blanching. However, it's a small price to pay for the dividends.

Steaming foods is the better blanching pretreatment method because it adds less water to foods and dissolves fewer nutrients than boiling.

When the blanching process is completed, either blot food or gently roll pieces in a towel to soak up excess moisture. After foods are blanched and blotted dry, no other pretreatment is required prior to placing them into the dryer.

Blanching fruits and vegetables has these purposes:
- sets color
- stops ripening process (enzymatic action)
- prevents changes in flavor
- facilitates drying process
- reduces drying time
- reduces contamination from molds and bacterial growth

Chemical Solutions for Fruits

Chemical solutions may be used to treat fruit to prevent discoloration, molds, and bacteria. See **Chart 16–2** following for details of treating specific fruits to prevent darkening.

Chart 16–2

Chemical Solutions for Treating Fruits

Solution	Purpose	Mixture Preparation	Time in Mixture
Ascorbic acid	Prevent discoloration[4]	1–1½ tsp. to 1 C. cold water	Soak fruit 2–3 min.
Saline	Prevent molds & bacteria	4–6 tsp. to 1 gal. cold water	Soak fruit 10 min.
Sulfur	Prevent molds & bacteria	1–1½ tsp. to 1 gal. water	Soak fruit 10–20 min.

Ascorbic acid: Darkening will occur with some fruits, such as apples, apricots, peaches, pears, and nectarines. The treatment for reducing the oxidation is an antioxidant chemical in the form of pure crystalline ascorbic acid. This product is generally available in any pharmacy. This is a temporary treatment, helping keep the original color intact while in the dryer. Either dip fruits in the ascorbic acid mixture or sprinkle onto all surfaces with a sprinkle bottle. Drain thoroughly and dry by blotting with paper or cloth towel.

---

[4] For apples, use up to 3 teaspoons per cup of cold water. Apples darken so quickly they require special handling.

Saline solution: Formerly a popular method for pretreating fruits, but today's health conscious generation doesn't like the idea of too much salt in their diet.

Sulfuring: The purpose of sulfuring of fruits is to inhibit the growth of molds and bacteria that cause souring. The easiest method for applying sulfur to fruits is to make a mixture of sulfur (available at any pharmacy) and cold water and soak for 10-20 minutes. Commercial dehydrating plants utilize sulfuring as a prime method of treatment.

Alternatives to Chemical Solutions

Nature's own chemical preservatives and some kitchen actions are effective in helping preserve color, facilitate drying, and prevent contamination as explained in the next sections.

Fruit juice: Many people prefer lemon, lime, or pineapple juice instead of a chemical bath. Simply dip fruit in unsweetened juice of lemon or pineapple, drain in a colander, blot with paper towels, and put into dryer.

Vitamin C: Crush 3–4 vitamin C tablets (500 mg each) into 1 quart cold water. Soak fruits in solution for 10 minutes.

Removing skins or peels: Drop fruits into boiling water for 30–60 seconds, rinse in cold water, then peel by hand.

Cracking or "nicking" skins or peels: When fruit skins or peels are thick, but not to be removed, put them in boiling water for 15–45 seconds. Immediately dunk into cold water and the skin should crack. If they're too thick to crack, then make several nicks in the skins with a sharp stainless steel knife.

Freezing: Put fruit into freezer overnight, then thaw by dropping into hot water just before processing.

Step 4: Drying Fruits & Vegetables

Warm, dry air is passed over, under, around, and through the food, pulling out the moisture, evaporating it, and reducing the food to between $1/6$–$1/3$ of its original size. Drying removes as much as 90% of the moisture from vegetables and only slightly less, approximately 80%, from fruits.

Whatever the heat source, all you need is a sustained temperature of 140°–150°F, a number of trays to hold the fruit or vegetable, and several hours of unattended drying time. Spread one layer of prepared and treated produce on each drying tray. Turn produce often to assure thorough drying. A temperature of 140°F for at least half the drying time is required to kill the inherent bacteria in drying foods.

The time required for successful drying depends on these variables:

- moisture in prepared and treated foods
- humidity
- temperature inside dryer
- size of pieces of foods
- rotation of trays and stirring of foods

In-home drying effectively preserves food with more flavor, color, appearance, texture, and the highest food value when compared to commercial processes. Little effort is required to perfect in-home drying, and equipment and time commitments are small.

Drying may be done in the sun, in an oven, or in an electric home dehydrator. Families without hungry children or nosy pets may be able to use heating ducts or furnace rooms as heat sources, or the tops of counters and open spaces. In earlier times, the sun was the prime heat source for drying, and probably in those days it was the family's entertainment. (As I recall, it was for my grandmother—it seemed she got a kick out of seeing us work!) In today's busy world, however, people buy an electric dryer and try to fit drying experiences during half-time or between doing the dishes and washing clothes.

Indoor Drying Methods

There are several in-home methods[5] for drying foods, and each is somewhat different, based on the area's temperature and humidity ranges, food you want to dry, and the time available for processing. The usual locations utilized for indoor drying are listed here.

Space: Hang strands of beans, pods of pepper, and baskets of herbs and flowers in whatever warm space available.[6]

Oven: Most electric and gas stoves will work, even though not an excellent method of drying. Temperature control is a little difficult, and they are inconvenient at times.

Heat register: Registers are not recommended due to the contaminants in the typical home heating ducts.

Commercial dryer: Many models are available. Shop carefully before buying. (In previous editions, a do-it-yourself plan for building a dryer was included. Prices of dryers are now less than what the parts formerly cost for a homemade unit. In fact, some of the parts may no longer be available!)

Microwave oven: Except for blanching and boiling foods prior to drying them, this method has proven too difficult to control for many of us. Also, cooking often occurs prior to drying. Then, too, there's the ubiquitous dry, hard spots in the foods! It's not a recommended drying method. In all fairness, however, there are experts who succeed where others fail.[7] We've tried the system, but haven't perfected it yet. If you're a serious drying devotée, you might want to get the book and try this method.

Outdoor Drying Methods

In some climates, outdoor drying is an easy and natural process. If you don't live in one of those climates or microclimates, contact your State Agricultural Extension Agent. Local agents usually have the best information on local drying methods for their area.

Solar heat: [8] Open-air processing in the heat of the direct sun. This works best where daytime temperatures are high and humidity ranges are low both day and night.

---

[5] The USDA has another out-of-print brochure which describes these alternatives with explicit details: *Farmers' Bulletin No. 984, Farm and Home Drying of Fruits and Vegetables.* If not available at the library, call your County Extension Agent.

[6] One of the best space dryers is made by **Product Source Int'l.,** 255 East 400 South, Suite #150, Salt Lake City UT 84111 ☎(801) 531-8996 or 🖷(801) 328-1243. It's called the **Food Pan*trie*™,** and is both an air-drying device and an effective sprouting system. An instructional video is provided.

[7] Isabel Webb, author of *Fruit Drying with a Microwave,* Sterling Publishing Co., Inc., 387 Park Avenue South, New York NY 10016, seems to have a very good system for microwave fruit drying.

[8] The USDA Federal Extension Service has a pamphlet, *Sun Dry Your Fruits and Vegetables (1958),* a step-by-step explanation of drying procedures for the southwestern and south central U.S.

Shade: [9] For geographic areas where the temperature, air movement, and humidity range allow food to complete the drying process without direct sun exposure (after an adequate "jump-start" either by solar or artificial heat).

Air: For geographic areas where the movement of air is adequate to complete the drying process (after a "jump start" in an oven or dryer, of course.)

Drying Tips

These tips apply both to indoor and outdoor drying methods.

- Do not mix vegetables and/or fruits while drying. All fruits and vegetables have different drying times and even different tests for doneness.
- Rotate trays as needed to assure even drying (or turn trays around in oven).
- Prevent scorching and discoloration by rotating food trays away from the heat source or lower the temperature a few degrees—but not below 140°F.
- Drying temperature for juicy foods should be started at less than 140°F and raised slowly. Too much heat too soon will harden the outer cells and prevent release of internal moisture. This is particularly important with the "juicy" fruits.
- Maintain temperature between 140°–150°F for maximum drying effectiveness and to reduce molds and bacterial growth.
- Check trays occasionally to separate pieces sticking together.
- Turn larger pieces over more often and keep them near the outside of the dryer.
- Move nearly dry pieces to center of trays and pile them up—but continue to turn them from time to time.

Doneness Testing

Appearance and feel are the in-home drying tests for determining when dried foods are ready for storage. See **Quick-Guides** for details.

Fruits are considered dry enough for storage when pieces have these qualities:
- no moisture can be squeezed from a dried sample when it's cut
- pieces are tough and pliable, like leather
- pieces separate after being squeezed together tightly

Vegetable tests for doneness are characterized in terms of
- brittle
- tough-to-brittle
- crispness

Note:
Vegetables must be drier than fruits for home storage purposes.

The **Quick-Guides** detail the doneness test for each fruit and vegetable, including any exceptions. Always perform the doneness test with a cooled test piece. When the test piece has passed the doneness test, remove entire batch from dryer and allow to cool thoroughly. Before packaging foods, check once more for pieces that are not dried properly. Those may be recycled through the dryer or eaten within a few days. Package only best quality foods for your storage.

---

[9] Mother called the last two methods "porch drying." It's how we dried the remainders of "daddy's garden." In those days, we laid butcher paper on the slats of the wood porch swing and used an electric fan to provide enough air to make both shade and air drying methods work. (That was also prior to air pollution!)

Step 5: Post-Drying Handling to Extend Shelf Life

There are several techniques that will help both improve the quality of dried foods and extend their shelf life in your food storage program. If you're encountering difficulty with either in-home dried foods or commercially dehydrated food, perhaps there are some resolutions in the following sections.

Conditioning Period

Prior to packaging, certain dried foods, usually fruits with large pits or those with skins left on and dense vegetables, require a "conditioning period"— a day or so in a closed bulk container. Conditioning allows the moisture remaining in some of the pieces to re-distribute more evenly throughout the dried batch. After the conditioning period, too-moist pieces should be removed and eaten immediately or reprocessed in the dryer.

Molds and Bacterial Elimination

Whether you dry food in the outdoor sun or in the kitchen oven, there are two methods you can use to assure that molds, yeast, and bacteria are killed after the drying process prior to packaging. Extreme temperatures above and below the life support range of molds, yeast, and bacteria effectively eliminate them.

Heating: after testing for doneness, spread dried foods on a baking sheet, approximately 2 inches thick. Heat dried foods in warm oven at 165°–175°F for 10–12 minutes to kill any organisms or mold spores that may have developed during the drying process. Deadly bacteria, molds, and food yeast can live only in atmospheres having a certain level of moisture and temperature, so this method eliminates them with high heat levels prior to final packaging for storage. Attention must be given to assure dried foods are not cooked or burned while heating them at this higher temperature range. Allow foods to cool thoroughly before packaging.

Freezing: after putting cool dried foods in food-grade, plastic, resealable bags, place them in a chest or upright freezer—*not freezer section of combination unit*—for 48 hours at 0°F or lower. When removing from freezer, allow to return to room temperature very slowly to avoid internal sweating.

Freezing is the better method for eliminating molds, yeast, and bacteria because fewer nutrients are lost through freezing than heating.

Packaging and Storing

Dried foods will begin absorbing humidity when removed from the dryer or exposed when opening the packaging for use. To prevent absorption of humidity, as soon as foods are properly cooled, package them immediately in heavy-duty, food-grade, air-tight, self-sealing plastic bags.[10]

---

[10] Packaging wholesalers may also have desiccant (moisture removing chemical) packs for insertion in plastic bags. The desiccant will absorb moisture and is renewable when heated in the oven.

Here are some general notes to help in packaging and storing in-home dried foods:

- Freezer-weight, zip-lock bags are excellent for packaging dried foods. Force excess air from bags as they are sealed.
- Procure heavy-duty, food-grade, storage-quality, sealable plastic bags from local commercial packaging wholesalers.
- Store dried food products in a cool, dry location out of direct sunlight. Use a kraft-paper bag inside larger plastic bags to shield dried foods from sunlight. Paper used outside the plastic bags provides nesting places for bugs and spiders.
- Store only one kind of food in each individual package to avoid mixing flavors and possible cross-contamination should molds or spoilage occur.
- Another method for storing dried products is to place dried food in a food-quality, plastic bag, then put it in an airtight glass or metal container.
- Discard moldy food. Don't take chances on botulism or a debilitating sickness over a few pennies or dollars. Don't feed moldy foods to the dog, either!
- The advantage of having small amounts in individual packages will eliminate big losses should a mold or bacterial condition occur.
- The problem of a few bugs in dried foods may be solved by spreading the infested dried food on a cookie pan, placing in a 300°F oven for 25–30 minutes. Bugs and eggs die, and the food is edible again. (Protein content is higher, too!)

Step 6: Rehydration for Use

To rehydrate dried fruits and vegetables, cover them with water and soak for approximately 30 minutes, adding more water if necessary. The **Quick-Guides** provide details for rehydrating each fruit and vegetable. Be aware of results as you rehydrate your dried food so you'll become more proficient in utilizing the fruits of your labors.

There are books on dehydrating and using dehydrated foods, as well as many listings of equipment dealers and suppliers, in the materials at the end of the book.

Suggestions for rehydrating foods:

- Add hot, boiling water to dried foods, then cover to speed rehydration. *Better rehydration occurs when water is added to foods—not when foods are added to water!*
- Rehydration with boiling water will usually cook dried foods adequately, though this depends on the manner in which the food was prepared, treated, and dried.
- When additional cooking is required, do not boil or simmer, just keep hot at low heat.
- Do not use excess water when rehydrating dried foods—nutrients will be lost.
- Soaking water remaining from rehydration can be used in another recipe.
- Use rehydrated fruits in recipes as if fresh—no extra sugar needed to sweeten them.
- Dried fruits may be eaten dry or chopped and diced for desserts and cereals.
- Always add salt *after* rehydration process is completed.
- Rehydration is not necessary when making soups, stews, or casseroles with dried vegetables. Remember to adjust liquid for their absorption.
- Store small portions in individual packages. Small portions will prevent big losses in your storage should infestation or mold occur. Portion control will also reduce waste after opening a package or rehydrating it for use.

In-home drying, whether building a homemade dryer in the garage or buying commercial equipment with today's technology, has literally become an electronic breeze!

Note:

Always force excess air from bags when packaging dried foods.

Unless there's a vacuum in the packaging, any unfilled space contains air and moisture!

Quick-Guide 16–1

Basic In-Home Fruit Drying Guide

Directions for selecting, preparing, preservation treatment, drying in electric dryer, doneness testing, storing, and rehydrating fruits:

Step 1: Select quality, ripe, firm, and undamaged fruit. Wash carefully.

Step 2: Prepare fruit for drying. Review listed suggestions as guidelines.[1]

Step 3: Treat to preserve color and taste, if specified.

Step 4: Maintain drying temperatures between 140°–150°F. Turn frequently or change tray positions to dry fruits evenly without scorching.

Step 5: Storage life in months for in-home dried fruits when stored at 70°F.[2]

Step 6: Rehydrating stored dried fruits to use by covering with hot, boiling water.

Step 1	Step 2	Step 3	Step 4	Step 5	Step 6
Fruit Selection	Preparation for Drying	Preservation Treatment[3] Prior to Drying	Drying & Doneness Test	Shelf Life	Rehydration for Use[4]
Apple	Pare, core, and cut in $1/8"$–$1/4"$ slices or rings. Leave peeling on if "chewy" apples preferred.	Immediately after cutting, either treat in ascorbic acid[5] bath @ 3 tsp. to 1 C. cold water solution or 100% lemon juice. Or, may blanch 4 min. instead.	Leathery to brittle	6	Equal hot water and apples. Soak 10 min. Soft, but holds shape. Dried apples are an excellent chewy snack.
Apricot	Peel, if desired. Cut in halves, remove pits. May be quartered. Turn inside out to speed drying.	Treat in ascorbic acid bath solution @ $1\frac{1}{2}$ tsp. to 1 C. cold water. Or, treat with other listed solutions.	Leathery & pliable	8	Equal hot water and apricots. Soak 15 min. Soft and dark. Dried apricots are an excellent snack.
Avocado	Peel, cut in half, and remove seed. Cut into thin strips.	Must treat to prevent from turning black. After slicing, dip immediately in 100% lemon juice.	Leathery & pliable	2	Will not rehydrate well—use equal hot water and avocado. Soak 10 min. Soft and mushy. Good only for guacamole and soup flavoring.
Banana	Peel and slice across or along length, or cut in quarters, halves or dry whole.	No treatment required.	Leathery & pliable, not sticky	4	Equal hot water and bananas. Soak 15 min. Soft, limp, and dark. Dried bananas are an excellent chewy snack.

[1] Check with State Agricultural Extension, County Extension Agent, or local food storage experts for particulars about special needs for drying fruits in your geographic area.

[2] Approximate period before deterioration of food becomes noticeable to the taste. After this period, even though the food quality, i.e., flavor, nutritive value, etc., is declining, fruits will still be edible and useful, as long as they are not contaminated. In-home dried fruits stored at 50°F will have a shelf life approximately 4 times as long as when stored at 70°F! The key to extending storage life of dried fruits is to keep them at the lowest possible temperatures. Freezing dried fruit in airtight packages will provide many years of shelf life.

[3] Treatment process includes the following methods to prevent molds & bacteria, discoloration, loss of flavor (souring), and to extend storage:

• **Sulfur solution treatment**—bathe fruit in solution of $1\frac{1}{2}$ tsp. sulfur to 1 C. cold water, drain in colander, blot dry with paper towels, then put into electric dryer.

• **Antioxidant solution treatment**—dip fruit in undiluted, unsweetened lemon, lime, or pineapple juice, depending on your preference for taste. Drain fruit in colander and blot dry with paper towels, then put into electric dryer immediately.

• **Ascorbic acid solution treatment**—dissolve 3–4 vitamin C tablets (500 mg ascorbic acid each tablet) in 1 qt. cold water solution. Soak fruit in solution for 10 minutes, drain in colander, blot dry with paper towels, then put into electric dryer immediately.

• **Blanching treatment**—place fruit in basket suspended above boiling water (blanch fruits w/steam instead of boiling water) as required. Always add any sweeteners after rehydration is completed.

[4] When rehydrating fruits for desserts, allow liquid to be absorbed and the fruit plumps up. Remove and blot dry. Place fruits in dryer immediately.

[5] Apples require a stronger antioxidant treatment to prevent darkening and loss of flavor. Use 3 tsp. sulfur to 1 C. cold water solution.

Food	Preparation	Treatment	Dryness Test		Notes
Berries—all with skin, exceptions in separate listings	Leave whole, remove stems. Crack skins by dropping into boiling water for 15–45 sec., depending on toughness. Plunge into cold water immediately to crack skin. Dry thoroughly. (Freezing will also crack skins.)	No treatment required for blueberries, huckleberries, currants, or cranberries.	Hard, without visible moisture when squeezed between fingers	6	Will not rehydrate well—use equal hot water and berries. Soak 10–15 min. Good for purées, drink flavoring, etc. Dried berries are excellent sweet-tart snacks.
Blueberry	See Berries for details.	No treatment required.	Leathery & pliable, like raisins	12	Equal hot water and blueberries. Soak 10–15 min. Dried blueberries are a sweet-tart snack.
Cherry	Remove stems, cut in half, and remove pits. Drain if juicy.	No treatment required.	Leathery & pliable, like raisins	12	Equal hot water and cherries. Soak 10 min. Soft, but holds shape. Dried cherries are an excellent snack.
Citrus peel (zest)	Clean orange or lemon peel thoroughly. Scrape off inner pith to avoid bitter taste. Cut into strips.	No treatment required.	Crispy	12	Use dried only. Prior to use, chop in blender to desired fineness. Use as spice; add to liquid in recipe.
Coconut	Drain milk. Break in half and remove meat from shell. Slice or grate.	No treatment required.	Leathery to crisp	1	Use dried only. Sprinkle on foods. Drop small amounts in blender to flavor drinks.
Cranberry	See Berries for details.	No treatment required.	Leathery & pliable, like hard raisins	6	Equal hot water and cranberries. Soak 10–15 min. Dried cranberries are a tart snack!
Date	Wash thoroughly and dry well. Best dried whole.	No treatment required.	Leathery, but slightly sticky	12	Equal hot water and dates. Soak 15 min. Dried dates are excellent sweet snack.
Fig	Wash thoroughly. Leave whole, dip in boiling water 1 min. to crack skin.	Steam 20 min.	Leathery, but slightly sticky	6	Equal hot water and figs. Soak 15 min. Dried figs are tough but excellent for snacking.
Grape	Use only seedless grapes for drying. Leave whole, but remove stems. Crack skins with sharp knife, blanching quickly or freezing.	No treatment required.	Pliable, dark brown or black color	6	Raisins—will not reconstitute to grapes! Use dried in baking, cooking, and on cereal. Raisins make an excellent sweet snack.
Grapefruit	Peel, break into sections, pierce with knife.	No treatment required.	Leathery & pliable	6	Equal hot water and grapefruit. Soak 15 min. Soft flesh, but holds shape. Dried grapefruit is a tart and bitter-sour snack.
Kumquat	Peel, break into sections, pierce with knife.	No treatment required.	Leathery & pliable	6	Equal hot water and kumquat. Soak 15 min. Soft flesh, but holds shape. Dried kumquat is an excellent chewy snack.
Lemon	Peel, break into sections, pierce with knife.	No treatment required.	Leathery & pliable	6	Equal hot water and lemon. Soak 15 min. Soft flesh, but holds shape. Pulverize dried lemon for lemonade drink mix.
Nectarine	Peel if desired. Cut in half, remove pits. Quarter or slice if desired.	Treat in ascorbic acid bath @ $1\frac{1}{2}$ tsp. to 1 C. cold water solution. Or, treat with any other solution.	Leathery & pliable	6	Equal hot water and nectarine. Soak 5 min. Soft, dark flesh holds shape. Dried nectarine is an excellent chewy snack.
Melon—all kinds	Cut open, remove all rind and seeds, and slice flesh into chunks.	No treatment required.	Leathery, but not sticky	2	Melons will not rehydrate. Dried melon is a sweet and chewy snack.
Orange	Peel, break into sections, pierce with knife.	No treatment required.	Leathery & pliable	6	Equal hot water and orange. Soak 15 min. Soft flesh, but holds shape. Dried orange is an excellent tart snack.

Basic In-Home Fruit Drying Guide (continued)

Step 1 Fruit Selection	Step 2 Preparation for Drying	Step 3 Preservation Treatment Prior to Drying	Step 4 Drying & Doneness Test	Step 5 Shelf Life	Step 6 Rehydration for Use
Papaya	Peel, slice, and remove seeds.	No treatment required.	Leathery to crisp	6	Equal hot water and papaya. Soak 5 min. Soft, dark flesh and holds shape. Dried papayas are an excellent chewy snack.
Peach	Peel, if desired, by quick blanching and re-moving by hand. Cut in half, remove pits. Quarter or slice if desired.	Treat in ascorbic acid bath @ $1^1/_2$ tsp. to 1 C. cold water solution. Or, may treat with any solution.	Soft, leathery & pliable	6	Equal hot water and peaches. Soak 5 min. Soft, dark flesh and holds shape. Dried peaches are a chewy, excellent snack.
Pear	Pare and remove core and other woody parts. Cut into $1/_8$", $1/_4$", or $1/_2$" slices or rings.	Treat in ascorbic acid bath @ $1^1/_2$ tsp. to 1 C. cold water solution. Or, may blanch for 2 min.	Soft, pliable to leathery	6	Equal hot water and pears. Soak 10 min. Soft, dark flesh and holds shape. Dried pear slices are an excellent snack.
Pineapple	Cut away outer skin. Cut into slices or chunks.	Blanch 1 min.	Leathery, but not sticky	8	Equal hot water and pineapple. Soak 10 min. Soft, mushy, but holds shape. Dried pineapple is an excellent tart snack.
Plum	Leave whole or cut into thin slices. Blanching not required, but drying is faster. When us-ing whole, steam for 5 min. to crack skins and speed drying.	No treatment required.	Leathery & pliable	8	Equal hot water and plums. Soak 20 min. Soft, slippery but holds shape. Dried plums are prunes and are an excellent snack. Prunes soaked in water make juice.
Strawberry	Remove stems and leaves. Cut in half or thirds.	Blanch 1 min.	Leathery & pliable	6	Equal hot water and strawberries. Soak 10 min. Soft, mushy, and holds shape. Dried strawberries are an excellent tart snack.
Tangerine	Peel, break into sections, pierce with knife.	No treatment required.	Leathery & pliable	6	Equal hot water and tangerine. Soak 15 min. Soft flesh, but holds shape. Dried tangerine is an excellent snack, but tart.
Watermelon	Cut open, remove all rind and white lining, slice flesh into chunks, remove seeds.	No treatment required.	Leathery, but not sticky	2	Watermelon will not rehydrate. Dried watermelon is a sweet and chewy snack.

BASIC FRUIT LEATHER

Fruit leather is made by making a purée of ripe fruit or fruit combinations, then drying it. You choose whether to leave peeling on. It is simple to make and is nutritious, tasty, and fun for kids of all ages. The ingredients are very simple:

1 batch ripe fruit, puréed (after treating for drying)

Pare fruit skins and imperfections, remove seeds, core, and stems. Purée ripe fruit (or fruit combinations) in a blender until smooth. Pour fruit purée onto center of dryer sheets, spread thinly, $1/_8$" – $1/_4$" with spatula. Use waxed paper inserts for trays or cookie sheets when oven-drying. Keep purée at least $1/_2$" from sides of tray. Dry for 12 hr. or more. When leathery and not sticky, allow to cool fully, roll up in waxed paper or plastic wrap. Leave long or cut into shorter lengths and store in heavy-duty, food-grade, freezer-quality, sealable plastic bags.

Quick-Guide 16-2

Basic In-Home Vegetable Drying Guide

Directions for selecting, preparing, preservation treatment, drying in electric dryer, doneness testing, storing, and rehydrating vegetables:

Step 1: Select quality, ripe, firm, undamaged vegetables and wash carefully.
Step 2: Prepare vegetables for drying. Review suggestions for guidelines.[6]
Step 3: Treat all vegetables by blanching to preserve color and taste and eliminate molds and bacteria. Then spread in single layer on dryer tray.
Step 4: Maintain drying temperatures between 140°–150°F. Turn frequently or change tray positions to dry vegetables evenly w/o scorching.[7]
Step 5: Storage life in months for in-home dried vegetables when stored at 70°F.[7]
Step 6: Rehydrating stored dried vegetables according to chart suggestions.

Step 1	Step 2	Step 3	Step 4	Step 5	Step 6
Vegetable Selection	Preparation for Drying	Blanching Treatment[8] Prior to Drying	Drying & Doneness Test	Shelf Life	Rehydration for Use[9][10]
Asparagus	Use uppermost 3"–4" of spear.	Blanch 5 min. or steam 15–20 min.	Tough to brittle	2	Barely cover asparagus with hot water. Soak 15–20 min. Stems will remain tough after rehydrating.
Bean—bush varieties	Shell[11] mature beans.	Blanch 15–20 min. or steam until tender.	Shatters when crushed	4	For each C. dried beans use 2 C. cool water. Soak 2½ hr. or until all water is absorbed. Beans must be fully cooked before eating.
Bean—snap	Trim and slice lengthwise, at diagonal, or cut in 1" pieces.	Blanch 6 min. or steam 15–20 min. until tender.	Brittle & crisp, dark green to green-brownish color	4	Use twice the water as beans. Bring to boil, cover, reduce heat and simmer 30 min. Use as fresh: soups, stews, and casseroles.
Bean—green and yellow	Trim and slice lengthwise, at diagonal, or cut in 1" pieces.	Blanch 6 min. or steam 15–20 min. until tender.	Brittle & crisp, dark green to brownish color	4	Use twice the water as beans. Bring to boil, cover, reduce heat and simmer 30 min. Use as fresh: soups, stews, and casseroles.
Bean—lima	Shell mature beans.	Blanch 5 min. or steam 10–15 min.	Hard & brittle	4	For each C. beans use 2 C. cool water. Soak until all water is absorbed. Beans must be fully cooked before eating.

[6] Check with State Agricultural Extension Division, County Extension Agent, or local food storage experts for particulars about special needs for drying vegetables in your geographic area.

[7] Approximate period before deterioration of food becomes noticeable. After this period, even though the food quality, i.e., flavor, nutritive value, etc., is declining, vegetables will still be edible and useful, as long as they are not contaminated. In-home dried foods stored at 50°F will store for approximately 4 times as long as when kept at 70°F! The key to extending storage of dried foods is to keep them at the lowest possible temperatures. Freezing properly dried and packaged vegetables will extend shelf life many years.

[8] Blanching treatment—blanch vegetables in boiling water as suggested to prevent molds & bacteria, discoloration, loss of flavor (souring), and extend shelf life. Some vegetables may be steamed instead.

[9] Dried vegetables can be pulverized into powder in the blender for making baby food, flours, purées, or soup thickeners.

[10] Add salt, sugar, or other seasonings only after rehydration is completed.

[11] Try mother's "burlap-bag shelling" method: place mature pea and bean pods in an old pillowcase and tie shut. Insert the pillowcase into a burlap bag or potato sack (we called them "gunnysacks"). Then bang around for 25–30 minutes to dry the pods and expel the peas and beans from the pods. Then pop the ensemble into a clothes dryer at low or medium heat. Let them bang from the pods.

Basic In-Home Vegetable Drying Guide (continued)

Step 1 Vegetable Selection	Step 2 Preparation for Drying	Step 3 Blanching Treatment Prior to Drying	Step 4 Drying & Doneness Test	Step 5 Shelf Life	Step 6 Rehydration for Use
Beets	Use small, tender beets, free from wood-like fibers. Trim tops, but leave crown.	Blanch 40–45 min. or steam until cooked through and tender. Cool, trim roots and crown, peel. Cut into $1/8$" shoestring strips, $1/4$" cubes or thin slices.	Tough to brittle, dark red color	4	Equal hot water and beets. Soak 1 hr. Tender and limp, but good flavor and color.
Broccoli	Trim "trees" and cut as if serving fresh. Peel stalk and cut into $1/4$" rounds.	Blanch 4–5 min.	Crisp & brittle, dark color	1	Equal hot water and broccoli. Soak 30 min. Tender and limp flowerettes, but good flavor and color. Stem probably tough.
Cabbage	Remove outer leaves. Quarter head, remove core. Shred into shoestring-size strips.	Blanch 4–5 min. or steam 5–6 min. until completely wilted.	Brittle	1	Use $1 1/2$ cool water as cabbage. Soak 15–20 min. Flavor good and no strong odor. Best use is sauté or baked. Steam causes dried cabbage to be soggy and off-color.
Carrots	Use crisp, tender carrots, without woody tissue. Peel, trim roots and tops. Cut $1/4$" slices or strips.	Blanch 4 min. or steam 8–10 min.	Tough to brittle, deep orange color	6	Equal hot water and carrots. Soak 30 min. Flavor and color good, real carrot texture.
Cauliflower	Remove flowerettes from core. Split stems.	Blanch 3 min. or steam 10 min. until tender.	Crispy, tends to turn brownish	1	Equal hot water and cauliflower. Soak 15–20 min. Flavor and color good, but texture soft.
Celery	Remove leaves and bottom. Cut stalks into small pieces.	Blanch 1 min.	Dry & brittle	2	Equal hot water and celery. Soak 20 min. Flavor and color good, but has soft texture.
Corn—cut	Husk corn. Remove ends and silk.	Blanch 10 min. or steam 20–30 min. to set milk in kernels. Cut off kernels with sharp knife (don't cut into cob) before putting into dryer.	Dry & brittle[12]	4	Use twice water to corn. Bring to boil in saucepan, cover, reduce to low heat and simmer 30 min., adding water if needed. Flavor and texture good as canned.
Corn—whole ear	Use tender, sweet corn. Remove husk and silks.	Blanch whole ear 10 min. or steam for 20–30 min.	Dry & brittle	6	Add corn to boiling pot of water. Cover and reduce to simmer until corn is tender.
Cucumber	Peel and slice thinly.	Blanch 1 min.	Crispy	4	Equal cool water and cucumbers. Soak 1 hr. Color good, but rehydrated cucumbers are tough and tasteless. Use in dip or spread mix.
Eggplant	Peel and cut in $1/2$" slices or $1/2$" cubes.	Blanch 4–5 min.	Leathery to brittle	2	Equal cool water and eggplant. Soak 30 min. Color darker and texture tough, but tastes like eggplant. Use in soups.

[12] For excellent cornmeal, grind dried corn in wheat grinder or blender. Pulverize dried corn for soup thickener.

Vegetable	Preparation	Pretreatment	Dryness		How to Use
Garlic	Remove outer layers and split buds.	No treatment required.	Brittle	2	Do not rehydrate for cooking. Use dried garlic in recipes. Drop dried bud in vinegar or olive oil, or place in any other food.
Horseradish	Trim off tops and slice thin or grate.	No treatment required.	Brittle	4	Do not rehydrate for cooking. Equal warm water and horseradish 30 min. for use in dip or spread mix.
Kale	Wash and cut into strips.	Blanch 4 min.	Crisp & brittle	2	Steam leaves 5–6 min. Good flavor and tender, but off-color.
Leek	Remove outer leaves. Slice, cube, or chop $1/8"$–$1/4"$.	No treatment required.	Brittle	4	Equal hot water and leeks. Soak 15 min. Has appearance and taste of steamed leeks.
Mushroom	Leave buttons whole, slice larger sizes. Use stems if tender.	Blanch 3 min.	Leathery to brittle	2	No rehydration needed. Texture and flavor good. Use in casseroles, soups, and stews.
Okra	Cut off tips and slice $1/2"$.	Blanch 5 min.	Leathery to brittle	4	Use twice the water as okra. Bring to boil, cover, reduce heat and simmer 30 min.
Onions	Remove outer leaves. Slice, cube, or chop $1/8"$–$1/4"$.	None required.	Brittle	4	Equal hot water and onions. Soak 15 min. Appearance and taste of steamed onions.
Parsnip	Use small, tender parsnips, free from woody fibers. Trim tops, peel but leave crown.	Blanch 5 min. or steam until cooked through and tender. Allow to cool, then trim roots and crown. Cut into $1/8"$ shoestring strips, $1/4"$ cubes or thin slices.	Tough to brittle	4	Equal hot water and parsnips. Soak 1 hr. Tender and limp, but good flavor and color.
Pea—green	Shell young, tender sweet peas.	Blanch 3 min. or steam 10 min.	Shatters when crushed	4	Use twice the water as peas. Bring to boil, cover, reduce heat and simmer 30 min. Dried peas are an excellent snack.
Pepper—all "hot" types	Use only mature peppers. Dry whole, diced, slivers, halves, or quarters.	No treatment required.	Pliable to brittle, depending on type	8	Mince, crush, or turn to powder in blender for use as seasoning in recipes.
Pepper—all sweet types	Cut and remove seeds. Cut peppers in $1/8"$–$1/4"$–$1/2"$ strips, rings, or diced.	Scald in boiling water 3–5 minutes. Spread 2 layers deep.	Pliable to brittle	8	Equal hot water and sweet peppers. Soak 15–20 min. Flavor and color like steamed. Soft flesh and tough skin.
Potato	Peel and cut into shoestring strips $1/8"$–$1/4"$ or slice $1/8"$ thick.	Rinse first in cold water. Blanch 5 min. Soak in lemon water ($1/4$ C. lemon juice and 1 qt. cold water) for 45–60 min. to prevent turning black during drying process.	Brittle	4	Equal cold water and potatoes. Soak 25–30 min. Texture and flavor of raw potato. Use for mashed potatoes, in soups, and stews.
Pumpkin	Cut and remove seeds. Slice into 1" strips. Peel, then slice strips crosswise $1/4"$.	Blanch 3 min. or steam 8–13 minutes until slightly soft.	Tough to brittle	1	Equal water and pumpkin. Bring to boil in covered pot. Reduce heat to low, simmer 10 min. Color good, slightly mushy texture.
Rhubarb	Wash and cut into 1" strips.	Blanch 3 min.	Tough to brittle	4	Equal hot water and rhubarb. Soak 15–20 min. Flavor and color good, soft texture.
Spinach and other leafy greens	Choose young, tender leaves. Wash again. Cut into $1/4"$–$1/2"$ strips.	Blanch 2 min. or steam 4–5 min. until thoroughly wilted. Spread several layers deep.	Brittle	2	Steam leaves 5–6 min. Good flavor and tender, but off-color.

Basic In-Home Vegetable Drying Guide (continued)

Step 1	Step 2	Step 3	Step 4	Step 5	Step 6
Vegetable Selection	Preparation for Drying	Blanching Treatment Prior to Drying	Drying & Doneness Test	Shelf Life	Rehydration for Use
Squash—Hubbard	Cut and remove seeds. Slice into 1" strips. Peel, then slice crosswise 1/4" thick.	Blanch 3 min. or steam 8–13 min. until slightly soft.	Tough to brittle	1	Equal water and Hubbard squash. Bring to boil in pot. Cover, reduce heat to low, simmer 10 min. Off-color and soft texture.
Sweet potato	Wash and peel. Slice 1/4" thick or dice.	Blanch 3 min.	Tough to brittle	1	Equal cold water and potatoes. Soak 25–30 min. Texture and flavor of raw potato.
Swiss chard	Wash and cut into strips.	Blanch 2 min.	Crisp & brittle	2	Steam leaves 5–6 min. Good flavor and tender, but off-color.
Tomato—for stewing	Choose red-colored tomatoes. Dip in boiling water to remove skins. Chill in cold water and peel. Cut into 1/2–3/4" sections.	Blanch 3 min.	Leathery & pliable	3	Equal hot water and tomatoes. Soak 30 min. Flavor of tomato paste. Flesh is mushy and skin is tough. Color is darker. Use in soups, stews, casseroles and sauces.
Tomato—for sun-dried	Select small paste tomatoes. Slice in half lengthwise or cut larger ones into quarters.	None required, but watch carefully at end of drying cycle to prevent scorching.	Leathery & pliable	6	Equal hot water, vinegar, and tomatoes. Soak until chewy. Drain and cover with vinegar/olive oil, marinate in fridge 24 hr. Add to Mexican and Italian tomato sauces.
Turnips	Trim tops and roots. Slice into 1/4" rounds.	Blanch 5 min.	Tough to brittle	2	Equal hot water and turnips. Soak for 1 hr. Good flavor and color, texture soft and limp.
Zucchini & summer squash	Leave peeling on and slice into thin slices across.	Blanch 3 min.	Pliable to brittle, depending on variety	1	Equal hot water and zucchini or summer squash. Soak 15 min., then steam 8 min. Good flavor and color, but limp and mushy.

BASIC SUNSTYLE DRIED TOMATOES

3 lb. tomatoes of choice (plum, sauce, or medium salad)
2 tsp. salt

Wash and dry tomatoes carefully. Cut tomatoes lengthwise, across or in half. Place cut side up on dryer trays, 1 layer deep. Sprinkle salt evenly on tomatoes. Turn every 2–3 hr. As tomatoes near fully-dried stage, watch carefully to prevent scorching. Cool thoroughly. Store dry in freezer-quality, heavy-duty, food-grade, sealable plastic bags or place in jars with oil and garlic. Store in cool, dry and dark location for up to 3 months or refrigerate for 9–12 months.

GOURMET SUNSTYLE DRIED TOMATOES

2–4 C. olive oil   3–6 garlic buds

Dry as directed in Basic SunStyle Dried Tomatoes. Stuff slices of dried tomatoes into clean storage jars with tight-fitting lids. Peel and cut garlic buds in half, drop into jars. Pour olive oil into jars to cover dried tomatoes, tighten lids. Leave at room temperature 1–2 weeks for blending of flavors. Either store in cool, dry, and dark location for 2–3 months or put in refrigerator for up to 12 months.
For gifts, use decorative jars with rubber gaskets.

Chapter 17

Energy and Fuels Storage

Fuels will be very important should an emergency arise—food must still be prepared, dishes washed, people bathed and warmed. Electricity, natural gas, and other energy sources could be interrupted by an earthquake, flood, hurricane, or other natural disaster—not to mention rationing of energy-producing commodities due to trucking strikes, economic or other national disaster. The family with fuel to provide adequate energy for cooking, cleaning, sterilization, lighting, and warmth will be much better prepared than those families who ignore this important storage category. However, in your eagerness to accomplish this priority, don't forget the essentials of safety which are important in the storage of highly flammable materials.

- Do not store gas, kerosene, or similar liquid fuels where children can reach them.
- Do not store fuel near foods—an offensive taste will generally result in the food.
- Do not mix fuel storage with storage space for medicines, food, or water—the latter items will all become contaminated.

The following pages list some typical camping equipment utilizing energy or fuel and their respective consumption rates. This will guide your determination of fuel(s) needed.

TWO-MANTLE GAS LANTERN

A gallon of Coleman™-type fuel utilized with a two-mantle gas lantern has a burning time of approximately 40 hours. Light output is approximately the same as a 200W light bulb. Assuming an operating or burning time of 5 hours per day, the following approximate amounts of fuel would be consumed:

Chart 17–1

Two-Mantle Gas Lantern Fuel Consumption

Period	Fuel Consumed per 5 Hours
Day	1 quart
Week	2 gallons
Month	8 gallons
Year	100 gallons

White gas may be substituted in some camping equipment, but read and follow the specific instructions of the equipment manufacturer. A gas lantern gives a high intensity light and lots of heat, too—though the pressurized gas delivery system is quite noisy when operating.

KEROSENE LANTERN

Given today's technology, a kerosene lantern seems a bit old-fashioned and out of place! However, a kerosene lantern with a 1-inch wick will burn approximately 45 hours per quart of kerosene, saving lots of natural resources and utilizing approximately one-fourth as much fuel as a gas lantern. Kerosene lanterns are an effective and fairly safe lighting source. There are now scented lamp oils which replace kerosene. This lamp oil is generally available in retail stores. Make sure the oil is approved for use in your lamp.

There is a difference in lighting quantity and quality, as the kerosene lantern is quite dim when compared to the two-mantle gas lantern. The light output of a kerosene lantern is comparable to a 40W-60W light bulb.

As a rule of thumb, the typical kerosene lantern burns approximately 1 ounce of fuel per hour. Burning at the rate of 5 hours each day, the following approximate amounts of kerosene would be used:

Chart 17–2

Kerosene Lantern Fuel Consumption

Period	Fuel Consumed per 5 Hours
Day	$1/2$ pint
Week	2 quarts
Month	2 gallons
Year	25 gallons

FLASHLIGHT

A two-battery, "D"-cell flashlight with conventional dry cell batteries will provide light for the approximate times illustrated in the following chart. Long-life batteries have substantially longer life than conventional batteries.

Chart 17–3

Life of Conventional "D" Cell Dry Batteries

Type of Use	Battery Condition	Approximate Battery Life in Hours
Continuous	new old	5–6 2–4
Intermittent	new old	7–8 3–5

Shelf life of batteries is important. Age, temperature, manufacturer, humidity, bulb size, and other factors can shorten battery life and, ultimately, the effective performance of any battery. Choose batteries for a flashlight with as much consideration as any other item of basic equipment. Rotate batteries just as any other item in your in-home storage or preparedness inventory.

Rechargeable, long-life flashlights are available, as well as rechargeable batteries. Our research indicates rechargeable batteries have a much shorter life than conventional batteries, but the convenience of recharging them outweighs this shortcoming. Obviously, rechargeable units are not very useful when there's no electricity! Solar-powered models work best for long-term use.

There are, however, self-powered compact flashlights, making it possible to have light without the hassle of batteries. Light is produced by means of an internal generator, powered by pulling or squeezing a lever or pulling a trigger.

TALLOW CANDLES

Tallow candles burn brighter, longer, and are fairly smoke-free when compared to wax candles. Tallow candles are generally available in specialty stores only, unless you make your own. Wax candles are available almost anywhere housewares are sold.

The following chart gives details for approximate burning times:

Chart 17–4

Tallow Candle Burning Rate

Height	Diameter	Approximate Burning Time in Hours
6"	$1/2$"	3
6"	1"	8
9"	2"	48

Store tallow candles in a cool, dry location. Candles stored in the freezer will burn slower and without dripping.

EMERGENCY CANDLES

There are two types of emergency candles available for camping, storage, and emergency purposes. The type made of hardened wax in a can has the capability of utilizing several wicks simultaneously. The other type is a liquid paraffin-filled bottle with a wick for easy lighting. The liquid paraffin burns without odor or smoke. This candle has a minimum 100-hour burning time and indefinite shelf life.

TWO-BURNER GAS CAMP STOVE

Both burners of a Coleman™-type gas camp stove in use 4 hours per day will consume approximately the following amounts of Coleman™ fuel:

Chart 17–5

Two-Burner Camp Stove Fuel Consumption

Period	Fuel Consumed per 3 Meals
Day	5 pints
Week	3 gallons
Month	10 gallons
Year	100 gallons

Caution: use all types of burning fuel only in a well-ventilated space.

EMERGENCY TIN CAN STOVE

Make the tin can stove by turning a 1-gallon metal can (#10 can) upside-down and inserting a heating unit. An old metal bucket of any kind will serve the same purpose. A small tuna can ($1^1/_2$ inches tall) with a rolled-up section of newspaper soaked with paraffin wax coiled tightly in it will provide heat for cooking (and a little warmth).

- **How to make an emergency tin can stove:** cut one end from a 1-gallon tin can or #10 can and discard. Punch 4–6 holes in side of can, both at the top and bottom (near the seam), to allow the heat to draft upward more efficiently. Place heating source unit on a non-flammable surface, start fire, set tin can stove over the burning heat source and use as a camp stove. Bricks, rocks, or any heat-safe material will hold flame at appropriate height for cooking purposes.

- **How to make the tin can stove heating unit:** fold a double-size newspaper page length-wise, accordion-style, and force-fit into a tuna can. Pour paraffin or wax over the folded paper in the can. The paper acts as a wick. The wax burns hot and clean, providing adequate heat for emergency cooking, if positioned properly. This heat source will burn approximately 1–2 hours.

Alternate method for making the heating unit: cut corrugated paper cardboard into strips the height of the can, roll tightly, push into the can, then soak with wax and use as described.

CHARCOAL BRIQUETTES

Three or four briquettes in a small (8 x 8-inch) hibachi or charcoal grill will generate enough heat to cook a simple meal and at the same time provide a little heat. Store approximately 25 pounds of charcoal briquettes for each week's use. Store an adequate supply of charcoal starter, too.

Charcoal is a very useful fuel. It can be made from twigs and limbs of fruit, nut, and other hardwood trees, from black walnuts, or even peach and apricot pits. It makes a hot fire which gives off little or no smoke. Make your own charcoal using the following steps:

BASIC CHARCOAL

- Take a metal bucket or can with lid and punch $1/2$-inch holes all around and on ends.

- Put wood, sticks, or woody material into can and cover with lid.

- "Cook" over hot fire. The holes in the can allow the gases and flame to escape while reduced oxygen keeps the wood from burning completely to ashes.

- When the flame from the holes in the can turns to bright yellow-red, remove can from the fire and allow to cool.

- Store charcoal in paper bags or cardboard cartons in a dry environment.

Caution:

When using charcoal in an enclosed space, vent the grill by setting it on the fireplace hearth or placing it near a partially-opened window.

Death could result if space is improperly ventilated.

COAL

Two to four tons of coal, sparingly used, normally meets the cold weather needs of a family for a year. While a standard brick-lined fireplace is comfortable during times of plenty, it is not the most efficient way to heat a home when electricity or natural gas are not available.

Either a pot-belly or "Ben Franklin"-type stove or an old-fashioned coal or wood kitchen range would be more practical for warming large spaces. They also double their value as a means for cooking food. If coal were the only heating source, approximately one ton per month would be consumed in a standard stove or fireplace, depending on the severity of the winter weather, efficiency of stove or fireplace, and temperature maintained in the house.

Coal should preferably be stored in the dark and away from circulating air. After a period of time, air tends to break the coal into small pieces. Smaller pieces are consumed at a faster rate and higher intensity than larger lumps.

The best method for storing coal is in a hole lined with plastic sheeting. After putting coal in the hole, cover with more plastic and then cover with dirt. The plastic helps to keep the air out and also helps prevent loss in recovering it.

If coal is to be stored above ground, place it on the north side of the house where it will be out of the sun. Smaller quantities can be stored in potato sacks or large cans. These types of containers are more convenient when storing coal in a garage or basement space.

Caution:

Coal cannot be utilized safely with prebuilt metal or metal-lined fireplaces. Be sure to check the fireplace manufacturer's recommendations for fuel utilization in metal fireplaces.

NEWSPAPER FUEL

You can make a substitute for firewood from your daily newspapers—it's like having firewood delivered to your door at no extra cost! There are several commercial newspaper log-making machines which simplify and speed up the process of folding and rolling newspapers.

Four newspaper logs last approximately one hour and produce heat equivalent to a comparably sized stick of wood. Newspaper fuel overcomes problems of smoldering, flying ashes, and popping of wood.

The average daily newspaper will make 2–3 logs. The typical city Sunday edition will make up to 7 logs. Newspaper logs provide, on a pound-for-pound basis, approximately the same heat as wood and are an efficient energy source.

BASIC NEWSPAPER LOGS

- Use 6 sections (five double sheets in each section) for each newspaper log.

- Fold double sheets to single page size.

- Fold each single page section in half width-wise.

- Turn 90° and fold in half again.

- Stack the sections, alternating cut with folded sides. Allow bottom or outside section to extend out from the roll by 3–4 inches. This makes a convenient way to light the roll.

- Roll papers very tightly, securing the center and ends of the newspaper roll with a tightly twisted piece of wire.

The following method provides a cleaner-burning version of the *Basic Newspaper Log* by using water to help break down the paper, much like *papier maché.* This log burns more effectively because the compressed paper is now expanded. These logs are fatter and will burn more brightly. Adding the detergent speeds the saturation rate of the newsprint. A few crystals of copper sulfate added to the water will create beautiful flame highlights.

BASIC "CLEAN-BURNING" NEWSPAPER LOGS

- Divide the newspaper into sections.

- Fold sections to half size, approximately 12 x 15 x $1/_2$ inch thick.

- Fill laundry tub $3/_4$ full with water and add 2 tablespoons detergent to speed saturation. Place newspaper sections in tub and allow to soak in this mixture for approximately 2 hours, or until newspapers have absorbed maximum amount of water.

- While wet, roll the sections individually onto a 1-inch metal or wood rod, squeezing out the excess water while smoothing down the ends and edges.

- Tie with a metal tie-wrap near ends and middle to hold roll intact while drying.

- Slide the rolls off the rod and stand them on end to dry, tipping the rolls slightly to allow air to circulate through the center of the roll. The "log" should be approximately 12 inches long and 2–4 inches in diameter. They are ready to use when completely dry.

CANNED COOKING FUELS

Canned fuels have been utilized and accepted as an excellent short-term emergency and utility heating source. Canned fuels have proven essential to the military and the Boy Scouts. Most buffets and many restaurants utilize canned heat as a warming or heating device, so most people are familiar with this source of heat and fuel.

FIRE STARTERS

No discussion of fuels storage would be complete without including the means of starting a fire. Be sure to have a supply of matches, newspapers, and/or kindling to facilitate starting the fire. Store both waterproof and windproof matches for emergencies. Keep them in sealed plastic bags as protection from the elements and moisture. In this fire-starter category are kitchen (stick) and book matches, cigarette lighters with a metal wheel rubbing against a flint to produce sparks, and magnesium fire starters—which work even when conditions are suboptimal and material is wet.

GAS DETECTORS

When you are utilizing combustible fuel sources, oxygen is consumed and either carbon monoxide or other deadly fumes result as a by-product of combustion. Explosive gases from butane, propane, and natural gas can accumulate in concentrations capable of destroying life and property.

When storing and utilizing these fuels, it would be wise to have gas detectors installed in those areas to protect you and your family. The alarm will notify you of danger with a high-decibel warning until the air is clear.

Home-built, Hand-powered, Multi-size, Large Jar Vacuum Sealer

After drying your foods—fruit, meats, and vegetables—vacuum-seal them to preserve them for long-term storage. Most of the effective home vacuum systems and supplies are relatively expensive. With the instructions for building this vacuum sealer, you can utilize free containers from the foodservice industry for food storage.

Build your own hand-powered vacuum-sealing system that will seal any bottle or jar up to 1-gallon size. This device will also pump water, marinate meats, and pump air into your tires—all without electricity! The pump is hand-powered, but can be operated optionally with a small electric hand drill.

This vacuum sealer system requires no pinholes through which to draw the vacuum and pulls a stronger vacuum (up to 28 inches of mercury) with approximately 30 cranks than most electric or hand-held models accomplish (from 23 to 26 inches of mercury). Save the expense and bother of purchasing nitrogen, dry ice, and expensive electric-powered machines by making this vacuum sealer at home. With the profusely illustrated do-it-yourself instructions, you can build a device to vacuum-seal any size jar that will hold a vacuum—and you can reuse their original lids many times without failure. (The commercial versions only seal canning jars.)

Write or call Rev. Tom Halverson, c/o Pass the Pen Evangelistic Association, Rt. Box 273, Guthrie MN 56461 ☎(218) 751-1522. This organization is a non-profit ministry. Instructions for building the non-electric jar vacuum sealing pump are $10. The assemble-it-yourself kit with everything needed to build your own pump, except the pump itself, is $79. The fully-constructed vacuum-sealing pump is $149. You can purchase vacuum-sealable lids for the 1-gallon foodservice jars @ 10 lids for $7. Included also is information about how to find cheap—or even free—gallon jars. Prices subject to change without notice.

WEBSITES OF SELECTED PREPAREDNESS SUPPLIERS

This listing is comprised of those suppliers for which we have Internet addresses or websites. We welcome additional information about other suppliers to the preparedness industry.

Access Plus!	www.infowest.com/a/access ✉ access@infowest.com
Adobe Milling Co., Inc.	www.rmgl.com/rmpc/rmpc/html
Akin's Natural Foods Market	www.akins.com
Alco-Brite Co., Inc.	www.alcobrite..com ✉ alcoinfo@alco-brite.com
AlpineAire Foods	www.alpineaire.com
Alternative Energy Engineering	www.asis.com/aee
American Civil Defense Association / Store	www.tacda.org ✉ tacda2000@daccess.net
American Family Network	www.americanfamilynetwork.com ✉ apc@american-products.com
American Family Preparedness	www.amfam.org ✉ Probe@srv.net
American Freedom Magazine	www.amerifree.com
American Military	www.ammil.com ✉ sales@ammil.com
American Red Cross / Fresno-Madera Chapter	www.cybergate.com/redcross/store.html ✉ vtn4241@cybergate.com
American Supply Int'l., Inc.	www.amsupply.com
Aquacheck	www.aquacheck.com
Atlantic Spice Company	www.atlanticspice.com
B & A Products	www.baproducts.com ✉ Byron@baproducts.com
B & G Enterprises	www//thunder@plan-et.com ✉ bob@plan-et.com
Back to Basics	www.dnet.net/~basics/ ✉ basics@drake.dnet.net
Brigade Quartermasters, Ltd.	www.actiongear.com ✉ brigade@mindspring.com
Canteen, The	www.mojoski.com/canteen ✉ canteen@mojoski.com
Chadd Medical Supplies	www.berks.com/chadd/survival.htm ✉ Jack71@juno.com
Community Mill & Bean, Inc.	www.crusoeisland.com ✉ cmnb@mail.tds.net
Cornucopia, The	www.axiom.net/cornucopia ✉ sargent@axion.net
Country Store & Kitchen Specialties	www.HealthyHarvest.com ✉ country@aone.com
Crisis Management Systems	www.safetystore.com ✉ cms@safetystore.com
CropKing, Inc.	www.cropking.com
Crozet Natural Foods	http://monticello.avenue.gen.vaus/Library/JMRL/Crozet/cfcoop.html
Dewey Research Center on the Web	www.4drc.com ✉ edewey@4drc.com
Disaster Preparedness 101	www.primenet.com ✉ prepared@primenet.com
Earthquake Essentials of L.A.	www.quakesafe.com
Earthquake Supply Center	www.cflat.com/esc/index/html ✉ rattle1@microweb.com
Emergency Essentials	www.beprepared.com ✉ corporatesales@beprepared.com
Emergency Preparedness Ctr.–Deer Park (EPC)	www.cet.com/!epc ✉ epc@cet.com
EpiCenter	http://TheEpicenter.com ✉ bjnelson@The Epicenter.com
EPK—Emergency Products Kits	www.epks.com ✉ webmaster@epks.com
Evac One	www.evac-one.com/order.htm
Excalibur (Home dehydrator mfr.)	www.kctc.net/life/excalho
Family Food Storage Catalog	http://downtown-web.com/psi/foodinfo.htm ✉ foods@downtown-web.com
Farnsworth Business Services	www.digital-café.com/~webmaster/water00.htm ✉ ronf@digital-café.com
Faults Alarm, Inc.,	www.faultsalarm.com ✉ Faultsalarm@MSN.com
Food Pantrie Dryer / Sprouter / DUER Int'l. Inc.	http://downtown-web.com/psi ✉ psi/usa@downtown-web.com
Food Storage Buyer's Club	www.foodbuyersclub.com
Food Storage Central	www.foodstorage.net/order.htm ✉ foodstorage@foodstorage.net
Food Storage FAQ – Alan T. Hagan	http://waltonfeed.com/grain/faqs ✉ athagan@sprintmail.com
Foods Unlimited	www.universalweb.com/food ✉ ron@universalweb.com
Frontier Cooperative Herbs	www.frontierherb.com
Happy Hovel Foods	www.wwmagic.com/haphov ✉ haphov@seanet.com
Heart 'n Home Products	http://members.aol.com/hearthome4 ✉ hearthome4@aol.com

Selected Preparedness Provider Websites/E-Mail Addresses (Cont.)	
InfiNet Communications, Inc.	🖳www.mtmarketplace.com ✉mtmarket@mcn.net
J. J. Reidy & Co.	🖳www.tiac.net/users/jjreidy ✉jjreidy@tiac.net
Janet Kugel – Disaster Preparedness Consultant	🖳www.primenet.com/~prepared ✉prepared@primenet.com
Kitchen Science, Inc.	🖳www.bizcom.com/kitchenscience ✉kitchesc.ix.net.com
Lakeridge Food Storage	🖳www.shopsite.com/lfs ✉lfsfood@ix.netcom.com
LauraAnne J. Logar	🖳http://pages.prodigy.com/frugal-tightwad-foodstorage ✉TJZA00F
Lehman Hardware & Appliances, Inc.	🖳www.lehmans.com ✉GetLehmans@aol.com
Life Link	🖳www.lifelink.com ✉info@lifelink.com
Mail Order Catalog, The	🖳www.vege.com ✉catalog@usit.net
Maple Leaf Industries	🖳www.mapleleafinc.com ✉food@mapleleafinc.com
Martens Health & Survival Products, Inc.	🖳http://millenianet.com/survival ✉survival@millenianet.com
Mast Enterprises	🖳www.nidlink.com/~mastent/wheatfre.html
Mike Brown	🖳http://home.earthlink.net/~dlaw70/
Militia Of Montana (M.O.M.)	🖳www.logoplex.com/resources/mom ✉mom@logoplex.com
Millennium Group	🖳www.millenniumfoods.com ✉apt@itsnet.com
Monolithic Constructors, Inc.	🖳www.monolithicdome.com ✉Mail@monolithicdome.com
Mother Nature's General Store	🖳www.mothernature.com ✉mother@pond.com
National Honey Board	🖳www.nhb.org ✉mmc@csn.net
Nitro-Pak Preparedness Center	🖳www.nitro-pak.com ✉npprepare@aol.com
North Farm Cooperative	🖳www. Northfarm-coop.com/
Northern Hardware	🖳www.northern-online.com
Oasis Emergency Foods	🖳www.rmii.com/oasis ✉oasis@rmii.com
Oregon Freeze Dry, Inc.	🖳www.ofd.com/mh
Pines International	🖳www.wheatgrass.com
Preparedness Mart	🖳www.preparednessmart.com ✉mail@preparednessmart.com
Product Source International	🖳http://downtown-web.com/psi ✉psiusa@aros.net
Quake Gear	🖳www.globalstrategies.com/qg/contact ✉qg@globalstrategies.com
Rainy Day Supply	🖳www.cyberatl.net/~rdsupply ✉rdsupply@cyberatl.net
Ready Made Resources	🖳www.cococo.net/rmr ✉robert@avicom.net
Ready One Survival Products	🖳www.atyour.com/readyone/jsord1.htm
Real Goods	🖳www.realgoods.com
Safe-T-Proof	🖳www.safe-t-proof.com ✉info@safe-t-proof.com
Safe-Trek Outfitters	🖳http://montana.avicom.net/Safetrek.html
Safe-Trek Private Reserve Foods	🖳www.safetrek.com ✉safetrek@avicom.net
Safety Store	🖳www.safetystore.com ✉orders@safetystore.com
San Francisco Herb Co.	🖳www.sfherb.com
School of Self-Reliance	🖳home.earthlink.net/~nyerges/ ✉nyerges@earthlink.net
Secure Future Food & Supplies	🖳www.securefuture.com ✉sales@securefuture.com
Sensible Steam / Sensible Steam Consultants	🖳www.chatlink.com\~soltherm\tinypwr ✉104247.127@compuserve.com
Service Merchandise Co., Inc.	🖳www.servicemerchandise.com
Sierra Solar Systems	🖳www.sierrasolar.com
Soft Logic Inc.	🖳www.tecfen.com/itraders/emergency ✉slogic@tecfen.com
Solar Cookers International	🖳www.accessone.com/~sbcn ✉sbci@igc.apc.org
Solar Systems LTD	🖳www.middleman.com/solarsys ✉solarsys@middleman.com
SolarTrope Supply Corporation	🖳IMALL.com/emergency72hr ✉Ranger@vcol.net
South Summit Corporation	🖳www.southsummit.com ✉southsummit@topher.net
Sprout House, The	🖳www.hlthmall.com/healthmall/sproutman ✉sproutman@sproutman.com
Storehouse Products	🖳www.dcci.com/DCCI/storehouse ✉deyer@dcci.com
Suburban Water Testing Labs, Inc.	🖳www.h2otest.com ✉stump2@pipeline.com
Suntrek Home Energy	🖳www.suntrekenergy.com ✉suntrek@accessone.com
Survival Enterprises	🖳http://survival.simplenet.com ✉gunrunner@earthlink.net
Universal Safety Devices, Inc.	🖳www.altimat.org./2788
Walton Feed, Inc.	🖳http://waltonfeed.com 🖳www.lis.ab.ca./walton
Waterstar Technology	🖳www.tiac.net/users/jjreidy ✉jjreidy@tiac.net
West Coast Emergency Supplies	🖳www.emergencysupplies.com/wces ✉wces@open.org
Western Reserve Food & Supply Co.	🖳www.nmarket.com/wreserve/index.html ✉wrfood@cyberspace.net

FEMA NATIONAL EMERGENCY MANAGEMENT SYSTEM

The FEMA National Emergency Management System **(NEMS)** is the comprehensive mechanism for gathering, processing, and exchanging information in support of the emergency management community at the Federal, Regional, State, and local levels of government. FEMA/NEMS consists of physical facilities, telecommunications, and the requisite information and data systems required to sustain FEMA's vital emergency management mission as a Federal agency. In effect, FEMA is a correlating agency—now become a super-agency—which analyzes and reports the information to the President's cabinet. Resources are then mobilized as necessary to resolve emergency activities of Federal, State, military, and local authorities. FEMA is generally responsible for all emergency management resources of and in behalf of the Federal government—whether a natural disaster, man-caused disaster (including radiological, biological, or civil disobedience), or in time of war or threat of war.

There is a tremendously large collection of booklets, brochures, videos, and publicity materials designed to help individuals and families learn how to prepare for disasters. You may order a single copy of any publication that will help you meet your needs for a disaster preparedness program. To order any materials produced by **FEMA,** contact your local or State office of emergency management. Or, if not available locally, write to:

> **FEMA Publications**
> **PO Box 70274**
> **Washington, DC 20024**

The listings are listed in the following order:

1. **Programs for Schools & Home Schools**	6. **Flood & Flash Flood Disasters**
2. **General Purpose Publications**	7. **Hurricane Disasters**
3. **Multi-Hazard Disasters**	8. **Tornado Disasters**
4. **Earthquake Disasters**	9. **Winter Storm Disasters**
5. **Fire Disasters**	10. **Heat Wave Disasters**

These publications are aligned as follows:

- **first,** by type of natural disaster or hazard or type of publication
- **second,** by agency
- **third,** by title—it's easier to find a title than a number (especially when you don't have a clue about the federal numbering system!)
- **fourth,** by its alpha-numeric publication number

The information in this section is due to the special efforts of *Roy P. Huff, Jr., Assistant Emergency Management Coordinator,* Bexar County, the county in which San Antonio, TX is located. Roy has been a large part of planning and execution of emergency preparedness in a locale with 4 Air Force bases, 2 Army bases, and 2 major military hospital facilities. Roy spent 21 years in the Army, mostly in plans, operations, training, communications and always in leadership positions, actively planning and executing military support activities in cooperation with civil authorities. He graciously provided the FEMA manuals and handbooks for our analysis and review.

This *Appendix* is organized to simplify the information about each of the natural disasters to which we are most often exposed—and to which we are always vulnerable. Emergency preparedness is essential in the face of such potential dangers!

Quick-Guide II–1

Summary of Natural Disasters Publications

Title or Publication	Qty.	Cost each	Total Am't.
Disasters Materials for Schools & Home Schools			
Federal Emergency Management Agency (FEMA)			
Critical Time: Earthquake Response Planning & Schools *(video)*			
Earthquake Safety for Children *(FEMA-88a)*			
Guidebook for Developing a School Earthquake Safety Program *(FEMA-88)*			
Reducing Non-Structural Earthquake Damage—A Practical Guide for Schools *(video)*			
The Community Disaster Education Guide *(ARC 4331)*			
EMI Home Study Courses *(L-173)*			
The Emergency Program Manager—Home Study Course *(HS-1)*			
Emergency Preparedness, USA—Home Study Course *(HS-2)*			
Radiological Emergency Management—Home Study Course *(HS-3)*			
Preparedness for a Nuclear Crisis—Home Study Course *(HS-4)*			
Hazardous Materials: A Citizen's Orientation—Home Study Course *(HS-5)*			
Portable Emergency Data System *(PEDS)*—Home Study Course *(HS-6)*			
A Citizen's Guide to Disaster Assistance—Home Study Course *(HS-7)*			
General Purpose Disasters Materials			
Federal Emergency Management Agency (FEMA)			
A Guide to Federal Aid in Disasters *(DAP-19)*			
Emergency Preparedness Publications *(L-164)*			
FEMA Publications Catalog *(FEMA-20)*			
Preparing for Emergencies—A Checklist for People with Mobility Problems *(L-154M)*			
The American Red Cross			
Emergency Preparedness Checklist *(ARC 4471))*			
Emergency Preparedness Checklist *(ARC 4471S Spanish)*			
Helping Children Cope With Disaster *(ARC 4499)*			
When You Return to a Storm-Damaged Home *(DAP-16)*			
Your Family Disaster Plan *(ARC 4466)*			
Your Family Disaster Supplies Kit *(ARC 4463)*			
Federal Emergency Management Agency (FEMA)			
Are You Prepared? *(FEMA-166)*			
Are You Ready? Your Guide to Disaster Preparedness *(H-34)*			
Coping with Children's Reactions to Hurricanes and Other Disasters *(FEMA-185)*			
Coping with Children's Reactions to Hurricanes and Other Disasters *(FEMA-185 Spanish)*			
Disaster Driving *(L-116)*			
Don't Let Disaster Tear Your Family Apart *(FEMA Poster #11)*			
Emergency Food and Water Supplies *(FEMA-215)*			
Emergency Preparedness Checklist *(L-154)*			
Emergency Preparedness, USA—Home Study Course *(HS-2)*			
EMI Home Study Courses *(L-173)*			
Family Protection Display *(FEMA 8-0861)*			
Helping Children Cope With Disaster *(L-196)*			
Preparing for Emergencies—A Checklist for People with Mobility Problems *(L-154M)*			
Speakers Kit *(FEMA K-64)*			
When Disaster Strikes *(FEMA-79)*			
When You Return to a Storm-Damaged Home *(DAP-16)*			
Your Family Disaster Plan *(L-191)*			
Your Family Disaster Plan *(L-191S Spanish)*			
Your Family Disaster Supplies Kit *(L-189)*			
Your Family Disaster Supplies Kit *(L-189S Spanish)*			
National Weather Service (NOAA)			
Natural Hazard Watch & Warning Poster *(NOAA 8-6001)*			
NOAA Weather Radio *(NOAA PA 76015)*			
Watch Out, Storms Ahead *(NOAA PA 82004)*			
The Weather Channel			
Weather: Bringing it Home *(The Weather Channel)*			
Weather from Behind the Wheel *(The Weather Channel)*			

Title or Publication (Cont.)	Qty.	Cost each	Total Am't.
Your Family: Out of Harm's Way *(The Weather Channel)* *(slide presentation)*			
The American Red Cross			
Advanced First Aid Training *(Call your local ARC Chapter)*			
Community Disaster Education Guide *(ARC 4331)*			
Emergency Preparedness Checklist *(ARC 4471)*			
Emergency Preparedness Checklist *(ARC 4471S Spanish)*			
Family Survival Guide *(#329195)*			
Helping Children Cope With Disaster *(ARC 4499)*			
Natural Hazards Risk Profile: Hurricanes, Floods, Tornadoes, Lightning, Earth... *(ARC 4461P)*			
Preparing for Emergencies—A Checklist for People with Mobility Problems *(ARC 4497)*			
Safe Living in Your Manufactured Home *(ARC 4465)*			
Talking Points for Disaster Education Presentations—Earthquake, Flood ... *(ARC 4467T)*			
The Red Cross is Ready ... When The Time Comes *(ARC 2290)* *(video)*			
We're There When You Need Us—American Red Cross Disaster Services *(ARC 4450)*			
Your Family Disaster Plan *(ARC 4466)*			
Your Family Disaster Plan *(ARC 4466S Spanish)*			
Your Family Disaster Plan, Disaster Supplies Kit *(ARC 4498)*			
Your Family Disaster Supplies Kit *(ARC 4463)*			
Your Family Disaster Supplies Kit *(ARC 4463S Spanish)*			

Earthquake Disasters Materials

	Qty.	Cost each	Total Am't.
Federal Emergency Management Agency (FEMA)			
Blueprint for Earthquake Survival **(FEMA #6)** *(poster)*			
Coping with Children's Reactions to Earthquakes and Other Disasters *(FEMA-48)*			
Coping with Children's Reactions to Earthquakes and Other Disasters *(FEMA-66 Spanish)*			
Coping with Children's Reactions to Hurricanes and Other Disasters *(FEMA-185)*			
Coping with Children's Reactions to Hurricanes and Other Disasters *(FEMA-185 Spanish)*			
Earthquake Preparedness Information for People with Disabilities *(FEMA-70)*			
Earthquake Safety Checklist *(FEMA-46)*			
Emergency Preparedness Publications *(L-164)*			
Family Earthquake Safety-Home Hazard Hunt and Drill *(FEMA-113)*			
Learning to Live in Earthquake Country–Preparedness in Apartments & Mobile Homes *(L-143)*			
Preparedness for People with Disabilities *(FEMA-75)*			
Preparedness in High-Rise Buildings *(FEMA-76)*			
Safety Tips for Earthquakes *(L-111)*			
The Weather Channel			
Aftershock! from The Weather Channel *(video)*			
The American Red Cross			
Are You Ready for an Earthquake? *(ARC 4455)*			
Are You Ready for an Earthquake? *(ARC 4455S Spanish)*			
Are You Ready for an Earthquake? *(ARC P-942)*			
Earthquake! Do Something! *(ARC 5004)*			
Earthquake! Do Something! *(ARC 5006 / Urban version) (ARC 5007 / Rural version)*			
Earthquake! Do Something! *(ARC 5003S Spanish) (video)*			
Earthquake! Do Something! *(ARC 5005 Multi-language) (video)*			
Earthquake! Do Something! *(Poster # 4000)*			
Public Service Announcement: Earthquake *(ARC 4462)*			

Fire Disasters Materials

	Qty.	Cost each	Total Am't.
FEMA / U. S. Fire Administration			
After the Fire: Returning to Normal *(FA-46)*			
An Ounce of Prevention *(FA-76)*			
Check Your Hot Spots! *(K-63)*			
Curious Kids Set Fires *(K-71)*			
Curious Kids Set Fires *(K-74 Spanish)*			
Fire Safety Book *(FA-73)*			
Fire Safety Public Service Announcements: "Don't Let Children Play with Matches"; "Happy Birthday" "This is Fire"; "Let's Retire Fire"			
FEMA / U. S. Fire Administration (Cont.)			
Fire Safety Public Service Announcements *with Ahmad Rashad & Kathie Lee Gifford*			
Home Fire Safety—Act On It *(5-0200)*			

Home Fire Safety—Act On It (K-79 Fire Volunteers #5-0201)			
Home Fire Safety—Act On It (K-79 Media #5-0207)			
It's a Real Protector, It's A Smoke Detector (K-69E English)			
It's a Real Protector, It's A Smoke Detector (K-69S Spanish)			
Let's Retire Fire (K-72)			
On the Safety Circuit (K-78)			
Resources on Fire (FA-102)			
Safe at Home—Fire Do's & Don'ts (L-170)			
Safety Tips for Winter Storms (L-96)			
Smoke Detectors and Fire Safety: A Guide for Older Americans (L-126)			
Smoke Detectors: Don't Stay Home Without One (L-163)			
This is Fire (K-70)			
This is Fire (K-77 Spanish)			
Winter-Fire Safety Tips for the Home (L-97)			
Working Together For Home Fire Safety—A USFA Public-Private Partnership (K-75)			
Your Family Disaster Plan (L-191)			
Your Family Disaster Supplies Kit (L-189)			
The American Red Cross			
Are You Ready for a Fire? (ARC 4456)			
Are You Ready for a Fire? (ARC 4456S Spanish)			
Are You Ready for a Fire? (ARC P-943) (poster)			
Fire Prevention Week Campaign Kit			
Public Service Announcement: Fire! (ARC 2288)			

Flood & Flash Flood Disasters Materials

Federal Emergency Management Agency (FEMA)			
After a Flood: The First Steps (L-198)			
Alluvial Fans: Hazards and Management (FEMA-165)			
Answers to Questions About the National Flood Insurance Program (FIA-2)			
Dam Safety—Know the Potential Hazard (L-152)			
Guide to Flood Insurance Rate Maps (FIA-14)			
Manufactured Home Installation in Flood Hazard Areas (FEMA-85)			
Repairing Your Flooded Home (FEMA-234)			
Retrofitting Flood-Prone Residential Structures (L-153)			
National Weather Service (NOAA)			
Are You Ready for a Flood or Flash Flood? (NOAA PA 92059)			
Are You Ready for a Flood or Flash Flood? (NOAA PA 92060S Spanish)			
Are You Ready for a Flood or Flash Flood? (NOAA PA 92062)			
Flash Floods (NOAA A02770)			
Flash Floods and Floods...The Awesome Power! (NOAA PA 92050)			
The Awesome Power (video)			
The American Red Cross			
Are You Ready for a Flood or Flash Flood? (ARC P-945)			
Are You Ready for a Flood or Flash Flood? (ARC 4458)			
Are You Ready for a Flood or Flash Flood? (ARC 4458S Spanish)			
After a Flood: The First Steps (ARC 4476)			
Repairing Your Flooded Home (ARC 4477)			
Flash Floods and Floods ... The Awesome Power! (ARC 4493)			

Hurricane Disasters Materials

Federal Emergency Management Agency (FEMA)			
Coastal Construction Manual (FEMA-55)			
Hurricane Awareness—Action Guidelines for School Children (FEMA 8-0441)			
Hurricane Awareness—Action Guidelines for Senior Citizens (FEMA 8-0440)			
Hurricane Preparedness Program (FEMA-184)			
Hurricane Preparedness Program (FEMA-185 Spanish)			
Hurricanes-Floods-Safety Tips for Coastal and Inland Flooding (L-107)			
Safety Tips for Hurricanes (L-105)			

Title or Publication (Cont.)	Qty.	Cost each	Total Am't.
The Weather Channel			
Danger's Edge from The Weather Channel *(video)*			
Fource Four from The Weather Channel *(video)*			
National Weather Service (NOAA)			
Hurricane *(video)*			
Hurricane Hugo *(NOAA A 18529) (slide presentation)*			
Hurricane Preparedness *(NOAA PA 92062) (slide presentation)*			
Hurricane Tracking Chart *(NOAA PA 77020)*			
Hurricane! A Familiarization Booklet *(NOAA PA 91001)*			
Lessons from Hurricane Eloise *(NOAA 010141)*			
Storm Surge and Hurricane Safety with North Atlantic Tracking Chart *(NOAA PA 78019)*			
Survival in a Hurricane *(NOAA PA 70027)*			
Survival in a Hurricane *(NOAA PA 92058 Spanish)*			
The American Red Cross			
Are You Ready for a Hurricane? *(P-944)*			
Hurricane Preparedness *(ARC 009656)*			

Tornado Disasters Materials

Federal Emergency Management Agency (FEMA)			
Tornado Safety Tips *(L-148)*			
National Weather Service (NOAA)			
A Look at the "Tornado" and Other Local Storms *(NOAA AO 8135)*			
Are You Ready for a Tornado? *(NOAA PA 92057)*			
Are You Ready for a Tornado? *(NOAA PA 92058 Spanish)*			
Are You Ready for a Tornado? *(NOAA PA 92061)*			
Terrible Tuesday *(NOAA video)*			
The Safest Places in Schools *(NOAA 009605)*			
Tornado Safety in Residences *(NOAA A00796)*			
Tornadoes...Nature's Most Violent Storms *(NOAA PA 92052)*			
The Weather Channel			
The Enemy Wind *(video from The Weather Channel)*			
The American Red Cross			
Are You Ready for a Tornado? *(ARC P944) (poster)*			
Are You Ready for a Tornado? *(ARC 4457)*			
Are You Ready for a Tornado? *(ARC 4457S Spanish)*			
Tornadoes...Nature's Most Violent Storms *(ARC 5002)*			
Are You Ready for a Tornado? *(ARC P944) (poster)*			

Winter Storm Disasters Materials

Federal Emergency Management Agency (FEMA)			
Safety Tips for Winter Storms *(L-96)*			
National Weather Service (NOAA)			
Are You Ready for a Winter Storm? *(NOAA PA 91003)*			
Are You Ready for a Winter Storm? *(NOAA PA 91004 Spanish)*			
Are You Ready for a Winter Storm? *(NOAA PA 91005) (poster)*			
Winter Storms...The Deceptive Killers *(NOAA PA 91002)*			
The American Red Cross			
Are You Ready for a Winter Storm? *(ARC P-947) (poster)*			
Are You Ready for a Winter Storm? *(ARC 4464)*			
Are You Ready for a Winter Storm? *(ARC 4464S Spanish)*			
Winter Storms...The Deceptive Killers *(ARC 4467)*			

Thunderstorms & Lighting Disasters Materials

National Weather Service (NOAA)			
When Lightning Strikes *(NOAA AO-1979) (slide presentation)*			

Heat Wave Disasters Materials

National Weather Service (NOAA)			
Heat Wave *(NOAA PA 85001)*			

Subject Index

Making the Best of Basics
Family Preparedness Handbook

In today's world you can't afford to be unprepared. If you want the security of being able to live from your own personal resources for up to a year—or longer—regardless of external conditions, **Basics** will show you how.

With more than 350,000 copies of earlier editions sold, **Basics** has remained the standard on in-home storage and family preparedness. The 10th edition has been revised and updated, with more than 100 charts and tables, 200 recipes, and an expanded *Preparedness Resources Directory* with more than 2500 listings to help consumers find the necessities for long-term storage. It's the most comprehensive *single* volume ever compiled on in-home storage.

You'll find **Basics** the best publication available to help you determine which preparedness & survival products, food storage items, and other related goods and services you need. **Basics** offers more preparedness information than any other book of its kind—that's the main reason it's outsold all other preparedness books! That's also why it's called the *Family Preparedness Handbook*.

Basics is designed specifically for the urban family—though everyone can use it!—and includes:
- a **detailed step-by-step plan** for acquiring and maintaining your in-home food storage
- more than **100 charts** defining what foods and nonfoods to buy for your in-home storage
- a **Family Factor** to determine quantities of foods and other essential nonfood items
- **recipes** for using whole grains and stored foods
- a section on common **storage problems and solutions**
- a **Compendium of Preparedness Resources** with more than 2500 listings
- chapters on storing and making the best use of:
  - —**Water**
  - —**Drying Fruits** and **Vegetables**
  - —**Kitchen Gardening & Sprouting**
  - —**Wheat**, including bulgur, gluten, whole wheat flour, and sourdough
  - —**Energy & Fuels**
  - —**Honey** as a sweetener for recipes
  - —**Dairy Products** from **Powdered Milk**
  - —**Vitamin**, **Mineral**, and **Herbal Supplements** to maintain good health

COMPENDIUM OF PREPAREDNESS RESOURCES

Where do you find all the items one needs to get prepared? is the question most often asked when we talk with people about the concept of preparedness. Not to worry! There are thousands of companies in the US and Canada with products for those seeking security, self-reliance—or just being ready for whatever…! This chapter is a compendium (*a brief treatment of a subject*) of preparedness products suppliers—2500+ listings! This summary is extracted from *one* of the major sections of our new book, **Don't Get Caught with Your Pantry Down! …When the *Unexpected* Happens!**

Suppliers to the preparedness industry, including manufacturers, importers, processors, wholesalers, distributors, dealers, and retailers provide availability and choices for storage foods, foodstuffs, and the many preparedness items required. For many of these companies, the preparedness trade is their primary effort. The products they sell are, in the main, specifically designed for long-term storage and utilizing over an extended period.

In reality then, this chapter is about making connections—between the you and many preparedness products and services providers. This chapter will facilitate your connections to a sometimes obscure industry whose business is to help you become prepared for the uncertain future. There is so much to learn, appraise, consider, analyze, read, study, question, research, understand, then condense it to the essence and act upon it.

This information has been collected from a large variety of sources. No doubt, some of the information may become inaccurate or outdated due to the time required to collect data, organ-

> The future is before us and we are destined to live in it—
> ***prepared or not!***

ize, standardize, analyze it and put it into cogent order—then publish it. Time passes, businesses come and go—fail, sell, redirect their efforts, and merge—or grow beyond their expectations. Some respondents were perhaps a bit overzealous in their self-assessment, while others chose to ignore our request(s) for information altogether. Therefore, this work is a transitional database, but we're constantly seeking additional resources to include in this *Compendium*. The preparedness industry is not as large as it is diverse within itself.

This information is for reference and guidance purposes only. Use it with awareness and normal caution. Readers should receive both a valuable service and gain a measure of inspiration and encouragement to take responsibility for their personal preparedness from these providers. It's only in implementation of a preparedness plan that one is truly *making the best of basics.*

We are merely recorders and reporters of information from others, therefore we cannot be held liable for your private and personal transactions with any organization listed herein. Be aware there are special requirements for long-term storage items—be sure you are well-informed prior to selecting and paying for such items.

As in any other business or personal transaction, *know* what you need, *get* what you want, and *remember* the intelligent buyer's creed:

Caveat emptor!
(Let the buyer beware!)

HOW TO USE THE CONSUMER'S COMPENDIUM

The information in the **Consumer's Compendium** supplement is keyed to specific chapters in **Making the Best of Basics**—*Family Preparedness Handbook* (*Editions 9 & 10*) to help in your search for preparedness products and services. The chart is designed for those with or without experience in the preparedness industry's marketplace. *There are lots of choices here—more than 2500 of them in the following pages!*

Here's how the supplement is organized and how best to utilize it:

- **State alphabetical search:** find the **State** listed in alphabetical order.
- **Zip Code search:** within each State, find the desired (or nearest) **Zip Code.** Note they are placed on the extreme left margin for quicker, easier access and recognition.
- **Business/Category search:** the next three (3) columns to the right of the first column indicate the *type* of business or organization—whether **M**anufacturer or processor, **D**istributor/wholesaler, or **R**etailer—to help determine whether you may buy products direct, since some manufacturers and wholesalers do not sell direct to consumers.
- **Products/Services search:** the last eight (8) columns on the right identify the specific categories of products and/or services provided. The "**X**" marked in the column of a supplier listing indicates the *type* of business and the *products & services* offered. The "**C**" indicates that consulting services are offered. By searching with your finger up or down a specific column, you can locate suppliers for related products or services anywhere in the US & Canada.

Remember: This information is keyed to the chapters in *this* book!

Author's Note: **Listing herein is not to be considered an endorsement, nor is exclusion to be considered an intentional slight or rejection.**

(*For inclusion in future editions, complete the* Supplier / Provider Checklist at the back of this book.)

M = Manufacturer / Processor	D = Wholesaler / Trade distributor	R = Distributor / Retailer to public	M	D	R	04	05	12	13	14	15	16	17

Products & Services Suppliers
Selected Listings[1]

Symbols Code

☎ = Telephone	🖷 = Fax	🖥 = Website	✉ = E-mail

Product References Keyed to Chapters

04 water / air filtration & treatment	05 grains, seeds, mills & equip.	12 dairy / powdered milk supplies	13 honey / sweeteners
14 vitamins / minerals / herbs	15 sprouting / equip. & supplies	16 dried / dehydrated products	17 energy / fuels

M = Manufacturer / Processor	D = Wholesaler / Trade distributor	R = Distributor / Retailer to public	M	D	R	04	05	12	13	14	15	16	17

United States

Alabama

Listing	M	D	R	04	05	12	13	14	15	16	17
35209 **Alabama Outdoors**, 3054 Independence Drive, **Birmingham** AL ☎(205) 870-1919 — distributor of *Alco ♦Brite* gelled ethanol products				X							X
35244 **Miller Honey, Inc.**, 200 River Hills Business Park, **Birmingham** AL ☎(205) 991-7555	X	X	X				X				
35631 **Martin Industries Inc.**, **Florence** AL ☎(205) 767-0330 🖷(205) 740-5192 — manufacturer of wood-burning stoves, fireplace Inserts, gas space heaters, & fireplaces	X										X
35754 **Susan Snyder**, 84 Blue Sky Drive, **Laceys Spring** AL ☎(205) 498-2774 — distributor of *Magic Mill* products				X		X		X	X		
35803 **David & Jennifer Griffey**, 13902 Armond Drive, **Huntsville** AL ☎(205) 882-6685 — distributor of *Magic Mill* products				X		X	X	X		X	X
35814 **Evac One**, PO Box 5763, **Huntsville** AL ☎(205) 430-1700 or (800) 544-3822 🖷(205) 430-1717 🖥www.evac-one.com/order.htm				X	X						X
36032 **Bates Turkey Farm**, Rt. 1 Box 138, **Fort Deposit** AL ☎(205) 227-4505 🖷(205) 227-4386 — processor of turkeys; mail-order; overnight delivery of turkey products	X	X	X							X	
36106 **Frank Thomas**, 2175 Bowen Drive, **Montgomery** AL ☎(334) 272-4810 — distributor of *Magic Mill* products				X		X		X	X		
36602 **Grid Track**, 457½ Dauphin St., **Mobile** AL ☎(334) 433-8816 or (800) 580-5811 🖷(334) 433-0621 — hurricane tracking system for individuals	X	X	X								X
36611 **Pioneer Outfitters**, PO Box 11333, **Chickasaw** AL ☎(334) 452-9267 — specializing in hurricane preparedness; full-service emergency preparedness & food storage items;			C	X	X	X	X	X	X	X	X
36801 **Leah McMurray**, 523 Lee Road 735, **Opelika** AL ☎(534) 745-0446 — distributor of *Magic Mill* products				X		X	X		X	X	X

Alaska

Listing	M	D	R	04	05	12	13	14	15	16	17
99500 **Educational Training Company**, AK ☎(907) 747-3008 ✉*resq@ptialaska.net* — cold weather survival; 1-week course for learning cold weather survival techniques; preparedness consultant			C								
99503 **Natural Pantry**, 300 W. 36th Avenue, **Anchorage** AK ☎(907) 563-2727 🖷(907) 561-7063 — distributor of *Bosch & Kitchen Specialties* products			C	X	X	X	X	X	X	X	
99503 **Recreational Equipment, Inc. (REI)**, 1200-A W Northern Lights Blvd., **Anchorage** AK ☎(907) 272-4565 — outdoor/camping gear & equipment; *Mountain House* freeze-dried pouches; water filters; backpacks; GPS units			X	X						X	X
99508 **Roy's Nutrition**, 301 E. Northern Lights, **Anchorage** AK ☎(915) 277-3226			C	X	X	X	X	X	X	X	
99518 **Eagle Enterprises, Inc.**, 700 W. International Airport Rd. #B, **Anchorage** AK ☎(907) 562-2331 — distributor of *Alco ♦Brite* gelled ethanol products				X							X
99615 **Ken Houpt**, 808-B Lake Louise Dr., **Kodiak** AK ☎(907) 487-1902 — distributor of *Magic Mill* products				X		X		X	X		
99615 **Kim & Brian Swanson**, 112-D Five Fingers Court, **Kodiak** AK ☎(907) 487-4948 — distributor of *Magic Mill* products				X		X		X	X		
99686 **Two Ravens Expresso**, PO Box 365, **Valdez** AK ☎(907) 835-4445			C	X	X	X	X	X	X	X	
99701 **Sunshine Health Foods**, 418 Third St., Eagle Plaza Mall, **Fairbanks** AK ☎(907) 456-5433			C	X	X	X	X	X	X	X	
99708 **Whole Earth Grocery**, PO Box 80228, **College** AK ☎(907) 479-2052			C	X	X	X	X	X	X	X	
99780 **World Survival Institute** *(attn: Chris Janowski)*, Box 394C, **Tok** AK ☎(907) 883-4243 — wilderness survival seminars, workshops, & training; teaching videos for tracking, emergency medicine, more!	X		C								
99801 **KTOO-Radio Co-op**, 224 4th St., **Juneau** AK ☎(907) 586-1670			C	X	X	X	X	X	X	X	

---

[1] **ZIP** Code in **boldface type** indicates suppliers for which we did not have a correct Zip Code. We've added the nearest known Zip Code for the address.

Product References Keyed to Chapters (Cont.)

04 water / air filtration & treatment	05 grains, seeds, mills & equip.	12 dairy / powdered milk supplies	13 honey / sweeteners
14 vitamins / minerals / herbs	15 sprouting / equip. & supplies	16 dry / dehydrated / freeze-dried	17 energy / fuels

M = Manufacturer / Processor   D = Wholesaler / Trade distributor   R = Distributor / Retailer to public

Listing	M	D	R	04	05	12	13	14	15	16	17
99826 **Gustavus Co-op**, PO Box 251, **Gustavus** AK ☎(907) 697-2424			C	X	X	X	X	X	X	X	
99836 **Rideout Co-op**, PO Box 8063, **Port Alexander** AK ☎(907) 568-2263			C	X	X	X	X	X	X	X	

Arkansas

Listing	M	D	R	04	05	12	13	14	15	16	17
71730 **Health Unlimited**, 114 E. Grove St., **El Dorado** AR ☎(501) 862-7041			C	X	X	X	X	X	X	X	
71901 **Wayne's Health & Light**, 444 W. Grand Ave., **Hot Springs** AR ☎(501) 623-3038			C	X	X	X	X	X	X	X	
71953 **Ouachita Health Store**, Hwy. 71 S., **Mena** AR ☎(501) 394-4710			C	X	X	X	X	X	X	X	
72023 **Nutrition World**, 104 N. 1st St., **Cabot** AR ☎(501) 843-0010			C	X	X	X	X	X	X	X	
72042 **Cormier Rice Milling Co, Inc.**, PO Box 152, West Third Street, **Dewitt** AR ☎(501) 946-3561	X	X			X					X	
72129 **Mom's Health Foods**, PO Box 132 Highway 270, **Prattsville** AR			C	X	X	X	X	X	X	X	
72131 **Ozark Millenium Resources**, 6324 Heber Springs Road W., **Quitman** AR ☎(501) 589-2413 – preparedness consultant; in-home storage specialist; disasters or emergencies specialist			C		X			X		X	
72160 **Hartz Jacob Seed Co., Inc.**, Box 946, **Stuttgart** AR ☎(501) 673-8565 – organically grown soybeans, whole soybeans	X	X			X					X	
72160 **Producers Rice Mill, Inc.**, PO Box 461, **Stuttgart** AR ☎(501) 673-4444 ▤(501) 672-4473 – production, milling, &/or distribution of rice & processed rice products	X	X			X					X	
72160 **Riceland Foods, Inc.**, P. O. Box 927, **Stuttgart** AR ☎(501) 673-5485 ▤(501) 673-3366 – production, milling, &/or distribution of rice & processed rice products	X	X			X					X	
72205 **Beans & Grains & Things**, 300 S. Rodney Parham, **Little Rock** AR ☎(501) 221-2331			C	X	X	X	X	X	X	X	
72301 **Natural Foods**, PO Box 671, Hwy. 65 S., Rogers Hts. Shopping Ctr., **Clinton** AR ☎(501) 745-8835			C	X	X	X	X	X	X	X	
72315 **Main St. Natural Foods**, 808 E. Main, **Blythville** AR ☎(501) 762-1212			C	X	X	X	X	X	X	X	
72401 **Health 'n Action**, 2830 East Highland, **Jonesboro** AR ☎(501) 931-5483			C	X	X	X	X	X	X	X	
72401 **Rachel Sartin**, 3703 South Culberhouse, **Jonesboro** AR ☎(501) 935-0357 – distributor of *Magic Mill* products			X		X			X		X	
72560 **Healing Arts Emporium**, H C 32, Box 97-B, **Mountain View** AR ☎(501) 269-4177			C	X	X	X	X	X	X	X	
72601 **Kathy Scarborough**, 126 North Willow, **Harrison** AR ☎(501) 741-8980 – distributor of *Magic Mill* products			X		X			X		X	
72632 **Ozark Country Market**, Route 6, Box 128 Hwy. 62 West, **Eureka Springs** AR ☎(501) 253-8136			C	X	X	X	X	X	X		
72650 **Davidson's**, PO Box 588, **Marshall** AR – homesteading/survival pamphlets; emergency and preparedness products; mail-order supplier			X								
72701 **Ozark Cooperative Warehouse**, PO Box 1528, **Fayetteville** AR ☎(501) 521-4920 ▤(501) 521-9100 ✉ozarkcoop@aol.com Territory: *AL, AR, FL, GA, KS, LA, MS, OK, Eastern & Central TX*		C		X	X	X	X	X	X	X	
72703 **New Market Naturals**, 1039 Overcrest Street, **Fayetteville** AR ☎(501) 521-7786 or (800) 873-4321 – distributor of water filtration devices & systems for every application	X	X	X								
72756 **Roger's Health Food Store**, 310 N. 13th Street, **Rogers** AR ☎(501) 751-7824			C	X	X	X	X	X	X	X	
72764 **Mary's Natural Foods**, 220 S. Thompson, **Springdale** AR ☎(501) 751-4224			C	X	X	X	X	X	X	X	
72768 **Carabeef Ranch Arkansas**, Route 1 Box 74, **Sulphur Springs** AR ☎(501) 822-3587 – low-fat water buffalo meat, without hormones or antibiotics; delivered fresh-frozen & vacuum-packed	X	X	X								
72768 **Shiloh Farms, Inc.**, PO Box 97, **Sulphur Springs** AR ☎(501) 298-3297 ▤(501) 298-3359 – organically grown soybeans, soy flour	X	X	X		X					X	
72801 **Reimer's Country Cupboard**, 122 E. 4th Street, **Russelville** AR			C	X	X	X	X	X	X	X	
72823 **Polk Salad Granny's Health Food**, 105 NE 1st St., **Atkins** AR ☎(501) 641-7405			C	X	X	X	X	X	X	X	
72901 **Redi-Pak Disaster Preparedness Packs**, 1320 N. B St. #112, **Ft. Smith** AR ☎(888) 543-3224	X	X	C	X						X	X
72958 **Apple Valley Farm Co-op**, Rt. 2 Box 280-D, **Waldron** AR ☎(501) 637-4276			C	X	X	X	X	X	X	X	

Arizona

Listing	M	D	R	04	05	12	13	14	15	16	17
85008 **The Salvation Army**, 2707 E. Van Buren Street, **Phoenix** AZ ☎(602) 804-0326 – distributor of *Emergency Essentials* products				X	X	X	X	X		X	X
85011 **American Red Cross**, PO Box 17090, **Phoenix** AZ ☎(602) 264-9481 – authorized distributor of *Emergency Essentials* products				X	X	X	X	X	X	X	X
85012 **BBQs Galore**, 311 E. Camelback Rd., **Phoenix** AZ ☎(602) 266-9965 – distributor of *Alco ♦Brite* gelled ethanol products				X							X
85018 **The Plains Corporation**, 3627 E. Indian School Rd. #209, **Phoenix** AZ ☎(602) 957-0096 or (800) 875-0096				X			X				X
85023 **Dave's Magic Mill**, 3434 West Greenway Rd. # 4, **Phoenix** AZ ☎(602) 863-1080 – distributor of *Magic Mill* products				X	X			X		X	
85023 **Marco Industries, Inc.**, 3431 W. Thunderbird #144, **Phoenix** AZ ☎(800) 726-1612 ▤(602) 789-7048				X			X				
85028 **Kettle Moraine, Ltd.**, 3116 E. Shea Blvd. #152, **Phoenix** AZ ☎(602) 787-0741 ▤(602) 787-0746 – *Republic Radio International* broadcasting; auathorized distributor of *Alpine Aire* preparedness products				X	X					X	X
85032 **Luella Ranney**, 3502 E. Montreal Place, **Phoenix** AZ ☎(602) 992-0954 – distributor of *Magic Mill* products				X		X		X		X	

M = Manufacturer / Processor	D = Wholesaler / Trade distributor	R = Distributor / Retailer to public	M	D	R	04	05	12	13	14	15	16	17
85036 KareMor International (Corporate), PO Box 21858, **Phoenix** AZ ☎(800) 582-5273 – *VitaMist & SlenderMist*—vitamins & nutrients in an oral spray for faster, more effective & efficient absorption			X	X	X					X			
85060 Firing Pin Enterprizes, Box 80696, **Phoenix** AZ – booklets about food storage, emergency preparedness, & survival				X									
85201 SunAmp Power Co., 1902 N. Country Club, **Mesa** AZ ☎(800) MR-SOLAR			X	X									X
85204 Seagull Book & Tape, 409 E. 1ˢᵗ Ave., **Mesa** AZ ☎(602) 835-5827 or (800) 944-6257 – distributor of *Magic Mill* products; preparedness books				X			X	X	X			X	
85204 Stradling's Bakery Center / Food Specialties, 730 E. Southern Ave., **Mesa** AZ ☎(602) 962-4977 – distributor of *Bosch & Kitchen Specialties* products; preparedness consultant; in-home storage specialist				X	X	X						X	
85204 William & Betty Speakman, 1009 E. 8ᵗʰ Ave., **Mesa** AZ ☎(602) 969-9589 – distributor of *Magic Mill* products				X		X				X	X		
85207 Weather Shack, 8840 E. Main St., **Mesa** AZ ☎(602) 984-1177 – distributor of *Alco ♦Brite* gelled ethanol products				X									X
85210 Grover Co., 130 W. Hampton Ave., **Mesa** AZ ☎(602) 827-8011 or (800) 852-8011 ☏(602) 827-8014 – whole grains; special flours & grinds; sprouting seeds, powdered milk, & more; also, garden supplies			X	X	X	X	X	X	X	X	X	X	X
85210 Janca's Jojoba Oil & Seed Co., 1407 South Date St., **Mesa** AZ – fragrances for in-home soapmaking			X	X						X			
85213 Fletchers Frontier Sy. / Wendy Fletcher, 521 N. Alba Circle, **Mesa** AZ ☎(602) 641-2803 ☏(602) 830-7888 – discounted quality cooking accessories for the camp cook; food storage & emergency preparedness products				X		X	X	X	X		X	X	X
85222 The Health Food Store, 1236 East Florence #7, **Casa Grande** AZ				C	X	X	X	X	X		X	X	
85224 Larren Ross, 2907 North Cheri Lynn Ct., **Chandler** AZ ☎(602) 732-0452 or (800) 975-8513 — distributor of *Ready Reserve* brand long-term food storage products; preparedness consultant				X	X	X	X	X		X	X		
85234 Bee Prepared, 32 West Rawhide, **Gilbert** AZ ☎(602) 892-4092 – vest for wearing the 72-hour kit!; pattern for making your own or finished units				X	X			X					
85236 SSL, Inc., PO Box 2050, **Higley** AZ ☎(602) 588-1259 ☏(602) 988-1259 – broad range of products recommended for making life quicker & easier than going to the store; also available: grain grinders, blenders, pasta makers, rice cookers, juicers, books & videos, spices & herbs, soup bases, wheat & other grains; preparedness consultant; in-home storage specialist			X	X	X	X	X	X	X	X	X	X	X
85258 Deodorant Stones of America, 9420 E. Doubletree Ranch #C-101, **Scottsdale** AZ ☎(602) 451-4981 – manufactured & imported deodorant crystals for body, feet, socks, & jocks; excellent for storage			X	X									
85258 Viking Int'l. Trading, 9188 E. San Salvador Dr. #203A, **Scottsdale** AZ ☎(602) 451-0575 or (800) 451-4452 – distributor of *AlpineAire* freeze-dried foods				X	X		X	X		X		X	
85260 Photocomm. Inc., 7681 E. Gray Rd., **Scottsdale** AZ ☎(800) 544-6466 ☏(602) 951-6329				X									X
85267 FutureMed, Inc., PO Box 13837, **Scottsdale** AZ ☎(800) 800-8849 – catalog of self-healing resources; mail-order discount vitamins, minerals, & herbs; alternative medicine supplies				X						X			
85274 Grover Sales, PO Box 41989, **Mesa** AZ – authorized wholesale distributor of *Vacu-Dry* dehydrated food products			X	X									X
85281 The Handy Pantry, 2129 E. Cedar, **Tempe** AZ ☎(602) 967-4467 or (800) 735-0630 ☏(602) 921-4232. – sprouts, sprouting kits, seeds & sprouting books			X	X						X	X		
85301 Shar's Bosch Kitchen Ctr., 6204 N. 43ʳᵈ Ave., **Glendale** AZ ☎(602) 863-1080 ☏(602) 863-1090 – distributor of *Bosch & Kitchen Specialties* products				X		X	X	X		X	X		
85302 Sunlight Energy Corp., 4411 W. Echo Ln., **Glendale** AZ ☎(800) 338-1781				X	X								X
85321 Gamaliel, Box 1160, **Why** AZ – author describes how & when you volunteered to play the IRS game; achieve sovereignty as an individual legally				C									
85362 Annie's Country Store, PO Box 234, **Yarnell** AZ ☎(520) 427-3441				C	X	X	X	X	X	X			
85364 Provisions 2000, Inc., 2271 W. 12ᵗʰ Lane, **Yuma** AZ ☎(520) 329-7158 or (800) 549-4526 🖥http://home.sprynet.com/sprynet/prov2000 ✉*heavenbond@aol.com* – *AlpineAire* freeze-dried foods distributor; preparedness products					X	X	X	X	X		X	X	X
85546 SolarJack, 325 E. Main St., **Safford** AZ ☎(602) 428-1092 ☏(602) 428-1291				X	X								X
85629 Family Preparedness, 1256 Calle Ensayador, **Sahuarita** AZ ☎(602) 625-4546 – distributor of *Alco ♦Brite* gelled ethanol products				X									X
85635 Health Haven, 1692 S. Hwy. 92, **Sierra Vista** AZ				C	X	X	X	X	X	X			
85637 Sonoita Buying Club, **Sonoita** AZ				C	X	X	X	X	X	X			
85701 Tucson Cooperative Warehouse, 350 S. Toole Avenue, **Tucson** AZ ☎(800) 350-2667 or out*side AZ only* ☎(602) 884-9951☏(602) 792-3258 Territory: *AZ, Southern CA, CO, NM, NV, West TX, UT*			X	C	X	X	X	X	X	X	X		
85705 American Health Food, 3994 N. Oracle, **Tucson** AZ ☎(800) 858-2143 ☏(520) 888-0969 – mail order sales of brand name vitamins, minerals, & herbals				X						X			
85705 Arise & Shine Herbal Products, 3225 N. Los Altos Ave., **Tucson** AZ ☎(602) 293-0891 or (800) 688-2444 – natural solutions products for internal detoxification			X	X	C					X			
85705 Morning Sun Foods Inc., **Queen Creek** AZ ☎(602) 987-8706 – dehydrator/processor of fruits & vegetables			X	X	X								X

Product References Keyed to Chapters (Cont.)

04 water / air filtration & treatment	05 grains, seeds, mills & equip.	12 dairy / powdered milk supplies	13 honey / sweeteners
14 vitamins / minerals / herbs	15 sprouting / equip. & supplies	16 dry / dehydrated / freeze-dried	17 energy / fuels

Entry	M	D	R	04	05	12	13	14	15	16	17
M = Manufacturer / Processor **D = Wholesaler / Trade distributor** **R = Distributor / Retailer to public**											
85713 **A Gardener's Resource**, 2358 W. Ocelot, **Tucson** AZ ☎(520) 792-2803 🖷(520) 792-8023 🖳http://members.aol.com/GRDNSOURCE ✉*GRDNSOURCE@aol.com* – food storage products; food growing systems: greenhouses & hydroponics units & building supplies; garden equip.	X	X		X		X		X			X
85737 **MariSu Terry**, 1607 E. Broken Bow, **Tucson** AZ ☎(602) 825-9650 – distributor of *Magic Mill* products			X		X			X	X		
85738 **Arbico (USA)**, PO Box 4247, **Tucson** AZ ☎(520) 825-9785 or (800) 827-2847 – mail order for biological pest control; organic fertilizers			X								
85748 **Quality Fresh Farmers Market**, 170 North Harrison, **Tucson** AZ ☎(520) 298-2088			C	X	X	X	X	X	X	X	
85748 **Ted's Country Store**, 2760 North Tucson Blvd., **Tucson** AZ			C	X	X	X	X	X	X	X	
85936 **KSP Spices**, PO Box 892, **St. Johns** AZ ☎(520) 337-2904	X	X								X	
85939 **Debby Brimhall**, 825 Cholla Blvd., **Taylor** AZ ☎(602) 536-7932 – distributor of *Magic Mill* products			X		X	X	X	X	X	X	
86001 **Southwest Windpower, Inc.**, 1855 W. Kaibab Ln., **Flagstaff** AZ ☎(520)779-9463 🖷(520)779-1485	X	X									X
86003 **North Rim Country Store** / Canyoneers, Inc., PO Box 2997, **Flagstaff** AZ – distributor of *Alco ♦Brite* gelled ethanol products			X								X
86004 **Connolly's Continental Market**, 5200 E. Cortland Blvd., **Flagstaff** AZ ☎(520) 526-1781			C	X	X	X	X	X	X		
86004 **Southwest Windpower**, 2131 N. 1st St., **Flagstaff** AZ ☎(520) 799-WIND or (520) 779-9463	X	X									X
86021 **Garden Gate Specialties Health Food Store**, PO Box 550, **Colorado City** AZ ☎(520) 875-2808			X	X	X	X	X	X	X	X	
86022 **David Broadbent**, HC 65 Box 416, **Fredonia** AZ – consultant: food storage & preparedness			C		X		X				
86022 **Parashaunt, Inc.**, HC 65 Box 441, **Cane Beds** AZ ☎(800) 958-2408 🖷(520) 875-2702 – manufacturer of *Premier A-Live* live food concentrates	X	X	X					X			
86040 **Page Fast Glass**, 830 Vista Ave., **Page** AZ – distributor of *Alco ♦Brite* gelled ethanol products			X								X
86040 **Page Pellet & Stove**, 788 Sage, **Page** AZ – distributor of *Alco ♦Brite* gelled ethanol products			X								X
86303 **Farmers Market Organic Community Co-op**, 433 S. Montezuma, **Prescott** AZ ☎(520) 776-0792			C	X	X	X	X	X	X	X	
86323 **Hitney Solar Products**, PO Box 365, **Chino Valley** AZ ☎(602) 636-1001	X	X									X
86330 **Energy Efficient Products Inc.**, **Prescott** AZ ☎(602) 778-6700 🖷(602) 778-6703 – wood stoves, gas stoves, & fireplaces; other energy conservation items			X								X
86330 **Betty Brown**, 878 Tom Mix Trail, **Prescott** AZ ☎(520) 776-9848 – distributor of *Magic Mill* products			X		X			X	X		
86335 **Rim Rock Mercantile & Supply**, 3275 E. Beaver Creek Rd., **Rim Rock** AZ ☎(520) 567-4841 – distributor of *Alco ♦Brite* gelled ethanol products			X								X
86340 **Pure Planet**, PO Box 3054, **West Sedona** AZ			C	X	X	X	X	X	X	X	
California											
90001 **Life Link**, CA ☎(800) 543-3457 🖷(310) 375-3835 🖳www.lifelink.com ✉*info@lifelink.com* – disaster & emergency preparedness information, services, & supplies; online store; disasters specialist			C	X	X	X	X			X	
90004 **Silver Solutions**, 137 N. Larchmont Blvd. #195, **Los Angeles** CA ☎(888) 505-6005 🖷(213) 467-1107 – manufacturer of & master distributor for silver colloidal generators; distributor of the *Twig Stove*; lightweight, compact, ultimate camping stove that cooks entire meal with only a few twigs or some newspaper	X	X		X		X	X		X		X
90017 **Country Life Health Shop**, 888 South Figueroa St., **Los Angeles** CA ☎(213) 489-4118			C	X	X	X	X	X	X	X	X
90021 **Basic Foods Co.**, 1211 E. Olympic Blvd., **Los Angeles** CA ☎(310) 623-6686 🖷(310) 477-3494 – bulk food ingredients; soy proteins & meat analogs; wholesale only; *$20 min. order fob L.A.*	X	X								X	
90024 **Comet Rice Ingredients**, 10990 Wilshire Blvd., **Los Angeles** CA ☎(310) 478-0069	X	X			X					X	
90041 **School of Self-Reliance**, PO Box 41834, **Eagle Rock** CA ☎(213) 255-9502 🖳home.earthlink.net/~nyerges/ ✉*nyerges@earthlink.net* – teaching appreciation for Nature through respect and understanding: outdoor guidance, wilderness training, wild food outings, Native American skills, plant identification walks, & plant use training	X	X	X					X			
90042 **New Health Store**, 5831 N. Figueroa St., **Los Angeles** CA ☎(213) 254-4942			C	X	X	X	X	X	X	X	X
90045 **Robin Dexter**, 6399 West 80th Street, **Los Angeles** CA ☎(310) 645-5209 – distributor of *Magic Mill* products			X		X		X		X		
90064 **DD Sales** c/o Doug Dix, 11301 W. Olympic Blvd. #S23, **Los Angeles** CA ☎(310) 572-3464 – discount knives—all brands; spray blend of pepper & CS gas, used by law enforcement agencies worldwide	X	X									X
90064 **Whole Foods Market**, 11666 National Blvd., **Los Angeles** CA ☎(310) 996-8840 🖷(310) 996-9511		X	X		X	X	X	X	X	X	X
90066 **Pure Fresh & Organic**, 13230 Warren Ave., **Los Angeles** CA ☎(310) 398-8855			C	X	X	X	X	X	X	X	X
90066 **Wild Oats**, 3474 S. Centinela Ave., **Los Angeles** CA ☎(310) 636-1300 🖷(310) 636-1307		X	X		X	X	X	X	X	X	X
90069 **International Yogurt Company**, 628 N. Doheny Dr., **West Hollywood** CA ☎(310) 274-9917 – yogurt & kefir cultures; cheeses, sour cream, & buttermilk cultures & supplies	X	X	C								

M = Manufacturer / Processor — D = Wholesaler / Trade distributor — R = Distributor / Retailer to public	M	D	R	04	05	12	13	14	15	16	17
90069 **Wild Oats**, 8611 Santa Monica Blvd., *West Hollywood* CA ☎(310) 854-6927 🖷(310) 854-6229			X	X	X	X	X	X	X	X	
90069 **Wilshire Fireplace Shop**, 8400 Melrose Ave., *Los Angeles* CA ☎(310) 657-8183 — distributor of *Alco ◆Brite* gelled ethanol products			X								X
90083 **Innovative Products & Concepts**, PO Box 83250, *Los Angeles* CA ☎(310) 641-6928 — broad-based research & development organization; seeking to license, create, or marketing to preparedness dealers	X	X	C								
90210 **Organiclean™**, 270 N. Canon Drive #1297, *Beverly Hills* CA ☎(888) VEG-WASH — non-polluting, non-injurious, natural cleaning agent for fruits & vegetables	X	X						X			
90210 **Whole Foods Market**, 239 No. Crescent Dr., *Beverly Hills* CA ☎(310) 274-3360 🖷(310) 274-81498			X	X	X	X	X	X	X	X	
90230 **Farm Store**, 4243 Overland Blvd., *Culver City* CA ☎(310) 559-7901			C	X	X	X	X	X	X	X	
90242 **Sunflower Health Food Store**, 12844 Paramount Blvd., *Downey* CA ☎(310) 861-6383			C	X	X	X	X	X	X	X	
90245 **Greenery Natural Kitchen**, 100 North Sepulveda Blvd., *El Segundo* CA ☎(310) 640-1330			C	X	X	X	X	X	X	X	
90248 **Lo-Volt Lighting**, 606 W. 184th St., *Gardena* CA ☎(213) 321-9693 🖷(310) 323-3907	X	X									X
90248 **Major Surplus & Survival, Inc.**, 35 W. Alondra Blvd., *Gardena* CA ☎(310) 324-8855 or (800) 441-8855 — supplier of preparedness products; distributor of *Emergency Essentials, AlpineAire* products, *Survival Tabs & Storehouse Foods*, manufactured by *Food Reserves, Inc.; Alco ◆Brite* gelled ethanol products	X	X	X	X	X	X	X	X	X	X	X
90250 **Solec International, Inc.**, 12533 Chadron Ave., *Hawthorn* CA ☎(310) 970-0065 🖷(310) 970-1065	X										X
90266 **Hunt Co.**, 1456 12th St., #2, *Manhattan Beach* CA ☎(310) 546-5293 🖷(310) 568-3743 — *AlpineAire Foods* distributor		X	X	X		X		X		X	X
90274 **Malaga Cove Ranch Market**, 43 Malaga Cove Plaza, *Palos Verdes* CA ☎(301) 375-2683			C	X	X	X	X	X	X	X	
90277 **Heartwood Publications**, 5808 S. Pacific Coast Hwy. #14, *Redondo Beach* CA — homesteading & survival pamphlets & products			X								
90277 **Whole Foods Market**, 405 N. Pacific Coast Hwy., *Redondo Beach* CA ☎(310) 376-6931 🖷(310) 376-7651			X	X	X	X	X	X	X	X	
90401 **Alpha-Omega Labs**, 1431 Ocean Ave. #1611, *Santa Monica* CA ☎(310) 393-5747 🖷(310) 395-0545 — manufacturers of vitamin, mineral, & herbal products in creams, lotions, salves, & ointments for the skin	X	X						X			
90403 **Wild Oats**, 1425 Montana Ave., *Santa Monica* CA ☎(310) 576-4707 🖷(310) 576-4710			X	X	X	X	X	X	X	X	
90405 **Living Arts**, 2434 Main St., *Santa Monica* CA ☎(800) 2 LIVING — sources for mind & body processes	X							X			
90503 **Green Foods Corporation**, 620 Maple Avenue, *Torrance* CA ☎(310) 618-0678 — mail-order sprouts & barley grass powder	X	X	X					X			
90505 **Cookin' Stuff**, 22217-2 Palos Verdes Blvd., *Torrance* CA ☎(310) 371-2220 — distributor of *Magic Mill* products			X		X		X		X		
90505 **Quinoa Corp.**, 24248 Crenshaw Blvd., *Torrance* CA ☎(310) 530-8666 — organization dedicated to the propagation of *Quinoa* grain; information & product	X	X	C		X						
90602 **Herbie's House of Health**, 13306 E. Whittier Blvd., *Whittier* CA ☎(310) 698-6574			C	X	X	X	X	X	X	X	
90603 **Charlene Krause**, 6168 James Alan, *Cypress* CA ☎(714) 995-9217 — distributor of *Magic Mill* products			X	X							
90603 **Ready One Survival Products**, 15756 La Forge St. #509, *Whittier* CA 🖳www.atyour.com/readyone/jsord1.htm			X	X	X	X	X		X	X	X
90630 **Bev Tilson**, 5752 Lime Ave., *Cypress* CA ☎(714) 827-7374 — distributor of *Magic Mill* products			X		X		X		X		
90670 **Earthquake Preparedness Society**, 14525 Valley View Ave. #B, *Santa Fe Springs* CA ☎(800) 628-9111 — founded by off-duty & retired fire & police personnel; dedicated to preparing people for natural disasters			X	X	X	X	X		X	X	
90670 **Trojan Battery Co.**, 12380 Clark St., *Santa Fe Springs* CA ☎(800) 423-6569 🖷(310) 941-6038		X	X								X
90670 **West Coast Fire Place**, 12025 E. Florence Ave. #103, *Santa Fe Springs* CA ☎(310) 944-3500 — distributor of *Alco ◆Brite* gelled ethanol products			X								X
90701 **The Fireplace Man** / Hansen Wholesale, *Cerritos* CA ☎(800) 365-3267 Fax(310) 860-3744		X	X								X
90720 **Linda Berkley**, 2841 Piedmont Ave., *Los Alamitos* CA ☎(310) 594-4860 — distributor of *Magic Mill* products			X		X		X		X		
90734 **GSG & Associates**, PO Box 6448, *San Pedro* CA ☎(310) 548-7267 🖷(310) 548-5802			X								X
90804 **Green Kamut Corp.**, 1965 Freeman Ave., *Long Beach* CA ☎(310) 498-5769 or (800) 452-6884 — manufacturer of *Green Kamut*, a shelf-stable, enzyme-rich vegetable juice extract	X	X	C					X			
90806 **Star Fireplace**, 2335 Long Beach Blvd., *Long Beach* CA — distributor of *Alco ◆Brite* gelled ethanol products			X								X
90808 **Reyngolds Imports/Exports**, 3362 Knoxville Ave., *Long Beach* CA ☎(310) 212-4221 — exclusive importer offers night vision devices & radiation testers at excellent prices		X	X								
90815 **Personal Security Service**, 6444 E. Spring St. #110, *Long Beach* CA ☎(310) 987-0554 — emergency preparedness supplies; security devices; pepper spray for self-protection		X	X							X	X
90945 **Colonel Sanchez Foods**, PO Box 5848, *Santa Monica* CA ☎(310) 313-6769 🖷(213) 732-2271 — manufacturer of tofu & tofu foods products	X	X					X			X	
91103 **Pat McKay Animal Nutrition**, 396 W. Washington Blvd., *Pasadena* CA ☎(818) 296-1120 or (800) 975-7555 🖷(818) 296-1126 ✉*patmckay@earthlink.net* — cat/dog nutrition of frozen raw meats, vegetables, & fish fit for human consumption; ozone generators for animals	X	X	C					X			

Product References Keyed to Chapters (Cont.)

04 water / air filtration & treatment	05 grains, seeds, mills & equip.	12 dairy / powdered milk supplies	13 honey / sweeteners
14 vitamins / minerals / herbs	15 sprouting / equip. & supplies	16 dry / dehydrated / freeze-dried	17 energy / fuels

M = Manufacturer / Processor	D = Wholesaler / Trade distributor	R = Distributor / Retailer to public

Listing	M	D	R	04	05	12	13	14	15	16	17
91105 Extend-A-Life, Inc., 1010 S. Arroyo Pkwy., #7, **Pasadena** CA ☎(818) 441-1223 🖷(818) 441-1293 — inventory control system for tracking & maintaining emergency provisions; customized *Employee Purchase Program*; pre-packaged emergency kits, bulk provisions, first aid supplies & kits	X	X	X				X			X	X
91105 Faults Alarm, Inc., 620 South Raymond Ave. #2, **Pasadena** CA ☎(818) 449-6585 or (800) 995-9253 🖷(818) 449-0864 🖳www.faultsalarm.com ✉Faultsalarm@MSN.com — earthquake securing services; fastening hardware for home or business; seismic electrical disconnect system		X	X				X		X	X	X
91106 Wild Oats, 603 South Lake Ave., **Pasadena** CA ☎(818) 792-1778 🖷(818) 792-1778		X	X		X	X	X	X	X	X	X
91206 Whole Foods Market, 26 North Glendale Avenue, **Glendale** CA ☎(818) 240-9350 🖷(818) 240-2681		X	X		X	X	X	X	X	X	X
91301 Agoura Hills Hay & Grain, 28327 Agoura Rd., **Agoura Hills** CA ☎(818) 889-1989 — distributor of *Alco ♦Brite* gelled ethanol products			X		X					X	X
91301 Safe-T-Proof, 638 Lindero Canyon Road #257, **Oak Park** CA ☎(818) 865-3121 or (888) 677-2338 🖷(818) 865-3126 🖳www.safe-t-proof.com ✉info@safe-t-proof.com — manufacturer of earthquake preparedness products, supplies & kits; fasteners; safety courses & consulting	X	X	X							X	
91304 Sun-Mate Corporation, 8110 Remmet Avenue, **Canoga Park** CA ☎(808) 883-7766 — solar-powered products, emergency solar products; photovoltaics equipment; everything for the energy-independent	X	X									X
91313 Multi-Pure Corporation, PO Box 4179, **Chatsworth** CA — manufacturer of *Multi-Pure* water filtration & purification systems for home or emergency use	X	X	X	X							
91320 Naps International, 587-F N. Ventura Park Rd. #508, **Newbury Park** CA ☎(805) 494-6657		X									X
91320 Survivor Industries, 2551 Azurite Circle, **Newbury Park** CA ☎(805) 498-6062 or (800) 263-6818 — manufacturer; *Mainstay* emergency food bars & emergency water rations packs; survival kits for home & industry	X	X	C	X						X	
91324 Tina Hur, 18744 Vintage Street, **North Ridge** CA ☎(818) 341-5048 — distributor of *Magic Mill* products		X	X		X					X	
91324 Whole Foods Market, 9350 Reseda Boulevard, **Northridge** CA ☎(818) 701-5122 🖷(818) 701-1871		X	X		X	X	X	X	X	X	X
91331 Trail Foods, 12455 Branford St. Unit #6, **Arleta** CA ☎(818) 897-4370 🖷(818) 897-0148 — authorized retail distributor of *Mountain House* brand freeze-dried products		X	X							X	
91350 Hoods Woods Outdoor Education Center, **Green Valley** CA ✉Diogenes@survival.com — wilderness courses and programs to help people meet the changing priorities for wilderness adventure			C								
91351 Quake Kare, Inc., 27940 Solamint Rd. #11-107, **Canyon Country** CA ☎(805) 250-4951 — specialists in earthquake preparedness, emergency & disaster survival kits & supplies for car home, school, & office	X	X	X							X	
91360 Genesis Specialty Products, Inc., 1195 Burtonwood Avenue, **Thousand Oaks** CA ☎(805) 371-9044 or (800) 664-7448 🖷(805) 379-9792 ✉cbuxbaum@aol.com — manufacturer of 5-yr. shelf-stable food & water rations; safety, first aid, disaster, & emergency response provisions and supplies for commercial, resale, & individual use; portable kits	X	X	X	X						X	
91360 Whole Foods Market, 451 Avenida de los Arboles, **Thousand Oaks** CA ☎(805) 492-5340		X	X		X	X	X	X	X	X	X
91362 MCO, 3203 Bordero, **Thousand Oaks** CA — 30 detailed plans for building sun-, water-, & wind-powered home & outdoor appliances; $2.00		X	X								X
91364 Nature's Warehouse, 21932 Ventura Blvd., **Woodland Hills** CA ☎(818) 999-4714			C	X	X	X	X	X	X	X	
91386 Quake Savers, PO Box 1203, **Santa Clarita** CA ☎(805) 250-4951 🖷(805) 250-4951 — disaster preparedness supplies & equipment	X	X	X	X	X					X	X
91401 Van Nuys Stove, 6179 Van Nuys Blvd., **Van Nuys** CA ☎(818) 781-3500 — distributor of *Alco ♦Brite* gelled ethanol products			X								X
91403 Tulanian's Fireplaces & Patios, 14619 Ventura Blvd., **Sherman Oaks** CA ☎(818) 784-7248 — distributor of *Alco ♦Brite* gelled ethanol products			X								X
91403 Whole Foods Market, 4520 Sepulveda Blvd., **Sherman Oaks** CA ☎(818) 382-3700 🖷(818) 382-3710		X	X		X	X	X	X	X	X	X
91405 J. J. Automotive, 7526 Woodman Place, **Van Nuys** CA — distributor of *Alco ♦Brite* gelled ethanol products			X								X
91406 En Garde Health Products, 7702 Bldg. #10, Balboa Blvd., **Van Nuys** CA ☎(818) 901-8505 or (800) 955-4633 🖷(818) 996-0489 — mail-order catalog of innovative & all-natural health supplements			X					X			
91409 Richmoor Corporation, PO Box 8092 **Van Nuys** CA ☎(818) 787-2510 🖷(818) 780-6407 — producer of *Richmoor* and *Natural High* brands of freeze-dried/dehydrated natural lightweight camping foods	X	X								X	
91411 Earthquake Essentials of L.A., 14918 Burbank Blvd., **Sherman Oaks** CA ☎(818) 787-3737 🖷(818) 787-2008 🖳www.quakesafe.com — full-service emergency preparedness organization; food, water, & survival kits; equipment security & fasteners			X								
91423 Whole Foods Market, 12905 Riverside Dr., **Sherman Oaks** CA ☎(818) 762-5548 🖷(818) 762-0406		X	X		X	X	X	X	X	X	X
91605 Healthwise *(attn: Linda)*, 7246 Bellaire, **North Hollywood** CA ☎(818) 982-9966 — distributor of *Magic Mill* products			X		X		X			X	
91711 Natural High Health Foods, 843 West Foothill Boulevard, **Claremont** CA ☎(909) 621-5163			C	X	X	X	X	X	X	X	
91730 Honeyville Grain, Inc., 11600 Dayton Drive, **Cucamonga** CA ☎(909) 980-9500 🖷(909) 980-6503	X	X	X		X	X	X			X	X

	M	D	R	04	05	12	13	14	15	16	17
91745 Simpler Life Emergency Provisions, Inc., 1320 Johnson Drive, **City of Industry** CA ☎(818) 961-8858 or (800) 266-6737 🖷(818) 961-5648 – distributor of preparedness products: food, water, warmth, lighting, medical, hygiene, sanitation, Search & Rescue (SAR), shelter, & support; consulting with businesses at risk	X	X	X	X					X	X	X
91755 Quake Gear, 510 Edgley Drive, **Monterey Park** CA ☎(818) 288-0376 🖷(818) 288-5153 www.globalstrategies.com/qg/contact qg@globalstrategies.com – one-stop shopping center for emergency & disaster preparedness information & products	X	X	X	X					X	X	X
91766 Woodland Products Co., 1480 E. Grand Avenue, **Pomona** CA ☎(909) 623-3434 – distributor of *Alco ♦Brite* gelled ethanol products		X									X
91908 Virgin Earth / Dr. Joel Wallach, PO Box 1222, **Bonita** CA ☎(800) 755-4656 🖷(619) 479-2649 – humate soil conditioner & plant food re-mineralizes the soil	X	X						X			
91910 Boney's Marketplace, 362 F St., **Chula Vista** CA ☎(619) 476-1032			C	X	X	X	X	X	X	X	X
91935 China Diesel Imports, Inc., 15749 Lyons Valley Rd, **Jamul** CA ☎(909) 657-0379 🖷(909) 657-8120	X	X									
91941 Gardner Distributors (*attn: Doug*) 6880 Tower St., **LaMesa** CA ☎(619) 287-9291 🖷(619) 589-7115 – *Bosch/Kitchen Specialties* equipment products dealer			C	X	X		X			X	X
91941 The Warm Hearth, 8748 La Mesa Blvd., **La Mesa** CA ☎(619) 465-0890 – distributor of *Alco ♦Brite* gelled ethanol products		X									
91977 Heliotrope General, 3733 Kenora Dr., **Spring Valley** CA ☎(800) 552-8838 🖷(619) 460-9211	X	X									
92003 American Homestead Mercantile Co., PO Box 1354, **Bonsall** CA – mail-order homesteading & preparedness products			X	X	X	X				X	X
92007 Cardiff Seaside Market, 2087 San Elijo Ave., **Cardiff** CA ☎(619) 753-5445			C	X	X	X	X	X	X	X	X
92008 Martens Health & Survival Products, Inc., 2205 Faraday Ave. #A, **Carlsbad** CA ☎(619) 438-0866 or (800) 824-7861 🖷(619) 438-7910 http://millenianet.com/survival survival@millenianet.com – distributor of *Ready Reserve* dehydrated foods			X	X	X			X	X	X	X
92024 Community Market, 745 First Street, **Encinitas** CA ☎(619) 753-4632			C	X	X	X	X	X	X	X	X
92028 Korn's Survival Gear, 623 W. Beech Street, **Fallbrook** CA ☎(619) 728-7012	X	X									X
92029 Horizon Industries, 2120 W. Mission Rd., **Escondido** CA ☎(619) 480-8322		X			X						
92029 Oasis Breads, 440 Venture St., **Escondido** CA ☎(619) 747-7390 🖷(619) 747-4854 www.hlthmall.com/healthmall/oasis oasisbrd@connectnet.com – mail-order breads for *wheat allergics:* flourless, sprouted breads w/o shortening, oil, eggs, dairy, refined sugars, or preservatives; also, wheat breads; Rye, Pumpernickel, Raisin-Oat Bran, & *Kamut*			C	X	X	X	X	X	X	X	X
92037 UCSD Food Co-op, Student Center B-023, **La Jolla** CA ☎(619) 546-8339			C	X	X	X	X	X	X	X	X
92037 Whole Foods Market, 8825 LaJolla Drive, **LaJolla** CA ☎(619) 642-6700 🖷(619) 642-6730			X	X	X	X	X	X	X	X	
92040 Priscilla J. Schreiber, 12264 Linroe Dr., **Lakeside** CA ☎(619) 390-5776 🖷(619) 390-5074	X	X									X
92040 Towns Light Source, 11924 Lakeside, **Lakeside** CA ☎(619) 443-1481 or (888) 854-7850 🖷(619) 443-5084 http://members.aol.com/townslight/welcome.html townslight@aol.com – national distributor of the manually-powered, no-battery-required, emergency light imported from Russia		X	X	X							X
92054 Disaster Preparedness, 1405 El Camino Real #110 **Oceanside** CA ☎(619) 966-3600 or (800) 800-7922 🖷(619) 966-3602		X	X	X							X
92054 McCall's Natural Choice, 713 Arbolitos Blvd., **Oceanside** CA			C	X	X	X	X	X	X	X	X
92065 Home Canning Supply & Specialties, 2117 Main St., **Ramona** CA ☎(619) 788-0520 🖷(619) 789-4745 canning & food preservation supplies; bulk, regular, & low-methoxyl pectin with or without chemical preservatives			X								X
92065 Marian Petrovic, 24010 Necter Way, PO Box 2070, **Ramona** CA ☎(619) 789-1504 – distributor of *Magic Mill* products			X				X			X	X
92069 Kamut Brand Wheat, 295 Distribution Street, **San Marcos** CA 🖷(619) 752-1322	X	X	C		X						
92070 Julian Stoveworks, 30351 Highway 78, **Santa Ysabel** CA – distributor of *Alco ♦Brite* gelled ethanol products		X									X
92075 Quest For The Best, PO Box 1775, **Solana Beach** CA ☎(619) 944-2934 or (800) 326-8589 – books & products meeting a high standard of truth; send LSASE for list							X				
92075 Your Natural Grocer, 124 Santa Fe Dr. #103, **Solana Beach** CA ☎(619) 481-7244			C	X	X	X	X	X	X	X	X
92082 Jaffe Bros. Natural Foods, Inc., PO Box 636, **Valley Ctr.** CA ☎(619) 749-1133 🖷(619) 749-1282 – organic, untreated natural foods: fruits, peas, beans, seeds, grains & flours, brown rice, whole wheat & no-wheat pasta, dehydrated vegetables; in-shell & shelled nuts & butters; jams & oils; condiments, baking aids; milk powders	X		C		X						X
92102 Gold Mine Natural Food Co., 1947 30th Street, **San Diego** CA ☎(619) 296-9756 or (800) 475-3663 – natural products via mail order			X				X			X	X
92104 M & B Market, 3019 Lincoln Ave., **San Diego** CA ☎(619) 291-1635			C	X	X	X	X	X	X	X	X
92105 Maria's Farmers Market, 3944 Beech St., **San Diego** CA ☎(619) 291-1635			C	X	X	X	X	X	X	X	X
92109 Gamma Plastics, Inc., 4606 Santa Fe St., **San Diego** CA ☎(800) 842-6543 🖷(619) 272-5659 – *Gamma Seal Lid*, an easy-open/close, pest-proof, re-sealable, stackable, leakproof, & child-resistant lid for sealing 3.5- to 7-gal. plastic buckets; facilitates food products usage yet protects contents	X	X									
92111 Greentree Grocers, 3560 Mt. Acadia Blvd., **San Diego** CA ☎(619) 560-1975			C	X	X	X	X	X	X	X	X
92117 Solar Electric, Inc., 4901 Morena Blvd. #305, **San Diego** CA ☎(800) 842-5678 solar@cts.com		X	X								X

Table legend: **M** = Manufacturer / Processor   **D** = Wholesaler / Trade distributor   **R** = Distributor / Retailer to public

Product References Keyed to Chapters (Cont.)

04 water / air filtration & treatment	05 grains, seeds, mills & equip.	12 dairy / powdered milk supplies	13 honey / sweeteners
14 vitamins / minerals / herbs	15 sprouting / equip. & supplies	16 dry / dehydrated / freeze-dried	17 energy / fuels

M = Manufacturer / Processor	D = Wholesaler / Trade distributor	R = Distributor / Retailer to public

Key columns: **M D R** | chapters **04 05 12 13 14 15 16 17**

Listing	M	D	R	04	05	12	13	14	15	16	17
92118 **Neighbors United Food Cooperative**, 30th Street & Imperial Avenue, **San Diego** CA			C	X	X	X	X	X	X	X	
92118 **Whole Foods Market**, 711 University Avenue, **San Diego** CA			X	X		X	X	X	X	X	X
92120 **Farmers Outlet**, 10407 Friars Road, **San Diego** CA ☎(619) 563-9165			C	X	X	X	X	X	X	X	
92121 **United Solar Sys. Corp.**, 5278 Eastgate Mall, **San Diego** CA ☎(619) 625-2080 🖷(619) 625-2083	X	X									X
92123 **Boneys Marketplace**, 3332 Sandrock, **Sierra Mesa** CA ☎(619) 565-1714			C	X	X	X	X	X	X	X	
92124 **Farmers Outlet**, 205 South El Camino Real, **Encinitas** CA ☎(619) 436-5567			C	X	X	X	X	X	X	X	
92160 **Double M Enterprises**, PO Box 601542, **San Diego** CA ☎(619) 682-7594 🖷(619) 286-0427 🖳www2.4dcomm.com/doublem ✉doublem@4dcomm.com — quality emergency, preparedness, survival products & resources			X	X	X	X	X			X	X
92223 **Ready Reserve Foods**, PO Box 697, **Beaumont** CA ☎(714) 796-0098 or (800) 453-2202 — distributor of *Ready Reserve* brand long-term food storage products; full line of emergency preparedness items including over 100 different dry food products for long term storage	X	X	X	X	X	X	X	X	X	X	X
92240 **Church of Universal Knowledge** / Dr. Jesse F. Partridge, DD., DMT, PO Box 547, **Desert Hot Springs** CA ☎(619) 329-4682 — books, magnets, negative-ion generators; alternative healthcare products		X					X				
92284 **Gerald & Pat McGowan**, 56523 Carlyle Dr., **Yucca Valley** CA ☎(619) 365-3240 — distributor of *Magic Mill* products		X			X		X		X		
92285 **American Family Products, Int'l.** / Fruehe, PO Box 3192, **Landers** CA ☎(619) 364-2416		X					X				
92301 **GSE Solar Systems**, 17451 Raccoon Ave. #12, **Adelanto** CA ☎(619) 246-7733 🖷(619) 246-5770	X	X									X
92314 **Community Market**, PO Box 800, **Big Bear City** CA ☎(909) 585-2641			C	X	X	X	X	X	X	X	
92324 **Prophecy Preparedness**, 2097 E. Washington St. #1E-309, **Colton** CA ☎(909) 824-8941 — specializing in alternative healthcare supplies		X				X		X			
92335 **Roxanna Scumecz**, 16089 East Valley Blvd. #E, **Fontana** CA ☎(909) 355-6849 — *Magic Mill* kitchen products distributor		X			X				X	X	
92345 **Inland Fireplace & Wood Stove**, 16922 Main St. #K, **Hesperia** CA ☎(619) 956-7252		X									X
92320 **JLN & Associates** *(attn: Jack Nemceff)*, Box 307, **Calimesa** CA ☎(909) 275-3894 — *SamAndy Foods* products distributor			X	X	X	X	X		X	X	X
92352 **Lake Arrowhead Patrol**, *(attn: Jack Polley)*, PO Box 1078, **Lake Arrowhead** CA ☎(909) 336-3000 — *SamAndy Foods* products distributor			X	X	X	X	X		X	X	X
92354 **Loma Linda Market**, 24954 Prospect St., **Loma Linda** CA ☎(909) 824-4565 — distributor of *Magic Mill* products			C	X	X	X	X	X	X	X	
92369 **Lightwaves Ent.**, PO Box 102, **Patton** CA ☎(909) 382-6000 or (800) 633-3246 🖷(909) 425-0124		X	X								X
92369 **Personal Commode**, PO Box 102, **Patton** CA ☎(909) 425-0124 — *Eco-Toilet*, ultra-light, reusable, disposable, requires no water or chemicals; can be used anywhere	X	X	X								X
92392 **G.G.S.**, 14962 Bear Valley Rd. G198, **Victorville** CA ☎(619) 949-0479 🖷(619) 949-0479 — professional survival equipment; addressing basic needs, regardless of climatic condition or geographic location	X	C	X							X	X
92404 **Bernardino Fireplace & Wood Stoves**, 2240 E. Highland Ave., **San Bernardino** CA		X									X
92408 **Ready Reserve Foods**, 1442 S. Gage St., **San Bernardino** CA ☎(800) 453-2202 🖷(909) 796-2196 or (909) 796-0098 — producer of *Ready Reserves Foods*™ brand dehydrated foods packaged in heavy-duty cans for long-term storage; emergency rations; complete line of emergency & preparedness items; distributor of *Alco ♦Brite* gelled ethanol products; *Ready Reserve Report*, free monthly newsletter	X	X	C	X	X	X	X	X	X	X	X
92503 **Mumm's Mill**, 9194 Magnolia Ave., **Riverside** CA ☎(909) 359-7675 — distributor of *Magic Mill* products		X	X	X			X			X	X
92504 **Be Ready Disaster Preparedness**, 1405 El Camino Real #110, **Oceanside** CA ☎(619) 966-3600 🖷(619) 966-3602		X	X	X	X	X			X	X	
92505 **Hearth & Home**, 10485 Magnolia, **Riverside** CA — distributor of *Alco ♦Brite* gelled ethanol products		X									X
92544 **Hemet Fireplace**, 1960 East Florida, **Hemet** CA ☎(909) 658-2778 — distributor of *Alco ♦Brite* gelled ethanol products		X									X
92552 **The Staff of Life**, PO Box 7750, **Moreno Valley** CA ☎(909) 653-3261 or (800) 982-8368 — enzymes & colloidal silver health solutions		X					X	X			X
92570 **China Farm Machinery Co.**, 23985 Rolling Meadows Dr., **Perris** CA ☎(909) 657-0379 🖷(909) 657-8120 — importers of Chinese machinery; equip. & parts in stock; diesels generators, inverters, & propane fridges	X	X									X
92586 **Crains Health Food Center**, 28063 Bradley Rd., **Sun City** CA ☎(909) 679-4817			C	X	X	X	X	X	X	X	
92590 **Alternative Solar Prod.**, 27420 Jefferson #104-B, **Temecula** CA ☎(800) 229-7652 🖷(909) 308-2388	X	X									X
92600 **Whole Foods Market**, 14945 Holt Avenue, **Tustin** CA ☎(714) 731-3400 🖷(714) 505-7160			X	X		X	X	X	X	X	X
92626 **The Fresh Air Company**, 2330 Vanguard Way #Q-105, **Costa Mesa** CA ☎(800) 860-4244 — complete air purification systems for home & office	X	X									

Legend: **M = Manufacturer / Processor** · **D = Wholesaler / Trade distributor** · **R = Distributor / Retailer to public**

Listing	M	D	R	04	05	12	13	14	15	16	17
92627 The Tidy Tire Kit, Inc., 262 E. 19th St., **Costa Mesa** CA ☎(714) 645-3416 or (800) 843-9897 — emergency kits for people, cars, bikes, & survival; customized kits; quick safety signals; medical kits	X	X									
92629 Mark Chavez, 34051 Copper Lantern #A, **Dana Point** CA ☎(714) 240-2519 — distributor of *Magic Mill* products		X		X		X	X		X		
92644 Koosun Chung, 1341 Gallaway Street, **Garden Grove** CA ☎(714) 636-4315 — distributor of *Magic Mill* products		X		X		X	X	X	X		
92647 Earthquake Essentials of Orange County, 16089 Goldenwest St., **Huntington Beach** CA ☎(714) 841-1212 🖷(714) 841-6759		X	X	X	X				X	X	X
92651 Wild Oats, 283 Broadway, **Laguna Beach** CA		X	X	X	X	X		X	X	X	X
92663 Michael Shannon, 110 26th Street, **Newport Beach** CA ☎(714) 673-2735 — distributor of *Magic Mill* products		X		X			X		X		
92687 Wild Foods Company Inc., 22349 LaPalma Avenue #113, **Yorba Linda** CA ☎(714) 692-5331 — manufacturer of *Edible Wild Food Cards*® for easy identification of plants; *Wild Foods Nutritional Wheel*® offers quick & easy way to balance or supplement diet with free wild foods found in the local environment	X	X	C					X			
92692 Wild Oats, 27142 La Paz Road, **Mission Viejo** CA ☎(714) 460-0202 🖷(714) 460-0053 — natural & organic dairy, fruit, meats & vegetable foods; vitamins & supplements; bulk & pre-pack foods		X	X	X	X	X		X	X	X	X
92677 Farm to Market, Town Center Drive, **Laguna Niguel** CA ☎(714) 363-0123			C	X	X	X	X	X	X	X	X
92680 Sundance Honey Company, 18072 Bigelow Park, **Justin** CA ☎(714) 731-1959	X	X	X				X				
92683 Nite Owl & Associates, PO Box 1578, **Westminster** CA ☎(714) 301-0435 — natural disasters survival; personal & group disaster preparation		X	X							X	X
92697 Wilshire Fireplace Shops, 1522 Newport Blvd., **Costa Mesa** CA ☎(714) 650-2640 — distributor of *Alco ♦Brite* gelled ethanol products		X									X
92704 Tek-Tron Enterprises, Inc., **Santa Ana** CA ☎(714) 641-1988 🖷(714) 641-2005	X										X
92705 Emergency Lifeline Corp., 1510 E. Edinger Avenue #D, **Santa Ana** CA ☎(714) 558-8940 — authorized distributor of *Emergency Essentials* products	X	X	X	X	X	X	X	X	X	X	X
92708 Disaster Preparedness 101, c/o Janet Kugel, Independent Disaster Preparedness Consultant, 16958 Helena Circle, **Fountain View** CA ☎(714) 921-2273 🖳www.primenet.com/~prepared ✉*prepared@primenet.com* — disaster impact reduction for businesses & schools; identify hazards, assessing needs, development planning & implementation, & placement of products & services to solve problems; certification & training classes		C	X			X	X		X		X
92711 A.C.I., PO Box 10463, **Santa Ana** CA ☎(800) 245-1827	X	X									X
92804 Emergency Preparedness Training Institute, 800 S. Brookhurst St. #2B, **Anaheim** CA ☎(714) 776-4277 ✉*cprteacher@earthlink.net* — all safety training needs anywhere in So. CA; CPR; infant & adult First Aid; for individuals or organizations											
92806 WesMar Enterprises, 919 S. Nordica, **Anaheim** CA ☎(714) 961-8181 🖷(714) 956-7951 — "*The Protector*," full-body poncho, 1-person pup tent, survival blanket, lean-to, & ground cover—all in one!	X	X	C								X
92807 Chi's Enterprises, Inc., 5140 East La Palma Avenue #103, **Anaheim** CA ☎(714) 777-1542		X					X				
92815 Sioux Honey Association, PO Box 668, **Anaheim** CA ☎(714) 776-4112	X	X	X				X				
92817 American Holistic Health Association, PO Box 17400, **Anaheim** CA ☎(714) 779-6152 — free referral service for health & wellness resources to enhance health & well-being; send SLASE	X	C						X			
92821 Aquacheck, 1300 W. Pioneer St. #C, **Brea** CA ☎(310) 697-8915 or (800) 504-5508 *24-hr. order line:* (714) 739-7755 🖳www.aquacheck.com		X	X								
92865 SolarTrope Supply Corp., 739 W. Taft Ave., **Orange** CA ☎(800) 515-1617 or (714) 637-6226		X	X								X
93001 Fireside Mart, 1984 E. Main St., **Ventura** CA ☎(805) 653-6270 — distributor of *Alco ♦Brite* gelled ethanol products		X									X
93011 Emergency 72-Hour, PO Box 1978, **Camarillo** CA ☎(805) 484-7272 🖷(805) 484-9783 🖳IMALL.com/emergency72hr ✉*Ranger@vcol.net* — distributor of 72-hr. kits, emergency supplies, rations, & protective devices; of *Alco ♦Brite* products distributor		X	X								X
93012 Siemens Solar Industries, 4650 Adohr Ln., **Camarillo** CA ☎(805) 388-6568 🖷(805) 388-6395		X	X								X
93030 Solarmode, 2834 Teal Club Rd., **Oxnard** CA ☎(805) 382-8318		X	X								X
93035 Perfect Health Products Div., 5423 Driftwood St., **Oxnard** CA ☎(805) 382-2021 or (800) 444-4584 — herbs, vitamins, minerals, & whole foods; sprouting, dehydrating, juicing, cooking, grinding & blending equipment; air & water purifiers, vision therapy, cookware, cleansing tools, & more!		X	X	X				X	X	X	X
93101 Solar Systems LTD, 32 West Anapamu #257, **Santa Barbara** CA ☎(805) 563-2687 🖳www.middleman.com/solarsys ✉*solarsys@middleman.com*		X	X								X
93101 TMJ Imports, 1324 State St. #J108, **Santa Barbara** CA 🖷(805) 963-8848 🖳www.acdc-power.com — portable power supplies & accessories; power inverters for car, truck, or boat		X	X								X
93101 Fireside Shoppe, 536 Olive, **Santa Barbara** CA — distributor of *Alco ♦Brite* gelled ethanol products		X									X
93105 Teeccino Caffe, Inc., 1720 Las Canoas Road, **Santa Barbara** CA ☎(805) 966-0999 or (800) 498-3434 🖷(805) 966-0522 — caffeine-free, coffee-tasting Mediterranean herbal product	X	X	X						X	X	

Product References Keyed to Chapters (Cont.)

04 water / air filtration & treatment	05 grains, seeds, mills & equip.	12 dairy / powdered milk supplies	13 honey / sweeteners
14 vitamins / minerals / herbs	15 sprouting / equip. & supplies	16 dry / dehydrated / freeze-dried	17 energy / fuels

Listing	M	D	R	04	05	12	13	14	15	16	17
M = Manufacturer / Processor **D = Wholesaler / Trade distributor** **R = Distributor / Retailer to public**	M	D	R	04	05	12	13	14	15	16	17
93111 **Soft Logic Inc.**, 5276 Hollister Avenue #305, **Santa Barbara** CA ☎(805) 683-9451 📠(805) 683-9461 📧www.tecfen.com/itraders/emergency ✉*slogic@tecfen.com* — distributors of smoke hoods, survival kits, & survival blankets	X	C									X
93117 **Bragg Live Foods**, 7340 Hollister Ave., **Santa Barbara** CA ☎(800) 446-1990 📠(805) 968-1001 — manufacturer of *Bragg* liquid amino acids & organic apple cider products	X	X	C					X			
93117 **Tecfen Corporation**, 5860-C Hollister Ave., **Santa Barbara** CA ☎(805) 967-1153 📠(805) 967-1295 ✉*tecfen@tecfen.com* — smoke hoods, flint fire starter, safety goggles, backpacking stove, survival kits, 3-day kits; *international sales only*	X	C	X								X
93277 **Caron L. Thompson**, 2340 Blackmon Court, **Visalia** CA ☎(209) 733-5942 – *Magic Mill* distributor			X	X	X		X		X		X
93301 **Two Sweep Stove Shop**, 1100 24ᵗʰ Street, **Bakersfield** CA ☎(805) 633-1731 – distributor of *Alco ♦Brite* gelled ethanol products			X								X
93307 **Valley Spa & Stoves**, 120 Union Ave., **Bakersfield** CA ☎(805) 393-3616 – distributor of *Alco ♦Brite* gelled ethanol products			X								X
93308 **AmeriCal Awning Co.**, 823 Wilson Ave., **Bakersfield** CA – distributor of *Alco ♦Brite* gelled ethanol products			X								X
93405 **Chuck Wagon Outfitters**, 250 Avila Beach Dr., **San Luis Obispo** CA – distributor of *Alco ♦Brite* gelled ethanol products			X								X
93428 **Sooty Goose**, 801 C. Main St., **Cambria** CA ☎(805) 927-5019 – distributor of *Alco ♦Brite* gelled ethanol products			X								X
93449 **Hydro Heaven Spas & Stove**, 821 Oak Park Rd., **Pismo Beach** CA – distributor of *Alco ♦Brite* gelled ethanol products			X								X
93535 **Earthquake Survival Services**, 1036 E. Avenue J #E, **Lancaster** CA – author, lecturer, seminars, audio recordings; disaster volunteer with L. A. County Sheriff's Department			C								
93555 **Dan Allen**, 401 S. Chinalake Blvd., **Ridgecrest** CA – 60 delicious recipes for breads, cakes, pies, cookies; 15 of each +10 prize-winning recipes; send $3 & SASE			X		X						
93561 **K-Mart**, 710 West Tehachapi, **Tehachapi** CA ☎(805) 822-7496 – distributor of *Alco ♦Brite* gelled ethanol products			X								X
93561 **Sally Davis**, 21404 Quail Springs Road, **Tehazhapi** CA ☎(805) 822-8364 – *Magic Mill* distributor			X		X		X	X	X		
93611 **BBQ King**, 5095 E. Shepherd Ave., **Clovis** CA ☎(209) 299-2332 – distributor of *Alco ♦Brite* gelled ethanol products			X								X
93613 **ABC Central California**, 2820 Willow Ave., **Clovis** CA ☎(209) 291-7700 – distributor of *Magic Mill* products			X		X			X	X		
93620 **Evergreen Nursery**, 1636 Center Ave., **Dos Palos** CA ☎(209) 392-6640 – distributor of *Alco ♦Brite* gelled ethanol products			X								X
93643 **Offline**, PO Box 231, **North Fork** CA ☎(209) 877-7080		X	X								X
93644 **Climate Control Systems**, 40120 Hwy. 49, **Oakhurst** CA ☎(209) 683-8367 – distributor of *Alco ♦Brite* gelled ethanol products			X								X
93710 **Kristinas Natural Ranch Market**, 761 East Barstow Ave., **Fresno** CA ☎(209) 224-2222			C	X	X	X	X	X	X	X	
93721 **American Red Cross / Fresno-Madera Counties Chapter**, 1841 Fulton Street, **Fresno** CA ☎(209) 486-0701 📠(209) 486-5826 📧www.cybergate.com/redcross/store.html ✉*vtn4241@cybergate.com*			X								X
93727 **Survival & Emergency Food Products**, 4111 N. Perry, **Fresno** CA ☎(209) 292-5528 – distributor of *SamAndy* food storage & preparedness products		X	X	X	X				X	X	X
93923 **Wolf Canyon Foods, Inc.**, 27863 Berwick Dr., **Carmel** CA ☎(408) 626-1323 📠(408) 626-1325 – freeze-dried foods processor; *wholesale only*; fruits, vegetables, beans, rice, meats, & special products: dried cottage cheese, scrambled egg, & non-fat yogurt; available whole, sliced, diced, granules, & powder	X	X								X	
93940 **Heath Shop-Monterey**, 486 Del Monte Center, **Monterey** CA – distributor of *Alco ♦Brite* gelled ethanol products			X								X
93940 **Joan Miller**, 1052 Paloma Road, **Del Ray Oaks** CA ☎(408) 394-5761 – distributor of *Magic Mill* products			X		X			X	X		
94022 **New Spirit Naturals**, 130 Lyell, **Los Altos** CA ☎(415) 949-2412 – distributor of *Green Magic*, synergistic blend of 15 all-natural ingredients providing the essence of nutrition	X	X						X			
94025 **Shelter Systems**, 224 W. O'Connor, **Menlo Park** CA ☎(415) 323-6202 – instant domes & greenhouses set up in 20 minutes; many models; color catalog for $1.00	X	X									X
94040 **Marcella Lynch**, 1325 Isabella Avenue, **Mountain View** CA ☎(415) 969-9838 – distributor of *Magic Mill* products			X		X			X	X		
94040 **Safety Central**, 1100 W. El Camino Real, **Mountain View** CA ☎(415) 965-3509 – distributor of *Alco ♦Brite* gelled ethanol products			X								X
94040 **The Stove Works**, 575 W. El Camino Real, **Mountain View** CA ☎(415) 909-9001 – distributor of *Alco ♦Brite* gelled ethanol products			X								X

M = Manufacturer / Processor	D = Wholesaler / Trade distributor	R = Distributor / Retailer to public	M	D	R	04	05	12	13	14	15	16	17
94043 Kroeger & Associates, 231 Sierra Vista, **Mountain View** CA ☎(415) 969-1982 — distributor of *Alco♦Brite* gelled ethanol products				X								X
94044 Pacifica Farmers Market, 450 Manor Plaza, **Pacifica** CA ☎(415) 355-0668					C	X	X	X	X	X	X		
94060 Phipps Country, PO Box 349, **Pescadero** CA ☎(800) 279-0889 🖷(415) 879-1622 — organically grown soybeans, whole soybeans			X	X								X
94087 Wild Oats, 1265 South Mary St., **Sunnyvale** CA ☎(408) 730-1310 🖷(408) 730-9223				X	X	X	X	X	X	X	X	
94103 San Francisco Herb Co., 250 14th Street, **San Francisco** CA ☎(414) 861-7174 or (800) 227-4530 🖷(415) 861-4440 🖳www.sfherb.com — importer & distributor dealing uniquely in spices, spice blends, dehydrated vegetables, shelled nuts & seeds, bulk tea & bags, bulk herb tea blends, sprouting seeds, gelatin caps, kelp, & herbs; mail-order bulk & pre-packed units			X	X	X				X		X	
94107 Good Life Grocery, 1524 20th St., **San Francisco** CA ☎(415) 282-9204					C	X	X	X	X	X	X	X
94107 Tilia, Inc., 340 Townsend St., **San Francisco** CA ☎(800) 777-5452 — *Foodsaver®* kitchen vacuum-sealing equipment & supplies		X	X									
94109 Earthquake Outlet, 900 North Point St. #E1 Rose Ct. (Ghirardelli Sq.), **San Francisco** CA ☎(415) 674-9091 🖷(415) 674-9093 — disaster preparedness for human survival; medical aid & care; sanitation/hygiene; rescue/escape; & non-structural hazards; comprehensive preparedness products inventory				X	X	X	X		X	X	X	
94109 Searchlight Market, 1964 Hyde St., **San Francisco** CA ☎(415) 673-1010					C	X	X	X	X	X	X	X
94109 Whole Foods Market, 1765 California St., **San Francisco** CA ☎(415) 674-0500 🖷(415) 674-0505			X	X	X	X	X	X	X	X	X	
94110 Good Life Grocery, 448 Cortland Ave., **San Francisco** CA ☎(415) 648-3221					C	X	X	X	X	X	X	X
94114 Jawad Market, 98½ Sanchez St., **San Francisco** CA ☎(415) 861-1027					C	X	X	X	X	X	X	X
94117 Ashbury Market, 205 Frederick Street, **San Francisco** CA ☎(415) 566-3134					C	X	X	X	X	X	X	X
94117 Haight Street Natural Foods, 1621 Haight St., **San Francisco** CA ☎(415) 487-1540					C	X	X	X	X	X	X	X
94117 Haight-Ashbury Produce, 1615 Haight St., **San Francisco** CA ☎(415) 861-5672					C	X	X	X	X	X	X	X
94117 Sunrise Market, 588 Haight St., **San Francisco** CA ☎(415) 431-2311					C	X	X	X	X	X	X	X
94118 Village Market, 4555 California St., **San Francisco** CA ☎(415) 221-0445					C	X	X	X	X	X	X	X
94119 Valencia Farmers Market, 1299 Valencia St., **San Francisco** CA ☎(415) 282-6863					C	X	X	X	X	X	X	X
94122 Crisis Management Systems, 4115 Irving St., **San Francisco** CA ☎(415) 661-8500 or (888) 723-3897 🖷(415) 661-8500 🖳www.safetystore.com ✉cms@safetystore.com — planning, training, assessment; business preparedness & recovery; disaster management experts		X	X	X						X	X	X
94122 Safety Store, 4115 Irving St., **San Francisco** CA ☎(888) 723-3897 🖷(415) 661-8500 🖳www.safetystore.com ✉orders@safetystore.com — mail-order only for emergency & disaster preparedness products for home, business, & pet safety				X	X	X	X		X	X	X	
94123 Wild Oats, 2324 Chestnut Street, **San Francisco** CA ☎(415) 921-2992 🖷(415) 921-2244			X	X	X	X	X	X	X	X	X	
94124 Bayshore Farmers Market, 300 Bayshore Blvd., **San Francisco** CA ☎(415) 647-1806					C	X	X	X	X	X	X	X
94127 Tower Market, PO Box 27587, **San Francisco** CA ☎(415) 664-1600					C	X	X	X	X	X	X	X
94203 Mountain House Freeze Dried Foods Dealer, 1120 Fulton Ave., **Sacramento** CA ☎(916) 488-4888			X								X	
94301 Whole Foods Market, 774 Emerson Street, **Palo Alto** CA ☎(415) 326-8676 🖷(415) 326-0539			X	X	X	X	X	X	X	X	X	
95050 Barbara Salsbury, 1135 MaryAnne Drive, Santa Clara CA ☎/🖷(408) 984-8611 — author of several books on food storage, emergency preparedness, & consumerism; expert advisor to consumers		X	X	X (C)								X
94523 Foods Unlimited, 15 Cornell Court, **Pleasant Hill** CA ☎(510) 938-5015 or (800) 823-5122 🖷(510) 938-5015 🖳www.universalweb.com/food ✉ron@universalweb.com — *Bosch Kitchen Machine* distributor			X			X		X		X	X	
94530 El Cerrito Natural Foods, 10367 San Pablo Ave., **El Cerrito** CA ☎(510) 526-0672					C	X	X	X	X	X	X	X
94538 San Francisco Herb & Natural Food Company, 47444 Kato Road, **Fremont** CA ☎(800) 227-2830 or (510) 770-1215 🖷(510) 770-9021 — herbs for manufacturing purposes: whole, cut & sifted, tea-bag cut, or powder form; *institutional sales only*		X	X						X		X	
94546 Valley Stove & Chimney, 3180 Castro Valley Blvd., **Castro Valley** CA ☎(510) 538-7883 — distributor of *Alco♦Brite* gelled ethanol products			X									X
94550 Dom's Outdoor Outfitters, 1870 First St., **Livermore** CA ☎(800) 447-9629 🖷(510) 447-0195 — authorized retail distributor of *Mountain House* brand freeze-dried products		X	X								X	
94550 Helen Totten, 486 Encino Drive, **Livermore** CA ☎(510) 449-6370				X	X	X	X	X		X		X
94559 Vallergas Market, 301 1st St., **Napa** CA ☎(707) 253-1666					C	X	X	X	X	X	X	X
94565 Eric Jones, 2243 Westwood Court, **Pittsburgh** CA ☎(510) 709-0389 — distributor of *Magic Mill* products			X			X			X		X	
94565 Secure Future Food & Supplies, 640 Bailery Rd. #188, **Pittsburg** CA 🖳www.securefuture.com ✉sales@securefuture.com — distributor of *Ready Reserve* brand long-term food storage products		X	X	X	X	X	X			X	X	X
94574 Don Brehm, 787 Silverado Trail South, **St. Helena** CA ☎None — distributor of *Magic Mill* products								X		X	X	
94577 Allergy Research Group, 400 Preda St., **San Leandro** CA ☎(800) 545-9960			X						X			

Product References Keyed to Chapters (Cont.)

04 water / air filtration & treatment	05 grains, seeds, mills & equip.	12 dairy / powdered milk supplies	13 honey / sweeteners
14 vitamins / minerals / herbs	15 sprouting / equip. & supplies	16 dry / dehydrated / freeze-dried	17 energy / fuels

M = Manufacturer / Processor D = Wholesaler / Trade distributor R = Distributor / Retailer to public

Company & Address	M	D	R	04	05	12	13	14	15	16	17
94578 Top Notch, 1225 MacArthur, **San Leandro** CA ☎(510) 481-5100 — distributor of *Alco ◆Brite* gelled ethanol products		X							✓		X
94585 B & K2, Fairfield CA ☎(707) 427-3770 ▤(707) 427-1743 ✉*bnk2@community.net* — wood, pellet, & gas stoves; fireplaces	X										X
94587 Delta Spice Works, Inc., 33453 Western Ave., **Union City** CA ☎(800) 394-7742 ▤(510) 487-8011 — seasonings & blends for the food storage industry; custom blends for soups, sauces, & specialty recipes; custom recipe development & blended food ingredients; non-animal beef & poultry blends; organic blends	X	X						X			
94602 California Disaster Preparedness & Supply, 4988 Hedge Lane, **Oakland** CA ☎(510) 339-0513 ▤(510) 339-9394 — preparedness products & food storage items; mail-order prescriptions filled for long-term storage purposes		C	X	X							X
94608 Macrobiotic Grocery, 1050 40ᵗʰ Street, **Oakland** CA ☎(510) 653-6510			C	X	X	X	X	X	X	X	
94608 Sierra Designs, 1255 Powell Street, **Emeryville** CA ☎(510) 450-9555 — gear for backpacking, skiing, climbing, & biking; tents & sleeping bags for the discriminating	X	X									X
94611 Cole's Honey Co., PO Box 11150, **Piedmont** CA ☎(510) 654-3803	X	X	X				X				X
94611 The Book Tree, 6121 LaSalle, **Oakland** CA (510) 339-0513 Fax (510) 339-9394		X									
94703 Wild Oats, 1581 University Ave., **Berkeley** CA ☎(510) 549-1714 ▤(510) 549-9985			X	X	X	X	X	X	X	X	
94705 Whole Foods Market, 3000 Telegraph Avenue, **Berkeley** CA ☎(510) 649-1333 ▤(510) 649-1474 — natural & organic dairy, fruit, meats & vegetable foods; vitamins & supplements; bulk & pre-pack foods			X	X	X	X	X	X	X	X	
94706 Earthquake Outlet, 981 San Pablo Avenue, **Albany** CA ☎(510) 526-3587 ▤(510) 526-3589 — disaster preparedness concerns: human survival; medical aid & care; sanitation/hygiene; rescue/escape; & non-structural hazards; disaster preparedness products; distributor of *Alco ◆Brite* gelled ethanol products		X	X	X					X	X	X
94707 Traveling Light, 1563 Solano Ave. #284, **Berkeley** CA — manufacturer of the ultra-light *Outback Oven*; accessories & cookware; pre-packaged entrees, breads, & desserts	X	X		X							X
94710 Tubmakers, Berkeley CA ▤(510) 843-2000 ▤(916) 843-5722 ✉*info@tubmakers.com* — pellet & wood stoves		X	X								X
94901 Earthquake Supply Center, 509-B Francisco Blvd. East, **San Rafael** CA ☎(415) 459-5500 or (800) 728-8531 ▤*www.eflat.com/esc/index/html* ✉*rattle1@microweb.com*		X	X	X						X	X
94901 Whole Foods Market, 340 Third Street, **San Rafael** CA			X	X	X	X	X	X	X	X	
94903 Solar Depot, Inc., 61 Paul Dr., **San Raphael** CA ☎(800) 822-4041 or (415) 499-1333	X										X
94904 Kuhn-Rikon Duromatic Pressure Cookers, Greenbrae CA ☎(800) 662-5882 — US distributor of Swiss-made pressure cooker with integrated lid-locking system	X										
94904 Woodlands Market, 735 College Ave., **Kentfield** CA ☎(415) 457-8160			C	X	X	X	X	X	X	X	
94924 Bolinas People's Store, PO Box 808, **Bolinas** CA ☎(415) 868-1433			C	X	X	X	X	X	X	X	
94925 David's Finest Produce, 341 Corte Madera Town Center, **Corte Madera** CA ☎(405) 927-2431			C	X	X	X	X	X	X	X	
94928 Solar Electric Eng., Inc., 175 Cascade Court, **Rohnert Park** CA ☎(707) 586-1987 ▤(707) 586-0690	X	X									X
94931 Larsen's Feed, 7400 Gravenstein Hwy., **Cotati** CA ☎(707) 795-4106 — distributor of *Alco ◆Brite* gelled ethanol products		X									X
94941 Roots & Legends, 38 Miller Ave., **Mill Valley** CA ☎(415) 381-5631 — Chinese herbs & patent medicines		X						X			
94941 Whole Foods Market, 414 Miller Ave., **Mill Valley** CA ☎(415) 381-1200 ▤(415) 381-1036			X	X	X	X	X	X	X	X	
94942 The Whole Herb Company, 250 E. Blithdale Avenue, **Mill Valley** CA ☎(415) 383-6485 — wholesale only; bulk dried herbs		X	C					X		X	
94949 Freeze Dry Products USA, Inc., 68 Leveroni Court, **Novato** CA ☎(415) 883-1340 — bulk freeze-dried fruits & vegetables; dehydrated vegetables; 100-lb. min. + freight; *wholesale only*		X	X							X	
94960 Emerald Energy Products / Pine Street Prod., 124 Pine St., **San Anselmo** CA ☎(415) 456-7741 — dynamic & balanced food formulas to enhance well-being & increase vitality & info		X						X			
94960 Wild Oats, 222 Greenfield Ave., **San Anselmo** CA ☎(415) 258-0660 ▤(415) 457-4317			X	X	X	X	X	X	X	X	
95006 Bogart Engineering, 19020 Two Bar Rd., **Boulder Creek** CA ☎(408) 338-0616	X	X									X
95008 EPK—Emergency Products Kits, 1901 South Bascom #1525, **Campbell** CA ☎(800) 377-3722 ▤(408) 377-3263 ▤*www.epks.com* ✉*webmaster@epks.com* — preparedness information center; corporate, retail, wholesale, & fund-raising programs; custom-made kits		X	X	X	X					X	X
95008 Whole Foods Market, 1690 S. Bascom Avenue, **Campbell** CA ☎(408) 371-5000 ▤(408) 371-8784			X	X	X	X	X	X	X	X	
95014 PowerStar Products, Inc., 10011 N. Foothill Blvd., **Cupertino** CA ☎(800) 645-4004	X	X									X
95014 Whole Foods Market, 20830 Stevens Creek Blvd., **Cupertino** CA ☎(408) 257-7000 ▤(408 257-1475			X	X	X	X	X	X	X	X	
95017 Harris Hydroelectric, 632 Swanton Rd., **Davenport** CA ☎(408) 425-7652	X	X									X
95032 Whole Foods Market, 15980 Los Gatos Blvd., **Los Gatos** CA ☎408) 358-4434 ▤(408) 358-4433			X	X	X	X	X	X	X	X	
95037 LauraAnne J. Logar, 17140 Oak Leaf Drive, **Morgan Hill** CA ☎(408) 778-2139 ▤*http://pages.prodigy.com/frugal-tightwad-foodstorage* ✉*tjza00f@prodigy.com* — author of "*Making Food Storage Fast, Fun & Easy*"; in-home storage specialist; visit the website for information		X									

M = Manufacturer / Processor	D = Wholesaler / Trade distributor	R = Distributor / Retailer to public	M	D	R	04	05	12	13	14	15	16	17
95043 Sanderson's Rebuilt Vacuums, 20295 Panoche Rd., **Paicines** CA ☎(408) 628-3362 — re-manufactured vacuum cleaners for alternate energy systems			X	X									X
95060 Cutting Edge Enterprises, 1803 Mission St. #546, **Santa Cruz** CA			X	X									X
95060 Nature's Bounty, 811 Pacific Ave., **Santa Cruz** CA ☎(408) 458-9055					C		X	X	X	X	X	X	
95060 New Leaf Market, 2351 Mission St., **Santa Cruz** CA ☎(408) 426-1306					C		X	X	X	X	X	X	
95062 Falcon Trading Co., 1055 17ᵗʰ Avenue, **Santa Cruz** CA ☎(800) 655-3252 or (408) 462-1280 — wholesale distributor of natural organic & packaged foods			X	C				X	X	X	X	X	
95062 SunRidge Farms, 1055 17ᵗʰ Avenue, **Santa Cruz** CA ☎(408) 462-1280 — bulk supplier of organic beans & legumes since 1977; free bean & legumes recipes			X	X				X				X	X
95062 Wood Stove & Sun, 510 Soquel Ave., **Santa Cruz** CA ☎(408) 425-5123 — distributor of *Alco♦Brite* gelled ethanol products					X								X
95063 Daisyfresh Dairy Cultures, Box 36, **Santa Cruz** CA — supplier of cultures for cheesemaking & yogurt			X	X	C			X					X
95073 Sunnyside Produce, 2520 Main St., **Soquel** CA ☎(408) 476-8904					C		X	X	X	X	X	X	
95117 Unique Products, 1129 Andrea Drive, **San Jose** CA ☎(408) 243-2826 🖷(408) 246-8909 — garden tools					X								X
95123 BeeHive Country Store, 5897 Winfield Blvd., **San Jose** CA ☎(408) 225-3531					C		X	X	X	X	X	X	X
95128 Valley Fireplaces, 1330 N. Bascom, **San Jose** CA					X								X
95129 Linda Young Soon Bak / YS Good, 1039 Danbury, **San Jose** CA ☎(408) 996-1484 — *Magic Mill* distributor					X			X			X		
95153 Eureka Resource, Box 53565, **San Jose** CA — homesteading & survival pamphlets & products					X								
95307 Favorite Things (*attn: Glynda DePee*) 2449 Faith Home Road, **Ceres** CA ☎(209) 537-6939 — distributor of *Bosch & Kitchen Specialties* products			X	X	X			X			X		
95336 Taylor West, PO Box 2005, **Manteca** CA ☎(209) 239-7788 or (800) 595-7788 — outside hot water furnace heats entire home & hot water; burns almost any combustible material & heats for days			X	X									X
95338 High Country Health Foods, PO Box 187, **Mariposa** CA ☎(209) 966-5111					C		X	X	X	X	X	X	
95338 The Healthy Life Company, PO Box 1913, **Mariposa** CA ☎(209) 742-6397 — medical-grade ozone purifiers, hydrogen peroxide; orthopedic pillows; medical supplies & more			X	X					X				X
95354 Survival Enterprises, 1029 8ᵗʰ Street, **Modesto** CA ☎(209) 527-4330 🖷(209) 527-4343 🖳http://survival.simplenet.com ✉gunrunner@earthlink.net — distributor of emergency & disaster supplies & products			X	X	X							X	X
95360 Valley Sun Products of California, Inc., PO Box 549, **Newman** CA ☎(800) 426-5444 🖳www.valleysun.com — sun-dried tomato products			X	X								X	
95401 Buck Stove Pool & Spa, 225 W. Collage Ave., **Santa Rosa** CA ☎(707) 527-7277 — distributor of *Alco♦Brite* gelled ethanol products					X								X
95403 Good Stuff Market & Deli, 1760 Piner Road, **Santa Rosa** CA ☎(707) 544-6067					C		X	X	X	X	X	X	
95403 Hearth & Color Shop, 3450 Airway Drive, **Santa Rosa** CA 🖷(707) 526-3322 🖷(707) 526-7963 ✉buchart@hearthshop.com			X	X									X
95405 Skandera Kitchen Products, 1932 Creekside Road, **Santa Rosa** CA ☎(707) 526-3268 — *Magic Mill, Kitchen Specialties, & Bosch Kitchen Machines*					X			X			X	X	
95407 New Wave Pool & Spa, 3774 Santa Rosa Ave., **Santa Rosa** CA — distributor of *Alco♦Brite* gelled ethanol products					X								X
95409 Preparedness Resources, 626 Middle Rencon Road, **Santa Rosa** CA ☎(707) 538-0937 🖷(707) 539-3672					C			X	X	X	X	X	
95410 OMNI Instruments, PO Box 96, **Albion** CA ☎(707) 468-0878			X	X									X
95437 Dwyer's Stove Works, 200 East Redwood, **Fort Bragg** CA ☎(707) 964-7337 — distributor of *Alco♦Brite* gelled ethanol products					X								X
95437 G.E.M. Cultures, 30301 Sherwood Road, **Ft. Bragg** CA ☎(707) 964-2922 — cultures for homemade soyfoods and tempeh			X	X				X			X		
95437 Purity Market, 242 N. Franklin St., **Fort Bragg** CA ☎(707) 964-0747					C		X	X	X	X	X	X	
95444 Willow Wood Market, PO Box 416, **Graton** CA ☎(707) 823-0233					C		X	X	X	X	X	X	
95448 Timber Crest Farms, 4791 Dry Creek Road, **Healdsburg** CA ☎(707) 433-8251 🖷(707) 433-8255 — mail-order unsulfured dried foods: *Sonoma Brand* dried tomatoes, dried fruits, nuts, & specialty foods			X	X				X				X	
95449 Real Goods Solar Living Ctr. – Hopland, Hwy. 101 S., **Hopland** CA ☎(707) 744-2100 🖷(707) 744-1342 — retail store & catalog mail-order products for energy independence & a safe home, solar equipment & supplies, efficient lighting equipment, natural pest control, books; renewable energy; & lots more			X	X								X	X
95453 Nature's Food Center, 601 N. Forbes, **Lakeport** CA ☎(707) 263-5359					C		X	X	X	X	X	X	
95454 The Good Food Store, PO Box 340, **Laytonville** CA ☎(707) 984-6118					C		X	X	X	X	X	X	
95461 Harbin Resident Co-op, PO Box 782, **Middletown** CA ☎(707) 987-3913					C		X	X	X	X	X	X	
95472 Bill's Farm Basket, 10315 Bodega Highway, **Sebastopol** CA ☎(707) 829-1777					C		X	X	X	X	X	X	X

Product References Keyed to Chapters (Cont.)

	M	D	R	04	05	12	13	14	15	16	17
04 water / air filtration & treatment — 05 grains, seeds, mills & equip. — 12 dairy / powdered milk supplies — 13 honey / sweeteners — 14 vitamins / minerals / herbs — 15 sprouting / equip. & supplies — 16 dry / dehydrated / freeze-dried — 17 energy / fuels	M = Manufacturer / Processor	D = Wholesaler / Trade distributor	R = Distributor / Retailer to public								

Listing	M	D	R	04	05	12	13	14	15	16	17
95472 Vacu-Dry, 7765 Healdsburg Avenue, **Sebastapol** CA ☎(707) 829-4600 🖷(707) 829-4643 — major dehydrator/processor of fruits & vegetables, blends, & mixes; *contract sales only to industrial buyers*	X									X	
95473 General Hydroponics, PO Box 1576, **Sebastopol** CA ☎(800) 37-HYDRO or (707) 824-9376 🖷(707) 824-9377 www.genhydro.com ✉GenHydro@monitor.net — major manufacturer of hydroponics equipment & supplies; dealers worldwide	X	X	C								X
95482 Naturally Pure Alternatives, 575 Live Oak Ave., **Ukiah** CA ☎/🖷(707) 462-1000 or ☎(800) 645-5225 — water-quality testing facility; for those interested in knowing quality of water being used		X	X	X							
95482 Real Goods – Ukiah, 966 Mazzoni Street, **Ukiah** CA ☎(707) 468-9486 or (800) 762-7325 🖷(707) 468-0301 🖳www.realgoods.com — retail store & catalog mail-order; products for energy independence & a safe home, solar equipment & supplies, efficient lighting equipment, natural pest control, books; renewable energy; & lots more!		X	X	X						X	X
95488 West Port Community Store, PO Box 7, **West Port** CA ☎(707) 964-2872			C		X	X	X	X	X	X	X
95490 Jeff's Gas Appliances, 549 Central St., **Willits** CA ☎(707) 459-5223	X	X									X
95490 Photron, Inc., PO Box 578, **Willits** CA ☎(800) PHOTRON 🖷(707) 459-2165	X	X									X
95521 E. & O. Market, 1451 Glendale Drive, **Arcata** CA ☎(707) 822-1157			C		X	X	X	X	X	X	
95521 North Coast Co-op, 977 9th St., **Arcata** CA ☎(707) 826-8669			C		X	X	X	X	X	X	X
95521 Sun Frost, PO Box 1101, **Arcata** CA ☎(707) 822-9095	X	X									X
95521 Tofu Shop Specialty Foods, 100 Ericson Ct. #150, **Arcata** CA ☎(707) 822-7401			C		X	X	X	X	X	X	X
95521 Whole Food Express, 811 I St., **Arcata** CA ☎(707) 822-5947			C		X	X	X	X	X	X	X
95521 Wildberries Marketplace, 747 13th St., **Arcata** CA ☎(707) 822-0095			C		X	X	X	X	X	X	X
95540 C. Crane Co., 558 10th St., **Fortuna** CA ☎(800) 522-TUNE	X	X									X
95560 Alternative Energy Engineering, PO Box 339, **Redway** CA ☎(707) 923-7216 or (800) 777-6609 🖳www.asis.com/aee	X	X	X								X
95602 Mountain Peoples Warehouse, 12745 Earhart Avenue, **Auburn** CA ☎(916) 889-9531 **Territory: CA, ID, NV, OR, UT, HI** — full line distributor of natural & conventional fresh, dried, & bulk foods	X	C			X	X	X	X	X	X	X
95603 Farmers' Rice Cooperative, PO Box 15223, **Sacramento** CA ☎(916) 373-5555 🖷(916) 372-1288 — production, milling, &/or distribution of rice & processed rice products	X	X			X			X			
95603 Green Heart Market, 140 Cleveland, **Auburn** CA ☎(916) 885-5478			C		X	X	X	X	X	X	X
95604 American Red Cross, PO Box 4219, **Auburn** CA ☎(916) 885-9392			X	X	X	X			X	X	X
95611 Abersold Foods, PO Box 3927, **Citrus Heights** CA ☎(800) 275-1437 🖷(800) 497-4329 — producer of dry milk options; *Vegalicious & Snowy Tofu* powder						X					X
95624 Advanced Electronics, 8525 Elk Grove Blvd. #106, **Elk Grove** CA ☎(916) 687-7666	X	X	X	X	X	X			X	X	X
95661 The Rice Company, 1624 Santa Clara #23C, **Roseville** CA ☎(916) 784-7745 🖷(916) 784-7681 — production, milling, &/or distribution of rice & processed rice products	X	X			X			X			
95662 The General Store, 6725 Smithart Street, **Orangevale** CA ☎(916) 721-4508 🖷(916) 721-4508						X	X				X
95663 Wellness Institute for Personal Transformation, 8300 Rock Springs Rd., **Penryn** CA ☎(916) 663-3910 or (800) 655-3846 🖷(916) 663-9178 — professional neuro-cellular re-patterning; non-profit corporation for lectures, seminars, & workshops	X							X			
95667 Noah's Ark Natural Foods, 535 Placerville Drive, **Placerville** CA ☎(916) 621-3663 — also distributor of *Magic Mill* products			C		X	X	X	X	X	X	X
95682 Placerville Energy Center, 3971 Durock Rd. #8, **Shingle Springs** CA ☎(916) 677-5755 — distributor of *Alco ♦Brite* gelled ethanol products	X										X
95687 Nutrition Shoppe, 1005 Alamo Drive, **Vacaville** CA ☎(707) 447-2306			C		X	X	X	X	X	X	X
95689 Big Trees Market, 25020 Shake Ridge Road, **Volcano** CA ☎(209) 295-7525			C		X	X	X	X	X	X	X
95691 Rice Growers Assoc. of CA, 1550 Harbor Blvd. #200, **West Sacramento** CA ☎(916) 371-6941 — production, milling, &/or distribution of rice & processed rice products 371-6941 🖷(916) 372-7158	X	X			X			X			
95695 Clear Water Trader, 637 Fairview Drive, **Woodland** CA ☎(916) 661-1507 or (800) 440-9904		X	X	X						X	X
95730 Tahoe Community Market, PO Box 863, **Tahoe City** CA ☎(916) 583-3156			C		X	X	X	X	X	X	X
95736 Weimar Country Store, 206041 West Paoli Lane, **Weimer** CA ☎(800) 525-9191	X				X			X		X	
95746 Hardware Trader, 7807 Kirk, **Granite Bay** CA — emergency preparedness supplies; paratrooper flashlight for emergencies	X	X									X
95776 Pacific International Rice Mills, Inc., 845 Kentucky Avenue, **Woodland** CA ☎(916) 666-1691	X	X			X			X			
95814 Solar Cookers International, 1919 21st Street #101, **Sacramento** CA 🖳www.accessone.com/~sbcn ✉sbci@igc.apc.org	X	X									X
95814 The Solar Syndicate, 114 K St., **Sacramento** CA 🖷(800) 701-4449 🖷(916) 447-6426 — wood stoves, gas stoves, fireplaces, pellet stoves & much more…	X	X									X
95818 Harvest Market, 171 Boatyard Drive, **Fort Bragg** CA ☎(707) 964-7034			C		X	X	X	X	X	X	X
95824 Excalibur, 6083 Power Inn Road, **Sacramento** CA ☎(800) 875-4254 🖳www.kctc.net/life/excalho — manufacturer of *Excalibur* dehydrators & grain grinders; kitchen utensils for processing fruits & vegetables	X	X	X		X					X	

M = Manufacturer / Processor — D = Wholesaler / Trade distributor — R = Distributor / Retailer to public	M	D	R	04	05	12	13	14	15	16	17
95825 **Santa Fe Marketplace**, 611 Munroe St., **Sacramento** CA ☎(916) 482-4199			C	X	X	X	X	X	X	X	X
95826 **Solar Depot, Inc.**, 8605 Folsom Blvd., **Sacramento** CA ☎(800) 321-0101 or (916) 381-0235		X	X								X
95829 **Pg. 1 Building Products**, PO Box 292850, **Sacramento** CA ☎(916) 381-4242 – distributor of *Alco ♦Brite* gelled ethanol products		X									X
95831 **Natural Value Products**, **Sacramento** CA 🖷(916) 427-3784 ✉*NaturalVal@aol.com* – mail-order; premium quality natural & organic products discounted; shipped direct from the manufacturer		X			X				X	X	X
95851 **Farmers' Rice Co-op**, 2325 Natomas Park Dr., **Sacramento** CA ☎(916) 568-4351 🖷(916) 920-3321 – cooperative for milling & marketing organic & conventional rice products	X	X	C	X		X		X		X	X
95912 **California Family Food**, PO Box 1230, **Arbuckle** CA ☎(916) 476-3326 🖷(916) 476-3524 – production, milling, &/or distribution of rice & processed rice products	X	X		X						X	
95912 **California Pacific Rice, LTD.**, PO Box 725, **Arbuckle** CA ☎(916) 476-3235 🖷(916) 476-3536 – production, milling, &/or distribution of rice & processed rice products	X	X		X						X	
95912 **Shannon's Farmers Market**, PO Box 29, **Arbuckle** CA ☎(916) 473-3190			C	X	X	X	X	X	X	X	X
95926 **Greenfire, Inc.**, 347 Nord Ave. #1, **Chico** CA ☎(800) 895-8307 – hydroponics equipment & *Earth Juices* distributor		X	X								X
95928 **Today's Traditions**, 2560 Dominic Dr. #1, **Chico** CA ☎(916) 893-2646			C	X	X	X	X	X	X	X	X
95938 **Far West Rice, Inc.**, PO Box 370, **Durham** CA ☎(916) 891-1339 🖷(916) 891-0723 – production, milling, &/or distribution of rice & processed rice products	X	X		X						X	
95945 **Olive Drab Enterprises**, PO Box 3282, **Grass Valley** CA ☎(916) 346-8470 – survival & preparedness products; military surplus items; first aid kits & supplies; block magnesium & magnesium fire starters; water filters, & more!	X	X	X	X	X	X	X		X	X	X
95945 **Solar Quest**, 11743 Maltman Dr., **Grass Valley** CA ☎(800) 959-6354 🖷(916) 477-5631		X	X								X
95945 **Underground Shelters of America**, PO Box 3282, **Grass Valley** CA ☎(916) 346-8470 – underground direct burial shelter for food storage, concealment, documents, extra room, root or wine cellar	X	X	C								X
95947 **Cheryl Flint**, 6120 Diamond Mt. Rd., **Greenville** CA ☎(916) 284-7077			X	X			X		X		
95949 **Freedom Food**, 10624 Sharmiden Way, **Grass Valley** CA ☎(916) 268-1826 ✉*freedom@inreach.com* – distributor of *AlpineAire* freeze-dried foods			C	X	X	X	X		X	X	
95959 **AlpineAire Foods (Corp. Ofc.)**, PO Box 926, **Nevada City** CA ☎(916) 272-1971 or (800) 322-6325 🖷(916) 272-2624 🖳www.alpineaire.com – producer & wholesale distributor; complete line of freeze-dried & dehydrated foods; backpacking foods; soy beans, dry beans, millet, & cornmeal; emergency food items; just add water; more than 200 items available in cans and backpacking pouches; distributor of *Alco ♦Brite* gelled ethanol products	X	X	C	X	X	X	X		X	X	X
95959 **Ananda Power Technologies, Inc.**, 14618 Tyler Foote Rd., **Nevada City** CA ☎(916) 292-3834 🖷(916) 292-3330 ✉*apt@aptsolar.com*		X	X								X
95959 **Earth Song**, 135-A Argall Way, **Nevada City** CA ☎(916) 265-9392			C	X	X	X	X	X	X	X	X
95959 **Harmony Ridge Market**, PO Box 2013, **Nevada City** CA ☎(916) 265-5761			C	X	X	X	X	X	X	X	X
95959 **Herb Shop**, 107 N. Pine, **Nevada City** CA ☎(916) 265-6854			C	X	X	X	X	X	X	X	X
95959 **Sierra Solar Systems**, 109 Argall Way, **Nevada City** CA ☎(800) 51-SOLAR 🖳www.sierrasolar.com –140-page guidebook/catalog has complete information for complete systems of solar-electric, wind, hydropower, & solar pumping; catalog for $5.00, refundable		X	X								X
95966 **Skipper A. Clark**, 96 Canyon Highlands, **Oroville** CA ☎(916) 534-3924 🖷(916) 534-1796			C	X	X	X	X		X	X	X
95971 **Mac's Country Woodstoves**, 91 Bradley St., **Quincy** CA ☎(916) 283-2929 – distributor of *Alco ♦Brite* gelled ethanol products		X									
95974 **Lundberg Family Farms**, 5370 Church Street, **Richvale** CA ☎(916) 882-4551 🖷(916) 882-4500 – production, milling, &/or distribution of rice & processed rice products	X	X		X						X	
95987 **Williams Rice Milling Co.**, PO Box 1539, **Williams** CA ☎(916) 473-2862 🖷(916) 473-2406 – production, milling, &/or distribution of rice & processed rice products	X	X		X						X	
96002 **Enterprize Health Foods**, 2968 Churn Creek Road, **Redding** CA ☎(916) 222-4402 – distributor of *Magic Mill* products		X		X				X		X	
96002 **Rainbow Pellet Hearth & Home**, 20181 Charlanne Dr., **Redding** CA ☎(916) 223-6833 – distributor of *Alco ♦Brite* gelled ethanol products		X									X
96002 **Rainbow Pellet Hearth & Home**, **Redding** CA ☎(916) 223-6833 or 🖷(916) 223-0543		X									X
96009 **Beverly Swarm**, 107 South 1st Street, PO Box 506, **Bieber** CA ☎(209) 781-5187 – *Magic Mill Kitchen* equipment & products dealer		X		X				X		X	
96021 **Low's Feed Corral**, 5605 Hwy. 99 W., **Corning** CA ☎(916) 824-2816 – distributor of *Alco ♦Brite* gelled ethanol products		X									X
96028 **Fall River Wild Rice**, Osprey Drive, **Fall River Mills** CA – grower of rice; processed rice products	X	X		X						X	
96044 **Electron Connection**, PO Box 203, **Hornbrook** CA ☎(916) 475-3401 ✉*econnect@snowcrest.net*		X	X								X
96044 **Lil' Otto Hydroworks!**, PO Box 203, **Hornbrook** CA ☎(916) 475-3401		X	X								X
96049 **East Earth Trade Winds**, PO Box 493151, **Redding** CA ☎(800) 258-6878 – Chinese herbs & patent medicines		X					X				

Product References Keyed to Chapters (Cont.)

04 water / air filtration & treatment	05 grains, seeds, mills & equip.	12 dairy / powdered milk supplies	13 honey / sweeteners
14 vitamins / minerals / herbs	15 sprouting / equip. & supplies	16 dry / dehydrated / freeze-dried	17 energy / fuels

Listing	M	D	R	04	05	12	13	14	15	16	17
M = Manufacturer / Processor — D = Wholesaler / Trade distributor — R = Distributor / Retailer to public											
96067 **Berryvale Grocery**, 305 Mt. Shasta Blvd., **Mt. Shasta** CA ☎(916) 926-3666			C		X	X	X	X	X	X	X
96067 **Lassen Lane Grocery**, 905 Lassen Lane, **Mt. Shasta** CA ☎(916) 926-1712			C		X	X	X	X	X	X	X
96080 **North Valley Carpet & Woodstoves**, 440 Antelope Blvd. #2, **Red Bluff** CA ☎(916) 527-7288			X								X
– distributor of *Alco ♦Brite* gelled ethanol products											
96093 **Mountain Marketplace**, PO Box 1639, **Weaverville** CA ☎(916) 623-2656			C		X	X	X	X	X	X	X
96122 **South Side Grocery**, 165 Commercial St., **Portola** CA ☎(916) 832-1142			C		X	X	X	X	X	X	X
96146 **Squaw Valley Community Market**, PO Box 3536, **Olympic Valley** CA ☎(916) 581-2014			C		X	X	X	X	X	X	X
96158 **Fallen Leaf Groceries**, PO Box 9512 South Lake Tahoe, **Soquel** CA ☎(916) 541-4671			C		X	X	X	X	X	X	X
96160 **FACT**, PO Box 3928, **Truckee** CA ☎(916) 582-9139 🖷(916) 582-9139		X	X	X	X			X		X	X
96161 **Truckee Community Market**, 11357 Donner Pass Road, **Truckee** CA ☎(916) 587-7426			C		X	X	X	X	X	X	X
96161 **Truckee River Stove**, 12036 Donner Pass Rd., **Truckee** CA ☎(916) 587-9131			X								X
– distributor of *Alco ♦Brite* gelled ethanol products											
96678 **MicroTek Publishers**, 8910 Sunset Ave. #H, **Fair Oaks** CA ☎(916) 966-7718 🖷(916) 966-7768	X	X	X								
– publisher of "*Outback Skills & Survival Techniques*"; dual-indexed First Aid & outback skills booklet; includes lifesaving techniques & details; simple illustrations; what to do & how to survive emergencies											

Colorado

Listing	M	D	R	04	05	12	13	14	15	16	17
80003 **Schultz Honey & Wax, Inc.**, 6625 Pierce St., **Arvada** CO ☎(303) 425-1896	X	X	X				X				
80004 **A & B Surplus**, 10959 W. 62nd Place, **Arvada** CO ☎(303) 238-2078		X	X							X	X
– preparedness products; military surplus											
80004 **Mountain Magic**, 12371 W. 64th Ave., **Arvada** CO ☎(303) 424-1319 or (800) 979-2665		X	X							X	X
– *Multi-Pure* water treatment products; products & appliances for better health	C										
80012 **Maxam Wholesale**, 14190 East Jewell Avenue #6, **Aurora** CO ☎(303) 745-4111 🖷(303) 752-0475		X	X							X	X
– discount retail & catalog order store; bargain-priced preparedness items											
80014 **The Urban Homemaker**, 2527 S. Dawson Way, **Aurora** CO ☎(303) 750-7230 or (800) 552-7323 🖷(303) 750-7193 ✉*UrbanHome@AOL.com*			C	X	X	X	X	X	X	X	X
– old-fashioned skills for contemporary people; food storage products, bread baking equipment & supplies, mixers & grain mills, juicers & dehydrators, & water purification systems											
80014 **Wild Oats**, 12131 East Iliff Ave., **Aurora** CO ☎(303) 695-8801 🖷(303) 695-7739		X	X		X	X	X	X		X	X
80026 **Ken Lewis**, 1560 Belvidere Circle, **Lafayette** CO ☎(303) 666-4601			X			X		X		X	
– consultant on survival training, outdoor & urban survival seminars											
80030 **Pro Environment Grills**, 3705 West 73rd Ave., **Westminster** CO			X								X
– distributor of *Alco ♦Brite* gelled ethanol products											
80104 **InforTel, Ltd.**, PO Box 1777, **Castle Rock** CO ☎(303) 688-8380 🖷(303) 688-8387			X								
– emergency escape smoke hood; 20 minutes of breathable air											
80110 **Carina, Inc.**, 3298 S. Acoma St., **Englewood** CO ☎(303) 781-4328			X								X
– distributor of *Alco ♦Brite* gelled ethanol products											
80110 **Fireplace Equipment of Colorado**, 1295 S. Sheridan #B, **Sheridan** CO ☎(303) 428-6576		X	X								X
80110 **Stove Designs, Inc.**, 69 W. Floyd Ave., **Englewood** CO ☎(303) 781-4328			X								X
– distributor of *Alco ♦Brite* gelled ethanol products											
80111 **Wild Oats**, 6000 S. Holly, **Greenwood Village** CO ☎(303) 796-0996 🖷(303) 796-7126		X	X		X	X	X	X		X	X
80121 **Wild Oats**, 5910 S. University, **Littleton** CO ☎(303) 798-9699 🖷(303) 797-3856		X	X		X	X	X	X		X	X
80124 **Essentials for Health**, 769 Mercury Circle, **Littleton** CO ☎(303) 799-3889	X	X	X								
– *Multi-Pure* water filtration & purification systems for home or emergency use to remove contaminants											
80124 **Karinya for Body, Mind, & Spirit**, 13526 Omega Circle, **Littleton** CO ☎(303) 706-9050 or (800) 454-1356 🖷(303) 706-9050 🖳www.karinya.com ✉*karinya@usa.net*		X	X					X			
80206 **Christian Home Educators of Colorado**, 3739 East 4th Avenue, **Denver** CO ☎(303) 388-1888			X								
– homeschool supplies & newsletter for Coloradoans											
80206 **Northwest Soft Spa**, 270 Columbine, **Cherry Creek** CO ☎(303) 355-9842			X								X
– distributor of *Alco ♦Brite* gelled ethanol products											
80206 **Wild Oats**, 201 University, **Denver** CO ☎(303) 320-9071 🖷(303) 320-4616		X	X		X	X	X	X		X	X
80206 **Wild Oats**, 2260 East Colfax Ave., **Denver** CO ☎(303) 320-1664 🖷(303) 320-6489		X	X		X	X	X	X		X	X
80210 **Just In Case**, 3290 S. Steele St., **Denver** CO ☎(303) 782-0499			C		X	X	X	X		X	
80210 **Wild Oats**, 1111 S. Washington, **Denver** CO ☎(303) 733-6201 🖷(303) 733-6013		X	X		X	X	X	X		X	X
80211 **Advanced Living Technology**, 2438 Meade St., **Denver** CO ☎(303) 480-9226 or (800) 317-9969		X	X			X		X		X	X
80215 **Great Books Educational Supplies**, 9797 West Colfax Avenue #3-SS, **Lakewood** CO ☎(303) 274-0680 or (800) 555-1610 🖷(303) 274-0288			X								
– Colorado's #1 home school supply store; home school subjects bookstore											
80215 **The Green Herb**, 2099 N. Wadsworth, **Lakewood** CO ☎(800) 283-7962			X					X			
80218 **Green's Market**, 1312 East 6th Ave., **Denver** CO ☎(303) 778-8117			C		X	X	X	X	X	X	X

M = Manufacturer / Processor — D = Wholesaler / Trade distributor — R = Distributor / Retailer to public	M	D	R	04	05	12	13	14	15	16	17
80218 Wild Oats, 900 E. 11th Ave., **Denver** CO ☎(303) 832-7701 🖷(303) 831-0438			X	X	X	X	X	X	X	X	
80219 Laura McGuire, 1846 Xavier St., **Denver** CO ☎(303) 935-5777 — distributor of *Magic Mill* products			X		X			X		X	
80224 Nada Chair, 1449 S. Leyden, **Denver** CO ☎(303) 759-4257 — device to aid in proper posture, but not a chair; fits in backpack or purse; great relief for a sore back		X									
80229 Dean Bennett Sy. Co., 1770 E. 69th Ave., **Denver** CO ☎(303) 286-1500 or (800) 621-4291 🖷(303)286-0001 — wholesale distributor; full-line domestic & ranch water well supplies & equipment; windmills; gas pump jacks; hand-operated shallow & deep well pumps; electric pumps for use with generators	X	X	X								X
80300 For The Health Of It, 2525 Arapahoe # E4-153, **Boulder** CO ☎(303) 589-4780			X		X			X		X	
80301 Atwater Carey Ltd., 5505 Central Ave., **Boulder** CO ☎(303) 444-9326 or (800) 359-1646		X	X								X
80301 Backpacker's Pantry, 6350 Gunpark Drive, **Boulder** CO ☎(303) 581-0518 or (800) 641-0500 — manufacturer of traditional & all-natural lightweight foods for emergency, camping, or outdoors; breakfast, lunch, & dinner entrees; *not recommended for long-term food storage*	X	X	X							X	
80301 Chinook Medical Gear, Inc., 2805 Wilderness Place, **Boulder** CO ☎(303) 444-8683 or (800) 766-1365 🖳(303) 444-8689 — mail order supplier of medical necessities for the outdoors, wilderness, & travel; instruments & tools for survival in the outdoors—no matter where you go!	X	X	X	X	X					X	
80301 JABCO, 1630 30th Street #504, **Boulder** CO — emergency preparedness checklists; send $3.00 for all three checklists	X										
80301 SweetWater, Inc., 4725 Nautilus Court South, **Boulder** CO ☎(800) 557-9338 — manufacturer of the *Guardian*™ water purifier, 99.99% effective in screening out Giardia & Cryptosporidium, & other protozoa, parasites, worms, & bacteria	X	X	X	X							
80302 Dr. Deborah Banker, MD, 1905 9th St., **Boulder** CO ☎(303) 449-6162 🖷(303) 449-2402 — ophthalmologist/general practitioner; lecturer, natural health & vision improvement; author of *"Self-Help Vision Care"*, home-study program for lifestyle changes to restore total body balance; reduce dependency on eyeglasses		X / C						X			
80302 Peppercorn, 1235 Pearl St., **Boulder** CO ☎(303) 449-5847 or (800) 447-6905 🖷(303) 440-6188 — delightful choices of food preparation equipment, items, & supplies; books for every culinary style		X	X							X	
80302 Phil Carl & Ingrid Koster, 891 12th St., **Boulder** CO ☎(303) 444-3849 or (303) 444-3849 🖷(800) 927-2527 X6296 ✉*gateway@indra.com* — *Cell-Tech* high-energy, low-risk home business opportunity		X						X			
80302 Sequel Outdoor Clothing, 14116-B Pearl St., **Boulder** CO ☎(303) 449-4252 🖳105201.533@compuserve.com — US-made innovative & sturdy outerware, backpacks, & outdoors accessories	X	X	X								X
80302 Wild Oats / Vegetarian, 1825 Pearl St., **Boulder** CO ☎(303) 440-9599 🖷(303) 442-0530			X	X	X	X	X	X	X	X	
80302 Wild Oats, 1651 Broadway, **Boulder** CO ☎(303) 442-0909 🖷(303) 786-9939			X	X	X	X	X	X	X	X	
80302 Zane International, 2026 10th St., **Boulder** CO ☎(303) 444-7226		X	X								X
80303 Wild Oats, 2584 Baseline Road, **Boulder** CO ☎(303) 499-7636 🖷(303) 499-1467			X	X	X	X	X	X	X	X	
80306 Jade Mountain, Inc., PO Box 4616, **Boulder** CO ☎(303) 449-8266 or (800) 442-1972 *toll-free for orders* 🖷(303) 449-8266 ✉*75442.1622@compuserve.com* or *jade-mtn@indra.com* — manufacturer & distributor of 4,000+ preparedness & appropriate technology products	X	X	X / C								X
80306 UniTea Herbs, PO Box 8005 #318, **Boulder** CO — herbal teas that are good for people & the planet	X	X	X				X		X		X
80401 Lionheart Ltd., 676B Moss St., **Golden** CO ☎(303) 277-0305 — authorized distributor of *Survival Tabs & Storehouse Foods*, manufactured by *Food Reserves, Inc.*		X	X							X	
80433 Inglenook Energy Center, 26437 Conifer Rd., **Conifer** CO ☎(303) 674-0630 — distributor of *Alco ♦Brite* gelled ethanol products		X									X
80439 Faber Foods, 1153 Bergen Pkwy. #M-105, **Evergreen** CO ☎(303) 670-0967 or (800) 237-3255 — bulk producer of *meusli* health food	X	X	X							X	
80487 Northwest Furnishings, Franklin Mall #833 Lincoln, **Steamboat Springs** CO ☎(303) 879-2024 — distributor of *Alco ♦Brite* gelled ethanol products		X									X
80503 Madhava Honey, 4689 Ute Hwy., **Longmont** CO ☎(303) 444-7999	X	X	X					X			
80523 Appropriate Technology Sourcebook, W-110 Eng. Resource Center @ Colorado State University, **Ft. Collins** CO ☎(800) 648-8043 🖳www.colostate.edu/orgs/ati — producer of *Appropriate Technology Sourcebook*; complete guide for environmentally sustainable living		X									X
80524 Jax, Inc., 1200 N. College Ave., **Fort Collins** CO ☎(303) 221-0544 — distributor of *Alco ♦Brite* gelled ethanol products		X									X
80524 The Cupboard / Carey Hewitt, 152 S. College Ave., **Fort Collins** CO ☎(303) 493-8585		X				X		X		X	X
80525 Christian Survival Intelligence Network, PO Box 271802, **Ft. Collins** CO ☎(406) 587-5571 🖳www.jcave.com~whenonr/CSIN/announce.htm — network for Christian tribulation		X									
80525 Classic Hearth, Inc., 5832 S. College Ave., **Fort Collins** CO ☎(303) 266-4090 — distributor of *Alco ♦Brite* gelled ethanol products		X	X								X

Product References Keyed to Chapters (Cont.)

04 water / air filtration & treatment	05 grains, seeds, mills & equip.	12 dairy / powdered milk supplies	13 honey / sweeteners
14 vitamins / minerals / herbs	15 sprouting / equip. & supplies	16 dry / dehydrated / freeze-dried	17 energy / fuels

Address	M	D	R	04	05	12	13	14	15	16	17
80525 Wild Oats, 1611 S. College Ave., **Fort Collins** CO ☎(970) 482-3200 🖷(970) 482-3396		X	X	X	X	X		X	X	X	
80525 Wild Oats, 216 W. Horsetooth Road, **Fort Collins** CO ☎(970) 225-1400 🖷(970) 225-1429		X	X	X	X	X		X	X	X	
80534 American Freedom Magazine, PO Box 430, **Johnstown** CO ☎(970) 587-5175 or (800) 205-6245 🖷(970) 587-5450 🖳www.amerifree.com – published in collaboration with the USA Freedom Network			X								
80534 USA Patriot Network, 39 S. Parish, **Johnstown** CO ☎(970) 587-5175 or (800) 205-6245 – long-term food storage & preparedness products & emergency/disaster supplies & equipment; food dryers & more!			X		X			X		X	
80537 Healthy Habits, PO Box 6021, **Loveland** CO ☎(970) 667-6897 – practitioner of Naturopathy; radio talk show host; consultant in alternative health			X					X			
80538 Patty Fust, 821 Scotch Elm Dr., **Loveland** CO ☎(970) 667-5953 – distributor of *Magic Mill* products			X		X			X	X		
80501 National Honey Board, 390 Lashley St., **Longmont** CO ☎(800) 356-5941 🖷(303) 776-1177 🖳www.nhb.org ✉mmc@csn.net – information, formulas, recipes, & more	X	C	C				X				
80540 Sun Pure Water Sys., 400 Main St. N., **Lyons** CO ☎(303) 823-0118 or (800) 590-0090 🖷(303) 823-9215	X	X	X	X							X
80615 Mid-West Indoor Air Quality Control, 227 Park Avenue, **Eaton** CO ☎(970) 353-6828 or (800) 873-7115 🖷(907) 454-0963	X	X									
80631 Betterway Whole Food Club, 1117 8ᵗʰ St., **Greeley** CO ☎(303) 356-1847		C	X	X	X	X		X	X	X	X
80631 Gary Jantz, 1710 9ᵗʰ Street, **Greeley** CO ☎(970) 351-7118 – distributor of *Magic Mill* products			X		X			X	X		
80632 Traditional Prenatal Care, PO Box 674, **Greeley** CO ☎(970) 346-2680 – home birth kits, midwifery referrals; inexpensive kits for alternative births			X								
80814 Earth Quest Technologies, PO Box 753, **Divide** CO – antibiotic/anti-viral alternative: colloidal silver kills more than 650 viruses, bacteria & fungi & germs don't become immune or resistant; safe, non-toxic, reduces length & severity of infectious disorders			X					X			
80820 Allergy Resources (attn: *Christine Beaman*), 6 Main St., **Guffy** CO ☎(719) 689-2969 – distributor of *Magic Mill* products			X		X			X	X		
80825 Christian Family Resources, 15011 Hwy. 287/40 W., **Kit Carson** CO ☎(719) 962-3228 🖷(719) 962-3228 – long-term preparedness products & storage items; specialists in homeschooling; distributor of *Emergency Essentials, AlpineAire, K-Tec, Bosch, Katadyn, Maple Leaf, Provident Pantry, Sproutmaster, & Country Grain* products; SW radios; home-schooling books & products; colloidal silver generators & silver sets; deluxe beef jerky		C	X	X	X	X	X	X	X	X	X
80829 Red Eagle Mountain Bed & Breakfast, 616 Ruxton Ave., **Manitou Springs** CO – distributor of *Alco♦Brite* gelled ethanol products			X								X
80863 Pikes Peak Paradise, 236 Pinecrest Rd., **Woodland Park** CO ☎(719) 687-6656 – distributor of *Alco♦Brite* gelled ethanol products			X								X
80866 B & G Enterprises, 70 Spruce Dr. Box 4415, **Woodland Park** CO ☎(719) 687-6510 or (888) 223-1755 🖷(719) 687-0990 🖳www//thunder@plan-et.com ✉bob@plan-et.com			X								
80903 Market LaRue, 501 East Kiowa, **Colorado Springs** CO ☎(719) 636-3663		C	X	X	X	X		X	X	X	X
80904 R & A Natural Food, 2631 W. Colorado, **Colorado Springs** CO ☎(719) 632-2516		C	X	X	X	X		X	X	X	X
80906 G & H Market, 1785 S. 8ᵗʰ St., **Colorado Springs** CO ☎(719) 733-6201		C	X	X	X	X		X	X	X	X
80909 Panacea – Mother Nature's Pharmacy, 3624 Citadel Dr. North, **Colorado Springs** CO ☎(719) 389-1292 – distributor of gold & silver colloidal formulas		X	X					X			
80915 Jane Deland, 6410 Sayres Road, **Colorado Springs** CO ☎(719) 550-0242 – distributor of *Magic Mill* products			X		X			X	X		
80918 Firehouse, 4553 Austin Bluff Parkway, **Colorado Springs** CO ☎(719) 597-2030 – distributor of *Alco♦Brite* gelled ethanol products			X								X
80918 Wild Oats, 5075 N. Academy Blvd., **Colorado Springs** CO ☎(719) 548-1667 🖷(719) 548-9535		X	X	X	X	X		X	X	X	
80931 International Tesla Society, Inc., PO Box 5636, **Colorado Springs** CO ☎(719) 475-0918 🖷(719) 475-0582		C	X		X	X			X		X
80935 G. G. Grains, Ltd., PO Box 17332, **Colorado Springs** CO ☎(719) 633-3793 or (800) 747-2467 🖳www.tejasmall.com/suindex		X	X		X				X		
80935 Oasis Emergency Foods, PO Box 17433, **Colorado Springs** CO ☎(800) 214-1164 🖷(719) 574-9255 🖳www.rmii.com/oasis ✉oasis@rmii.com – distributors of *AlpineAire* freeze-dried foods		X	X	X						X	
81101 Alpinvale Sweeps Stoves, 723 Main St., **Alamosa** CO ☎(719) 589-6938 – distributor of *Alco♦Brite* gelled ethanol products			X								X
81122 ICA, 166 Turner Dr., **Durango** CO ☎(303) 259-4100 or (800) 525-9556 🖷(303) 259-9396			X								
81122 Lewis Mercantile, 271 N. Mountain View Dr., **Bayfield** CO ☎ – distributor of *Alco♦Brite* gelled ethanol products			X								X
81147 Abraham Solar Equipment, 124 Creekside Pl., **Pagosa Springs** CO ☎(800) 222-7242	X										X
81224 McDell's Market, PO Box 1309, **Crested Butte** CO ☎(303) 349-6492		C	X	X	X	X		X	X	X	X

Legend: M = Manufacturer / Processor | D = Wholesaler / Trade distributor | R = Distributor / Retailer to public

Listing	M	D	R	04	05	12	13	14	15	16	17
81301 International Collectors Associates (attn: Don McAlvaney), PO Box 5150, Durango CO ☎(970) 259-4100 or (800) 525-9556 🖷(970) 259-9396 — investment consultation firm; specializing in precious metals & foreign government bonds to protect assets	X	X	C							X	
81301 Kroeger's True Value Hardware, 8 Town Plaza, Durango CO ☎(303) 247-0660 — distributor of Alco ◆Brite gelled ethanol products			X								X
81301 Sequel Outdoor Clothing, 108 E. 5ᵗʰ St., Durango CO ☎(970) 385-4421 🖷(970) 385-4710 📧105201.533@compuserve.com — US-made innovative & sturdy outerware, backpacks, & outdoors accessories; mail-order catalog available	X	X	X								X
81302 Sierra Supply (attn: Bill Henry), PO Box 1390, Durango CO ☎(970) 259-1822 🖷(970) 259-1822 — dependable merchandise for uncertain times; distributor of current contract military surplus items						X	X	X	X	X	X
81324 Adobe Milling Co., Inc., PO Box 374, Dove Creek CO ☎(970) 677-2620 or (800) 542-3623 🖷(303) 677-2667 🖳www.rmgl.com/rmpc/rmpc/html — producer/processor of CO high country beans: Anasazi brand beans, black, bolita, & beans; bean recipe books		X				X				X	
81324 Azbro, Inc., PO Box 374, Dove Creek CO ☎(970) 677-2775 — producer & grower of high mountain-grown beans		X				X				X	
81401 Johnson Electric Ltd., 2210 Industrial Dr. #A, Montrose CO ☎(303) 249-0840 — solar electric products	X										X
81401 Michelle Farnese, 21516 Uncompahgre Rd., Montrose CO ☎(303) 249-1110 — distributor of Magic Mill products		X				X		X	X		
81413 Manna Natural Foods Market, PO Box 693, Cedaredge CO ☎(970) 856-7372			C	X	X	X	X	X	X	X	
81428 Sunnyside Market, PO Box 245, Paonia CO ☎(303) 527-3737			C	X	X	X	X	X	X	X	
81501 Sundrop Grocery, 321 Rood Ave., Grand Junction CO ☎(303) 243-1175			C	X	X	X	X	X	X	X	
81520 Mountain Home Basics, PO Box 42, Clifton CO ☎(970) 434-9549 or (800) 572-9549 📧n0mva@aol.com — specialty distributor of kitchen equipment for processing food storage in-home		X				X				X	
81601 Good Health Grocery, 730 Cooper Avenue, Glenwood Springs CO ☎(303) 945-0235			C	X	X	X	X	X	X	X	
81601 Cozy Corner Co., 7870 Hwy. 82, Glenwood Springs CO — distributor of Alco ◆Brite gelled ethanol products		X									X
81611 Clark's Market, 300 Puppysmith Street, Aspen CO ☎(303) 925-8046			C	X	X	X	X	X	X	X	
81621 B-UtilityFree, Inc., 74 Sunset Dr., Basalt CO ☎(970) 927-1331 or (800) 766-5550 🖷(920) 927-1325 📧utilfree.infosphere.com — catalog/sourcebook is the most complete reference for energy-efficient and renewable energy products for a self-sufficiency lifestyle; solar, wind, & alternative power generation and products for maximization	X	X	X								X
81623 Solar Energy International, PO Box 715, Carbondale CO ☎(970) 963-8855 📧sei@solarenergy.org	X										X
81623 SunSense Solar Electric Systems, PO Box 301, Carbondale CO ☎(970) 963-1420	X										X
81625 Northwest Title, 530 Breeze St., Craig CO ☎(970) 824-9427 — distributor of Alco ◆Brite gelled ethanol products		X									X
81657 Wild Oats, 141 East Meadow Dr., Vail CO ☎(970) 476-1199 🖷(970) 476-8697		X	X	X	X	X	X	X	X		

Connecticut

Listing	M	D	R	04	05	12	13	14	15	16	17
06033 The Gluten-Free Pantry, 22 Kreiger Lane #1206, Glastonbury CT ☎(860) 633-3826 — distributor of Magic Mill Kitchen equipment & products			X			X		X	X		
06078 Body Magnetics, 871 Thrall Ave., Suffield CT ☎(203) 668-5137			X					X			
06239 Lemra Products, 16 Maple St., Danielson CT ☎(860) 774-7024 — manufacturer of home canning equipment			X								
06247 Eastford Food Co-op Buying Club, 119 Main Street, Hampton CT 📧cgklab			C	X	X	X	X	X	X	X	
06360 Wholistic Food Options, 231 Salem Turnpike, Norwich CT ☎(860) 848-7199 📧gldhardt@nai.net			C	X	X	X	X	X	X	X	
06365 Preston Trading Post, Preston CT ☎(860) 886-1484 🖷(860) 886-4906 — stoves, fireplaces & more…	X	X									X
06410 Buzzotto's Wholesale, Cheshire CT ☎(203) 272-3511 — distributor of Parmalat shelf-stable, whole milk dairy products	X						X				
06437 Laura Garceau, 106 Water St., Guilford CT ☎(203) 453-1336 — distributor of Magic Mill Kitchen equipment & products			X			X		X	X		
06472 Farm River Nursery, 470 Forest Rd., Northford CT ☎(203) 484-0174 — distributor of Alco ◆Brite gelled ethanol products			X								X
06479 Dean's Stove Shop, 75 W. Main St., Plantsville CT ☎(203) 621-5311 — distributor of Alco ◆Brite gelled ethanol products			X								X
06492 Best Value Home Center, 654 N. Colony Rd., Wallingford CT ☎(203) 369-6644 — distributor of Alco ◆Brite gelled ethanol products			X								X
06776 V & V Woodstoves, 449 Danbury Rd. Rt. 7, New Milford CT ☎(860) 354-1068 🖷(860) 354-2435 📧svecchione@aol.com — stoves; distributor of Alco ◆Brite gelled ethanol products	X	X									X
06830 Fresh Fields, 90 E. Putnam Avenue, Greenwich CT ☎(203) 661-0631 🖷(203) 661-9375			X	X	X	X	X	X	X	X	

Product References Keyed to Chapters (Cont.)

04 water / air filtration & treatment	05 grains, seeds, mills & equip.	12 dairy / powdered milk supplies	13 honey / sweeteners
14 vitamins / minerals / herbs	15 sprouting / equip. & supplies	16 dry / dehydrated / freeze-dried	17 energy / fuels

Listing	M	D	R	04	05	12	13	14	15	16	17
M = Manufacturer / Processor — D = Wholesaler / Trade distributor — R = Distributor / Retailer to public											
06902 **Jack Rabbit Energy Systems,** 425 Fairfield Ave., **Stamford** CT ☎(203) 961-8133 🖷(203)358-9250	X	X									X

Delaware

Listing	M	D	R	04	05	12	13	14	15	16	17
19808 **The Fireplace Shoppe,** 1726 Newport Bap **Wilmington** DE ☎(302) 999-1200	X	X									X
19904 **Byler's Store, Inc.,** 1368 Rose Valley Road, **Dover** DE ☎(302) 674-1689 🖷(302) 674-3083		X			X			X			

District of Columbia

Listing	M	D	R	04	05	12	13	14	15	16	17
20008 **Fresh Fields,** 2323 Wisconsin Avenue NW, **Washington** DC ☎(202) 333-5393 🖷(202 333-5392			X	X	X	X	X	X		X	X
20016 **Fresh Fields,** 4530 40th Street NW, **Washington** DC ☎(202) 237-5800 🖷(202) 237-1115			X	X	X	X	X	X		X	X

Florida

Listing	M	D	R	04	05	12	13	14	15	16	17
32050 **William McCall,** PO Box 572, 4197 Cotton Lane, **Middleburg** FL ☎(904) 282-6393 — distributor of *Magic Mill* products			X		X			X		X	
32084 **Gary Allen,** 303 Anastasia Blvd. #B, **St. Augustine** FL ☎(904) 825-2869 🖷(904) 825-2869 — distributor of *Magic Mill* products		C	X		X			X		X	
32085 **JRH Enterprises,** PO Box 3986, **St. Augustine** FL ☎(904) 797-9462 — books, tapes & videos; dehydrated & freeze-dried foods; *Ready Reserve* foods at discount; emergency medical classes & kits; bulk grains; MREs; emergency preparedness consulting		C	X	X	X				X	X	X
32091 **T.A.C.D.A. Store—The American Civil Defense Association,** PO Box 910, **Starke** FL ☎(904) 964-5397 or (800) 425-5397🖷(904) 964-9641 🖳www.tacda.org ✉tacda2000@daccess.net — non-profit mail-order for dehydrated storage foods, water barrels, grain grinders, & radiation dosimeters; *Journal of Civil Defense,* monthly magazine; *TACDA Alert Newsletter,* 8 times/yr. advocating *"Peace through Preparedness"* for preparedness, protection, & peace; America's voice for disaster preparedness		C	X	X	X	X		X			X
32114 **The Salvation Army,** 124 Bay Street, **Daytona Beach** FL ☎(904) 255-2417 — authorized distributor of *Emergency Essentials* products	X	C	X	X	X	X	X	X		X	X
32132 **Tropical Blossom Honey Co., Inc.,** 106 N. Ridgewood Ave., **Edgewater** FL ☎(904) 428-9027	X	X	X				X				
32177 **Anne Keckler,** Rt. 1 Box 6991, **Palatka** FL ☎(904) 325-9194 — distributor of *Magic Mill* products			X		X			X		X	
32301 **New Leaf Market,** 1235 Apalachee Pkwy, **Tallahassee** FL ☎(904) 942-2557		C	X	X	X	X	X	X		X	
32308 **Betty Lou Ferris,** 1900 Centre Point Blvd. #187, **Tallahassee** FL ☎(904) 216-1436 — distributor of *Magic Mill* products			X		X			X		X	
32405 **Shipes Studio,** 2509 E. 15th St., **Panama City** FL ☎(904) 785-5261 🖷(904) 785-3738 — *Purification for Life*® fiterless air purification systems distributor	X	X		X							
32425 **Doxology Technology,** RFD Box 877, **Bonifay** FL ☎(904) 547-3877 🖷(904) 547-7474 — specializing in marketing of new products & inventions	X	X	X								X
32447 **Dragon's Lair Enterprises,** PO Box 6143, **Marianna** FL ☎(904) 762-4124 — publishes monthly newsletter *"Rumblings from Dragon's Lair"* about homesteading & survival;		C						X			
32501 **Ever'mans Natural Foods Co-op,** 1200 N. 9th Ave. **Pensacola** FL ☎(904) 438-0402		C	X	X	X	X	X	X		X	
32578 **Carol Whittenburg,** 435 Old Post Road, **Niceville** FL ☎(904) 897-3046 — distributor of *Magic Mill* products			X		X			X		X	
32583 **Chimney Cricket,** 2784 Avalon Blvd., **Milton** FL ☎(904) 623-0318 — distributor of *Alco ◆Brite* gelled ethanol products			X								X
32601 **SolarDyne Corp.,** 20 S. Main St., **Gainesville** FL ☎(904) 372-0333 🖷(904) 373-1653			X								X
32609 **Brasington's Trail Shop, Inc.,** 2331 NW 13th St., **Gainesville** FL ☎(904) 372-0521 — distributor of *Alco ◆Brite* gelled ethanol products			X								X
32667 **Revita,** PO Box 167, **Micanopy** FL ☎(904) 466-3402 — distributor of *LiquaHealth,* the most nutritious food in the world			X		X			X			
32703 **ABC Florida Apopka / Roger Simpson,** 3909 East Semoram Blvd., **Apopka** FL ☎(407) 869-9006 — distributor of *Magic Mill* products			X		X			X		X	
32704 **Oxygen for Life / John E. Miller,** PO Box 2441, **Apopka** FL ☎(800) 529-8258 — distributor of oxygen products; advanced liquid nutrition for a healthier lifestyle			X		X			X			
32714 **Ultimate Preparedness,** 931 North SR 434 #1201-194, **Altamonte Springs** FL — for those who want to be spiritually prepared as well; books, vitamin supplements, & videos			X					X			
32720 **Michael Blubaugh,** 1373 W. Taylor Road, **Deland** FL ☎(904) 738-7077			X		X			X		X	
32756 **Richard & Bonnie Carlson,** PO Box 814, **Mt. Dora** FL ☎(352) 357-0400 — distributor of *Magic Mill* products			X		X			X		X	
32782 **Alpha-Omega Laboratories,** PO Box 6426, **Titusville** FL ☎(407) 269-6059 🖷(407) 267-0707 — manufacturer of vitamin, mineral, & herbal products formulations; creams, lotions, salves, & ointments for the skin	X	X						X			
32782 **Survival Associates, Inc.,** PO Box 6426, **Titusville** FL ☎(407) 269-6059 🖷(407) 267-0707 — *Survival Food Tabs*™ distributor; convenient, compact, lightweight, life-saving food ration for emergencies	X							X		X	

M = Manufacturer / Processor	D = Wholesaler / Trade distributor	R = Distributor / Retailer to public	M	D	R	04	05	12	13	14	15	16	17
32789 ABC Florida Winter Park, 655 North Wymore Road, **Winter Park** FL ☎(407) 644-4255 — distributor of *Magic Mill* products					X	X				X		X	
32789 Chamberlain's Health Foods, 430 North Orlando, **Winter Park** FL ☎(407) 647-6661					C	X	X	X	X	X	X	X
32794 Living Air System, PO Box 948035, **Maitland** FL ☎(407) 628-1848 — distributor of *Air Solutions* air purification system; mountain-fresh air; portable, no filter changes					X	X							X
32801 Dr. Brett Thomas, 235 East Amelia Street, **Orlando** FL ☎(407) 850-0056 — 600+ mail-order items for health & survival; food storage; wilderness supplies; water purification systems					X			X				
32809 American Military, 7611 South Orange Blossom Trail, **Orlando** FL ☎(407) 696-8006 or (800) 417-7696 ☏(407) 695-7526 ⌨www.ammil.com ✉sales@ammil.com					X	X					X	X
32811 Boyd's LDS Books, 4888 S. Kirkman Rd., **Orlando** FL ☎(407) 292-0502 or (800) 232-0571					X	X						
32818 Purest Foods Market, 7321 W. Colonial Drive, **Orlando** FL ☎(407) 522-91969 ☏(407) 522-9131					C	X	X	X	X	X	X	X
32904 Heartsong, 1893 West New Haven Ave. #190, **Melbourne** FL ☎(407) 255-2407 or (800) 779-2407 — distributor of *Bosch & Kitchen Specialties* products				X								
32905 Mr. Fireplace, 3340 Dixie Bay Hwy. NE, **Palm Bay** FL					X							X
32931 Sunseed Food Co-op, Inc., 275 W. Cocoa Beach Causeway, **Cocoa Beach** FL ☎(407) 784-0930					C	X	X	X	X	X	X	X
32960 Greens Plus, 730 14th St., **Vero Beach** FL ☎(800) 643-1210 (USA) or (800) 387-4761 (CAN)					X		X		X			
33014 Survival Made Simple, *(attn: Linda Slomian)*, 15505 Bull Run Rd #255, **Miami Lakes** FL — *SamAndy Foods* products distributor					X	X	X	X		X	X	X
33067 Whole Foods Market, 800 University Dr., **Coral Gables** FL					X	X		X	X	X	X	X
33071 MountainView Country Seasonings, 10619 W. Atlantic Boulevard #122, **Coral Springs** FL ⌨www.mountainview-m.com/mcs.htm — gourmet, all-natural ingredients seasoning blends for meats, fish & fowl without added salt		X	X							X		
33143 Fireplaces Etc., 6701 Red Rd., **Coral Gables** FL ☎(305) 667-1686 — distributor of *Alco ♦Brite* gelled ethanol products					X							X
33150 Hydrocap, 975 NW 95th St., **Miami** FL ☎(305) 696-2504			X									X
33156 Evenings Delite, 9621 S. Dixie Hwy., **Miami** FL ☎(305) 666-3315 — distributor of *Alco ♦Brite* gelled ethanol products					X							
33161 Institute Herb Co., 1190 NE 125th St. #12, **North Miami** FL ☎(305) 899-8704 — Chinese herbs & patent medicines					X							
33166 ABC Florida Miami / Paublo, 1 South Royal Poinciana Blvd., **Miami Springs** FL ☎(305) 805-9900 — distributor of *Magic Mill* products					X	X			X		X	
33176 ABC Supply House Inc., 14227 B South Dixie Hwy., **Miami** FL ☎(305) 378-9587 — distributor of *Magic Mill* products			X	X		X		X		X		
33180 Whole Foods Market, 3565 NE 207th St., **No. Miami Beach** FL ☎(305) 933-1543 ☏(305) 933-2567					X	X	X	X	X	X	X	X
33181 Sprout Delights Inc., 12551 Biscayne Blvd., **Miami** FL ☎(305) 893-9394 — mail-order seeds for sprouting					X					X		
33304 Wild Oats, 2501 East Sunrise Blvd., **Ft. Lauderdale** FL ☎(954) 566-9333 ☏(954) 566-7743					X	X	X	X	X	X	X	X
33309 Evenings Delite, 3839 NW 9th Ave., **Fort Lauderdale** FL — distributor of *Alco ♦Brite* gelled ethanol products					X							X
33312 Life Extension Foundation, 2490 Griffin Road, **Fort Lauderdale** FL ☎(305) 966-4886 or (800) 841-5433 ☏(305) 989-8269 — membership provides access to the numerous directories; weekly newsletters; monthly issues of reports; more!		X	X					X				
33511 Health Source *(attn: Robert Worzalla)*, 660 Oakfield Drive, **Brandon** FL ☎None — distributor of *Magic Mill* products					X		X		X		X	
33514 Waterwise, Inc., PO Box 45977, **Center Hill** FL ☎(800) 874-9028 ☏(352) 787-8123 — tap water purification appliance		X	X	X	X							
33550 Love America, Inc., PO Drawer 1176, **Mango** FL ☎(813) 620-1776 — distributor of *Alco ♦Brite* gelled ethanol products					X							X
33565 Family Preparedness / James Darough, 1833 N. Forbes Rd. # 8, **Plant City** FL ☎(813) 754-4375 — distributor of *Alco ♦Brite* gelled ethanol products					X							X
33567 Roush Military Surplus, Inc., 2410 West Baker Street, **Plant City** FL ☎(813) 759-0459 — hurricane survival kits, military survival items, camping supplies, & more!			X	X							X	
33592 The Steam Outlet, PO Box 1426, **Thonotassassa** FL — simple & inexpensive home construction plans for: steam boilers & generators, converting 4-cycle engines to steam; wood stoves powering electrical generators; automatic steam cycle; outboard boat engine; & wind generators		X	X	X								X
33604 Water Survival Institute, 8113 North Ola Avenue, **Tampa** FL ☎(813) 932-7045 — specializing in water purification pumps			X	X								X
33614 AmeriNet Broadcasting, 3615 W. Waters Ave. #308, **Tampa** FL ☎(813) 879-5505 or (800) 482-2560 — freedom radio with personality, featuring the Baker boys, Jeff & Rod					X	X	X	X	X	X	X	X
33614 Live Oak Farms, 3615 West Waters Ave. #308, **Tampa** FL ☎(813) 977-1128 or (800) 482-2560 — complete line of food storage & other preparedness products			X	C	X	X	X	X	X	X	X	

Product References Keyed to Chapters (Cont.)

	M	D	R	04	05	12	13	14	15	16	17
04 water / air filtration & treatment / **14 vitamins / minerals / herbs** — **05 grains, seeds, mills & equip.** / **15 sprouting / equip. & supplies** — **12 dairy / powdered milk supplies** / **16 dry / dehydrated / freeze-dried** — **13 honey / sweeteners** / **17 energy / fuels**											
M = Manufacturer / Processor — D = Wholesaler / Trade distributor — R = Distributor / Retailer to public	M	D	R	04	05	12	13	14	15	16	17
33615 Mother Nature's General Store, Inc., 5521 Baywater Drive, **Tampa** FL ☎(800) 290-8140 🖷(813) 854-4752 💻www.mothernature.com ✉*mother@pond.com*			C	X	X	X	X	X	X	X	
33625 Arron Sivan, 15005 Red Cliff Drive, **Tampa** FL ☎None available – distributor of *Magic Mill* products			X		X			X	X		
33629 Here's to Your Health!, 3825 Henderson. #205, **Tampa** FL ☎(813) 282-1522 🖷(813) 282-1132			X					X			
33634 Anchor Glass Container Corp., 4343 Anchor Plaza Pkwy., **Tampa** FL – manufacturer of glass bottles for canning & packing	X										
33802 New Era Co-op, PO Box 347, **Lakeland** FL			C	X	X	X	X	X	X	X	
33990 Lifeline Products (attn: Kathy Myers), 912 SE 18th Terrace, **Cape Coral** FL ☎/🖷(941) 772-2938			X				X				
34275 M. F. Enterprise, 510 Olive Avenue #210, **Nokomis** FL ☎(941) 486-1505 – emergency preparedness kits			X			X					
34430 Father's Treats (attn: Brenda Surface), PO Box 2051, **Dunnellon** FL ☎(888) 673-1646 – no-sugar gourmet fruit bars; coffee substitute; liquid minerals; oils for the internal body		X	X					X	X		
34472 Action Products Intl., Inc., 344 Cypress Rd., **Ocala** FL ☎(904) 687-2202 or (800) 772-2846 – freeze-dried trail snacks: ice cream; ice cream sandwiches, vanilla, strawberry, & chocolate; *wholesale only*	X	X								X	
34615 Infinity², 906 Drew Street, **Clearwater** FL ☎(813) 446-6167 – nutrition & strength professionals; live blood analysis			X					X			
34616 A Place for Cooks / Tom Dinicola, 1447 S. Fort Harrison Ave., **Clearwater** FL ☎(813) 446-5506 – distributor of *Magic Mill* products			X		X			X	X		
34635 Preferred Marketing Group, PO Box 385, **Indian Rocks Beach** FL ☎(800) 272-5254 – a biodegradable product that replaces non-abrasive cleaning products; concentrated			X								
34641 Solar Bright Corp., 3665 E. Bay Dr. #204-256, **Largo** FL ☎(800) 780-1759	X	X									X
34646 Chris Steiner, 10049 Bahama Court, **Seminole** FL ☎(813) 596-4820 ✉*BBS:596-5372* – electronic files of survival & preparedness subjects;; suppressed political information available	X	X	X								
34668 A Plus Fireplaces, 8133 Ridge Rd., **Port Richey** FL ☎(813) 847-6248 – distributor of *Alco ♦Brite* gelled ethanol products			X								X
34711 Emergency Water Storage / Aspects of Self-Reliance, 1330 Milholland Ave., **Clermont** FL ☎(904) 394-2043 or (800) 398-2829 🖷(904) 394-1994 – manufacturer of *SOFTANK*, 55-gal. water storage bag; reusable, foldable, collapsible, & lightweight; suitable for either in-ground or above-ground emergency water storage	X	X	X/C	X		X			X		
34748 Bread of Life Co-op, 1157 Emma Lane, **Leesburg** FL ☎(352) 728-5871 🖷(352) 728-5851 ✉*ForHIM3@aol*(c/o El Shaddai Ministries of Florida, Inc.)			C	X	X	X	X	X	X	X	
34769 Fireplace Works, Inc., 3182 Sugarmill Lane, **St. Cloud** FL ☎(407) 957-8619 – distributor of *Alco ♦Brite* gelled ethanol products			X								X
34952 Autumn Moon Fireplace, 10207 SE Leonard Rd., **Port St. Lucie** FL ☎(407) 335-1457 🖷(407) 335-7909 – distributor of *Alco ♦Brite* gelled ethanol products			X								X

Georgia

	M	D	R	04	05	12	13	14	15	16	17
29901 Hearth of Gold, Gainesville GA ☎(770) 536-6299 or (800) 433-HEAT 🖷(770) 534-8348 – fireplaces, wood stoves, gas logs, & more…	X	X									X
30059 Carol Kirby, 4500 Queen Anne Court, **Mapleton** GA ☎(770) 944-2001 – distributor of *Magic Mill* products			X		X			X	X		
30071 Emergency Preparedness Association, 5039 Running Fox Trail, **Norcross** GA ☎(404) 729-0630 – distributor of *Alco ♦Brite* gelled ethanol products			X								X
30076 Centuries Olde Herbals, 920 Laurel Mill Dr., **Roswell** GA								X		X	
30084 Aline Bennett, 4471 Doyle Street, **Tucker** GA ☎(404) 908-0444 – distributor of *Magic Mill* products			X		X			X	X		
30125 Rainy Day Supply (attn: Sharon Miller), 2315 Collard Valley Road, **Cedartown** GA ☎(770) 748-3297 or (888) 412-3434 🖷(770) 748-7826 💻www.cyberatl.net/~rdsupply or www.beprepared.net ✉*rdsupply@cyberatl.net* – distributor of food storage items and preparedness products; specializing in home food storage & emergency supplies; helping provide security for your family in time of natural, man-caused, or personal disasters			C		X		X	X		X	
30131 Kandy Kimbrough, 1383 Haw Creek Drive, **Cumming** GA ☎(404) 781-8272 – distributor of *Magic Mill* products			X		X			X	X		
30152 Brigade Quartermasters, Ltd., 1025 Cobb International Blvd., **Kennesaw** GA ☎(770) 428-1248 or (888) 276-4700 🖷(770) 426-7211 💻www.actiongear.com ✉*brigade@mindspring.com*			X					X			
30188 The Canteen, 1375 Chatley Way, **Woodstock** GA ☎(770) 592-1698 or (888) 226-8336 🖷(770) 516-1200 💻www.mojoski.com/canteen ✉*canteen@mojoski.com*	X	X	X				X				X
30201 Brad & Sue Becker, 561 Dogwood Hills Lane, **Alpharetta** GA ☎(770) 475-2386 – distributor of *Magic Mill* products			X		X			X	X		
30201 Deborah Gale White, 3785 Hamby Rd., **Alpharetta** GA ☎(770) 475-1416			X		X			X	X		

M = Manufacturer / Processor D = Wholesaler / Trade distributor R = Distributor / Retailer to public	M	D	R	04	05	12	13	14	15	16	17
30209 **Joy Woodruff**, 210 Briar Patch Dr., **Covington** GA ☎(770) 787-8790 – distributor of *Magic Mill* products			X	X				X	X		
30215 **Janet Willis**, 421 Brooks Woolsey Road, **Fayetteville** GA ☎(770) 460-1525 – distributor of *Magic Mill* products			X	X				X	X		
30247 **Hutton SolarPower**, 1775 MacLeod, **Lawrenceville** GA ☎(770) 729-9413	X										X
30247 **Ramco International**, **Lilburn** GA ☎(800) 875-3750 🖳(770) 972-3008 – manufacturer of wood-burning stoves	X										X
30263 **The Herb Shop**, 4 Dixon Street, **Newnan** GA ☎(404) 254-0004			X					X			
30277 **Donald Jones**, 9 Meadow Way, **Sharpesburg** GA ☎(404) 251-1558 – distributor of *Magic Mill* products			X	X				X	X		
30316 **Parmalat**– Atlanta Dairies, **Atlanta** GA ☎(404) 688-2671 – distributor of *Parmalat* shelf-stable, whole milk dairy products	X						X	X			
30328 **Liahona**, (*attn: Michael Burnett*), 6303 Barfields Road #208, **Atlanta** GA ☎(404) 252-6873 – distributor of *Magic Mill* products			X	X				X	X		
30340 **Daniel Chung**, 5302 Buford Hwy. A–1, **Doraville** GA ☎None available – distributor of *Magic Mill* products			X	X				X	X		
30340 **Maxam Wholesale**, 3400 Oakcliff Road #A2, **Doraville** GA ☎(404) 455-1991 🖳(404) 455-1966 – discount retail & catalog order store; must be a business to order; many bargain-priced preparedness items			X							X	X
30603 **Dixie Canner Equipment Co.**, PO Box 1348, **Athens** GA ☎(706) 549-1914	X										
30606 **Beth Holland**, 125 Wood Valley Lane, **Athens** GA ☎(706) 546-7214 – distributor of *Magic Mill* products			X	X				X	X		
30606 **Helen J. Howington**, 180 St. James Drive, **Athens** GA ☎(706) 549-2787 – distributor of *Magic Mill* products			X	X				X	X		
30606 **Phyllis Steinborn**, 125 Timber Lane Drive, **Athens** GA ☎(706) 548-5030 – distributor of *Magic Mill* products			X	X				X	X		
30720 **Jan C. Wilkinson**, 1302 Beverly Drive, **Dalton** GA ☎(706) 278-3586 – distributor of *Magic Mill* products			X	X				X	X		
30721 **Elizabeth Woodwards**, 116 Showford Road, **Dalton** GA ☎(706) 259-3887 – distributor of *Magic Mill* products			X	X				X	X		
31069 **Stove Mart**, 1404 Parkway Dr., **Perry** GA ☎(912) 987-2380			X								X
31206 **Charlene Sharp**, 2785 Virginia Drive, **Macon** GA ☎(912) 788-0415 – distributor of *Magic Mill* products			X	X				X	X		
31404 **Parker's Pantry**, (*attn: James Parker*), 11 Timberline Dr., **Savannah** GA ☎(912) 692-1112 – *SamAndy Foods* products distributor			X	X	X	X			X	X	X
31503 **Sioux Honey Association**, 2195 Industrial Blvd., **Waycross** GA ☎(912) 283-6515	X	X	X					X			
31701 **Freedom Financial Consultants**, 700 Pine Ave., **Albany** GA ☎(912) 435-6637 or (800) 633-2462 – financial consulting firm offering a full range of offshore financial services for asset protection, privacy, etc.	C										
31905 **U. S. Cavalry**, 4411 Victory, **Columbus** GA ☎(706) 682-0547 🖳(706) 682-3999 – retailer & mail order (4,200+ items); survival & outdoor clothing & equipment; preparedness products			X	X						X	X
Hawaii											
96701 **Curtis Taylor**, 98-456 Kaimu Loop, **Aiea** HI ☎(808) 488-6142 🖳(808) 484-5334 – distributor of *Bosch, Kitchen Specialties, & Magic Mill* products			X	X				X	X		
96712 **Planet Guardians Co-op**, 66-082 Kam Highway, **Halelwa, Oahu** HI ☎(808) 637-6713			C	X	X	X	X	X	X	X	
96732 **Nature's Outlet Ltd.**, 415 Dairy Rd. #E133, **Kahului, Maui** HI ☎(808) 871-2001			C	X	X	X	X	X	X	X	
96739 **Aloha Village Store**, PO Box 390730, **Kailua-Kona, Hawaii** HI ☎(808) 322-9941			C	X	X	X	X	X	X	X	
96740 **Altech Heating Hawaii**, 73-1236 Ahikawa St., **Kailua-Kona** HI ☎(808) 325-7100 – distributor of *Alco ◆Brite* gelled ethanol products			X								X
96746 **Papaya's Natural Foods**, 4-831 Kihio Highway, **Kapaa, Kauai** HI ☎(808) 823-0190			C	X	X	X	X	X	X	X	
96750 **Ohana Co-op**, PO Box 1663, **Kealekekua, Hawaii** HI ☎(808) 322-2425			C	X	X	X	X	X	X	X	
96768 **Down To Earth**, 1169 Makawao Ave., **Makawao, Maui** HI ☎(808) 572-1488			C	X	X	X	X	X	X	X	
96782 **Good Health Store**, 98-1254 Kaahumanu, **Pearl City, Oahu** HI ☎(808) 487-0082			C	X	X	X	X	X	X	X	
96788 **Pahoa Natural Groceries**, PO Box 1429, **Pahoa, Hawaii** HI ☎(808) 965-8322			C	X	X	X	X	X	X	X	
96814 **Vim N. Vigor Foods**, 1450 Ala Moanna Blvd. #1294, **Honolulu, Oahu** HI ☎(808) 941-1995			C	X	X	X	X	X	X	X	
96817 **ABC Hawaii**, 228 Pali Highway, **Honolulu** HI ☎(808) 595-4689 – distributor of *Magic Mill* products			X	X				X	X		
96817 **Inter-Island Solar Supply**, 345 N. Nimitz Hwy., **Honolulu** HI ☎(808) 523-0711 🖳(536-5586	X	X									X

Product References Keyed to Chapters (Cont.)

| 04 water / air filtration & treatment | 05 grains, seeds, mills & equip. | 12 dairy / powdered milk supplies | 13 honey / sweeteners |
| 14 vitamins / minerals / herbs | 15 sprouting / equip. & supplies | 16 dry / dehydrated / freeze-dried | 17 energy / fuels |

| M = Manufacturer / Processor | D = Wholesaler / Trade distributor | R = Distributor / Retailer to public | M | D | R | 04 | 05 | 12 | 13 | 14 | 15 | 16 | 17 |

Idaho

Listing	M	D	R	04	05	12	13	14	15	16	17
83211 **K-IDA-AG**, 2540 Smith Road, **American Falls** ID ☎(800) 727-5884 or (206) 226-5884 — organic minerals for depleted soils; produces chemical-free organic food with energy previously unavailable	X	X	X								X
83226 **Regenpag Gardens**, #2 Regenpag, **Challis** ID ☎(800) 848-8977 — distributor of *Alco ♦Brite* gelled ethanol products			X								X
83226 **River 1, Inc.**, PO Box 81 Highway 93, **Strand Lane**, Challis ID ☎(208) 879-5300 — distributor of *Alco ♦Brite* gelled ethanol products			X								X
83228 **Storage Transport / Franklin Metal**, 500 N. Main Hwy., **Clifton** ID ☎(208) 747-3310 🖷(208) 852-3020 — stackable storage containers	X	X									
83228 **Westover Salvage/Portable**, PO Box 32, **Clifton** ID ☎(208) 747-3310 🖷(208) 852-2003 — storage containers for food storage	X	X									
83250 **Retsel Corporation**, PO Box 37, Highway 30 North, **McCammon** ID ☎(208) 254-3737 — manufacturer of the Idaho-made *Little Ark, Mil-Master, & Mil-Rite* grain & seed mills; available in stone or stainless steel burr grinding kits			X		X						
83254 **OK Tire**, 178 N. 4th St., **Montpelier** ID ☎(208) 847-0615 — distributor of *Alco ♦Brite* gelled ethanol products			X								X
83254 **Squirrel's Nest**, 916 Washington, **Montpelier** ID ☎(208) 847-1111 — distributor of *Walton Feed & Bosch* products			X	X	X	X	X		X	X	X
83254 **Walton Feed, Inc.**, 135 North 10th, **Montpelier** ID ☎(208) 847-0465 or (800) 847-0465 🖷(208) 847-0467 🖳http://waltonfeed.com or 🖳www.lis.ab.ca./walton — major supplier of food storage products & preparedness items; large assortment of organic grains & seeds; distributor of *Magic Mill* products; authorized distributor of *Emergency Essentials* products; authorized wholesale distributor of *Vacu-Dry* dehydrated food products; distributor of *Alco ♦Brite* gelled ethanol products	X	C	X	X	X	X	X	X	X	X	X
83274 **Cox Honey Farms, Inc.**, 456 S. State St., **Shelley** ID ☎(208) 357-3226	X	X	X				X				
83301 **A Happy Camper**, 1485 Poleline Rd. East, **Twin Falls** ID ☎(208) 736-8048 — distributor of *Alco ♦Brite* gelled ethanol products			X								X
83301 **Dwight & Myrna Bell**, 761 2nd Avenue N., **Twin Falls** ID ☎(208) 734-6400 — distributor of *Magic Mill* products			X		X			X	X		
83301 **Make A Difference Food**, 1414 Heyburn East, **Twin Falls** ID ☎/🖷(208) 734-6516 — food storage & preparedness products; disasters consulting		C	X	X	X	X	X	X	X		
83313 **Glenn's Grocery**, PO Box 403, **Bellevue** ID ☎(208) 788-4211		C	X	X	X	X	X	X			
83316 **Valley Co-Op, Inc.**, 130 11th Ave. S., **Buhl** ID ☎(208) 543-4356 — distributor of *Alco ♦Brite* gelled ethanol products			X								X
83318 **Kitchen Kneads**, 329 E. 5th North, **Burley** ID ☎(208) 678-7098 — authorized distributor of *Emergency Essentials* products			X	X	X	X	X	X	X	X	
83355 **Positive Way Basics**, 152 E. Main St., **Wendell** ID ☎(208) 536-6184 — distributor of *Alco ♦Brite* gelled ethanol products			X								X
83355 **Positive Way Basics**, PO Box 728, **Wendell** ID ☎(208) 536-6184 — specializing in 72-hr. kits			X	X							
83401 **Food Storage Outlet**, 6405 E. Twin Creek Dr., **Idaho Falls** ID ☎(208) 522-5399			X	X	X	X	X		X		X
83401 **Noah's**, 378 Gorfield St., **Idaho Falls** ID ☎/🖷(208) 523-5334 — distributor of preparedness products & emergency supplies		C	X	X	X	X			X	X	X
83402 **The Preparedness Store**, 196 W. Elva, **Idaho Falls** ID ☎(208) 625-4546 — distributor of *Magic Mill* products; distributor of *Alco ♦Brite* gelled ethanol products			X		X			X		X	X
83403 **C-A-L Stores**, 665 E. Anderson St., **Idaho Falls** ID ☎(208) 523-3359 — distributor of *Alco ♦Brite* gelled ethanol products			X								X
83404 **American Family Preparedness**, 1650 S. Woodruff Ave., **Idaho Falls** ID ☎(208) 525-8655 🖳www.amfam.org ✉Probe@srv.net			X	X	X	X	X		X	X	X
83440 **Eldon C. & Julina Hart**, PO Box 7, **Rexburg** ID ☎(208) 356-3309 — distributor of *Magic Mill* products			X		X			X	X		
83442 **Mrs, Bateman's Products**, 125 South State Street, **Rigby** ID ☎(208) 574-6822 or (208) 745-9033 🖳www.bakingbutter.com ✉bateman@bakingbutter.com — manufacturer of powdered baking butter for the commercial industry											
83442 **EVP Enterprises**, PO Box 74, **Rigby** ID — 30-page manual with diagrams & instructions for building inexpensive food dryers; directions & recipes for drying	X	X	X							X	
83467 **Nature's Pantry**, 401 Main St., **Salmon** ID ☎(208) 756-6067		C	X	X	X	X	X	X			
83536 **Center for Action / Col. "Bo" Gritz**, c/o HC 11 Box 307, **Kamiah** ID ☎(208) 935-2918 — preparing for emergencies when you can't depend on "911" or the gov't. for protection for what lies ahead		C									
83539 **Miracle of Ozone**, Box 731, **Kooskin** ID ☎(208) 926-7151 🖷(208) 926-7154			X	X							

M = Manufacturer / Processor	D = Wholesaler / Trade distributor	R = Distributor / Retailer to public	M	D	R	04	05	12	13	14	15	16	17
83605 D & B Supply, 3303 East Lindon, **Caldwell** ID ☎(208) 459-7446 – distributor of *Alco ◆Brite* gelled ethanol products					X								X
83605 Maskal Forages, Inc., 1318 Willow, **Caldwell** ID					X	X						
83611 Cascade Co-op, PO Box 87, **Cascade** ID ☎(208) 382-3800					C	X	X	X	X	X	X	X	
83629 Ponderosa Sports & Merc., Inc., 6854 Hwy. 55, **Horseshoe Bend** ID ☎(208) 793-3121 🖷(208) 793-3133 – specializing in preparedness food, equipment & supplies; MREs, freeze dried foods, heatermeals, balanced food mix, first aid kits & supplies, magazines, military surplus, survival manuals & supplies, and more!					X	X	X	X	X	X	X	X	X
83634 Kuna Trading Post & Pardner's Distributing, 478 W. 3ʳᵈ, **Kuna** ID ☎(208) 922-4292 – distributor of *Alco ◆Brite* gelled ethanol products					X								X
83642 American Family Products, Int'l (Corp. Ofc.), 550 N. Meridian Road, **Meridian** ID ☎(208) 888-5205 or (800) 843-9439 – manufacturer of dried whey beverage superior to dried milk; high protein, low-calorie, no cholesterol, low lactose, no preservatives, & fortified with *Acidophilus & Bifidus* cultures			X	X	X			X				
83642 Harvest House / Kim M. Blake, 2252 E. Green Meadow Court, **Meridian** ID ☎(208) 887-1003 – distributor of *Magic Mill* products					X		X			X		X	
83652 Darcher Ranch Market, PO Box 9102, **Nampa** ID ☎(208) 467-2302					C	X	X	X	X	X	X	X	
83687 Gering & Son, 2020 Third Street North, **Nampa** ID ☎/🖷(208) 466-9003 – dry-pack canner for #10 cans; reflanger for cutting off old ring and putting new sealing ring on used cans			X	X	X								X
83701 Koppal's Brownsville, PO Box 198, **Boise** ID – distributor of *Alco ◆Brite* gelled ethanol products					X								X
83702 Boise Co-op, 1674 Hill Road, **Boise** ID ☎(208) 342-6652					C	X	X	X	X	X	X	X	
83703 U-DIG-IT Folding Hand Shovel, 3953 Brookside Lane, **Boise** ID ☎(208) 939-8656 – stainless steel folding hand shovel for backpacker, biker, gardener, sportsman, boater, or preparedness			X	X	X								
83704 Chases Natural Foods Market, 5326 Overland Road, **Boise** ID ☎(208) 343-2182					C	X	X	X	X	X	X	X	
83704 First Aid America, 6720 Emerald Street, **Boise** ID ☎(208) 375-9458					X	X							
83705 Bench Mart, 625 Vista Ave., **Boise** ID ☎(208) 338-7200 – distributor of *Alco ◆Brite* gelled ethanol products					X								X
83706 Quality Lifestyles, 3598 S. Minuteman Way, **Boise** ID ☎(208) 344-7553 – Pycnogenol, Melatonin, DHEA products					X				X				
83714 Boise Army Navy, 4924 Chinden Blvd., **Boise** ID ☎(208) 322-0660 – distributor of *Alco ◆Brite* gelled ethanol products					X								X
83714 Zamzow's, 4741 Glenwood, **Boise** ID ☎(208) 322-5250 – distributor of *Alco ◆Brite* gelled ethanol products					X								X
83805 Earth Shelter Building School, Route 4 Box 618, **Bonners Ferry** ID ☎(208) 267-7349 – author & consultant: earth shelters; root cellars; emergency shelters			X	X	C								X
83809 Everybody's Kitchen Machines, PO Box 1, **Careywood** ID ☎(208) 683-2459 – bread baking classes, wheat-free cooking classes; beans & grains cookie classes & info					C		X						
83809 Farnsworth Business Services, 950 Crosswhite Road, **Careywood** ID ☎(208) 683-3448 🖷(208) 683-3065 💻www.digital-café.com/~webmaster/water00.htm ✉ronf@digital-café.com – supplier of water treatment units; air purification units for home or business; vitamin supplements			X	X	X				X				
83814 Best Yet Pellet Stoves, 2929 Government Way, **Coeur-d'Alene** ID ☎(208) 667-8436 – distributor of *Alco ◆Brite* gelled ethanol products					X								X
83814 Global Insights, Inc., 5872 Government Way Bldg. 1 #10, **Coeur d'Alene** ID ☎(208) 762-8223 or (800) 729-4131 *Customer Service* (702) 885-0700 🖷(208) 762-8223 – publisher of *Global Insights Catalog*; preparedness subjects & products					X								
83814 Mast Enterprises, 2615 N. Fourth St. #616, **Coeur d'Alene** ID 💻www.nidlink.com/~mastent/wheatfre – information & products for those allergic to wheat & other grains; allergen-free grains, books, & recipes					X		X		X				
83814 Survival Supply Co., PO Box 4582, **Coeur d'Alene** ID ☎(208) 776-5620 🖷(208) 765-4295 – mail-order supplier for outdoor & emergency needs; hiking, camping, food storage, & backpacking					X	X	X	X	X		X	X	X
83822 Oldtown Hardware, 21 E. Hwy. #2, **Oldtown** ID ☎(208) 437-5512 – distributor of *Alco ◆Brite* gelled ethanol products					X								X
83835 Dave Frazier, 88 West Commerce, **Hayden Lake** ID ☎(208) 772-2911 – distributor of *Magic Mill* products					X		X			X		X	
83839 Summertime Products Ltd., Box 457, **Kingston** ID ☎(208) 682-3003 or (800) 626-0108					X	X							X
83854 Pelletman Heating Product, 2625 East Solstice Way, **Post Falls** ID ☎(208) 773-5610 – distributor of *Alco ◆Brite* gelled ethanol products					X								X
83856 International Association For Oxygen Therapy, PO Box 1360, **Priest River** ID ☎(208) 448-2504 – research, publication & subscription services in the oxidative sciences, Naturopathy, & natural health care;					X				X				
83861 St. Marie's Wild Rice, PO Box 293, **St. Maries** ID – catalog mail-order for specialty rice products; specializing in wild rice			X	X		X							
83864 Backwoods Solar Electric, 8530 Rapid Lightning Creek Rd., **Sand Point** ID ☎(208) 263-4290			X	X									X
83864 Northwest Energy Storage, 10418 Hwy. 95 N., **Sand Point** ID ☎(800) 718-8816			X	X									X

Product References Keyed to Chapters (Cont.)

04 water / air filtration & treatment	05 grains, seeds, mills & equip.	12 dairy / powdered milk supplies	13 honey / sweeteners
14 vitamins / minerals / herbs	15 sprouting / equip. & supplies	16 dry / dehydrated / freeze-dried	17 energy / fuels

M = Manufacturer / Processor — **D = Wholesaler / Trade distributor** — **R = Distributor / Retailer to public**

Entry	M	D	R	04	05	12	13	14	15	16	17
83869 **Old West Hardware**, 324 Main St., **Spirit Lake** ID ☎(208) 623-3740 — distributor of *Alco ♦Brite* gelled ethanol products		X									X
Illinois											
60504 **Fireplace & Patio, Aurora** IL ☎(708) 820-8664 🖷(708) 820-8743 — 3 locations; stoves, fireplaces & more…		X	X								X
60005 **Glashaus Inc.**, 415 West Golf Road #13, **Arlington Heights** IL ☎(708) 640-6918 — manufacturer of boiling water canning system & equipment; electric self-contained heating unit	X	X	X								X
60062 **Chef's Catalog**, 3215 Commercial Avenue, **Northbrook** IL ☎(800) 338-3232 — name brands-only equipment, supplies, appliances, tools, gourmet gifts, cookware, implements & appliances		X			X					X	X
60067 **Whole Foods Market**, 1311 North Rand Road, **Palatine** IL ☎(847) 776-8080 🖷(847) 776-8083		X	X			X	X	X	X	X	X
60073 **Ives-Way Prod., Inc.** *(attn: Glenn Ouris)* 2030 North Nicole Lane, **Round Lake Beach** IL ☎(847) 740-0658 — manufacturer of hand-operated & motorized can sealers; many models from which to choose	X		X								
60077 **Pure Sweet Honey Farms**, 8950 Gross Point Rd., **Skokie** IL ☎(847) 470-2504	X	X	X				X				
60090 **Collins Fireplace & Patio Shop, Inc., Wheeling** IL ☎(708) 541-4780 or 🖷(708) 541-0424 — stoves, fireplaces & more…		X	X								X
60143 **Fellowes®**, 1789 Norwood Avenue, **Itasca** IL — products available at office supply chains & stores; *Bankers Box* #57036 corrugated paper storage boxes with lid perfect for storing lightweight materials, such as medical supplies, parts, cords, spray paint, etc.	X										X
60174 **Ingersoll & Associates**, 6 N. 971 Riverside Dr., **St. Charles** IL ☎(888) 259-4040 🖷(847) 742-9170		X					X				
60201 **Whole Foods Market**, 1930 Ridge Avenue, **Evanston** IL ☎(847) 733-1600 🖷(847) 733-1670		X	X			X	X	X	X	X	X
60305 **Whole Foods Market**, 7245 Lake Street, **River Forest** IL ☎(708) 366-1045 🖷(708) 366-1044		X	X			X	X	X	X	X	X
60423 **Valco Stove Corp., Frankfort** IL ☎(708) 479-2456 🖷(815) 469-6401 — manufacturer of wood-burning stoves	X										X
60419 **Live Free, Int'l.**, PO Box 375, **Dolton** IL ☎(773) 821-LIVE — freedoms consulting/publishing; *Liberty Club* & *Freedom & Wellness Internationale*® non-profit members clubs	X	X	C	X	X			X		X	X
60521 **D. R. G. Alternatives, Inc.** 40 South Spring Lake, **Hinsdale** IL ☎(630) 654-4624 🖷(630) 654-4623 — preparedness and food storage products; consulting & seminars; books, tapes, & videos; more!		X (C)	X					X		X	X
60563 **Whole Foods Market**, 1163 Ogden Avenue, **Naperville** IL ☎(708 369-9800 🖷(708) 369-9836		X	X			X	X	X	X	X	X
60567 **Nu-World Amaranth**, PO Box 2022, **Naperville** IL ☎(630) 369-6819 — national distributor of amaranth and other grains; bulk flour & seeds; puffed amaranth		X	X		X					X	
60622 **Whole Foods Market**, 1000 West North Avenue, **Chicago** IL ☎(312) 587-0648 🖷(312) 587-0606		X	X			X	X	X	X	X	X
60645 **The House of Cans, Inc.**, 7060 N. Lawndale Ave., **Lincolnwood** IL ☎(847) 677-2100 — home canning equipment & supplies; metal cans & lids		X									X
60649 **Midway Labs, Inc.**, 1818 E. 71ˢᵗ St., **Chicago** IL ☎(312) 667-PVME 🖷(312) 667-6577	X										X
60657 **Whole Foods Market**, 3300 N. Ashland, **Chicago** IL ☎(312) 244-4200 🖷(312) 244-4074		X	X			X	X	X	X	X	X
60661 **N. Turek & Sons Supply Co.**, 333 South Halsted St., **Chicago** IL ☎(312) 263-3560 — distributor of *Alco ♦Brite* gelled ethanol products		X									X
60954 **Van Drunen Farms**, 300 W. 6ᵗʰ St., **Momence** IL ☎(815) 472-3100 🖷(815) 472-3850 — producer & processor of freeze-dried, individually quick-frozen (**IQF**) & drum-dried fruits, vegetables, & meats; custom-processing for industrial customers; organic herbs; frozen herbs & vegetables; sugar-infused fruits; organic farming; *minimum order, 1 case of any product*	X	X								X	
61101 **Goodwin Energy Products**, 1320 Blue Ridge Avenue, **Rockford** IL ☎(815) 963-7089 — distributor of *Magic Mill* products; *Safe-Trek Foods* distributor			C		X			X		X	
61283 **Midwest Bio-Systems**, Route 1 Box 121, **Tampico** IL ☎(815) 542-6426 — providing solutions for organic waste management & developing comprehensive soil fertility programs; equipment & supplies; responsible waste management & environmentally sound farming consulting		X	C								X
61548 **Farm Country General Store** *(attn: Larry)*, Rt. 1, Box 63, **Metamora** IL ☎None — distributor of *Magic Mill* products		X	X		X			X		X	X
61721 **Earth Sheltered Homes / Davis Caves**, PO Box 69, **Armington** IL ☎(309) 392-2574 — bright, spacious, comfortable & secure; built to survival shelter specifications (4 ft. of earth cover); nationwide builder; blueprints available for $15.00 and includes floorplan book	X	X	C								X
61875 **Seymour Organic Foods**, 205 S. Main, **Seymour** IL ☎(217) 687-4810 🖷(217) 687-4830 — distributor of organic foods; soy products: flakes, flour, whole soybeans, milk drinks & powders, yogurt, infant formula, oil & shortenings; tofu products: powder, textured soy protein (TVP), whole soybeans		X	X		X					X	
61937 **Edna Schrock**, Rt 2 Box 81, **Lovington** IL ☎(217) 543-3645 — *Magic Mill* products distributor						X		X		X	
62034 **IMS-PLUS**, 208 W. Main St., **Glen Carbon** IL ☎(618) 288-3498 🖷(618) 288-3498 ⌨www.imsplus.com ✉imsplus@imsplus.com — military surplus, camping, & survival gear; military clothing & uniforms; fuel bars & tablets; T-shirts		X	X					X		X	X

M = Manufacturer / Processor — D = Wholesaler / Trade distributor — R = Distributor / Retailer to public	M	D	R	04	05	12	13	14	15	16	17
62239 Gateway Food Products Co., 1728 N. Main Street, **Dupo** IL ☎(314) 231-9932 🖷(618) 286-3444 – soy products	X	X								X	
62341 Dadant & Sons, Inc., 51 S. 2nd St., **Hamilton** IL ☎(217) 847-3324 – beekeeping equipment & supplies	X	X	X				X				
62401 Hodgson Mill, 1901 S. 4th St. #26, **Effingham** IL ☎(800) 525-0177 🖷(217) 347-0198 – custom-ground flours; available in health food and grocery markets; soy products	X	X	X			X				X	
62461 Harder Supply, RR 1 Box 97, **Shumway** IL – homesteading/survival pamphlets & products; mail-order supplier			X								
62525 ADM (Archer Daniels Midland), 4666 Faries Pkwy., **Decatur** IL ☎(217) 424-2593 🖷(217) 362-3959 – soy products producer: hydrolyzed vegetable protein (HVP), meat alternatives, fiber, flakes, flours, grits, protein concentrates, milk drinks, milk powder products, yogurt, oil & shortenings, textured protein (TVP)	X	X				X				X	
62573 The Mad Prophet's Granary, PO Box 604, **Warrensburg** IL ☎(217) 672-3356 🖷(217) 875-6114 – long-term storage and emergency supplies; authorized regional dealer for *SamAndy®* dehydrated food & equipment; seeking retail dealers; aloe products & vitamins		C				X		X	X		
62812 Sarge's Surplus, *(attn: Larry Bozic)*, 320 S. Main, **Benton** IL ☎(618) 435-3524 – *SamAndy Foods* products distributor			X	X	X	X			X	X	X
62824 White Oak Ventures, PO Box 357, **Clay City** IL ☎(618) 676-1076 or (888) 999-4001 – *Safe-Trek Foods* distributor; food storage & preparedness products			X	X	X	X				X	X
62864 Chimney Shop, 1226 Salem Rd., **Mt. Vernon** IL ☎(618) 242-4328 – distributor of *Alco ♦Brite* gelled ethanol products			X								X

Indiana

M = Manufacturer / Processor — D = Wholesaler / Trade distributor — R = Distributor / Retailer to public	M	D	R	04	05	12	13	14	15	16	17
46074 Eiseles Honey Bee Supply, 2129 W. 186th St., **Westfield** IN ☎(317) 896-5830	X	X	X				X				
46151 Wind Mountain Rock Shop, 8265 Beech Grove Lane, **Martinsville** IN ☎(317) 996-3176 – surgical scissors, knives, cutlery, and other kitchen supplies			X								
46173 Stan Solomon Productions, 3349 Georgetown Rd., **Indianapolis** IN ☎(800) 844-7826 or (318) 387-7555 🖷(317) 387-7554 ✉*Solomon@IEI.NET* – distributor of *Survival Tabs*, SW radios & generators; books & videos; and supplemental health foods	X	X						X			X
46227 Nature's Cupboard, 8924 US Hwy. 31 S., **Indianapolis** IN (800) 290-9200 or (317) 888-0557 🖷888-8985 – general-purpose preparedness & food storage products	X	X				X		X	X	X	X
46250 Judith A. Toroni, 9305 Budd Run Drive, **Indianapolis** IN ☎(317) 841-9358 – distributor of *Magic Mill* products & additional information			X			X			X	X	
46254 Georgetown Health Foods, 3976 Georgetown Rd., **Indianapolis** IN ☎(317) 293-9525 – distributor of *Magic Mill* products & additional information			X			X			X	X	
46383 Fireside Specialties, 512 Randle St., **Valparaiso** IN ☎(219) 464-2924 – distributor of *Alco ♦Brite* gelled ethanol products			X								X
46567 The Country Baker, 8751 N. 850 E., **Syracuse** IN ☎(219) 834-2134 – *Bosch distributor*; *GrainMaster* grain grinder; *Zojirushi* home bread & pastry bakery; rice cooker; food dehydrator; juicers; stainless steel cookware			X	X	X	X	X		X	X	X
46581 Clark New Vision Int'l. & Resource Supplies, PO Box 1984, **Warsaw** IN ☎(219) 491-5707 – camping supplies, water filters & purifiers, storage foods; preparedness consultant		C		X	X	X	X	X	X	X	X
46637 Solar Tech, Inc., 19089 Summers Drive, **South Bend** IN ☎(219) 272-8087 🖷(219) 277-1314	X	X									X
46807 Security Foods, div. of Grogan, Inc., 4305 Beaver Avenue, **Fort Wayne** IN			X	X	X	X	X		X	X	X
46970 Marburger Foods, PO Box 387, **Peru** IN ☎(317) 473-3086 🖷(317) 473-8554 – manufacturer of meat alternatives	X					X		X	X	X	
47305 Alltrista Consumer Products Co., 301 S. High St., **Muncie** IN ☎(317) 281-5000 or (800) 240-3340 – manufacturer of *Ball* canning jars & metal self-sealing lids; free *"Ball Home Canning Basics"* booklet	X										
47305 Ball Corporation, 345 S. High St., **Muncie** IN ☎(317) 747-6100 – manufacturer of home canning equipment, jars, & lids	X										
47302 Natural Readiness Foods, 4400 E. Maple Manor Pkwy., **Muncie** IN ☎(765)288-5850 or (888) 377-5449 – distributor of *AlpineAire, Maple Leaf, Mountain House, Provident Pantry, Ready Reserve,* & *Walton Feed* food storage products; distributor of *Emergency Essentials* preparedness products		C	X	X	X	X	X	X		X	X
47374 Long Life Foods, PO Box 8081, **Richmond** IN ☎(317) 939-0110 or (800) 601-2833🖷(317) 939-0065 – long shelf-life food rations for outdoor & emergency preparedness			X	X	X	X	X			X	X
47374 Resourceful Foods Co., PO Box 8100, **Richmond** IN ☎(800) 782-7478 🖷(317) 966-6774			X	X	X	X	X			X	X
47501 The Long Term Store, Route 1 Box 109, **Washington** IN ☎(812) 254-4964 – preparedness consultant; in-home storage specialist; disasters or emergencies specialist		C	X								
47804 General Housewares, PO Box 4066, **Terre Haute** IN ☎(812) 232-1000 – manufacturer of home canning equipment	X										X

Product References Keyed to Chapters (Cont.)

04 water / air filtration & treatment	05 grains, seeds, mills & equip.	12 dairy / powdered milk supplies	13 honey / sweeteners
14 vitamins / minerals / herbs	15 sprouting / equip. & supplies	16 dry / dehydrated / freeze-dried	17 energy / fuels

M = Manufacturer / Processor D = Wholesaler / Trade distributor R = Distributor / Retailer to public

Listing	M	D	R	04	05	12	13	14	15	16	17
Iowa											
50036 **Greg T. Rinhart,** 703 Kale Road, **Boone** IA ☎(515) 432-4480 — distributor of *Magic Mill* products			X		X			X	X		
50265 **ABC Iowa / Missouri,** 1005 Grand Ave., **West Des Moines** IA ☎(515) 223-1091 — distributor of *Magic Mill* products			X		X			X	X		
50313 **GSF** (attn: Bill), 6280 NE 14th Street, **Des Moines** IA ☎(515) 289-1097 — distributor of *Magic Mill* products			X		X			X	X		
50456 **Allison Hill,** 3480 Olive Ave., **Manly** IA ☎(515) 454-2241 — distributor of *Magic Mill* products			X		X			X	X		
50525 **Country Stoves** (attn: Rick), 1898 250th St., **Clarion** IA — distributor of *Alco•Brite* gelled ethanol products			X								X
50529 **Pat Crozier,** 1510 1st Street SW, **Clarion** IA ☎(515) 532-2185 — distributor of *Magic Mill* products			X		X			X	X		
50595 **Murray McMurray Hatchery, Webster City** IA ☎(800) 456-3280 — 140+ varieties of baby chicks, bantams, turkeys, guineas, peafowl, game birds, waterfowl; also, eggs, incubators, books, equipment & medications; supplier for eggs, meat, & exhibition poultry	X	X									
50702 **Custom Blacksmithing,** 827 Commercial St., **Waterloo** IA ☎(319) 291-2095 — distributor of *Alco•Brite* gelled ethanol products			X								X
51025 **Holstein Mfg., Inc., Holstein** IA ☎(712) 368-4342 — manufacturer of wood-burning stoves, barbecue equipment, & sawdust furnaces	X										X
51102 **Sioux Honey Association,** PO Box 388, **Sioux City** IA ☎(712) 258-0638	X	X	X				X				
51240 **Lee Seed Farm,** 2242 Highway 182, **Inwood** IA ☎(712) 753-4403 — soybean candies, soy nuts, whole soybeans	X	X			X					X	
51366 **JPD,** PO Box 27, **Webb** IA ☎(712) 838-7705 — *K-TEC* kitchen products distributor; preparedness consultant; in-home storage specialist			C		X		X	X			
52556 **Wellness Now,** PO Box 1362, **Fairfield** IA ☎(800) 555-9894 or (515) 472-7601 🖷(515) 472-1556 💻www.wellnessnow.com ✉herbsrus@kdsi.net — distributor of health-related complementary nutritional products; iridology, therapeutic nutrition, kinesiology, & health consultations by telecom; personal care supplies, & more!		X	X (C)					X			
52774 **Root Acres,** Box 118-B, **Welton** IA ☎(319) 659-5576 — high-germinating organic seeds for sprouting at reasonable prices via mail order; free recipes with orders			X		X				X		
Kansas											
66001 **Midwest Fireplace, Stoves & Spas, Olathe** KS ☎(913) 764-5575 ✉midwest@hearth.com		X	X								X
66002 **American White Wheat Producers Association,** PO Box 326, **Atchison** KS ☎(913) 367-4422 — producers' association for marketing *Natural s'Wheat* products: white wheat whole berries, cracked wheat, flakes, flour, & bulgur; whole or kibbled *Sofgrain*	X	X	X		X						
66018 **Caprine Supply,** 33001 W. 83rd St., **DeSoto** KS ☎(913) 585-1191 — cheesemaking supplies	X	X	X			X					
66044 **Pines International,** 1992 East 1400 Road, **Lawrence** KS ☎(913) 841-6016 or (800) 697-4637 🖷(913) 841-1252 💻www.wheatgrass.com ✉sales@wheatgrass.com — concentrated whole food products; wheat grass, wheat & barley grass, juice powders; certified organic herbs; wheat grass pastas; alfalfa & alfalfa blends with superfoods	X	X	X		X			X	X		
66044 **Wild Oats,** 1040 Vermont, **Lawrence** KS ☎(913) 865-3737 🖷(913) 865-2840			X	X	X	X	X	X	X	X	
66053 **Jeffery Earl,** 6620 West 303rd Street, **Louisburg** KS ☎(913) 837-5809 — distributor of *Magic Mill* products			X		X			X	X		
66062 **Harvest Moon Natural Foods,** 2113-A East 151 St., **Olathe** KS ☎(913) 782-7562			C	X	X	X	X	X	X	X	
66205 **Wild Oats,** 5101 Johnson Dr., **Mission** KS ☎(913) 722-4069 🖷(913) 722-2178			X	X	X	X	X	X	X	X	
66207 **Manna Nutrition Store,** 5309 W. 94th Terrace, **Prairie Village** KS ☎(913) 381-6604			C	X	X	X	X	X	X	X	
66208 **Good Earth Natural Food,** 3934 W. 69th Terrace, **Prairie Village** KS ☎(913) 432-8040			C	X	X	X	X	X	X	X	
66413 **Tenth Generation,** 807 West Banks, **Burlingame** KS — distributor of *Private Reserve* brand dehydrated foods			X								
66436 **Kansas Wind Power,** 13569 214th Road, **Holton** KS ☎/🖷(913) 364-4407 (913) 364-4407 💻www.smallfarm.com/kanswind — wind/solar electric systems; energy-saving equipment; propane-operated equipment—refrigerators, lights, tankless water heaters; inverters, pumps, motors, fans, grain mills, bed warmers, composting toilets, solar cookers, solar stills, books, radios; discount prices!; catalog $4	X	X	X	X					X	X	X
66507 **Kenneth Flagler,** Rt. 1 Box 180, **Mapleville** KS ☎(913) 437-6170 — distributor of *Magic Mill* products			X		X			X	X		
66601 **Midwest Fireplace / Stoves & Spas, Topeka** KS ☎(913) 267-9600 ✉midwest@hearth.com		X	X								X

M = Manufacturer / Processor	D = Wholesaler / Trade distributor	R = Distributor / Retailer to public	M	D	R	04	05	12	13	14	15	16	17

66604 Health Food Mart, 1507 SW 21st, **Topeka** KS — R=C; 04 X, 05 X, 12 X, 13 X, 14 X, 17 X
– complete health/natural foods line; vitamins, minerals, herbs, books, dietetics, teas, proteins, nuts, juicers

66612 Topeka Health Foods, 514 W. 10th, **Topeka** KS ☎(913) 233-591 — R=C; 04–17 X

66748 Harvest Health, 714 Bridge St., **Humbolt** KS — R=C; 04–17 X

66801 P.D.S.I., PO Box 1461, **Emporia** KS ☎(800) 941-2889 — M X, D X, R X; 13 X, 17 X
– distributor of *Aerobic 07*; for oxygen health to clean water, food, immune system, and more

67021 The Coleman Co., Inc., / *Institutional Department*, PO Box 2931, **Wichita** KS ☎(800) 633-7155 — M X, D X; 17 X
– emergency preparedness equip. & products for personal comfort; heat & lighting; appliances; electrical generators

67203 Whole Foods, 2172 N. Amedon, **Wichita** KS ☎(316) 832-1227 — R=C; 04–17 X

67206 Green Acres, 8141 E. 21st St., **Wichita** KS ☎(316) 634-1500 — R=C; 04–17 X

67213 Wheatland Pantry c/o Eileen Dumford, 915 West Douglas, **Wichita** KS ☎(316) 264-5519 — R X; 05 X, 14 X, 16 X
– distributor of *Magic Mill* products

67214 Food For Thought, 2819 E. Central, **Wichita** KS ☎(316) 683-6028 — R=C; 04–17 X

67214 Nature's Mercantile, 2900 E. Central, **Wichita** KS ☎(316) 685-3888 — R=C; 04–17 X

67226 Warming Trends, 3101 N Rock Rd. #130, **Wichita** KS ☎(316) 636-9677 — R X; 17 X
– distributor of *Alco♦Brite* gelled ethanol products

67344 Marlene's Mills, Rt. 1 Box 195, **Elk City** KS ☎(316) 627-2230 — R X; 05 X, 14 X, 16 X
– distributor of *Magic Mill* products

67401 General Nutrition Center, 2259 South 9th Street, **Salina** KS ☎(913) 823-0800 — R=C; 04–17 X

67401 Prairieland Food Co-op, 138 S. 4th, **Salina** KS ☎(913) 823-8041 — R=C; 04–17 X

67401 The Vita Villa, 1009 E. Crawford, **Salina** KS ☎(913) 827-7547 — R=C; 04–17 X

67504 PMS Foods, Inc., PO Box 1099, **Hutchinson** KS ☎(316) 663-5711 or (800) 835-5006 — M X; 17 X
– wholesale only; flavored soy products; meat analogs; barbecue sauce; flavored TVP

67521 Protech Wheat, PO Box 95, **Brownell** KS ☎(913) 481-2391 ✎(913) 481-2391 — M X, D X, R X; 13 X, 15 X
– grower-direct organic wheat delivered to consumers

67530 The General Store, 1320 10th, **Gt. Bend** KS ☎(800) 836-7712 — D X, R X; 04 X, 05 X, 12 X, 16 X, 17 X

67672 Great Plains Seed, Inc., 706 Barclay Avenue, **Wakeeney** KS ☎(913) 743-5778 — M X, D X, R X; 12 X, 16 X
– source of wheat, whole grains, peas, beans, & rice

67863 Heartland Mill, Inc., Rt. 1 Box 2, **Marienthal** KS ☎(316) 379-4472 or (800) 232-8533 — M X, D X, R X
– custom-ground all-organic flours

67901 Nature's Cupboard, 1010 S. Kansas, **Liberal** KS — R=C; 04–17 X

Kentucky

40050 Lone Wolf Enterprises, 650 Scobie Lane, **New Castle** KY ☎/✎(502) 845-1002 — M X, D X

40160 U. S. Cavalry Store (Corp. Ofc.), 2865 Centennial Avenue, **Radcliff** KY ☎(502) 351-1164 or (800) 777-7172 ✎(502) 352-2266 💻www.uscav.com ✉hq@uscav.com — R X; 04 X, 05 X, 12 X, 13 X, 15 X, 16 X, 17 X
– retailer & mail order (4,200 items); survival & outdoor clothing & equipment; preparedness products

40160 U. S. Cavalry, 601 N. Duke, **Radcliff** KY ☎(502) 351-7000 ✎(502) 351-8714 — R X; 04 X, 05 X, 12 X, 13 X, 15 X, 16 X, 17 X
– retailer & mail order (4,200 items); survival & outdoor clothing & equipment; preparedness products

40207 U. S. Cavalry, 5000 Shelbyville Road, **Louisville** KY ☎(502) 895-9033 ✎(502) 895-9747 — R X; 04 X, 05 X, 12 X, 13 X, 15 X, 16 X, 17 X
– retailer & mail order (4,200 items); survival & outdoor clothing & equipment; preparedness products

40224 Tova Industries, Inc., PO Box 24410, **Louisville** KY ☎(512) 267-7333 ✎(502) 267-7119 — M X, D X; 17 X
– producer of more than 600 dry food products; custom formulation; dietary products; beverages, cake & bread mixes, soup bases, desserts, gravies, dressings; herbs & spices; dehydrated vegetables

41139 Linda Quade, 910 Vance Street, **Flatwoods** KY ☎(606) 836-2675 — R X; 05 X, 14 X, 16 X
– distributor of *Magic Mill* products

42103 Lilybeth Parrent, 908 Richland Drive, **Bowling Green** KY ☎(502) 782-5088 — R X; 05 X, 14 X, 16 X
– distributor of *Magic Mill* products

42240 Sunworthy Solar Electric, 4105 Witty Ln., **Hopkinsville** KY ☎(502) 889-0624 ✉louis1@ldd.com — M X, D X; 17 X

42262 U. S. Cavalry, 16298 Ft. Campbell Rd., **Oak Grove** KY ☎(502) 439-4945 ✎(502) 351-8714 — R X; 04 X, 05 X, 12 X, 13 X, 15 X, 16 X, 17 X
– retailer & mail order (4,200 items); survival & outdoor clothing & equipment; preparedness products

42327 Sam Kercheval, 360 Main Street, **Calhoun** KY ☎(502) 273-5606 — R X; 05 X, 14 X, 16 X
– distributor of *Magic Mill* products

Louisiana

70002 Nature Lovers Health Foods, 3014 Cleary Ave., **Metarie** LA ☎(504) 887-4929 — R=C; 04–17 X

70043 Nutritional Foods East, 8921 W. Judge Perez Dr., **Chalmette** LA ☎(504) 271-3292 — R=C; 04–17 X

70053 Total Health Foods, 419-F La Palco Blvd., **Gretna** LA ☎(504) 392-0548 — R=C; 04–17 X

70058 Health Hut, 2034 Woodmere Blvd., #A, **Harvey** LA ☎(504) 340-1332 — R=C; 04–17 X

70062 The Health & Energy Center, 2440 Veterans Blvd., **Kenner** LA ☎(504) 466-8858 — R=C; 04–17 X

70068 Naturally Yours Health Foods, 421 W. Airline Hwy. #E., **La Place** LA ☎(504) 652-2975 — R=C; 04–17 X

70115 All Natural Foods, 5517 Magazine St., **New Orleans** LA ☎(504) 891-2651 — R=C; 04–17 X

Product References Keyed to Chapters (Cont.)

04 water / air filtration & treatment	05 grains, seeds, mills & equip.	12 dairy / powdered milk supplies	13 honey / sweeteners
14 vitamins / minerals / herbs	15 sprouting / equip. & supplies	16 dry / dehydrated / freeze-dried	17 energy / fuels

M = Manufacturer / Processor   D = Wholesaler / Trade distributor   R = Distributor / Retailer to public

Listing	M	D	R	04	05	12	13	14	15	16	17
70118 **Eve's Market**, 7700 Cohn, **New Orleans** LA ☎(504) 861-4514			C	X	X	X	X	X	X	X	
70118 **Food for Thought**, 3309 S. Carrollton Ave., **New Orleans** LA ☎(504) 488-7900			C	X	X	X	X	X	X	X	
70119 **Whole Foods Market**, 3135 Esplanade, **New Orleans** LA ☎(504) 943-1626 🖨(504) 947-7901		X	X	X	X	X	X	X	X	X	
70126 **Nutritional Foods East**, 3926 Old Gentilly Rd., **New Orleans** LA ☎(504) 945-5760			C	X	X	X	X	X	X	X	
70130 **Back to the Garden**, 207 Dauphine, **New Orleans** LA ☎(504) 524-6915			C	X	X	X	X	X	X	X	
70130 **The Appleseed Shoppe**, 346 Camp St., **New Orleans** LA ☎(504) 529-3442			C	X	X	X	X	X	X	X	
70156 **Natural Nutrition Center**, 906 South Lewis Street, **New Iberia** LA ☎(318) 365-9037			C	X	X	X	X	X	X	X	
70360 **Pro Nutrition**, 1222 St. Charles, **Houma** LA ☎(504) 852-8055			C	X	X	X	X	X	X	X	
70433 **Columbia Street Whole Foods Market**, 415 North Columbia St., **Covington** LA ☎(504) 893-5500			C	X	X	X	X	X	X	X	
70433 **Springs of Life**, 518 N. Columbia St., **Covington** LA ☎(504) 892-6277			C	X	X	X	X	X	X	X	
70460 **Ruby's Natural Foods**, 1030 Hwy. 190 West, **Slidell** LA ☎(504) 641-1620			C	X	X	X	X	X	X	X	
70501 **Louisiana Data Products**, 1101 NW Evangeline Thruway, **Lafayette** LA ☎(800) 826-5767 — authorized retail distributor of *Mountain House* brand freeze-dried products	X	X								X	
70503 **Sandra's Health Food**, 111-A Rena Drive, **Lafayette** LA ☎(318) 988-0108			C	X	X	X	X	X	X	X	
70506 **Nature's Best**, 111 Arnold Blvd., **Lafayette** LA ☎(318) 981-9087			C	X	X	X	X	X	X	X	
70527 **Falcon Rice Mill, Inc.**, PO Box 771, **Crowley** LA ☎(318) 783-3825 🖨(318) 783-1568 — production, milling, &/or distribution of rice & processed rice products	X	X			X					X	
70527 **Supreme Rice Mill, Inc.**, **Crowley** LA ☎(318) 783-5222 🖨(318) 783-3204 — production, milling, &/or distribution of rice & processed rice products	X	X			X					X	
70546 **Jennings Co-op**, 638 E. Academy Ave., **Jennings** LA ☎(318) 824-8886			C	X	X	X	X	X	X	X	
70548 **Liberty Rice Mill, Inc.**, PO Box 218, **Kaplan** LA ☎(318) 643-7176 🖨(318) 643-1929 — production, milling, &/or distribution of rice & processed rice products	X	X			X					X	
70556 **Broussard Rice Mill, Inc.**, 102 South 13th Street, **Mermentau** LA ☎(318) 824-2409 — production, milling, &/or distribution of rice & processed rice products	X	X			X					X	
70601 **Lumen Foods/ Herbologics Ltd.**, 409 Scott St., **Lake Charles** LA ☎(318) 436-6748 — soy products; meat alternatives, protein concentrates, milk drinks, milk powder & products, TVP		X				X					
70602 **Farmers' Rice Milling**, PO Box 3704, **Lake Charles** LA ☎(318) 433-5205 🖨(318) 433-1735 — production, milling, &/or distribution of rice & processed rice products	X	X			X					X	
70634 **Ideal Health Mart**, 610 North Pine, **Deridder** LA ☎(318) 463-7210			C	X	X	X	X	X	X	X	
70730 **Myra Pollard**, 2158 Turner Road, **Ethel** LA ☎(504) 683-3995 — distributor of *Magic Mill* products		X			X					X	
70737 **Horn Of Plenty**, 623 E. Ascension, **Gonzales** LA ☎(504) 644-6080			C	X	X	X	X	X	X	X	
70791 **Zachary Health Store**, 5250 East Mae St., Box 539, **Zachary** LA ☎(504) 654-6513			C	X	X	X	X	X	X	X	
70806 **Vitality Food Shoppe**, 3140 Government, **Baton Rouge** LA ☎(504) 925-5142			C	X	X	X	X	X	X	X	
70809 **Vitality Food Shoppe**, 5475-B Essen Lane, **Baton Rouge** LA ☎(504) 767-6740			C	X	X	X	X	X	X	X	
70815 **Vitality Food Shoppe**, 750 Oak Villa, **Baton Rouge** LA ☎(504) 925-5780			C	X	X	X	X	X	X	X	
71104 **Sunshine Health Foods**, 2328 Line Ave., **Shreveport** LA ☎(318) 425-3042			C	X	X	X	X	X	X	X	
71108 **Good Life Health Foods & Emergency Supplies**, 6132 Hearne Ave., **Shreveport** LA ☎(318) 635-4753 🖨(318) 636-5084			C	X	X	X	X	X	X	X	
71108 **Goodlife Health Food Store**, 6132 Hearne Ave., **Shreveport** LA ☎(318) 635-4753 — distributor of *Alco ♦Brite* gelled ethanol products		X									X
71111 **Sunshine Health Foods**, 532 Benton Road, **Boosier City** LA ☎(318) 746-9788			C	X	X	X	X	X	X	X	
71294 **Health Food Store**, PO Box 1363, **West Monroe** LA ☎(318) 325-2423			C	X	X	X	X	X	X	X	
71449 **Nuclear Defense Shelters & Equip.**, RR 1 # 725, Hwy. 6 W., **Many** LA ☎(318) 256-2021 🖨(318) 256-0879 — contractors/consultants for nuclear defense shelters & equipment; design, engineering, & construction of reinforced concrete blast/fallout shelters, chemical/biological filter systems, & related shelter hardware	X	X	C								X
Maine											
04479 **Dover Stove Co., Inc.**, **Sangerville** ME ☎(207) 876-3265 — manufacturer of wood-burning stoves & furnaces	X										X
04609 **Sunrise Home & Hearth**, **Bar Harbor** ME ☎(207) 667-3205 🖨(207) 667-3315	X	X									X
04614 **American Sun Co**, PO Box 789, **Blue Hill** ME ☎(207) 374-5700 — fireplaces, stoves, & other energy-saving products	X	X									X
04841 **Mazzeo's Stoves & Fireplaces**, **Rockland** ME ☎(207) 596-6496 🖨(207) 594-7845	X	X									X
04937 **Marshall Engineering**, 337 Norridgewock Road, **Fairfield** ME — become water self-sufficient at a fraction of the cost of a well with proven, fully automatic, solar-powered water system; details of plans & photos available	X	X	X								X

M = Manufacturer / Processor	D = Wholesaler / Trade distributor	R = Distributor / Retailer to public	M	D	R	04	05	12	13	14	15	16	17

Maryland

Entry	M	D	R	04	05	12	13	14	15	16	17
20601 Tri-County Energy, Waldorf MD ☎(301) 843-1771 (301) 932-7972 — stoves, fireplaces, & more…	X	X									X
20616 American Supply Int'l., Inc., PO Box 1207, **Bryans Road** MD ☎(301) 870-0200 (301) 843-9654 www.amsupply.com		X				X					
20740 Beautiful Day, 5010 Berwyn Rd., **College Park** MD ☎(301) 345-6655	C	X	X	X	X	X	X	X			
20740 Smile Herb Shop, 4908 Berwyn Road, **College Park** MD ☎(301) 474-4288 (301) 441-3734		X						X			
20814 Pathway Apothecary Pharmacy, 5415 Cedar Lane, **Bethesda** MD ☎(301) 530-1112		X						X			
20816 Fresh Fields, 2569 River Road, **Bethesda** MD ☎(301) 984-4860 (301) 984-4870		X	X	X	X	X	X	X	X		
20841 Richard Coats, 23101 E. Slydell Road, **Boyds** MD ☎(301) 428-2910 — distributor of *Magic Mill* products		X	X					X		X	
20852 Fresh Fields, 1649 Rockville Pike, **Rockville** MD ☎(301) 984-4880 (301) 816-1897		X	X	X	X	X	X	X	X		
20879 Staff of Life Products (*attn: Robert Schellhase*), 19217 Autumn Maple Lane, **Gaithersburg** MD ☎(301) 391-6860 (301) 946-2562 — distributor of *Magic Mill* products		X	X					X		X	
21001 Hodges True Value Hardware, 1517 S. Philadelphia Blvd., **Aberdeen** MD — distributor of *Alco ♦Brite* gelled ethanol products		X									X
21014 Bay State Pellet Distributor, 223 Rolling Knoll Dr., **Bel Air** MD ☎(410) 893-6667 — distributor of *Alco ♦Brite* gelled ethanol products		X									X
21014 Courtland Hardware, Inc., 6 N. Bond St., **Bel Air** MD ☎(410) 838-5161 — distributor of *Alco ♦Brite* gelled ethanol products		X									X
21036 Total Health Int'l., Inc., PO Box 44, **Dayton** MD ☎(410) 531-5911 (410) 531-5911		X	X					X		X	
21157 Miller's, Westminster MD ☎(410) 857-0333 or (800) 634-3473 — chimney sweeping, wood, pellet & gas stoves	X	X									X
21162 County Stoves, Inc., 11433 Pulaski Hwy., **White Marsh** MD ☎(410) 335-8831 — distributor of *Alco ♦Brite* gelled ethanol products		X									X
21201 Pastores Distributors, Baltimore MD ☎(410) 633-0400 — distributor of *Parmalat* shelf-stable, whole milk dairy products	X	X			X						
21206 Christ the King Bookstore (*attn: Leonard Wood*), 5525 Belair Rd., **Baltimore** MD — *SamAndy Foods* products distributor		X	X	X	X	X			X	X	X
21209 Fresh Fields, 1330 Smith Avenue, **Baltimore** MD ☎(410) 532-6700 (410) 532-7002		X	X	X	X	X	X	X	X		
21221 Bay State Pellets, 7110 Golden Ring Rd. #113, **Baltimore** MD ☎(410) 893-6667 — distributor of *Alco ♦Brite* gelled ethanol products		X									X
21401 Fresh Fields, 2504 Solomons Island Drive, **Annapolis** MD ☎(410) 573-1800 (410) 573-1801		X	X	X	X	X	X	X	X		
21713 Debra Youngbar, 215 Maple Ave., **Boonsboro** MD ☎(301) 432-4824 — distributor of *Magic Mill* products		X	X					X		X	
21721 The Maples Fruit Farm, Inc., PO Box 167, **Chewsville** MD ☎(301) 733-0777 — dried fruits, grains, coffees & teas		X	X								
21740 Elin Craig, 16026 Spade Road, **Hagerstown** MD ☎(301) 733-8385 — distributor of *Magic Mill* products		X	X					X		X	
21742 Bake Crafters c/o Michael Byrd, 21927 Martin Circle, **Hagerstown** MD ☎(301) 714-1892 — distributor of *Magic Mill* products		X	X					X		X	

Massachusetts

Entry	M	D	R	04	05	12	13	14	15	16	17
01001 DC Solar, MA ☎(800) DC-SOLAR (508) 759-5059	X	X									X
01004 Wellspring Natural Food Co., PO Box 2473, **Amherst** MA ☎(800) 578-5301 — mail-order organic & natural soy foods; miso, milk drinks, Tamari, tempeh, tofu & tofu, whole soybeans		X	X	X	X	X	X	X	X	X	
01005 Higgins Energy Alternatives, Barre MA ☎(508) 355-6343 (508) 355-4582 — wood stoves, pellet stoves, gas stoves, coal stoves, & more…	X	X									X
01035 Bread & Circus, Route 9 / Russell Street, **Hadley** MA ☎(413) 586-9932 (413) 584-4588		X	X	X	X	X	X	X	X		
01035 Olde Hadleigh Hearth & Home, S. **Hadley** MA ☎(800) 331-HEAT (413) 538-9845	X	X									X
01093 Nash Energy, 106 State Rd., **Whately** MA ☎(413) 665-8500 — distributor of *Alco ♦Brite* gelled ethanol products		X									X
01098 Fowler Solar Electric, 226 Huntington Rd., **Worthington** MA ☎(800) 914-4131	X	X									X
01220 Catamount Pellet Fuel Corp., 60 Printworks Dr., **Adams** MA ☎(413) 743-8212 — distributor of *Alco ♦Brite* gelled ethanol products		X									X
01230 The Sprout House, 314 Main Street, **Great Barrington** MA ☎(413) 528-5200 or (800) 777-6887 (413) 528-5201 www.hlthmall.com/healthmall/sproutman sproutman@sproutman.com — *Sproutman* organic sprouting seeds & supplies; kits; books on sprouting; fresh sprouts overnight via mail	X	X	X						X	X	
01240 Get a Life, PO Box 2218, **Lenox** MA ☎(800) 967-7279 — supplier of Yoga products		X	X					X			

Product References Keyed to Chapters (Cont.)

04 water / air filtration & treatment	05 grains, seeds, mills & equip.	12 dairy / powdered milk supplies	13 honey / sweeteners
14 vitamins / minerals / herbs	15 sprouting / equip. & supplies	16 dry / dehydrated / freeze-dried	17 energy / fuels

Listing	M	D	R	04	05	12	13	14	15	16	17
M = Manufacturer / Processor — D = Wholesaler / Trade distributor — R = Distributor / Retailer to public											
01242 CSCF Distributor, 139 Walker St., **Lenox Dale** MA – distributor of *Alco ♦Brite* gelled ethanol products		X									X
01330 New England Cheesemaking Supply Co., Inc., PO Box 85 Main St., **Ashfield** MA ☎(413) 628-3808 🖷(413) 628-4061 🖳www.cheesemaking.com *info@cheesemaking.com* – suppliers to the home cheesemaking industry; catalog available for $1.00	X	X								X	
01341 South River Miso Co., 888 Shelburne Falls Road, **Conway** MA ☎(413) 369-4057 🖷(413) 369-4299	X	X	X			X	X			X	
01469 Sterilite Corporation, **Townsend** MA – plastic storage products available at chain & discount stores, office supply chains & stores	X										X
01520 J.J. Reidy & Co., 1260 Main St., **Holden** MA ☎(508) 829-6550 🖷(508) 829-6550 🖳www.tiac.net/users/jjreidy ✉*jjreidy@tiac.net* – unit produces water by condensing water vapor from the air; only system with unlimited drinking water available!	X	X	X	X							
01520 Wachusett Food Co-op, 21 Avery Heights Drive, **Holden** MA ☎(508) 829-4797 ✉*72103.50@compuserve.com*			C		X	X	X	X	X	X	X
01520 Waterstar Technology, 1260 Main St., **Holden** MA ☎(508) 829-6550 🖷(508) 829-6550 🖳www.tiac.net/users/jjreidy ✉*jjreidy@tiac.net* – drinking water from the air we breathe!; multi-patented technology extracts drinking water from the air	X	X	X	X		X	X				X
01585 Herbs From God's Garden, 103 New Braintree Rd., **West Brookfield** MA ☎(508) 867-6214		X						X			
01720 Emerson Ecologics Inc., 436 Great Rd., **Acton** MA ☎(800) 654-4432		X						X			
01742 Concord Spice & Grain, 89-93 Thoreau St., **Concord** MA ☎(508) 369-1535			C		X	X	X	X	X	X	X
01742 The Storm Shelter, 60 Thoreau St. #269-W, **Concord** MA – solar & rechargeable products for emergency and everyday use	X	X									X
01760 Fireplace Shop, **Natick** MA ☎(508) 655-1070	X	X									X
01760 Natick Outdoor Store, 38 N. Ave., **Natick** MA ☎(508) 653-9400 – distributor of *Alco ♦Brite* gelled ethanol products		X									X
01844 Environmental Solar Systems, Inc., 119 W. St., **Methuen** MA ☎(800) 934-3848	X	X									X
01906 Wild Harvest, 357 Broadway (Route 1), **Saugus** MA ☎(617) 233-5341			C		X	X	X	X	X	X	X
01944 Northeast Organics Inc., Box 7, 1 Beaver Dam Road, **Manchester-by-the-Sea** MA ☎(508) 526-7888 or (800) 924-7347 🖷(508) 526-9818 – manufacturer of fish-based liquid fertilizer supplement for healthy & stress-reduced crops	X	X									
01949 Yankee Fireplace & Stove, **Middleton** MA ☎(800) 445-2760 or (508) 774-2760 🖷(508) 777-2634	X	X									X
02021 Stove Depot & Fireplace, 1049 Turnpike St., **Canton** MA – distributor of *Alco ♦Brite* gelled ethanol products		X									X
02035 All Natural Distributors, 11 Perry Drive **Foxboro** MA ☎(508) 543-1160 Fax⊗508) 543-5974 – distributor specializing in New England-based organic & macrobiotic products		X			X	X	X	X	X	X	X
02115 Bread & Circus, 15 Westland Avenue, **Boston** MA ☎(617) 375-1010 🖷(617) 375-1069			X		X	X	X	X	X	X	
02138 Bread & Circus, 186 Alewife Brook Parkway **Cambridge** MA ☎(617) 491-0040 🖷(617) 497-9469			X		X	X	X	X	X	X	
02139 Bread & Circus, 115 Prospect Street, **Cambridge** MA ☎(617) 492-0070 🖷(617) 492-9045			X		X	X	X	X	X	X	
02139 Harvest Cooperative Supermarket, 591 Massachusetts Ave., **Allston** MA ☎(617) 661-1580			C		X	X	X	X	X	X	X
02146 Bread & Circus, 15 Washington Street, **Brookline** MA ☎(617) 738-8187 🖷617) 566-8268			X		X	X	X	X	X	X	
02155 Wild Harvest, 2151 Mystic Valley Parkway, **Medford** MA ☎(617) 395-4998			C		X	X	X	X	X	X	X
02161 Bread & Circus, 916 Walnut Street, **Newton** MA ☎(617) 969-1141 🖷(617) 964-5773			X		X	X	X	X	X	X	
02181 Bread & Circus, 278 Washington Street, **Wellesley Hills** MA ☎(617) 235-7262 🖷(617) 431-9730			X		X	X	X	X	X	X	
02368 Russo Products, **Randolph** MA ☎(617) 963-1182 – manufacturer of wood-burning & coal-burning stoves	X										X
02553 Gardener's Kitchen, PO Box 322, **Monument Beach** MA – supplier of lids, rings, & seals for jar sizes #70, #86, #63 "flats" & rings; press-on ID labels for contents		X									
02652 Atlantic Spice Company, PO Box 205, **North Truro** MA ☎(508) 487-6100 or (800) 316-7965 🖷(508) 487-2550 🖳www.atlanticspice.com – spices, spice blends, selected dehydrated vegetables, shelled nuts & seeds, bulk tea & bags, black teas, bulk herb tea blends, sprouting seeds, gelatin caps, kelp, herbs, & spice containers	X	X	X					X		X	
Michigan											
48009 EV NAT Incorporated, 320 East Maple #262, **Birmingham** MI ☎(810) 754-5478 or (888) 235-7032 🖷(810) 754-5478 ✉*evnatinc@flash.net* – distributor of *Ready Reserve* brand long-term food storage products; preparedness consultant			C		X	X	X			X	X
48076 Mister Medic, Inc., PO Box 760490, **Lathrup Village** MI ☎(248) 968-1616 🖷(248) 968-9865 – emergency medical kits & equipment; water treatment supplies	X	C	X								
48089 Radnoy Corporation, 13231 Brainwood Ave., **Warren** MI ☎/🖷(800) 522-1862 or ☎(810) 758-7132 – longest-lasting hand-held flashlight; operates 2800 hours on 2 "D" batteries	X	X	X								X

M = Manufacturer / Processor · D = Wholesaler / Trade distributor · R = Distributor / Retailer to public	M	D	R	04	05	12	13	14	15	16	17
48101 C. B. Clark Services, *(attn: Connie Clark)*, 17151 Corse Rd., **Allen Park** MI ☎(313) 383-6744 — *SamAndy Foods* products distributor			X	X	X	X	X			X	X
48103 Daily Grind Flour Mill, 220 Felch Street #3, **Ann Arbor** MI ☎(313) 665-3845 🖷(313) 665-1541 — cooperative-owned flour mill; milled to order 100% organic whole grains, flours, & ground grain meals; whole wheat & spelt pretzels; packaged pastas	X	X	X			X					
48104 Whole Foods Market, 2398 East Stadium Blvd., **Ann Arbor** MI ☎(313) 971-3366 🖷(313) 971-7717			X	X		X	X	X	X	X	X
48105 Tri-Oxy, 6028 E. Joy, **Ann Arbor** MI ☎(313) 996-8458 🖷(313) 996-8458 💻www.inet-images.com/tri-oxy ✉*kevinconnie@provide.net* — ozone-based water purification systems; air purification systems			X	X				X			X
48127 New Light Services, 6612 Rockdale, **Dearborn Heights** MI ☎(313) 277-4637 — *K-Tec* kitchen machines distributor; mills, mixers, & health products; homeschooling curriculum			X	X	X		X				
48141 Wideview Scope Mount Corp., 26110 Michigan Ave., **Inkster** MI ☎(605) 341-3220 — distributor of *Alco ◆Brite* gelled ethanol products			X								X
48158 The Pathway Home, 201 E. Main Street, **Manchester** MI ☎(313) 428-1050 — herbs, teas, & spices packaged in plastic bags; larger quantities quoted on request			X			X	X	X		X	
48170 Patricia Trillich, 41194 Ann Arbor Trail, **Plymouth** MI ☎(313) 455-8967 — *Magic Mill* products distributor			X		X			X		X	
48185 D. Mouradian, PO Box 85355, **Westland** MI ☎(313) 554-1090 — catalog order supplier of preparedness products			X	X	X					X	X
48207 Rafal Spice Company, 2521 Russell, **Detroit** MI ☎(313) 259-6373 🖷(313) 259-6220 — spices, herb teas, & herb-related products			X	X				X		X	
48210 Cheryl A. Sartor, 7457 American, **Detroit** MI ☎(313) 834-8052 — *Magic Mill* products distributor			X		X			X		X	
48310 Young Park, 4139 Gloucester, **Sterling Height** MI ☎(810) 977-0263 — *Magic Mill* products distributor			X		X			X		X	
48336 Janice Parks, 23609 Spring Brook, **Farmington Hill,** MI ☎(810) 478-0366 *Magic Mill* distributor			X		X			X		X	
48353 Hartland Buying Club, PO Box, 428, **Hartland** MI ☎(810) 632-7952			C	X	X	X	X	X	X	X	X
483530 Betty L. Edmunds – Co-op Consultant, PO Box 428, **Hartland** MI ☎(810) 632-7952 — consumer consultant; specialist in setting up & operating retail & neighborhood food-buying co-ops			C								
48357 Charles & Shirley Courtney, 94 Locust, **Highland** MI ☎(313) 426-3160 — *Magic Mill* products distributor			X		X			X		X	
48629 Vera Parsons, 106 Hazen-Ella Drive, **Houghton Lake** MI ☎(517) 422-3333 — *Magic Mill* products distributor			X		X			X		X	
48842 Innovations Unlimited, 5700, Loch Woode Ct., **Holt** MI ☎(517) 694-5348 — soy nut butter, soy nuts	X	X				X				X	
48854 Sycamore Creek Company, 200 State St., **Mason** MI ☎(888) 769-4231 🖷(517) 676-6721 — soy nut butter, soy nuts, whole soybeans	X	X	X			X				X	
48864 Purity Foods, Inc., 2871 W. Jolly Rd., **Okemos** MI ☎(517) 351-9231 or (800) 997-7358 — producer of *Vita-Spelt* flour products; flours, blends, & mixes; available through better health food stores	X	X	X			X				X	
48893 Dorothy E. Adams, 9256 West Drew Road, **Weidman** MI ☎(517) 644-3481 — *Magic Mill* products distributor			X		X			X		X	
48906 Freedom Energy Co / Donald W. Sheets, 15902 Turner Road, **Lansing** MI ☎(517) 372-0347 — solar power products distributor		X	X								X
48909 Lorann Oils, PO Box 22009, **Lansing** MI — oils & fragrances for soapmaking; soapmaking supplies; catalog of food, apothecary & home crafting		X	X					X			
48910 M & B Construction, 1530 Bailey St., **Lansing** MI ☎(517) 485-9062 — *Hardy* brand outside wood furnace for homes w/forced air heating systems; designed for long, cold winters		X	X								X
49015 Dorene Janette Smith, 138 Orleans Ave., **Battle Creek** MI ☎(616) 660-1763 — *Magic Mill* products distributor			X		X			X		X	
49017 Something Better Natural Foods, 614 Capital Ave. NE, **Battle Creek** MI ☎(616) 965-1199 — processor of hydrolyzed vegetable protein (HVP), lecithin, meat alternatives, soy flour, soy grits, soy milk drinks, soy milk powder & products, soy nuts, textured soy protein, whole soybeans	X	X	X			X				X	
49103 Apple Valley Market, 9067 US 31, **Berrien Springs** MI ☎(800) 237-7436 🖷(616) 471-3594 — meat alternatives from soy products: flour, grits, protein concentrates, sauce products, organically grown soybeans, milk powders, nut butter, oil & shortenings, Tamari, tempeh, tofu, teriyaki products, TVP, & whole soybeans		X	X			X				X	
49103 Natural Foods Market, 9067 US 31, **Berrien Springs** MI ☎(800) 237-7436 🖷(616) 471-3594 — mail-order natural foods & organics			X	X		X	X	X	X	X	X
49200 Storey Stove Company, Jackson MI ☎(517) 782-4033		X	X								X
49201 Rainbow Meadow, 6943 Clarklake Road, **Jackson** MI ☎(517) 764-4170 💻www.sojourn.com/~rainbow/soapsupp ✉*rainbow@sojourn.com* — supplier of soapmaking oils, supplies & equipment for in-home soapmaking	X	X						X			

Product References Keyed to Chapters (Cont.)

04 water / air filtration & treatment			05 grains, seeds, mills & equip.			12 dairy / powdered milk supplies		13 honey / sweeteners		
14 vitamins / minerals / herbs			15 sprouting / equip. & supplies			16 dry / dehydrated / freeze-dried		17 energy / fuels		

M = Manufacturer / Processor	D = Wholesaler / Trade distributor	R = Distributor / Retailer to public	M	D	R	04	05	12	13	14	15	16	17
49228 Derco, Inc., Blissfield MI ☎(517) 486-4337 🖷(517) 486-4559 – manufacturer of wood-burning stoves & commercial furnaces			X										X
49241 DWM Communications, PO Box 66, Hanover MI ☎(517) 563-9022 *credit card orders*: (517) 563-2613 🖷(517) 563-8974 ⌨www.glr.com/dwm ✉*tinytenna@aol.com* – US-made; SW/ham radio accessories; transmitters, receivers, antennas; books to improve SW performance			X	X	X								X
49301 Heaven Can Wait, 8831 Bailey Drive, Ada MI ☎(616) 676-9272 or (800) 969-9272				X						X			
49301 Vicki Degrazier, 5899 Two Mile Road NE., Ada MI ☎(616) 676-0598 – *Magic Mill* products distributor				X			X			X	X		
49302 Detaxing America, 9392 Whitneyville, Alto MI (616) 891-2217 – detaxing programs, unincorporated trusts, debt cancellation, bank & credit cards; potentials unlimited tapes				X									
49331 Bear's Military Surplus Distributing, PO Box 127, Lowell MI (616) 8971550				X	X	X	X	X	X	X	X	X	X
49411 Cold Stream Farm, 2030 Freesoil Rd., Freesoil MI ☎(616) 464-5809 – develop 4 acres of hybrid poplar and heat your home forever			X										X
49418 Kathryn Terpstra, 4240 Wilson, Grandville MI ☎(616) 534-7874 – *Magic Mill* products distributor				X			X			X	X		
49450 Country Life Natural Foods Store, PO Box 489, Pullman MI ☎(616) 236-5011 🖷(616) 236-8357 – mail-order source for wheat, whole grains, peas, beans, & rice; flours				X			X			X	X		
49512 Worldshop, 3665 29th Street, Grand Rapids MI ☎(616) 957-0555 ⌨www.worldshop.com – mail-order distributor of freeze-dried foods for the happy camper				X								X	
49677 Sherry Dillbeck, 315 West Franklin Ave., Reed City MI ☎(616) 832-4583 – *Magic Mill* distributor				X			X			X	X		
49738 Kathy Pflugrad, 201 Maple St., Grayling MI ☎(517) 348-4845 – specializing in vegetarian cookery for wilderness or emergency				C			X						X
49770 American Spoon Foods, Inc., PO Box 566, Petoskey MI ☎(616) 347-9030 or (800) 222-5886 🖷(800) 647-2512 ⌨www.spoon.com ✉*information@spoon.com*				X	X								X
49801 Khoury Factory Outlet, 1508 N. Stephenson Ave., Iron Mountain MI ☎(906) 779-1240 – distributor of *Alco ♦Brite* gelled ethanol products				X									X
49837 Roxanne & Lee Evison, 6501 Marble Lane, Gladstone MI ☎(906) 428-9316 – *Magic Mill* products distributor				X			X			X	X		
49935 Ginnies Inc., 812½ W. Cayuga St., Iron River MI ☎(906) 265-6292 – survival-packaged spices in foil-sealed pouches; 1-lb. basic spices for long-term storage				X								X	

Minnesota

M = Manufacturer / Processor	D = Wholesaler / Trade distributor	R = Distributor / Retailer to public	M	D	R	04	05	12	13	14	15	16	17
55014 Lancaster & Simpson, Ltd., 6292 Red Maple Lane, Lino Lakes MN ☎(612) 490-1132				X									
55024 The Campers Pantry, PO Box 293, Farmington MN ☎(612) 463-3765 – authorized retail distributor of *Mountain House* brand freeze-dried products			X	X								X	
55024 The Campers Pantry, PO Box 293, Farmington MN ☎(612) 463-3765 🖷(612) 463-3765 ⌨www.alcasoft.com/campers_pantry ✉*Cpantry@aol.com* – drehydrated & freeze-dried foods; *mail order only*			X	X	X							X	X
55032 Joan Mellum, 855 Stark Road West, Harris MN ☎(612) 689-9709 – *Magic Mill* products distributor				X			X			X	X		
55040 Joyce Shuman, 4782 County Road #5 N.W., Isanti MN ☎(612) 444-5269 – *Magic Mill* products distributor							X			X	X		
55075 The Sportsman's Guide, Inc., MN ☎(800) 882-2962 🖷(800) 333-6933 ⌨www.sportsmanguide.com – retail mail-order catalog of high-value merchandise to outdoor enthusiasts				X	X								X
55104 Whole Foods Market, 30 South Fairview, St. Paul MN ☎(612) 690-0197 🖷(612) 690-0382				X	X	X	X	X	X	X	X		
55164 Harvest State Coop, PO Box 64594, St. Paul MN – soy products producers—soy flour, soy oil & shortenings			X	X				X				X	
55313 Buffalo Family Food Co-op, 12 1st Avenue South, Buffalo MN ☎(612) 682-6433				C	X	X	X	X	X	X	X		
55318 American Harvest, Inc., 4064 Peavey Rd., Chaska MN ☎(612) 448-4400 or (800) 288-4545 – manufacturer of *American Harvest* food dehydrators; *Converga-Flow* technology; adjustable thermostat			X									X	
55337 Northern Hardware, 2800 Southcross Drive, Brunsville MN ☎(800) 533-5545 ⌨www.northern-online.com – regional chain of heavy hardware items—call for locations & mail-order catalog				X	X								X
55343 LaFlame Industry, 1109 South Landmark, Hopkins MN ☎(612) 933-5828 – distributor of *Alco ♦Brite* gelled ethanol products				X									X
55372 Viereck Fireplace Sales, Prior Lake MN ☎(612) 440-5620 ⌨www.hotfireplaces.com ✉*sales@hotfireplaces.com*				X	X								X
55379 David M. & Jackie Sebald, 1146 Harrison Street, Shakopee MN ☎(612) 445-2034 – *Magic Mill* products distributor				X			X			X	X		
55401 Summit Home Center, St. Paul & Minneapolis MN ☎(800) 825-2858 🖷(612) 731-6192				X	X								X

M = Manufacturer / Processor · D = Wholesaler / Trade distributor · R = Distributor / Retailer to public	M	D	R	04	05	12	13	14	15	16	17
55401 World Wide, Inc., PO Box 1224, **Minneapolis** MN ☎(612) 830-8700 — distributor of *Alco♦Brite* gelled ethanol products		X									X
55404 National Co-op Directory *(Referral Svc.)*, 919 21st Ave. South, **Minneapolis** MN ☎(612) 332-0417 — write for names & locations of nearest cooperative wholesaler, co-op retail store, or local neighborhood buying club	X	C	C								
55404 Roots & Fruits Cooperative Produce, 1929 E. 24th St., **Minneapolis** MN ☎(612) 722-3030 — wholesale co-op organic produce; cheese, dry goods, related products	X	C		X				X			
55408 East Calhoun Food Co-op, 3255 Bryant Ave. S., **Minneapolis** MN ☎(612) 827-4145			C	X	X	X	X	X	X	X	
55414 Blooming Prairie Natural Foods, 510 Kasota Ave. SE, **Minneapolis** MN ☎(800) 322-8324 *in MN* ☎(800) 322-8241 *outside MN Only* 🖷(612) 378-9780 **Territory:** *MN, Western MI, Eastern ND, SD, WI* — co-op distributor of whole, natural, & organic foods to the retail co-ops & food-buying clubs; *bulk & wholesale only*	X	C	X	X	X	X	X	X	X		
55420 Delta Light, PO Box 202223, **Minneapolis** MN ☎(612) 980-6503 — send SASE for information about light bulbs that never wear out!	X	X	X								X
55422 Our Daily Bread, 4350 Lakeland Ave. N., **Robbindale** MN ☎(612) 535-5514 🖷(612) 535-9822			C	X	X	X	X	X	X	X	
55440 Damark, 7101 Winnetka Ave. N., **Minneapolis** MN ☎(800) 729-9000 — discount mail-order; close-outs & factory-serviced housewares: electric breadmakers, juicers, kitchen wares, small appliances, water filters, mixers & blenders, tents & camping gear, inflatable boats & kayaks		X	X	X						X	X
55736 Ace Outdoor Furnace, Box 43, **Floodwood** MN ☎(218) 476-2180	X										X
55744 L & M Supply, Inc., 1200 E. Hwy. 169, **Grand Rapids** MN ☎(218) 326-9783 — distributor of *Alco♦Brite* gelled ethanol products			X								X
58701 Energy Plus, Duluth MN ☎(218) 722-7818 🖷(218) 722-2146 — all types heating equipment		X	X								X
55802 World Power Technologies, Inc., 19 N. Lake Ave., **Duluth** MN ☎(218) 722-1492 🖷(218) 722-0791 — small wind power systems generate electricity for battery charging and accessories to be self-sufficient		X	X								X
55949 The Dry Store, Rt. 2 Box 156, **Lanesboro** MN ☎(507) 467-2928 🖳www.polaristel.net/~drystore ✉drystore@means.net			X		X				X		
55965 Community Market & Deli, 110 St. Anthony St., **Preston** MN ☎(507) 765-5245 ✉kneegan@preston.polaristel.net			C	X	X	X	X	X	X	X	
56002 Mitor Industries, Inc., PO Box 4339, **Mankato** MN ☎(507) 387-1599 🖷(507) 387-7491 — mfr. of *Mitor* 3-way compact fluorescent portable luminaire; energy-saving & efficient lamp using $\frac{1}{3}$ the energy	X										X
56073 New Ulm Food Co-op, 1403 Broadway South, **New Ulm** MN ☎(507) 359-5583			C	X	X	X	X	X	X	X	
56093 Sproutamo Corporation, Box 308, **Waseca** MN ☎(507) 835-7712 🖷(507) 835-1628 — "no-rinse" sprouting with *Easy Sprout*™; innovative design & natural convection action provides ideal environment for sprouting seeds; available through participating dealers	X	X	X						X		
56175 Living Farms, Box 1127, **Tracy** MN ☎(507) 629-4431 🖷(507) 629-4253 — organic seeds, grains, beans & legumes for storage; may be purchased by the lb.			X		X				X		
56232 Western Prairie Food Co-op, 674 6th St., **Dawson** MN			C	X	X	X	X	X	X	X	
56303 Steve Ziemer, 1010 31st Ave. N., **St. Cloud** MN — authorized wholesale distributor of *Vacu-Dry* dehydrated food products		X	X							X	
56316 Aqua-Therm, Rt. 1 Box 1, **Brooten** MN ☎(800) 325-2760 — manufacturer of outdoor wood stoves	X										X
56331 Wellness Marketing, Box 112, **Freeport** MN ☎(612) 836-2445 — wellness products that help you feel energized & relaxed			X					X			
56345 Peterson Machine Shop Co., Little Falls MN ☎(320) 632-6949 — manufacturer of wood-burning stoves, fireplace inserts, & high dome fireplace units	X										X
56353 Koch Hardware Hank, 13845 125th Ave., **Milaca** MN ☎(612) 294-5544 — distributor of *Alco♦Brite* gelled ethanol products			X								X
56353 W. W. Enterprises, 11992 170th, **Milaca** MN ☎(612) 983-6381 — distributor of *Alco♦Brite* gelled ethanol products			X								X
56442 Custom Metal Fabrication Inc., **Crosslake** MN ☎(218) 692-2425 🖷(218) 692-2425 — manufacturer of wood-burning stoves	X										X
56461 Pass the Pen Evangelistic Association, Rt. 1 Box 273, **Guthrie** MN ☎(218) 751-1522 ✉102.545.244 — plans with 65 illustrations for a build-it-yourself, multi-size jar vacuum-sealing machine, made from used parts	X	C	X							X	X
56474 Stromberg's Chicks & Gamebirds Unlimited, Box 400, **Pine River** MN ☎(218) 587-2222 or (800) 720-1134 *toll-free number for orders* 🖷(218) 587-4230 — everything for every kind of fowl or poultry; equipment, tools, & supplies for the bird, fowl, & poultry industry		X	C				X				
56623 Dahl Wood Stoves, Inc., Hwy. 11 West, **Baudette** MN ☎(218) 634-1100	X										X
56623 Medical Corps, Rt. 3 Box 33A, **Baudette** MN — potassium iodide for emergency use during & after nuclear fallout			X					X			
56633 Berge's Stoves, Inc., **Cass Lake** MN ☎(218) 335-6362	X										X
56636 Gibbs Wild Rice, Box 277, **Deer River** MN ☎(218) 246-8595 or (800) 344-6378 🖷(218) 246-8123 — distributor of instant wild rice to retail & foodservice; white & wild blends; wild rice in collector tins			X				X			X	

Product References Keyed to Chapters (Cont.)

04 water / air filtration & treatment	05 grains, seeds, mills & equip.	12 dairy / powdered milk supplies	13 honey / sweeteners
14 vitamins / minerals / herbs	15 sprouting / equip. & supplies	16 dry / dehydrated / freeze-dried	17 energy / fuels

M = Manufacturer / Processor **D = Wholesaler / Trade distributor** **R = Distributor / Retailer to public**

Chapter columns: 04 05 12 13 14 15 16 17

Entry	M	D	R	04	05	12	13	14	15	16	17
56726 **Central Boiler**, Rt. 1, Box 220, **Greenbush** MN ☎(218) 782-2575 or (800) 248-4681 — manufacturer of whole-house hot water and heating units	X										X
56737 **Natural Way Mills**, R2, Box 37, **Middle River** MN ☎(218) 222-3677 — *Magic Mill* products distributor					X		X		X	X	
56763 **Heatmor**, Hwy. 11 East, Box 787, **Warroad** MN ☎(218) 386-2769	X	X									X
59201 **Basic Water Quality Testing**, MN ☎(612) 699-4040 or (612) 721-6123 — for non-municipal sources, test water for many substances & determining purification requirements; $25.00 per test	X	X	X	X							

Mississippi

Entry	M	D	R	04	05	12	13	14	15	16	17
38701 **Cargill Rice Milling**, Highway 82, West Cargill Drive, **Greenville** MS ☎(601) 378-0335	X	X			X					X	
39056 **Mike McMillan**, 303 Hester Street, **Clinton** MS ☎(601) 924-7042 — distributor of *Magic Mill* products					X		X		X	X	
39204 **The Sesame Seed**, 314 Raymond Rd., **Jackson** MS ☎(601) 373-9727			C		X	X	X	X	X	X	
39350 **Hardy Manufacturing Co.**, Rt. 4 Box 156, **Philadelphia** MS ☎(601) 656-5866	X										X
39401 **Health Hut**, 1004 Hardy St., **Hattiesburg**, MS ☎(601) 582-4333			C		X	X	X	X	X	X	
39479 **ABCO**, Box 306, **Seminary** MS — free information for building liquid piston engine from pipe fittings	X	X									X
39577 **Free Spirit Farm & Survival, Inc.**, PO Box 967, **Wiggins** MS ☎(601) 928-5081 or (888) 245-8061 ᕟ(601) 928-5081 ✉*freedom@netdoor.com* — retail store; providing food storage & emergency preparedness products			C		X	X	X	X	X	X	
39701 **Theresa E. Brown**, 30 Honeysuckle Lane, **Columbus** MS ☎(601) 329-9938 — distributor of *Magic Mill* products					X		X		X	X	

Missouri

Entry	M	D	R	04	05	12	13	14	15	16	17
63019 **David Kennedy**, PO Box 186, **Crystal City** MO — authorized regional dealer for *SamAndy*® dehydrated food & equipment; seeking retail dealers	X	X	X	X	X				X	X	X
63032 **Self-Reliance**, PO Box 306, **Florissant** MO		X									X
63043 **Jaeger Greenhouses**, 2411 Creve Coeur Mill Rd., **Maryland Heights** MO ☎(314) 739-5709 or (314) 739-1507 — distributor of *Kitchen Specialties* products; wheat and grain products; seminars & classes on breadmaking		X	C		X						
63101 **Busch Agricultural Resources, Inc.**, 1010 Market Street, **St. Louis** MO ☎(314) 622-3922 — production, milling, &/or distribution of rice & processed rice products	X	X			X					X	
63108 **Golden Grocer**, 335 N. Euclid, **St. Louis** MO ☎(314) 367-0405			C		X	X	X	X	X	X	
63119 **Natural Way**, 8110 Big Bend, **Webster Grove** MO ☎(314) 961-1880			C		X	X	X	X	X	X	
63124 **Wild Oats**, 8823 Ladue Road., **St. Louis** MO ☎(314) 721-8004 ᕟ(314) 721-8011		X	X		X	X	X		X	X	
63129 **New World**, 4037 Union Road, **St. Louis** MO ☎(314) 487-8310			C		X	X	X	X	X	X	
63138 **Anne E. Belley**, 939 Pridge Road, **St. Louis** MO ☎(314) 741-8704 — distributor of *Magic Mill* products					X		X		X	X	
63141 **Natural Way West**, 12345 Olive Blvd., **St. Louis** MO ☎(314) 878-3001			C		X	X	X	X	X	X	
63301 **Worthington Stove & Hearth**, St. Charles MO ☎(314) 947-3165 ᕟ(314) 947-1730	X	X									X
63376 **Nutrition Stop**, 4101 Mexico, **St. Peters** MO ☎(314) 928-7550			C		X	X	X	X	X	X	
63401 **Sedna Specialty Health Products**, PO Box 347, **Hannibal** MO ☎(314) 221-4747 or (800) 223-0858 ᕟ(314) 221-6504	X	X					X	X	X		X
63401 **The Withers Mill Co.**, PO Box 347, **Hannibal** MO ☎(341) 221-4747 or (800) 223-0858 ᕟ(314) 221-6504 — portable, solar-powered ionization system eliminates the need for chlorine & other harmful chemicals in swimming pools, spas, wells, & water storage supplies	X	X	X								X
63536 **Annette C. Horner**, 15 Outen Drive, **Downing** MO ☎(816) 379-2855 — distributor of *Magic Mill* products					X		X		X	X	
63565 **Davis Auto Supply**, 111 South 18th Street, **Unionville** MO — distributor of *Alco♦Brite* gelled ethanol products		X									X
64020 **Food Reserves, Inc.**, 110 Bismark Street, **Concordia** MO ☎(660) 463-2158 ᕟ(660) 463-2159 ✉*goodforyou@almanet.net* — manufacturer of *Survival Tabs*—"15 days' food supply under 1 lb."; long-term food storage products	X	X	X						X	X	
64024 **Barbara L. Baldwin**, 607 Garland, **Excelsior Springs** MO ☎(816) 630-3047 — distributor of *Magic Mill* products					X		X		X	X	
64052 **Staff of Life Health Foods**, 1415 W. Lexington, **Independence** MO ☎(816) 252-5335			C		X	X	X	X	X	X	
64063 **Nature's Market**, 535 SE Melanie, **Lee's City** MO ☎(816) 525-2625			C		X	X	X	X	X	X	
64064 **Soapmaking Kits**, PO Box 6751, **Lee's Summit** MO ☎(816) 525-0664 — supplies, books & videos for in-home soapmaking; soapmaking newsletter	X	X									
64088 **Osage Honey Farm Inc.**, 222 Santa Fe, **Sibley** MO ☎(816) 650-5637	X	X	X				X				
64111 **Clearly Nature's Own**, 4301 Main St., **Kansas City** MO ☎(816) 931-1873			C		X	X	X	X	X	X	

M = Manufacturer / Processor	D = Wholesaler / Trade distributor	R = Distributor / Retailer to public	M	D	R	04	05	12	13	14	15	16	17
64111 **Wild Oats**, 4301 Main St., **Kansas City** MO ☎(816) 931-1873 🖨(816) 931-7734					X	X		X	X	X	X	X	X
64116 **Model Stove Midwest, Inc.**, 2419 Burlington, **North Kansas City** MO ☎(913) 831-4203 – distributor of *Alco♦Brite* gelled ethanol products					X							X
64133 **Futura**, 9605 E. 67 Terrace, **Raytown** MO ☎(816) 358-6439 or (800) 530-5242					X			X		X		X
64133 **Pumpkin Seed Health Store**, 9055 East 350 Hwy., **Raytown** MO ☎(816) 358-1700					C	X	X	X	X	X	X	X
64507 **Kathryn Shelley**, 3514 Seneca, **St. Joseph** MO ☎(816) 232-4509 – distributor of *Magic Mill* products					X			X		X		X
64803 **Common Sense Products**, PO Box 2423, **Joplin** MO ☎/🖨(417) 325-5444 ✉*jlp.csp@juno.com* – home education & tutorial materials; homeschool products			X	C								
64836 **Oak Street Health & Herbs**, 425 Oak Street, **Carthage** MO ☎(417) 358-0990					C	X		X	X	X	X	X
64836 **Richard Cooley**, 626 S. Case Street, **Carthage** MO ☎(417) 358-3286 – distributor of *Magic Mill* products					X			X		X		X
64840 **Stirling Sharpeners**, PO Box 358, **Diamond** MO ☎(417) 325-4256 – all-metal kitchen & pocket knife sharpener			X	X	X							X
65109 **USA Features Co.**, 3702 W. Truman Blvd., #200–151, **Jefferson City** MO ☎(800) 693-9858 🖨(573) 635-8670 ✉*usafeature@juno.com*					X	X	X				X	
65233 **Judy Arnett**, 24863 Highway 98, **Boonville** MO ☎(816) 882-8009 – distributor of *Magic Mill* products					X			X		X		X
65570 **American Survival**, PO Box 458, **Success** MO ☎(417) 458-4647					C							X
65583 **Sunburst Health Store**, 1029 Mini Mall, **St. Robert** MO ☎(314) 336-3339					C	X	X	X	X	X	X	X
65613 **New Life Natural Food Store**, 106 W. Jackson, **Bolivar** MO					C	X	X	X	X	X	X	X
65615 **Tiny Power Steam Engine Co.**, PO Box 1605, **Branson** MO ☎(417) 334-2655 💻www.chatlink.com\~soltherm\tinypwr.htm ✉*146942@msn.com* – tiny power steam engines, castings only; 13 models available; facility open to the public; displays & steamboat			X	X								X
65616 **"Sensible Steam" Consultants**, c/o Skip Goebel, 152 von Goebel's Lane, **Branson** MO ☎(417) 336-2869 💻www.chatlink.com\~soltherm\tinypwr\htm ✉*146942@msn.com* or ✉*104247.127@compuserv.com* – steam-powered systems alternate energy; creating large amounts of controllable & usable heat—smallest steam system provides more than enough heat for food processing, drying & heating; may utilize unrefined or waste fuels			X	X	C							X
65641 **Mitchell's Ltd.**, Mitchell Plaza, **Eagle Rock** MO ☎(417) 271-3220 – distributor of *Alco♦Brite* gelled ethanol products					X							X
65655 **Hodgson Mill, Inc.**, **Gainesville** MO ☎(417) 679-4651			X	X	X			X			X	
65672 **Whole Foods General Store**, 217 N. Bus. 65, **Branson** MO ☎(417) 335-8300					C	X	X	X	X	X	X	X
65708 **Bass Equipment Company**, PO Box 352, **Monett** MO ☎(417) 235-7557 or (800) 798-0150 🖨(417) 235-4312 ✉*Rabbits4U@mo-net.com* – manufacturer of rabbit raising equipment & supplies			X	X	X							
65711 **Meadowbrook Natural Foods**, 100 Union St., **Mountain Grove** MO					C	X	X	X	X	X	X	X
65726 **Edwards Mill College of Ozarks**, **Point Lookout** MO ☎(417) 334-6411 – mail-order, custom-ground flours & meals; cornmeal, whole wheat flour, wheat germ, cracked wheat, & more!			X				X					
65737 **Fuller's Fire Protection**, Rt. 7 Box 669, **Reeds Springs** MO ☎(417) 272-3273 – distributor of *Alco♦Brite* gelled ethanol products					X							X
65737 **Ozark Renewables**, Rt. 2 Box 4305, **Reeds Spring** MO ☎(417) 338-8688				X								X
65760 **East Wind Nut Butters**, Rt. 3 Box 682, **Tecumseh** MO ☎(417) 679-4682 – cooperative worker-owned processor of organic nut butters			X	X	X			X			X	
65803 **Country Cupboard**, 1727 E. Division, **Springfield** MO ☎(417) 865-7350					C	X	X	X	X	X	X	X
65804 **Winslow Health & Diet Food**, 1501 S. Glenstone, **Springfield** MO ☎(417) 881-5643					C	X	X	X	X	X	X	X
65807 **Maschino's**, 1715 S. Campbell, **Springfield** MO – distributor of *Alco♦Brite* gelled ethanol products					X							X
65808 **Mike Brown**, PO Box 4884, **Springfield** MO ☎/🖨(417) 890-8636 💻http://home.earthlink.net/~dlaw70/ – author, patriot broadcaster, & consultant; alternative energy via steam engines; author of personal health books			X	X	C					X			X
Montana												
59011 **Magic Mill Products**, East of Big Timber, **Big Timber** MT ☎(406) 932-6579					X		X			X	X	
59047 **Big Sky Co-op**, Route 38, Box 2219, **Livingston** MT ☎(405) 222-7350					C	X	X	X	X	X	X	X
59047 **Juice Plus**, PO Box 1061, **Livingston** MT ☎(406) 222-8466 – fruits & vegetables encapsulated by a unique proprietary process to preserve the naturally-occurring vitamins, minerals, fiber, enzymes, and antioxidants			X	X				X				
59101 **Bar S Supply Company**, 2102 Old Hardin Rd., **Billings** MT ☎(406) 259-3391 – distributor of *Alco♦Brite* gelled ethanol products					X							X
59261 **Pride of the Prairie – Saco Dehy Inc.**, PO Box 268, **Saco** MT ☎(406) 527-3414 🖨(406) 527-3277 – organic wheat, barley, & oats; grown in high & dry mountains; proteins above 16%			X	X	X			X				
59270 **Kalberer's Heating, Inc.**, 218 3rd St. NE, **Sidney** MT ☎(406) 482-2630 – distributor of *Alco♦Brite* gelled ethanol products					X							X

Product References Keyed to Chapters (Cont.)

04 water / air filtration & treatment	05 grains, seeds, mills & equip.	12 dairy / powdered milk supplies	13 honey / sweeteners
14 vitamins / minerals / herbs	15 sprouting / equip. & supplies	16 dry / dehydrated / freeze-dried	17 energy / fuels

M = Manufacturer / Processor **D = Wholesaler / Trade distributor** **R = Distributor / Retailer to public**

Entry	M	D	R	04	05	12	13	14	15	16	17
59301 **Riverside Marketplace**, 21 South 9th Street, **Miles City** MT ☎(406) 232-5811			C	X	X	X	X	X	X	X	
59401 **Bernice Askeland**, 1601 2nd Ave. N., **Great Falls** MT ☎(406) 761-1604			X			X		X		X	
59401 **Good Food Country Store**, 1601 2nd Ave. North, **Great Falls** MT ☎(406) 761-1604			X						X	X	X
59401 **Health Food Shop**, 507 1st Ave. North, **Great Falls** MT ☎(406) 452-0361			C	X	X	X	X	X	X	X	
59401 **Mountain Market Place**, 109 N. 4th Street, **Hamilton** MT ☎(406) 452-0361			C	X	X	X	X	X	X	X	
59427 **Montana Wheat Growers, Inc.**, Cut Bank MT ☎(406) 338-5307	X	X	X	X	X	X	X	X	X	X	
59457 **Sun Food Store**, 108 6th Ave. N, **Lewiston** MT ☎(406) 538-2815			C	X	X	X	X	X	X	X	
59486 **Full of Grace**, PO Box 457, **Valier** MT ☎(406) 472-3323											
59601 **Real Food Store**, 1090 Helena Ave., **Helena** MT ☎(406) 443-5150			C	X	X	X	X	X	X	X	
59601 **Smitty's Fireplace Shop**, 4373 N. Montana Ave., **Helena** MT ☎(406) 442-2242 – distributor of *Alco ♦Brite* gelled ethanol products			X								X
59701 **Dancing Rainbow Natural Grocery**, 9 S. Montana Street, **Butte** MT ☎(406) 723-8811			C	X	X	X	X	X	X	X	
59715 **Gallatin Food Reserves**, 90 Safe-Trek Place, **Bozeman** MT ☎(800) 424-7870 ▤(406) 582-0614 – custom canning; products sourcing; distributor of *Private Reserve* brand dehydrated storage foods	X	X				X					X
59715 **Safe-Trek Outfitters**, 90 Safe-Trek Place, **Bozeman** MT ☎(406) 587-5571 or (800) 424-7870 ▤(406) 582-0614 www.safetrek.com or http://montana.avicom.net/Safetrek.html – distributor of food storage & preparedness products; full line of dehydrated & freeze-dried foods; books & videos; solar equipment & products; underground shelters; military surplus gear for NBC pollution; authorized distributor of *Survival Tabs & Storehouse Foods,* manufactured by *Food Reserves, Inc.;* authorized distributor of *Emergency Essentials* products; distributor of *Alco ♦Brite* gelled ethanol products			C	X	X	X	X	X	X	X	
59715 **Safe-Trek Private Reserve Foods**, 90 Safe-Trek Place, **Bozeman** MT ☎(406) 586-4840 or (800) 424-7870 ▤(406) 586-4842 www.safetrek.com ✉safetrek@avicom.net – *Private Reserve* wholesale food & dehydrated foods cannery; full-line distributor of food storage products	X	X	X	X	X	X	X	X	X	X	X
59716 **Hungry Moose Market**, PO Box 160673, **Big Sky** MT ☎(406) 995-3045			C	X	X	X	X	X	X	X	
59718 **Renaissance LTD.**, 90 Safe-Trek Place, **Bozeman** MT ☎(406) 586-4840 or (800) 424-7870 ▤(406) 586-4872 www.safetrek.com ✉safetrek@avicom.net – precious metals dealer; investment fund dealing in precious metals & commodity futures	X				X		X		X		
59722 **Fitness Health & Nutrition**, PO Box 3641, **Bozeman** MT ☎(406) 585-9898 or (406) 585-9204			C	X	X	X	X	X	X	X	
59725 **Mountain Valley Grocery**, 26 Bannack, **Dillon** MT ☎(406) 683-6772			C	X	X	X	X	X	X	X	
59752 **Wheat Montana Farms**, PO Box 647, **Three Forks** MT ☎(800) 535-2798 – certified chemical-free grains; wheat includes: *Hard Red Spring & Hard White Spring*; flours; 7-grain mixes; beans, barley, rice, alfalfa, & lentils; *Montana* honey; plastic pails	X	X	X		X		X			X	X
59758 **Pika Foods Co-op**, 121 Madison Ave., **West Yellowstone** MT ☎(406) 646-4969			C	X	X	X	X	X	X	X	
59771 **InfiNet Communications, Inc.**, PO Box 6339, **Bozeman** MT ☎(406) 585-9324 ▤(406) 585-0671 www.mtmarketplace.com ✉mtmarket@mcn.net – *Internet* marketing of preparedness products; organic grains; freeze-dried foods; precious metals; distributor of *Emergency Essentials* products & *AlpineAire Gourmet Freeze-dried Foods*	X		C	X	X	X	X	X	X	X	
59772 **America West Distributors**, PO Box 3300, **Bozeman** MT ☎(406) 585-0700 or (800) 729-4131 *toll-free number for orders* ▤(406) 585-0703 – distribution to 650 bookstores & 6500 individuals	X										
59802 **Covenant Products**, 13545 Lacasse Lane, **Missoula** MT ☎(406) 626-1863	X	X	X				X				
59802 **Ridge Runner Whole Foods Market**, 501 N. Higgins Ave., **Missoula** MT ☎(406) 721-8200			C	X	X	X	X	X	X	X	
59802 **Worden's Market, Inc.**, 451 N. Higgins Ave., **Missoula** MT			C	X	X	X	X	X	X	X	
59820 **My Pantry**, PO Box 116, **Alberton** MT – how to make pantry shelf mixes; instant soups: tomato, French onion, cream base; baking mixes: cookie, cake, biscuit; recipes for Moravian Christmas Loaf, Cuban & Indian yeast bread; 4 substitute coffee recipes			X		X					X	
59834 **Tom Tucker**, PO Box 364, **Frenchtown** MT ☎(406) 626-4410 ▤(406) 626-4410 – distributor of *Magic Mill* products			C		X		X		X		
59840 **Mountain Marketplace**, 105 North 4th, **Hamilton** MT ☎(406) 363-0601			C	X	X	X	X	X	X	X	
59840 **Solar Electricity**, PO Box 1499, **Hamilton** MT	X										X
59840 **Sunelco / The Sun Electric Company**, 100 Skeels St., **Hamilton** MT ☎(406) 363-6924 or (800) 338-6844 ▤(406) 363-6046 – distributor of complete selection of solar products from many sources; photovoltaics modules, inverters, controllers, water pumps; energy-renewable products; propane appliances; free planning & product catalog	X	X									X
59848 **Herb Store & More**, PO Box 35, **Lone Pine** MT ☎(406) 741-5670			C	X	X	X	X	X	X	X	
59853 **Militia Of Montana (M.O.M.)**, PO Box 1486, **Noxon** MT ☎(406) 847-2735 ▤(406) 847-2246 www.logoplex.com/resources/mom ✉mom@logoplex.com – dedicated to spreading the word & making sure that all members of the unorganized militia of the several States are well informed & well prepared to bring America back to her former greatness; authorized distributor of *Survival Tabs & Storehouse Foods,* manufactured by *Food Reserves, Inc.*	X	X	X	X	X	X	X	X	X	X	

M = Manufacturer / Processor — D = Wholesaler / Trade distributor — R = Distributor / Retailer to public	M	D	R	04	05	12	13	14	15	16	17
59870 **Omega II**, 370 Mountain Springs Rd., **Stevensville** MT ☎(406) 777-2181 — distributor of *Alco ♦Brite* gelled ethanol products	X										X
59870 **Ron or Kelly Bruce**, 266 Middleburnt Fork Rd., **Stevensville** MT ☎(406) 777-7202 — distributor of *Magic Mill* products	X				X		X	X			
59875 **Homestead Foods Equip. Pioneers**, 334 Meadowood Lane, **Victor** MT ☎(800) 838-3132 or (406) 642-6414 — equipping pioneers for the future; distributor of *AlpineAire* brand products for long-term food storage	X	X	X	X	X				X	X	X
59875 **Vision Freedom**, 1655 Red Crow Road, **Victor** MT ☎(406) 8961-5570 or (800) 422-7320 — 20/20 without glasses!; safe, rapid, & non-surgical	X	X	X								
59911 **Wild Mile Market & Deli**, PO Box 1133, **Big Fork** MT ☎(406) 837-3354			C	X	X	X	X	X	X	X	
59912 **Debra Faustini**, Box 1626, **Columbia Falls** MT — homeschool resource list; 150+ listings of catalogs, magazines, books & more; send $3.00 & **LSASE**			X								
59912 **Harvest Health Shoppe**, 426 Nucleus Ave., **Columbia Falls** MT ☎(406) 892-5644 🖷(406) 892-1002			C		X		X		X		
59917 **Glass, Etc.**, 604 1ˢᵗ Ave. East, **Eureka** MT ☎(406) 296-2875 — distributor of *Alco ♦Brite* gelled ethanol products			X								X
59932 **Bosch Kitchen Kneads & Mills** (*attn: Jean Remington*) 635 N. Juniper Bay Rd., **Somers** MT ☎(406) 857-3706	X	X	X					X		X	
59934 **Tom & Judy's Farm Market**, PO Box 64, **Trego** MT ☎(406) 882-4733			C	X	X	X	X	X	X	X	
59937 **Advanced Composting Systems**, 195 Meadows Rd., **Whitefish** MT ☎(406) 862-3855	X	C									X
59937 **Third Street Market**, 244 Spokane Avenue, **Whitefish** MT ☎(406) 862-5054			C	X	X	X	X	X	X	X	

Nebraska

Entry	M	D	R	04	05	12	13	14	15	16	17
68005 **Miller Honey Co.**, 301 Industrial Drive, **Bellevue City** NE ☎(402) 292-0482	X	X	X				X				
68018 **Vernon**, Rural Route 1 Box 179, **Colon** NE ☎(402) 443-4149 — *Bosch / Kitchen Specialties* distributor; preparedness consultant; in-home storage specialist			C	X	X		X	X		X	
68102 **Scoular Grain Company**, 2827 Dodge Street, **Omaha** NE ☎(402) 342-3500 🖷(402) 342-4493 ✉*GLICKTEI@SCOULAR.COM* — supplier of soybeans for tofu, soy milk, miso, & other food products; contracts direct with Midwest farmers	X	X			X					X	
68111 **Nordic Stove Mfg. Inc.**, **Omaha** NE ☎(402) 451-2575	X										X
68132 **Celiac Sprue Assoc. of America**, 805 North 50ᵗʰ Street, **Omaha** NE ☎(402) 558-0600 — distributor of *Magic Mill* products			X		X			X		X	
68310 **Gary Frantz**, 1800 Scott Street #45, **Beatrice** NE ☎(402) 223-3900 — distributor of *Private Reserve* brand dehydrated foods			X					X			
68501 **Body Enterprises**, PO Box 80577, **Lincoln** NE ☎(402) 435-8877 🖷(402) 435-8973		X						X			
68510 **Golden Carrot**, 6900 O St. #111, **Lincoln** NE ☎(402) 466-5713			C	X	X	X	X	X	X	X	
68524 **Brown's Best Foods**, 4343 NW 38ᵗʰ St., **Lincoln** NE ☎(402) 470-2021 or (888) 470-2021 🖷(402) 470-3549 — producer of pre-cooked beans, peas, & lentils; dehydrated quick-cooking & instant whole beans, peas, & lentils; other varieties on a custom basis; quick-cooking & instant bean flakes, granules, & powders	X	X			X					X	
68524 **Innovative Grain Technologies, Inc.**, 4343 NW 38ᵗʰ Street, **Lincoln** NE ☎(402) 470-2021 or (888) 470-2021 🖷(402) 470-3549 — producer of pre-cooked barley, corn, rice, rye, triticale, wheat & wild rice; quick-cooking, stabilized 7 roasted categories; flakes, pearled, grits, kibbled—all are available; custom-processing available	X	X			X					X	
68601 **Mother Nature's Emporium**, 2715 13ᵗʰ Street, **Columbus** NE ☎(402) 564-5666			C	X	X	X	X	X	X	X	
69160 **Cabela's Sporting Goods**, 812 13ᵗʰ Ave., **Sidney** NE ☎(308) 254-5505 — distributor of *Alco ♦Brite* gelled ethanol products			X								X
69301 **Grandma Beth's Cookies**, 1221 Toluca, **Alliance** NE ☎(308) 762-8433			X		X		X	X		X	
69361 **Nutter's #101**, 2621 5ᵗʰ Ave. #1, **Scottsbluff** NE ☎(308) 632-1013 🖷(308) 632-1014 ✉*scottsbluff@nutters.com*			X								X

Nevada

Entry	M	D	R	04	05	12	13	14	15	16	17
89008 **Mountain Mercantile**, 169 Clover St., **Caliente** NV ☎(702) 726-3891 — distributor of *Alco ♦Brite* gelled ethanol products			X							X	X
89014 **American Family Prod., Int'l. / R. Perkins**, 310 Redondo Street **Henderson** NV ☎(702) 454-2773	X	X				X				X	
89019 **REXARCH**, Box 19250, **Jean** NV — air wells condense atmospheric humidity, electro-culture; "free energy" generators, & antigravity products			X								X
89024 **Coyote Design Group**, 80 Arrowhead Lane, **Mesquite** NV ☎(702) 346-7330 — distributor of *Alco ♦Brite* gelled ethanol products			X								X
89041 **Pahrump Wood-N-Pellet Stoves**, 360 E. Kings Way, **Pahrump** NV ☎(702) 727-0233 — distributor of *Alco ♦Brite* gelled ethanol products			X								X
89101 **The Food Pantry**, 1801 Elm Ave., **Las Vegas** NV ☎(702) 384-1646			X			X	X			X	
89102 **Desert Outfitters, Inc.**, 2101 S. Decatur #5 & 6, **Las Vegas** NV ☎(702) 362-2561 — rentals & sales of camping & prospecting equipment & supplies			X								X

Product References Keyed to Chapters (Cont.)

04 water / air filtration & treatment	05 grains, seeds, mills & equip.	12 dairy / powdered milk supplies	13 honey / sweeteners
14 vitamins / minerals / herbs	15 sprouting / equip. & supplies	16 dry / dehydrated / freeze-dried	17 energy / fuels

M = Manufacturer / Processor D = Wholesaler / Trade distributor R = Distributor / Retailer to public

Listing	M	D	R	04	05	12	13	14	15	16	17
89102 Econ, 300 Wall St., **Las Vegas** NV ☎(702) 384-4682 — distributor of *Alco ♦Brite* gelled ethanol products			X								X
89102 Fireplace BBQ Shop, 1212 South Rainbow, **Las Vegas** NV ☎(702) 870-8995 — distributor of *Alco ♦Brite* gelled ethanol products			X								X
89102 Phil's Fine Cutlery, 4616 West Sahara Ave. #145, **Las Vegas** NV ☎(702) 646-6990 — specializing in small & large commercial knives; automatic knives, pocket knives & blades			X								X
89102 Vital 4 Life, 1204 Hunt Street, **Las Vegas** NV ☎(702) 258-8908 🖷(702) 384-5704 — *"Vitamist"* spray vitamins		X	X					X			
89102 Wild Oats, 6720 West Sahara, **Las Vegas** NV ☎(702) 253-7050 🖷(702) 253-0718		X	X		X		X	X	X	X	
89104 Superior Water Sys., 1211 So. Eastern Ave., **Las Vegas** NV ☎(702) 477-7736 🖷(702) 477-7759 — licensed contractor installs only American-made products; sales, service & installation		X	X								X
89107 Dyer's Kitchen Kneads, 441 S. Decatur Blvd., **Las Vegas** NV ☎(702) 878-4641 — *Bosch & Kitchen Specialties* distributor; in-home storage specialist		X			X					X	
89109 C & F Distributors, PO Box 80205, **Las Vegas** NV ☎(702) 643-3664 — distributor of *Alco ♦Brite* gelled ethanol products		X									X
89109 Environmental Marketing, Inc., 2961 Industrial Rd. #603, **Las Vegas** NV	X	X									X
89109 Taylor'd Enterprises,. 2961 Industrial Rd. #187, **Las Vegas** NV ☎(702) 361-7461 — retail general store searches the market for military surplus, vehicles, generators, propane products, Dutch ovens, all cast-iron cookware, wood burning stoves, MREs, food storage containers—or whatever		X	X			X	X			X	X
89110 American Family Prod., Int'l. / J. Perkins, 920 Crazyhorse Way, **Las Vegas** NV ☎(702) 452-6500		X				X				X	
89121 A Kitchen Center, 3280 E. Tropicana Ave. #Q, **Las Vegas** NV ☎(702) 456-6730 🖷(702) 456-8982 — *Bosch & Kitchen Specialties* kitchen products distributor; *Magic Mill* dealer		X	X	X	X	X			X	X	
89121 Wild Oats, 3455 East Flamingo, **Las Vegas** NV ☎(702) 434-8115 🖷(702) 434-1738		X	X		X		X	X	X	X	
89130 Alternative Birthing, 4300 Ivory Circle, **Las Vegas** NV ☎(702) 878-1972 — emergency birth kits designed by professional midwives; sealed from the elements for long shelf life; a must for every family wanting to be fully prepared; catalog of additional supplies for birthing experiences		C									
89431 Buck Stove & Home Center, 1380 Greg Street #207, **Sparks** NV ☎(702) 358-4444 — distributor of *Alco ♦Brite* gelled ethanol products		X									X
89431 Glass Mountain Block, Inc., **Sparks** NV ☎(702) 358-1200 — manufacturer of wood-burning stoves	X										X
89503 Zee Medical, 1401 West 4th St., **Reno** NV ☎(702) 329-8522 🖷(702) 329-8062 — individual, family, group, business, & commercial survival & first aid kits		X									
89701 Global Insights, 675 Fairview Dr. #246, **Carson City** NV ☎(702) 885-0700 or (800) 729-4131 — natural foods, kitchenware, stainless steel pressure cookers, grain mills, & more		X						X	X		
89701 Tookie Johns, 1501 Appaloosa, **Carson City** NV ☎(702) 883-5259 — distributor of *Magic Mill* products		X			X			X	X		
89705 Health Technologies, 3759 Gross Circle, **Carson City** NV ☎(702) 267-2550 or (800) 882-9577 🖷(702) 267-4840		X						X			
89706 Apex Stoves & Energy Distributors, **Carson City** NV ☎(702) 883-2102 🖷(702) 883-7512	X	X									X
89706 Prep America Corp., 2533 N. Carson Street #2083, **Carson City** NV ☎(702) 883-1516 or (800) 909-7737 🖷(702) 883-4874 — specializing in emergency and disaster supplies and products		X								X	
89801 Liberty Food Storage, 2186 Chism Drive, **Elko** NV ☎(702) 738-3882 or (800) 793-9300 — *SamAndy Foods* distributor		X							X	X	
89801 Natural Nutrition, 1900 Idaho Street #106, **Elko** NV ☎None — distributor of *Magic Mill* products		X			X			X	X		
New Hampshire											
03062 Brookstone, 17 Riverside Street, **Nashua** NH ☎(800) 351-7222 — mail order; 60+ retail stores; items for the special needs of 72-hour kits		X	X								X
03076 Beaver Valley Farm, 17 Main St., **Pelham** NH — distributor of *Alco ♦Brite* gelled ethanol products		X									X
03079 Stove Shop, 354 N. Broadway, **Salem** NH ☎(603) 893-0456 — distributor of *Alco ♦Brite* gelled ethanol products		X									X
03118 Associated Grocers of New England, **Manchester** NH ☎(603) 669-3250 — distributor of *Parmalat* shelf-stable, whole milk dairy products		X				X					
03261 Radius Defense, Inc., 222 Blake Hills Road, **Northwood** NH — builder of underground shelters to protect families from tornadoes, earthquakes, nuclear & chemical accidents or weapons, terrorism, forest fires, or famines	X										X
03261 Subterranean Technologies, Inc., 138-I Blakes Hill Road, **Northwood** NH ☎(603) 942-7527 — designer/builder of high-efficiency, completely self-contained, fiberglass earth houses & disaster shelters	X										X

M = Manufacturer / Processor — D = Wholesaler / Trade distributor — R = Distributor / Retailer to public	M	D	R	04	05	12	13	14	15	16	17
03443 Stow Mills Distributor, Keene NH ☎(603) 256-3000 – distributor of *Parmalat* shelf-stable, whole milk dairy products	X					X					
03450 Solar Survival, Box 250, Harrisville NH	X	X									X
03755 The Dartmouth Co-op, Rt. 120, Hanover NH			C	X	X	X	X	X	X	X	X
03784 Energex, 20 Airpark Rd., West Lebanon NH – distributor of *Alco ♦Brite* gelled ethanol products			X								X
03784 Woodstock Soapstone Co., West Lebanon NH ☎(603) 298-5955 🖷(603) 298-5958 – manufacturer of wood-burning stoves	X										X
03804 Skyline Engineering, PO Box 134, Temple NH ☎(603) 878-1600 🖷(603) 878-4643		X	X								X
New Jersey											
07003 Purple Dragon Co-op, 165 Willow St., Bloomfield NJ ☎(201) 429-0391			C	X	X	X	X	X	X	X	
07004 The Fireplace Place, 264 Route 46, Fairfield NJ – distributor of *Alco ♦Brite* gelled ethanol products			X								X
07008 Kathleen Salardino, 87 Fitch Street, Carteret NJ ☎(908) 969-3387 – distributor of *Magic Mill* products			X		X			X	X		
07008 White Rose Wholesale, Carteret NJ ☎(908) 541-5555 – distributor of *Parmalat* shelf-stable, whole milk dairy products	X	X				X					
07024 IntraCell Nutrition, Inc., Box 3070, Fort Lee NJ ☎(800) 572-3663 – manufacturer of *Foodform*® *Manna*			X					X			
07036 Brunal Supply Co., Inc., 36 E. Edgar Rd., Linden NJ – distributor of *Alco ♦Brite* gelled ethanol products			X								
07041 Bread & Circus, 187 Millburn Avenue, Millburn NJ ☎(201) 376-4668 🖷(201) 376-8664			X	X	X	X	X	X	X	X	
07042 Bread & Circus, 701 Bloomfield Avenue, Montclair NJ ☎(201) 746-5110 🖷(201) 746-8119			X	X	X	X	X	X	X	X	
07044 Luke's Oil Service, Inc., 286 Grove Ave., Verona NJ ☎(201) 239-2611 – distributor of *Alco ♦Brite* gelled ethanol products			X								X
07047 The Vitamin Shoppe, 4700 Westside Ave., North Bergen NJ ☎(800) 223-1216 🖷(800) 852-7153 – mail-order health & beauty catalogue; 14,000 items in stock; homeopathic remedies; body-building & sports; vitamins, minerals, & herbs; pure & natural cosmetic products; health equipment & supplies			X			X	X				
07060 Home Energy Conservation, North Plainfield NJ ☎(908) 754-5750 🖷(908) 754-5455 – distributor of *Alco ♦Brite* gelled ethanol products; stoves, fireplaces & more…		X	X								X
07417 Kathy Bratt, 946 Old Road, Franklin Lakes NJ ☎(201) 891-9264 – distributor of *Magic Mill* products			X		X			X	X		
07436 Tina Bruno, 34 Pawnee Ave., Oakland NJ ☎(201) 337-4492 – distributor of *Magic Mill* products			X		X			X	X		
07458 Campmor, PO Box 700-D, Saddle River NJ ☎(800) 230 CAMPMOR ⌨www.campmor ✉customer-service@campmor.com – authorized retail distributor of *Mountain House* brand freeze-dried products		X	X								X
07624 Community Enterprises *(attn: Jerry Ikalowych)*, **60 Harrington Ave., Closter** NJ ☎(201) 768-8119 – *SamAndy Foods* products distributor	X		C	X	X	X			X	X	X
07628 Micro Balanced Prod. Corp., 25 Aladdin Ave., Dumont NJ ☎(201) 387-0200 or (800) 528-4546 – exclusive importer of aluminum-free deodorant application; also, foot deodorant product	X	X						X			
07675 Nam Choi, 614 Stanley Place, River Vale NJ – distributor of *Magic Mill* products			X		X	X			X		
07712 Peet Bros. Co., 1308-512V Doris Ave., Ocean NJ ☎(800) USA-PEET 🖷(908) 517-0669		X	X								X
07712 Wood Stoves, 1643 Hwy. 35, Ocean NJ – distributor of *Alco ♦Brite* gelled ethanol products			X								X
07719 Belmar Bay's Hell's Kitchen, 619A 10ᵗʰ Avenue, Belmar NJ ☎(908) 280-8611 🖷(908) 280-5508			X					X			
08053 Linda Stauffer, 142 Thornwood Drive, Marlton NJ ☎(609) 596-0340 – distributor of *Magic Mill* products			X		X			X	X		
08055 Stoveworks Inc., Medford NJ ☎(609) 654-1384 🖷(609) 654-2114 ✉sw@hearth.com		X	X								X
08071 Libby Sez…, 611 East Holly Ave., Pitman NJ ☎(609) 589-7255 – preparedness consultant & in-home storage specialist			C		X						
08075 Reckitt & Colman, Inc., PO Box 1614, Delran NJ ☎(800) 456-9477 or (201) 573-5700 – manufacturer of *Red Devil Lye* (for homemade soapmaking)	X										
08094 American Pellet Stoves, 1016 N. Main St., Willamstown NJ ☎(609) 629-3891 – distributor of *Alco ♦Brite* gelled ethanol products			X								X
08094 Stoveworks Inc., Williamstown NJ ☎(609) 875-0666 🖷(609) 875-1891 ✉sw@hearth.com		X	X								X
08096 Bob's Fireside Shop, 252 S. Broadstreet, Woodbury NJ – distributor of *Alco ♦Brite* gelled ethanol products			X								X
08110 I. Goldberg, 115 Twinbridge Dr. #G, Pennsauken NJ ☎(609) 662-8600 – distributor of *Alco ♦Brite* gelled ethanol products			X								X

Product References Keyed to Chapters (Cont.)

	M	D	R	04	05	12	13	14	15	16	17
04 water / air filtration & treatment — **05** grains, seeds, mills & equip. — **12** dairy / powdered milk supplies — **13** honey / sweeteners — **14** vitamins / minerals / herbs — **15** sprouting / equip. & supplies — **16** dry / dehydrated / freeze-dried — **17** energy / fuels. M = Manufacturer / Processor; D = Wholesaler / Trade distributor; R = Distributor / Retailer to public											
08221 **Lee Thorne**, 18 W. Sea View Ave., **Linwood** NJ ☎(609) 927-7931 — distributor of *Magic Mill* products		X			X			X		X	
08232 **AkPharma Inc.**, PO Box 111, **Pleasantville** NJ ☎(800) 257-8650 — manufacturer of *BEANO*, food enzyme dietary supplement; digestive aid to prevent intestinal gas	X							X			
08250 **Energy Alternatives**, Highstown NJ ☎(800) 637-0179 ✉capthare@injersey.com — stoves, fireplaces & more…		X	X								X
08540 **The Whole Earth Center**, 360 Nassau St., **Princeton** NJ ☎(609) 924-7429			C	X	X	X	X	X	X	X	
08648 **Energy Warehouse**, 2783 Rt. 1, **Lawrenceville** NJ ☎(609) 882-6006 — distributor of *Alco ♦Brite* gelled ethanol products		X									X
08701 **Lifestyle Fascination**, 1935 Swarthmore Ave. #3023 **Lakewood** NJ ☎(800) 669-0987 🖷(908) 364-4448 — mail-order catalog for mechanical & electrical gadgets o make things easier, safer, & more convenient		X									X
08755 **Dover Pools, Inc.**, 1740 Lakewood Rd., **Toms River** NJ ☎(908) 244-2190 — distributor of *Alco ♦Brite* gelled ethanol products		X									X
08802 **Tracking, Nature & Wilderness Survival School**, PO Box 173, **Asbury** NJ ☎(908) 479-4681 🖷(908) 479-6867 ✉TrackInc@aol.com — Tom Brown Jr.'s School for tracking, nature, and wilderness survival training			C								
08807 **Albers Fireplaces**, 976 US Highway 22, **Bridgewater** NJ ☎(908) 526-6650 — distributor of *Alco ♦Brite* gelled ethanol products		X									X
08818 **Dr. Leonard's Healthcare Catalog**, 42 Mayfield Ave., **Edison** NJ ☎(908) 225-0880 — mail-order healthcare catalog; hundreds of appliances, equipment, & supplies for body care & support		X						X			
08822 **H₂O Leisure**, 11 Route 31, **Flemington** NJ — distributor of *Alco ♦Brite* gelled ethanol products		X									X

New Mexico

	M	D	R	04	05	12	13	14	15	16	17
87008 **Davis True Value**, 12168 N. Hwy. 14, **Cedar Crest** NM ☎(505) 281-4072 — distributor of *Alco ♦Brite* gelled ethanol products		X									X
87104 **AAA Solar Service & Supply**, 2021 Zearing NW, **Albuquerque** NM ☎(800) 245-0311	X										X
87104 **B.K.'s Health Pantry**, 119 San Pasquale SW, **Albuquerque** NM ☎(505) 243-0370			C	X	X	X	X	X	X	X	
87104 **Solo Power Solar Electric Systems**, 1011A Sawmill Rd NW, **Albuquerque** NM ☎(800) 279-7656 — composting toilets; energy-saving products; solar power systems	X	X	X								X
87104 **Zoneworks Corp.**, 1011 Sawmill Rd. NW, **Albuquerque** NM ☎(800) 279-6342	X										X
87107 **Array Technologies, Inc.**, 3204 Stanford NE, **Albuquerque** NM ☎(505) 881-7567 🖷(505) 881-7572	X	X									X
87107 **Direct Power & Water Corp.**, 3455-A Princeton NE, **Albuquerque** NM ☎(505) 889-3585 🖷(505) 889-3548	X	X									X
87108 **La Montanita Food Co-Op**, 200 Amherst Drive SE, **Albuquerque** NM ☎(505) 266-6694			C	X	X	X	X	X	X	X	
87109 **Carrizo Solar Corp.**, 3700 Osuna Rd. NE, **Albuquerque** NM ☎(800) 776-6718 or (505)764-0345	X	X									X
87109 **Health & Nutrition Center**, 5901-U Wyoming Blvd. NE, **Albuquerque** NM ☎(505) 828-2066			C	X	X	X	X	X	X	X	
87109 **Wild Oats**, 6300-A San Mateo NE, **Albuquerque** NM ☎(505) 823-1933 🖷(505) 857-9221		X	X	X	X		X	X	X	X	
87110 **Health Haven**, 1307 San Mateo NE, **Albuquerque** NM ☎(505) 265-4830			C	X	X	X	X	X	X	X	
87110 **Loma Vista Chile**, Albuquerque NM ☎(505) 881-9611 — manufacturer/processor of *Loma Vista* brand chilies, beans, posole, and Mexican meal foods ingredients	X	X					X			X	
87110 **South West Stoves**, 1609 San Mateo NE, **Albuquerque** NM ☎(505) 268-2431 — distributor of *Alco ♦Brite* gelled ethanol products		X									X
87111 **Rio Grande Outfitters**, 4200 Wyoming NE, **Albuquerque** NM ☎(505) 323-1000 — dedicated to the outdoorsman; survival kits, supplies, & rations; water purification systems; food storage products; seminars on wilderness first aid & survival; *AlpineAire* brand products for long-term food storage			C	X	X			X		X	
87112 **Keller's Farm Store**, 2912 Eubank NE, **Albuquerque** NM ☎(505) 294-1427			C	X	X	X	X	X	X	X	
87112 **Wild Oats**, 11015 Menaul Blvd. NE, **Albuquerque** NM ☎(505) 275-6660 🖷(505) 275-7102		X	X	X	X		X	X	X	X	
87120 **Keller's Farm Store #2**, 6100 Coors NW, **Albuquerque** NM ☎(505) 898-6121			C	X	X	X	X	X	X	X	
87123 **Fountain of Health**, 521 Wyoming NE, **Albuquerque** NM ☎(505) 256-7871			C	X	X	X	X	X	X	X	
87125 **SoloPower**, 1011-A Sawmill Rd. NW, **Albuquerque** NM ☎(800) 279-7656	X	X									X
87176 **Cygnus X Enterprises**, PO Box 37124, **Albuquerque** NM ☎(888) 294-6879 ⌨www.flash.net/cgi-bin/cgiwrap/cygnusx1	X	X									X
87501 **Cookworks I**, 322 S. Guadalupe St., **Santa Fe** NM ☎(505) 820-6776 — distributor of *Alco ♦Brite* gelled ethanol products		X									X
87501 **Dankoff Solar Products, Inc.**, 100 Ricardo Rd., **Santa Fe** NM ☎(505) 820-6611	X	X									X
87501 **Wild Oats**, 1090 St. Francis Dr., **Santa Fe** NM ☎(505) 983-5333 🖷(505) 986-6087		X	X	X	X		X	X	X	X	
87501 **Wild Oats**, 333 W. Cordova Road, **Santa Fe** NM ☎(505) 986-8667 🖷(505) 986-8711		X	X	X	X		X	X	X	X	
87505 **Wild Oats**, 1708 Llano St., **Santa Fe** NM ☎(505) 473-4943 🖷(505) 473-5292		X	X	X	X		X	X	X	X	
87529 **Cid's Food Market**, PO Box 59, **El Prado** NM ☎(505) 758-1148			C	X	X	X	X	X	X	X	

M = Manufacturer / Processor D = Wholesaler / Trade distributor R = Distributor / Retailer to public	M	D	R	04	05	12	13	14	15	16	17
87544 **Health Food Shop**, 1320 17th Street, **Los Alamos** NM ☎(505)662-4900			C	X	X	X	X	X	X	X	X
87571 **Amigos Food Co-op**, PO Box 6291, **Taos** NM ☎(505) 758-8493			C	X	X	X	X	X	X	X	X
87574 **Tesuque Village Market**, PO Box 231, **Tesuque** NM			C	X	X	X	X	X	X	X	X
87832 **The Free American**, US Hwy. 380 Box 2943, **Bingham** NM ☎(505) 423-3250 ✉*freeamerican@etsc.net* – authorized distributor of *Survival Tabs & Storehouse Foods* by *Food Reserves, Inc.*; *AlpineAire Foods* distributor	X	X						X		X	
87901 **Sierra Feed**, 2598 S. Broadway, **Truth Or Consequences** NM ☎(505) 894-3994 – distributor of *Alco ♦Brite* gelled ethanol products				X							X
88023 **B & E Hardware**, 401 North Central, **Bayard** NM ☎(505) 537-3281 – distributor of *Alco ♦Brite* gelled ethanol products				X							X
88025 **naturas Sacredplay**, PO Box 32, **Buckhorn** NM – *Wise Herb Blends*™, organic green allies for promoting & maintaining health for the inner & outer body	X	X	X					X			
88211 **L & M Marketing**, PO Box 1663, **Artesia** NM ☎(800) 260-5339 – distributor of *AlpineAire* brand products for long-term food storage				X	X	X	X			X	X
88310 **Stove Enterprises, Alamogordo** NM ☎(505) 437-6546 🖷(505) 434-3722 – food-grade 55-gal. steel barrels with open top & lid, new liner & sealing gasket; $25.00 ea. f.o.b. source				X							
New York											
10001 **Bread & Circus**, Queensboro Br. Approach (under the 59th Street Br. between 59th & 60th), **Manhattan** NY				X	X	X	X	X	X	X	X
10304 **Fire Glow, Inc.**, 1565 Richmond Rd., **Staten Island** NY ☎(718) 979-9191 – distributor of *Alco ♦Brite* gelled ethanol products				X							X
10990 **BayGen USA**, 80 Amity Road, **Warwick** NY ☎(914) 258-5660 or (800) WIND-234 🖷(914) 258-3213 🖳http://freeplay.pair.com ✉*freeplay@pair.com* – *Freeplay*® radio with SWR, AM, & FM reception; 2 models: 3–12 Mhz & 12 Mhz! only; wind-up radio (Baylis generator—wind approx. 25-30 sec. & it plays 30 min.!); no additional power is needed; 9 volt convertor available	X	X	X								X
10583 **Mrs. Green's Natural Market**, 780 White Plains Rd., **Scarsdale** NY ☎(914) 462-0111			C	X	X	X	X	X	X	X	X
10604 **Krasdale Wholesale, White Plains** NY ☎(914) 697-5219 – distributor of *Parmalat* shelf-stable, whole milk dairy products				X			X				
10901 **Mordecai Roth**, 397 Spook Rock, **Suffern** NY ☎(914) 368-2532 🖷(914) 368-2533 – distributor of *Magic Mill* products	X	X				X					
10913 **Henny Koh**, 193 Burrows Lane, **Blauvelt** NY ☎(914) 365-2215 – distributor of *Magic Mill* products				X		X		X		X	
10940 **Chimney Sweep Enegry Co.**, Rd. # 10 Box 230 Shaw Rd., **Middletown** NY ☎(914) 361-3672 – distributor of *Alco ♦Brite* gelled ethanol products				X							X
10940 **Northstar Energy Systems, Middletown** NY ☎(914) 692-6701 🖷(914) 692-6702 – wood stoves, pellet stoves, gas stoves, central heating & more…	X	X									X
10950 **Fireplace Specialists**, 465 Old Dutch Hollow Rd., **Monroe** NY ☎(914) 986-4732 – distributor of *Alco ♦Brite* gelled ethanol products				X							X
10977 **Kay Lee**, 5 Raymond Ave., **Chestnut Ridge** NY ☎(914) 356-3391 – distributor of *Magic Mill* kitchen products				X		X		X		X	
11030 **Bread & Circus**, 2101 Northern Boulevard, **Munsey Park** NY ☎(516) 869-8900 🖷(516) 869-9250				X	X	X	X	X	X	X	X
11363 **Kim Hwang**, 40-04 248th Street, **Little Neck** NY ☎(718) 631-8515 – distributor of *Magic Mill* products				X		X		X		X	
11364 **Awilda V. Claros**, 78-38 223rd Street, **Hollis Hills** NY ☎(718) 479-0456 – distributor of *Magic Mill* products				X		X		X		X	
11560 **Miracle Exclusives, Inc.**, PO Box 349, **Locust Valley** NY ☎(516) 676-0220 – exclusive importer of the *Samap* hand-operated grain mill from France	X	X				X					
11733 **Shawn Cordz**, 236 Sheep Pasture Road, **Setauket** NY ☎(516) 246-5073 – distributor of *Magic Mill* products				X		X		X		X	
11735 **Burlington Bio-Medical Corp.**, 222 Sherwood Ave., **Farmingdale** NY ☎(516) 694-9000 🖷(516) 694-9177 ✉*BABL@prodigy.com* – *Inca*® *Food Protect•R*™ spray for fresh foods to prevent oxidation & deterioration & spoilage	X			X				X			
11746 **Saint Jude Herb Center**, Box 563, **Huntington Station** NY				X	X		X	X	X		X
12043 **National Stove Works, Inc., Cobleskill** NY ☎(518) 296-8517 – manufacturer of wood-burning stoves	X										X
12074 **Natural Bounty, Gallaway** NY			C	X	X	X	X	X	X	X	X
12095 **H & K Van Valken Burgh, Inc.**, 250 N. Comrie Ave., **Johnstown** NY ☎(518) 762-7613 – distributor of *Alco ♦Brite* gelled ethanol products				X							X
12106 *Vita*/Bioforce of America, Ltd., **Kinderhook** NY – manufacturer of *Bambu*, organic Swiss coffee substitute						X					X
12134 **Adirondack Alternate Energy**, 98 Northville Rd., **Edinburg** NY ☎(518) 863-4338				X							X
12538 **Culinary Institute of America**, 433 Albany Post Road, **Hyde Park** NY ☎(914) 451-1716 – distributor of *Magic Mill* products				X		X		X	X		

Product References Keyed to Chapters (Cont.)

04 water / air filtration & treatment	05 grains, seeds, mills & equip.	12 dairy / powdered milk supplies	13 honey / sweeteners
14 vitamins / minerals / herbs	15 sprouting / equip. & supplies	16 dry / dehydrated / freeze-dried	17 energy / fuels

M = Manufacturer / Processor | D = Wholesaler / Trade distributor | R = Distributor / Retailer to public

Entry	M	D	R	04	05	12	13	14	15	16	17
12538 Markus Sarbinger, 433 Albany Post Road, **Hyde Park** NY ☎(914) 451-1716 — distributor of *Magic Mill* products			X	X			X	X			
12566 Homegrown Booklets, 67 Awosting Rd., **Pine Bush** NY ☎(914) 744-2245 — homesteading & survival pamphlets & products			X								
12590 Sunrise Energy Systems, 6 Old Route 9, **Wappingers Falls** NY ☎(914) 298-5645 — distributor of *Alco ♦Brite* gelled ethanol products			X								X
12603 Hudson Valley Federation, 6 Noxon Road, **Poughkeepsie** NY ☎(914) 473-5400 🖷(914) 473-5458 Territory: *NY, NJ, Western CT, Eastern PA*	X	C	X	X	X	X	X	X	X		
12992 Rob Roy Earthwood Building School, 366 Murtagh Hill Road, **West Chazy** NY ☎(518) 493-7744 — back-to-the-earth books, plans, & instructions for building homes, saunas, & other buildings from rammed earth, cordwood, underground, & poles; solar electric construction; alternative house-building information	X	C									X
12993 Champlain Valley Milling Corp., PO Box 454, **West Port** NY ☎(518) 962-4711 — food coop; soy flour producers	X					X					
13126 Oswego Supply, 157 E. 1ˢᵗ St., **Oswego** NY ☎(315) 342-4567 — distributor of *Alco ♦Brite* gelled ethanol products			X								X
13146 Community Mill & Bean, Inc. – *Mail-order Division*, 267 Rt. 89 South, **Savannah** NY ☎(315) 365-2664 🖷(315) 365-2690 — mail-order organic & conventional grains, seeds, & flours; custom grinding to customer order			X		X	X	X	X	X	X	
13146 Community Mill & Bean, Inc. (formerly *Crusoe Island Grocery Store*), 267 Route 89 South, **Savannah** NY ☎(315) 365-2664 or (800) 755-0554 🖷(315) 365-2690 💻www.crusoeisland.com ✉cmnb@mail.tds.net — *Old Savannah* brand organic products; flours, dry beans, grains & seeds for cooking, milling & sprouting			X C	X	X	X	X	X	X	X	
13208 Suzanne Pannfino, 236 Cleveland Ave., **Syracuse** NY ☎(315) 471-4301 — distributor of *Magic Mill* products			X		X		X		X		
13212 Mary Ellen Conway, 116 Waterbury Drive, **North Syracuse** NY ☎(315) 458-3736 — distributor of *Magic Mill* products			X		X	X	X		X		
13215 Storehouse Freeze-Dried Foods, PO Box 81, **Syracuse** NY ☎(315) 492-4728 🖷(315) 469-5629 ✉mandolina@sesva.exc.edu — processor & packager of freeze-dried foods for long-term home storage; main meal entrees, vegetables, & fruits nitrogen-packed in quart-sized #3 tall cans	X	X	X C							X	
13316 The Generator Outlet, Box 163-E Babcock Rd., **Camden** NY ☎(315) 245-3916			X								X
13408 Ed McCabe, Consultant, RD #1 Box 22-A, **Morrisville** NY ☎(800) 284-6263 — founder/director of the non-profit *Foundation for the Advancement of Oxygen Therapies*; expert on oxygen therapies & products; lobbyist for clinical use of ozone & other oxygen products in the US			C					X			
13413 SCEPTER—Survival Centre for Emergency Preparedness Technology, 52 Genesee St. 2ⁿᵈ Floor, **New Hartford** NY ☎(315) 732-1190 🖷(315) 735-3244			C X							X	X
13416 Tammy Ford, Rt. 1 Box 57, **New Port** NY ☎(315) 845-8549 — distributor of *Magic Mill* products			X	X	X						
13601 Sundance Leisure, 1928 US Route 22, **Watertown** NY ☎(315) 788-2207 — distributor of *Alco ♦Brite* gelled ethanol products			X								X
13694 Barbara Doe, 15 Brookview, **Waddington** NY ☎(315) 388-7825 — distributor of *Magic Mill* products			X		X		X		X		
13753 Delhi Agway, 5 Lower Main St., **Delhi** NY ☎(607) 746-2349 — distributor of *Alco ♦Brite* gelled ethanol products	X	X	X		X						X
13780 Deer Valley Farms, RFD 1, **Guilford** NY			X					X			
13820 Agway, Inc., 10 Winney Hill Road, **Oneonta** NY ☎(607) 432-4611 — distributor of *Alco ♦Brite* gelled ethanol products	X	X	X		X						X
13830 Christian Homesteading Movement, Oxford NY — training for homesteading: organic gardening, medicinal herbs, wild foods, survival shelters, log cabins, snares & deadfalls, midwifery, & non-electric living; making tinctures, salves, & dried medicinal herbs		C	X			X	X	X	X		X
13905 Blue Ox Corporation, 31 Brown St., **Binghamton** NY ☎(607) 797-2356 — distributor of *Alco ♦Brite* gelled ethanol products			X								X
14150 Sun-Mar Corp., 600 Main Street, **Tonawada** NY ☎(905) 332-1314 🖷(905) 332-1315 — composting toilets, electrical & non-electric; for remote locations & environmental considerations	X	X									X
14207 The Sausage Maker, 26 Military Road, **Buffalo** NY ☎(716) 876-5521 🖷(716) 875-0302 — mail-order sausage & meat smoking supplies, training videos, equipment, etc.			X							X	
14224 Black Hat Chimney & Fireplaces, 3155 Seneca St., **West Seneca** NY ☎(716) 674-0367 — distributor of *Alco ♦Brite* gelled ethanol products			X								X
14304 Strenkoski Bros. Construction Co., Inc., 8888 Porter Rd., **Niagara Falls** NY ☎(716) 298-8221 — distributor of *Alco ♦Brite* gelled ethanol products			X								X
14471 Bread & Roses Natural Foods, 7½ W. Main St., **Honeoye** NY ☎(726) 229-4652			C	X	X	X	X	X	X		

M = Manufacturer / Processor	D = Wholesaler / Trade distributor	R = Distributor / Retailer to public	M	D	R	04	05	12	13	14	15	16	17
14517 **Once Again Nut Butter, Inc., Nunda** NY ☎(716) 468-2535 🖷(716) 468-5995 – mail-order certified organic nut butters & honey, roasted nuts & fruit honeycreme spreads			X	X	X			X					X
14589 **Williamson Hardware, Williamson** NY ☎(315) 589-4011 ✉*wmsonace@frontiernet.net* – stoves, fireplaces & more…			X	X									X
14616 **Dewey Research Center on the Web,** 3800 Dewey Avenue #125, **Rochester** NY ☎(800) 208-9576 🖷(716) 865-8994 🖳www.4drc.com ✉*edewey@4drc.com* – **Internet** marketer of *AlpineAire Foods*; author of *"Emergency Survival Manual"*			X	X						X			
14724 **French Creek General Store,** Rt. 2 Box 130, **Clymer** NY – distributor of *Alco ♦Brite* gelled ethanol products			X	X	X					X		X	X
14757 **Gourmet & Bulk Foods** *(attn: Jud White),* RR 1 Box 145, **Mayville** NY ☎(716) 753-3767 – *SamAndy Foods* products distributor			X	X	X	X	X				X	X	X
North Carolina													
23792 **Richard Dorian,** 2307 Old Kanuga Road, **Hendersonville** NC ☎(704) 698-8386					X		X						
27310 **Old Mill of Guilford,** 1340 N NC 68 Hwy., **Oak Ridge** NC ☎(910) 643-4783 – active custom grinding mill; whole grain yellow & white corn, 14% wheat, grain flours, & mixes			X	X	X					X			
27374 **G'Morning Glory! Food Co-op,** PO Box 1718, **Welcome** NC ☎(704) 243-7653 – food buying co-op; contact for information about becoming a member or participating				C	X				X	X			
27410 **Jennifer Schmidt,** 528 Lindley Road, **Greensboro** NC ☎(910) 294-5994 – distributor of *Magic Mill* products				X	X				X	X			
27514 **Wellspring Grocery,** 81 South Elliot, **Chapel Hill** NC ☎(919) 968-1983 🖷(919) 967-0228				X	X	X	X	X	X	X	X	X	
27533 **Turner Equipment Co., Inc.,** PO Box 1260, **Goldsboro,** NC ☎(919) 736-4550 or (800) 672-4770 – affordable greenhouses & accessories, supplies, & equipment; books & precision instruments				X									X
27607 **Wellspring Grocery,** 3540 Wade Avenue, **Raleigh** NC ☎(919) 828-5805 🖷(919) 828-5825				X	X	X	X	X	X	X	X	X	
27607 **Wild Bill's,** 1210 Ridge Rd., **Raleigh** NC ☎(919) 828-3022 – distributor of *Alco ♦Brite* gelled ethanol products				X									X
27613 **Elite Force, Inc.,** 8809 Running Oak, **Raleigh** NC ☎(800) 948-0754 or (919) 781-0609 🖷(919) 781-8771 – distributor of military & outdoor clothing & equipment; equipment & supplies for all uniformed personnel; authorized distributor of *Survival Tabs,* a product of *Food Reserves, Inc.*			X	X					X		X	X	
27701 **River Runners Emporium,** 201 Albemarle St., **Durham** NC ☎(919) 688-2001 – distributor of *Alco ♦Brite* gelled ethanol products				X									X
27705 **Wellspring Grocery,** 621 Broad, **Durham** NC ☎(919) 286-0371 🖷(919) 286-7819				X	X	X	X	X	X	X	X	X	
28105 **The Healthy Kitchen,** 9707 Clifton Meadow Dr., **Mathews** NC ☎(704) 568-4307 – distributor of *Tilia* vacuum-sealing equipment & supplies				X						X			
28114 **Byron Staie,** 149 Haney Drive, **Mooresboro** NC ☎(704) 657-6931				X	X								
28137 **Go Solar Enterprises,** PO Box 422, **Richfield** NC ☎(704) 463-1405			X										X
28213 **Carolina Adventist Book Center,** 2701 East W. T. Harris Blvd., **Charlotte** NC ☎(704) 599-0699 – distributor of *Magic Mill* products				X		X				X	X		
28303 **U. S. Cavalry,** 6215 Yadkin Rd., **Fayetteville** NC ☎(910) 864-3220 🖷(910) 864-1269 – retailer & mail order (4,200 items); survival & outdoor clothing & equipment; preparedness products				X								X	
28377 **Taylor Waterstoves Mfg.,** PO Box 518, **Elizabethtown** NC ☎(910) 862-2576 or (800) 545-2293			X										X
28601 **Hickory Stoves,** Hickory NC ☎(704) 322-7328 🖷(704) 322-7329			X	X									X
28711 **Heart 'n Home Products,** PO Box 442, **Black Mountain** NC ☎(888) 875 BAKE or (704) 669-8773 🖷(704) 669-7056 🖳http://members.aol.com/hearthomc4 ✉*hearthome4@aol.com* – *Bosch & Kitchen Specialties* products, *Walton Feed* products, *Retsel* mills, & *Champion Magic Vac* products				C	X	X	X	X	X	X	X	X	X
28711 **Milford's Lightweight Foods,** 315 Flat Creek Road, **Black Mountain** NC ☎(704) 669-5760 – distributor of *Mountain House & AlpineAire* lightweight trail & camping foods; freeze-dried products				X	X							X	
28721 **Old Grouch's Military Surplus,** 15 S. Main St., **Clyde** NC ☎(704) 627-0361 – distributor of *Alco ♦Brite* gelled ethanol products				X									X
28722 **Good Earth Publications,** RR 2 Box 1875, Green Creek Dr., **Columbus** NC ☎(704) 863-2288 – homesteading & survival pamphlets & products				X									
28731 **Green Pastures,** PO Box 1367, **Flat Rock** NC ☎(704) 698-8386 – dry juice powder			X	X						X			
28739 **Richard Dorian,** 2307 Old Kanuga Road, **Hendersonville** NC ☎(704) 698-8386 – distributor of *Magic Mill* products				X		X				X	X		
28745 **Aurora Productions,** PO Box 445, **Lake Junaluska** NC ☎(800) 972-TAPE 🖷(704) 926-9399 ✉*auroraprod@earthlink.net* – audio recordings of preparedness, self-reliance, freedom, & patriot speakers at preparedness expositions			X	X	X								
28748 **Red Moon Herbs,** PO Box 780, **Leicester** NC ☎(704) 683-1414 – fresh wild-crafted & organic tinctures; vinegars, salves, & oils; how to make organic tinctures, vinegars, salves, & oils; herbal classes & consultations in the wise woman tradition; preparedness consultant				C					X				

Product References Keyed to Chapters (Cont.)

04 water / air filtration & treatment	05 grains, seeds, mills & equip.	12 dairy / powdered milk supplies	13 honey / sweeteners
14 vitamins / minerals / herbs	**15 sprouting / equip. & supplies**	**16 dry / dehydrated / freeze-dried**	**17 energy / fuels**

Entry	M	D	R	04	05	12	13	14	15	16	17
28760 Diamond Brand Camping Center, Hwy. 25, **Naples** NC ☎(704) 684-6262 – distributor of *Alco ♦Brite* gelled ethanol products			X								X
28777 Buck Stove Mfg., **Spruce Pine** NC ☎(704) 765-6144 ✆(704) 765-0462	X										X
28786 Back to Basics, 111 Church Street, **Waynesville** NC ☎(704) 452-2866 ⌨www.dnet.net/~basics/ ✉basics@drake.dnet.net – programs and products for self-reliance; 1-day homesteading class; how to set up the homestead; organic gardening; food storage; consultations; books; audio cassettes for self-instruction in homesteading	X	C	X	X	X	X	X	X	X	X	X
28787 Gourmet Gardens Herb Farm, 14 Bankstown Road, **Weaverville** NC ☎(704) 658-0766		X						X	X		
28792 Assembly Required, 142 East Third Avenue, **Hendersonville** NC			X				X	X		X	X
28800 Great Eastern Sun, Inc., 92 McIntosh Road, **Asheville** NC ☎(704) 665-7790 ✆(704) 667-8051 – miso, soy sauce & soy sauce products, Tamari & Tamari products	X	X			X					X	
28801 T. S. Morrison & Co., 39 N. Lexington Ave., **Asheville** NC ☎(704) 253-2348 – country store with lots of preparedness products & non-electric items		X			X						
28804 Life Spring Natural Lifestyle Shoppers Club, 16 Lookout Drive, **Asheville** NC ☎(800) 752-2775 – $10.00 membership; subscription to *Natural Lifestyle Magazine;* monthly newsletter *Lifespring* with coupons; retailer & mail-order distributor of natural foods, water purification systems, grain mills, natural foods books, more!			X	X	X	X	X	X	X	X	X
28804 Natural Lifestyle, 16 Lookout Dr., **Asheville** NC ☎(704) 254-8053 or (800) 752-2775 ✆(707) 752-3386 – natural foods & foodstuffs & products for natural living offered at special prices to Shopper's Club members; *Multi-Pure* water purification products distributor; miso, soy milk drinks, tofu & tofu products			X	X	X	X	X	X			X
28806 Appalachian Stoves & Fabricators Inc., **Asheville** NC ☎(704) 253-0164 ✆(704) 254-7803 – manufacturer of wood-burning stoves, gas fireplaces, & gas logs	X										X
28806 Matters of Energy Diodes Int'l., 92 Belmont Ave., **Asheville** NC ☎(800) 483-4633 – diode products to correct & counterbalance negative effects of detrimental electromagnetic radiation			X						X	X	
28806 Mountain Ark Trading Company, 799 Old Leicester Highway, **Asheville** NC ☎(704) 252-1221 or *Order Desk* (800) 643-8909 ✆(704) 252-9479 – processor, importer, & national distributor of quality natural foods for macrobiotic nutrition	X	X	X	X	X	X	X	X	X	X	X
28904 Product Concepts Company, PO Box 596, **Hayesville** NC ☎(704) 389-3301 – *FloGo*™ patented sub-micron filtration system produces 200+ gal. of pure, clean water	X	X	X	X							

North Dakota

Entry	M	D	R	04	05	12	13	14	15	16	17
58038 Country Products (div. Agway, Inc.), Box 169, **Grandin** ND ☎(701) 484-5313 ✆(701) 484-5657 – processor of soy nuts	X				X						
58201 The Garden c/o Jay Sutliffe, 1911 S. Washington Street, **Grand Forks** ND ☎(701) 746-5920 – distributor of *Magic Mill* products			X		X			X		X	
58442 Miller Honey Co., Farms Highway 56 South, **Gackle** ND ☎(701) 485-3350	X	X	X				X				
58501 ABC Dakota, 15903 Shyanne Circle, **Bismark** ND ☎(701) 258-6531 – distributor of *Magic Mill* products			X		X			X		X	
58701 Magic Mill Kitchen Center, 115 Main St. S., **Minot** ND ☎(701) 852-4818 – distributor of *Magic Mill* products			X		X						

Ohio

Entry	M	D	R	04	05	12	13	14	15	16	17
43001 Wilderness Survival Institute, ☎(614) 489-9001 – wilderness survival training for men & women of all ages; 3-day workshops in remote OH location	X	C									
43026 Back in Time, 6248 Roberts Road, **Hilliard** OH ☎(614) 771-7042 or *toll-free*☎(888) 850-9066			X	X	X	X	X			X	X
43026 Vanner-Weldon, Inc., 4282 Reynolds Dr., **Hilliard** OH ☎(614) 771-2718 ✆(614) 771-4904	X										X
43040 Vicki Glassburn, 1089 Fairfield Drive, **Marysville** OH ☎(513) 644-0488 – distributor of *Magic Mill* products			X		X			X		X	
43064 Melissa Heiselt, 6881 Harriott Rd., **Powell** OH ☎None – distributor of *Magic Mill* products			X		X			X		X	
43085 Jackie's Kitchen Tech., 6907 Rieber St., **Worthington** OH ☎(614) 433-0181 or (800) 404-4112 – distributor of *K-Tec* products, flour mills & breadmaking kitchen machines; kitchen products; small appliances, non-electric items; no food items sold		C	X		X					X	
43125 Staber Industries, Inc., 4411 Marketing Pl., **Groveport** OH ☎(800) 848-6200			X								X
43213 Federation of Ohio River Co-ops, 320 Outerbelt St. #D, **Columbus** OH ☎(614) 861-2446 ✆(614) 861-7638 Territory: *IN, KY, MD, NC, OH, PA, SC, TN, VA, WV*		C		X	X	X	X	X	X	X	X
43220 Darla's Kitchen, 4114 Kenridge Dr., **Columbus** OH ☎(614) 451-3435 or (614) 451-3403 – distributor of *Magic Mill* products; hand-operated grinder, dehydrator, food supplements		C						X		X	
43332 Ridgeway Hatcheries, Box 306, **LaRue** OH ☎(800) 323-3825 – books & supplies, baby chicks, ducklings, goslings, turkeys, pheasants, guineas, quail; live arrival guaranteed	X	X									
43515 Fire-Born Knives, PO Box 186, **Delta** OH ☎(419) 822-4159 – custom-made knives & camping gear	X	X									X

M = Manufacturer / Processor / D = Wholesaler / Trade distributor / R = Distributor / Retailer to public	M	D	R	04	05	12	13	14	15	16	17
43604 Theresa Metcalf, 1302 N. Superior Street, **Toledo** OH ☎(419) 243-3706 — distributor of *Magic Mill* products			X	X				X		X	
43844 Perry & Patsy Coghlan, 39352 TR 83, **Warsaw** OH ☎(614) 824-3337 — distributor of *Magic Mill* products			X	X				X		X	
44092 Cheryl Lee Adams, 29284 Willow Lane, **Willoughby Hills** OH ☎(216) 944-0454 — distributor of *Magic Mill* products			X	X				X		X	
44093 The Emporium, c/o Pilgrim Goose Hatchery, PO Box 95, **Williamsfield** OH — homesteading & survival pamphlets & products			X								
44103 Cucina Mia, PO Box 603468, **Cleveland** OH ☎(800) 766-0300 — catalog/mail-order for Italian style cookware; everything Italian for the kitchen			X								
44118 Goosefoot Acres, Inc., PO Box 18016, **Cleveland** OH ☎(216) 932-2145 or (800) 697-4858 🖷(216) 932-2187 ✉*petergail@aol.com* — author of resourceful living books on wild plants; distributor of *Dandy Blend*, substitute for instant coffee	X	X	C							X	
44119 Jack Walters, PO Box 19175, **Cleveland** OH ☎(216) 383-1777 💻www.nmarket.com/wreserve — distributor of *Ready Reserve* brand long-term food storage; products integrated preparedness package contains a combination of dehydrated, and no-cook long-term storage foods, water storage			X	X	X	X	X		X		X
44119 Western Reserve Food & Supply Co., PO Box 19175, **Cleveland** OH (216) 383-1777 or (888) 366-3482 www.nmarket.com/wreserve/index.html ✉*wrfood@cyberspace.net* — dehydrated & *AlpineAire* freeze-dried foods, MRE's; preparedness products	X	C	X	X						X	X
44138 Vita-Mix, 8615 Usher Rd, **Cleveland** OH ☎(800) 848-2649 🖷(800) 848-2649 — healthy & easy to prepare whole, natural foods quickly & inexpensively; make super-nutritious juices, breads, sauces, low-fat ice creams, & everything in between!; easy clean-up & no attachments	X										X
44143 National Testing Laboratories, Inc. (NTL), 6151 Wilson Mills Road, **Cleveland** OH — water-testing facility		X	X								
44216 Darlene Pickle, 8596 Hickory Lane Ave. NW, **Clinton** OH ☎(216) 854-5359 — distributor of *Magic Mill* products			X	X				X		X	
44258 A. I. Root Co., PO Box 706, **Medina** OH ☎(800) 289-7668 🖷(330) 725-5624 — beekeeping equipment & supplies manufacturer; books & videos; bee hives & parts; supers, frames & foundations; tools, harvesting equipment & clothing; smokers; medications & chemicals; containers & labels	X	X	X					X			
44258 CropKing, Inc., PO Box 310, **Medina** OH ☎(216) 725-5656 🖷(216) 722-3958 💻www.cropking.com — manufacturer & suppliers of greenhouses & hydroponics growing systems for vegetable production	X	X	X				X				X
44309 Akro-Mills (div. **Myers Industries Company**), PO Box 989, **Akron** OH — manufacturer of plastic storage containers; available at chain, discount, office supply & hardware stores	X										
44452 Mellinger's, Inc., 2310 W. S. Range, **N. Lima** OH ☎(216) 549-4861 or (800) 321-7444 🖷(216) 549-3716 — extraordinary seed & garden supply business; food, storage, preparedness, & emergency products			X	X					X	X	
44460 L. B. Brunk & Sons, Inc., **Salem** OH ☎(330) 332-4297 🖷(330) 332-9768 — manufacturer of wood-burning stoves	X										X
44484 Laura Larosa, 4179 Allenwood Drive SE, **Warren** OH ☎(216) 856-2449 — distributor of *Magic Mill* products			X	X				X		X	
44512 Youngstown Propane, 1409 Boardman Canfield Rd., **Youngstown** OH ☎(216) 758-2341 — distributor of *Alco ◆Brite* gelled ethanol products			X								X
44618 Bonita Bullach, 1999 Alabama Ave. SW, **Dalton** OH ☎(216) 837-9458 — distributor of *Magic Mill* products			X	X				X		X	
44633 Naomi Miller, 9140 County Road 329, **Holmesville** OH ☎(216) 279-4031 — distributor of *Magic Mill* products			X	X				X		X	
44636 Lehman's, One Lehman Circle, **Kidron** OH ☎(330) 857-5757 🖷(330) 857-5785 💻www.lehmans.com ✉*info@lehmans.com* — serving the Amish and others without electricity with products for simple, self-sufficient living; equipment & supplies utilized in a past era—but still useful for today; *Bosch & Kitchen Specialties* products; & much more!	X	C	X	X			X	X	X	X	X
44641 Spotted Pony Traders, 8451 Ravenna Ave., **Louisville** OH — deer, elk, bison leather, leather clothing, & cloth; beads, furs, patterns, & craft supplies; $1.00 for catalog	X	X									
44654 Erma Schrock, 3360 SR 39, **Millersburg** OH ☎(216) 893-2371 — distributor of *Magic Mill* products			X	X				X		X	
44667 Orrville Products, **Orrville** OH ☎(330) 683-4010 🖷(330) 684-2619 — manufacturer of wood-burning stoves & fireplaces	X										X
44677 Lee Rufener, 7070 Fox Lake Road, **Smithville** OH ☎(216) 669-2213 — distributor of *Magic Mill* products			X	X				X		X	
44691 Rubbermaid Incorporated, Wooster OH — home storage containers available at grocery, department, chain & discount & office supply stores	X										X
44805 Evelyn Gibson, 1528 Country 1575, **Ashland** OH ☎(800) 388-6844 — distributor of *Magic Mill* products			X	X				X		X	
44862 Emergency Preparedness Supplies, PO Box 260, **Ontario** OH ☎(419) 985-2573 or (800) 500-4853 — food storage & preparedness products; *Baygen* crank radio			C	X	X	X	X	X	X	X	X

Product References Keyed to Chapters (Cont.)

04 water / air filtration & treatment	05 grains, seeds, mills & equip.	12 dairy / powdered milk supplies	13 honey / sweeteners
14 vitamins / minerals / herbs	15 sprouting / equip. & supplies	16 dry / dehydrated / freeze-dried	17 energy / fuels

Listing	M	D	R	04	05	12	13	14	15	16	17
44883 The C. S. Bell Co., PO Box 291, **Tiffin** OH ☎(419) 448-0791 — manufacturer of a hand-operated grist mill with permanent cone-shaped steel burrs	X	X	X		X						
44903 Alison J. Rall, Rt. 4, 262 Wolf Road, **Mansfield** OH ☎(419) 589-2793 — distributor of *Magic Mill* products			X		X			X	X		
45202 The Bromwell Company, Cincinnati OH ☎(513) 621-0620 ✉*bromwells@hearth.com* — fireplace equipment: gas logs & more…	X										X
45209 Autumn Harvest c/o Christina Thompson, 3750 Drakewood Dr., **Cincinnati** OH ☎None — distributor of *Magic Mill* products			X		X			X	X		
45238 New Pioneer Hardware, PO Box 389164, **Cincinnati** OH ☎(513) 956-8236 — simpler products enabling people to live simpler lives; catalog $2; heavy-duty products for reliability; open-pollinated seeds; windmills, water pumps, non-electric equipment, small-scale, farming implements; books: homesteading, animal care, & building; mail order		X	X		X						X
45242 Right Away Foods, div. **The Wornick Company**, 10825 Kenwood Road, **Cincinnati** OH ☎(513) 794-9800 🖷(513) 794-9543 — TX manufacturing plant; *contract sales to institutional buyers only through* **The Wornicke Company** *office*	X									X	
45242 Shelf Stable Foods, div. **The Wornick Company**, 10825 Kenwood Road, **Cincinnati** OH ☎(513) 794-9800 🖷(513) 794-9543 — OH manufacturing plant; *contract sales to institutional buyers only through* **The Wornicke Company** *office*	X									X	
45242 Wornick Company, The, 10825 Kenwood Road, **Cincinnati** OH ☎(513) 794-9800 🖷(513) 794-9543 — corporate & sales office of largest MRE manufacturer; *contract sales to institutional buyers only*	X									X	
45246 ZestoTherm, Inc., 311 Northland Boulevard, **Cincinnati** OH ☎(513) 772-3066 🖷(513) 772-3269 — MRE & packaged wet foods heaters	X	X								X	X
45373 Hobart Corporation USA, 701 S. Ridge Ave., **Troy** OH ☎(513) 332-3000 — manufacturer of *Kitchen Aid* kitchen machine, with attachments for coarse grinding hard grains only	X				X						
45406 In-Tec Equipment Co., Box 123, D.V. Station, **Dayton** OH ☎(513) 276-4077 — distributor of Danish *DIAMANT D525* steel grinding grain mill; capable of both hand and power operation; equally effective in wet grinding; spare parts available; also, scythe; seed & grain cleaner & grader	X	X			X						
45440 Charlotte Lewis, 137 Eastwick Court, **Beaver Creek** OH ☎(513) 429-2483 — distributor of *Magic Mill* products			X		X			X	X		
45459 The Freedom & Wellness Group, 485 West Alex-Bell Pk., **Centerville** OH ☎/🖷(513) 436-0693 — health food supplies, colloidal silver generators, ozone machines, survival & personal independence products; more!			C					X			
45631 Enviro Flame Heating, Inc., 386 State Rt. 160, **Gallipolis** OH ☎(614) 446-7400 — distributor of *Alco ♦Brite* gelled ethanol products			X								X
45801 United States Plastic Corp., 1390 Neubrecht Road, **Lima** OH ☎(800) 537-9724 🖷(419) 228-5034 — plastic containers!; buy direct from most comprehensive national supplier of plastic food storage containers	X	X	X								X

Oklahoma

Listing	M	D	R	04	05	12	13	14	15	16	17
73013 Edmond Health Foods, 1530 S. Blvd., **Edmond** OK ☎(405) 341-6443			C	X	X	X	X	X	X	X	
73018 Natural Health Food Center, 1722 S. 4th, **Chickshaw** OK ☎(405) 224-1854			C	X	X	X	X	X	X	X	
73061 Noble Country Health Foods, PO Box 189, **Morrison** OK ☎(405) 724-3593			C	X	X	X	X	X	X	X	
73069 Bergey Windpower Co., Inc., 2001 Priestley Ave., **Norman** OK ☎(405) 364-4212 🖷(405) 364-2078	X										X
73069 Dodson's Nutritional Foods, 301 W. Main, **Norman** OK ☎(405) 329-4613			C	X	X	X	X	X	X	X	
73069 Earth Natural Foods #1, 309 S. Flood, **Norman** OK ☎(405) 364-3551			C	X	X	X	X	X	X	X	
73106 Nutritional Food Center, 1024-28 Classen Blvd., **Oklahoma City** OK ☎(405) 232-8404			C	X	X	X	X	X	X	X	
73108 Sam's Surplus Store, Inc., 2409 South Agnew Ave., **Oklahoma City** OK ☎(405) 636-1486 — distributor of *Alco ♦Brite* gelled ethanol products			X								X
73110 Stat Plus Emergency Medical, 523 Peppertree Lane, **Midwest City** OK ☎(405) 733-5180 — everything for emergency medical treatment			C								
73112 Healthway Natural Foods, 6207 N. Meridian, **Oklahoma City** OK ☎(405) 721-2121			C	X	X	X	X	X	X	X	
73116 Akin's Natural Foods Market, 2924 NW. 63rd Street, **Oklahoma City** OK ☎(405) 843-3033			C	X	X	X	X	X	X	X	
73116 Bachle Fireplace Equiment, 2838 W. Wilshire Blvd., **Oklahoma City** OK ☎(405) 842-8872 — distributor of *Alco ♦Brite* gelled ethanol products			X								X
73118 Earth Natural Foods #2, 1101 NW. 49th, **Oklahoma City** OK ☎(405) 840-0502			C	X	X	X	X	X	X	X	
73127 Shari Cregan, 1504 N. Harvard Ave., **Oklahoma City** OK ☎None — distributor of *Magic Mill* products			X		X			X	X		
73144 Prepared Enterprises, PO Box 19572, **Oklahoma City** OK ☎(800) 579-4118 or (405) 682-8836 — distributor of *SamAndy* & *AlpineAire Foods*			X	X	X	X	X	X	X	X	X
73160 Best Products, 9516 S. Sheeds # 136, **Moore** OK — distributor of *Alco ♦Brite* gelled ethanol products			X								X

Where: **M** = Manufacturer / Processor **D** = Wholesaler / Trade distributor **R** = Distributor / Retailer to public

M = Manufacturer / Processor D = Wholesaler / Trade distributor R = Distributor / Retailer to public	M	D	R	04	05	12	13	14	15	16	17
73165 **Live Oak Farms** / Tutor, 3920 SE 104th, **Oklahoma City** OK ☎(405) 794-7365 or (888) 359-5596 🖷(405) 794-7365 🖳www.universalweb.com/food ✉ron@universalweb.com — distributor of *Live Oak Farms* preparedness products	X			X				X		X	
73505 **Whole Foods of Lawton, Inc.**, 2353 W. Gore Blvd., **Lawton** OK ☎(405) 248-3182			C	X	X	X	X	X	X	X	X
73521 **Plaza Health Foods**, 1100 N. Main #3-L, **Altus** OK ☎(405) 477-0039			C	X	X	X	X	X	X	X	X
73533 **Natural Food & Vitamin Shop**, 1517 N. Hwy. 81, **Duncanville** OK ☎(405) 252-1084			C	X	X	X	X	X	X	X	X
73628 **S & K BBQ**, PO Box 66, **Cheyenne** OK ☎(405) 497-2354 — distributor of *Alco ♦Brite* gelled ethanol products	X										X
73644 **Family Health Food Store**, 121 N. Main, **Elk City** OK ☎(405) 225-5040			C	X	X	X	X	X	X	X	X
73644 **Family Health Food Store**, 208 W. Broadway, **Elk City** OK ☎(405) 225-5040			C	X	X	X	X	X	X	X	X
73701 **Natural Food Center Inc.**, 131 W. Garriott, **Enid** OK ☎(405) 234-5000			C	X	X	X	X	X	X	X	X
74003 **Billie's Health Food Center**, 313 SE Osage, **Bartlesville** OK			C	X	X	X	X	X	X	X	X
74012 **Martha's Health Food Store**, 310 W. Kenosha, **Broken Arrow** OK ☎(918) 258-0877			C	X	X	X	X	X	X	X	X
74055 **Daily Bread**, 10412 East Bridgewater Pl., **Owasso** OK ☎(918) 272-7598 — distributor of *Magic Mill* products	X			X				X		X	
74066 **Raby's Wood Stoves Inc.**, **Sapula** OK ☎(918) 224-1488 🖷(918) 224-6471	X	X									X
74108 **Mary Erb**, 15520 East 11th Street, **Tulsa** OK ☎(918) 234-3774 — distributor of *Magic Mill* products	X			X				X		X	
74115 **Earl's Health Food Store**, 3701 E. Admiral Plaza, **Tulsa** OK ☎(918) 834-1374			C	X	X	X	X	X	X	X	X
74120 **The Natural Choice**, 1314 East 15th Street, **Tulsa** OK			C	X	X	X	X	X	X	X	X
74135 **Akin's Natural Foods Market**, 3321 E. 31st St. in Newport Square, **Tulsa** OK ☎(918) 742-6630			C	X	X	X	X	X	X	X	X
74145 **Akin's Natural Foods Market**, 7807 E. 51st Street, **Tulsa** OK ☎(918) 663-4137 🖷(918) 664-9681 or *mail orders*: ☎(800) 800-3133 🖳www.akins.com			C	X	X	X	X	X	X	X	X
74354 **Nature's Plenty**, 19 Goodrich Blvd., **Miami** OK			C	X	X	X	X	X	X	X	X
74403 **Nature's Health Food Center**, 325 Eastside Blvd., **Muskogee** OK ☎(918) 683-4111			C	X	X	X	X	X	X	X	X
74464 **Linda's Health Foods**, 215 N. Muskogee, **Tahlequah** OK ☎(918) 456-8412			C	X	X	X	X	X	X	X	X
74701 **Family Health Food Store**, 1020-A West Main, **Durant** OK ☎(405) 924-3214			C	X	X	X	X	X	X	X	X
74820 **House of Health**, 700 E. Main St., **Ada** OK ☎(405) 436-4143			C	X	X	X	X	X	X	X	X
74820 **Power Nutrition Center**, 910 Arlington Center, **Ada** OK ☎(405) 332-1130			C	X	X	X	X	X	X	X	X
74931 **B & A Products**, Rt. 1 Box 100, **Bunch** OK ☎(918) 696-5998 🖷(918) 696-5999 🖳www.baproducts.com ✉*Byron@baproducts.com* — preparedness products; consultant & author	X	X	X C	X	X	X	X	X	X	X	X

Oregon

	M	D	R	04	05	12	13	14	15	16	17
97005 **Deanna DeLong**, 3450 SW 108th Avenue, **Beaverton** OR ☎(503) 641-1916 🖷(503) 644-9236 ✉*delong@teleport.com* — distributor of *Multi-Pure* water filtration & purification systems for home or emergency use	X	C	X								X
97005 **Ludemans Inc.**, **Beaverton** OR ☎(503) 646-6409 🖷(503) 646-8034 — stoves, fireplaces & more…	X	X									X
97005 **Preservation Pantry**, 3450 SW 108th Ave., **Beaverton** OR ☎(500) 443-7948 *PIN #1916* 🖷(503) 644-7400 — expert in home food dehydration, preservation & storage; bread mixers, grain mills & grinders; household & kitchen implements; sprouts, seeds & equipment; books, tapes, & videos on dehydration & food storage			C	X	X	X	X			X	X
97006 **Brian & Marla Wells**, Box 5572, **Aloha** OR ☎(503) 590-9355 or (500) 449-9355 🖷(503) 590-9357 — distributor of *Multi-Pure* water filtration & purification systems for home or emergency use	X	C	X								
97021 **Azure Standard**, 79709 Dufur Valley Road, **Dufur** OR ☎(541) 467-2230 — wholesale distributor of bulk & natural foods, raw nuts, beans, & seeds, pastas, juices, baking mixes & products, cereals, cheeses, dried fruit, dairy products, grains & flours, grocery products, vitamins & minerals	X	C	X	X	X	X	X	X	X		
97031 **Little Bit Ranch Supply**, 2727 W. Cascade Ave., **Hood River** OR ☎(541) 386-1299 — distributor of *Alco ♦Brite* gelled ethanol products	X										X
97034 **Nature's Fresh NW! Blue Heron Cafe**, 333 S. State St., **Lake Oswego** OR ☎(503) 635-3374			C	X	X	X	X	X	X	X	X
97035 **Bear's Basic Essentials**, PO Box 1457, **Lake Oswego** OR ☎(503) 670-0314 ✉*Bear1888@aol.com*	X	X	X	X					X	X	X
97042 **Bio Water Products**, Box 911, **Mulino** OR ☎(503) 829-9529 — *Bio Water* catalyst & related products; Pycnogenol & bio-moist herbal rejuvenating cream with Pycnogenol	X	X	X					X			
97045 **Bea Lydecker's Naturals, Inc.**, 15443 S. Latourette Rd., **Oregon City** OR ☎(503) 631-7389 or (800) 258-8589 🖷(800) 258-8589	X							X			
97053 **Liahona**, 33587 Rodney Rd., **Warren** OR ☎(503) 397-5825 — full-line distributor of preparedness products & storage foods			C	X	X	X	X		X	X	X
97060 **Bake N' Bread**, 2639 SE Lewellyn Ave., **Troutdale** OR — *Bosch & Kitchen Specialties* products distributors	X				X		X		X		
97070 **Liberty Organization, Inc.**, 9325 S. W. Barber St., **Wilsonville** OR ☎(503) 685-9600 — distributor of *Alco ♦Brite* gelled ethanol products	X										X
97103 **Community Store**, 1389 Duane St., **Astoria** OR ☎(541) 325-0027			C	X	X	X	X	X	X	X	X

Product References Keyed to Chapters (Cont.)

04 water / air filtration & treatment	05 grains, seeds, mills & equip.	12 dairy / powdered milk supplies	13 honey / sweeteners
14 vitamins / minerals / herbs	15 sprouting / equip. & supplies	16 dry / dehydrated / freeze-dried	17 energy / fuels

M = Manufacturer / Processor D = Wholesaler / Trade distributor R = Distributor / Retailer to public

Entry	M	D	R	04	05	12	13	14	15	16	17
97119 Adrienne Sissoyev, 407 Church St., **Gastin** OR ☎(503) 985-3265 – distributor of *Magic Mill* products		X			X		X	X		X	
97124 Eagle Investments, A2019 NE Josephine, **Hillsboro** OR ☎(503) 693-8952 – the toddy people, distributors of the forbidden cure survival kit of colloidal minerals		X	X				X	X			
97148 T & E's, 110 Maple St., **Yamhill** OR ☎(503) 662-3322 – distributor of *Alco ♦Brite* gelled ethanol products		X									X
97201 Nature's Fresh Northwest!, 5909 SW Corbett, **Portland** OR ☎(503) 244-3934			C		X	X	X	X	X	X	X
97201 Nature's Fresh Northwest!, 6344 SW Capitol Hwy., **Portland** OR ☎(503) 244-3110			C		X	X	X	X	X	X	X
97202 American Family Network, 2727 SE Raymond Street, **Portland** OR ☎(503) 238-1166 *outside OR:* (800) 668-8181 🖷(503) 238-0237 🖳www.americanfamilynetwork.com ✉apc@american-products.com			C		X		X	X		X	X
97202 American Products Co., (div. LTA Mktg. Co.), 2727 SE Raymond St., **Portland** OR ☎(503) 238-1166 or (800) 668-8181 *(outside OR)* 🖷(503) 238-0237		X				X	X		X		X
97202 Nature's Fresh Northwest!, 3016 SE Division, **Portland** OR ☎(503) 233-7374			C		X	X	X	X	X	X	X
97206 R-U-Prepared?, 4326 SE Woodstock #393, **Portland** OR – 72-hr. kits & emergency kits for autos, contains life-saving items; solar radio; re-useable heat packs, more!		X	X							X	X
97212 Nature's Fresh Northwest!, 3449 NE 24th, **Portland** OR ☎(503) 281-7489			C		X	X	X	X	X	X	X
97213 Indoor Environmental Products, 2316 NE 55th Ave., **Portland** OR ☎(800) 335-0761 – *Alpine Aire* system air purification		X									X
97214 Organically Grown Co-op, 233 SE 3rd, **Portland** OR ☎(503) 232-0674			C		X	X	X	X	X	X	X
97220 International Yogurt Company, 5858 NE 87th Ave., **Portland** OR ☎(503) 256-3754 – yogurt & kefir cultures; cheeses, sour cream, & buttermilk cultures & supplies	X	X	X			X			X		
97222 Bob's Red Mill Natural Foods, Inc., 6209 SE Int'l. Way, **Portland** OR ☎(503) 654-3215 🖷(503) 653-1339 – soy flour, soy grits, whole soybeans		X				X	X	X		X	
97224 Country Fresh Farms Intl., Inc. (Corporate Ofc.), 15055 SW Sequoia Parkway #180, **Portland** OR ☎(503) 620-0700 🖷(503) 639-0710 – no-cholesterol whey milk substitute, excellent for lactose-intolerant persons; available in 5 flavors; tastes like fresh milk without the calories; no calcium caseinate; nitrogen-flushed for 5-yr. shelf life	X	X	C			X					
97224 Finlandia Sauna, **Portland** OR ☎(800)) 354-3342 🖷(503) 684-1120 – manufacturer of electric sauna heaters & wood-burning sauna stoves	X	X	C								X
97230 Ruhl Bee Supply, 12713 Whitaker Way, **Portland** OR – beekeeping & honey production supplies & equipment	X	X	X				X				
97236 Kitchen Center, 16409 SE Division St., **Portland** OR ☎(503) 761-9264 – *Bosch* kitchen products distributor		X	X								X
97301 Heliotrope Natural Foods, 2060 Market St. NE, **Salem** OR ☎(503) 362-5499 or (800) 670-5487			C		X	X	X	X	X	X	X
97301 Home Fire Stove, **Salem** OR ☎(503) 364-6339 🖷(503) 364-1083 ✉nissentj@open.org @aol.com	X	X									X
97301 Kitchen Ctr. / Robert Dinubillo, 4260 Center St. NE, **Salem** OR ☎(503) 362-1552 🖷(503) 362-0419 – *Bosch* kitchen products distributor		X				X	X	X	X	X	X
97308 Food Storage Central. PO Box 561, **Salem** OR ☎(503) 585-0478 🖳www.foodstorage.net/order.htm ✉foodstorage@foodstorage.net – *Food Storage ON-LINE™*; distributor of *AlpineAire* freeze-dried products for long-term food storage		X	X	X	X	X				X	X
97321 Oregon Freeze Dry, Inc., PO Box 1048, **Albany** OR ☎(800) 547-0244 or (800) 547-0244 🖷(541) 967-6527 🖳www.ofd.com/mh – processor of freeze-dried desserts, entrees, fruits, meats, vegetables; *available only through authorized distributors*	X									X	
97321 Weldon McKinney, 1610-A NW Scenic Drive, **Albany** OR ☎(541) 926-5435 – distributor of *Magic Mill* products		X			X			X		X	
97330 Roger Brownell, 1140 NW Lester Ave., **Corvallis** OR ☎(503) 753-8314 or (800) 682-3712 – distributor of *Magic Mill* products		X			X			X		X	
97335 Satellite Pools & Spas, 1524 South Main St., **Lebanon** OR ☎(503) 259-4488 – distributor of *Alco ♦Brite* gelled ethanol products		X									X
97341 Harry Caylor, PO Box 282, **Depoe Bay** OR ☎(503) 765-4326 or (800) 765-4407 – distributor of *Multi-Pure* water filtration & purification systems for home or emergency use		X	X								
97365 Oceana Natural Foods Co-op, 159 SE 2nd St., **Newport** OR ☎(541) 265-3893			C		X	X	X	X	X	X	X
97366 South Beach Heating, 3335 Ferry Slip Rd., **South Beach** OR ☎(503) 867-3533 – distributor of *Alco ♦Brite* gelled ethanol products		X									X
97383 Embassy of Heaven Church, 8777 Basl Hill Road SE, **Stayton** OR ☎(503) 769-5034 – spiritual preparedness; spiritual retreats; publishes books on internal cleansing			C					X			
97385 West Coast Emergency Supplies, 803 Dalmatian SW, **Sublimity** OR ☎(503) 769-9414 or (800) 769-9419 🖷(503) 769-9414 🖳www.emergencysupplies.com/wces ✉wces@open.org – distributor of complete line of food storage & preparedness products		X	X	X	X	X			X	X	X
97386 Sweet Home Stove Sales, 610 Main St., **Sweet Home** OR ☎(503) 367-5197 – distributor of *Alco ♦Brite* gelled ethanol products		X									X

M = Manufacturer / Processor	D = Wholesaler / Trade distributor	R = Distributor / Retailer to public	M	D	R	04	05	12	13	14	15	16	17
97386 Town & Country Spices, 1101 Main St., **Sweet Home** OR			X	X							X	
– more than 200 spices, herbs & teas; save 50-80%; catalog sent for **SASE**												
97401 Oasis Fine Foods Marketplace, 2580 Willakenzie, **Eugene** OR ☎(541) 334-6382					C	X	X	X	X	X	X	X
97401 Practical Preparedness Catalog, PO Box 70131, **Eugene** OR ☎(541) 746-6828 🖷(541) 747-2509				X			X	X	X		X	X
– *AlpineAire Foods* distributor; mail-order preparedness products & camping supplies; underground survival shelters												
97401 Real Goods Store, 77 W. Broadway, **Eugene** OR ☎(541) 334-6960 🖷(541) 334-6962 ✉*garyb@efn.org*			X	X			X	X			X	X
– retail store & catalog mail-order; products for energy independence & a safe home, solar equipment & supplies, efficient lighting equipment, natural pest control, books; renewable energy; & lots more!												
97401 Rising Moon, 1432 Willamette, **Eugene** OR ☎(800) 766-6679 ✉*sales@risingmoon.com*			X	X								X
– tofu & tofu products												
97401 Surata Soyfoods Co-op, 325 W. 3rd Ave., Bldg A, **Eugene** OR ☎(541) 485-6990 or (541) 343-8434					C	X	X	X	X	X	X	
97402 Craft Stove Center, 1875 West 6th Ave., **Eugene** OR ☎(503) 485-0533				X								X
– distributor of *Alco ◆Brite* gelled ethanol products												
97402 Delta One, 3232 W. 16th Ave., **Eugene** OR			X	X								X
97402 Grain Millers, Inc., PO Box 21339, **Eugene** OR ☎(800) 443-8972				X			X					
– grains & flours freshly ground												
97402 Organically Grown Co-op, 1800 Prairie Road #B, **Eugene** OR ☎(541) 589-5320					C	X	X	X	X	X	X	X
97405 Sundance Natural Foods, 749 East 24th Ave., **Eugene** OR					C	X	X	X	X	X	X	X
97416 Field Of Dreams Enterprises, 811 Main Camas Rd., **Camas Valley** OR ☎(541) 445-2923 🖷(541) 445-2923 ✉*pgriffin@users.wizzard.net*				X					X			
97424 Sunshine General Store, 824 W. Main, **Cottage Grove** OR ☎(541) 942-8836					C	X	X	X	X	X	X	X
97440 Down to Earth Distributors, Inc., PO Box 1419, **Eugene** OR ☎(800) 234-5932 🖷(503) 485-7141			X	X								X
– organic gardening supplies, kitchen utensils, baskets, glassware, & other natural products												
97440 Flint Firestarters, PO Box 924, **Eugene** OR ☎(541) 345-3400			X	X	X							X
– survival tool for emergencies, camping, hunting, fishing, & backpacking; fire, signal, & light in one item												
97444 MariSu Terry, 27944 Boomer Bend, **Gold Beach** OR ☎(541) 247-7387					X				X	X		
– distributor of *Magic Mill* products												
97448 Frontier Fire Starter, PO Box 44, **Junction City** OR ☎(541) 998-3703			X	X	X							X
– magnesium fire-starter; basic survival tool												
97457 International Power Foods & Prod., PO Box 1537, **Myrtle Creek** OR ☎(503) 863-7368 or (800) 557-0303			X	X	X					X		X
– ozone water & air purification systems; nutritional products; ozone generators, colonic boards & equipment; more!												
97459 Kozy Wood Heating, 2257 Broadway, **North Bend** OR				X								X
– distributor of *Alco ◆Brite* gelled ethanol products												
97470 Orley's Spas & Stoves, 1244 N. E. Walnut St., **Roseburg** OR ☎(503) 672-8599				X								X
– distributor of *Alco ◆Brite* gelled ethanol products												
97470 The Vitamin Shoppe c/o Jim Wilson, 250 NE Garden Valley Blvd., **Roseburg** OR ☎(503) 673-6315				X		X				X	X	
– distributor of *Magic Mill* products												
97479 Sutherlin Natural Foods, PO Box 829/109 East Central, **Sutherlin** OR ☎None				X		X				X	X	
– distributor of *Magic Mill* products												
97501 Health Food Mart Inc. c/o Jim Ford, 259-D Barnett Road, **Medford** OR ☎(503) 772-3231				X		X				X	X	
97501 Kitchen Kneads (attn: Maria Neville) 2430 Neville Street, **Medford** OR 🖷(541) 772-8191				X	X	X					X	
– distributor of *Bosch & Kitchen Specialties* products												
97501 Kitchen Kneads, 2138 W. Main Street #104, **Medford** OR ☎(503)772-7098			X	X	X	X	X	X	X	X	X	X
– *Magic Mill* distributor; authorized distributor of *Emergency Essentials* products												
97502 AlpineAire Distributors, PO Box 3100, **Central Point** OR ☎(541) 826-9279 or (800) 453-7453 for orders only 🖷(541) 826-1023				X		X			X			
– books; preparedness products; spiritual preparedness; publications												
97504 Mainline Electric, 4324 Fern Valley Rd., **Medford** OR ☎(800) 221-9302 🖷(503) 535-8833			X	X								X
97520 Cantwell's Market, 310 Oak St., **Ashland** OR ☎(541) 488-2120 🖷(541) 482-3805					C	X	X	X	X	X	X	X
97520 Michael Linden, Box 62, **Ashland** OR ☎(800) 746-7413				X						X	X	X
– sprouting guides; *Cell-Tech* distributor												
97520 Rosetta Aware House, Box 3028 **Ashland** OR ☎(503) 488-1379 🖷(503) 482-4984 ✉*aware@mind.net*				X	X				X			X
97523 Energy Outfitters, 136 S. Redwood Hwy., PO Box 1888 **Cave Junction** OR ☎(800) GO-SOLAR				X	X							X
97524 Butte Creek Mill, PO Box 561, **Eagle Point** OR ☎(541) 826-3531 🖷(541) 830-8444			X	X	X		X					X
– water-powered stone-ground wheat, corn, barley, millet, oat flours; *Butte Creek* brand flours & mixes; mail order												
97526 Stor-Tite Containers, 124 NE Morgan Lane, **Grants Pass** OR ☎(541) 476-4977 🖷(805) 942-0999			X	C		X					X	X
– 5-gal. re-useable **HDPE** pails w/screw-on/off lids; has air-tight seal & positive locking action; nitrogen or CO_2 regulator hose & nozzle set for packing long-term storage products at home												
97527 Solar Chef, 220 Southridge Way, **Grants Pass** OR ☎(800) 378-4198			X	X								X
97603 Aladdin Valley Rental, 3580 Shasta Way, **Klamath** OR ☎(503) 882-6686				X								X
– distributor of *Alco ◆Brite* gelled ethanol products												
97701 Fireside Spa & Patio, **Bend** OR ☎(541) 382-2597 🖷(541) 382-3017 ✉*fireside@transport.com*			X	X								X

Product References Keyed to Chapters (Cont.)

04 water / air filtration & treatment	05 grains, seeds, mills & equip.	12 dairy / powdered milk supplies	13 honey / sweeteners
14 vitamins / minerals / herbs	15 sprouting / equip. & supplies	16 dry / dehydrated / freeze-dried	17 energy / fuels

M = Manufacturer / Processor   D = Wholesaler / Trade distributor   R = Distributor / Retailer to public

Chapter columns: M · D · R · 04 · 05 · 12 · 13 · 14 · 15 · 16 · 17

Listing	M	D	R	04	05	12	13	14	15	16	17
97701 Solar Tech, Solar Tech 27250 Willard Rd, **Bend** OR ☎(503) 388-2053 or: (541) 388-2053	X	X									X
97741 Cascade Satellite Stove & Spa, 53 SW D St., **Madras** OR ☎(541) 475-7949		X									X
97801 Pendleton Flour Mills, Inc., Box #1427, **Pendleton** OR ☎(503) 276-6511 ▤(503) 276-9151 — custom-grinding of flours and mixes; whole grains	X	X	X		X					X	
97801 Pendleton Grain, 1000 SW Dorian, **Pendleton** OR ☎(503) 276-7611 — custom-ground flours & mixes; whole grains & seeds	X	X	X		X					X	
97838 Gardner's LDS Books c/o Dale Gardner, Rt. 3, Box 3289-C, **Hermiston** OR — preparedness products and long-term storgae items			X			X			X	X	
97838 HSC Feed Co., 300 W. Feed Mill Rd, **Hermiston** OR ☎(800) 700-2295 ▤(503) 564-0354 — grains & flours custom-ground for the public	X	X	X		X					X	
97914 Cambridge Enterprises / Powell's Office Supply, PO Box 1019, **Ontario** OR ☎(503) 889-7528 — preparedness products distributor; preparedness books & office supplies						X	X	X	X	X	X

Pennsylvania

Listing	M	D	R	04	05	12	13	14	15	16	17
15241 Joseph's Storehouse, 255 Franklin Dr., **Pittsburgh** PA ☎(412) 941-4009 — *SamAndy Foods* products distributor			X			X	X	X	X	X	X
15501 Fike Plumbing & Heating, #5, Box 246, **Somerset** PA ☎(814) 445-2027 — distributor of *Alco ♦Brite* gelled ethanol products			X								X
15940 Heating World, Inc., 6590 Admiral Perry Hwy., **Loretto** PA ☎(814) 886-4106 — distributor of *Alco ♦Brite* gelled ethanol products			X								X
16134 Shrocks, 3706 Bush Rd., **Jamestown** PA ☎(800) 830-0498 — specialist in remote alternative power generation systems; diesel engines 5 to 35 KW, alternators, turnkey generators	X	X									X
16222 Ken & Ann Fisher, RD 2, Box 86, **Dayton** PA ☎(814) 257-8216 — distributor of *Magic Mill* products			X		X			X	X		
16404 Kalkbrenner's Archery, Rt. 4, **Centerville** PA — distributor of *Alco ♦Brite* gelled ethanol products			X								X
16506 Stoves & Such, Inc., 5455 West Ridge Rd., **Erie** PA ☎(814) 833-4871 — distributor of *Alco ♦Brite* gelled ethanol products			X								X
16823 Pennwood Corporation, Pleasant Gap PA ☎(800) 598-3995 ▤9814) 359-2763 — stoves, fireplaces, & more…	X	X									X
16923 Genesee Foods, RD 2 Box 105, **Genesee** PA ☎(800) 445-0094 or (814) 228-3200 **Territory:** *DE, MD, NJ, NY, OH, PA*	X	C	X			X	X	X	X	X	X
17022 W. D. Espenshade, Inc., 380 W. Bainbridge St., **Elizabethtown** PA ☎(717) 367-6496 — distributor of *Alco ♦Brite* gelled ethanol products			X								X
17030 Clearview Hatchery, Box 399, **Gratz** PA — chicks, ducklings, goslings, turkeys, guineas, bantams, hatching eggs, books, medication; poultry supplies, & equip.			X								
17071 Smith's, Box 83C, **New Germantown** PA — Amish-made tools and supplies; mail-order supplier			X								
17078 North Forge Home Heating, Rt. 3 Box 96-A, **Palmyra** PA ☎(717) 838-4559 — distributor of *Alco ♦Brite* gelled ethanol products			X								X
17522 Bowman's Stove & Patio, **Ephrata** PA ☎(717) 733-4973 ▤(717) 738-0815 ▢www.bowmansstove.com — distributor of *Alco ♦Brite* gelled ethanol products		X	X								X
17529 Sunline Solar, 4052 Ridge Rd., **Gordonville** PA ☎(717) 656-1644		X	X								X
17538 John C. Bucher, 118 Main Street, **Salunga** PA ☎(717) 898-0349 — distributor of *Magic Mill* products			X		X			X	X		
17740 Terry's Wood & Coal Stoves, 216 Bastress St., **Jersey Shore** PA ☎(717) 398-2199 — distributor of *Alco ♦Brite* gelled ethanol products			X								X
17862 Walnut Acres, Inc., Penn's Creek PA ☎(717) 837-0601 — distributor of *Magic Mill* products; organic products; custom-ground flours	X	X	X		X	X	X	X	X		
18011 Coal Heat, Inc., 120 N. Main St., **Alburtis** PA ☎(215) 966-3556 — distributor of *Alco ♦Brite* gelled ethanol products			X								X
18067 Keller Coal & Oil Co., 1514 Main St., **Northampton** PA ☎(610) 262-3975 — distributor of *Alco ♦Brite* gelled ethanol products			X								X
18252 Stoves & Stuff, Tamaqua PA ☎(717) 386-5656 ▤(717) 386-4030		X	X								X
18301 Cramers Cashway, 320 N. Courtland St., **E. Stroudsburg** PA ☎(717) 424-5953 — distributor of *Alco ♦Brite* gelled ethanol products			X								X
18322 Stove & Fireplace Shop, Route 209, **Brodheadsville** PA ☎(717) 992-4422 — distributor of *Alco ♦Brite* gelled ethanol products			X								X
18036 Suzanne Wampler, 7707 Cymun Drive, **Coopersburg** PA ☎(610) 967-1234 — distributor of *Magic Mill* products			X		X			X	X		

M = Manufacturer / Processor	D = Wholesaler / Trade distributor	R = Distributor / Retailer to public	M	D	R	04	05	12	13	14	15	16	17
18042 **Archive Co.**, 32 N. Second St., **Easton** PA – distributor of *Alco♦Brite* gelled ethanol products			X										X
18420 **Sue Stoddard**, Rt. 407, **Fleetville** PA ☎(717) 945-7161 – distributor of *Magic Mill* products			X			X			X		X		
18603 **Ironwolf Enterprises**, 203 E. 2ⁿᵈ St., **Berwick** PA ☎(800) 752-WOLF or (717) 752-8800 🖷(717) 759-1800 – equipment for the serious survivalist; preparedness products			X	C	X							X	X
18651 **Woody's Fireplace, Inc.**, **Larksville** PA ☎(717) 283-2534			X	X									X
18951 **Wood Heat**, **Quakertown** PA ☎(610) 346-7894 🖷(610) 346-6866 💻www.woodheat.com ✉staff@woodheat.com			X	X									X
18954 **Mother Nature's General Store**, **Southampton** PA ☎(800) 290-8140 💻www.mothernature.com ✉mother@pond.com – for **Internet** shoppers; appliances, bath & dental supplies, body building, housewares, diet products, groceries, homeopathic, massage oils & aromatherapy, pet supplies, vitamins, upplements & herbs; herbal teas					X	X	X	X	X	X	X	X
18964 **Dawn Bergy**, 480 Homestead Ave., **Souderton** PA ☎(215) 723-5953 – distributor of *Magic Mill* products			X			X			X		X		
18966 **Bunn's Natural Food Shoppe**, 1007 Street Road, **Southampton** PA ☎(215) 355-1165			C	X	X	X	X	X	X	X	
18969 **Laurie Brubaker**, 254 Indian Creek Road, **Telford** PA ☎(215) 723-2386 – distributor of *Magic Mill* products			X			X			X		X		
18974 **Nishemeny Valley Natural Foods**, Ginco Industrial Park, 5 Louise Drive, **Ivyland** PA ☎(215) 443-5545 Territory: *CT, DE, DC, NJ, NY, PA, VA*			C			X	X	X	X	X	X	X	X
18974 **Seasons Hearth & Patio, Inc.**, 1060 Greeley Ave., **Warminster** PA ☎(215) 442-0600 – distributor of *Alco♦Brite* gelled ethanol products			X										X
19007 **Life Support International, Inc.**, 200 Rittenhouse Circle #4 West, **Bristol** PA ☎(215) 785-2870 – manufacturer of canned drinking water (10 oz. aluminum cans)			X	X	X							
19013 **Grate Fireplaces**, 3301 W. 4ᵗʰ St., **Trainer** PA ☎(215) 494-2021 – distributor of *Alco♦Brite* gelled ethanol products			X										X
19019 **Bread & Circus**, 2001 Pennsylvania Avenue, **Philadelphia** PA				X	X	X	X	X	X	X	X	
19019 **Bread & Circus**, 929 South Street, **Philadelphia** PA *Opening 1998*				X	X	X	X	X	X	X	X	
19020 **The Blazing Hearth**, 1963 Street Rd., **Bensalem** PA ☎(215) 633-8993 – distributor of *Alco♦Brite* gelled ethanol products			X										X
19087 **Bread & Circus**, 821 Lancaster Avenue, **Wayne** PA ☎(610) 688-9400 🖷(610) 688-9401				X	X	X	X	X	X	X	X	
19096 **Bread & Circus**, 339 E. Lancaster Avenue, **Wynnewood** PA ☎(610) 896-3737 🖷(610) 896-9129				X	X	X	X	X	X	X	X	
19365 **Twila Ranck**, Rt. 1 Box 347, Lincoln Highway, **Parksburg** PA ☎(717) 442-1255 – distributor of *Magic Mill* products			X			X			X		X		
19403 **Robert Houchins**, 100 South Trooper Road, **Jeffersonville** PA ☎(610) 539-6965 🖷(610) 539-8591 – Rife research with bioactive frequency; a mechanical treatment for ailments and therapy for well-being			X	X C					X			
19426 **Fitz Waterwheel Co.**, 118 Sycamore Ct., **Collegeville** PA ☎(215) 489-6256			X	X									X
19440 **Wood Burners**, Market & Broad St., **Hatfield** PA ☎(215) 362-2443 – distributor of *Alco♦Brite* gelled ethanol products			X										X
19454 **Bread & Circus**, 1210 Bethlehem Pike, **North Wales** PA ☎(215) 646-6300 🖷(215) 542-2190				X	X	X	X	X	X	X	X	
19506 **Suburban Water Testing Labs, Inc.**, 4600 Crookston Road, **Temple** PA ☎(800) 433-6595 💻www.h2otest.com ✉stump2@pipeline.com			X	X								
19512 **Berkmont Industries, Inc.**, **Boyertown** PA ☎(610) 754-7399 – manufacturer of coal & wood-burning stoves			X										X
19543 **Hartz Farm Store—Natural Foods**, 211 Twin County Road, **Morgantown** PA ☎(610) 286-5268			X			X			X	X	X	
Rhode Island													
02888 **Stovepipe Fireplace Shop**, 654 Warwick Ave., **Warwick** RI ☎(603) 635-2597 – distributor of *Alco♦Brite* gelled ethanol products			X										X
02818 **Adventure Group, Inc.**, East Greenwich RI ☎(401) 885-6899 – distributor/mail-order freeze-dried foods for campers, backpackers, sailors, emergency mgt. groups, & adventurists			X	X		X					X	
02906 **Bread & Circus**, 261 Waterman Street, **Providence** RI ☎(401) 272-1690 🖷(401) 272-0280				X	X	X	X	X	X	X	X	
South Carolina													
29334 **Southern Bowhunter**, 1719 E. Wade Hampton Blvd., **Duncan** SC – distributor of *Alco♦Brite* gelled ethanol products			X										X
29601 **The Country Factory**, **Greenville** SC 💻http://cybercity.piedmont.net/countryfactory – **Internet** access only				X								
29607 **Foresight Products**, 100 Questover Drive, **Greenville** SC – more than 600 storage & survival products; send $2.00 for catalog				X	X	X	X			X	X	X
29607 **James Edwards**, 150 Mountain Brook Trail, **Greenville** SC ☎(803) 246-8963 – distributor of *Magic Mill* kitchen products				X	X	X			X		X	

Product References Keyed to Chapters (Cont.)

04 water / air filtration & treatment	05 grains, seeds, mills & equip.	12 dairy / powdered milk supplies	13 honey / sweeteners
14 vitamins / minerals / herbs	15 sprouting / equip. & supplies	16 dry / dehydrated / freeze-dried	17 energy / fuels
M = Manufacturer / Processor	D = Wholesaler / Trade distributor	R = Distributor / Retailer to public	

Entry	M	D	R	04	05	12	13	14	15	16	17
29616 United Metal Services, Greenville SC ☎(864) 288-4174 — manufacturer of wood-burning stoves	X										X
29676 Pat Kaufman, 698 Brittany Lane, **Salem** SC ☎(None) — distributor of *Magic Mill* kitchen products					X	X			X	X	
29732 Fran Cope, 3155 India Hook Road, **Rock Hill** SC ☎(803) 366-1275 — distributor of *Magic Mill* kitchen products					X	X			X	X	
26949 Deborah H. Stumbo, 107 Cedar Lake Court, **Greenwood** SC ☎(803) 229-5596 — distributor of *Magic Mill* kitchen products					X	X			X	X	
29926 The Antique Hardware Store, 1 Matthews Ct., **Hilton Head** SC ☎(800) 422-9982 — homesteading/survival pamphlets & products; mail-order supplier		X									
South Dakota											
57006 Priscilla A. Pulscher, Rt. 4 Box 232, **Brookings** SD ☎(605) 693-4592 — distributor of *Magic Mill* products					X	X			X	X	
57033 Solar Pathfinder, 25720 465th Ave., **Hartford** SD ☎(605) 528-6473 ✉*solarpf@aol.com*	X										X
57201 Carol Kannegieter, 118 East Kemp, **Watertown** SD ☎(605) 886-4626 — distributor of *Magic Mill* products					X	X			X	X	
57350 Emma Tschetter, Rt. 1 Box 206, **Huron** SD ☎(605) 352-7661 — distributor of *Magic Mill* products					X	X			X	X	
57401 Kay Vikander, 114 North Lincoln, **Aberdeen** SD ☎(605) 229-4947 — distributor of *Magic Mill* products					X	X			X	X	
57701 Heart & Hearth, 306 Main St., **Rapid City** SD — distributor of *Alco ✦Brite* gelled ethanol products		X									X
Tennessee											
37033 Deanna L. Haley, 248 Low Branch Road, **Centerville** TN ☎(615) 729-0368 — distributor of *Magic Mill* products					X	X			X	X	
37088 American Bee Supply, Box 555 Rt. 7 Sparta Pike, **Lebanon** TN	X	X	X				X				
37166 Black Kat Books & Herbals, PO Box 271, **Smithville** TN ☎(615) 597-1270 📠(615) 597-1270 ✉*BLACKKAT@mail.infoave.net*		X						X			
37202 Service Merchandise Co., Inc., PO Box 25130, **Nashville** TN ☎(800) 251-1212 🖥www.servicemerchandise.com — national discount chain; equipment & supplies for processing & in-home production of food storage		X	X								X
37210 Aladdin Industries, Inc., 703 Murfreesboro Road, **Nashville** TN — manufacturer of Aladdin clean-burning kerosene lamps for household lighting; many table and hanging models; maximum lighting intensity equal to 60W light bulb	X		X								X
37216 Cynthia Bohannon, 1204 McHesney Ave., **Nashville** TN ☎None — distributor of *Magic Mill* products and information					X	X			X	X	
37315 Village Market c/o Frances Johnson, 5000 College Drive West, **Collegedale** TN ☎(615) 396-3121 — distributor of *Magic Mill* products					X	X			X	X	
37329 Ready Made Resources, 125 County Rd. 585, **Englewood** TN ☎(423) 746-9814 or (800) 627-3809 📠(423) 746-9814 🖥www.cococo.net/rmr ✉*robert@avicom.net* — long-term food storage, water purifiers, herbal & medical products; books & videos, dehydrators, grain mills, solar & non-electrical equipment, trail mixes, & more!; *AlpineAire* brand products; cooking equipment & supplies		C	X					X		X	X
37387 The Marugg Co., PO Box 1418, **Tracy City** TN — homesteading/survival pamphlets & products; mail-order supplier		X									
37388 Sandra Anderson, 330 Turkey Creek Drive, **Tullahoma** TN ☎(615) 455-8049 — distributor of *Magic Mill* products					X	X			X	X	
37422 Self-Care Catalog, PO Box 182290 **Chattanooga** TN ☎(800) 345-3371	X	X						X			
37604 ADH Emergency Supplies, 3101 Brownsville Road, #6-118, **Johnson City** TN — cold-weather/survival gear; emergency electronics, radio; emergency medical & first-aid supplies, kits, & equipment; hunting & fishing gear	X	C	X							X	X
37612 Anne Parker, 599 Tyne Gray Road, **Afton** TN ☎(423) 798-0255 — distributor of *Magic Mill* products					X	X			X	X	
37659 Herb Peddler c/o Gary Smith, 133 E. Main Street, **Jonesboro** TN ☎(423) 753-0083		X	X	X	X	X	X	X			X
37688 Under The Sun Natural Foods 1076 Winchester Road, **Shady Valley** TN ☎(423) 739-9266 — mail-order organic/non-organic bulk food items, nuts, seeds, grains, dried fruit, beans, vitamins, etc.; no minimums		X	X		X			X		X	
37901 Harvest Direct, PO Box 988, **Knoxville** TN ☎(423) 523-2304 📠(423) 523-3372 ✉*harvest@slip.net* — meat alternatives, soy flour, organic soybeans, soy milk drinks, soy milk powder & products, & tofu products		X	X		X					X	
37912 Carolyn Kohler, 5935 Talent Road, **Knoxville** TN ☎(615) 688-6749 — distributor of *Magic Mill* products					X	X			X	X	

M = Manufacturer / Processor	D = Wholesaler / Trade distributor	R = Distributor / Retailer to public	M	D	R	04	05	12	13	14	15	16	17
37912 **Freedom & Liberty Foundation** (attn: Robert Pelton), PO Box 12619, **Knoxville** TN ☎(423) 523-9523 – author & publisher of *"The Official Pocket Survival Manual"*			X	X	C								
37919 **Natural Pantry**, 6600 Kingston Pike, **Knoxville** TN ☎(615) 584-4714					C	X	X	X	X	X	X		
37922 **Shoney's Main Office**, 9720 Truckers Lane, **Knoxville** TN ☎(615) 690-6331 – distributor of *Alco ✦Brite* gelled ethanol products					X								X
38117 **Honeysuckle Health Foods**, 4741 Poplar Ave., **Memphis** TN					C	X	X	X	X	X	X		
38134 **Bartlett Health Food Store**, 5800 Stage Road, **Bartlett** TN ☎(901) 385-2995					C	X	X	X	X	X	X		
38464 **L & N Supply**, 106 N. Military Ave., **Lawrenceburg** TN ☎(615) 766-0486				X	X								
38483 **The Mail Order Catalog**, PO Box 180, **Summertown** TN ☎(615) 964-2241 or (800) 695-2241 ≜(615) 964-3518 ▯www.vege.com ✉catalog@usit.net – vegetarian & Vegan food products; cookbooks; alternative health; meat alternatives, soy products				X						X			
38555 **Cumberland Gen'l.Store**, #1 Hwy. 68, **Crossville** TN ☎(615) 484-8481 / (800) 334-4640 ≜(615) 456-1211 – old-time, non-electric & country-style products; send $4.00 for catalog				X	X	X				X			X	X
Texas													
75001 **Marsh Lane Health Foods**, 14344 Marsh Lane, **Addison** TX ☎(214) 243-5558					C	X	X	X	X	X	X		
75006 **Santa Cruz Natural Foods**, 2650 Midway Road #128, **Carrollton** TX ☎(214) 733-0961					C	X	X	X	X	X	X		
75007 **Real Foods**, 3044 Old Denton Rd. #117, **Carrollton** TX ☎(214) 446-1806					C	X	X	X	X	X	X		
75007 **S L.L.C.**, 3030 N. Josey Lane, **Carrollton** TX ☎(972) 625-6789 – emergency supplies; *Survival Tabs* distributor; alternative medical supplies & equipment; colloidal silver				X	X				X	X			X
75014 **SamAndy Food & Equipment Co.**, PO Box 141741, **Irving** TX ☎(800) 331-0358 ≜(214) 717-1332 – manufacturer & distributor of *SamAndy Foods*; authorized distributor of *Emergency Essentials* products; emergency supplies; first aid, water purification, survival tools, free monthly newsletter			X	X	C	X	X	X	X	X	X	X	X
75023 **Huls & Associates**; 949 W. Spring Parkway, **Plano** TX ☎(214) 634-4448 or (888) 417-5918 ≜(972) 517-6214 ▯www.rampages.onramp.net/~dcraigh/water.htm ✉dcraigh@onramp.net – *PurAqua* water treatment systems				X	X		X	X		X			X
75028 **Julia Lewis**, 2813 Oxford Lane, **Flower Mound** TX ☎(972) 355-3783 – distributor of *Magic Mill* products				X		X			X		X		
75041 **Rain Fresh Water Co.**, 3134 National Circle Dr., **Garland** TX ☎(214) 826-2899 ≜(214) 823-3813				X	X	C	X						X
75043 **Family Food Health Store #3**, 6026 Broadway, **Garland** TX ☎(214) 240-5072					C	X	X	X	X	X	X	X	
75056 **Marcus' Enterprises**, 5264 Ragan, **The Colony** TX ☎(972) 625-6789 – authorized distributor of *Survival Tabs & Storehouse Foods,* manufactured by *Food Reserves, Inc.*				X	X						X		
75060 **Herbal Alternatives**, 503 East Second Street, **Irving** TX ☎(214) 579-7042 or (800) 860-7042 – retail store; fresh dried herbs & blends in bulk; homeopathic aids, tinctures, essential oils & flower remedies; books										X			
75067 **Abundant Life Health Food**, 1128 W. Main, **Lewisville** TX ☎(214) 221-1210					C	X	X	X	X	X	X	X	
75067 **Great Health Food Store**, 2420 South Stemmons #B, **Lewisville** TX ☎(214) 315-0042					C	X	X	X	X	X	X	X	
75067 **Lewisville Health Foods**, 724 W. Main #320, **Lewisville** TX ☎(214) 221-6786					C	X	X	X	X	X	X	X	
75074 **Baker's Outpost Survival & Preparedness Center**, 1108 Summit #9, **Plano** TX ☎(972) 423-0211 ≜(972) 516-0333					C	X	X					X	X
75074 **Washitaw Natural Products**, 1000 14th Street #268, **Plano** TX ☎(972) 578-0625 – a heritage of herbs, formulas for the body's systems					X		X		X	X			X
75080 **Armed Forces Merchandise Outlet**, 111 N. Central Expressway., **Richardson** TX ☎(972) 235-9781 or (800) 282-3327				X	X		X	X		X			X
75080 **Whole Foods Market**, 60 Dal-Rich Village, **Richardson** TX ☎(972) 699-8075 ≜(972) 699-9419				X	X	X	X	X	X	X	X		
75081 **Garrett Jensen**, 1004 Mount Vernon Dr., **Richardson** TX ☎(214) 918-9094 or (800) 898-9910 – *Living Air* purification system				X									X
75081 **Jensen**, 1004 Mount Vernon Dr., **Richardson** TX ☎(214) 918-9094 or (800) 898-9910 ≜(214) 918-9694 – distributor of *AlpineAire* brand products for long-term food storage				X	X							X	X
75085 **South Summit Corporation**, PO Box 851293, **Richardson** TX ☎(972) 495-5270 ≜(972) 495-9579 ▯www.southsummit.com ✉southsummit@topher.net – outdoor gear & emergency preparedness products; complete line of dehydrated & freeze-dried foods				X	X	X	X	X	X	X	X	X	
75087 **Richard Lopez**, 519 I-H 30 #300, **Rockwall** TX ≜(972) 722-9548 – camping, personal protection devices, storage food containers, & ammo				X					X			X	X
75091 **Blue Star Environmental**, 801 Carleton Drive, **Richardson** TX ☎(972) 918-9094 or (800) 898-9910 ≜(972) 918-9694 ✉bluestarenv@earthlink.net – air, water, and nutritional products; *Survival Straw*, a complete water purification system in a straw				X	X	X			X			X	X
75093 **Whole Foods Market**, 2201 Preston Road, **Plano** TX ☎(972) 612-6729 ≜(972) 867-0414				X	X	X	X	X	X	X	X		
75115 **Health Food Center**, 719 N. Hampton Rd. #211, **Desoto** TX ☎(214) 223-6493					C	X	X	X	X	X	X	X	
75116 **Health Food Center**, 714 W. Wheatland Rd., **Duncanville** TX ☎(214) 296-4613					C	X	X	X	X	X	X	X	
75149 **Best Prices Storable Foods**, 1737 Cascade Street, **Mesquite** TX ☎(214) 742-7777 or (972) 288-0262 ▯http://web2.airmail.net/foodstr2 – *Maple Leaf* products distributor; bonded dealer of food storage items & preparedness supplies			X	C	X	X	X	X	X	X	X	X	

Product References Keyed to Chapters (Cont.)

04 water / air filtration & treatment	05 grains, seeds, mills & equip.	12 dairy / powdered milk supplies	13 honey / sweeteners
14 vitamins / minerals / herbs	15 sprouting / equip. & supplies	16 dry / dehydrated / freeze-dried	17 energy / fuels

M = Manufacturer / Processor — D = Wholesaler / Trade distributor — R = Distributor / Retailer to public	M	D	R	04	05	12	13	14	15	16	17
75149 Stun-Ning Sales, 949 West Kearney #104, **Mesquite** TX ☎(214) 329-7886 or (800) 466-7886 — *distributor of protective products: pepper sprays, stun guns, air taser, police baton, & other security devices*	X	X									
75150 Family Health Food Store #2, 1111 N. Town East Blvd., **Mesquite** TX ☎(214) 270-4505			C		X	X	X	X	X	X	X
75165 Kirkpatrick's Health Foods, 207 S. College, **Waxahachie** TX ☎(214) 937-0010			C		X	X	X	X	X	X	X
75165 T. W. Burleson & Son, Inc., **Waxahachie** TX — *honey products distributor*	X	X	X				X				
75201 Great Earth Vitamins, 1530 Main Street #101, **Dallas** TX ☎(214) 744-1017			C		X	X	X	X	X	X	X
75206 Whole Earth Provision Co., 5400 E. Mockingbird Lane, **Dallas** TX ☎(214) 824-7444 — *outfitters for travel & outdoors: camping, climbing, expedition gear, travel guides, clothing & shoes*		X	X								X
75206 Whole Foods Market, 2218 Lower Greenville Ave., **Dallas** TX ☎(214) 824-1744 📠(214) 824-2730		X	X	X	X	X	X	X	X	X	X
75207 Pendery's, 1221 Manufacturing St., **Dallas** TX ☎(214) 741-1870 or (800) 533-1870 — *poly-bagged dried & dehydrated herbs, spices, and fruits & vegetables*	X	X						X		X	
75209 Phil's Natural Grocery, 7919 Inwood, **Dallas** TX ☎(214) 357-7445			C		X	X	X	X	X	X	X
75216 Pyramid Survival, 1431 S. Marsalis Ave., **Dallas** TX ☎(214) 946-8451 📠(214) 942-2651 — *food storage & preparedness equipment dealer*		X	X	X	X	X				X	X
75218 Rainbow Harvest Health Foods, PO Box 180502, **Dallas** TX ☎(214) 327-1492			C		X	X	X	X	X	X	X
75218 White Rock Co-op, 8606 Angora, **Dallas** TX ☎(214) 327-3133			C		X	X	X	X	X	X	X
75219 Fresh Start Market & Deli, 4108 Oaklawn, **Dallas** TX ☎(214) 528-5535			C		X	X	X	X	X	X	X
75219 Perfect Setting, 4270 Oak Lawn, **Dallas** TX ☎(214) 373-6302 — *distributor of Alco ♦Brite gelled ethanol products*			X								X
75220 Essential Water & Air, 10921 Shady Trail #102, **Dallas** TX ☎(214) 350-1967 📠(214) 350-0585 — *distributor of reverse osmosis water treatment units; shower filters; counter-top matrix block water filters*	X	X	X	X							
75220 Great Earth Vitamins, 4345 West NW Highway 111, **Dallas** TX ☎(214) 352-7318			C		X	X	X	X	X	X	X
75223 Nature's Storehouse, 1104 Parkview Avenue, **Dallas** TX ☎(214) 826-5725			C		X	X	X	X	X	X	X
75224 Ann's Health Foods, 2320 S. Zang, **Dallas** TX ☎(214) 942-9483			C		X	X	X	X	X	X	X
75225 Take Charge of Your Health, 3825 Greenbrier, **Dallas** TX ☎(214) 696-4952 — *nutrition counselor offering a complete line of health & nutritional products*		X	X			X		X			
75229 Parker Power Systems, Inc., 11265 Goodnight Ln. #1021, **Dallas** TX ☎(214) 484-9044 or (800) 281-9044 📠(214) 484-4318 — *emergency portable Generac, Honda, Kawasaki, Kohler, Onan, & Winco generators, equipment, & mobile lighting*		X	X				X		X		X
75230 Seagull Book & Tape, 112 Preston Valley Center, **Dallas** TX ☎(972) 934-9988 or (800) 299-9988 — *Magic Mill products distributor*	X	X	X						X		
75231 Nature's Harvest, 6780 Abrams Rd. #109, **Dallas** TX ☎(214) 341-1517			C		X	X	X	X	X	X	X
75231 Whole Foods Market, 7205 Skillman Street, **Dallas** TX ☎(214) 341-5445 📠(214) 341-3350		X	X	X	X	X	X	X	X	X	X
75232 Scott's Delight Food Co-op, 1428 Misty Glen, **Dallas** TX ☎(214) 331-1520			C		X	X	X	X	X	X	X
75234 Real Foods, 13000 Josey Lane #110, **Farmer's Branch** TX ☎(214) 484-2206			C		X	X	X	X	X	X	X
75234 The Container Store, 2000 Valwood Parkway, **Dallas** TX ☎(800) 733-3532 📠(800) 786-5868 — *chain of retail stores; plastic & paper containers, shelving systems, kitchen organizers, supplies, & utensils; more!*			X								X
75236 Gourmet Award, Dallas TX ☎(214) 298-2957 — *Parmalat shelf-stable, whole milk dairy products distributor for SE Regional area*	X					X					
75236 Maxam Wholesale, 3920 S. Walton Walker Blvd., **Dallas** TX ☎(214) 333-2111 📠(214) 333-2137 — *discount retail & catalog order store; must be a business to order; many bargain-priced preparedness items*	X	X	X							X	X
75238 North Lake Health Food, 210 North Lake Center, **Dallas** TX ☎(214) 341-8804			C		X	X	X	X	X	X	X
75244 Hearthside Shop, 14221 Inwood, **Farmers Branch** TX — *distributor of Alco ♦Brite gelled ethanol products*			X								X
75244 Hutton Solar Power, 4112 Billy Mitchell Drive, **Dallas** TX ☎(214) 239-0580	X	X									X
75409 Reintree Farms, 11900 County Road 509, **Anna** TX ☎(214) 924-2665 — *Alpine Industries air purification systems*		X	X	X	X				X	X	
75501 Sunnyside Natural Food Market, 4030 Summerhill Square, **Texarkana** TX ☎(214) 792-4385			C		X	X	X	X	X	X	X
75551 Natural Foods, Etc., 305 E. Main St., **Atlanta** TX ☎(214) 796-2879			C		X	X	X	X	X	X	X
75601 Jack's Natural Foods #1, 1614 Judson Rd., **Longview** TX ☎(903) 753-4800			C		X	X	X	X	X	X	X
75602 Daystar Cooperative, 1822 Institute Drive, **Longview** TX ☎(903) 753-2385			C		X	X	X	X	X	X	X
75604 Jack's Natural Foods #2, 2199 Gilmer Rd., **Longview** TX ☎(214) 759-4262			C		X	X	X	X	X	X	X
75647 Granary Street Natural Foods, 621 West Upshur, **Gladewater** TX ☎(903) 759-2744			C		X	X	X	X	X	X	X
75657 Helen R. DeLong, Rt. 4, Box 572, **Jefferson** TX ☎(903) 665-2726 — *distributor of Magic Mill products*			X		X			X		X	
75662 Kilgore Health Foods, 414 E. Main, **Kilgore** TX ☎(903) 983-1521			C		X	X	X	X	X	X	X
75668 Swope Enterprises, PO Box 1290, **Lone Star** TX ☎(800) 447-9772 📠(903) 562-1609 💻www.publiconline.com/=swopeenterpris — *nutritional products, books, tapes, & videos to promote quality of life*	X	X						X			

M = Manufacturer / Processor	D = Wholesaler / Trade distributor	R = Distributor / Retailer to public	M	D	R	04	05	12	13	14	15	16	17
75703 **Karen's Health Foods**, 4507 Troup Highway, **Tyler** TX ☎(903) 581-5961					C	X	X	X	X	X	X	X	
75757 **S & A Distributors**, PO Box 788, **Bullard** TX ☎(903) 825-7471 🖷(903) 825-7471 – distributor of *AlpineAire* freeze-dried foods for long-term storage					X	X	X	X	X			X	X
75935 **Center Health Food**, 811 Nacogdoches, **Center** TX ☎(409) 598-4987					C	X	X	X	X	X	X	X	X
75961 **Morning Glory Health Foods**, 3500 North Street, **Nacogdoches** TX ☎(409) 564-0159					C	X	X	X	X	X	X	X	X
76006 **Farmer Fresh Produce & Natural Grocery**, 3018 Pitkin Dr., **Arlington** TX ☎(817) 261-1319					C	X	X	X	X	X	X	X	X
76012 **Health Cupboard**, 1730 W. Randol Mill #150, **Arlington** TX ☎(817) 460-2652					C	X	X	X	X	X	X	X	X
76015 **Good Health Place**, 820 Secretary Drive, **Arlington** TX ☎(817) 265-5261					C	X	X	X	X	X	X	X	X
76017 **Tina Toler**, 5903 Crepe Myrtle Dr., **Arlington** TX ☎(817) 478-4852 – distributor of *Magic Mill* products					X	X			X		X		
76020 **Nature's Health Store**, 103 E. Main St., **Azle** TX					C	X	X	X	X	X	X	X	X
76021 **Health Hut**, 623 Harwood Rd., **Bedford** TX ☎(817) 581-7180					C	X	X	X	X	X	X	X	X
76023 **S. D. F. Co.**, Rt. 2 Box 359, **Boyd** TX ☎(817) 433-5229 🖷(817) 433-5229 ✉*dacdon@aol.com* – *SafeTrek Foods* distributor					X	X	X	X	X	X		X	X
76031 **Lee Products**, 4308 E. Highway 67, **Cleburne** TX ☎(817) 641-9893 – distributor of *Alco♦Brite* gelled ethanol products					X	X							X
76048 **Health In Store**, 700 Highway 377 E., **Granbury** TX ☎(817) 573-4971					C	X	X	X	X	X	X	X	X
76095 **The Preparedness Store**, PO Box 211503, **Bedford** TX ☎(817) 354-8946 – home, office, & travel emergency kits & disasters supplies, food & water storage, first aid kits; books & tapes					C	X	X	X	X		X	X	X
76107 **Fireplace Accents**, 4630 Camp Bowie Blvd., **Fort Worth** TX – distributor of *Alco♦Brite* gelled ethanol products					X	X							X
76112 **Nature's Way Health Store**, 6544-A Meadowbrook Dr., **Fort Worth** TX ☎(817) 451-2653					C	X	X	X	X	X	X	X	X
76116 **Food Fresh** (Earth Friendly Goods), 3701 Stoney Creek Rd., **Ft. Worth** TX ☎(800) 257-2848 – keeps foods fresher, longer in refrigerator by absorption/desorption, depending on temperature & humidity			X	X									X
76117 **Approved First Aid, Inc.**, 2527-B & C Minnis Drive, **Fort Worth** TX ☎(817) 654-2234 or (800) 472-8419 🖷(817) 838-7914			X	C									
76117 **Hartsell Health Foods**, 2227-G Haltom Rd., **Fort Worth** TX ☎(817) 838-7505					C	X	X	X	X	X	X	X	X
76118 **ExelTech**, 2225 E. Loop 820 N., **Ft. Worth** TX ☎(800) 886-4683			X	X									X
76133 **Richardson's Health Foods**, 5051 Granbury Rd., **Fort Worth** TX ☎(817) 294-1180					C	X	X	X	X	X	X	X	X
76135 **Nature's Resources**, 6304-A Lake Worth Blvd., **Fort Worth** TX ☎(817) 238-9812					C	X	X	X	X	X	X	X	X
76180 **Nature's Ally Health Foods**, 7513 Grapevine Highway, **Fort Worth** TX ☎(817) 485-6041					C	X	X	X	X	X	X	X	X
76185 **James Samudio**, PO Box 100421, **Fort Worth** TX ☎(817) 927-5952 🖷(817) 924-1307 ✉*74632.505@compuserv.com* – *Magic Mill* products & *Pampered Chef* distributor					X	X	X	X	X	X	X	X	X
76201 **Cupboard Health Foods**, 932 University, **Denton** TX ☎(817) 387-5386					C	X	X	X	X	X	X	X	X
76230 **Healthy Foods**, 412 W. Wise, **Bowie** TX ☎(817) 872-4992					C	X	X	X	X	X	X	X	X
76262 **Abundant Life Health Foods**, 500 N. Hwy. 377, **Roanoke** TX ☎(817) 430-4624					C	X	X	X	X	X	X	X	X
76308 **Sunshine Natural Foods**, 2907 Bob, **Wichita Falls** TX ☎(817) 767-2093					C	X	X	X	X	X	X	X	X
76401 **Health Focus Foods**, 2900 W. Washington, **Stephenville** TX ☎(817) 965-7880					C	X	X	X	X	X	X	X	X
76401 **Health Food Center**, 931 W. Washington, **Stephenville** TX ☎(817) 965-5555					C	X	X	X	X	X	X	X	X
76504 **Discover Natural Foods**, 1218 South 33rd, **Temple** TX ☎(817) 773-7711					C	X	X	X	X	X	X	X	X
76541 **U. S. Cavalry**, 830 South Fort Hood St., **Killeen** TX ☎(817) 634-4765 🖷(817) 634-0850 – retailer & mail order (4,200 items); survival & outdoor clothing & equipment; preparedness products					X	X	X	X	X		X	X	X
76541 **Wildflowers Natural Food**, 4101 East Rancher 403, **Killeen** TX ☎(817) 699-9250					C	X	X	X	X	X	X	X	X
76554 **Straight Meat Co.**, 1902 N. Hwy. 95, **Little River** TX ☎(817) 982-4222 or (800) 753-4212 – farm-raised & grain-fed beef; no antibiotics, hormones or *MSG;* quick-frozen, individually packaged			X	X	X								X
76651 **Monolithic Constructors, Inc.**, One Dome Park Place, **Italy** TX ☎(214) 483-7423 🖷(214) 483-6662 🖥www.monolithicdome.com ✉*Mail@monolithicdome.com* – concrete in-ground or above-ground homes & shelters; video tape & newsletter			X	X	C								X
76705 **Solar Utility Network**, 323 S. Lacy Dr., **Waco** TX ☎(817) 799-4909 or (800) 713-4909 🖷(817) 799-4909 – solar electric/thermal systems, energy conservation products & appliances; distributors of 50 manufacturers			X	C									X
76707 **Connor Health Foods**, 2625 West Waco Dr., **Waco** TX ☎(817) 756-2201					C	X	X	X	X	X	X	X	X
76710 **AAMA**, 217 Schroeder Dr., **Waco** TX ☎(817) 859-5259 – distributor of *Alco♦Brite* gelled ethanol products					X								X
76801 **Natural Health Food Store**, 1029 Riverside Dr., **Brownwood** TX ☎(915) 643-4356					C	X	X	X	X	X	X	X	X
76901 **Tumlinson Health Foods**, 3121 K-Mart Plaza, **San Angelo** TX ☎(915) 949-4080					C	X	X	X	X	X	X	X	X
76903 **Dickson's Pure Honey**, 4331 Hatchery Rd., **San Angelo** TX ☎(915) 655-9233			X	X	X				X				
77001 **Herberia Pancho Villa**, 1910 Tidwell, **Houston** TX ☎(713) 692-4031					C	X	X	X	X	X	X	X	X
77009 **Sweet Herbs & Produce**, 2520 Airline Drive, **Houston** TX ☎(713) 868-7004					C	X	X	X	X	X	X	X	X
77024 **Gulf Pacific Rice Co., Inc.**, 950 Echo Lane #100, **Houston** TX ☎(713) 464-0606 🖷(713) 467-0325 – production, milling, &/or distribution of rice & processed rice products			X	X			X						X

Product References Keyed to Chapters (Cont.)

04 water / air filtration & treatment	05 grains, seeds, mills & equip.	12 dairy / powdered milk supplies	13 honey / sweeteners
14 vitamins / minerals / herbs	**15 sprouting / equip. & supplies**	**16 dry / dehydrated / freeze-dried**	**17 energy / fuels**

			M	D	R	04	05	12	13	14	15	16	17
M = Manufacturer / Processor		**D = Wholesaler / Trade distributor**			**R = Distributor / Retailer to public**								

Entry	M	D	R	04	05	12	13	14	15	16	17
77037 **Botanica San Miguel**, 11036 Airline, **Houston** TX ☎(713) 999-5109			C	X	X	X	X	X		X	X
77037 **LDS Bookstore**, *(attn: Ming Dingamense)*, 9311 N. Freeway #A-108, **Houston** TX ☎(713) 448-2788 – distributor of *SamAndy Foods* products			X	X	X	X	X		X	X	X
77041 **Nicky's**, 10607 Brookshire Lane, **Houston** TX ☎(713) 896-6753 🖷(713) 896-4278 – specializing in binoculars, night vision equipment, & outdoors/camping gear		X	X							X	X
77042 **El Campo Rice, Ltd.**, 11111 Wilcrest Green #400, **Houston** TX ☎(713) 784-3600 🖷(713) 784-3602 – production, milling, &/or distribution of rice & processed rice products	X	X			X					X	
77042 **Whole Foods Market**, 11145 Westheimer Road, **Houston** TX ☎713) 784-7776 🖷(713) 954-3768		X	X	X	X	X	X			X	X
77057 **Whole Foods Market**, 6401 Woodway, **Houston** TX ☎(713) 789-4477 🖷(713) 789-9419		X	X	X	X	X	X			X	X
77060 **American Rice, Inc.**, 16825 Northchase Dr. #160, **Houston** TX ☎(713) 872-7423 🖷(713) 872-2031 – production, milling, &/or distribution of rice & processed rice products	X	X			X					X	
77060 **Coastal Distributing Services**, **Houston** TX ☎(713) 999-6600		X	X			X	X		X		X
77063 **Electronic Parts Outlet**, 3753-B Fondren, **Houston** TX ☎(800) 403-3741 or (713) 784-0140 ⌨www.epo.houston.com	X										X
77069 **Betsy's Health Foods**, 5730 FM 1960 West, **Houston** TX ☎(713) 440-9081			C	X	X	X	X	X		X	X
77070 **Nature's Market**, 10924 FM 1960 West, **Houston** TX ☎(713) 469-7665			C	X	X	X	X	X		X	X
77074 **Southwest Health Food**, 8316 SW Freeway, **Houston** TX ☎(713) 981-7707			C	X	X	X	X	X		X	X
77081 **Botanica Elegua Yerberia**, 6043 Bissonett, **Houston** TX ☎(713) 660-6767			C	X	X	X	X	X		X	X
77089 **Tri Health Foods** c/o Herman Mobley, 11025 Fuqua Street, **Houston** TX ☎None – distributor of *Magic Mill* products		X			X				X	X	
77092 **C & J Ltd.**, 12121 NW Freeway #394, **Houston** TX ☎(713) 466-4476 – distributor of *SamAndy Foods* products		X	X	X	X	X			X	X	X
77098 **Whole Earth Provision Co.**, 2934 S. Shepherd, **Houston** TX ☎(713) 526-5226 – outfitters for camping, climbing, expedition gear, travel guides, clothing & shoes for the outdoorsperson		X	X	X						X	X
77098 **Whole Foods Market**, 2900 South Shepherd, **Houston** TX ☎(713) 520-1937 🖷(713) 520-0265		X	X	X	X	X	X			X	X
77219 **Common Sense Nutrition** / John Paul Williams, PO Box 130331, **Houston** TX ☎(713) 692-0055 – *Certified Nutritionist & Registered Massage Therapist*; wholesale distributor of organic green drinks		X	X					X			
77251 **Uncle Ben's, Inc.**, PO Box 1752, **Houston** TX ☎(713) 670-2106 🖷(713) 670-2111 – production, milling, &/or distribution of rice & processed rice products	X	X			X					X	
77252 **Riviana Foods Inc.**, P0 Box 2636, **Houston** TX ☎(713) 525-9599 🖷(713) 529-1661 – production, milling, &/or distribution of rice & processed rice products	X	X			X					X	
77252 **Rivland**, PO Box 2636, **Houston** TX ☎(713) 529-3251 🖷(713) 529-1661 – production, milling, &/or distribution of rice & processed rice products	X	X			X					X	
77254 **Evert-Fresh Corp.**, PO Box 590974, **Houston** TX ☎(713) 529-4593 🖷(713) 529-4594 – patented re-useable, "anti-fogging" & "breathing" plastic fridge storage bag prolongs life of fruits & vegetables	X										X
77255 **Dixie USA, Inc.**, PO Box 55549, **Houston** TX ☎(713) 688-4993 for information or (800) 347-3494 *order hotline* 🖷(713) 688-4881 or(800) 688-2507 ⌨www.dixieusa.com ✉*info@dixieusa.com* – quality Emergency Medical Service products for ambulance, industry, facility, & individual care		X	X								
77301 **Conroe Health Food**, 919 W. Lewis, **Conroe** TX ☎(409) 756-1052			C	X	X	X	X	X		X	X
77301 **Healthy Choices**, 1712 North Frazier, **Conroe** TX ☎(409) 441-0141			C	X	X	X	X	X		X	X
77305 **WBL**, PO Box 3334, **Conroe** TX ☎(409) 539-5624 or (800) 243-0676 🖷(409) 539-5624 – *Trail Pack Meals* for emergency industry; typical grocery store foods w/pull-tabs; for emergencies & disasters	X	X	X							X	
77322 **Mickie Roland**, 13614 Old Texaco Road, **Conroe** TX ☎(409) 231-2729 – distributor of *Magic Mill* products		X			X				X	X	
77351 **Life Forces Resource Center**, 101 Rainbow Dr. #6789, **Livingston** TX ☎(719) 783-9539		X						X			
77388 **Heavenly Health Foods**, 1811 Spring Cypress, **Spring** TX ☎(713) 355-6110			C	X	X	X	X	X		X	X
77414 **Health Food Cottage**, 2211 Ave. G, **Bay City** TX ☎(409) 245-3833			C	X	X	X	X	X		X	X
77429 **DayStarter Southeast / Jordan**, 20818 Hempstead, **Cypress** TX ☎(713) 469-3294		X			X						
77479 **Wilderness Furnishings**, 5420 Manor Drive, **Sugar Land** TX ☎(713) 980-1777 or (800) 343-3545 🖷(281) 261-9184 ⌨www.wildfur.com – catalog mail-order for outdoor & camping gear; expedition, camping, backpacking, & emergency products		X									
77506 **Chadd Medical Supplies**, 1245 Carroll, **Pasadena** TX ☎(713) 920-2845 🖷(713) 920-1917 ⌨www.berks.com/chadd/survival.htm ✉*Jack71@juno.com*		X									
77506 **Nutrition Kneads** c/o Kay Gailbraith, 1001 Randall, **Pasadena** TX ☎(800) 569-2708 ☎/🖷(713) 473-4835 ✉*brlygreen@aol.com* or *barleygreen@msn.com* – distributor of *Bosch & Kitchen Specialties* products; *Magic Mill* products distributor		X	X	X	X			X		X	
77511 **Affiliated Rice Milling, Inc.**, 715 N. Second Street, **Alvin** TX ☎(713) 331-6176 🖷(713) 585-0336 – production, milling, &/or distribution of rice & processed rice products	X	X			X					X	
77575 **Carol Bond Health Foods**, 904 N. Main, **Liberty** TX ☎(409) 336-9001			C	X	X	X	X	X		X	X

M = Manufacturer / Processor	D = Wholesaler / Trade distributor	R = Distributor / Retailer to public	M	D	R	04	05	12	13	14	15	16	17
77578 **Kimberly A. Horvath**, 9718 King Circle North, **Manvel** TX ☎(713) 388-2476 – distributor of *Magic Mill* products					X	X				X		X	
77642 **Mr. T's Health Food Store**, 3339 Gulfway Drive, **Port Arthur** TX ☎(409) 982-3933					C	X	X	X	X	X	X	X	X
77642 **Kitchen Center** / Shirley Wiggins, 4137 Stoney Brook Lane, **Port Arthur** TX ☎(409) 722-2167 – distributor of *Bosch & Kitchen Specialties* & *Magic Mill* products					X	X				X		X	
77701 **American Health Foods**, 3847 Stagg Drive, **Beaumont** TX ☎(409) 833-7488					C	X	X	X	X	X	X	X	X
77701 **Beaumont Rice Mills, Inc.**, 1800 Pecos Street, **Beaumont** TX ☎(409) 832-2521 📠(409) 832-6927 – production, milling, &/or distribution of rice & processed rice products		X	X				X				X		
77707 **Doguet's Rice Milling**, 795 South Major Drive, **Beaumont** TX ☎(409) 866-2297 📠(409) 866-1646 – production, milling, &/or distribution of rice & processed rice products		X	X				X				X		
77802 **Brazos Natural Foods**, 4303 South Texas Avenue, **Bryan** TX ☎(409) 846-4459					C	X	X	X	X	X	X	X	X
77802 **Southern Ladies' Co-op**, 4301 Carter Creek Pkwy, **Bryan** TX					C	X	X	X	X	X	X	X	X
78003 **Alamo Area GMX**, PO Box 1295, **Bandera** TX ☎(888) 460-8306 or (830) 8306 📠(830) 460-7983 – *GMX* magnetic water treatment systems; magnetic systems for all fluids flow; "green" energy-saving products		X	X	X									X
77824 **Madisonville Health Foods**, 300-B East Main, **Madisonville** TX ☎(409) 348-9196					C	X	X	X	X	X	X	X	X
77840 **Linders' Health Foods**, 1405-B Harvey, **College Station** TX ☎(409) 693-1990					C	X	X	X	X	X	X	X	X
77903 **Health Food House**, 4206 N. Ben Jordan, **Victoria** TX ☎(512) 573-4711					C	X	X	X	X	X	X	X	X
77908 **Buffalo Hardware Co., Inc.**, 2614 Westheimer, **Houston** TX ☎(713) 524-1011 📠(713) 524-8758		X	X										X
77964 **Blais Health Food**, Route 4, Box 197-B, **Helletsville** TX ☎(512) 798-5498					C	X	X	X	X	X	X	X	X
77979 **Port Health Foods**, 132 Commerce Street, **Port Lavaca** TX ☎(512) 552-3811					C	X	X	X	X	X	X	X	X
78001 **Nueces Natural Foods**, 111 W. Nopal, **Uvalde** TX ☎(512) 278-6701					C	X	X	X	X	X	X	X	X
78006 **The Homeschool Exchange**, PO Box 1378, **Boerne** TX ☎(210) 336-2021 📠(210) 336-3105 ✉*HSXCHANGE@AOL.COM* – buy/sell *monthly newspaper* for homeschooling families				X									
78006 **Watkins Products Distributor** (attn: *John & Peggy Taylor*), 8824 Fox Briar Ln., **Boerne** TX ☎(210) 698-1016 or (800) 484-9019 pin *1139*		X	X						X		X		
78028 **Champion Fishing Co., Ltd.**, 624 Clay Street, **Kerrville** TX ☎(210) 896-3474 📠(210) 896-7193 – national distributor; network marketing sales & distribution; fishing/outdoors gear, equipment, & supplies		X	X	X	X							X	X
78028 **River Valley Health Foods**, 130-B West Main, **Kerrville** TX ☎(210) 896-7383					C	X	X	X	X	X	X	X	X
78029 **Sprout Ease Co.**, Box 1876, **Kerrville** TX ☎(210) 896-0117 📠(210) 792-3267 – sprouting equipment & supplies; untreated & organic		X	X				X			X			
78040 **Laredo Health Foods**, 1218 Hidalgo, **Laredo** TX ☎(210) 723-1971					C	X	X	X	X	X	X	X	X
78102 **Old Home Health Foods**, 401 N. Adam, **Beeville** TX ☎(210) 358-4291					C	X	X	X	X	X	X	X	X
78130 **Julie Salsman**, 1183 Fox Run Circle, **New Braunfels** TX ☎(210) 620-1936 – distributor of *Magic Mill* products				X			X			X		X	
78151 **Busy Bee Apiaries & Shoppe**, Box 247, **Runge** TX		X	X	X				X					
78155 **Brenner's Health Foods**, 550 Hwy. 123 Bypass #154, **Seguin** TX ☎(512) 372-2011					C	X	X	X	X	X	X	X	X
78209 **Whole Foods Market**, 255 E. Basse, **San Antonio** TX ☎(210) 696-6331 📠(210) 641-6713			X	X	X	X	X	X	X	X	X	X	
78212 **F.E.A.S.T.**, 4719 Blanco Rd., **San Antonio** TX ☎(210) 342-4674 – home-schooling center for South Texas homeschoolers				X									
78216 **Enzyme Resource Gp.**, 9311 San Pedro #700, **San Antonio** TX ☎(210) 525-7905 📠(210) 525-7906 – enzymes for man & beast; improves digestion and assimilation		X	X						X				
78216 **National Outdoors, Inc.** (prev. *Nat'l. Army Surplus*), 7134 San Pedro, **San Antonio** TX ☎(210) 680-3322			X	X								X	X
78217 **Forever Living Prod.**, 10203 Kotzebue #103, **San Antonio** TX ☎(210) 820-3103 📠(210) 820-3183										X			
78217 **Genesis Marketing**, 2420 Freedom Drive, **San Antonio** TX ☎(210) 804-1400 📠(201) 804-1503		X	X							X			X
78217 **Maxam Wholesale**, 10001 Broadway #2, **San Antonio** TX ☎(210) 824-4444 📠(210) 824-4451 – discount retail & catalog order store; bargain-priced preparedness items		X	X	X								X	X
78218 **Garden–Ville Fertilizer Co., Inc.**, 7561 E. Evans Rd., **San Antonio** TX ☎(210) 688-9435 or (800) 788-8256 – food-grade diatomaceous earth; gardening tools, supplies, & equipment; organic pest control	X	X	X										X
78218 **Mountain Man Nut & Fruit Co.**, 5627 Brandemere Dr., **San Antonio** TX ☎(210) 637-5318 – purveyor of quality nuts, dried fruits & candies		X	X									X	
78218 **National Outdoors, Inc.**, 5470 Walzem, **San Antonio** TX ☎(210) 680-3322 – camping gear; military surplus clothing; hiking & outdoor shoes; camp foods & cooking equiment		X	X									X	X
78220 **Star Food Processing**, 3444 E. Commerce, **San Antonio** TX ☎(210) 223-4553 or (800) 882-6325 📠(210) 271-9276 – processor of shelf-stable entrees that are not only ready to eat, but are great-tasting; not ordinary MREs	X	X	X									X	X
78221 **National Outdoors, Inc.**, 616 SW Military Drive, **San Antonio** TX ☎(210) 680-3322 – camping gear; military surplus clothing; hiking & outdoor shoes; camp foods & cooking equiment		X	X									X	X
78223 **AGGrand** / M. Klann, PO Box 23090, **San Antonio** TX ☎(210) 333-5739 or (888) 333-4927 – liquid natural organic fertilizer sales			X										X
78229 **Pain & Stress Therapy Center**, 5282 Medical Dr. #160, **San Antonio** TX ☎(800) 669-CALM			X						X				
78230 **Nature's Way Health Foods**, 8059 Callaghan Rd., **San Antonio** TX ☎(210) 344-1482					C	X	X	X	X	X	X	X	X

Product References Keyed to Chapters (Cont.)

04 water / air filtration & treatment	05 grains, seeds, mills & equip.	12 dairy / powdered milk supplies	13 honey / sweeteners
14 vitamins / minerals / herbs	15 sprouting / equip. & supplies	16 dry / dehydrated / freeze-dried	17 energy / fuels

M = Manufacturer / Processor **D = Wholesaler / Trade distributor** **R = Distributor / Retailer to public**

Listing	M	D	R	04	05	12	13	14	15	16	17
78238 National Outdoors, Inc., 5600 Bandera Road, **San Antonio** TX ☎(210) 680-3322 — camping gear; military surplus clothing; hiking & outdoor shoes; camp foods & cooking equiment		X	X							X	X
78240 Cynthia K. Wilder, 7002 Forest Crest North, **San Antonio** TX ☎(210) 680-5388 — distributor of *Magic Mill* products			X		X			X		X	
78240 Drills, Skills, & More, 7002 Forest Crest N., **San Antonio** TX ☎(210) 680-5388 or (800) 352-2347			C	X	X	X	X	X	X	X	
78246 Promised Land Natural Foods, 1004 Central Parkway S., **San Antonio** TX ☎(210) 494-1458			C	X	X	X	X	X	X	X	
78247 Health Kitchen c/o Sandra Hicks, **San Antonio** TX ☎(210) 829-4884			X		X				X		
78247 Heat-It Manufacturing Co., Inc., 11811 Starcrest, **San Antonio** TX ☎(210) 494-5254 or (800) 323-9336 🖷(210) 490-3810 — manufacturer of canned fuel for heating & keeping foods warm; non-spilling, easy re-lights, no evaporation; long-burning at constant temperature, clean & odorless, ignite easily with proper handling, & does not flash	X	X	X								X
78257 Frances Brown, 25315 Fahrenthold, **San Antonio** TX ☎(210) 698-2698 🖷(210) 698-2698 — preparedness consultant; in-home storage specialist			C		X		X		X	X	
78257 Sandra Hicks, 25315 Fahrenthold, **San Antonio** TX ☎(210) 698-2698 🖷(210) 698-2698 — distributor of *Bosch & Kitchen Specialties* products			C	X	X			X		X	
78264 Pro Systems / Colloidal Silver Testing Services, Rt. 7 Box 510, **San Antonio** TX ☎(210) 626-2546 🖷(210) 626-2406 ⌨www.csprosystems.com	X	X	C					X			
78269 Storehouse Products, PO Box 690021, **San Antonio** TX ☎(210) 690-7632 ⌨www.dcci.com/DCCI/storehouse ✉deyer@dcci.com			X	X	X	X		X		X	
78501 Major Health Foods, 1001 S. 10ᵗʰ, **McAllen** TX ☎(210) 687-7759			C	X	X	X	X	X	X	X	
78501 Sunland Health Foods #1, 1111 S. 10ᵗʰ, **McAllen** TX ☎(210) 682-2661			C	X	X	X	X	X	X	X	
78504 Hector's Health Foods & Co., 4317 N. 10ᵗʰ St., **McAllen** TX ☎(210) 687-5920			C	X	X	X	X	X	X	X	
78539 Texas Plant & Soil Lab, Inc., RR 7 Box 213, **Edinburg** TX ☎(210) 383-0739 🖷(210) 383-0730 — soil, plant, & water testing & analysis by specialists in soil, fertility, plant nutrition, & crop products											
78550 Health Garden, 712 North 77 Sunshine Strip, **Harlingen** TX ☎(210) 428-2206			C	X	X	X	X	X	X	X	
78552 Genuine Natural Foods, Route 3, Box 218, **Harlingen** TX ☎(512) 428-8604			C	X	X	X	X	X	X	X	
78572 South Tex Organics, 6 Betty Drive, **Mission** TX ☎(210) 585-1040 🖷(210) 581-1040 — organically grown citrus fruits & vegetables shipped anywhere	X	X	X								
78617 Karen Haynes, 8609 Elroy Road, **Del Valle** TX ☎(512) 247-2124 — distributor of *Magic Mill* products			X		X			X		X	
78627 Ryan Health Foods, Box 859, **Georgetown** TX			C	X	X	X	X	X	X	X	
78641 Lone Star Honey, 106 Willis Street, **Leander** TX ☎(512) 259-0524	X	X	X				X				
78652 Benford, PO Box 643, **Manchaca** TX ☎(512) 280-9119 — distributor of *Aqua-Vista* water systems	X	X	X								
78666 Rainwater Collection Over Texas, 201 Thurman Rd., **San Marcos** TX ☎(512) 353-4949 or (800) 222-3614 🖷(512) 353-5855 — water independence by harvesting rainfall; systems & supplies; consultation & design; water conservation products	X	X	X	X							X
78666 The Cornucopia, 1104 Thorpe Lane #J, **San Marcos** TX ☎(512) 353-5044 or (888) 353-5044 🖷(512) 353-5045 ⌨www.axiom.net/cornucopia ✉sargent@axion.net		X	X					X			
78676 Hill Country Natural Foods, RR 2325, PO Box 1523, **Wimberley** TX ☎(512) 856-3291			C	X	X	X	X	X	X	X	
78703 Whole Foods Market, 601 North Lamar, **Austin** TX ☎(512) 476-1206		X	X	X	X	X		X	X	X	
78704 Mother Nature's Health Store, 121 W. Oltorf, **Austin** TX ☎(512) 442-6826			C	X	X	X	X	X	X	X	
78704 Sun Harvest Market #15, 4006 South Lamar, **Austin** TX ☎(512) 444-3079			C	X	X	X	X	X	X	X	
78704 Water Works, 2206 Matterhorn Lane, **Austin** TX ☎(512) 326-4636 🖷(512) 326-9934 — rainwater catchment systems; water purification systems; *PurTest* water testing system	X	X	X	X							X
78705 Whole Earth Provision Co., 2410 San Antonio St., **Austin** TX ☎(512) 478-1577 — outfitters for travel & outdoors: camping, climbing, expedition gear, travel guides, clothing & shoes		X	X		X			X			X
78714 Desert Blend Beef Jerky, PO Box 142103, **Austin** TX ☎(512) 990-7000 or (800) 975-3759 http://members.aol.com/desertblnd/index.html ✉desertblnd@aol.com — blended beef jerky; excellent for short-term storage	X	X	X							X	
78724 White Egret Farm, 15704 FM 969, **Austin** TX ☎(512) 276-7408 — natural, unprocessed goat milk, goat cheeses, & natural meats	X	X	X			X				X	
78735 Hill Country Herbs & General Store, 6300-A Highway 290 West, **Oak Hill** TX ☎(512) 892-5221			C	X	X	X	X	X	X	X	
78737 Judy's Country Store, 108 Royal Way #1001, **Austin** TX			C	X	X	X	X	X	X	X	
78745 Harry Hodson, 507 Gate Tree Lane, **Austin** TX ☎(512) 444-5461 — distributor of *Magic Mill* products			X		X			X		X	
78746 Bon Fresh Food Market, 3801 Bee Caves Rd., **West Lake Hills** TX ☎(512) 327-3801			C	X	X	X	X	X	X	X	
78746 Whole Foods Market Corp. Ofc., 601 N. Lamar St. #300, **Austin** TX ⌨www.wholefoods.com — corporate offices for the only national whole & natural foods retail chain	X	X	X	X	X	X	X	X	X	X	X

M = Manufacturer / Processor — D = Wholesaler / Trade distributor — R = Distributor / Retailer to public	M	D	R	04	05	12	13	14	15	16	17
78748 ChemSOLVE, 11629 Manchaca Road, **Austin** TX ☎(512) 280-7680 🖷(512) 280-7651 ✉Chemsolve@aol.com — manufacturer of "*Aguadulce*" water-testing packages; tests water quality, solvents, & complete analysis	X	X	X	X							
78753 Break N' Bread / Ricki King, 12005 Presa, **Austin** TX ☎(512) 835-6096 🖷(512) 835-4528 ✉*ricki@io.com* — distributor of *Magic Mill* products		X		X				X		X	
78757 Sun Harvest Market #4, 2917 W. Anderson Lane, **Austin** TX ☎(512) 451-0669			C	X	X	X	X	X	X	X	
78758 Austin Innovations, 2222 W. Rundberg #400, **Austin** TX ☎(512) 339-6765 🖷(512) 837-0337 — *AgriSpo*n facilitator for fertilizer; increases microorganism activity & growth; natural & safe product	X	X									
78759 Whole Foods Market, 9607 Research Boulevard, **Austin** TX ☎(512) 345-5003 🖷(512) 345-5331		X	X	X	X	X	X	X	X	X	
78763 Amazing Reprints, Box 5931, **Austin** TX — homesteading/survival pamphlets & products; mail-order supplier			X								
78801 B & B Health Food, 301 E. Main St., **Uvalde** TX ☎(512) 278-2081			C	X	X	X	X	X	X	X	
78801 B & B Health Food, 707 Barton St., **Uvalde** TX ☎(512) 278-2081			C	X	X	X	X	X	X	X	
78861 Medina Agriculture Products Co., Inc., PO Box 309, Highway 90 West, **Hondo** TX ☎(210) 426-3011 🖷(210) 426-2288 🖳www.eden.com/~medina *medina@eden.com* — biological products for building productivity of the soil in gardens, farms; increases soil microorganisms levels	X	X	X								
78950 Heinsohn's, Rt. 2 Box 21, **New Ulm** TX ☎(409) 732-5081 or (800) 300-5081 🖷(409) 732-9666 ✉*Heinsohn@intertex.net*			C	X							
79007 Sara's Health Foods, 527 N. Main, **Borger** TX ☎(806) 273-5191			C	X	X	X	X	X	X	X	
79015 Ronald J. Kershen, 200 Mohawk Trail, **Canyon** TX ☎(806) 655-9520 — industry consultant on *Triticale*, the wheat-rye genetic mix grain; expert grower & grain dealer			C	X							
79036 Bennet Flooring, 408 West Broadway, **Fritch** TX — distributor of *Alco ♦Brite* gelled ethanol products		X									X
79045 Arrowhead Mills, Inc., 110 S. Lawton, **Hereford** TX ☎(806) 364-0730 🖷(806) 364-8242 — traditional & organic grains, legumes, seeds, & processed derivatives; mixes; *bulk & wholesale only*	X	D	R	X				X			
79109 Eat Right Health Foods, 2425 I 40 West, **Amarillo** TX ☎(806) 353-7476			C	X	X	X	X	X	X	X	
79410 Alternative Food Company, 2611 Boston, **Lubbock** TX ☎(806) 747-8740			C	X	X	X	X	X	X	X	
79415 The Fireplace Place, 2316 Clovis Rd., **Lubbock** TX — distributor of *Alco ♦Brite* gelled ethanol products		X									X
79549 Health Food Center, 1910 37th St., **Snyder** TX ☎(915) 573-0251			C	X	X	X	X	X	X	X	
79603 Olympic Natural Foods, 3124 N. 1st, **Abilene** TX ☎(915) 677-9581			C	X	X	X	X	X	X	X	
79605 Louise W. Wayte, 410 S. LaSalle, **Abilene** TX ☎(915) 692-3424 — distributor of *Magic Mill* products		X		X				X		X	
79605 Natural Food Center, 2534 S. 7th, **Abilene** TX ☎(915) 673-2726			C	X	X	X	X	X	X	X	
79701 American Wellness Assoc., 312 E. Illinois Ave., **Midland** TX ☎(915) 570-8644 🖷(915) 682-3415 — grain grinders & mills; juicers; equipment for health maintenance			C	X				X			
79701 Water Power Machinery Company, Box 9723, **Midland** TX ☎(915) 697-6955 — hydroelectric systems; AC/DC components, 200W to 5 MW		X	X								X
79732 Wanda's Health Foods, 4555 E. University A-4, **Odessa** TX ☎(915) 366-1800			C	X	X	X	X	X	X	X	
79762 Wilderness Cabin, 3309 Sherbrook, **Odessa** TX ☎(888) 238-3263 *PIN 9724* — homemade soups, dips, & breads	X	X	C							X	
79902 El Paso Health Food Center, 2700 Montana, **El Paso** TX ☎(915) 565-4667			C	X	X	X	X	X	X	X	
Utah											
84003 Security Food & Supply, 1060 S.500 E., **American Fork** UT ☎(801) 756-1199 or (800) 755-1199			X			X	X	X		X	X
84004 Inner Light International, 134 E.200 N., **Alpine** UT ☎(801) 222-0990 or (800) 876-5403 🖷(801) 783-8647 — manufacturer & distributor of 45+ problem-specific holistic nutritional formulas; in use by 4,000+ doctors	X	X	X					X			
84010 All Design, 621 W. 800 S., **Bountiful** UT ☎(801) 292-0413 — distributor of *Alco ♦Brite* gelled ethanol products			X								X
84010 Gregory's Clinton Wheat Shop, 930 South 500 West, **Bountiful** UT ☎(801) 295-3405 — distributor of *Bosch* kitchen equipment: grain grinders, juicers, & health appliances; custom-ground flours			X	X	X	X	X			X	X
84010 Resourceful Foods (formerly **Safeguard Foods**), 40 W. 500 S., **Bountiful** UT ☎(801) 292-1772			X	X	X	X	X			X	X
84014 Della Mae Kiel, 483 E. 400 N., **Centerville** UT ☎(801) 298-9459 — distributor of *Magic Mill* products			X		X			X		X	
84014 Farr West Business Consulting Co. Trust, 144 West Parrish Lane #124, **Centerville** UT ☎(801) 299-9390 🖷(801) 299-9362 — specialists in federal income, estate trust, & gift taxes; asset protection; tax & estate planning/business strategies			C								
84014 Kitchen Science, Inc., 426 S. 300 E., **Centerville** UT ☎(801) 298-1385 or (888) 298-1385 🖷(801) 299-9166 🖳www.bizcom.com/kitchenscience ✉*kitchesc.ix.net.com* — *K-TEC* kitchen machines distributor specializing in breadmaking skills, products & equipment	X	X		X							

Product References Keyed to Chapters (Cont.)

04 water / air filtration & treatment	05 grains, seeds, mills & equip.	12 dairy / powdered milk supplies	13 honey / sweeteners
14 vitamins / minerals / herbs	15 sprouting / equip. & supplies	16 dry / dehydrated / freeze-dried	17 energy / fuels

M = Manufacturer / Processor — **D = Wholesaler / Trade distributor** — **R = Distributor / Retailer to public**

Chapter columns: 04 · 05 · 12 · 13 · 14 · 15 · 16 · 17

Listing	M	D	R	04	05	12	13	14	15	16	17
84020 Back to Basics Products, Inc., 11660 S. State Street, **Draper** UT ☎(801) 571-7349 🖷(571) 6061 — manufacturer of kitchen tools, sprouting equipment, high- & low-pressure canning products, hand-operated food processing tools; distributor of juicers, bread auto-baking equip., dehydrators, yogurt-makers, & electric grain mills	X	X	X	X					X	X	X
84020 The Long Rifle Trading Co., PO Box 898, **Draper** UT ☎(801) 528-8859 — knives & accessories for preparedness		X						X			
84032 Bear Creek Country Kitchens, 325 W. 600 S., **Heber City** UT ☎(801) 654-5449 or (800) 516-7286 🖷(801) 654-2660 — manufacturer of dehydrated soups and vegetable dips	X	X	X							X	
84032 Bestpak, LLC, 855 South 600 West, **Heber City** UT ☎(801) 654-1441 — wholesale only; packing house and custom-labeling dehydrated foods	X	X								X	
84032 Mama La Guardia Foods, PO Box 466, **Heber City** UT ☎(801) 654-6404 — producer of dehydrated soup mixes	X	X	X							X	
84032 Nitro-Pak Preparedness Center, 151 No. Main St., **Heber City** UT ☎(800) 866-4876 or (801) 654-0099 🖷(801) 654-3860 💻www.nitro-pak.com ✉npprepare@aol.com — distributor of *Survival Tabs, Perma Pak* dehydrated foods, *Mountain House* freeze-dried products in #10 cans, *AlpineAire Foods* freeze-dried foods, *K-Tec* products, *Emergency Essentials* products; *Alco ♦Brite* gelled ethanol	X	C	X		X	X	X	X	X	X	X
84032 Preparedness Products, 325 W. 600 S., **Heber City** UT ☎(801) 654-5400				X	X	X	X	X		X	X
84037 Bosch Kitchen Center, 1120 Raymond Road, **Kaysville** UT ☎(801) 544-0404 — *Bosch & Kitchen Specialties* products; authorized distributor of *Emergency Essentials* products				X	X	X	X	X	X	X	X
84041 TRAX, 2470 North Fairfield Road, **Layton** UT ☎(801) 771-1820 🖷(801) 771-4271 — books & tapes on politics, socio-economics, health & alternative medical subjects								X			
84042 Exodus Provisions, 875 East 65 South, **Lindon** UT ☎(801) 859-7026 or (800) 795-2274 🖷(801) 859-7036 ✉mhelmant@hotmail.ldm — pedal-powered survival vehicle for transporting entire family's survival & preparedness provisions	X	X			X		X		X		X
84042 K-TEC (Corporate Office), 420 N. Geneva Road, **Lindon** UT ☎(801) 785-3600 — manufacturer of mills, breadmakers, kitchen machines & a complete line of accessories; dehydrators; kitchen equipment: juicers & cookers; grains, beans & legumes; products for in-home chefs & bakers	X	X			X	X			X		
84042 K-Tec Factory Store, 420 N. Geneva Road, **Lindon** UT ☎(801) 222-0888 ☎(801) 785-7100					X		X				X
84043 Lehi Roller Mills Co., Inc., 833 E. Main, **Lehi** UT ☎(801) 768-4401 🖷(801) 768-4557					X	X	X				
84047 Survival Outdoor Surplus, 30 Ivory Dr., **Midvale** UT ☎(801) 565-1445 — distributor of *Alco ♦Brite* gelled ethanol products					X						X
84049 Family Supply, PO Box 1210, **Midway** UT ☎(801) 654-3314 🖷(801) 654-7497				X	X		X	X	X		X
84049 Mountain Merchants, PO Box 1327, **Midway** UT ☎(800) 868-9795 🖷(801) 868-0524 — brand-name producer of powdered milk & 8 soups	X	X	X		X						X
84501 Global Environmental Energy Technologies (GEET), PO Box 439, **Price** UT ☎(801) 281-4577 — fuel processor system transmutes low-quality liquids into non-polluting, more efficient fuel for internal combustion engines; patented combination of basic scientific principles & consistent with laws of thermodynamics	X	X (C)	X								X
84054 Preparedness Products, 130 South Redwood Road #F, **North Salt Lake City** UT ☎(801) 292-3481 — video *"Practical Preparedness"*; how to survive disasters illustrated with typical problems & how to solve them; practical helps in every aspect of long- or short-term preparation; meeting the challenges of disasters	X	X	X								
84057 H₂Ovations, 935 N. Industrial Park Dr., **Orem** UT ☎(801) 225-6010 🖷(801) 225-2677		X	X	X			X	X	X		X
84057 Water Bionomics Ind., 935 N. Industrial Park Drive, **Orem** UT ☎(801) 229-1209 🖷(801) 229-2768 — water treatment & purification systems for home or business		X	X	X							X
84058 Bosch Kitchen Center / Alma Hair, 1133 S. State, **Orem** UT ☎/🖷(801) 224-1616 or (800) 584-9943			X		X				X		
84058 Emergency Essentials Store, 352 N. State, **Orem** UT ☎(801) 222-9667			X	X	X	X	X	X	X	X	X
84058 Emergency Essentials (Corp. Ofc. & warehouse, 165 S. Mountain Way Drive, **Orem** UT ☎(801) 222-9596 or (800) 999-1863 🖷(801) 222-9598 💻www.beprepared.com ✉corporatesales@beprepared.com — wholesale distributor of emergency & preparedness products; MREs; food storage & specialty products; 72-hr. kits; electronics; food storage containers; distributor of *Alco ♦Brite* gelled ethanol products	X	X	X	X	X	X	X	X	X	X	X
84058 High Country Gourmet Ent., 225 S. Mountain Way Dr., **Orem** UT ☎(801) 426-4383 🖷(801) 426-4385 — *Old World Cuisine,* the ultimate food storage programs; vegetarian low-sodium dehydrated soups	X	X	X	X			X			X	
84058 Holistic Health Horizons, 1449 South 800 East, **Orem** UT ☎(801) 224-8358 — name brand vitamins, supplements, herbs, bulk herbs, capsule blanks, capsule fillers, nutritional health informaiton			X					X			
84058 Jeannie Sorensen, 1538 W. 860 S., **Orem** UT ☎(801) 266-0227 — distributor of *Magic Mill* products			X								
84058 Marshall Distributing. c/o Len Marshall, 2625 W. Directors Row, **Salt Lake City** UT ☎(801) 973-8855 — distributor of *Magic Mill* products			X		X			X		X	
84058 Neighborhood Necessities, 920 E. 1400 S., **Orem** UT ☎(801) 226-3486 — food-buying club; membership information & participation			X	X	X	X	X			X	X
84058 Out-N-Back, 1797 South State Street, **Orem** UT ☎(801)224-0454 — authorized distributor of *Emergency Essentials* products & *Alco ♦Brite* gelled ethanol products			X	X	X	X	X	X	X	X	X

M = Manufacturer / Processor D = Wholesaler / Trade distributor R = Distributor / Retailer to public	M	D	R	04	05	12	13	14	15	16	17
84058 Pearson Emergency, Inc. Escape Pods, 654 North 550 East, **Orem** UT ☎(801) 225-4235 – manufacturer of emergency escape pod, specially-designed trailer (transportable pod) for safety & security	X	X	X								X
84058 The Preparedness Source, 1448 W. Business Park Drive, **Orem** UT ☎(800) 949-3663 or (801) 224-3663 🖷(801) 221-0336 – everything for those wanting to be prepared, whether for outdoors, survival, or preparedness	X	X	X	X	X	X	X	X	X	X	X
84059 J & D Distributing, PO Box 1375, **Orem** UT ☎(801) 224-0713 or (800) 847-2890 – CD-ROM software; 1,090,000 recipes from 4700 cookbooks & 200,000 cooks; organized into 52 categories	X	X	X								
84059 Preparedness Plus, PO Box 1985, **Orem** UT ☎(801) 226-4188 or (888) 839-0334 🖷(801) 225-6219 ✉*preplus@enol.com* – *Maple Leaf* foods distributor; specializing in organic products for food storage; distributorships available	X	C	X	X	X	X	X	X	X	X	X
84062 Wholesale Foods, 580 W. State Street, **Pleasant Grove** UT ☎(801) 785-3400 – authorized distributor of *Emergency Essentials* products			X	X	X	X	X	X	X	X	X
84062 Wholesale Foods, 580 W. State Street, **Pleasant Grove** UT ☎(801) 785-3400			X	X	X	X	X		X	X	X
84065 Christensen's Arizona Nutritionals, 1962 W. 13400 S., **Riverton** UT ☎(801) 254-3032 or (800) 556-7515		X	X			X	X	X	X		
84070 All Grain Mills, 10498 S. Weeping Willow, **Sandy** UT ☎(801) 566-4990 – manufacturer of electric powered; stone grinding surface, kitchen flour mill	X		X	X							
84070 Bosch Kitchen Center, Brian Hansen, 8926 S. 700 E., **Sandy** UT ☎(801) 562-3333		X	X	X							
84070 Kitchen Center / Brian Hansen, 8926 S 700 E, **Sandy** UT ☎(801) 562-1212 – distributor of *Bosch & Kitchen Specialties* products		X		X							
84070 Preparedness Systems Inc., 9382 S 679 W, **Sandy** UT ☎(801) 562-2338		X				X					X
84070 The Drying Pantry, 9756 Kristin Drive, **Sandy** UT ☎(801) 571-9115 – manufacturer & distributor of the non-electric dryer & sprouting system	X	X	X						X	X	
84078 Diamond Mountain Distributing, PO Box 642, **Vernal** UT ☎(801) 789-2304 – distributor of *Bosch & Kitchen Specialties* products; preparedness consultant; in-home storage specialist		C	X	X	X		X		X		
84078 The Stove Shoppe, 560 N. Vernal Ave., **Vernal** UT ☎(801) 789-6600 – distributor of *Alco ♦Brite* gelled ethanol products		X									X
84088 A-Associates Solar, 1393 West 9000 South, **West Jordan** UT ☎(801) 569-0779	X	X									X
84088 Volcano Corporation, 3450 W. 8550 S., **West Jordan** UT ☎(801) 566-5496 🖳(801) 566-1993 – manufacturer of outdoor cookstove & accessories	X	X	X								X
84091 Macey's Grocery Stores, PO Box 159, **Sandy** UT ☎(801) 561-5400 – authorized distributor of *Emergency Essentials* products			X	X	X	X	X	X	X	X	
84093 Future Harvest, 9120 South Meadow Court, **Sandy** UT ☎(801) 943-0775 – authorized distributor of *Emergency Essentials* products			X	X	X	X	X	X	X	X	X
84094 Vern Madsen Service, 9400 S. 1190 E., **Sandy** UT ☎(801) 572-4400 – distributor of *Alco ♦Brite* gelled ethanol products		X									X
84097 Lakeridge Food Storage, 896 E. 640 N., **Orem** UT ☎(801) 235-0919 or (800) 336-7127 🖷(801) 221-8207 🖳www.shopsite.com/lfs ✉*lfsfood@ix.netcom.com* – complete line of dehydrated foods, fruits & vegetables; dairy products & adjuncts; check out **Internet** site	X	C	X	X			X	X	X	X	X
84097 Matt Thomas, 971 North 475 East, **Orem** UT ☎(801) 224-0777 or (800) 594-8973 – authorized *Perma Pak* distributor; food storage & emergency preparedness products	X	C	X	X	X	X			X	X	
84101 Utah Barrel, Inc., 370 West 9ᵗʰ South, **Salt Lake City** UT ☎(801) 363-1933 🖷(801) 531-9548 – used barrels for food & water storage	X	X	X		X	X		X		X	
84102 Wild Oats, 812 E. 200 South, **Salt Lake City** UT ☎(801) 355-7401 🖷(801) 355-9586			X	X	X	X	X	X	X	X	
84103 Rainy Day Gourmet, 1136 E. 3ʳᵈ Ave., **Salt Lake City** UT ☎(801) 530-1042 🖷(801) 532-1754 – tasty dehydrated soups; quick & easy, fat-free & vegetarian, all-natural, low sodium; only 20 min. prep	X	X	X	X		X			X		X
84104 Honeyville Grain, Inc., 1756 S. 4250 W., **Salt Lake City** UT ☎(801) 972-2168 🖷(801) 972-8412		X	X		X	X	X		X		
84104 Steve Jones, Nuclear Survival Consultant, 1402 S. 1000 W., **Salt Lake City** UT ☎(801) 972-0863 or (800) 850-5947 – consultant on nuclear preparedness & survival; mfr. of do-it-yourself, cheap, simple radiation dosimeter anyone can assemble from household items & use; instructions available; disasters or emergencies specialist	X	X	C								
84105 QuakeSafe, 2004 S. 800 E., **Salt Lake City** UT ☎(801) 488-3605 or (800) 950-2795 🖷(801) 467-0597 – manufacturer of patented line of water heater seismic restraint devices; tested to exceed 9.0 earthquake	X	X	X								
84106 Wild Oats, 2454 S. 700 East, **Salt Lake City** UT ☎(801) 359-7913 🖷(801) 485-7919			X	X	X	X	X	X	X	X	
84107 Karemore International Distr. / Ronald K. Gee, RPT, 6095 S. 300 E. #100, **Murray** UT ☎(801) 266-4402 – natural nutritional supplements; essential oils for natural healing	X	X	X					X			
84107 Pantry Supply Store, 250 E. 6400 S., **Murray** UT ☎(801) 268-9915 – retail store; distributor of *Perma Pak* dehydrated foods & emergency products & supplies, *Backpackers Pantry Food, Bosch/Kitchen Specialties* products, & *Emergency Essentials* preparedness and emergency products			C	X	X	X			X	X	X
84107 Perma Pak Distribution (Corporate), 3999 South Main #S-3, **Salt Lake City** UT ☎(800) 230-3663 – manufacturer of *Perma Pak* brand long-term food storage products & preparedness products	X	X	X	X	X	X	X	X	X	X	

Product References Keyed to Chapters (Cont.)

04 water / air filtration & treatment	05 grains, seeds, mills & equip.	12 dairy / powdered milk supplies	13 honey / sweeteners
14 vitamins / minerals / herbs	15 sprouting / equip. & supplies	16 dry / dehydrated / freeze-dried	17 energy / fuels

Entry	M	D	R	04	05	12	13	14	15	16	17
84107 Stat Medical Supply, div. of **Tolin Medical, Inc.**, 4555 South 300 West #500, **Murray** UT ☎(801) 261-4363 or (800) 223-6176 🖷(801) 261-4396 – distributor of complete line of emergency medical treatment equipment & supplies	X	X									X
84107 Thomas Transport Packs, PO Box 7104, **Murray** UT ☎(801) 262-6503 or (800) 445-3640 – space-efficient medical equipment pack with clear & coded pockets to provide rapid recognition and access to medical equipment & supplies; designed by experienced trauma MD	X	X									
84108 Don Wagstaff, 2265 E. Murray, **Salt Lake City** UT ☎(801) 277-3888 – distributor of *Magic Mill* kitchen products			X	X	X	X	X	X		X	
84109 Utah Wheat Grass, 3653 S. 2300 E., **Salt Lake City** UT ☎(801) 273-0644	X	X	X					X			
84109 Wilson's Magic Mill *(attn. Delsa Wilson)*, 3686 S. 2455 E., **Salt Lake City** UT ☎(801) 278-6950 – distributor of products & appliances for better health: *Magic Mill*, *Bosch*, *Zojirushi*, *Omega Juicer*, vacuum-sealing system, non-electric grinders, & more; storage foods & specialties; in-home storage specialist	X	X	X	X	X	X	X	X	X	X	X
84111 DUER International, Inc. / *Food PANtrie*™ Dryer & Sprouter, 255 E. 400 S. #150, **Salt Lake City** UT ☎(801) 531- 8996 🖷(801) 328-1243 🖳http://downtown-web.com/psi ✉psi/usa@downtown-web.com – manufacturer of *Food PANtrie*™, non-electric hanging dryer & sprouter	X	X	X							X	
84111 Product Source International / **Family Food Storage Catalog**, 255 E. 400 S. #150, **Salt Lake City** UT ☎(801) 531-8996 🖷(801) 328-1243 🖳http://downtown-web.com/psi ✉psiusa@aros.net or ✉foods@downtown-web.com – inventor & producer of the *Food PANtrie*™ sprouter & dehydrator; requires no electricity	X	X	X/C	X	X			X	X	X	X
84111 Mormon Food Storage List, 255 E. 400 S. #150, **Salt Lake City** UT ☎(801) 531-8996 🖷(801) 328-1243 – over 900 food storage items at institutional prices; available to all who want to purchase foods at reasonable prices and are preparing for the future; not affiliated with the *Church of Jesus Christ of Latter-day Saints (Mormon)*	X	C				X	X	X		X	X
84115 Blue Chip Group, Inc., 464 W. 3440 S., **Salt Lake City** UT ☎(801) 269-9699 🖳(801) 269-9666 – manufacturer & wholesale distributor of food products for long-term storage	X	X/C	X	X	X	X	X	X	X	X	X
84115 Emergency Essentials–Retail Store, 3272 S. W. Temple, **Salt Lake City** UT ☎(801) 467-1297			X	X	X	X	X			X	X
84115 Gagik Galstyan *(attn: Garry)*, 393 E. 3360 S. #29, **Salt Lake City** UT ☎(801) 486-7375	X	X									
84115 Home Preparedness, 2330 S. Main #3, **Salt Lake City** UT ☎(801) 487-3737 or (800) 435-1373 🖷(801) 487-3737		C	X	X	X					X	X
84115 Kitchen Specialties (Corp. Ofc.), 3767 S. 150 E., **Salt Lake City** UT ☎(801) 263-8900 🖷(801) 263-8902 – exclusive US distributor of German-made *Bosch Universal Kitchen System*; manufacturer of American-made *WhisperMill*™ flour maker; kitchen, cooking, & baking specialties; home convenience appliances	X	X	C	X	X	X	X	X	X	X	X
84115 Magic Mill Products & Appliances (Corp. Ofc.), 3767 S. 150 E., **Salt Lake City** UT ☎(801) 281-4943 🖷(801) 263-8902 – call for current catalog & dealer information	X	X	C	X	X	X	X	X	X	X	X
84115 Miller Honey Co., 3000 S. West Temple, **Salt Lake City** UT ☎(801) 486-8479	X	X	X				X				
84115 Solar Power Co., 2020 S. Main, **Salt Lake City** UT ☎(801) 484-1818 or (800) 297-9797 🖷(801) 467-8034	X	X									X
84115 Universal Safety Devices, Inc., 116 E. Helm Ave., **Salt Lake City** UT ☎(801) 288-0626 or (888) 201-2621 🖷(801) 273- 7673 🖳www.altimat.org./2788 – earthquake & water detection devices; intelligent home systems detect natural, propane, CO$_2$ & Radon gas	X	X	C								
84116 Future Group, PO Box 16372, **Salt Lake City** UT ☎(800) 678-4344 – portable dome shelters for temporary shelter or permanent living, cover, greenhouse, camping, or disaster shelter	X	X	C								X
84116 Good For You, 1550 W. 500 N., **Salt Lake City** UT ☎(801) 595-1151 – aerobic oxygen in concentration of non-toxic stabilized electrolytes with oxygen to destroy bacteria; for health & maintenance, athletic training, energy & stamina; keeps fruits & veggies fresh; mouthwash & prevents tooth decay	X	C						X			
84117 Wild Oats, 4695 S. Holladay Boulevard, **Salt Lake City** UT ☎(801) 278-8242 🖷(801) 278-0239		X	X	X	X	X	X	X			
84118 Advanced Water Storage, 5918 So. Salem Ave., **Salt Lake City** UT ☎(801) 968-9044 or (800) 800-5944	X	X	X	X							
84118 Alternative Energy Systems, 5918 So. Salem Ave., **Salt Lake City** UT ☎(801) 968-9044 or (800) 800-5944 – home, shop, & greenhouse stoves & boilers; solar electric & hot water heating; back-up generators	X	X	X								X
84118 Arizona Nutritionals / Karen Geis, 3040 Eugene Hill Way, **Taylorsville** UT ☎(801) 969-1892		X						X			
84119 ZCMI Department Stores, 2200 S. 900 West, **Salt Lake City** UT ☎(801) 579-6000 – distributor of *Emergency Essentials* products; locations throughout the Intermountain West			X	X	X	X	X			X	X
84121 Linda's Home Products, 7246 S. 1600 E., **Salt Lake City** UT ☎(801) 924-8948 🖷(801) 943-8860 – full-line distributor of *Bosch, Kitchen Specialties & Magic Mill* products			X	X	X	X	X			X	X
84121 Peterson's Bosch Kitchen Center, 6265 S. Highland Drive, **Salt Lake City** UT ☎(801) 272-9922 – distributor of *Bosch & Kitchen Specialties* products for a healthier lifestyle; in-home storage specialist			X	X	X	X	X		X	X	X
84123 General Army Navy, 4974 S. Redwood Road, **Salt Lake City** UT ☎(801) 966-5556 – distributor of *Emergency Essentials* products; locations throughout the Intermountain West			X	X	X	X	X			X	X
84130 Deseret Book, PO Box 30178, **Salt Lake City** UT ☎(801) 534-1515 – distributor of *Emergency Essentials* products; locations throughout the Intermountain West			X	X	X	X	X			X	X
84130 LDS Books Club, PO Box 30400, **Salt Lake City** UT ☎(801) 972-0488 – distributor of *Emergency Essentials* products; locations throughout the Intermountain West			X	X	X	X	X			X	X

M = Manufacturer / Processor   D = Wholesaler / Trade distributor   R = Distributor / Retailer to public

M = Manufacturer / Processor — D = Wholesaler / Trade distributor — R = Distributor / Retailer to public	M	D	R	04	05	12	13	14	15	16	17
84152 **American Red Cross**, PO Box 526279, **Salt Lake City** UT ☎(801) 467-7339 — distributor of *Emergency Essentials* products			X	X	X	X	X		X	X	X
84157 **The Preparedness Group, Inc.**, PO Box 573688, **Murray** UT ☎(801) 263-0250 or (888) 263-0250 🖷(801) 263-6906 ✉*BowRob@sisna.com* — publisher of *"Ready or Not!",* monthly newsletter about how to become prepared in all aspects of your life, and how to function more efficiently; distributor of preparedness items & food storage products			X	X	X	X	X	X		X	X	X
84245 **Colonia Sales**, 104 S. 100 W., **La Verkin** UT ☎(801) 635-2470			X	X			X		X		
84302 **Big J Milling & Elevator Co.**, 733 W. Forest St., **Brigham City** UT ☎(801) 723-3459	X	X		X							
84306 **Wheatland Seed Co.**, 14585 N. Highway 38, **Collinston** UT ☎(801) 458-2249 — organic & conventionally-grown seeds & grains	X	X		X							
84314 **Honeyville Grain, Inc.**, **Honeyville** UT ☎(801) 279-8668	X	X		X		X	X		X		
84318 **Emergency Safety & Supply**, 16 E. 100 S., **Hyde Park** UT ☎(801) 563-6657 — distributor of *Alco ♦Brite* gelled ethanol products			X								X
84319 **Hansen's Heirlooms**, 443 W. 200 S., **Hyrum** UT ☎(801) 245-5746 — old-fashioned spinning wheels, weaving looms, books, fleeces, & instruction in techniques	X	X	X								X
84321 **Central Milling Company, Inc.**, 122 E. Center St., **Logan** UT ☎(801) 752-6625 — grain processor; bulk and retail sales	X	X	X	X							
84321 **Life Foods**, 1360 E. 2100 N., **Logan** UT ☎(801) 753-1782			X	X						X	
84323 **Field & Forest Distributing**, PO Box 240, **Logan** UT ☎(801) 753-0910 or (800) 934-2879 *orders* — herbal products for preparedness		X	X					X			
84328 **Life Sprouts**, PO Box 150, **Paradise** UT ☎(801) 245-3891 or (800) 241-1516 — manufacturer of *Sprout Master* brand sprouting system; distributor, traditional & organic sprouting seeds; open-pollinated seeds for gardening; organic honey; distributor of *Alco ♦Brite* gelled ethanol products	X	X	X	X			X	X	X	X	X
84333 **Gilt Edge Flour Mill, Inc.**, PO Box 7, **Richmond** UT ☎(801) 258-2425	X	X	X	X							
84335 **R & R Mill Co.**, 45 W. 100 North, **Smithfield** UT ☎(801) 563-3333 ✉*8015634093* — mfr. *Corona* grain & corn mill; interchangeable stone & steel grinding surfaces; other kitchen equipment & prod.	X	X	X	X							
84335 **Smithfield Implement Co.**, 99 N. Main St., **Smithfield** UT ☎(801) 563-3333 🖷(801) 563-4093 — mail-order preparedness products			X	X	X	X	X	X		X	X	X
84337 **Olsen Enterprizes** c/o Joyce Olsen, 141 West 5th South, **Tremonton** UT ☎(801) 257-3877 — distributor of *Magic Mill* kitchen products			X	X			X		X		
84341 **Emergency Safety & Supply**, 1209 N. Main, **Logan** UT ☎(801) 787-1339 — distributor of *Alco ♦Brite* gelled ethanol products			X								X
84341 **Kitchen Kneads**, 1211 N. Main Street, **Logan** UT ☎(801) 752-9220 — authorized distributor of *Emergency Essentials* products			X	X	X	X	X	X	X	X	X
84400 **Wheeler Enterprises**, **Ogden** UT ☎(801) 782-2383 🖳www.relia.net/wheeler ✉*bryanw@relia.net* — authorized *Perma Pak* distributor; food storage & emergency preparedness products			X	X	X	X	X		X	X	X
84405 **Keith Carrigan**, 3720 River Valley Drive, **Ogden** UT ☎(801) 621-2616 — authorized *Perma Pak* distributor; preparedness consultant			X	X	X	X	X	X		X	X
84405 **Pure Health Products**, 1150 West 24th St., **Ogden** UT ☎(801) 394-6561 🖷(801) 394-1169 — water distillation system for the home; provides pure water for about $0.20/gal		X	X	X							
84501 **Christi Jardine**, 1187 W. 430 N., **Price** UT ☎(801) 637-0271 — *Magic Mill* products distributor			X	X		X		X			
84532 **Flora Najafi**, Castle Valley Star Rt., Box 1809, **Moab** UT ☎(801) 259-8453 — distributor of *Magic Mill* kitchen products			X	X			X		X		
84601 **Consider The Kitchen**, 250 North University, **Provo** UT ☎(801) 374-0393 — distributor of *Bosch & Kitchen Specialties* products			X	X			X		X		
84601 **Millennium Group**, 726 North 1890 West #34, **Provo** UT ☎(801) 375-2264 or (800) 500-9893 🖷(801) 356-1523 🖳www.millenniumfoods.com ✉*apt@itsnet.com* — *Millennium Gourmet Food Reserves* brand dehydrated foods & mixes	X	X	X	X						X	
84601 **Pure Ultraviolet, Inc.**, 1140 Aviation Drive, **Provo** UT ☎(801) 377-4200 — distributor of water purification products		X	X	X							
84603 **Paul J. Young & Associates**, PO Box 1904, **Provo** UT ☎(801) 489-0089 — Living Trusts to protect assets from unnecessary taxation, litigation & probate			C								
84603 **The Food Place**, PO Box 482, **Provo** UT ☎(801) 374-1858 — in-home storage specialist; disasters or emergencies specialist	X	X	X					X		X	
84604 **Food Storage Buyer's Club**, 2250 N. University Parkway #4834, **Provo** UT 🖳www.foodbuyersclub.com — members-only **Internet** wholesale food storage supermarket providing members with latest products at special wholesale pricing; self-service, **Internet** access-only organization featuring *Buyer's Club Choice* brand products	X	X	C	X	X	X			X	X	
84605 **DVO Enterprises**, PO Box 50882, **Provo** UT ☎(800) 435-8030 — food planner software; helps determine which foods are needed in food storage, what quantities, how to utilize what's in storage, how long it will last, organize your recipes, & more!	X	X	X								

Product References Keyed to Chapters (Cont.)

04 water / air filtration & treatment	05 grains, seeds, mills & equip.	12 dairy / powdered milk supplies	13 honey / sweeteners
14 vitamins / minerals / herbs	15 sprouting / equip. & supplies	16 dry / dehydrated / freeze-dried	17 energy / fuels

M = Manufacturer / Processor	D = Wholesaler / Trade distributor	R = Distributor / Retailer to public

Listing	M	D	R	04	05	12	13	14	15	16	17
84627 Maple Leaf Industries Retail Store, 480 South 50 East, **Ephraim** UT ☎(800) 671-5323 or (800) 671-5323 🖷(801) 283-4200 🖵www.mapleleafinc.com ✉*food@mapleleafinc.com* — complete retail store of food storage items		X	X C	X	X	X	X	X	X	X	X
84627 Maple Leaf Industries, 480 South 50 East, **Ephraim** UT ☎(800) 671-5323 or (800) 671-5323 🖷(801) 283-4200 🖵www.mapleleafinc.com ✉*food@mapleleafinc.com* — wholesale warehouse distributor of food storage products & emergency preparedness items; bulk products; brand name & custom packing & canning operation	X	X	X	X	X	X	X	X	X	X	X
84642 The Cook Book Shoppe / Vicki Tate, 302 East 200 North, **Manti** UT ☎(801) 835-8283 — consultant; author of *"New Cookin' With Home Storage"*		X	X	X	X	X		X		X	
84648 Nutribiz Plus, 205 South Main St., **Nephi** UT ☎(801) 623-4837 🖷(801) 623-4138 — preparedness & emergency products; reverse-osmosis purified water; distributor of *Magic Mill* kitchen products		X				X		X		X	X
84651 Magic Mixes, 588 E. Park Dr., **Elk Ridge** UT ☎(801) 423-1991 ✉*magicmixes@Juno.Com* — *Maple Leaf* products distributor; preparedness consultant		X	X	X	X	X			X	X	X
84651 Young Living Essential Oils, 250 South Main Street, **Payson** UT ☎(801) 465-5400 🖷(801) 465-5424 *Orders only:* ☎(800) 763-9963 *for Customer Service:* (801) 236-6200 — herbal formulas & aromatherapy for balancing the body, mind & spirit; essential oils therapy; education & training	X	C						X			
84653 Diana Ballard, 119 W. Salem Canal Rd., **Salem** UT ☎(801) 423-2324		X	X								
84660 Latter-day Family Resources, 140 N. Main St., **Spanish Fork** UT ☎(801) 798-2106 or (800) 290-2283 🖷(801) 798-2067		X						X			
84663 Christopher Family Herbals, 188 South Main, **Springville** UT ☎(801) 489-8787	X	X	C					X			
84663 Christopher Publications, PO Box 412, **Springville** UT ☎(801) 489-4254 or (800) 372-8255 — books, audio, & video materials by master herbalist Dr. David Christopher & the late Dr. John Christopher	X	X	X					X			
84663 Dr. Christopher's Herb Shop, 188 S. Main, **Springville** UT ☎(801) 489-8787		X	X					X			
84663 Maxam Wholesale, 110 South Main, **Springville** UT ☎(801) 489-0160 🖷(801) 489-0080 — discount retail & catalog order store; must be a business to order; many bargain-priced preparedness items	X	X	X							X	X
84663 Murdock Pharmaceuticals, 1400 Mountain Springs Pkwy., **Springville** UT ☎(800) 962-8873	X	X	X					X			
84663 Nature's Way Products, 10 Mountain Springs Pkwy., **Springville** UT (800) 544-4542								x			
84663 The Herb Shop, 188 S. Main, **Springville** UT ☎(801) 489-8787 or (800) 453-1406 🖷(801) 489-7207 — herbal first aid kits, herbs, herbals, herb & health books, video & audio tapes, juicers & small appliances for health		X						X			
84663 The School of Natural Healing, PO Box 412, **Springville** UT ☎(800) 372-8255 — earn the Master Herbalist degree from the institution founded by Dr. John Christopher in 1953	X							X			
84701 The Preparedness Place, 68 South Main, **Richfield** UT ☎(801) 896-4455 🖷(801) 896-4477 — complete array of *Maple Leaf* preparedness & food storage products; consults on food preparation		X	X	X	X	X			X	X	X
84701 Thompson's, 363 Valley View Drive, **Richfield** UT ☎(801) 896-9094 or (800) 927-9381		X	X			X	X	X	X		X
84720 American Brain Storm Innovations, PO Box 10, **Glendale** UT ☎(801) 648-2222 — consultant on organic gardening & greenhouses; preparedness consultant	X	C									X
84720 Lisa Lunt, 446 West 1100 North, **Cedar City** UT ☎(801) 865-0302 — distributor of *Magic Mill* kitchen products		X				X		X	X		
84745 Ilene Church, PO Box 847, **La Verkin** UT ☎(801) 635-2470 — distributor of *Magic Mill* kitchen products		X				X		X	X		
84745 Do It Homestead Inc., *(attn: Charlie Collins),* 101 Smith Mesa, **La Verkin** UT ☎/🖷(801) 877-1061 🖵www.netins.net/showcase/solarcatalog ✉*MrSolar@netins.net* — solar, wind, & alternative power; expert & consultant; check out the website for details!	X	X									X
84765 Pure Health Products, 1150 West 24th St., **Ogden** UT ☎(801) 394-6561 or (801) 543-2317	X	X	X					X			
84765 The Fresh Air Company, 705 Lava Flow Drive, **Santa Clara** UT ☎(801) 674-0655 — ozone generator & ionizer; remove dust, pollen, smoke, chemicals, molds, mildew, etc. without filters or chemicals	X	X	X								X
84770 Access Plus!, 620 S 400 E #106, **St. George** UT ☎(801) 673-6224 🖵www.infowest.com/a/access ✉*access@infowest.com*		X	X	X	X	X	X	X			
84770 Bosch Kitchen Ctr. / Leavitt's, 150 N. 400 E., **St. George** UT ☎(801) 628-6698 🖷(801) 628-6308 — preparedness consultant; in-home storage specialist; free cooking classes											
84770 Emergency Essentials Retail Store, 695 Bluff Street, **St. George** UT ☎(801) 656-9233		X	X	X	X	X	X	X	X	X	X
84770 Family Resource Warehouse, 465 S. Bluff #333, **St. George** UT ☎(801) 865-0908 — family preparedness products; home schooling supplies; gardening supplies		X	X	X						X	X
84770 Leavitt's Kitchen Center, 150 N. 400 E., **St. George** UT ☎(801) 628-6698 🖷(801) 628-6308 — distributor of *Bosch & Kitchen Specialties* products		X				X		X			
84770 Olive Osmond, PO Box 2575, **St. George** UT ☎(801) 656-1317		X				X		X			
84770 Preparedness Mart, 1060 East Tabernacle #6, **St. George** UT ☎(801) 673-0437 or (800) 773-0437 🖵www.preparednessmart.com ✉*mail@preparednessmart.com* — specializing in *Maple Leaf* food storage products, camping supplies, & military surplus items		X	X C	X	X	X				X	X

	M	D	R	04	05	12	13	14	15	16	17
84784 Alco-Brite Co., Inc., PO Box 840926, **Hildale** UT ☎(435) 874-1025 or (800) 473-0717 🖷(435) 874-1026 💻www.alcobrite.com ✉*alcoinfo@alco-brite.com* — manufacturer of jelled alcohol fuel product; emits harmless CO_2 & water vapor; stove appliances for cans	X	X	X								X

Vermont

	M	D	R	04	05	12	13	14	15	16	17
05001 King Arthur Flour, 62 Olcott Park Drive, **White River Jct.** VT ☎(802) 649-3711 — distributor of *Magic Mill* kitchen products			X	X	X	X	X	X		X	
05055 Sands, Taylor & Wood Co., Norwich VT ☎(800) 777-4434 — producer of *King Arthur's Stone-Ground Flours*, reputed to be one of the finest flours for baking	X	X			X						
05058 Chelsea Green Publishing Co., PO Box 130 Rt. 113, **Post Mills** VT — lifestyle books: homesteading, self-reliance, & self-sufficiency; environmental & healthy living books	X		X								
05091 Countryman Press, PO Box 175, **Woodstock** VT ☎(800) 245-4151 — preparedness books & information			X								
05161 Vermont Country Store, Rt. 100 South, **Weston** VT ☎(802) 824-3184 🖷(802) 362-0285 — retail store & catalog order; dehydrated & freeze-dried foods; dried beans & rice; crackers; soaps & lotions; catalog			X		X	X	X			X	X
05255 Friends of the Sun, Manchester Center VT ☎(802) 362-4070 ✉*friends@hearth.com* — stoves, fireplaces & more…		X	X								X
05304 Northeast Cooperatives, 49 Bennett Drive, **Brattleboro** VT ☎(800) 236-5880 or (802) 257-5856 🖷(802) 257-7039 Territory: *CT, MA, ME, NH, NY, RI, VT*		C	X	X	X	X	X	X	X	X	
05346 S & H Alternative Energy Products, RD 3 Box 312, **Putney** VT ☎(802) 722-3704		X	X								X
05401 Origanum Natural Foods, Inc., 227 Main St., **Burlington** VT ☎(802) 863-6103		C	X	X	X	X	X	X	X	X	
05402 Windstream Power Systems, Inc., 1 Mill St., **Burlington** VT ☎(802) 658-0075 🖷(802) 658-1098		X	X								X
05602 Solar Works, Inc., 64 Main St., **Montpelier** VT ☎(802) 223-7804 🖷(802) 223-8980		X	X								X
05661 HearthStone / NHC, Inc., **Morrisville** VT ☎(802) 888-5232 🖷(802) 888-7249 — manufacturer of wood-burning stoves & residential gas-fired heaters	X										X
05867 Maple State Battery, **Sutton** VT ☎(802) 467-3662		X	X								X

Virginia

	M	D	R	04	05	12	13	14	15	16	17
22003 Margaret Bechtel, 7225 Wilburdale Drive, **Annandale** VA ☎(703) 642-2911 — distributor of *Magic Mill* products			X		X			X		X	
22015 Nature's Finest, PO Box 10311, **Burke** VA — catalog of fragrances and scents for soapmaking & the home			X						X		
22043 Bread & Circus, 7511 Leesburg Pike, **Falls Church** VA ☎(703) 448-1600 🖷(703) 847-1441		X	X	X	X	X	X	X	X	X	
22079 Gregory Spann, 9005 Macsvega Court, **Lorton** VA ☎(703) 339-6467 — distributor of *Magic Mill* products			X		X			X		X	
22091 Bread & Circus, 11660 Plaza Americana Drive, **Reston** VA ☎(703) 736-0600 🖷(703) 736-0674		X	X	X	X	X	X	X	X	X	
22110 J. E. Rice, Co., 9124 Mathis Ave., **Manassas** VA ☎(703) 361-3141 — distributor of *Alco ♦Brite* gelled ethanol products			X								X
22124 Diane Hulcher, 11154 Conestoga Court, **Dakton** VA ☎(703) 273-9117 — distributor of *Magic Mill* products			X		X			X		X	
22152 Bread & Circus, 8402 Old Keene Mill Road, **Springfield** VA ☎(703) 644-2500 🖷(703) 644-7447		X	X	X	X	X	X	X	X	X	
22153 Resources LifeChange, 7418 Golden Horseshoe, **Springfield** VA — protect yourself against deadly new diseases & microbial mutations by building immune & endocrine systems			X				X				
22180 Bread & Circus, 143 Maple Avenue East, **Vienna** VA ☎(703) 319-2000 🖷(703) 319-2001		X	X	X	X	X	X	X	X	X	
22192 Lawn Leisure & Pellet Stoves, 2612 Dynasty Loop, **Woodbridge** VA ☎(703) 494-8909 — distributor of *Alco ♦Brite* gelled ethanol products			X								X
22201 Bread & Circus, 2700 Wilson Boulevard, **Arlington** VA ☎(703) 527-6596 🖷(703) 527-6568		X	X	X	X	X	X	X	X	X	
22303 Eagle Investments / The Toddy People!, PO Box 4341, **Alexandria** VA ☎(800) 329-6987 — *Mineral Toddy* has 60 colloidal minerals from ancient plant deposits, chemical-free & non-polluted		X	X					X			
22303 Heritage Health Products, PO Box 4341, **Alexandria** VA ☎(800) 678-9265 🖷(970) 484-3953 — colloidal nutrition from ancient plant sources; liquid vitamins & minerals; oxygen products			X				X	X			
22312 Bread & Circus, 6548 Little River Turnpike, **Alexandria** VA ☎(703) 914-0040 🖷(703) 914-8803		X	X	X	X	X	X	X	X	X	
22601 American Stove Co., 214 E. Triccadilly St., **Wincherster** VA ☎(703) 722-4382 — distributor of *Alco ♦Brite* gelled ethanol products			X								X
22602 Mary's Cupboard, 1033 Mountain Falls Rd., **Winchester** VA ☎(540) 877-9725 — authorized regional dealer for *SamAndy*® dehydrated food & equipment			X	X	X	X	X		X	X	X
22801 Christian Light Education, PO Box 1212, **Harrisburg** VA ☎(540) 434-0750 🖷(540) 433-8896 — full curriculum for grades 1-12; library books for homeschool		C									
22801 Wilderness Voyagers, 1544 E. Market St., **Herrisonburg** VA — distributor of *Alco ♦Brite* gelled ethanol products			X								X
22821 Teri Jacobsen, Rt. 2 Box 48 A, **Dayton** VA ☎(703) 879-2965 — distributor of *Magic Mill* products			X		X			X		X	

Product References Keyed to Chapters (Cont.)

04 water / air filtration & treatment	05 grains, seeds, mills & equip.	12 dairy / powdered milk supplies	13 honey / sweeteners
14 vitamins / minerals / herbs	15 sprouting / equip. & supplies	16 dry / dehydrated / freeze-dried	17 energy / fuels

M = Manufacturer / Processor **D = Wholesaler / Trade distributor** **R = Distributor / Retailer to public**

#	Listing	M	D	R	04	05	12	13	14	15	16	17
22901	Bread & Circus, 1416 Seminole Trail, **Charlottesville** VA ☎(804) 973-4900 🖷(804) 973-4650		X	X	X	X	X	X	X		X	
22932	Crozet Natural Foods, PO Box 634, **Crozet** VA ☎(804) 823-5583 — http://monticello.avenue.gen.vaus/Library/JMRL/Crozet/cfcoop.html			C	X	X	X	X	X		X	X
22972	Carol Wayner, 13092 Wayner Drive, **Somerset** VA ☎(703) 672-5601 — distributor of *Magic Mill* products			X		X			X		X	
23083	Bruce Burdge, 24750 Selma Road, **Jetersville** VA											
23320	TDS Incorporated, 816 Greenbrier Circle, **Chesapeake** VA ☎(804) 424-2482 — personal water purification system requires no pumping; single pass w/o iodine, no residue, & lightweight	X	X									X
23323	Karen Dayton, 629 Hopewell Drive, **Chesapeake** VA ☎(804) 485-0830 — distributor of *Magic Mill* products			X		X			X		X	
23437	JoAnne Thompson, 7973 Carr Lane, **Suffolk** VA ☎(757) 539-4412 — distributor of *Magic Mill* products			X		X			X		X	
23451	K. C. Appliances, PO Box 1379, **Virginia Beach** VA — device built in strict accordance with Edgar Casey readings; utilized to assist the body in returning to & maintaining energy balance; unique approach to noninvasive homeostasis	X	X									
23452	Home Health, 949 Seahawk Cir. **Virginia Beach** VA ☎(800) 284-9123 — natural herbal & homeopathic remedies and a variety of products for promoting good health at home	X						X				
23464	Marguerite E. Umphers, 1913 Dulles Court, **Virginia Beach** VA ☎(804) 479-2684 — distributor of *Magic Mill* products			X		X			X		X	
23505	Pamela Crane, 300 Gunn Court, **Norfolk** VA ☎(804) 583-4583 — distributor of *Magic Mill* products			X		X			X		X	
23608	Russell Minter, 885 Elder Road, **Newport News** VA ☎(804) 875-1319 — distributor of *Magic Mill* products			X		X			X		X	
24073	Moonlight Solar, 2932 Vicker Switch Rd., **Christiansburg** VA ☎(540) 381-4971	X										X
24501	The Fireplace, **Lynchburg** VA ☎(804) 528-0851 🖷(804) 528-4796	X	X									X

Washington

#	Listing	M	D	R	04	05	12	13	14	15	16	17
98002	Rainbow Cleaners, 335 E. Main St., **Auburn** WA ☎(206) 939-3372 or (206) 248-0143 — *Sea Mist Industries* air purification system & living environment cleaner utilizing the "water trap" method		X									X
98003	Federal Way Fuel, 1225 S. 30056, **Federal Way** WA ☎(206) 874-2765 — distributor of *Alco ◆Brite* gelled ethanol products		X									X
98004	Bellevue Fireplace, 208 105th Ave. NE, **Bellevue** WA — distributor of *Alco ◆Brite* gelled ethanol products		X									X
98007	Weldon Sant, 3080 148th Avenue SE, **Bellevue** WA ☎(206) 747-4745 — distributor of *Magic Mill* kitchen products	X	X			X			X		X	
98020	Edmonds Garden Center, 610 5th So., **Edmonds** WA ☎(206) 778-4877 — distributor of *Honda* electric generators; gardening equipment by *Troy-bilt, Toro, Stihl, & Echo*			X								
98026	Remedies at Law, 9115-236th Street NW #B, **Edmonds** WA ☎/🖷(425) 778-2012 — protection for family, business, & property; emphasis on dispute resolution; services provided by a "non-union" attorney			X / C								
98027	Sue Fazekas, Ph.D., 660 Wildwood Blvd. #B-8, **Issaquah** WA ☎(206) 557-8872 🖷(206) 557-0894 — author of disaster survival book "*Earthquake, Fire & Storm…Your Guide for Emergency Preparedness*"	C	X	C								X
98032	Hearth Interface Corp., 21440 68th Ave., **Kent** WA ☎(800) 446-6180 🖷(206) 872-3412	X	X									X
98033	**Noah Industries,** *(attn: Marvin Harshberger)*, HC 68 Box 304, **Kirkland** WA ☎(520) 899-1025 — *SamAndy Foods* products distributor			X		X	X	X	X		X	X
98037	Rich's Woodstoves & Spas, 16504 Hwy. 99, **Lynnwood** WA ☎(206) 745-2749 or (800) 354-3633 — richs@hearth.com — distributor of *Alco ◆Brite* gelled ethanol products		X									X
98038	Comfort Zone West, 23719 SE West 248th Street, **Maple Valley** WA ☎(206) 432-8083 or (800) 468-5945 🖷(206) 432-8134 www.comfortzoneww.com vannoyinc@aol.com	X	X									X
98042	Dan's Outback, 28433 152nd Avenue SE, **Kent** WA ☎(206) 630-7625 🖷(206) 227-3299		X	X					X		X	X
98042	For Your Health Pharmacy, 13215 SE 240th St., **Kent** WA ☎(800) 456-4325		X							X		
98043	Raytel Corporation, 6510 216th SW #D, **Mountlake Terrace** WA ☎(206) 776-7413 — air purification equipment, negative ionizers, oxygen generators for home, car, & travel; EMF monitor s	X	X	X								X
98052	Elco Northwest Wood 'n Energy, 16151 Cleveland St., **Redmond** WA — distributor of *Alco ◆Brite* gelled ethanol products		X									X
98058	Dan's Outback, 14254 SE 176th St. # J-6, **Renton** WA ☎(206) 630-7625 🖷(206) 227-3299		X	X			X				X	X
98064	Gearhead Company, PO Box 5948, **Kent** WA ☎(206) 846-4109 🖷(206) 846-4077		X	X								
98065	Survival Basics, Inc., **Snoqualmie** WA ☎(360) 557-6599 — distributor of food storage products	X	X	X		X	X	X			X	X

M = Manufacturer / Processor	D = Wholesaler / Trade distributor	R = Distributor / Retailer to public	M	D	R	04	05	12	13	14	15	16	17
98101 **Safe-Pak Supply Canada Inc. (US Ofc.)**, 720 Olive Way # 930, **Seattle** WA ☎(206) 447-9174 🖷(206) 447-9180 🖳http://204.174.18.3/survival ✉safe_pak@mindlink.bc.ca – US outlet for *Safe-Pak Canada;* first aid, emergency preparedness & related customized products			X	X	X								
98103 **Hydro-Tech**, 3929 Aurora Ave., **Seattle** WA ☎(206) 547-2202 – preparedness products; alternative energy & plant growth technology				X			X		X				
98105 **Wild Oats**, 5440 Sand Point Way NE, **Seattle** WA ☎(206) 525-9515 🖷(206) 525-0191				X	X	X	X	X	X		X	X	X
98107 **Ample Power Co.**, 1150 NW 52nd St., **Seattle** WA ☎(800) 541-7789			X										X
98108 **Emergency Preparedness Service**, 5511 6th South, **Seattle** WA ☎(206) 762-0889 – distributor of *Alco ♦Brite* gelled ethanol products				X									X
98108 **Emergency Preparedness Services**, 511 6th Avenue S., **Seattle** WA ☎(206) 762-0889 – authorized distributor of *Emergency Essentials* products			X	X	X	X	X	X	X	X	X		
98108 **Mountain Peoples Northwest Warehouse**, 4005 Sixth Avenue S., **Seattle** WA ☎(800) 336-8872 (*outside WA*) or (800) 762-0211 (*WA only*) Territory: AK, northern ID, MT, western WY, OR, WA – full line wholesale distributor of natural & conventional fresh, dried, & bulk foods			X	X	X	X	X	X	X	X	X		
98108 **Progressive International Corp.**, 8300 Military Road South, **Seattle** WA ☎(206) 762-8300 or (800) 426-7101 🖷(206) 762-4548 – distributor of kitchen equipment for processing in-home food storage production			X	X	X							X	X
98109 **Joyce Showalter**, PO Box 19392, **Seattle** WA ☎(206) 283-4510 or (800) 733-1107 – distributor of *Multi-Pure* water filtration/purification systems for home/emergency contaminants removal			X	X	X								
98111 **Nordstrom**, PO Box 870, **Seattle** WA – distributor of *Alco ♦Brite* gelled ethanol products				X									X
98115 **The Food Cupboard**, 9414 Roosevelt Way NE, **Seattle** WA ☎(206) 524-6800					X	X	X	X	X		X	X	X
98122 **Eclectic Enterprises**, 1500 24th Avenue, **Seattle** WA ☎(206) 328-5809 🖷(206) 328-1039											X		
98134 **Fisher Mills, Inc.**, Box C3765, **Seattle** WA ☎(206) 622-4430 or (800) 426-0101 🖷(206) 682-3676			X	X	X		X					X	
98136 **The EpiCenter**, 6523 California Ave. SW #161, **Seattle** WA ☎(206) 937-5658 🖷(206) 937-5658 🖳http://TheEpicenter.com ✉bjnelson@The Epicenter.com – emergency preparedness center; earthquake supplies; MREs; highway safety products; much more…!				X	X	X	X	X		X	X	X
98144 **Professional Marketing Group**, 912 Rainier Avenue S., **Seattle** WA ☎(206) 322-7303 or (800) 227-3769 🖷(206) 322-4351 – dehydrators, vacuum-packing equipment & supplies, storage & food containers; other household equipment			X	X	X		X					X	X
98148 **Safety First Products, Inc.**, PO Box 48262, **Seattle** WA ☎(206) 227-6205 🖷(206) 236-6302 – author of *"Earthquake, Fire, Storm…Your Guide for Emergency Preparedness";* evacuation masks and breathing system for escape from fire disaster										X		
98155 **Rich Osborne**, 18764 18th Ave. N. E., **Seattle** WA ☎(206) 363-2579 – distributor of *Multi-Pure* water filtration/purification systems for home/emergency; removes contaminants			X	C	X								
98160 **TechSolutions International**, PO Box 60282, **Seattle** WA 🖷(206) 542-9340 🖳www.halcyon.com/tsirlr/ARK ✉tsirlr@halcyon.com – custom-designed "building in a box" specialized shelters for temporary housing, field operations, or other use			X	X	C								X
98168 **NW Cooperage Co., Inc.**, 7152 1st Ave. So., **Seattle** WA ☎(206) 763-2345 or (800) 451-3471 – new & re-conditioned 55-gal. steel & plastic drums for storing food & water supplies				X									
98168 **The Grainery** c/o Pat Spendlove, 13629 1st Ave. South, **Seattle** WA ☎(206) 244-5015 – distributor of *Magic Mill* kitchen products				X		X			X		X		
98177 **Light Energy Company**, 1056 NW 179th Place, **Seattle** WA ☎(206) 542-7612 or (800) 544-4826 – portable, battery-operated phototherapy units; safe, red LED light for pain relief & therapeutic applications			X	X	X						X		
98199 **Aanon Publishing**, PO Box 99763, **Seattle** WA(206) 283-0595 – program provides courage in following dreams & accomplishing personal objectives				X							X		
98201 **Country Save Corporation**, 3410 Smith Avenue, **Everett** WA ☎(206) 258-1171 🖷(206) 252-7095 – cleaning products: 100% phosphate-free, septic tank safe, & biodegradable detergents & non-chlorine bleach			X	X									X
98203 **Everett Fireplace Shop**, 5612 Evergreen Way, **Everett** WA ☎(206) 353-3722 – distributor of *Alco ♦Brite* gelled ethanol products				X									X
98223 **Cornehl Sales**, 5702 172 N. E., **Arlington** WA ☎( ) 435-2530 – distributor of *Alco ♦Brite* gelled ethanol products				X									X
98223 **Nelson Distributing**, 208 S. W. Ave., **Arlington** WA – distributor of *Alco ♦Brite* gelled ethanol products				X									X
98223 **The Home School Books & Supplies**, 104 S. West Ave., **Arlington** WA ☎(360) 435-0376 or (800) 788-1221 🖷(360) 435-1028 🖳www.TheHomeSchool.com – one-stop shopping for home schooling education; complete catalog for home schoolers				X									
98225 **Crystal Air** / David & Elisabeth Miller, 1225 E. Sunset Dr. #415, **Bellingham** WA ☎(800) 906-2624 🖷(360) 914-9178 – filterless air purifiers; *AquaLab* water treatment systems; *Flozone, Vortec,* & *Infinity Tech* water filters, & more!			X	X	X C		X		X			X
98226 **Northwest Pellet Stove & Fuel**, 4721 N. W. Road, **Bellingham** WA ☎(206) 676-7609 – distributor of *Alco ♦Brite* gelled ethanol products				X									X

Product References Keyed to Chapters (Cont.)

04 water / air filtration & treatment	05 grains, seeds, mills & equip.	12 dairy / powdered milk supplies	13 honey / sweeteners
14 vitamins / minerals / herbs	15 sprouting / equip. & supplies	16 dry / dehydrated / freeze-dried	17 energy / fuels

	M	D	R	04	05	12	13	14	15	16	17
98226 Shomer-Tec, 3861 Mustang Way, **Bellingham** WA ☎(360) 733-6210 — authorized distributor of *Survival Tabs & Storehouse Foods*, manufactured by *Food Reserves, Inc.*	X	X						X		X	
98226 Vibrational Ventures, 1225 E. Sunset Dr. #415, **Bellingham** WA ☎(800) 906-2624 — products for air, water, & body purification; several forms of oxygen therapies to help the body heal itself		X	X					X			
98240 Eco-Logic Homes, PO Box 598, **Custer** WA ☎(206) 366-3660 — designer & custom builder of environmentally friendly housing & energy solutions; earth berm shelters	X	X	C								X
98244 Canyon Industries, Inc., PO Box 574, **Deming** WA ☎(360) 592-5552 — hydroelectric systems; turbines & complete systems 100W to 5 MW; manufacturing turbines since 1976	X	X									X
98260 Frosty Hollow, Box 53, **Langley** WA		X	X				X				
98264 Joyce Pugh, 1402 Main Street, **Lynden** WA ☎(206) 354-4835 — *Magic Mill* products distributor; author of *"Gettin' By"*		X			X		X		X		
98264 The Commonwealth Trust Company, 413 19th Street #144, **Linden** WA ☎(206) 647-5242 — trust protects assets from taxes, regulation, probate costs, & tax lien seizures; control tax liability & obtain privacy		X									X
98270 Nobach Sales, PO Box 284, **Marysville** WA ☎(206) 659-6415 — distributor of *Alco ♦Brite* gelled ethanol products		X									X
98280 Rainshadow Solar, PO Box 242, **Orcas** WA ☎(206) 376-5336 — independent electrical power systems; reliable, independent, & renewable electrical systems from natural resources		X	X								X
98292 Country Living Prod., 14727 56th Avenue NW, **Stanwood** WA ☎(360) 652-0671 🖷(360) 652-8913 — manufacturer of the *Country Living Grain Mill*	X	X	C		X						X
98328 Water Magic, PO Box 1790, **Eatonville** WA ☎(360) 832-8456 🖷(360) 832-8457 ✉*mindsurgeo@aol.com* — water treatment systems for home or business	X	X	X								
98335 The Iron Rod, PO Box 2255, **Gig Harbor** WA ☎(206) 851-3293 🖷(206) 851-4258		X	X					X			
98368 Jan Berg, 61 Simcoe Road, **Port Townsend** WA ☎(206) 385-4542			C					X			
98370 First Choice Supply, 16083 Hwy. 305, **Poulsbo** WA ☎(206) 779-1917 — distributor of *Alco ♦Brite* gelled ethanol products		X									X
98370 The Ozone Center™, 19689 7th Ave. NE #120, **Poulsbo** WA ☎(360) 394-4394 — environmental disinfecting systems; ozone equipment for water purification & air decontamination	X	X	C	X				X			
98377 BOHICA Concepts, PO Box 546, **Randle** WA ☎(360) 497-7075 — distributor of politically incorrect publications		X									
98386 Sir Plus, 929 Water Street, **Port Townsend** WA ☎(206) 385-9311 — surplus & prime survival gear, equipment & supplies		X	X							X	X
98390 R.E.I., 1700 45th St. E., **Sumner** WA ☎(800) 426-4840 (US or CAN) 🖥www.rei.com — national retail chain; outdoor/camping products; distributor of *Mountain House* freeze-dried pouches; tents & sleep gear; water filters; backpacks; camp gear; GPS units; binoculars; lanterns; trail clothing; cooking gear	X	X	X							X	X
98420 Wallace's Woodstoves, **Tacoma** WA ☎(206) 535-2255		X	X								X
98422 E'OLA Products, 5914 26th Street NE, **Tacoma** WA ☎(206) 927-3771 — all-natural herbal weight-loss supplement that also increases vitality with first-day results	X	X						X			
98444 A & A Wood & Pellet Stove, 752 S. 108th St., **Tacoma** WA ☎(206) 531-2203 — distributor of *Alco ♦Brite* gelled ethanol products		X									X
98499 Lakewood Natural Foods, 5808 100th St. SW, **Tacoma** WA ☎(206) 584-3929			C	X	X	X	X	X	X	X	X
98499 The Bunker, 11013 Pacific Hwy. SW #702, **Tacoma** WA ☎(206) 984-0122			X	X	X	X	X			X	X
98499 Toad's Survival Innovations, 12134 Pacific SW, **Lakewood** WA ☎(800) 446-TOAD or (253) 582-1319 🖷(253) 582-1338 ✉*toadsurvival@earthlink.net* — full-line distributor of preparedness products & storage foods			C	X	X	X	X		X	X	X
98502 Teri Null, 8327 Mason Street NW, **Olympia** WA ☎(360) 866-1430 — *Magic Mill* products distributor		X			X			X		X	
98512 Evergreen Food Ingredients, 2210 Black Lake Blvd. SW, **Olympia** WA ☎(360) 754-1718 — pre-cooked & dried beans, peas, lentils, & grains; *wholesale only*		X	C		X						X
98576 Intent Outfitters, PO Box 46, **Rainier** WA ☎(360) 894-3885 — tent that can be worn as a coat, slept in like a sleeping blanket, or sheltered by a tent		X	X								X
98597 Happy Hovel Foods, 204 E. Yelm Ave., **Yelm** WA ☎(360) 458-4445 or (800) 637-7772 🖷(360) 458-7977 🖥www.wwmagic.com/haphov ✉*haphov@seanet.com* — organic/natural food; self-sufficiency products; saving power/water; catalog & **Internet** sales of preparedness prod.		X	C	X	X	X	X	X	X	X	X
98597 Suntrek Home Energy, 303-C Creek Street NE, **Yelm** WA ☎(360) 458-8980 or (800) 364-9941 🖷(360) 364-9941 🖥www.suntrekenergy.com ✉*suntrek@accessone.com* — retail eco-store & home energy center; design & consulting		X	X								X
98597 The Optimum Energy Preparedness Center, 106 38483 Yelm Ave. West, **Yelm** WA ☎(360) 458-4602 or (800) 565-1403 🖷(360) 458-9102 — preparedness products: water filters/storage, alternative lighting/cooking, evacuation supplies, hand pumps, & more!	X			X	X	X	X	X	X	X	X
98597 Thunder Market & Good Food, PO Box 1228, **Yelm** WA ☎(206) 458-2905				X	X	X	X	X	X	X	X

Legend: M = Manufacturer / Processor   D = Wholesaler / Trade distributor   R = Distributor / Retailer to public

M = Manufacturer / Processor	D = Wholesaler / Trade distributor	R = Distributor / Retailer to public	M	D	R	04	05	12	13	14	15	16	17
98640 Jack's Country Store, Bay Ave. & Hwy. 10, **Ocean Park** WA ☎(360) 665-4988 🖨(360) 665-4989					X	X	X					X	
98660 Charles Houchens, 111 West 44th Street, **Vancouver** WA ☎(360) 695-8561			X	X	X								X
– manufacturer of *Pioneer* magnesium fire-starter; basic survival tool; useful for fire-making, signaling, & for light													
98662 Country Store & Kitchen Specialties, 9336 NE 76th Street, **Vancouver** WA ☎(360) 256-9131 or (800) 896-9131 🖨(360) 687-0939 💻www.HealthyHarvest.com ✉country@aone.com			X	C	X	X	X	X	X	X	X	X	X
– distributor of *Bosch & Kitchen Specialties* products; everything for being prepared; from custom-packing to off-the-shelf products; preparedness products & emergency supplies; custom packaging													
98662 Healthy Harvest, 9336 NE 76th, **Vancouver** WA ☎(206) 256-9131 🖨(206) 687-0939			X	X	C	X	X	X				X	X
– dehydrated foods brand name & packager of custom products													
98801 Wenatchee Natural Foods, 222 N. Wenatchee, **Wenatchee** WA ☎None			X		X				X		X		
– distributor of *Magic Mill* kitchen products													
98902 Magic Kitchen Ctr. / Arla Crosier, 1103 So. 3 Ave., **Yakima** WA ☎(509) 453-8827			X		X	X	X	X			X	X	
– distributor of *Magic Mill* kitchen products													
98903 South First Surplus, 2318 S. First Street, **Yakima** WA ☎(509) 452-0868			X										X
– distributor of *Alco ◆Brite* gelled ethanol products													
98908 J & S Marketing, PO Box 8297, **Yakima** WA ☎(509) 965-9274			X			X	X				X	X	
– general preparedness products dealers; in-home storage specialist; disasters or emergencies specialist													
98926 Snow Creek Mountain Enterprise, 902 E. Capitol Ave., **Ellensburg** WA ☎(509) 962-5236			X	X	X	X	X				X	X	
– *SamAndy Foods* products distributor													
99003 The Staff Of Life, PO Box 369, **Chattaroy** WA ☎(800) 251-0673			X	X				X					
– plant concentrate assures complete digestion, reduces chronic illness, & strengthens the immune system													
99006 Deer Park Emergency Preparedness Center (EPC), N. 23 Weber Rd. #C-4, **Deer Park** WA ☎(509) 276-9747 🖨(509) 276-1347 💻www.cet.com/!epc ✉epc@cet.com			C	X	X	X	X				X	X	
99006 Deer Park Feed & Seed, W. 12 First St., **Deer Park** WA ☎(509) 276-8408			X		X						X	X	
– distributor of *Alco ◆Brite* gelled ethanol products													
99101 Cover-Yur-Basics, 1376 Main, **Addy** WA ☎(509) 935-0375 🖨(509) 935-0375			C	X	X	X	X	X	X				
– preparedness consultant; in-home storage specialist													
99114 Aladdin Steel Products Inc., **Colville** WA ☎(509) 684-3745 🖨(509) 684-2138			X	X									X
manufacturer of non-catalytic wood-burning stoves													
99124 Tillman's Trustworthy Hardware, Hwy. 155, **Elmer City** WA ☎(509) 633-3445			X										X
– distributor of *Alco ◆Brite* gelled ethanol products													
99150 Northwest Waterstoves, 1838 Aeneas Creek Road, **Naka** WA ☎(509) 779-4488			X	X									X
– manufacturer of outdoor water stoves for whole-house heating & hot water supply													
99156 American Family Products, Int'l., PO Box 1677, **Newport** WA ☎(509) 447-2277			X			X							
99166 Republic Farm & Garden, PO Box 552801 South Park, **Republic** WA ☎(509) 775-3323			X										X
– distributor of *Alco ◆Brite* gelled ethanol products													
99185 Wilbur Drug, West 2nd Main, **Wilbur** WA ☎(509) 647-2034			X										X
– distributor of *Alco ◆Brite* gelled ethanol products													
99205 Champion Pellet Stove Repair, N. 3927 Hawthorne, **Spokane** WA			X										X
– distributor of *Alco ◆Brite* gelled ethanol products													
99207 Lifetime Pools, 6125 N. Division, **Spokane** WA ☎(509) 489-1560			X										X
– distributor of *Alco ◆Brite* gelled ethanol products													
99207 Loretta Frey, 2506 N. Hogan, **Spokane** WA ☎(509) 484-9276 🖨(509) 484-1885			X			X	X		X			X	X
– distributor of *Magic Mill* kitchen products													
99207 Safe Quest Mktg., 58 E. Rowan, **Spokane** WA ☎(509) 484-1552 or (800) 270-8619 🖨(509)484-1552			X						X				
99207 Turbo Burn, Inc., E.4225 Joseph, **Spokane** WA ☎(509) 487-3609 🖨(509) 483-0148			X	X									X
– multi-fuel central heating system for homes as a by-product of water heating													
99212 Jay's Bosch Kitchen Center c/o Linda Holliday, E. 8123 Sprague Ave., **Spokane** WA ☎(509) 924-6241 🖨(509) 924-0081			X			X				X	X		
– distributor of *Bosch & Kitchen Specialties* products													
99218 Inland Harvest Bulk & Natural Foods, 10113 Newport Hwy., **Spokane** WA ☎(509) 468-8090 🖨(509) 468-1084			X	X	X	X	X	X	X		X		
99336 Kitchen Center, 8300 W. Gage Blvd., **Kennewick** WA ☎(509) 783-9292 🖨(509) 736-3692			X	X	X					X		X	
– distributor of *Bosch & Kitchen Specialties* products													
West Virginia													
25064 Alder Marketing, PO Box 847, **Dunbar** WV ☎(304) 776-1393 🖨(304) 776-1179			C	X				X					X
– preparedness & emergency preparation products; vacuum-sealers; long-term storage items; book, & more!													
25267 Panther Primitives, Box 32, **Normantown** WV			X	X									X
– 140-page catalog of Early American items including full-sized tipis, kegs, cookware, much more													
25427 Star View Satellite & Stove, Rt. 6 Box 1100, **Hedgesville** WV ☎(304) 754-8044			X										X
– distributor of *Alco ◆Brite* gelled ethanol products													

Product References Keyed to Chapters (Cont.)

04 water / air filtration & treatment	**05 grains, seeds, mills & equip.**	**12 dairy / powdered milk supplies**	**13 honey / sweeteners**							
14 vitamins / minerals / herbs	**15 sprouting / equip. & supplies**	**16 dry / dehydrated / freeze-dried**	**17 energy / fuels**							

Listing	M	D	R	04	05	12	13	14	15	16	17
26003 **Natural Roads Food Co-op**, 118 N. Park St., **Wheeling** WV ☎(304) 242-9893 ✉*elias@ovnet.com*			C	X	X	X	X	X	X	X	
26101 **Sun Selector**, PO Box 1545, **Parkersburg** WV ☎(304) 485-7150 📠(304) 422-3931		X									X
26651 **Prime Cable Plus**, 820 Broad Street, **Summersville** WV – distributor of *Alco♦Brite* gelled ethanol products		X									X

Wisconsin

Listing	M	D	R	04	05	12	13	14	15	16	17
53032 **Northwest Tipi**, 2001 S. Main St. Rd., **Horicon** WI ☎(414) 485-4744 – call evenings for information about the Indian Tipi (teepee) designed for the backpacker, canoeist, survivalist, or year-round naturalist; 3-yr. Guarantee on Indian lodges; practical & inexpensive alternate shelter	X	X	X								X
53094 **Fire Glow**, W. 4283 Ebemezer Dr., **Watertown** WI ☎(414) 261-5330 – distributor of *Alco♦Brite* gelled ethanol products		X									X
53105 **Frahm Enterprises, Inc.**, 256 S. Pine St., **Burlington** WI ☎(414) 763-8141 – distributor of *Alco♦Brite* gelled ethanol products		X									X
53115 **Simple Energy Inc.**, 303 Butternut Dr., **Delavan** WI ☎/📠(414) 728-1950 or (800) 642-2299 – outdoor products & emergency electronics		X	X								X
53147 **Hearthside Shop**, 116 E. Geneva Square, **Lake Geneva** WI – distributor of *Alco♦Brite* gelled ethanol products		X									X
53186 **Fireplace Systems, Inc.**, 1251 Sentry Dr., **Waukesha** WI ☎(414) 245-0055 – distributor of *Alco♦Brite* gelled ethanol products		X									X
53201 **Lee Engineering Co.**, 2023 W. Wisconsin Avenue, **Milwaukee** WI ☎(414) 272-4050 – manufacturer of the *Lee* home grain mill; produces cool flours; not intended for oily seeds, nuts or smallest grains	X	X	X		X						
53214 **Chr Hansen's Laboratory**, 9015 W. Maple St., **Milwaukee** WI ☎(414) 476-3630 – cheesemaking supplies; colorants; contract ingredients & foods processor supplies	X	X	X			X					
53543 **Chimney Specialists, Inc.**, 869 North Main, **Highland** WI ☎(800) 395-6660 – distributor of *Alco♦Brite* gelled ethanol products		X									X
53562 **Saco Foods**, 6120 University Ave., **Madison** WI ☎(608) 238-9101 ✉*sacofoods@aol.com* – producer of buttermilk powder and other baking adjuncts for long-term storage	X					X					
53581 **Pine River Food Co-op**, PO Box 464 Main Street, **Richland Center** WI ☎(608) 647-7299			C	X	X	X	X	X	X	X	
53593 **Pure Sweet Honey Farm, Inc.**, 514 Commerce Pkwy., **Verona** WI ☎(608) 845-9601	X	X	X				X				
53704 **Ayurvedic Health 2000, Inc.**, 5310 Wall St. #600, **Madison** WI ☎(608) 243-1243 or (800) 509-5609 – publisher of *Health 2000 Report*; utilizes Ayurvedic principles for weight loss & control the natural way		X						X			
53705 **Whole Foods Market**, 3313 University Ave., **Madison** WI ☎(608) 233-9566 📠(608) 233-8066		X	X			X	X	X	X	X	
53714 **North Farm Cooperative**, 204 Regas Road, **Madison** WI ☎(800) 236-5880 or (608) 241-2667 📠(608) 241-0688 💻www. Northfarm-coop.com/ or 💻http://users.aol./nfcoop ✉*nfcoop@northfarm-coop.com* Territory: *IL, MI, MN, MT, ND, WI, Eastern WY* – wholesale distributor of natural foods to retail stores and food-buying coops		X	C	X	X	X	X	X	X	X	
53954 **Portage Food Buying Club**, W. 7065 County Hwy. P, **Pardeeville** WI ☎(608) 742-8411			C	X	X	X	X	X	X	X	
54213 **Lake Michigan Wind & Sun**, 3971 E. Bluebird Rd., **Forestville** WI ☎(414) 837-2267 📠(414) 837-7523		X	X								X
54220 **Mirro Company**, 1512 Washington Street, **Manitowoc** WI ☎(414) 684-4421 – manufacturer of home canning equipment; *Mirro, Earthgrown, & Foley* brands pressure cookers	X										
54221 **Wisconsin Aluminum Foundry Co.**, PO Box 246, **Manitowoc** WI ☎(414) 682-8286 – manufacturer of pressure cookers & home canning equipment	X										X
54227 **Lakeshore Whole Foods Cooperative** *(Buying Club)*, 13922 Melnik Road, **Maribel** WI ☎(414) 755-4136 📠(414) 755-4061			C	X	X	X	X	X	X	X	
54406 **Real Goods Hearth & Home Ctr.**, 286 Wilson St., **Amherst** WI ☎(715) 824-3982 📠(715) 824-5021 – retail store & catalog mail-order; products for energy independence & a safe home; solar equipment & supplies, efficient lighting equipment, natural pest control, books; renewable energy; & lots more!		X	X							X	X
54449 **Marshfield Food Cooperative** *(Buying Club)*, PO Box 601, **Marshfield** WI ☎(715) 387-3650			C	X	X	X	X	X	X	X	
54475 **Northwoods Food Cooperative** *(Buying Club)*, PO Box 21, **Medford** WI			C	X	X	X	X	X	X	X	
54639 **CROPP Cooperative**, Main St, **La Farge** WI ☎(608) 625-2602 📠(608) 625-2600 ✉*organic@mwt.net* – growers' cooperative dedicated to sustainable agriculture & high quality organic dairy, eggs, & produce	X	X	C			X	X	X		X	X
54667 **Alternative Power Renewable Energy Center**, 701 S. Main, **Westby** WI ☎(608) 634-2984		X									X
54701 **Consumers Cooperative Assoc.**, 1201 Hastings Way, **Eau Claire** WI ☎(715) 876-8710 📠(715) 836-8712			C	X	X	X	X	X	X	X	
54701 **Energy Store Leisure Home Center**, Eau Claire WI ☎(800) 722-FIRE ✉*directfire@hearth.com*	X	X									X
54703 **National Presto Industries, Inc.**, 3925 N. Hastings Way, **Eau Claire** WI ☎(715) 839-2121 – pressure cookers: services & parts for *Steamline, Maid of Honor, Kook Kwik, Best Made, & Merit* models	X										X
54741 **Community Co-op Shopping Center**, 241 N. Front, **Fairchild** WI ☎(715) 334-4141			C	X	X	X	X	X	X	X	
54751 **Menomonie Food Co-op**, 1707 Stout Street, **Menomonie** WI ☎(715) 235-6533			C	X	X	X	X	X	X	X	
54840 **North Country Metals, Inc.**, **Grantsburg** WI ☎(715) 463-5334 – manufacturer of wood-burning stoves	X										X

M = Manufacturer / Processor / D = Wholesaler / Trade distributor / R = Distributor / Retailer to public	M	D	R	04	05	12	13	14	15	16	17
54847 Iron River Grocery Cooperative, PO Box 8, **Iron River** WI ☎(715) 372-4264			C	X	X	X	X	X	X	X	
54865 Great Northern Solar, Rt. 1 Box 71, **Port Wing** WI ☎(715) 774-3374	X	X									X
54880 North Farm Co-op Warehouse, 1505 N. 6th Street, **Superior** WI ☎(715) 525-5675 🖷(715) 392-4517 Territory: *IL, IN, MI, MN, MO, OH, WI*	X		C	X	X	X	X	X	X	X	
54884 Ken & Agnes Heath, 7138 W. Fadness Road, **Winter** WI ☎(715) 266-4821 – *Magic Mill* products distributor		X			X			X		X	
54896 Winter Cooperative IGA, Box 6, **Winter** WI ☎(715) 266-2611			C	X	X	X	X	X	X	X	
54935 Debbie Shaw, 93 E. Sutton Street, **Fond Du Lac** WI ☎(414) 924-6706 – *Magic Mill* products distributor		X			X			X		X	
54956 Solid Flue Chimney Savers, 9590 North Oakwood Ave., **Neenah** WI – distributor of *Alco ♦Brite* gelled ethanol products		X									X
54968 Water Street Market Cooperative, 511 W. Water St., **Princeton** WI ☎(414) 295-4321			C	X	X	X	X	X	X	X	
54984 Helen Jakubowski, Rt. 1, Box 311, **Wild Rose** WI ☎(414) 622-3450 – *Magic Mill* products distributor		X			X			X		X	
Wyoming											
82051 High Country Stoves, 415 S. 5th Street, **Laramie** WY ☎(307) 745-4488 🖷(307) 745-4466 ✉*hi-cntry@vcn.com*	X	X									X
82070 Prairie Soaps, 306 Buchanan, **Laramie** WY – natural ingredients, hand-made soaps w/o synthetic dyes, scents, or preservatives; send **SASE** for brochure		X					X				
82214 Walker Texaco, 15 E. Wanlen, **Guernsey** WY – distributor of *Alco ♦Brite* gelled ethanol products		X									X
82501 Porter's Mtn View Supply, 750 E. Sunset Drive, **Riverton** WY – distributor of *Alco ♦Brite* gelled ethanol products		X									X
82636 Smith RV Sales, 3500 E. Yellowstone Hwy., **Evansville** WY ☎(307) 234-5617 – distributor of *Alco ♦Brite* gelled ethanol products		X									X
82701 Hiday Enterprises / Soot Busters Chimney Service, 5011 US Hwy. 16, **Newcastle** WY ☎(307) 746-2386 – distributor of *Alco ♦Brite* gelled ethanol products		X									X
82701 Weston County True Value, 326 W. Main, **New Castle** WY – distributor of *Alco ♦Brite* gelled ethanol products		X									X
82717 The Pellet Stove Place, 605 E. Lake Way, **Gillette** WY ☎(307) 682-3849 – distributor of *Alco ♦Brite* gelled ethanol products		X									X
82720 Susan Sanders, PO Box 265, 1210 Hwy. 24 West, **Hulett** WY ☎(307) 467-5651 – *Magic Mill* products distributor		X						X		X	
83001 Teton Rental, 1055 South Hwy. 89, **Jackson** WY – distributor of *Alco ♦Brite* gelled ethanol products		X									X

Canadian Products & Services Suppliers
Selected Listings

Symbols Code

☎ = Telephone	🖨 = Fax	💻 = Website	✉ = E-mail

Product References Keyed to Chapters

04 water / air filtration & treatment	05 grains, seeds, mills & equip.	12 dairy / powdered milk supplies	13 honey / sweeteners
14 vitamins / minerals / herbs	15 sprouting / equip. & supplies	16 dried / dehydrated products	17 energy / fuels
M = Manufacturer / Processor	D = Wholesaler / Trade distributor	R = Distributor / Retailer to public	

Listing	M	D	R	04	05	12	13	14	15	16	17
Alberta											
T0C 1S0 Jeanette Ogilvie, RR #4, Lacombe AB ☎(403) 782-2056 — *Magic Mill* products distributor; call for additional information		X			X			X		X	
T0M 0R0 Sunergy Systems, PO Box 70, Cremona AB ☎(403) 637-3973		X									X
T1J OE7 Bosch Kitchen Ctr. c/o Ted Hill, 1269 2nd Ave. S., **Lethbridge** AB ☎(403) 329-8227 ☎(403) 320-7227 — *Bosch & Kitchen Specialties* products distributor		X	X	X	X	X	X	X	X	X	X
T2H 0X9 Bosch Kitchen Centre / Hill's Pantry #4, 7640 SE Fairmount Dr., **Calgary** AB ☎(403) 258-1337 — *Bosch & Kitchen Specialties* products distributor		X	X	X	X	X	X	X	X	X	X
T8A 3G6 Dri Harvest Foods Ltd., 96 Groveland Rd, **Sherwood Park** AB ☎(403) 464-4373	X	X								X	
TOC 1SO Jeanette Ogilvie, RR #4, Lacombe AB ☎(403) 782-2056		X					X				X
Foods Ltd., 111 1st St. S., **Vauxhall** AB ☎(403) 654-2116	X	X								X	
British Columbia											
V0H 1R0 Okanagan Dried Fruits Ltd., 1406 Maple, **Okanagan Falls** BC ☎(604) 497-8051 or 497-8273	X	X								X	
V0H 1R0 Sun Stream Fruit Ltd., 258 Oliver Ranch Rd., **Okanagan Falls** BC ☎(604) 497-5525	X	X								X	
V0R 1L0 Pacific Energy Woodstoves Ltd., **Cobble Hill** BC ☎(604) 743-2543 — manufacturer of wood-burning stoves	X										X
V1E 1B7 Nutter's, Centenoka Park Mall #441, 360 TransCanada Hwy. SW, **Salmon Arm** BC ☎(604)833-0144 🖨(604) 833-0149 ✉*salmonarm@nutters.com* — **Saskatchewan locations:** Assiniboia, Estevan, Humboldt Kindersley, Melfort, Moose Jaw, North Battleford, Prince Albert, Saskatoon, Swift Current, Weyburn, Yorkton — **Manitoba locations:** Brandon, Dauphin			X		X	X	X	X	X	X	X
V1T 2B8 Sunseed Natural Foods & Vegetarian Café, 2919 30th Ave., **Vernon** BC ☎(604) 542-7892	X	X				X			X	X	
V2C 6T6 Nutter's, 500 Notre Dame Drive, **Kamloops** BC ☎(604) 828-9960 🖨(604) 828-9961 ✉*kamloops@nutters.com*											
V3C 5M5 Safe-Pak Supply Canada, Inc., 1638 Kebet Way, **Port Coquitlam** BC ☎(604) 942-1788 🖨(604) 942-8830 💻http://mindlink.bc.ca/safe_pak/info ✉*safe_pak@mindlink.bc.ca* — manufacturer & distributor of *SafePak Survival* packs; first aid, emergency preparedness & related customized products; 72-hr. kits for home, auto, outdoors, or on the water	X	X									X
V5A AV8 StatPower, 7725 Lougheed Hwy., **Burnaby** BC ☎(800) 668-0003 🖨(604) 420-1591	X	X									X
V5Z 1B8 EcoSpace Inc., 704 West 7th Avenue #23, **Vancouver** BC ☎(604) 708-0307 💻(604) 708-0781 — specializing in emergency kits, supplies, and emergency preparedness training to facilitate personal readiness for an earthquake and other emergencies	X	X									X
V6G 1C8 Capers, 1675 Robson St., **Vancouver** BC☎(604) 687-5288 🖨(604) 687-5063 — natural & organic dairy, fruit, meats & vegetable foods; vitamins & supplements; bulk & pre-pack foods			X		X	X	X	X	X	X	X
V6K 1N9 Capers, 2285 West 4th Ave., **Vancouver** BC ☎(604) 739-6676 🖨(604) 739-6694 — natural & organic dairy, fruit, meats & vegetable foods; vitamins & supplements; bulk & pre-pack foods			X		X	X	X	X	X	X	X
V7V 1L1 Capers, 2496 Marine Drive, **West Vancouver** BC ☎(604) 925-3316 🖨(604) 925-9306 — natural & organic dairy, fruit, meats & vegetable foods; vitamins & supplements; bulk & pre-pack foods			X		X	X	X	X	X	X	X
V8T 5A5 Columbia Fire & Safety, 768 Spruce Street, **Victoria** BC ☎(250) 386-6773 or (800) 661-5090 🖨(250) 386-3941 💻www.columbia-safety.com/quakeaid ✉*safety@visual.net*	X	X	X								X
V8Z 1C8 Osburn Mfg., Inc., **Victoria** BC ☎(250) 475-3800 🖨(250) 475-1028 — manufacturer of wood-burning stoves, inserts, & gas stoves	X	X									X
Backwoods Corner, Prince George BC ☎(604) 562-2185 🖨(604) 562-2911 💻www.irl.bc.ca/backwood ✉*IRLBackwoods Corner*		X	X							X	X
Denic Service & Sales, Ltd., 3014 Edgemont Blvd., **North Vancouver** BC ☎(604) 929-6696 💻www.webdirect.net/denic ✉*tsteffen@direct.ca* — preparedness how-to book		X									
Energy Alternatives, Parksville BC ☎(604) 248-6828	X	X									X
Vancouver Gas Fireplaces, 1521 West 8 Ave., **Vancouver** BC ☎(604) 732-3470 🖨(604) 732-5722 💻www.axionet.com/vangas ✉*rkoby@vangasfireplaces.com*		X	X								X

M = Manufacturer / Processor D = Wholesaler / Trade distributor R = Distributor / Retailer to public	M	D	R	04	05	12	13	14	15	16	17
Manitoba											
R3C 2C6 **Arbico / CAN**, Box 17 Group 242, RR2, **Winnipeg** MB ☎(204) 697-0863 or (800) 665-2494 — mail order biological pest controls; organic fertilizers			X								
R3C 3Z3 **Winnipeg Square Sunshine Fruit & Nut Co.**, 360 Main, **Winnipeg** MB ☎(204) 942-8153		X	X					X	X	X	
R3H 1A4 **LM Reliance**, **Winnipeg** MB ☎(204) 633-4403 ⊟(204) 694-5132 — manufacturer of HDPE pail, bottles & shipping containers	X										
R7A YA4 **McFayden**, 30 Ninth St., **Brandon** MB ☎(204) 725-7314 — herbs, vegetables, fruits, small fruits; tools, books & supplies			X								
New Brunswick											
E0E 1P0 **Energy Systems & Design**, PO Box 1557, **Sussex** NB ☎(506) 433-3151	X	X								X	
E0G 2N0 **The Herb Farm**, **Norton** NB — catalog $5.00; herbs for teas & drinks	X										
Newfoundland											
Northwest Territory											
Nova Scotia											
B0M 1X0 **Ropak CAN, Inc.**, **Spring Hill** NS ☎(902) 597-3787 ⊟(902) 597-8318 — manufacturer of polyethylene containers	X										
B1P 6J1 **DynaGen Systems, Inc.**, 80 Marine Dr. #A, Sydport Industrial Park, **Sydney** NS ☎(902) 567-0133 or (888) 396-2436 ⊟(902) 567-0633 ⊑www.etcom.uccb.ns.ca/dynagen/dynagen — emergency & stand-by power for residential & business applications; engine-driven technology	X	X								X	
Ontario											
K0E 1Y0 **Harvest Foodworks**, 445 Hwy. 29, RR 1, **Toledo** ON ☎(613) 275-2218 ⊟613) 275-1359 ⊑*www.harvest.on.ca* ✉*thefolks@harvest.on.ca* — great-tasting, low-fat, muscle-replenishing, vegetarian, easy-to-cook meals for camping, hiking, biking, canoeing, hunting, fishing, skiing, boating, mountain climbing or any activity in the Great Outdoors	X	X				X			X	X	
K0G 1M0 **Wood 'N' Energy**,1 Main Street, **McDonalds Corners** ON ☎(613) 278 2023 or (800) MID-FIRE ⊟(613) 278 2708 ✉*wood@superaje.com* — wood cookers, classic ranges & gas hearth installations	X	X								X	
K7H 2T1 **Embers**, 63 North Street, **Perth** ON ☎(613) 264-0878 ⊟(613) 264-9076 ✉*embers@superaje.com* — stoves, fireplaces & more…			X							X	
K7K 6C7 **Bubble Action Pumps Ltd.**, 121 Counter St., **Kingston** ON ☎(613) 542-4045 ⊟(613) 542-0198	X	X								X	
KOE 1KO **Caleen Weatherhead**, RR 1 **Iroquois** ON ☎(613) 652-1552 — distributor of *Magic Mill* products			X			X	X		X	X	
L0C 1A0 **Richter's**, **Goodwood** ON — catalog $2.00; herbs for teas & drinks	X										
L0C IAO **Richter's Herbs**, **Goodwood** ON — herbal teas for better health	X	X	X					X			
L1N 4M4 **Donghee Nam**, 1624 Brock Street S., **Whitby** ON ☎(905) 668-6620 — distributor of *Magic Mill* products			X			X			X	X	
L2G 4P1 **Sunnygold Australia Pty. Ltd.**, 6710 Drummond Rd., **Niagara Falls** ON ☎(905) 374-6433	X	X								X	
L4K 4S1 **World Famous Sales Of Canada Inc.**, 333 Confederation Pkwy., **Concord** ON ☎(905) 738-4777 — distributor of *Mountain House* freeze-dried foods in cans for long-term food storage		X	X	X	X					X	
L6T 3T2 **Buckhorn CAN, Inc.**, **Brampton** ON ☎(905) 791-6500 (800) 461-7579 ⊟(905) 791-9942 — manufacturer of transportation & processing polyethylene containers	X										
L6T 5C3 **Polybottle Group Ltd.**, **Brampton** ON ☎(905) 450-3600 ⊟(905) 450-0027 — manufacturer of stock & custom plastic containers including wide & narrow mouth	X										
L7G 5L6 **Dominion Seed House**, Box 2500, **Georgetown** ON — Canadian herbs & vegetables	X										
L7L 5V2 **Sun-Mar Corp.**, 5035 North Service Road C9-10, **Burlington** ON — composting toilets, electrical & non-electric; for remote locations & environmental considerations	X	X								X	
L7R 3M1 **Frank's Magic Crops, Inc.**, 480 Guelph Line, **Burlington** ON — hydroponics & *Earth Juice* distributor								X			
L8P 3A2 **House Of Java**, 166 S James St., **Hamilton** ON ☎(905) 527-7559		X									

Product References Keyed to Chapters (Cont.)

04 water / air filtration & treatment	05 grains, seeds, mills & equip.	12 dairy / powdered milk supplies	13 honey / sweeteners
14 vitamins / minerals / herbs	15 sprouting / equip. & supplies	16 dry / dehydrated / freeze-dried	17 energy / fuels

Entry	M	D	R	04	05	12	13	14	15	16	17
M = Manufacturer / Processor / **D = Wholesaler / Trade distributor** / **R = Distributor / Retailer to public**	M	D	R	04	05	12	13	14	15	16	17
L9Y 4H7 **Heritage Energy Systems, Collingwood** ON ☎(705) 445-7655 — manufacturer of wood-burning stoves & fireplace inserts	X	X									X
M2H 3B4 **Lien Thuan Co. Ltd.**, 734 Gordon Baker, **Toronto** ON ☎(416) 493-3075			X								
M4M 2T4 **Homemade Fine Food**, 388 Carlaw, **Toronto** ON ☎(416) 466-4224		X	X		X					X	
M4P 2H5 **Simuva Foods Inc.**, 2482 Yonge, **Toronto** ON ☎(416) 481-3616		X	X							X	
M8Z 2S6 **Eden Mfg. Co. Ltd., Toronto** ON ☎(416) 231-4005 🖨(416) 239-9638 — processor of drink mixes, jelly powders, soup bases & mixes, army rations, non-dairy coffee creamers; camping & trail foods	X									X	
M8Z 2S6 **Eden Mfg. Co. Ltd., Toronto** ON ☎(416) 231-4005 🖨(416) 239-9638 — processor of drink mixes, jelly powders, soup bases & mixes, army rations, non-dairy coffee creamers & camping & trail foods	X										
M9C 4V3 **The Wilderness Kitchen**, PO Box 255, Station 'A', **Etobicoke** ON ☎(888) 553-2553 🖨(416) 231-3938 ▫www3.sympatico.ca/j.pledger ✉j.pledger@sympatico.ca — one-stop shop for trip supplies; comprehensive list of foods & goods for wilderness travelers; custom-designed supply packs; complete range of staple foods for wilderness trips; *AlpineAire* freeze-dried foods		X	X						X	X	X
M9L 1Z9 **Quality Containers, Ltd., Weston** ON ☎(416) 749-6247 🖨(416) 749-3293 — manufacturer of tin cans & slip cover, friction top & open top containers	X										
N0H 2O9 **Sarah Curtosi**, Box 9, **Thornburg** ON ☎(519) 599-7127 — distributor of *Magic Mill* products			X		X		X	X			
N1H 6J2 **Harthex Fireplaces, Guelph** ON ☎(519) 837-3200 — manufacturer of wood-burning & coal-burning stoves	X	X									X
N3B 1M3 **Elmira Stove Works, Elmira** ON ☎(519) 669-1281 — manufacturer of wood-burning & coal-burning cook stoves	X	X								X	
N6J 1G5 **Southcrest Bulk Foods**, 360 Springbank Dr., **London** ON ☎(519) 472-0610		X	X		X					X	
NOH 209 **Sarah Curtosi**, Box 9, **Thornburg** ON ☎(519) 599-7127 — distributor of *Magic Mill* products			X		X		X		X	X	X
Freeze-Dry Foods Limited, 579 Speers Road, **Oakville** ON ☎(905) 844-1471 🖨(905) 844-8140 ▫www.freeze-dry.com ✉email@freeze-dry.com	X	X	X			X	X	X		X	
Samar Canada, 39 Glen, **Cameron** ON ☎(905) 881-5353		X									
Sunworks Inc., 1466 Highway 34, **Hawkesbury** ON ☎(800) 277-0709 (*from 514, 613, 819 Area Codes*) or (613) 632-0456 🖨(613) 632-2606 ✉pdksun@hawk.igs.net — distributor of wood & pellet stoves, geothermal heat pumps & other Earth-friendly energy products		X	X								X

Prince Edward Island

Quebec

Entry	M	D	R	04	05	12	13	14	15	16	17
H2G 1X3 **Les Epices Pietro**, 2260 Des Carrieres, **Montréal** PQ ☎(514) 276-1427			X								
H3N 1P3 **Marché Africana**, 999 Ogilvy, **Montréal** PQ ☎(514) 278-3466			X								
H3Z 1A7 **Balcorp Limited**, 4103 Sherbrooke W., **Westmount** PQ ☎(514) 939-0909			X								
H4N 1G8 **Amira Entreprise Inc.**, 1425 Mazurette Rue, **Montréal** PQ ☎(514) 382-9823			X								
H4N 1G8 **Kesra Trading Inc. / Cananut**, 1415 Mazurette, **Montréal** PQ ☎(514) 388-8003			X								
H4N 1J8 **Tootsi Impex**, 855 Du Marché Central Rue, **Montréal** PQ ☎(514) 381-9790			X								
H4P 1M2 **Hampstead Foods**, 5470 Ferrier Rue, **Montréal** PQ ☎(514) 731-7621			X								
H4S 1Y5 **Rose Hill Foods Inc. / Major Canada Inc.**, 5778 Cypihot, **Montréal** PQ ☎(514) 856-1000			X								
H7L 3S4 **Les Produits Alimentaires Berthelet Inc.**, 1805 Berlier, **Chomedey** PQ ☎(514) 334-5503			X								
H7P 599 **W. H. Perron**, 2914 Labelle Blvd., **Laval** PQ ☎(514) 332-3619 — herbs, vegetables, fruits & small fruits; tools, books, & supplies			X								
H9P 1H7 **Twinpak, Inc., Dorval** PQ ☎(514) 684-7070 🖨(514) 685-3643 — wholesaler/distributor of plastic; manufacturer of polypropylene containers, foil & film laminated stocks	X										
J0E 2N0 **Les Poincons de Waterloo Inc., Waterloo** PQ ☎(514) 539-3916 — manufacturer of wood-burning stoves	X	X									X
J0H 1A0 **Plante Carole**, 500 Bonin, **Acton Vale** PQ ☎(514) 546-3279			X								
J0K 3L0 **Harnois Ind.**, 1044 Principale, C.P. 150, **St. Thomas de Joliette** PQ ☎(514) 756-1041 🖨(514) 756-8389 — manufacturers & suppliers of greenhouses and growing systems	X	X									
Concentrated Food, Inc., 8500 Henrri Bourassa, **Montréal** PQ ☎(514) 333-3838			X								
Daltons (1834) Inc., 50 Montcalm, **La Prairie** PQ ☎(514) 659-5451			X								
Les Aliments Trophy, Inc., 5595 Ch. St. Francois, **Montréal** PQ ☎(514) 339-5458			X								
R I P Corp., 4632 Bd. Thimens Blvd., **Saint Laurent** PQ ☎(514) 745-1005			X								

M = Manufacturer / Processor	D = Wholesaler / Trade distributor	R = Distributor / Retailer to public	M	D	R	04	05	12	13	14	15	16	17
Saskatchewan													
KOE 1KO **Betty Reimer,** 320-1 Springs Drive, **Saskatchewan** SK ☎(306) 627-3625 — distributor of *Magic Mill* products					X	X			X	X		
Yukon Territory													
International Suppliers													
Cran-Mar Distributors, 15 Redkiln Road, **Hamilton Parish** Bermuda CR 02 ☎(441) 293-2933 — distributor of *Magic Mill* products					X	X			X	X	X	X
Dr. Dorcus Velez, PO Box 11370, **St. Thomas** VI 00801 ☎(809) 776-4200 — distributor of *Magic Mill* products					X	X			X	X	X	X
Ian Diack, 23 Flatman Crescent, **Geraldine** NZ 8751 ☎(011) (643) 693-8322 — distributor of *Magic Mill* products					X	X			X	X	X	X

If you are a supplier to the preparedness or food storage industry or are selling any type of emergency products, there's a free listing in our publications for you! Place your company in the *Preparedness Resources Directory©* by marking all categories and items you provide. Write in **OTHER** category any pertinent items or services you provide not listed on this sheet. Also, specify brands for additional listings under manufacturer listings. Include all business locations, phones, Fax, toll-free #s, E-mail, and Website. Use a different form for each business entity. Please complete this form, tear out, and mail or fax to the above address. We neither sell products nor endorse them. **There is no charge for this listing!**

Use additional sheets for details or send literature, if desired—information is kept on file for referrals!

SUPPLIER / PROVIDER CHECKLIST

Check all that apply: ❑ *manufacturer/processor* ❑ *wholesaler/distributor* ❑ *direct distribution/retail*

01	**72-hour disaster kits:** ❑ individual ❑ family ❑ commercial/business ❑ other
02	**books, tapes & videos:** ❑ food preparation ❑ in-home storage ❑ preparedness & survival ❑ cookbooks
03	**bread mixers:** ❑ hand-operated ❑ electric ❑ non-electric ❑ equipment & supplies
04	**camping:** ❑ tents ❑ cots ❑ bedding ❑ sleeping bags ❑ backpacks ❑ outdoors tools & kits ❑ equipment
05	**clothing, protective:** ❑ hot-weather ❑ cold-weather ❑ survival gear
06	**complementary medicine & supplements:** ❑ vitamins ❑ minerals ❑ herbs ❑ health foods *Brand(s):*
07	**consulting, lecturing, & seminars:** ❑ in-home food storage ❑ emergency preparedness ❑ food preparation
08	**dehydrated foods:** ❑ bulk ❑ single cans ❑ pre-pack units ❑ Other:
09	**dehydrators & dryers:** ❑ electric ❑ non-electric ❑ equipment ❑ supplies *Brand(s):*
10	**emergency electronics:** ❑ field radio ❑ walkie-talkie ❑ two-way radio ❑ other
11	**emergency medical:** ❑ first aid supplies ❑ instruction ❑ kits ❑ publications
12	**food storage plans:** ❑ bulk ❑ pre-pack units ❑ single cans *Brand(s):*
13	**freeze-dried foods:** ❑ bulk ❑ pre-pack units ❑ single cans *Brand(s):*
14	**grains:** ❑ wheat ❑ other grains ❑ beans & legumes ❑ bulk ❑ pre-pack units ❑ **conventional** ❑ **organic**
15	**grain mills & grinders:** ❑ electric ❑ non-electric *Specify brand(s):*
16	**household & kitchen implements:** ❑ equipment ❑ supplies ❑ specialty items *Brand(s):*
17	**hunting & fishing:** ❑ fishing equipment ❑ game supplies ❑ hunting guns ❑ ammunition
18	**light, heat, & cooking:** ❑ fuels ❑ batteries ❑ equipment ❑ supplies ❑ **generators:** ❑ *gas* ❑ *diesel* ❑ *solar*
19	**MREs:** ❑ individual packs ❑ bulk units ❑ 3-day units ❑ 7-day units ❑ 14-day units ❑ 30-day units
20	**pastas, soups, & drinks:** ❑ mixes ❑ pre-pack units ❑ equipment ❑ supplies
21	**personal care:** ❑ supplies ❑ kits ❑ equipment ❑ specific items:
22	**personal protection devices:** ❑ chemicals ❑ bows & arrows ❑ handguns & ammunition ❑ knives
23	**powdered milk:** ❑ bulk product ❑ individual packs ❑ pre-pack storage units
24	**sanitation:** ❑ equipment ❑ supplies *(specifics):*
25	**specialty foods products:** ❑ natural/organic foods ❑ dietary foods *Brand(s):*
26	**sprouts / seeds:** ❑ bulk ❑ pre-pack units ❑ kits ❑ supplies ❑ **conventional** ❑ **organic**
27	**storage & food containers:** ❑ equipment ❑ supplies ❑ containers ❑ desiccants ❑ oxygen absorbents
28	**sweeteners:** ❑ honey ❑ sugar: white, brown, & powdered ❑ other sweeteners
29	**water / treatment:** ❑ pre-pack rations ❑ treatment devices ❑ equipment ❑ containers *Brand(s):*
30	**OTHER** *(be specific!)*: **over ➜**

Business Name: _____

Address: _____

City: _____ **State:** ____ **ZIP:** _____ - _____

Phone: (____)_____ **FAX:** (____)_____ **Toll-free #** (____)_____

E-mail: _____ **Web site:** _____

Authorized by (*required*):	*Please print name so we are correct!*	*Check here if you prefer your name not be published!* .... ❑

Ed10